Human Growth and Development

Beverly Allred Schroeder
Michigan State University

WEST PUBLISHING COMPANY

ST. PAUL   NEW YORK   LOS ANGELES   SAN FRANCISCO

COPYEDITING *Susan Baranczyk*
DESIGN *Diane Beasley*
COVER DESIGN *Pollock Design Group*
COVER IMAGE Courtyard, West End Library, Boston, 1901, *by Maurice Prendergast. From the Metropolitan Museum of Art, New York. Reprinted with permission.*
INDEXING *E. Virginia Hobbs*
COMPOSITION *Carlisle Communications, Ltd.*
Production, prepress, printing, and binding by West Publishing Company.

COPYRIGHT © 1992   By West Publishing Company
50 W. Kellogg Boulevard
P. O. Box 64526
St. Paul, MN 55164–0526

Printed in the United States of America

99 98 97 96 95 94 93 92   8 7 6 5 4 3 2 1 0

Library of Congress Cataloging-in-Publication Data

Schroeder, Beverly,
    Human growth and development / Beverly Schroeder.

        p.   cm.
    Includes bibliographical references and index
    ISBN 0–314–92703–4 (hard)
    1. Human growth.   2. Developmental biology.   3. Child
        development.
    I. Title.
QP84.S38 1992
612.6–dc20

                                                    91–30165
                                                    CIP ∞

Photo Credits

1, Bill Anderson, Monkmeyer; 3, Historical Picture Service, Chicago; 4, Historical Picture Service, Chicago; 5, Historical Picture Service, Chicago; 6, *continued on next page*

Art Credits

Cartographics Figure 1-1, p. 8; Figure 1-2, p. 20; Figure 1-4, p. 26; Figure 2-4, p. 47; Figure 2-5, p. 49; Figure 2-6, p. 50; Figure 2-7, page 64; Figure 5-1, p. 155; Figure 5-2, p. 156; Figure 9-1, p. 248; Figure 12-1, p. 338; Figure 14-1, p. 387;

Georg Klatt Figure 2-1, 40; Figure 2-2, 41;

Cyndy Wooley Figure 2-3, p. 45; Figure 3-1, p. 72; Figure 3-2, p. 88; Figure 3-3, p. 90; Figure 4-1, p. 100; Figure 4-2, p. 106; Figure 4-3, p. 107; Figure 4-4, p. 121;

Martha Campbell cartoons: pp. 192, 193, 200, 204, 206.

In keeping with the life span theme
I would like to dedicate this book to
my parents, Bill and Claudia Allred
My husband, Keith Schroeder
and
my sons, Thad and Seth Eubank

Brief Table of Contents

Table
of
Contents

Preface

Seventeen years ago, when I first started teaching human growth and development courses, there was no life span human development text. My colleagues and I used a child development text and supplemented it with a couple of paperbacks that loosely discussed adult development. The view then of life span development resembled the old fairy tale in which the heroine and hero, after many trials and tribulations, entered adulthood, got married, and lived happily ever after. There was no recognition that humans change, grow, and develop past that point.

The study of human development is relevant to everyone. Each person comes from a family of some kind, no matter how it is defined. Each person is connected to someone or some group. We are both different and alike. We experience each stage, age, or episode of our lives in our own unique way. We assume different family roles while being the same person. For example, I am simultaneously a wife, mother, daughter, sister, aunt, niece, stepmother, step-grandmother, granddaughter, cousin, sister-in-law, and daughter-in-law. We also assume different roles outside of the family; I am, for example, a neighbor, researcher, writer, lecturer, friend, church member, school board committee member, officer of a professional organization, and library volunteer. Each role we assume, each person we come in contact with, makes some impact, no matter how minor, on how we develop. Each stage of development is unique in its own right, even as it grows out of the previous stage, and bears on the next one.

I wrote *Human Growth and Development* to address these various dimensions of the lifespan. I organized the text chronologically, encompassing the physical, cognitive, and psychosocial components of development in each stage. I prefer this approach because studying each developmental stage naturally leads to a holistic discussion of humankind. Similarly, I explored the growing research literature on humor, not just because it is interesting and new, but because the development of humor marks us so distinctly as human beings.

Two special devices have been included in the various chapters that encourage the student to view human development in a more personal manner. "Critical Issues" encourage students to think about issues that are interesting to researchers and to all of us, such as Infant Mortality; Is Day Care Harmful to Infants?; Television; Adolescent Homosexuality; Teen Employment; Premenstrual Syndrome; Elder Abuse, and so on. "Human Development in the News" takes human development out of the ivory tower by examining the everyday issues that we read and hear about and that are a part of our own lives: Do the Unborn Have Rights?; Curing Cystic Fibrosis; Program Aids Families in Abuse Crisis; Older Workers Good Investment, and so on.

Human development is the most interesting story I know. I hope you agree and I hope you will learn from and enjoy this book as much as I learned from and enjoyed writing it.

● ACKNOWLEDGEMENTS

Writing a text has its own lifespan. To finally produce this book was like giving birth except that gestation for a pregnancy is only nine months whereas the gestation period for this text was six years. During that time many people have provided much support and advice. I would like to thank my former colleagues at Lansing Community College, especially Dr. William Heater and David Novak, who encouraged me to begin this process in the first place. I would also like to thank the many research assistants who did much of my library research over the years, including Helen Hagens, Fran and Brad Wilson, Mary Clissold, and Sue Saguiguit. Barbara Sharp, my step-daughter, willingly learned my word processing program so that she could type several of my bibliographies. I'm deeply indebted to my dear friend Elizabeth Johnston who sacrificed several weekends to critique final revisions of the last few chapters. The copy editor, Susan Baranczyk, was much appreciated and enlightening. The suggestions and critiques from the reviewers have been extremely beneficial in improving my manuscript. Those individuals include:

Julius Gregg Adams, State University of New York, College at Fredonia
William B. Bates, St. Cloud State University
Alice Burnett, Northern Illinois University
Roger V. Burton, State University of New York, College at Buffalo
Charlotte Callens, Prince Georges College
John B. Cannon, University of Lowell
Mary Anne Christenberry, Augusta College
Virgil E. Christensen, Mankato State University
Steve Coccia, Orange County Community College
Marilyn Coleman, University of Missouri–Columbia
Ann Daluiso, Grossmont College
Steven M. Davis, New Mexico Junior College
R. Dale Dick, University of Wisconsin–Eau Claire
Lorraine T. Dorfman, The University of Iowa
Richard Fabes, Arizona State University
Roger W. Fink, Towson State University
Peter Flynn, Northern Essex Community College
Jerry L. Gray, Washburn University
Ruth A. Gynther, Auburn University
Martha Haslam, Laredo Junior College
Thomas M. Hess, North Carolina State University
Frederic E. Keller, Miami-Dade Community College
Joseph C. LaVoie, University of Nebraska at Omaha
John F. Lavach, College of William and Mary
Robert B. McLaren, California State University–Fullerton
David Morrill, University of Southern Maine
Joan S. Rabin, Towson State University
Thomas C. Patton, Graceland College

Jean M. Samii, Saint Francis College
Toby Silverman–Dresner, William Patterson College
Jane A. Simons, Des Moines Area Community College
Beverly A. Slichta, Trocaire College
Patrick S. Williams, University of Houston–Downtown
Dewey Wise, Mississippi Gulf Coast Community College

The editorial staff, Clark Baxter and Nancy Crochiere, at West have been very supportive and their "atta girls" have pulled me through many times. Thomas Modl, production editor, and his staff have been extremely patient and tolerant. I would also like to thank Anne Arnason for her efforts in the marketing area.

My deepest thanks and appreciation go to my husband, Keith, and children, Thad and Seth, for their patience and forbearance throughout this period of our lives. Thanks guys!

Beverly Allred Schroeder

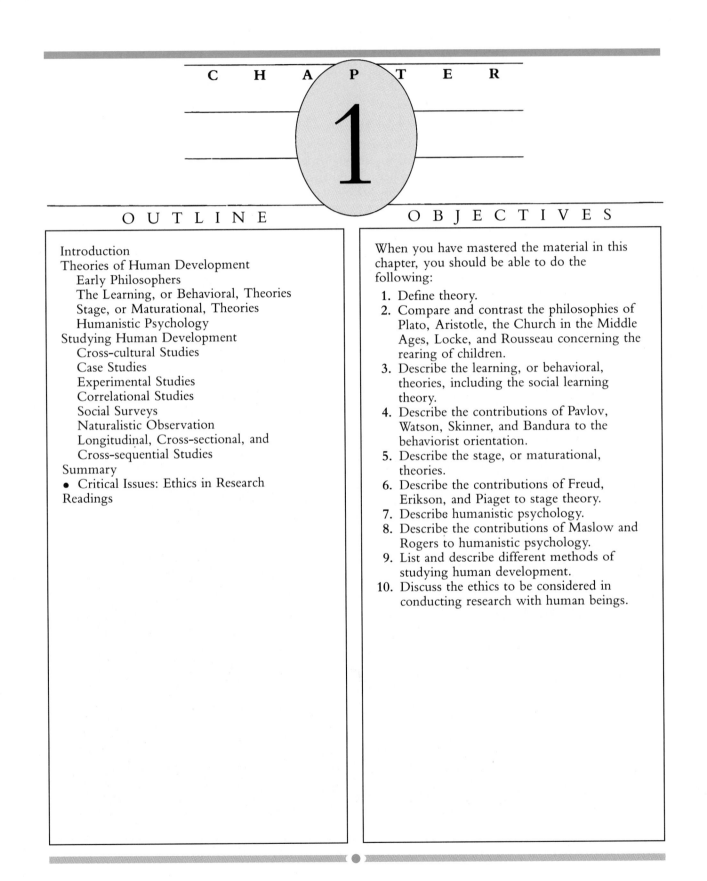

CHAPTER

1

OUTLINE

OBJECTIVES

When you have mastered the material in this chapter, you should be able to do the following:

1. Define theory.
2. Compare and contrast the philosophies of Plato, Aristotle, the Church in the Middle Ages, Locke, and Rousseau concerning the rearing of children.
3. Describe the learning, or behavioral, theories, including the social learning theory.
4. Describe the contributions of Pavlov, Watson, Skinner, and Bandura to the behaviorist orientation.
5. Describe the stage, or maturational, theories.
6. Describe the contributions of Freud, Erikson, and Piaget to stage theory.
7. Describe humanistic psychology.
8. Describe the contributions of Maslow and Rogers to humanistic psychology.
9. List and describe different methods of studying human development.
10. Discuss the ethics to be considered in conducting research with human beings.

The Desire to Know:
Theories and Research
Methods

Development
Those processes in an organism that are biologically programmed as well as those that are influenced and/or transformed by the environment.

The study of human development concentrates on the process and changes that occur from conception through adulthood and dying. Development has been defined as those processes in an organism that are biologically programmed as well as those that are influenced and/or transformed by the environment. Since human development is so complicated and multifaceted, understanding it necessitates a multidisciplinary approach; this encompasses not only psychology but also biology, sociology, history, anthropology, and philosophy. And while each of these disciplines contributes to the understanding of human development, none of them provide a complete picture. Viewing the individual as an ecological system provides further insight when examining the physical, cognitive, and psychosocial developmental areas. Developmental psychologists, who take an ecological approach, consider how human beings adapt to their environments. They focus on how various factors, settings, and contexts influence behavior and development.

● **THEORIES OF HUMAN DEVELOPMENT**

Theory
A logical framework that attempts to explain a broad range of phenomena within a particular science.

Hypothesis
A specific prediction that is derived from a theory and confirmed or disproven by empirical investigation.

A **theory** is a logical framework that attempts to explain a broad range of phenomena within a particular science. It is a way of organizing data, ideas, and hypotheses and a way to guide further research. A theory includes definitions and propositions that attempt to identify interrelationships of variables in a systematic way. In order to test a theory, the scientist must test a **hypothesis,** which is a specific prediction derived from a theory. There are different levels of certainty as to what extent the hypothesis can be supported and, in turn, support the theory.

Theories, even when not formalized or in writing, are entrenched in people's thought processes. Individuals may change their theories when a particular topic is discussed, when a new acquaintance interjects his or her ideas, or when a stimulating book introduces a new perspective on a particular topic. Well-researched, well-documented theories, as well as those that are aesthetically pleasing, are more apt to gain support than those that are poorly constructed or poorly documented.

A theory provides a framework, a way to clarify and organize existing observations, to explain and try to predict. Theories are not mutually exclusive. No theory is totally correct or complete in and of itself. It is not necessary to accept one and reject the others.

Early Philosophers

Plato

Some of the great philosophers have had varying theories on the nature of childhood and how children should be raised. Plato (428–347 b.c.), for example, felt that parents in Athens were morally decayed and unfit to raise children. He thought even admirable and capable individuals could not be trusted to raise future citizens of an ideal state because there were almost as many child-rearing techniques as there were parents. He therefore advocated that all children be separated from their parents early in life and that the state control child rearing and education (a philosophy that has been adopted in some contemporary cultures, such as the Israeli kibbutzim, the Soviet Union, and China). Every infant born in Athens was to have an equal opportunity regardless of social and economic position and sex unless he or she was a slave. Plato felt that both boys and girls should be able to attend school and have the same basic education.

Aristotle

Aristotle (384–322 B.C.), a disciple of Plato, thought education should be arranged to fit different personalities. He disagreed with Plato regarding state control of child rearing, which he felt was appropriate only for future leaders. He also felt that the family provided personal and social stability and that the privacy of home life should be encouraged. Different child-rearing techniques would be advantageous, because no single parenting technique seemed likely to be effective with all children.

The Church in the Middle Ages

During the Middle Ages, approximately the fifth to thirteenth centuries A.D., the Bible was the basis for the discussion of behavior and development in Western civilization. The interpretation by the leaders of the Church was that human beings were born sinful and wicked, so children's misbehavior was due to innate wickedness.

During the Middle Ages, childhood was not seen as a distinct period of life. Children were considered infants until five to seven years of age; then they became adults. No separate world of childhood existed. Children were viewed as small adults. This is illustrated in the artwork of the period, in which children are depicted in adult-style clothes with adult facial expressions and adult physical proportions (Aries 1962).

Until the eighteenth century, children were often viewed as small adults and were depicted in artwork with adult-style clothes, adult facial expressions, and adult physical proportions.

During this same period, the infant mortality rate was very high due to medical ignorance, poor health practices, neglect, harsh treatment, and infanticide. Because infant deaths were so common, parents did not allow themselves to become attached to their infants (de Mause 1974). The standard of living was very low, with a great deal of competition for food and shelter. The weak and helpless, including infants, could not compete successfully. Often female infants and infants who were deformed or illegitimate were put out to die. The practice of infanticide continues to the present day in some cultures (de Mause 1974).

Wealthier families sent infants to live with a wet nurse or hired one to live with them. The wet nurses took care of the infants the first two to five years of life. They not only breastfed the infants but also chewed their food for them later on (de Mause 1974).

During the mid-1700s across Europe, the emerging medical profession helped the mortality rate drop. The death rate went from about 400 deaths per 1000 births to less than 25 deaths per 1000 births. Mothers were encouraged to feed newborns only milk rather than the traditional butter and sugar, oil, boiled bread, gruel, or wine. By the late 1700s, philosophers initiated an active concern in the developing child, which contributed to a change in the perceived role of the child (de Mause 1974).

Locke

The philosophy of John Locke (1632–1704) was widely discussed in the mid-to-late 1700s. Locke said that children were essentially the same as adults and were governed by the same laws of association in learning. A newborn infant, said Locke, was like a blank slate, a *tabula rasa*. All ideas and learning came from the environment, which included experience and observation. Locke did believe that each child was born with a different personality and intelligence

John Locke

than other children, but he emphasized the role of the parent in teaching the child. He rejected the idea that children were born with knowledge. He saw *nurture,* or external forces, as the most important force in development (Locke 1964).

Locke opposed physical punishment as a method of teaching. Instead, he advocated praise and commendation; that is, praise children for good behavior—in order to reinforce that behavior—and ignore rather than punish bad behavior.

Rousseau

In the mid-1700s Jean-Jacques Rousseau (1712–1778) wrote *Emile,* one of the most notable philosophic discussions of children. While Locke emphasized nurture as the most important force in development, Rousseau emphasized the importance of *nature,* or internal forces. He saw children as natural in the sense that they would develop according to their own inner, inborn nature. This philosophy was in direct opposition to the "original sin" theory still adhered to by the Church (that is, that everyone was born evil). He even felt that the child's development would be better left alone than if adults meddled in it.

Jean-Jacques Rousseau

Rousseau thought education should foster children's natural goodness. Parents and teachers were to observe children closely and fit education to them, not attempt to force them to learn what was beyond them. He believed children learned through their own experience and only when they felt like learning. If children were screened from the negative aspects of society, thought Rousseau, their natural goodness assured that they would make wise choices about what they should learn (Rousseau 1965). It is important to note that Rousseau did not practice what he preached. His own illegitimate children were ignored by him and sent to orphan asylums.

Locke and Rousseau were the first scholars who recognized the importance as well as the uniqueness of childhood. Their views first raised the question of whether nurture or nature is primarily responsible for the shaping of development. The writings of Locke and Rousseau provide the roots of two major orientations that continue to emerge in contemporary theories of human development: the learning, or behavioral, theories (nurture) and the stage, or maturational, theories (nature). The Lockean view, with the emphasis on nurture, supports the learning theories, and the view of Rousseau, with the emphasis on nature, supports the stage theories.

Learning, or Behavioral, Theories

The **learning, or behavioral, theories** of development emphasize the importance of learning and the modifiability of the course of development. Objectively observable behavior is emphasized rather than inner mental experiences. **Behaviorism** focuses on the environment as a determinant of human and animal behavior. This environmentalist orientation is apparent in the work of men like Pavlov, Watson, Skinner, and Bandura (who is not a strict behaviorist). There are some major differences between these theorists, but they all support the environment as the major determinant in human learning and behavior.

Behaviorists believe that the laws of human behavior must be demonstrated scientifically. When looking at and studying human beings, they see the same laws working for everyone, from the fetus to the octogenarian. The basic laws of learning theory explore the relationship between one event and another, or

Learning theories
Theories of development that emphasize the importance of learning and the modifiability of the course of development.

Behaviorism
A learning theory that focuses on the environment as a major determinant of human and animal behavior.

between stimulus and response. Behaviorists attempt to control or modify behavior by manipulating the environment in some way. They believe that by objectively studying environmental stimuli and the resultant responses of a person to that stimuli, it is possible to understand that person and even predict his or her responses.

Pavlov

Ivan Pavlov (1849–1936), a Russian physiologist, introduced the idea of changing behavior through **classical conditioning,** a process of association between one stimulus and another. According to classical conditioning, after a neutral stimulus is paired with an *unconditioned stimulus* a number of times, learning takes place: the neutral stimulus becomes a *conditioned stimulus*. At that point the conditioned stimulus by itself will bring about the response that was once made only to the unconditioned stimulus. An association has been made between the two stimuli, and the response, which was at first an *unconditioned response,* has become a *conditioned response.* For example, using classical conditioning, Pavlov trained a dog to salivate at the sound of a bell (a neutral stimulus). After hearing the bell with every presentation of food over an interval of time, the dog eventually associated the sound of the bell with the arrival of food; and whenever the dog heard the bell, it began salivating in anticipation. The sound of the bell was the conditioned stimulus; the food was the unconditioned stimulus. In Pavlov's experiment, the salivation, which at first was an unconditioned response to the food that followed the ringing bell, became a conditioned response to the ringing bell all by itself.

Watson

John Watson (1878–1958), an American behaviorist, saw conditioning as a basis for most of human learning. He illustrated this in his and Raynor's now

Classical conditioning
According to Pavlov, learning whereby a neutral stimulus elicits a certain response by repeated association with another stimulus that already elicits that response.

Pavlov, a Russian physiologist, and his dogs. Pavlov demonstrated classical conditioning by training dogs to salivate at the sound of a bell.

classic study with a nine-month-old boy named "Little Albert" in 1920 (Watson and Raynor, 1920). Albert was conditioned to fear a white rat. Prior to conducting the study, Watson and Raynor first established that he was not afraid of the rat and would play with it. They also established that he was afraid of a loud clang produced by hitting a bar with a hammer. In order to condition Albert, a white rat (conditioned stimulus) was paired with the loud noise (unconditioned stimulus). Each time Albert touched the rat, the bar was struck with the hammer. After seven pairings, Albert would cry when the rat was presented. Albert had *learned* to fear the white rat. His fear also generalized to other white furry objects, such as a white rabbit and a Santa Claus beard. Unfortunately, before the researchers could extinguish Albert's fears through conditioning, his mother took him away.

Watson was not interested in the basic nature of children. His major philosophy of child rearing was expressed by the term *habit training*. As far as he was concerned, a child's total personality was essentially the outcome of the conditioning experiences unique to that child. Watson criticized sentimentality and encouraged objectivity, which is illustrated by the following statement:

> There is a sensible way of treating children. Treat them as though they were young adults. Dress them, bathe them with care and circumspection. Let your behavior always be objective and kindly firm. Never hug and kiss them, never let them sit in your lap. If you must, kiss them once on the forehead when they say good night. Shake hands with them in the morning. Give a pat on the head if they have made an extraordinarily good job of a difficult task. Try it out. In a week's time you will find how easy it is to be perfectly objective with your child and at the same time kindly firm. You will be utterly ashamed of the mawkish, sentimental way you have been handling it. (Watson 1928)

Granted, the lack of affection towards children advocated by Watson is no longer supported by most researchers and child development specialists today. He asserted that environmental conditioning insured the child's learning and development, and he gave the parents complete responsibility for their children's behavior. Watson's ideas about parents' responsibilities are now seen as unrealistic. Children are not considered just the products of their parents' training. Despite his controlled demonstrations, most of Watson's suggestions were based on his personal philosophy rather than empirical studies. However, his work did make us aware of the need to study children objectively and of the vital role of learning processes in shaping a child's development.

Skinner

In the 1950s, another American behaviorist, B. F. Skinner (1904–1990), developed a more sophisticated version of behaviorism than the concept developed by Watson. Skinner popularized the concept of **operant conditioning.** Operant conditioning is a process in which a voluntary response is more or less likely to occur depending on the consequences. An animal or human being learns that a particular behavior produces a particular response and then performs that behavior to achieve that response. A behavior may lead to one of three possible consequences; neutral, reinforcement, or punishment.

The *neutral* consequence neither increases nor decreases the probability that the behavior will occur again.

In *reinforcement,* a reinforcer increases the probability of the behavior it follows. Reinforcers are similar or roughly equivalent to rewards. Any stimulus is a reinforcer if it strengthens the preceding behavior. It can be positive or

Operant conditioning
According to Skinner, a process in which a voluntary response is more or less likely to occur depending on the consequences.

● FIGURE 1.1
Classical Conditioning
Pavlov introduced the idea of changing behavior through classical conditioning, a process of association between one stimulus and another.

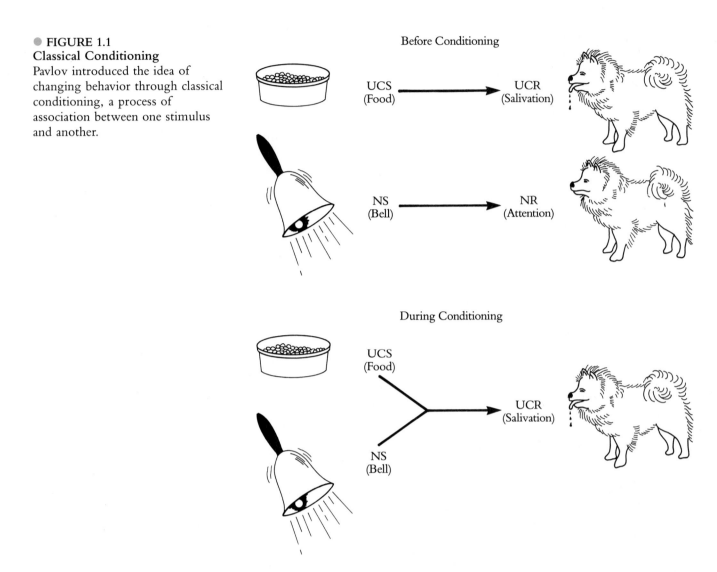

Before Conditioning

UCS (Food) ⟶ UCR (Salivation)

NS (Bell) ⟶ NR (Attention)

During Conditioning

UCS (Food)
NS (Bell) ⟶ UCR (Salivation)

After Conditioning

CS (Bell) ⟶ CR (Salivation)

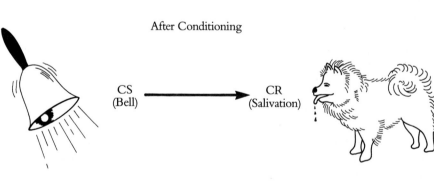

UCS = Unconditioned Stimulus   NR = Neutral Response
UCR = Unconditioned Responses   CS = Conditioned Stimulus
NS = Neutral Stimulus   CR = Conditioned Response

negative. A positive reinforcer is pleasant, such as a hug for setting the table or an *A* for an excellent report. A negative reinforcer involves removing an unpleasant stimulus as a result of a particular behavior. For example, when a keynote speaker's anxiety is reduced by extra preparation, the reduction of anxiety is a negative reinforcer.

Punishment, the third type of consequence, is an unpleasant event that makes the behavior less likely to be repeated. A punisher may be any unpleasant stimulus or event, such as grounding a twelve-year-old for not obeying curfew (Skinner 1953).

These principles of learning are applied in **behavior modification.** This approach is applied to the problem of altering maladaptive behavior or teaching people new responses. Behaviorists believe that maladaptive behavior is learned the same way that normal behavior is learned. Thus the best way to eliminate an unwanted behavior is usually to stop reinforcing it. Behavior modification may also involve deliberate intervention in the form of reward or punishment (Wolpe 1973, 1981). For example, autistic children who have never spoken before have learned a vocabulary of several hundred words through the operant conditioning technique of positive reinforcement (Lovaas 1977). Other individuals have learned to quit smoking and nail biting or have learned better study habits or how to play the piano by using behavior modification techniques.

Behavior modification
A behaviorism-based technique for eliminating or changing specific behavior.

Bandura

Albert Bandura (1925–   ) supported Skinner concerning the potential value of applying principles of operant conditioning to human behavior, but he was bothered by Skinner's emphasis on external control. Bandura's views represent the **social learning theory,** that is, the theory that learning results from social interaction. Although social learning theory has grown out of behaviorism, it has moved a long way from other behaviorist viewpoints. Bandura believed that behaviorists overemphasized manipulative control, because they assumed that reinforcement influenced behavior without the conscious involvement of the individual (Bandura 1977). The principles of classical and operant conditioning contribute to the understanding of how humans adapt themselves to their environment through modifying their behavior. However, these principles fail to explain many other changes in behavior that result from social interaction with people. This is where social learning theory fills in the gap.

Social learning theory
The theory that learning is a result of social interaction, including observing and imitating others.

Bandura and Walters (1963) argue that personality is dependent on the context in which behavior is originally learned and on the current situation. Principles of social learning include *observational, or vicarious, learning*, that is, learning by watching what others do and what happens to them when they do it, and *self-reinforcement,* that is, rewarding oneself for reaching a goal or punishing oneself for failing to do so.

Most of the behavioral theories are based on animal studies, while Bandura based his theory on human behavior that involved, at its core, human cognitive processes. Bandura postulated that an individual's cognitive processes take a central role in regulating learning, rather than human learning and behavior being at the mercy of external stimuli. The cognitive processes he refers to are simply those intellectual processes that involve awareness, learning, mental development, and perception. The mental, or cognitive, operations regulate what children attend to, how they describe or think about what they see, and whether they repeat it to themselves and lodge it in memory (Bandura 1977).

Social learning theory views the individual as approaching, exploring, and dealing with things that are perceived as being within his or her ability. The individual learns to avoid things that seem stressful or beyond his or her capabilities. The social learning theorists stress that other people play a primary role in a child's development. What those others do and say and the way they behave become sources of information for the child. The child uses this information in making judgments and in creating expectations about himself or herself and the world.

In social learning theory, much of human behavior stems from observation and imitating the behavior of others. For children, models can include parents, siblings, television, peers, historical figures, media personalities, and characters portrayed in children's literature. Bandura (1977) stresses that children learn new responses from watching a model and imitating any behavior they see rewarded and avoiding any they see punished. But learning from a model is not simply imitation. A cognitive process is taking place. Children as well as adults, when watching others, form concepts about possible behavior, and these concepts will later guide their own actions. As they experience their own actions and observe the consequences, they can change their concepts and act in different ways.

Bandura and his colleagues (Bandura, Ross, and Ross 1963) illustrated this process in their study on imitation and aggression with preschoolers. In their now classic study, they showed each of four groups of three- and four-year-olds a film. The researchers showed one group of children a man and another group a woman who were punching, hitting, yelling at, and hammering a large inflatable rubber clown. They showed the third group of children a cartoon in

Bandura and his colleagues illustrated how preschoolers imitated aggression they saw perpetrated against an inflated "Bobo" doll.

Helen Keller

Helen Keller (1880–1968) was a bright normal child who began walking at twelve months of age and began talking at a fairly young age. When she was 19 months old she suffered from a high fever that almost killed her and, in its wake, left her blind and deaf. Her family did not know how to deal with her. Her inability to communicate and her baffled attempts to deal with her world frustrated her and led her to throw uncontrollable violent tantrums. The tantrums became more frequent as she got older. She later talked about that period as her "prison house." Fortunately, when she was seven years old her parents engaged a teacher, Anne Sullivan, who had been trained at the Perkins Institute for the Deaf and the Blind. Miss Sullivan had been nearly blind until she was 15 years old, but eye surgery had restored her vision. While a student at Perkins she learned the manual alphabet from some the deaf students. After graduating from Perkins, she went to Alabama to work with Helen Keller.

At first the situation between teacher and pupil did not go well. Helen quickly imitated the manual hand signs that Sullivan spelled in her hand, but she did not connect them with the object that they symbolized. She thought finger spelling was just a game and she soon tired of it since she saw no point to it. The situation worsened because Helen's family indulged her slightest whim and let her do what she pleased. She had no limits. Cooperation almost ceased and no progress was made. Miss Sullivan persuaded the Kellers to let her take Helen to a little garden house a quarter of a mile from the family home. She wanted to gain Helen's cooperation and to teach Helen how to trust and obey her in order to get Helen to focus on learning rather than fighting. It worked for awhile. However, the family did not like the separation and had them move back within a month. After they moved back, the family again indulged Helen's every whim and the battles began again. During this time Miss Sullivan continued to hand spell and place objects in Helen's hand, even though Helen indicated no sign of associating a connection between an object and the name that was immediately spelled in her hand. Two weeks after they moved back into the house, a landmark breakthrough occurred. They were walking past the well-house while someone was pumping water. Sullivan put Helen's hand under the spout and spelled "water" in her hand, just as she had done so many times in other situations.

However, this time was different! Helen remembers it this way:

> As the cool stream gushed over one hand, she (Miss Sullivan) spelled into the other the word "water," first slowly, then rapidly. I stood still, my whole attention fixed upon the motions of her fingers. Suddenly I felt a misty consciousness as of something forgotten—a thrill of returning thought; and somehow the mystery of language was revealed to me. I knew then that W A T E R meant the wonderful cool something that was flowing over my hand . . . I left the well-house eager to learn. Everything had a name, and each name gave birth to a new thought. As we returned to the house every object which I touched seemed to quiver with life. (Lash, 1980, p. 55)

This marked the beginning of Helen Keller's education. She became the first blind and deaf person to successfully pursue a higher education.

Helen Keller's learning process is not unique, but it is more obvious because she had to overcome her handicaps. What form of learning theory did Anne Sullivan use to teach Helen Keller? Classical conditioning? Operant conditioning? Behavior modification? Social learning?

which a cat punished, hit, and hammered the clown. The final group were shown no aggressive model at all. All of the children were then given attractive toys to play with, and shortly thereafter the toys were removed. After a period of time the children were allowed to play with a set of toys that included the large inflatable rubber clown. The children from the first three groups imitated the aggressive behavior they had viewed earlier. The children who had not seen any aggressive acts were far less aggressive than those children who had seen the aggression. Among the children who had seen the human actors, the girls were more likely to imitate the adult female's aggressive acts, and the boys were more likely to imitate the adult male's behavior. The greatest number of aggressive acts came from those children who had viewed the cartoon. Therefore, according to social learning theory, such acts arise from a stored cognitive representation of earlier observed behavior.

In summary, the theories of Locke, Pavlov, Watson, Skinner, and Bandura represent an orientation in which external influences and stimuli are viewed as the major contributors to human learning and development.

Stage, or Maturational, Theories

Rousseau's writings mark an introduction to the second major category of theories dealing with human growth, the **stage, or maturational, theories.** In this view human beings are not simply blank slates when they come into this world but instead are born with certain innate characteristics. While outer forces are the determining factors to the behaviorists, the stage theorists stress the internal, self-directing quality of a child's maturation. The environment still plays a part in molding a child, but it is not totally responsible. This orientation stresses that human development is an orderly progression through a series of predictable changes, which in turn lead to characteristic ways of dealing with experiences at various ages. In the twentieth century this orientation is supported by the research of Freud, Erikson, and Piaget.

Freud

Sigmund Freud's (1856–1939) major aim was to clarify understanding of the adult personality by tracing development from early childhood. Freud saw the child developing through a series of conflicts stemming from within his or her own nature. He developed an extensive and elaborate theory of the nature of human personality based on fundamental instincts and drives. He postulated that the personality has three components: *the id, the ego, and the superego.*

Unconscious impulses, sexual impulses, the hunger drive, and aggressive urges are housed in the **id.** The id strives for immediate gratification. For example, the toddler in the grocery store who wants a candy bar "right now!" is all id.

The **superego** is the moral arm of the personality. According to Freud, the superego functions as a watchdog, preventing the dominant id within us from motivating us toward socially unacceptable behavior. It sits in judgment on the activities of the id, encouraging good feelings when something is done well and encouraging miserable feelings when the rules are broken. The superego represents religious teachings, moral standards, and the ethics and mores of our parents and culture. It supposedly develops slowly over the course of one's childhood and adolescence.

Between the id and the superego is the **ego.** Freud saw the ego as the reality component of the personality. It functions as the referee between the id's desire for immediate gratification and pleasure and the demands of society (Freud 1938). Freud felt that these three personality components, and the way they balance and counterbalance each other, become established by the end of adolescence.

Another component of Freud's theory is the sequential, or stage, component of development. Its central emphasis is the pattern or progression of the organism through different and increasingly adaptive developmental stages called **psychosexual stages.** Freud proposed that the onset of each psychosexual stage and some forms of behavior occurring in each stage are controlled by maturational factors. Freud's proposal of developmental stages was the first theoretical attempt to describe developmental change as an orderly and predictable process combining maturational and environmental influences. The most

Maturational theories
See Stage theories.

Stage theories
Theories that emphasize the internal, self-directing quality of an individual's maturation, with sequential steps of development that form a logical hierarchy with one another.

Id
According to Freud, the part of an individual's personality that houses unconscious impulses, sexual impulses, the hunger drive, and aggressive urges.

Superego
According to Freud, the portion of one's personality that represents religious teachings, moral standards, and the ethics and mores of our parents and culture.

Ego
According to Freud, the rational, reality component of the personality, which coordinates the impulses from the id and the societal pressures imposed by the superego.

Psychosexual theory
Freud's theory of human personality development, which is based on fundamental instincts and drives. It involves three components of the personality (the id, ego, and superego) and five developmental stages (oral, anal, phallic, latency, and genital).

significant aspect of Freud's theory was the assumption that the early stages provided the foundation for adult behavior.

The first psychosexual stage, the **oral stage,** marks the first year of life. The primary focus of stimulation during this period is the mouth and oral cavity. Oral stimulation is received through eating, sucking, mouthing, and biting. According to Freud, people who remain fixated at this stage, as adults, may seek constant *oral gratification* through smoking, drinking, and/or overeating.

The second psychosexual stage of development, which lasts roughly from the second to the fourth year, is the **anal stage.** There is a heightened sensitivity to the stimulation of the mucous membrane surrounding the anal area of the body. The major issue then becomes the control of the expulsion or elimination of fecal material, a lesson in self-control that the child learns during toilet training. It is during the anal period that the child confronts the need for conformity to social expectations. According to Freud, people who remain fixated at this stage may become *anal retentive,* holding everything in, obsessive about neatness and cleanliness. On the other hand, they may become just the opposite, *anal expulsive,* which is messy and disorganized.

Freud's third stage, the **phallic, or Oedipal, stage,** occurs roughly between the fourth and the sixth year. Psychic energy is invested in the genitals, and pleasure is achieved through organ manipulation. Freud's theory holds that the children this age wish to possess the parent of the opposite gender through general affectionate relations and get rid of the parent of the same gender. In other words, they want the parent of the opposite gender to give them *total* attention and affection. By this time the child has a fairly sound identity of himself or herself, with the realization that he or she is biologically and psychologically separate from others. He or she is not only facing increased conflicts with the parents but is also establishing gender-role identity.

The **latency stage,** beginning around age seven, involves the inhibition or nonrecognition of the sensitivity of the erogenous zones, with sexual feelings subsiding. Much of the energy formerly invested in sexual desires is displaced or channeled to other behaviors. The individual's development seems to slow down. Energy is now focused on developing affection for the parents and on the establishment of social ties with children of the same gender.

The **genital stage** is synonymous with adolescence and begins at puberty. It marks the beginning of mature adult sexuality. Sexual energy is located in the genitals and is eventually directed toward sexual intercourse. When the genital period ends, the mature adult personality has been set in place. Changes in personality structure are difficult to achieve after this point.

Freud's theory has had mixed reviews over the years. There are very few true Freudians anymore, and many of his supporters have modified his original theory. However, Freud has made many contributions to our understanding of human development. He noted that unconscious motives affect our behavior and that we use defense mechanisms to avoid conflicts. **Defense mechanisms** are thought patterns that distort one's perceptions in order to avoid unbearable inner conflicts. He also proposed the idea that certain aspects of human development occur in predictable stages. One of the major disadvantages of his theory is that it is difficult or impossible to test many of the ideas in psychoanalysis. The observations are descriptive and poetic rather than scientific. Many of his ideas about unconscious motivations are impossible to confirm or disprove. It cannot be denied, however, that Freud left a powerful legacy to psychology.

Oral stage
Freud's first stage of psychosexual development, in which the primary focus of stimulation is the mouth and oral cavity. This stage lasts from birth to one year.

Anal stage
Freud's second stage of psychosexual development, in which there is a heightened sensitivity to the stimulation of the mucous membrane surrounding the anal area of the body. This stage lasts roughly from the second to the fourth year.

Phallic stage
Freud's third stage of psychosexual development, sometimes called the *Oedipal stage,* in which psychic energy is invested in the genitals and pleasure is achieved through manipulating the genitals. This stage lasts roughly from the fourth to the sixth year.

Latency stage
Freud's fourth stage of psychosexual development, in which sexual feelings subside as the child attempts to resolve the Oedipal conflict. This stage begins around age seven.

Genital stage
Freud's fifth stage of psychosexual development, which is viewed as synonymous with adolescence. It marks the beginning of mature adult sexuality.

Defense mechanism
A thought pattern that distorts one's perception in order to avoid an unbearable inner conflict.

Sigmund Freud

Psychosocial theory
Erikson's theory of human development, which encompasses the social, cultural, and sexual aspects of development.

Trust vs. mistrust
Erikson's first psychosocial crisis, during which the infant will either establish a sense that the world is a safe place or develop a sense of suspicion and fear of those in his or her environment.

Erikson

Erik Erikson (1902–   ) a protégé of Freud, developed an elaborate, life-spanning **psychosocial stage theory.** Erikson placed a much greater emphasis on social and cultural forces than did Freud. He proposed that the way in which individuals cope with their social experiences shapes their life. According to this theory, individuals cross eight different conflict or crisis points over the span of their life. These crises points or conflicts must be resolved in order for healthy development to occur.

Erikson perceived that the first major conflict faced by an individual occurs during his or her first year. That initial conflict is the establishment of **trust** rather than **mistrust.** Parents must maintain an environment that is consistently supportive, nurturing, and loving so that the child develops basic trust. The consistency makes it possible for the infant to predict responses to needs and to develop trust in the parents. If the care of the infant is inconsistent, rejecting, and inadequate, over a period of time the infant will develop a sense of mistrust. This mistrust will create an attitude of suspicion and fear toward other people and toward the self. It will delay or prevent cognitive development and the achievement of future stages of psychosocial development.

If the sense of basic trust has been established, the child must develop autonomy, in order for healthy ego and personality development to continue. This is the beginning of the second psychosocial conflict, **autonomy versus**

shame and doubt, which develops between the ages of one and three. Children during this period begin to learn independence, which represents the will of the children to be themselves. The self-control learned during this time can provide a long-term sense of pride. If parents or caregivers are overcontrolling or non-supportive, the children may feel a loss of self-control involving a sense of shame and compulsive doubt about themselves. They will feel they are incapable of doing things by themselves.

Between the ages of three and five, for children who have a sense of basic trust and feel autonomous or competent, the third conflict emerges: **initiative versus guilt.** During this time children learn to initiate activities and enjoy their accomplishments, which enables them to acquire direction and purpose. If initiative is discouraged, they will feel guilty for their attempts at independence.

Erikson's theory holds that the elementary school years, when a child is approximately six to twelve years of age, are crucial for the child's sense of **industry.** This encompasses the ability to master the social skills necessary to compete and function successfully in the society in which the child lives. Cultural expectations take precedence over other needs, with the ability to master certain skills and abilities becoming paramount. Industriousness leads to a feeling of completeness or satisfaction. Children who are not given the opportunity to master their own world or who have their efforts blocked experience a sense of **inferiority,** that is, a perceived lack of importance or inability to deal with the demands of his or her world. The preadolescent child who strives for recognition and is unsuccessful may feel inferior through later stages of life.

Erikson labeled the period during adolescence as **identity versus role confusion.** Adolescents are expected to begin defining their interests in terms of a career, further education, trade skills, and raising a family. Biologically and culturally, this period is recognized as the end of childhood and the beginning of adulthood. Identity, or the definition of self, is perceived as selecting and defining a role and preparing to handle a chosen position. If the environment is not supportive and the adolescent finds it difficult to establish a role, then he or she will develop an ill-defined self-identity, or role confusion. A lack of role definition or role satisfaction may result from pressures to define a role at an early age and/or the inability to resolve previous crises.

Intimacy versus isolation describes Erikson's stage of young adulthood. Young adults are expected not only to develop and meet career goals but to establish relationships with others of the same and the opposite sex. The intimacy discussed by Erikson is a general type between people, regardless of gender or personal arrangements. Intimacy represents a commitment on the part of individuals to each other so that a warm and meaningful relationship is established. An individual must have some degree of autonomy and basic trust as well as a sense of identity in order to enter into an intimate relationship. This stage is intertwined with the preceding one (identity versus role confusion) because role confusion can lead to unsuccessful and superficial relationships. When there is little or no intimacy, a sense of ostracism, or isolation, occurs. When feelings are not communicated or shared, a feeling of being left out and low self-esteem result. The inability to develop a close, meaningful relationship results in despair, loneliness, and a form of isolation that sometimes lasts for a lifetime.

The adult who is well on his or her way to a successful career and intimate personal relationships generates plans that define future goals and his or her life role. **Generativity versus stagnation** represents the middle adult stage. Gen-

Autonomy vs. shame and doubt
Erikson's second psychosocial crisis, in which the toddler will either learn independence and pride or feel a loss of self-control involving a sense of shame and compulsive doubt about himself or herself.

Initiative vs. guilt
Erikson's third psychosocial crisis, in which children learn to initiate activities and enjoy their accomplishments, which enables them to acquire direction and purpose. If initiative is discouraged, they will feel guilty for their attempts at independence.

Industry vs. inferiority
Erikson's fourth psychosocial crisis, which occurs during the elementary years. The child either gains confidence to master social skills or perceives a lack of importance or inability to deal with the demands of his or her world.

Identity vs. role confusion
Erikson's fifth psychosocial stage, when adolescents begin defining themselves in terms of social, sexual, and occupational identities or they struggle to identify their role, resulting in an ill-defined concept of their identity.

Intimacy vs. isolation
Erikson's sixth psychosocial crisis, involving young adults forming a commitment to each other so that a warm and meaningful relationship is established. When there is little or no intimacy, a sense of ostracism or isolation occurs, which can lead to unsuccessful and superficial relationships.

TABLE 1.1 Erikson and Freud

PERIOD OF TIME	ERICKSON'S CONFLICTS	DESCRIPTION	FREUD'S STAGES
First Year	Basic Trust vs. Mistrust	Parents and family help the child develop a sense of trust in himself or herself by providing a supportive, nurturing environment.	Oral
1–3 Years	Autonomy vs. Shame and Doubt	As the child develops bowel and bladder control, he or she develops a healthy attitude about being independent. He or she develops a sense of control without a loss of self-esteem. If the child feels his or her attempts at independence are wrong, he or she will develop shame and self-doubt instead of autonomy.	Anal
3–5½ Years	Initiative vs. Guilt	The child discovers ways to initiate actions on his or her own and to acquire direction and purpose in activities. If her initiatives are successful, he or she avoids feelings of guilt.	Phallic
5½–12 Years	Industry vs. Inferiority	The child learns to develop a sense of competency and mastery in intellectual, social, and physical skills. Failure to do so results in feelings of inadequacy and inferiority.	Latency
Adolescence	Identity vs. Role Confusion	The young person must develop a sense of role identity socially, vocationally, and sexually. He or she must develop an integrated image of himself or herself as a unique person. Failure to do so leads to confusion as to who he or she is socially, vocationally, and/or sexually.	Genital
Early Adulthood	Intimacy vs. Isolation	The young adult forms close relationships and friendships with others. He or she is willing to give of himself or herself to another person in an intimate way. Failure to do so leads to isolation socially as well as psychologically.	
Middle Adulthood	Generativity vs. Stagnation	The adult becomes concerned with others and wishes to leave something of himself or herself to future generations. He or she helps and guides children, including his or her own and others. The adult not concerned with others becomes self-centered and stagnates.	
Later Adulthood	Ego Integrity vs. Despair	An elderly adult who can look back on his or her life with a deep sense of satisfaction experiences ego integrity. The individual who looks back on his or her life with disgust and the desire to change how he or she lived will experience a sense of despair.	

erativity emphasizes continuity with the preceding stages as well as with the next generation. Individuals who cannot support this continuity to the next generation may become overly absorbed in self and personal needs while ignoring the needs of others. These individuals become stagnated.

Erikson's final stage is **ego integrity versus despair.** The older person who exhibits ego integrity recognizes that after a lifetime of successfully resolving conflicts, he or she has led a meaningful, productive, and worthwhile life. A healthy individual can look back upon the past years and feel satisfied, regardless of what happened. If earlier crises have been successfully met, the individual finds that life has had meaning, and he or she is able to adjust to the aging process and eventual death. When an individual has not resolved earlier crises successfully, he or she cannot view life in a meaningful perspective. He or she develops a feeling of despair at the realization that there is no time to start a new life and try alternative routes to integrity. The individual realizes that things are not as they should be and that the emptiness he or she has experienced will continue. The older person who experiences a sense of despair is not ready to face death and feels bitter about his or her life.

Erikson built on Freud's insights. However, unlike Freud, Erikson emphasized that the process of personality development occurs throughout the life span. He also had a more optimistic view of human development than did Freud. Freud, who based his theory on his work with patients, was more concerned with pathological outcomes, while Erikson perceived more healthy and positive resolutions to our "identity crises."

Generativity vs. stagnation
Erikson's seventh psychosocial stage, representing middle adulthood. Generativity emphasizes continuity with the preceding stages as well as with the next generation. Those who cannot support this continuity to the next generation may become overly absorbed in self and personal needs while ignoring the needs of others.

Ego integrity vs. despair
Erikson's final psychosocial stage, involving the elderly. The older person who exhibits ego integrity recognizes that he or she has led a meaningful, productive, and worthwhile life. When an individual has not resolved earlier crises successfully, he or she feels a sense of despair and cannot view life in a meaningful perspective. The individual is not ready to face death and feels bitter about his or her life.

Erik Erikson

Piaget

Jean Piaget (1896–1980), a Swiss biologist and psychologist, was also a stage theorist, but his work stresses stages of cognitive development. Piaget's theory concerns the mental operations by which children know and understand their world. Piaget's position is that cognitive, or mental, functions are not separate from the affective, or emotional, nor are they independent of biological and social interaction processes. Mental organization is perceived as undergoing significant changes at key points between infancy and adolescence. The sequences of development are invariant; each person experiences the periods and stages in the same order, even though his or her rate of progress may differ from that of others. The reason is that attainments in any stage are dependent on those achieved in prior stages. The prior achievements are integrated into more complex ways of thinking as development proceeds. Piaget has contributed strategies for observing perceptual and cognitive behavior, as well as a wealth of new supporting research data.

Piaget identified four stages of cognitive development. Although he did not attach ages to his stages, his first stage, **sensorimotor,** encompasses approximately the first two years of life. During this period infants develop concepts through their senses and motor abilities. Their understanding of objects in their world is limited to the actions they can perform on them. Infants learn to make use of the sensations coming at them from the outside world and to integrate these experiences through the manipulation and control of the muscles of their bodies. This stage begins at birth with simple reflexes of the neonate and continues until about two years of age with the beginning of symbolic thought, representing early language acquisition. *Object permanency,* that is, the knowledge that an object still exists when out of sight, is one of the major milestones of this stage.

Children between two and seven years enter the next stage, **preoperational thought.** There are two substages of preoperational thinking: *preconceptual,* at two to four years, in which thinking still lacks the logic of adult thinking and is still based a great deal on sensory experiences, and *intuitive,* at four to seven years, when mental operations are possible but there is an inability to see the principles underlying these operations.

A key part of the preoperational stage is symbolic thought, which involves the child's emerging capability to use symbols, especially language, in his or her thinking. Symbols make it possible to deal with people and things in another time and place. Children use symbols to portray the external world internally, such as talking about or playing with an object and forming a mental image of it.

Preoperational thought has other characteristics, which are often seen as limitations in thinking. One such characteristic is *egocentrism,* the inability to take another person's point of view or to put oneself in another's place. "The way they see it is the way it is." *Irreversible thinking* is the inability to retrace a mental operation. For example, a boy who was asked if he had a brother said yes, but when asked if his brother had a brother, he said no. *Centering* is the process of seeing only one aspect or dimension of a problem at a time. For example, a preschooler has difficulty comprehending that his grandfather can simultaneously be his mother's father. *Transductive reasoning* links an event with another unrelated event, often resulting in erroneous deductions regarding cause-and-effect relationships. For example, a child thought he was responsible for his grandfather's death because he had kicked his grandfather in the shins the week before he died.

The **concrete operational** period occurs from approximately age seven to

---

Sensorimotor stage
Piaget's first stage of cognitive development, in which infants develop concepts through their senses and motor abilities. The understanding of objects in their world is limited to the actions the infant performs on them.

Preoperational thought
Piaget's second stage of cognitive development. The preschool child engages in symbolic thought, which involves the child's emerging capability to use symbols, especially language, in his or her thinking. Preschoolers' reasoning is limited because of egocentrism, transductive reasoning, centering, and irreversible thinking.

Concrete operational stage
Piaget's third stage of cognitive development, in which the elementary-age child can mentally manipulate tangible and concrete information by using logical rules.

CHAPTER 1   *The Desire to Know: Theories and Research Methods*

age twelve. This stage is characterized by the ability to mentally manipulate tangible and concrete information by using logical rules. The concrete operational child now possesses the structures necessary to reverse an operation and is sociocentric as opposed to egocentric. Piaget defined *operation* as "an action that can return to its starting point, and that can be integrated with other actions also possessing this feature of reversibility" (Piaget and Inhelder 1956, 36). The child is aware that others have a perspective on the world that is different from his or her own but may not be aware of what the content of that perspective is. They can solve problems that are abstract to a limited degree, but they are still dependent upon concrete and tangible information to formulate and test hypotheses. They are now capable of understanding *conservation,* that is, the concept that an amount of a substance is not affected by changes in shape or placement.

Piaget's final stage of intellectual development, called **formal operational,** begins at approximately twelve years and includes the adolescent years and beyond. A formal operational child acquires the ability to think logically about abstract propositions and things he or she has not experienced before. He or she is capable of accepting assumptions without any physical evidence to support the assumptions. He or she can develop hypotheses and test them, and is capable of reevaluating and restating the hypotheses if the outcomes of the testing are not congruent with other assumptions. The adolescent in the stage of formal operations now has the ability to consider many different solutions to a problem before acting on any one, which greatly increases the individual's efficiency. The formal operational thinker considers past experiences, present demands, and future consequences (Salkind 1981).

Piaget has made outstanding contributions to our understanding of children's thinking processes. He has insisted that the thought of infants and young children is not a miniature version of adult thought. His theory draws attention to the possibility that an unsuspected order may underlie some aspects of children's intellectual development. Although more recent researchers (Brainerd 1978, 1979; Ashton 1975; Dasen 1977; Flavell 1978, 1982, 1985) question some of Piaget's explanations, they were inspired enough by his work to do the necessary research to gain a better understanding of children's cognitive development. For example, Flavell (1985) feels Piaget may have underestimated the importance of perceptual learning and its role in cognitive growth. Some feel that Piaget underestimated the cognitive capabilities of infants and young children.

Formal operational stage
Piaget's fourth and final stage of cognitive development, in which the adolescent and adult acquires the ability to think logically about abstract propositions and things he or she has not experienced before.

Jean Piaget

Humanistic Psychology

Within the past thirty years **humanistic psychology** emerged in reaction to the two established and dominant psychological traditions of the psychoanalytical and behavior theories. Humanistic psychology stresses the uniqueness of each human being. It supports the idea that each individual has an inner drive to fulfill the best of his or her unique potential. This drive is present at every stage of life. Humanists take a holistic view of growth; they see each person as a whole being, unique and worthy of respect. The two major leaders of the humanistic approach are Abraham Maslow and Carl Rogers.

Maslow

According to Maslow (1908–1970), all humans have basic needs that are arranged in a hierarchy with a lower need having to be satisfied before a higher need could be satisfied. The basic needs are physiological needs, safety or se-

Humanistic psychology
Theory that stresses the uniqueness of each human being and supports the idea that each individual has an inner drive to fulfill the best of his or her unique potential.

curity needs, love and belonging needs, esteem needs, and self-actualization needs. Needs that are not satisfied have the greatest influence on behavior. If a person's lower needs are not met, he or she must spend time and energy to meet them. This process will stunt the normal need for love and self-esteem. However, if the lower needs are met, then the individual has the opportunity to achieve self-actualization (Maslow 1970).

Maslow theorized that once the basic survival needs are met, individuals will be able to show their growth needs for love, self-esteem, and self-actualization. *Self-actualization* is defined as the ultimate goal of human development. A self-actualized person fulfills his or her potential, creating the "actual" or creative self that each person can become. Self-actualized people are spontaneous, creative, ethical, and independent. Many have a few intimate friends with whom they are very close. They are not overly concerned with society's standards but are deeply concerned about other human beings. Maslow noted that they experience moments of great happiness that he calls *peak experiences*. These moments of insight and joy are feelings of harmony with nature, God, and/or other human beings. Abraham Lincoln, Albert Einstein, Jane Addams, and Eleanor Roosevelt were included in Maslow's list of self-actualizers (Maslow 1970).

Maslow (1970) believed that science should direct its efforts toward helping people achieve freedom, hope, strong self-identities, and self-fulfillment. He saw the role of the humanists as constructing a scientific system of values that help people live the "good life." Thus, the humanist approach is less research-oriented, which has drawn much criticism from the other dominant psychological traditions.

● **FIGURE 1.2**
Maslow's Hierarchy of Needs
All humans have basic needs that are arranged in a hierarchy with a lower need having to be satisfied before a higher need can be satisfied.

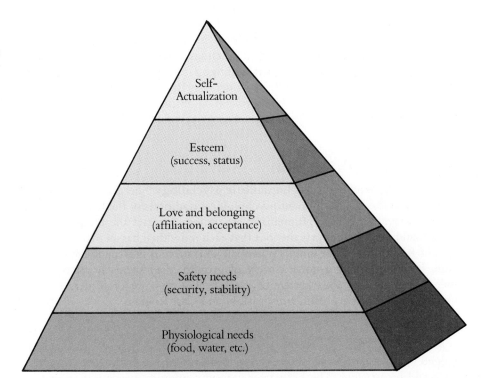

1. Self-actualized persons perceive reality more effectively than most people do and have more comfortable relations with it. They live close to reality and to nature, are able to judge others accurately, and can tolerate ambiguity or uncertainty more easily than others can.
2. Self-actualized persons accept themselves and their various characteristics with little feeling of guilt or anxiety, while at the same time readily accepting others.
3. Self-actualized persons show a great deal of spontaneity in both thought and behavior, although they seldom show extreme unconventionality.
4. Self-actualized persons are problem-centered, not ego-centered, often devoting themselves to broad social problems as a mission in life.
5. Self-actualized persons have a need for privacy and solitude at times and are capable of looking at life from a detached, objective point of view.
6. Self-actualized persons are relatively independent of their culture and environment but do not flaunt convention just for the sake of being different.
7. Self-actualized persons are capable of deep appreciation of the basic experiences of life, even things they have done or seen many times before.
8. Many self-actualized persons have had mystic experiences, such as having felt a deep sense of ecstasy, having felt limitless horizons opening up to them, or having felt very powerful and at the same time very helpless, but ending with a conviction that something significant had happened.
9. Self-actualized persons have a deep social interest and identify in a sympathetic way with humankind as a whole.
10. Self-actualized persons are capable of very deep, satisfying interpersonal relations, usually with only a few rather than many individuals.
11. Self-actualized persons are democratic in their attitudes toward others, showing respect for all people, regardless of race, creed, income level, and so on.
12. Self-actualized persons discriminate clearly between means and ends but often enjoy the means toward their ends more than impatient persons do.
13. Self-actualized persons have a good sense of humor, tending to be philosophical and nonhostile in their jokes.
14. Self-actualized persons are highly creative, each in his or her own individual way. They have "primary creativeness which comes out of the unconscious," and they produce truly original discoveries.
15. Self-actualized persons are capable of great love. They have "peak experiences" and moments of highest happiness and fulfillment, which may come in differing degrees of intensity during various activities, creative activity, aesthetic perception, appreciation of nature, and/or athletic events.

Source: Adapted from Maslow 1970, 149–180.

Rogers

Rogers' (1902–1987) theory of personality is based on the relationship between the self (the conscious view of oneself and the qualities that make up "I" or "me") and the organism (the sum of one's experience, including unconscious feelings, wishes, and perceptions). This relationship is known and felt only by the individual from his or her frame of reference. Fully functioning people experience harmony between the self and the organism. Rogers described these people as trusting, warm, and open to new experiences. Their beliefs about themselves are realistic, and they are not defensive or intolerant.

Rogers believed that unconditional positive regard from significant others helps people become fully functioning. As a result of this process, they learn to accept themselves for who they are. *Unconditional positive regard,* according to Rogers, is the love or support given to another person with no conditions attached (Rogers 1977).

● FIGURE 1.3
Maslow's Fifteen Criteria of Self-actualization

Rogers observed that many children are treated with *conditional positive regard,* that is, "I'll love you only if you do what I want you to do." Adults treat each other this way, too. When people are treated with conditional positive regard, they begin to suppress or deny feelings or actions that they feel are unacceptable to those they love. To suppress feelings and parts of oneself produces low self-esteem, inaccurate perceptions of reality, unhappiness, and defensiveness. One feels "out of touch with their feelings" or that they are "not being true to their real self."

The major criticism of humanistic psychology is that it is difficult to test many of its assumptions because the terms used by humanists are vague. It is difficult to identify a person who is self-fulfilled or self-actualized. Critics also feel that humanistic psychology is closer to philosophy than to science because it views human nature subjectively. It is a more positive view of human nature than other psychological orientations, but it is more difficult to prove.

It should be noted, however, that humanistic psychology has contributed added balance to psychology's view of human nature. Psychologists now look at the happier emotions and positive experiences such as love, creativity, altruism, and cooperation. Stress researchers see humor and hope as having healing powers. Child psychologists note how parental treatment can affect the self-esteem of a child. Crisis counselors use humanistic approaches to help homeless children and adults deal with the resulting loss of self-esteem. Finally, clinical research has found that empathy is a critical factor for successful therapy.

● STUDYING HUMAN DEVELOPMENT

In order to evaluate theories, understand human behavior, and be more critical of research findings, it is necessary to understand the basis of, as well as the methods or techniques of, research. Several methods and approaches to studying human development have emerged. An *experimental study,* which controls conditions so it can rule out all other influences except the one being investigated, is modeled after studies conducted in the physical sciences. **Correlational studies** assess the extent that two or more variables are related. **Naturalistic observation** describes behavior as it occurs in the natural environment, and is modeled after methods used in the biological sciences. *Cross-cultural studies, case studies,* and *interviews and surveys* are more common in sociology and developmental psychology. Regardless of which method is chosen, each has its own strengths and weaknesses.

The hypothesis of the study will help determine which type of study or method(s) will be used. As mentioned earlier, a hypothesis is a guess or prediction that may be confirmed or rejected by empirical investigation.

Cross-cultural Studies

Cross-cultural studies involve the comparison of individuals from two or more cultures. The principle behind these studies is to determine if certain behaviors or traits are a result of culture or of human nature. The answer would make it possible, then, to generalize about human development under different cultural circumstances.

Cross-cultural studies have been used to verify various theories of development, including Piaget's theory of cognition. Researchers and theorists have

Correlational study
A study in which researchers assess the extent to which variables appear to be related in some way. Correlation measures the strength and direction of the relationship between two or more variables.

Naturalistic observation
A research method that involves intense watching and recording of behavior as it occurs in the subject's natural habitat.

Cross-cultural study
A study that involves the comparison of individuals from two or more cultures. The principle behind this type of study is to determine whether certain behaviors or traits are the result of culture or of human nature. The results can make it possible, then, to generalize about human development under different cultural circumstances.

questioned if Piaget's stages and sequences of cognitive development are expressed by children in other areas of the world. Cross-cultural studies indicate that Piaget's stages of cognitive development are universal; however, an individual's experiences will determine the rate at which he or she will progress through these stages (Cole 1983; Rogoff et al. 1984).

Case Studies

The **case study** is a detailed description that focuses on one individual. It may be based on careful observation or formal psychological testing. Its purpose is to accumulate developmental information. Case studies are often used by clinicians who treat individual patients and by academic researchers. Case studies produce a more detailed view of the individual than other methods do.

The baby biography was an early form of the case study. A small number of parents and caregivers over the years recorded the development of their children or charges through observational diaries. One such parent was Charles Darwin, who kept a detailed record of the early behavior of his son, William Erasmus (Doddy). Piaget based his theory of cognitive development on his observations of his own three children. Such records are usually very subjective. They are not generally recognized today as a scientific study because baby biographers were probably influenced by their own expectations and by the fact that they were observing their own children. The individual who is the subject of the case study may be unlike most other individuals, even if from the same socioeconomic or age group. Because case studies must be interpreted in order to be meaningful, it is difficult to know how to choose one interpretation over another.

Experimental Studies

The **experimental method** is probably the most objective research method. It is a carefully controlled method in which the factors that are believed to influence the mind or behavior are controlled. The influential factors, or **independent variables,** are manipulated, and the **dependent variables,** the behaviors that may change due to the influence of the independent variables, are measured. For example, if a researcher hypothesized that violent television (independent variable) caused high levels of aggression (dependent variable) in the play of four-year-olds, she could use an experimental research method. In order to test the hypothesis, two groups of children would need to be selected: one group to view a violent TV show and one to view a nonviolent TV show. The group viewing the violent TV show would be called the *experimental group* because they would be exposed to a specific treatment, the *independent variable*. The children not exposed to violent television would be called the *control group*. Both groups would have to come from similar populations (that is, contain the same mix of sex, age, socioeconomic status, etc.), with the "only difference" between them being the viewing of violent television. After viewing their respective shows, both groups would be observed playing, with aggressive acts and nonaggressive acts being noted. This is the *postexperiment test*. In a well-designed experiment, any differences found between the two groups in the postexperiment test are likely to have been caused by the independent variable, in this case, the viewing of violent television.

Case study
A detailed description that focuses on one individual.

Experimental method
A carefully controlled method in which the factors that are believed to influence the mind or behavior are controlled.

Independent variable
A factor that is manipulated to determine its influence on some behavior of the population being studied.

Dependent variable
A factor that is measured in an experiment and is controlled by one or more independent variables.

Correlational Studies

In a correlational study the researcher assesses the extent to which two or more things, or *variables,* appear to be related in some way. Variables may be age, weight, height, income, IQ scores, number of aggressive acts—anything that can be measured, rated, or scored. The word *correlation* is often a synonym for *relationship,* but technically it is a numerical measure of the *strength and direction* of the relationship between two or more variables.

The two most common kinds of correlation are positive correlation and negative correlation. In a *positive correlation,* the high scores on one variable are associated with high scores on another variable, or the low scores on one variable are associated with low scores on another variable. For example, as a child's height increases so does his weight. In a *negative correlation,* the high scores on one variable are associated with low scores on another variable. For example, the older a car gets, the lower its value.

Correlation ranges from -1.00 to $+1.00$, with $+1.00$ being a perfectly positive correlation and -1.00 being a perfectly negative correlation. Therefore, a correlation of $+0.20$ is a weak positive correlation, while -0.85 is a strong negative correlation. A correlation is considered statistically significant if the relationship between variables is greater than what would occur by chance, even if it is not a perfect correlation. The value of correlation is in the degree of prediction possible, that is, the stronger the relationship, the more likely the variables will occur together. It is important to note that cause and effect can be verified only through experimental designs, not through correlational studies.

Social Surveys

Social survey
A quantitative way of collecting information directly from people. Survey data are usually collected by interview or questionnaire.

The **social survey** method is a quantitative way of collecting information directly from people. Survey data are collected in two major ways: interview and questionnaire. In the interview, a researcher asks prepared questions of a subject and records the answers. In the questionnaire method, a form is sent or given to the subject, who records his or her own answers and then returns the form to the researcher. Surveys have covered many topics, ranging from consumer preferences to sexual preferences. The Gallup poll is probably the most familiar national opinion poll.

The responses to social surveys allow researchers to arrive at broad generalizations about the larger population. However, social surveys have some limitations. The greatest difficulty in using the survey method is getting a sample that is representative of the larger population the researcher wishes to describe. If the survey fails to use proper sampling methods, then the researcher may obtain questionable results. Surveys cannot be used with infants, and only to a limited degree with preschool children. Adults who respond to surveys quite often distort the truth because their self-esteem is threatened, or they answer the way in which they think they are expected to answer.

Naturalistic Observation

Naturalistic observation involves intense watching and recording of behavior as it occurs in the subject's natural habitat. It is of extreme importance that researchers do not disturb or affect the events they are observing. They must remain as unobtrusive as possible so as not to alter the behavior they are observing. In recent years, movie cameras and video cameras have made this more possible. Observing individuals in their natural surroundings allows researchers to observe the natural "stream" of their behavior. For example, many university preschools use hidden cameras to observe socialization interaction patterns (Eubank 1976).

Longitudinal, Cross-sectional, and Cross-sequential Studies

In order to learn about the process and passage of change in human development, two major research methods or designs are used, *longitudinal* and *cross-sectional,* as well as a combination of both called *cross-sequential.*

The **longitudinal method** involves studying the same individuals over a period of time. The same individuals are measured more than once to see the changes that occur with age; these findings are then compared. This type of research allows researchers to learn how early childhood practices may influence the development of the adult, or which human characteristics are constant and which are likely to change. It avoids problems associated with *sample nonequivalence,* that is, comparing different groups of people rather than one original group of subjects. This method also makes the formulation of statements of correlational relationships more certain (Schaie and Hertzog 1982).

Although the longitudinal method has many advantages, it also has some disadvantages. To follow people or a sample over a period of time can be very expensive in terms of time and money. A **sample** is a group of subjects selected from a population for study in order to estimate the characteristics of the population. After a period of time the likelihood of people in the sample dropping from the study increases. Subjects drop out because of death, illness, mobility, loss of interest, or just because they are "tired" of the study. The remainder of people in the sample are likely to be more stable and cooperative than the total group, thus biasing the sample. The longer the study runs, the more likely it is that the staff also will change, thus impairing research continuity. In addition, newer statistical designs or measures make the original design weaker.

An alternative to the longitudinal method is the **cross-sectional method.** This method, which is more common than the longitudinal method, investigates development by comparing different groups of people of different ages simultaneously. These groups of people are similar in all other important ways, such as blend of socioeconomic status, ethnic background, education, and so on. A cross-sectional study involves less time and is less expensive than a longitudinal study. It does not demand continuity or long-term cooperation among subjects or research workers. Careful sampling procedures are necessary, however, to make the successive age levels of different subjects comparable. Comparability is difficult to achieve and is the main weakness of this method. It also neglects the continuity of development that occurs in a single individual.

Cross-sequential research combines the cross-sectional and longitudinal methods (Schaie and Herzog 1985). This method begins with a cross-sectional study, using several groups of people who are different ages. Then, months or years after the original testing, the same groups of people are tested again (just as in the longitudinal study). Simultaneously, a new group of people is tested at each age level in order to control for changes that may have occurred in the original group because of dropping out, because retesting affected their performance, or because their *cohort* had experiences that other cohorts did not. (A **cohort** is people of the same age group who share common experiences or

Longitudinal method
A research method that involves studying the same individuals over a period of time to see the changes that occur with age.

Sample
A group of subjects selected from a population for study in order to estimate the characteristics of the population.

Cross-sectional method
A research method that investigates development by comparing different groups of people of different ages simultaneously.

Cross-sequential research
Research combining the cross-sectional and longitudinal research methods. It begins with a cross-sectional study using several groups of people who are different ages. Then, months or years after the original testing, the same groups of people are tested again.

Cohort
People of the same age group who share common experiences or demographic traits, such as a school class or a whole generation.

FIGURE 1.4
Cross Sectional and Longitudinal Studies
In cross-sectional studies, individuals from different age groups are tested to ascertain how a particular ability or behavior changes. Longitudinal studies follow and test the same individuals over a period of time.

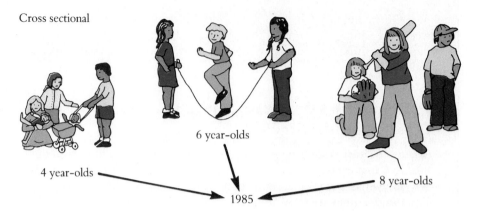

Cross sectional

4 year-olds

6 year-olds

8 year-olds

1985

Investigator assesses all three age groups at one time

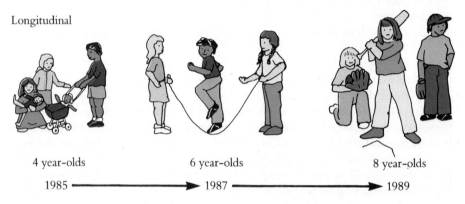

Longitudinal

4 year-olds

6 year-olds

8 year-olds

1985 ———————➤ 1987 ———————➤ 1989

Investigator assesses same children at three different times

demographic traits, such as a school class or a whole generation.) The cross-sequential method has been successfully applied to adult intelligence studies (Schaie 1983) and adult personality studies (Neugarten, Havighurst, and Tobin 1968). Although complicated and expensive, it provides insights that neither the cross-sectional method nor the longitudinal method provides.

Conclusion

In conclusion, psychologists and human development investigators have access to a number of ways to study behavior and development. Each method has its strengths and weaknesses. No one method is perfect. There is a time and place for each one. Access to, and choice of, different methods makes it possible for the investigator to present a convincing case for his or her hypothesis.

S U M M A R Y

- Developmental psychology concentrates on changes that occur from childhood to adulthood and on the processes and events that account for these changes. Development involves orderly sequences of change in the individual, which is dependent on growth and maturation while interacting with the environment.

- A theory is a logical framework that attempts to explain a broad range of phenomena within a particular science. It is a way of organizing data, ideas, and hypotheses and a way to guide further research. A theory includes definitions and propositions that attempt to identify interrelationships of variables in a systematic way.

- Over the centuries, attitudes concerning the child's place in society has moved in cycles. Plato thought that the state should raise children and that boys and girls should have equal education. Aristotle, Plato's pupil, thought parents should raise their own children, with the exception of children who were future leaders. The Bible was the basis for the discussion of behavior and development during the Middle Ages. John Locke (1632–1704) asserted that newborn children were like blank slates (*tabula rasa*) and that children were essentially the same as adults and were governed by the same laws of association in learning. Rousseau (1712–1778) emphasized the maturation and purity of the child.

- The writings of Locke and Rousseau provide the roots of two major theoretical orientations: the learning, or behavioral, theories and the stage, or maturational, theories.

- The theorists associated with behaviorism include Pavlov, Watson, Skinner, and Bandura. Basically, their theories emphasize the importance of learning in development and the modifiability of the course of development. The outside forces in the environment are the total determinants in shaping a child.

- The theorists associated with the stage, or maturational, theories include Freud, Erikson, and Piaget. The stage view stresses the internal, self-directing quality of a child's maturation. This orientation sees human development as an orderly progression through a series of predictable changes, which in turn lead to characteristic ways of dealing with experiences at various ages.

- Humanistic psychology, a "third force" psychology, stresses the uniqueness of each human being and supports the idea that each individual has an inner drive to fulfill the best of his or her potential. Maslow and Rogers are considered the major theorists of this approach.

- Various methods of studying children include cross-cultural studies; case studies; experimental studies; correlational studies; social surveys; naturalistic observation; and longitudinal, cross-sectional, and cross-sequential methods.

- Cross-cultural studies involve the comparison of individuals from two or more cultures. The principle behind these studies is to determine whether certain behaviors or traits are due to the culture or to human nature.

- The case study focuses on one individual.

- In an experimental study, the investigator manipulates one or more variables and then measures the resulting changes in the other variables.

- In a correlational study, the researcher assesses the extent to which variables appear to be related in some way. Variables may be events, scores, or anything else that can be tallied. Correlation measures the strength and direction of the relationship between two or more variables, which allows us to make predictions from one variable to the other but does *not* allow us to make any assumptions about one variable's *causing* the other.

- The social survey is a quantitative way of collecting data through interviews or questionnaires.

- Naturalistic observation involves intense watching and recording of behavior as it occurs in the subject's natural habitat.

- In order to learn about the process and passage of change, two major research methods or designs are used, longitudinal and cross-sectional. The longitudinal method studies the same group of people at intervals over a period of time. The same people are measured more than once to see the changes that occur with age. The cross-sectional method investigates development by comparing dif-

Ethics in Research

The Society for Research in Child Development (1972, 1973) and the American Psychological Association (APA) (1982) state that in studying humans, especially children, the researcher must take into consideration the ethical implications. Because doing research with human beings raises many ethical questions, researchers must balance the quest for knowledge with the rights of the individual. Whether naturalistic observation, case studies, or experimental studies are used, a common element of these methods is that all involve observing human subjects, and some may influence the conditions under which the subjects behave. Some research may be as simplistic as watching how people behave at a sports event or grocery store, while other research involves manipulation such as controlling the type of television adults or children view. Still other research, however, involves more drastic manipulation that can cause subjects to experience fear, stress, or extreme guilt. A research project should not be undertaken unless the investigator determines that the issue to be researched is important for advancing the understanding of behavior or development. No investigator should be allowed to ignore the rights and safety of the subjects involved in the study.

Any research study that involves human subjects is mandated to be reviewed by an independent review board. The approval of the review board is necessary before the research can begin. The responsibility of the review board is to examine the research procedures to ensure that they will not harm the subjects and to ensure that the researcher will use only those subjects who are fully informed and who willingly want to participate. The intellectual, emotional, and physical integrity of the subject must remain intact.

Numerous ethical issues have been identified by human development investigators, and efforts have been made to address them. One such issue is invasion of privacy. Observing people in their daily routine or taking physiological readings in a medical laboratory entails the invasion of privacy of individuals, especially in the case of AIDS patients. Results of such tests made public could lead to ostracism and the loss of a job and insurance benefits. Other sensitive issues have been studied, such as adult sexuality, morality, prejudice, and so on. These areas are regarded by most people as private and therefore not subject to public scrutiny.

How can people's right to privacy be protected? One way is to keep the subjects' names and responses anonymous, so their names or identities are not associated with the data. A second way is to keep the individual responses from being made public, instead, a summary of the results of the study may be published. Finally, informed consent is necessary. An individual should be able to withdraw from a project whenever he or she wishes and may not be forced to give a response. Before they participate, subjects should be told about the procedures to be used in the study. Parents or guardians should be fully informed when children or institutionalized adults are involved.

A second ethical issue involves deception. When is deception justified? Sometimes human subjects figure out the purpose of a study, which in turn can affect their behavior and ruin the study. Therefore, it may be necessary to deceive them. Ethically, if the research does dictate deception, then the investigator must explain this to the subjects after the study is completed. After the explanation is made—including the true nature of the study, the issues being investigated, and why the deception was used—a subject has the right to demand that data be destroyed and not used by the investigator. Critics of the use of deception claim that *debriefing* (that is, telling the subject the true purpose of the study after it is all over) does not always help. Deception deprives subjects of free choice (Baumrind 1985; Goldstein 1981). Under what circumstances should a subject be informed?

A third ethical problem concerns the possible harmful consequences that subjects may suffer as a result of a study. Some psychological studies may leave long-term negative effects on the subjects. In the past, subjects of studies were disillusioned or felt ashamed after they learned unpleasant truths about themselves. For example, in Stanley Milgram's study (1963), subjects found they were capable of administering extremely painful, and probably dangerous, electrical shocks to innocent people whom they did not know. These subjects suffered a great deal of psychological stress. Although they did not actually administer the electrical shocks, they left the experiment with the unpleasant realization that they were capable of hurting another human being just because they were told to do so (Milgram 1963). The psychological distress suffered by the subjects in this study prompted reform measures concerning the ethical responsibilities of researchers involved with human subjects.

Continued

Ethics in Research (continued)

It is difficult to deal with the issue of harmful consequences. The first question an investigator should ask is whether the potential benefits of the study are more important than the risks to the subjects. If the choice is to continue the study, then the subjects need to be informed of what the risks are, and if they decide to continue, the investigator must follow up and examine the subjects for some time after the study to see if they are suffering harmful consequences. Also, what about the control subjects who do not receive the treatment? They should be able to receive any potential benefits offered by the results of the study.

For example, a study has been proposed in which AZT (a powerful anti-viral medication) would be administered to pregnant mothers with AIDS to see if it will prevent transmission of AIDS to the unborn infants. Half of a group of HIV-infected women would receive AZT and the other half would receive a placebo (an ineffective medication) after the 14th week of gestation. This is a controversial study because the drug may have unknown effects on a fetus and because the women and infants in the control group would not receive any potential benefits (Angell, 1991). How else could this study be conducted? The subjects in this case cannot be informed of the possible risks, yet it may save their lives. What about the infants in the control group? Will they be sacrificed because they were not given the AZT at a possible critical period in their development? Are the ethical implications too high to even conduct a study in this manner? Perhaps in some cases other procedures that are not so risky could be used.

ferent groups of people of different ages simultaneously. Cross-sequential study combines the longitudinal and cross-sectional methods. The cross-sequential method begins with a cross-sectional study, using several groups of people who are different ages. Then, months or years after the original testing, the same groups of people are tested again.

READINGS

Appelbaum, M. I. and McCall, R. B. (1983). Design and analysis in developmental psychology. In P. H. Mussen (Ed.), *Handbook of child psychology* (4th ed.), Vol. 1. New York: Wiley.
Excellent reference source. Comprehensive overview of methodology, design, and approaches to special research problems.

Aries, P. (1962). *Centuries of childhood: A social history of family life.* New York: Alfred A. Knopf.
Historical description of childhood and their status in society.

Bandura, A. (1977). *Social learning theory.* Englewood Cliffs, NJ: Prentice-Hall.
Extensive description of the social learning theory.

Borstelmann, L. J. (1983). Children before psychology: Ideas about children from antiquity to the late 1800s. In P. H. Mussen (Ed.), *Handbook of child psychology* (4th ed.), Vol. 1. New York: Wiley.
Comprehensive historical view of children from ancient times until the twentieth century.

Cowan, P. (1978). *Piaget with feeling.* New York: Holt, Rinehart, and Winston.
Well-written, easy to understand overview of Piaget's theory.

Erikson, E. H. (1968). *Identity: Youth and crisis.* New York: Norton.
Full outline of Erikson's eight stages with emphasis on identity development.

Freud, S. (1963). *The sexual enlightenment of children*. New York: Collier Books.
Includes several of Freud's essays. He analyzes sexual implications of fantasies and lies children tell.

Ginsburg, H. and Opper, S. (1979). *Piaget's theory of intellectual development*. Englewood Cliffs, NJ: Prentice-Hall.
Helpful examples of each stage of Piaget's theory of cognitive development.

Hall, C. S. (1979). *A primer of Freudian psychology*. New York: New American Library.
Well-constructed discussion of Freud's theory.

Kessen, W. (1965). *The child*. New York: Wiley.
A history of childhood. A collection of historical original writings of various theorists, philosophers, and psychologists.

Lash, J. P. (1980). *Helen and teacher: The story of Helen Keller and Anne Sullivan Macy*. New York: Delacorte Press.

Maslow, A. (1968). *Toward a psychology of being*. New York: Van Nostrand Reinhold.
An account of human motivation based on observations of a few prominent people.

Miller, P. (1983). *Theories of developmental psychology*. New York: W. H. Freeman.
Overview of the major theories of human development including Piagetian, Freudian, social learning, and psychosocial.

Rogers, C. (1980). *On becoming a person*. New York: Dell.
Human potential from a humanistic therapist's perspective.

Salkind, N. (1981). *Theories of human development*. New York: Van Nostrand.
Discusses major theories of human development including Freud, Erikson, Piaget, Skinner, Bandura, and Gesell.

Schaie, K. W. (1983). *Longitudinal studies of adult psychological development*. New York: The Guilford Press.
Comprehensive and detailed collection of recent longitudinal studies as well as illustrating the use of cross-sequential studies.

Skinner, B. F. (1976). *About behaviorism*. New York: Random House.
Discussion and defense of behaviorism.

Human Development in the News: Women and Research

ANDREW PURVIS

One morning two years ago, a 60-year-old woman in Madison, Wis., asked her doctor what seemed like a simple question. The patient had just reached menopause and wanted to know whether she should start taking aspirin daily. She had seen newspaper and TV reports claiming that the pills lower the risk of heart attacks, and she knew such risks increase dramatically for women after they stop menstruating. "My answer was dead silence," says the woman's physician, Dr. Elizabeth Karlin, who teaches at the University of Wisconsin medical school. A week later, after scouring the literature, Karlin came to what she called an "appalling" conclusion: the finding, trumpeted in some newspapers as a lifesaver for everyone, was based entirely upon research on men. "There were simply no data to say this was safe for women."

Karlin had discovered an information gap that may be endangering millions of American women. A number of treatments now recommended for men and women—from cholesterol-lowering drugs and diets to AIDS therapies and antidepressants—have been studied almost exclusively in men. Little hard evidence exists about their efficacy or safety for women. The problem has begun to concern doctors, patients and now lawmakers. In June Congress's General Accounting Office released a report condemning the National Institutes of Health (NIH) for failing to promote studies that took adequate account of the differences between the sexes. The Congressional Caucus for Women's Issues, which commissioned the study, introduced a $237 million legislative package in July aimed at achieving "parity in medical research." Said caucus co-chair Patricia Schroeder of Colorado: "Doctors aren't getting the kind of guidance they need when they try to prescribe for women."

Medical testing done entirely with male subjects may be adequate when a disease strikes women and men in the same way, but a growing body of research shows that this is often not the case. Some preliminary studies on depression, for example, suggest that hormonal changes in many women may lead to a premenstrual deepening of depression. Further research on appropriate doses of antidepressants throughout the menstrual cycle is needed, says Dr. Jean Hamilton, a Washington-based neuropharmacologist, to determine if female patients are getting adequate medication.

Women's hearts also differ markedly from men's. Not only does cardiovascular disease strike women later in life, but blood cholesterol levels seem to play a somewhat different role in female patients. Dr. John Crouse, a lipids researcher at Bowman Gray School of Medicine in North Carolina, notes that women seem to be less vulnerable than men to high levels of LDL, the so-called bad cholesterol, and more vulnerable to low levels of HDL, the "good" cholesterol. Diets that reduce both levels, such as the one promoted by the American Heart Association, may actually harm women, Crouse argues. The dearth of data on women and heart disease may also have contributed to an alarming problem: women are significantly more likely than men to die after they undergo heart-bypass surgery. One reason, suggested a study last spring, is that doctors are slower to spot serious heart trouble in their female patients and slower to recommend surgery.

Many researchers complain that the billion-dollar federal onslaught on AIDS has also underrepresented women. At a time when women are the fastest-growing group afflicted by AIDS, there are troubling uncertainties about whether treatments or the disease itself are affecting women differently from men. Some studies, for example, have suggested that women with the virus die more quickly than men, and from a somewhat different range of opportunistic infections. "Drugs are developed with incomplete data on metabolic differences between the sexes," charges Congressman Henry Waxman, a major advocate for women's health. "This is not a question of affirmative action. It is a question of well-being."

Why have women been excluded from so many studies? In the case of heart disease, some researchers argue that it is too difficult to find enough subjects with the condition, since it develops later in women. Also, the hormone changes of the menstrual cycle are thought to complicate research, raising costs. Perhaps most important, doctors are worried that if women enrolled in a clinical trial became pregnant, experimental drugs could endanger the fetus.

Critics counter these arguments by asserting that it is worth the trouble and expense of recruiting women research subjects, given that women make up half the population—and half the taxpayers underwriting federal research. Concern for the fetus is often exaggerated, they say. "There is a tendency to think of women as walking wombs," says the University of Wisconsin's Karlin. Most female cardiac patients, she notes, are not planning to get pregnant.

Health concerns that primarily af-
Continued

fect women get particularly short shrift in the research community, many doctors say. Breast cancer, for example, has doubled in incidence since 1960 and is now killing 4,000 women each year. Yet last year the NIH spent just $77 million studying the ailment, including only $16 million on basic research. Two years ago, the NIH halted a major study on breast cancer and low-fat diets because of cost considerations. "I can't believe that decision," says Dr. Mary Guinan, assistant director for science at the Centers for Disease Control. "If we could tell women that their diet lowered their risk, we could save thousands of lives."

Research on contraception and menopause has also failed to garner many federal dollars. Though an estimated one-third of older women are taking hormone-replacement therapy to combat osteoporosis and other effects of menopause, many questions remain about how this treatment might alter the risks of breast cancer and heart disease. Says Guinan: "As doctors, we think we're helping women when we may actually be harming them." Meanwhile, no new contraceptive method has been approved in the U.S. since the 1960s. Overall, the NIH spends only 13% of its $7.7 billion budget on women's health issues, according to the Women's Caucus.

Officially, the NIH has had a policy since 1986 of requiring grant applicants to at least "consider" including women in their research. But that policy has been limply enforced. In September NIH acting director Dr. William Raub set up a special office to explore the problem.

For many experts, though, more study simply means more delay. Raub's likely successor, Dr. Bernadine Healy of the Cleveland Clinic—the first woman recommended to head the NIH—has called for "exercising relentless pressure" on researchers and policymakers to fully represent women in health studies. Until that is accomplished, it seems, doctors will have to decide for themselves which presents the greater risk to their female patients: the disease or a cure proven only for men.

Andrew Purvis, "A Perilous Gap," *Time,* Special Issue, Fall 1990, pp. 66–67.

OUTLINE

Heredity
    Mendel's Principles
    Genes
    Chromosomes
Genetically Unique
Inheritance of Abnormalities
    Dominant Pattern of Inheritance
    Recessive Pattern of Inheritance
    Sex-linked Pattern of Inheritance
    Chromosomal Abnormalities
Genetic Engineering
    Genetic Counseling
    Artificial Insemination
    Embryo Transfer
    In Vitro Fertilization
    Recombinant DNA
Interaction of Heredity and Environment
    Impact on Intelligence
    Impact on Personality
    Impact on Physical Characteristics
    Conclusion
Summary
• Critical Issues: Surrogate Parenting
Readings

OBJECTIVES

When you have mastered the material in this chapter, you should be able to do the following:

1. Describe the two preformationist theories.
2. Describe Mendel's principles.
3. Differentiate between recessive and dominant genes and between heterozygous and homozygous genes.
4. Discuss the function of chromosomes.
5. Describe meiosis and mitosis.
6. Differentiate between monozygotic and dizygotic twins.
7. Describe the rare phenomena of superfecundity and superfetation.
8. Describe each of the following abnormal patterns of inheritance and list examples of each: dominant, recessive, sex-linked, and chromosomal.
9. Define *genetic engineering* and discuss the various forms.
10. Discuss the nature-nurture controversy and the interaction of heredity and environment on intelligence, personality, and physical characteristics.
11. Discuss the issue of surrogate parenting and its impact on the infant and adults involved.

Before We Were Us:
Genetics

HEREDITY

The concept of heredity or genetics is not new. Heritability of physical traits and diseases was noted by early Greek philosophers. Plato argued that babies should be born only to those who possessed the most desirable traits and characteristics. In Sparta, the Greek city-state, soldiers offered their wives to the strongest and most powerful warriors in order that they might bear strong, fierce children (Sussman 1976). Hippocrates (460–377 B.C.), the father of medicine, observed that certain characteristics, such as blue eyes, crossed eyes, baldness, epilepsy, and blinding eye disease, were prevalent in some families but not in others (Nora and Fraser 1974). Aristotle wrote the first treatise on embryology, providing his own theory of genetics. His observations and arguments were so advanced that for nearly two thousand years almost nothing of significance was added. Aristotle was the first to formulate the alternative that either an embryo must be preformed, only enlarging during its development, or it must be actually differentiating from a formless being. He favored the preformed theory, which initiated a controversy that lasted for centuries (Arey 1974).

The invention of the compound microscope, in the seventeenth century, led to the discovery of sperm and ova and sparked Aristotle's controversy once again. Two groups of **preformationists** emerged: the spermists and the ovists. The *spermists* believed that each sperm cell contained a tiny performed embryo that would be nourished by the ovum and would grow only when deposited in the womb. The *ovists* argued that preformed human embryos appeared in the mother's ova, not in the father's sperm. They viewed the sperm cell as nothing more than fertilizer that triggered the growth of an embryo. However, biologists eventually discovered that both parents contribute equally to the creation of a child by passing genes to their offspring. One of the first such biologists was Father Gregor Johann Mendel, an Austrian monk.

Mendel's Principles

Gregor Johann Mendel (1822–1884) provided the world with the foundations of our modern-day understanding of genetics. Mendel formulated the principles of heredity by crossing varieties of peas in his monastery garden. His results were published in 1866 but remained unknown until other biologists made similar discoveries at the turn of the century. Mendel's central thesis was that independent units, which are today called **genes,** determine inherited characteristics and remain constant even when passed from one generation to another. He observed that genes are in pairs, with each parent donating one. Occasionally both genes are alike, but sometimes they are different and one will be **dominant** over the other. For example, in pea plants, the gene for red flowers is dominant over the gene for white flowers. Therefore, if a pea plant has one red gene and one white gene, the flowers will be red. The white gene is **recessive.** Another principle proposed by Mendel states that at the point that *gametes,* or sex cells, are formed in a parent, the pairs of genes he or she is carrying separate from each other (thus the reason why the dominant gene may not appear in each sperm cell or egg cell produced.) The separation is random, so it is impossible to predict if a particular gamete will contain a recessive or a dominant gene. With advances in research, most of Mendel's theory has been confirmed, with the exception that the interaction of dominant and recessive genes may take place in a variety of ways (Arey 1974; Scheinfeld 1972).

Preformationist
A theory in which a human being existed preformed in either the sperm or the ova.

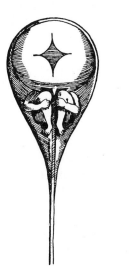

Hartsoeker's sperm cell. The spermists believed that each sperm cell contained a tiny preformed embryo that would be nourished by the ovum.

Genes
Independent units that determine inherited characteristics and remain constant even when passed from one generation to another.

Dominant gene
In a pattern of genetic inheritance, the one of a pair of genes that determines the trait and suppresses the expression of the other gene.

Recessive gene
In a pattern of genetic inheritance, the one gene in a pair of genes that is subordinate to the other, or dominant, gene. Two identical recessive genes must be present in order for a recessive trait to be expressed.

CHAPTER 2   *Before We Were Us: Genetics*

Genes

There are two genes for each human characteristic (one from each parent), each pair carrying identical codes or different codes. Each gene is composed of **DNA (deoxyribonucleic acid),** a complex substance that may assume thousands of chemical structures. The chemical structure of the DNA that makes up a gene is a hereditary code that determines the action or expression of that gene. All humans inherit genes that make them alike for many traits, such as having fingers, toes, and legs. There are different genetic inheritances among individuals for features such as eye color, skin color, hair texture, and blood type. An individual may have two genes with a code to signal the formation of brown eyes, or one gene carrying a code for brown and the other carrying a code for blue, or two genes bearing the code for blue. These gene codes are dominant or recessive. If both genes have a dominant code (i.e., they are **homozygous,** or alike), or if one has the dominant code and the other the recessive code (i.e., they are **heterozygous,** or different), the offspring will have the dominant feature. Therefore, a person with brown eyes may be homozygous for brown eyes. That person would then be both *genotypically* brown-eyed (**genotype** refers to one's genetic makeup for a trait) and *phenotypically* brown-eyed (**phenotype** refers to the visible expression of an inherited trait). Or an individual with brown eyes may be heterozygous for brown eyes. That is, while the phenotype of the genes may be a brown color, the genotype may be recessive and dominant. This means that one of the paired genes may carry a message for blue eye color. The dominant gene cancels out the effect of the recessive gene in the phenotype. The recessive gene remains in the genotype and can be transmitted, unaltered and uncancelled, to offspring. Genetic information determining brown eyes is dominant over such information for blue eyes, but if the combined genes are both recessive (homozygous), then the recessive feature, blue eyes, will appear (Arey 1974).

Chromosomes

Development begins at conception, when a sperm from the father penetrates an ovum from the mother, forming a **zygote.** A normal zygote contains forty-six chromosomes, twenty-three from the sperm and twenty-three from the ovum. The comparable chromosomes of the ovum and the sperm match up with each other and are arranged into twenty-three pairs. Twenty-two pairs of the chromosomes are called **autosomes,** and the twenty-third pair are called **sex chromosomes.** The rod-shaped autosomes contain approximately 20,000 to 100,000 genes, which in turn contain the "blueprints" for the structure and functioning of our bodies. The two types of sex chromosomes are X and Y. Normal females inherit the relatively large X chromosome from each parent. Males inherit an X chromosome from the mother and a smaller Y chromosome from the father. An adult female may transfer only X chromosomes to her offspring. An adult male, on the other hand, may transmit either an X chromosome or a Y chromosome to his offspring, thus determining the sex of the child.

The nucleus of every cell in the human body contains all forty-six chromosomes. We have two kinds of cells: **somatic, or body, cells,** which govern the formation of our bodies (including skin, bones, muscles, and organs) and **gametes, or sex cells,** which are the **sperm** in males and **ova** in females. The primary difference between somatic cells and gametes involves the way they

DNA (deoxyribonucleic acid)
A complex chemical substance found in a gene. It is a hereditary code that determines the action or expression of that gene.

Homozygous
A gene pair that gives the same hereditary directions for a particular trait (for example, either the same two dominant genes or the same two recessive genes).

Heterozygous
A gene pair that give different hereditary directions for a particular trait (for example, one dominant and one recessive gene).

Genotype
An individual's genetic makeup; that is, the totality of the genes inherited from the parent cells.

Phenotype
The visible expression of inherited traits, which depends on the genotype or how the environment has affected the expression of the genotype.

Zygote
A single cell formed from the union of two gametes, a sperm and an ovum. A normal zygote contains forty-six chromosomes, twenty-three from the sperm and twenty-three from the ovum.

Autosomes
The first twenty-two pairs of chromosomes in a human being.

Sex chromosomes
The twenty-third pair of chromosomes in a human being. Two X chromosomes determine a female, and an X and Y combination of chromosomes determines a male.

Somatic cells
Human cells that govern the formation of the human body, including the skin, bones, muscle, and organs.

Body cells
See Somatic cells

Gametes
Human cells that are the sperm in males and ova in females.

Sex cells
See Gametes

Sperm
Male gametes, or sex cells.

Ova
Female gametes, or sex cells.

Meiosis
A form of cell division involved in the production of gametes, or sex cells. Mature gametes, ova and sperm, have only one-half of the normal complement of chromosomes in their nuclei. Gametes undergo a reduction in the number of chromosomes carried in their nuclei so that when an ovum and sperm fuse, there will be forty-six chromosomes.

Mitosis
The process in which somatic, or body, cells divide. All somatic cells in normal human beings contain 46 chromosomes that can be arranged into twenty-three pairs. With fertilization, the comparable chromosomes of the ovum and sperm match up with each other and are arranged into twenty-three pairs of chromosomes. The cells of the embryo, the fetus, and finally the human body will be formed from divisions of this fertilized ovum.

Monozygotic twins
Identical twins, who develop from the same fertilized ovum and thus have the same genotype.

divide and the contents of their nuclei following division. Mature gametes have only one-half of the normal complement of chromosomes in their nuclei. In preparation for possible later fertilization, gametes undergo a reduction in the number of chromosomes carried in their nuclei; then, when an ovum and a sperm fuse, there will be forty-six chromosomes. This specialized cell division in the ova and sperm is called **meiosis.**

Somatic cells develop through a process of division called **mitosis.** All somatic cells in the human species contain 46 chromosomes that can be arranged into twenty-three pairs. The cells of the embryo, which become the fetus and finally the human body and its support structure (the chorion, amniotic sac, and placenta), are formed from divisions of the fertilized ovum. These cells contain the same chromosomal and genetic materials as the original parent cell. Cell division is extremely rapid during the prenatal period to allow for growth of the zygote into a neonate. Somatic cells divide continually throughout life to replace old, damaged, or discarded cells (Nora and Fraser 1974).

● GENETICALLY UNIQUE

Because each ovum and sperm contain a different combination of twenty-three chromosomes, each child receives a unique combination of forty-six chromosomes from his or her parents. With the number of possible combinations almost infinite, it is inevitable that two children in the same family will have different genetic traits. No two siblings will have the same genetic traits unless they are from the same fertilized ovum.

Monozygotic Twins

Children who develop from the same fertilized ovum are **monozygotic twins,** commonly called *identical twins.* Triplets may also develop in this manner, and very rarely other multiple births, such as the Dionne quintuplets, born

The Dionne quintuplets

TABLE 2.1 Inheritance Chart

PARENTS	GENOTYPE				PHENOTYPE
			B	b	
1st parent	Bb	B	BB	Bb	Each child has 75 percent chance of having brown eyes; a 25 percent chance of having blue eyes; and a 75 percent chance of being a carrier for blue eyes.
2nd parent	Bb	b	Bb	bb	
			B	B	
1st parent	BB	B	BB	BB	Each child has a 100 percent chance of having brown eyes and a 50 percent chance of being a carrier for blue eyes.
2nd parent	Bb	b	Bb	Bb	
			b	b	
1st parent	bb	B	Bb	Bb	Each child has a 100 percent chance of having brown eyes and a 100 percent chance of being a carrier for blue eyes.
2nd parent	BB	B	Bb	Bb	
			B	B	
1st parent	BB	B	BB	BB	Each child has a 100 percent chance of having brown eyes and no chance of being a carrier for blue eyes.
2nd parent	BB	B	BB	BB	
			b	b	
1st parent	bb	b	bb	bb	Each child has a 100 percent chance of having blue eyes and no chance of being a carrier for brown eyes.
2nd parent	bb	b	bb	bb	

B = Brown eyes (dominant)
b = blue eyes (recessive)

TABLE 2.2 Sex of Fraternal and Identical Twins
Approximately half the twins are of the same sex and the other half of the opposite sex. The different sex clearly identifies the twins as fraternal and solves the problem of definition in about one-third of twin births.

MALE-MALE IDENTICAL	FRATERNAL	MALE-FEMALE FRATERNAL	FEMALE-FEMALE IDENTICAL	FRATERNAL
1/6	1/6	1/3	1/6	1/6

Source: Elizabeth Noble, *Having Twins* (Boston: Houghton Mifflin, 1980), 21.

in Ontario, Canada in 1934. No other known surviving all–identical sets of quintuplets have been born to date.

Normally the human adult female releases only one mature ovum every menstrual cycle. Sometimes, after the one released ovum is fertilized, certain conditions cause the ovum to split, producing two embryos. About one quarter

1

Interphase

The chromosomes are uncoiled and not visible as such. There are four (two pairs) in the nucleus. Chromosome replication has occurred.

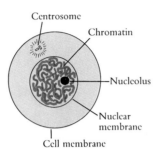

Centrosome

Chromatin

Nucleolus

Nuclear membrane

Cell membrane

2

Early prophase

The chromosomes have begun to condense and are now visible. Each chromosome consists of two sister chromatids joined at the centromere. The centrosome has divided to form centrioles, thus spindle formation has begun. The nucleolus has not yet dispersed.

Spindle fibers

Centriole

Centromere

Chromosome with two sister chromatids

3

Middle prophase

The chromosomes continue to coil and condense.

4

Late prophase

The chromosomes continue to coil and condense.

5

Metaphase

The nuclear membrane has broken down, and the nucleolus has dispersed. The chromosomes are short and thick and aligned at the equatorial region, attached to the spindle fibers by their centromeres.

Metaphase plate

6

Early anaphase

The centromeres divide and the sister chromatids, now called daughter chromosomes, move toward opposite poles, the centromere leading the way.

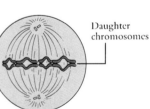

Daughter chromosomes

7

Late anaphase

The daughter chromosomes continue to move toward opposite poles.

8

Telophase

The chromosomes have ceased moving and a nuclear membrane reforms. The cell prepares to divide.

Cleavage furrow

9

Late telophase with cytokinesis

Each daughter cell has the same number of chromosomes as the original interphase nucleus, four (or two pairs).

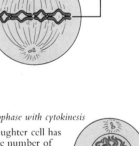

Daughter cells

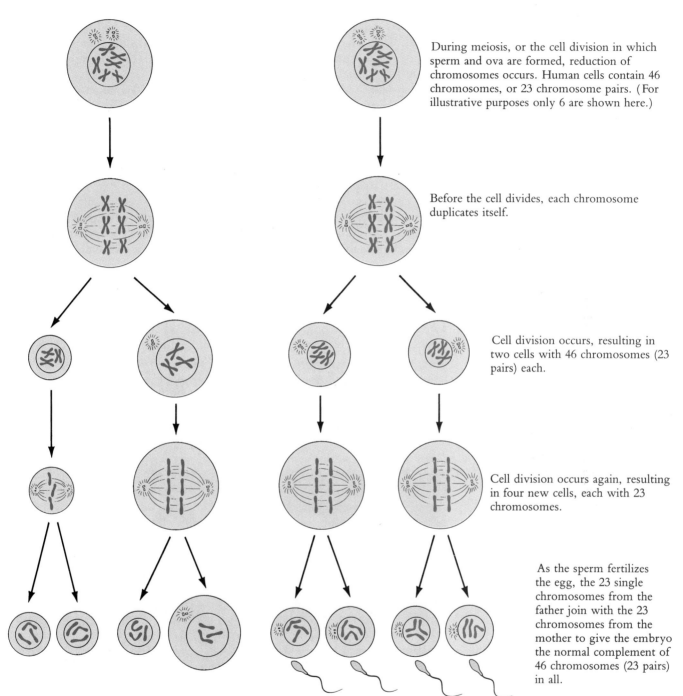

During meiosis, or the cell division in which sperm and ova are formed, reduction of chromosomes occurs. Human cells contain 46 chromosomes, or 23 chromosome pairs. (For illustrative purposes only 6 are shown here.)

Before the cell divides, each chromosome duplicates itself.

Cell division occurs, resulting in two cells with 46 chromosomes (23 pairs) each.

Cell division occurs again, resulting in four new cells, each with 23 chromosomes.

As the sperm fertilizes the egg, the 23 single chromosomes from the father join with the 23 chromosomes from the mother to give the embryo the normal complement of 46 chromosomes (23 pairs) in all.

of identical twins are "mirror twins." They have certain features that are related as in a mirror image, that is, on the opposite side. For example, a whorl or cowlick, a birthmark, or even internal organs such as the appendix may be on the reverse sides of twins. One twin may be left-handed and the other right-handed. Two of the Dionne quintuplets, Emile and Marie, were apparently mirror-imaged. (Emile died in 1954, and Marie died in 1970 of unrelated causes [Noble 1980; Scheinfeld 1972].)

Conjoined, or Siamese, twins are rare. The ratio of Siamese to normal twin births is approximately 1 in 1000. This phenomenon occurs once in approximately 50,000 births. Siamese twins are most commonly joined at their chests. The most likely explanation is the incomplete separation of the dividing cells following fertilization of a single egg. It is believed that unknown but definite environmental influences affect this incomplete fission. No clear hereditary factor appears to predispose an individual couple to have fused twins. Siamese twins are always identical, with 70 percent of them being female. The term *Siamese twins* comes from the famous Chang and Eng, conjoined twins from Thailand, who traveled with the Barnum Circus. Although they were joined at the chest, they married and fathered a total of twenty-two children between them (Noble 1980; Milunsky 1977).

By the end of the 1970s an unusual discovery was made concerning twins. Ultrasound scanning equipment made it possible for physicians to take detailed pictures of developing fetuses. Twins were being discovered as early as the first trimester. The surprising thing was the number of times that pregnancies with twins, discovered during the first two or three months of gestation, produced only a single baby at birth. The first explanation was that the pictures were being misinterpreted. However, it is now understood that twins are conceived two to four times more often than they are born. One explanation for this phenomenon is that one member of a pair of identical twins frequently succumbs before birth and may then *macerate,* or waste away, and reabsorb. This twin may also become compressed or mummify (Arey 1974; Harris 1983).

Chang and Eng, with their families.

Monozygotic twins

Dizygotic twins

In rare cases an accident during initial egg division may result in a chromosomal difference between identical twins, such as one developing with a loss of a chromosome or part of a chromosome. For example, in identical twins from an XY zygote, one twin may develop with the X and Y sex chromosomes, producing a male, whereas the other twin, losing the Y, may develop into an abnormal XO, which is a female with Turner's syndrome (Scheinfeld 1972). (See Section 2.5 for a discussion of Turner's syndrome.)

Dizygotic Twins

If two ova are fertilized, **dizygotic twins** (*fraternal twins*) will be conceived. Since dizygotic twins emanate from different ova as well as different sperm cells, the genetic relationship between these twins would be the same as between any other siblings. Fraternal twins occur in 1 out of 88 births; triplets occur in 1 out of 9,300 births; quadruplets, 1 in 500,000; and quintuplets, 1 in 50,000,000 (Milunsky 1977). It is unusual but possible for fraternal twins not to have the same father. For example, a sexually active young woman who produced two ova during the same menstrual cycle managed to get each ovum fertilized by a different man within a few hours. A complicated blood-typing procedure confirmed which man fathered which child. Interestingly, the mother had mistakenly linked the wrong twin with the wrong father (Terasaki et al. 1978; Conniff 1982). *Superfecundity* is the technical term for twins who are fathered by two different men. The first recorded case was in 1810. It was apparent because one father was black and the other white (Noble 1980).

Another rare phenomenon regarding twins is **superfetation,** the occurrence of a second egg being fertilized in the following reproductive cycle. It is theoretically possible for a woman to get pregnant again within the first three months of an established pregnancy, but it is rare because the hormones produced during pregnancy usually prevent ovulation. The theory is that low hormone levels at the beginning of these pregnancies do not adequately suppress ovulation. A marked difference in the twins at birth may be an indication of superfetation. In most twin births, the second twin is delivered within minutes of the first. There are exceptions, however. There are cases on record in which days and even months lapsed between the births. In Texas, a mother actually

Dizygotic twins
Fraternal twins, who develop from two ova fertilized at the same time by two sperm. The genetic relationship between these twins is the same as between any other siblings.

Superfecundity
The technical term for dizygotic twins who are fathered by two different men.

Superfetation
A rare occurrence when a second ovum is fertilized in the following reproductive cycle, producing fraternal twins with different gestation periods.

Just where do males come from, anyway? Reports last week in the journal Nature offer the most convincing answer yet. Researchers have known since 1959 that the Y chromosome makes an embryo develop testes rather than ovaries. Once that occurs, the sexual die is cast: other male traits, from beards to baldness, stem from hormones made by the testes. Now biologists think they've found the actual gene, on the Y chromosome, that nudges an embryo toward maleness.

People with two X chromosomes are usually female; an X and a Y make a male. But sometimes an XX is male and an XY is female. By studying these exceptions, researchers narrowed the search for the maleness gene to a smidgen of the Y—a piece that was absent from an XY female's Y, but present on an XX male's X. Researchers at the Imperial Cancer Research Fund in London used biochemical scissors to chop this smidgen of human DNA into 50 bits; they then mixed those bits with DNA segments from other mammals, male and female. Because a trait as basic as maleness is expected to have deep evolutionary roots and thus can be shared across species, the bit that found a match in every male was the best candidate for the masculinity gene. In a second study, using only mice, a team at Britain's National Institute for Medical Research discovered a virtually identical maleness gene, in the Y chromosomes of the test rodents.

Is it *the* maleness gene? If inserting it into an XX mouse turns "her" into "him," it would indeed prove to be the only gene needed for maleness. Understanding how this gene works might yield insights into how a mere fertilized egg becomes a complete newborn—boy *or* girl.

gave birth to twins in different years; one was delivered in December 1966 and the other in January 1967 (Noble 1980).

Identical twins are born at about the same rate all over the world. The exact reason why a fertilized ovum would split into two embryos is unknown. It seems to be a random phenomenon, and it may be related to certain environmental factors, or a transient lack of oxygen to the zygote. The incidence of this type of twinning is almost the same among different races and cultures. Universally, identical twins are born 3 and 4 per 1,000 births (Milunsky 1977; Noble 1980).

The occurrence of fraternal twins, unlike identical twins, correlates with race, age, family size, seasons, geography, hormones, and heredity (Milunsky 1977; Noble 1980). Nigerians have the greatest number, with 45 per 1,000 births. African-Americans have 20 per 1,000 births, and Europeans and white Americans have 18 per 1,000 births.

The older the mother, the more likely she is to have twins, reaching a peak between thirty-five and thirty-nine years. Twin-bearing families are more fertile, so the more children a woman has, the greater the probability of her conceiving twins. However, since the increase of family size parallels the increase in maternal age, the age of the mother is considered a more significant factor. Taller mothers and obese mothers are more likely to have twins than shorter mothers and thinner mothers.

Twinning is more common in rural areas than in urban areas. Some explanations include larger stature and superior physical fitness of the women, better nutrition, and less environmental pollution. Population characteristics and social customs of marriage and childbearing are also associated with geographical differences (Noble 1980). For example, women from cultures or countries in which the population tends to be taller and heavier would have more multiple births than those from populations which are lighter and shorter. Also, older women (30–39 years) tend to have more multiple births. Therefore, if the social customs include marrying at an older age, then twins are more likely. And if social customs encourage higher levels of sexual activity, then there is a greater chance of having twins.

Mothers of fraternal twins show high levels of *gonadotropin* hormones, which stimulate the ovaries. Gonadotropins have been used successfully to treat female infertility by stimulating the ovarian function. Multiple births resulting from this treatment are notorious. The use of oral contraceptives also increases the chance of a twin pregnancy. It is thought that higher levels of hormones, which stimulate increased production within the ovaries, are released after a woman discontinues the contraceptive pill. The likelihood is raised when a woman has taken the contraceptive pill for at least a year and conception occurs a month or two after the woman discontinues its use. Women who become pregnant within two months after discontinuing the contraceptive pill double their chances of having twins compared with women who wait a year or so before becoming pregnant (Noble 1980).

Mothers of multiples had an earlier onset of menstruation, have shorter menstrual cycles, and have earlier menopause. Those who conceive late in the ovulatory cycle have a threefold chance of bearing twins. Mothers of fraternal twins have four times the chance of conceiving another set. The gene favoring fraternal twins passes along the female line. If a woman has a history of fraternal twins in her family on her mother's side, or if she is a twin herself, the chances of conceiving twins are increased (Noble 1980).

A renowned case regarding multiple births in medical literature is that of Dr. Mary Austin, who, during thirty-three years of marriage, apparently had forty-four children: thirteen pairs of twins and six sets of triplets. A report in 1896 indicated that one of her sisters had given birth to forty-one children; another sister, to twenty-six children (Milunsky 1977).

Although in most cases the mother is physiologically responsible for producing multiple births, occasionally the father has been responsible for transmitting the tendency. For example, it was recorded in 1914 that a Russian peasant who had married twice had four sets of quadruplets, seven sets of

● FIGURE 2.3
Placentas of MZ and DZ Twins

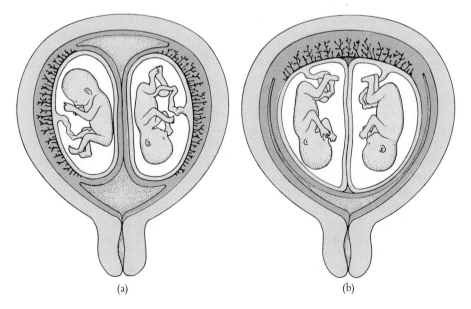

(a)   (b)

triplets, and sixteen pairs of twins with his first wife and two sets of triplets and six pairs of twins with his second wife. Of eighty-seven children, eighty-four survived birth (Milunsky 1977). Theoretically, the sperm may be more prone to cause the splitting of an egg, producing identical twins, triplets, or larger multiple births (Scheinfeld 1972).

Birth defects occur two to three times more often in twins, than in single births. Birth defects are more frequent in male than in female twins, and they are more frequent in black than in white twins. Both members of an identical pair have the same defects (for example, heart defects), indicating a hereditary influence. There is also an increased rate of death in twins at birth or soon thereafter, which relates mainly to a higher rate of prematurity. Identical twins have a greater risk of dying during the first month of life than nonidentical twins. The second delivered twin is at the greatest disadvantage in terms of survival and development. The use of instruments for delivery, length of anesthesia, and lack of oxygen associated with delay will all adversely affect the second twin.

● INHERITANCE OF ABNORMALITIES

Not only can various mental and physical characteristics be inherited, but many diseases and chromosomal abnormalities can be as well. Genetic defects are a result of dominant genes, recessive genes, sex-linked genes, or chromosomal abnormalities.

Dominant Pattern of Inheritance

At least twelve hundred illnesses or defects are caused by dominant genes. Each child has a 50 percent chance of inheriting such a disease from an affected parent. To inherit a defective gene, an individual must have an affected parent. Unaffected relatives will not have affected offspring. One example of a disease caused by a dominant gene is *Huntington's chorea,* a neurological disorder in which symptoms appear between eighteen and forty years of age. Some of the symptoms include jerks and twitches of the head, neck, arms, legs, and trunk; slurred speech; difficulty in eating; and personality changes. The accompanying deterioration of the body leads to death. Woody Guthrie, a popular folksinger, was a victim of Huntington's chorea.

Another example of a disease caused by a dominant gene is *Marfan's syndrome,* a degenerative disease that usually produces abnormally long limbs, heart malformation, hearing loss, eye weakness, and eventually certain death (Milunsky 1977). Abraham Lincoln is suspected of being a victim of this disease.

Sickle-cell trait is a heterozygous manifestation of the gene for the sickle-cell anemia disease and produces little disability compared with the homozygous form. (See later discussion of sickle-cell anemia.) An infant who is heterozygous for the gene (that is, an infant who produces both normal and sickle-cell hemoglobin in the red blood cells) has a much better chance of resisting malaria than a child who has only normal hemoglobin. A small child with the trait has a greater chance of surviving a first malaria attack and will develop antibodies against future attacks. However, the sickle-cell trait does not protect adults from malaria.

The trait is present in about one out of eleven African-Americans. Little or no symptoms are expressed except for a mild chronic anemia. However, some

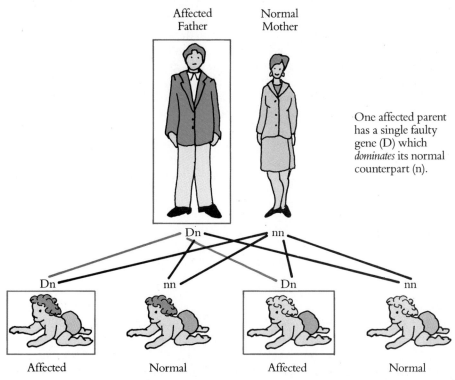

Affected
Father

Normal
Mother

One affected parent
has a single faulty
gene (D) which
dominates its normal
counterpart (n).

Dn   nn

Dn   nn   Dn   nn

Affected   Normal   Affected   Normal

● FIGURE 2.4
Dominant Pattern of Inheritance
In order for a child to be affected, one parent must have the disorder. For such a family there is a 50 percent chance that each child will have the disorder.

stress situations may be fatal, such as in the death of four African-American heterozygous army recruits at Fort Bliss, Texas, in 1970. Under lowered oxygen tension, such as in unpressurized aircraft or parachute drops, heterozygotes may develop symptoms similar to those of homozygotes or even infarction of the spleen (Nora and Fraser 1974).

Recessive Pattern of Inheritance

At least 950 defects or diseases are caused by recessive genes. When both parents are carriers, there is a one in four chance that a child will inherit the defect or disease; a one in two chance that the child will be a carrier; or a one in four chance that the child will not be affected at all. Parents of affected children are more likely to be related to each other than are parents of normal children (Nora and Fraser 1974).

Some of the diseases that are the result of the recessive pattern of inheritance include some forms of *muscular dystrophy,* a degenerative muscle disease that affects about 100,000 Americans, and *cystic fibrosis,* a disease that affects one in one thousand Caucasians and causes respiratory and digestive system malfunctions that shorten the life expectancy to around seventeen years (March of Dimes 1990).

Sickle-cell anemia is a blood disease prevalent in approximately fifty thousand Americans who are descendants of Mediterranean blacks or Spaniards. Anemia, which accompanies the malformed sickle-shaped blood cells, causes

Human Development in the News: Curing Cystic Fibrosis?

JEAN SELIGMANN

Only a year ago, researchers announced that they had identified the gene for cystic fibrosis. They hoped someday to be able to use the discovery therapeutically. Now that goal is much closer: last week two teams of scientists reported that they have been able to use a "normal" copy of the CF gene to override the effects of the defective one. Their work was done in the lab, using cells taken from CF patients, but there is good reason to believe the same process will work in human trials. Says Robert K. Dresing, president of the Cystic Fibrosis Foundation: "All the pieces are coming together quickly."

The stakes are high because CF is a killer. It's the most common fatal genetic disease among Caucasians; 30,000 Americans who inherited a defective CF gene from both parents have the illness. An additional 12 million—who don't have symptoms—carry a single defective gene. If two carriers conceive a child, there is a 25 percent chance their baby will be born with CF.

In children with the disease, epithelial cells lining the respiratory tract secrete a thick, sticky mucus that clogs their lungs and leads to chronic infections. To help youngsters cough up the mucus, parents must slap them on the back repeatedly in an unpleasant ritual. The disease also interferes with production of a pancreatic enzyme, which in the past caused malnutrition and short stature; today patients take a replacement enzyme. The average life span of a CF victim is 26, and few live beyond 40.

The discovery of the CF gene allowed researchers to make copies of both the normal version of the gene and the defective one, and to show for the first time that the abnormality can be corrected. In two separate projects, researchers from the University of Michigan, led by Dr. James Wilson, and the University of Iowa (collaborating with the Genzyme Corp.) took cells from CF patients and combined them in the lab with a normal version of the CF gene. To their great satisfaction, the formerly abnormal cells began functioning like normal ones. For example, one characteristic of CF is that chloride is not effectively transported through the cell membranes; in the lab experiments, the "chloride channels" opened up and the chemical passed freely in and out of the cell.

The use of genetic manipulation to intervene in disease is a dramatically expanding field of medicine. Two weeks ago scientists at the National Institutes of Health began the first federally approved attempt to treat a genetic abnormality in a human patient with "gene therapy" or genetic manipulation. The patient is a 4-year-old girl who has the same rare immune-system disorder that ultimately killed David, the Houston "boy in the bubble." NIH researchers removed viable immune-system cells from the little girl and combined them with human genes responsible for making the enzyme she lacked. Similar intervention for CF patients is at least several years off. If it works, says Dr. Michael Welsh, who headed the Iowa team, "cystic fibrosis might no longer be a fatal disease."

The new CF research shows that "this strategy works for an ever-increasing list of disorders where a defective gene is responsible," says University of Michigan's Dr. Francis Collins, who codiscovered the CF gene. "It gives credence to the idea that gene therapy will find a significant place in the medical armamentarium." But first, Welsh and Collins note, researchers must prove the safety and efficacy of the approach in animals, and resolve such issues as how to target the right receptor cells for the therapy, and avoid accidentally activating adjacent cells that might cause harm. Still, says Collins, "my hope is that this therapy will be available in the lifetime of people who now have the disease."

tissue and organ damage, with half of those having the disease dying by the time they are twenty years old.

Tay-Sachs, a disease prevalent among descendants of East European Jews, renders a victim unable to metabolize fats in the nervous system. A child with this disease usually dies between four and five years of age.

PKU, or phenylketonuria, is the inability to metabolize a specific protein. One in ten thousand children are born with this disease. PKU can be detected at birth and can be corrected by diet. If not corrected, it will damage the central nervous system and cause mental retardation.

Galactosemia, which affects one in thirty thousand people, is caused by the inability to metabolize milk sugar galactose. This disease can also be detected at birth or through amniocentesis and can be corrected by diet.

About seven million Americans suffer from *diabetes.* Although diabetes may be the result of a recessive pattern of inheritance, the exact pattern is hard to predict because the environment is so critical. With diabetes, the body does not produce enough insulin, so the victim metabolizes sugar abnormally.

Thalassemia, also known as Cooley's anemia, is common among descendants of Greeks and Italians. The symptoms include paleness and listlessness and low resistance to infection, which are due to abnormal blood cells. Treatment is by blood transfusion.

Albinism affects one in twenty thousand people, with 20 percent of the cases found in first-cousin marriages. This is a hereditary defect in the metabolism of melanin, causing the absence or major decrease of this pigment in the skin, mucosa, hair, and eyes.

Sex-linked Pattern of Inheritance

In most sex-linked genetic defects, an unaffected mother carries one faulty X chromosome and one normal X chromosome. The father carries normal X and Y chromosomes. The vast majority of sex-linked genetic defects occur in males, since they have only one X chromosome. The statistical odds for each male child are a 50 percent risk of inheriting the faulty X chromosome and hence the disorder from the mother and a 50 percent chance of inheriting normal X and Y chromosomes. For each female child, the statistical odds are a 50 percent

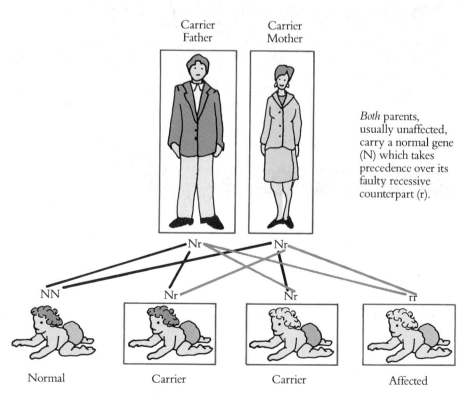

Carrier Father

Carrier Mother

Both parents, usually unaffected, carry a normal gene (N) which takes precedence over its faulty recessive counterpart (r).

Nr Nr

NN Nr Nr rr

Normal Carrier Carrier Affected

● FIGURE 2.5
Recessive Pattern of Inheritance
Both parents are carriers and each child has a 25 percent chance of having the disorder.

● FIGURE 2.6
Sex-linked Pattern of Inheritance
In most sex-linked genetic defects, an unaffected mother carries one faulty affected X chromosome and one normal x chromosome. The father carries normal x and y chromosomes. The vast majority of sex-linked genetic defects occur in males, since they have only one x chromosome.

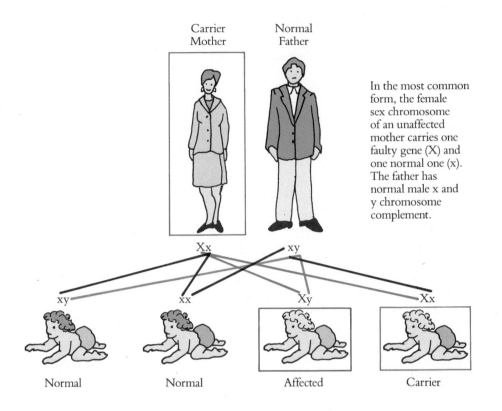

Carrier Mother   Normal Father

In the most common form, the female sex chromosome of an unaffected mother carries one faulty gene (X) and one normal one (x). The father has normal male x and y chromosome complement.

Xx   xy

xy   xx   Xy   Xx

Normal   Normal   Affected   Carrier

risk of inheriting one faulty X chromosome and hence becoming a carrier like the mother and a 50 percent chance of inheriting no faulty gene. A female can be a victim of the disease if the father has the disease, the mother is a carrier, and the child inherits the mother's faulty X chromosome. Affected males never transmit the gene to their sons but transmit it to their daughters, who will be carriers (Nora and Fraser 1974).

The most dramatic example of a sex-linked genetic abnormality is *hemophilia,* a defect that interferes with the normal clotting of blood. A small wound may cause a hemophiliac to bleed for hours when normally it would clot within five minutes. Internal bleeding is especially dangerous since it may go unnoticed and cause death. Queen Victoria, the most famous carrier of hemophilia, had four sons and five daughters. Her youngest son inherited the disease, and three of her daughters were carriers, transmitting hemophilia throughout various royal families in Europe.

Red-green color blindness is another example of a sex-linked genetic abnormality. A girl will inherit red-green color blindness if she receives the same gene from both parents. Therefore, her father must be red-green color-blind and her mother must carry the gene for the defect. A boy will be red-green color-blind only if he inherits the faulty X chromosome from his mother, as in hemophilia.

Hunter's syndrome, which affects one in 200,000 Americans, is also sex-linked. Retardation is a symptom but is minimal or absent. Claw hands and stiff joints are the primary symptoms.

The symptoms of *Duchenne muscular dystrophy,* another sex-linked disease, appears in boys by five years of age. The muscles, especially in the lower limbs, appear unusually well developed, yet the child is weak and unable to walk well,

pedal a tricycle, or walk up stairs. Usually by ten, he must use a wheelchair. About one-third of those with Duchenne muscular dystrophy are retarded. The heart and skeletal muscle are affected. Death usually occurs around twenty years of age.

There are approximately 150 other known sex-linked defects, including *juvenile glaucoma,* a hardening of the eyeballs, and *combined immune deficiency disease,* in which the body has no natural immunities. David the Bubble Boy suffered from combined immune deficiency disease until his death.

Chromosomal Abnormalities

Chromosomal abnormalities are another source of defects. *Down's syndrome,* or *Trisomy—21,* results when one of the chromosomes on the twenty-first pair contains extra chromosomal material. The most common cause of the extra material is a failure of the members of the twenty-first chromosome pair to separate during the process of mitosis. Another cause involves one portion of a chromosome breaking off and attaching to a chromosome of the twenty-first pair (March of Dimes 1990). Research indicates that mothers who have already given birth to a child with Down's syndrome are about three times as likely to have another child with Down's syndrome than are women of the same age who have not previously had a child with this condition. Although Down's syndrome has traditionally been associated with an older and faulty ovum, more recent research indicates that as many as 24 percent of all babies who have Down's were conceived when a faulty sperm fertilized a normal ovum (Emery 1983; Fuhrmann and Vogel 1983; Holmes 1979).

Down's syndrome, or Trisomy-21, results when one of the chromosomes on the twenty-first pair contains extra chromosomal material.

A variation of Down's syndrome is known as "mosaic" Down's syndrome. At some point during mitosis, one cell divides improperly, allotting 47 chromosomes to one new cell and 45 chromosomes to the other. Cells with 45 chromosomes cannot survive but those with 47 develop alongside normal cells with 46 chromosomes. People with mosaic Down's tend to have higher IQs than those with the usual Down's syndrome. (March of Dimes 1990).

Individuals with Down's syndrome have a variable degree of mental retardation (with IQ's ranging from 50–60), small stature, a small head, eyes that slant upward, a small or absent nose bridge, and an enlarged, protruding tongue. Many now survive into adulthood.

Another chromosomal abnormality is *Klinefelter's syndrome,* a disorder in which males have two X chromosomes and one Y chromosome. These males are not usually identified until puberty, when they fail to develop body and facial hair and other secondary sex characteristics. Such individuals have undeveloped testes and commonly develop into tall, thin men who, because of less testosterone, have enlarged breasts. They are sterile and may show some mental impairment. Males with Klinefelter's syndrome also may have personality and emotional problems. As infants they tend to be less active and less rebellious than normal boys. During their childhood, they seem to be more compliant and often have difficulty concentrating. When they are adults, they are more prone to a variety of behavioral problems, such as being depressed, obsessive, or anxious (Money, Klein, and Beck 1979).

Turner's syndrome is a condition in which women have only one X chromosome, that is, they are missing the additional sex chromosome. These women are usually short in stature, with "webbed" necks, broad chests, and low-set ears. Treatment with estrogen can help them look more normal (Baer 1977). Although they have female sex organs, they do not have ovaries and are sterile. Therefore, at puberty they fail to develop secondary sex characteristics. As a group, they are about average on tests of intelligence, although they frequently score below average on tests of spatial abilities, such as maze learning and mental rotation of figures. How well they perform on intelligence tests is related to the age they began estrogen treatment. The earlier they began, the higher their intelligence. About one in ten thousand women suffer from Turner's syndrome.

Approximately one male in one thousand has *XYY syndrome.* These males tend to be taller than the norm and are sterile. They also tend to have severe cases of acne during adolescence, and many of them score below average on intelligence tests, although their mental deficiencies are typically not profound.

Women with XXX or XXXX sex chromosomes, sometimes called *super- or metafemales,* may appear normal and sometimes have normal ovaries, but they are infertile. They are prone to have psychological and intellectual abnormalities, with a generally low IQ. (Baer, 1977 and Milunsky 1977)

The conditions described above are just some of the known defects related to chromosomal abnormalities.

● GENETIC ENGINEERING

Genetic engineering
A conscious manipulation that affects the frequency or expression of genes.

The study of genetics has raised many issues resulting from research. The term **genetic engineering** creates a science-fiction horror picture in the minds of many. However, genetic engineering can be broadly defined as a conscious manipulation that affects the frequency or expression of genes. The procedures

CHAPTER 2 *Before We Were Us: Genetics*

in this science were originally developed to increase food supplies for developing countries or to prevent defects in children or to help infertile individuals. Genetic counseling, artificial insemination, embryo transfer, in vitro fertilization, and recombinant DNA are all examples of genetic engineering.

Genetic Counseling

In recent years, a service called **genetic counseling** has helped prospective parents determine the likelihood that their children will have genetic defects. Although any couple who hope to have children might wish to talk with a genetic counselor about the hereditary risks their children may encounter, genetic counseling is particularly helpful for couples who have relatives with hereditary disorders, or for parents who already have a child with a disorder.

A genetic counselor may be a medical researcher, a geneticist, or a practitioner such as a pediatrician, obstetrician, or family doctor. The genetic counselor will usually begin by asking prospective parents why they have sought genetic counseling. This is to determine if the defect or defects that concern the couple are really hereditary in origin. If they are hereditary, the counselor will then take a complete family history from each parent. This history will include information about the diseases and cause of death of siblings, parents, and other blood relatives; the ethnicity and countries of origin of blood relatives who were immigrants; intermarriages that may have occurred in the past among close relatives (such as cousins); and previous problems the female client has had in the childbearing process, such as miscarriages, stillbirths, and so on.

The couple will also have to have a complete physical examination. If specific tests are available, prospective parents will be screened to determine if they carry the genes that are responsible for producing the hereditary defect or defects that prompted them to seek the counseling in the first place.

In establishing a reoccurrence risk, the genetic counselor must place the disease in one of four etiologic categories: diseases due to major mutant genes, chromosomal aberrations, major environmental agents, or multifactorial causes. From the overall profile, the genetic counselor will be able to determine the mathematical probability that the couple could have a child who will inherit the suspected defect, and then tell the couple if they can do anything to reduce that probability. The counselor must make sure that the parents know what the probability figure means in their case. They must then convert the probability into a decision, such as whether to have another baby, seek sterilization, marry, adopt, and so on.

The counselor may help the family reach a decision, but he or she should avoid making it for them. The counselor can point out various factors to be considered, such as the severity of the disease in relation to the risk of reoccurrence, the impact of the disease on the rest of the family, social and moral pressures they may experience, adoption or artificial insemination as an alternative, the pros and cons of sterilization, and the possibility of monitoring the next pregnancy by amniocentesis.

When confronted with the news that they are carriers of a genetic abnormality or with the prospect of having an abnormal child, people react in different ways. By letting the parents talk and express their emotions, by answering questions, and by acting as a resource, genetic counselors can help couples evaluate risks and then decide what action they wish to take.

At the present time, genetic tests cover diseases that affect fewer than one

Genetic counseling
A service that helps prospective parents determine the likelihood or risk that their children will have genetic defects.

million Americans. By 2005, scientists hope to finish mapping the 50,000 to 100,000 genes found in the human body, producing a genetic blueprint called a genome. By the time the genome puzzle is unlocked, almost every American will either have a detectable physical or mental defect or will know a family member who does. The positive side of genome mapping is that individuals will know if they have inherited a genetic defect. The negative side is that employers can use the information to discriminate against workers, insurance companies can refuse to accept certain clients or refuse to pay medical costs, or people may believe they are sick, even if they only have a small chance of actually acquiring a disease. There are many ethical issues associated with genetic counseling and genome mapping (Curtis and Barnes, 1989).

Artificial Insemination

The decline in the number of children available for adoption has made infertile couples seek other alternatives to have children. One such alternative is **artificial insemination.** This procedure involves injecting semen into the woman with a syringe to make her pregnant. This method is used if the husband is subfertile and needs more sperm to gain access to the egg or if the woman has erratic times of ovulation. When the spouse's sperm is used, the process is called AIH (artificial insemination Homologous).

If the husband is infertile, then a donor is used. This process is called AID (artificial insemination donor). Fresh semen can be used within thirty minutes after ejaculation, or it can be frozen and placed in a sperm bank for years if necessary. AID is responsible for the birth of some twenty thousand children in the United States each year (Fleming 1980).

Historically, there have been some legal, social, moral, and religious problems associated with donor insemination. Although it has been widely used since the 1940s, follow-up has been almost impossible due to secrecy on the part of the donor and recipient. Therefore, little is known about the reactions of these children. Most infertility specialists advise couples not to mention the AID process to anyone, not even the child (Waltzer 1982). Such advice, in itself, can raise some major ethical questions: What about the individual's right to know? How is this different from the dilemma facing adopted children and their birth parents?

An unexpected problem that has emerged because of donor confidentiality is the possibility of unwitting incest among their children. A 1979 study found that of 379 doctors who practiced AID, 90 percent did not have a policy on the maximum use of a specific donor. Occasionally, over the years, doctors have had to stop marriages between children who shared the same donor father (Andrews 1984).

Embryo Transfer

Embryo transfer, another form of genetic engineering, is basically a form of prenatal adoption. This procedure involves transplanting an embryo from the fallopian tube of the biological mother to the uterus of another woman who cannot conceive but who can carry the fetus to full term. Women who cannot conceive now have an opportunity to become mothers. Also, women who can conceive but cannot carry a fetus to full term are able to have someone else carry their fetus to full term. In this situation a woman becomes the biological mother

Artificial insemination
A procedure in which sperm from either a donor or the husband are injected into a woman's vagina with a syringe, with the intention of impregnating her.

Embryo transfer
A procedure that involves transplanting an embryo from the fallopian tube of the biological mother to the uterus of another woman who cannot conceive but who can carry the fetus to full term. This is a form of prenatal adoption.

of an infant who was not "born" to her but was conceived by her. Another scenario related to embryo transfer is the fertilization of an egg inside a donor's body by artificial insemination, using the sperm of an infertile woman's husband. After about five days, the zygote is removed and implanted in the infertile woman, and she maintains the pregnancy (Haas, 1975; Mawdsley, 1983; Handel, 1984).

The first successful embryo transfer, using a frozen zygote, was reported in India with the birth of a little girl. The research was surrounded with secrecy because the laws of India forbid this kind of experimentation and scientists on this project had been funded to work on new birth control methods (cited in Cohen et al., 1985). The work of the Indians was replicated by Australian scientists in 1983 (Wood et al., 1984). This procedure might be a solution to the moral dilemma associated with abortions. If a woman does not want to be pregnant, she can allow her embryo to be adopted without loss of life. However, this would have to be accomplished in the very early stages of the pregnancy.

In Vitro Fertilization

Yet another form of genetic engineering is **in vitro fertilization.** Two British physicians, Dr. Patrick Steptoe and Dr. Robert Edwards, were responsible for this medical breakthrough. In this procedure, an egg from a woman is fertilized in a petri dish by her husband's sperm, then implanted in her womb approximately four days after fertilization. The first surviving child to be conceived in this manner was Louise Joy Brown, who was born July 25, 1978, in Oldham, England. She now has a younger sister who was conceived by this same procedure. The first American infant conceived through in vitro fertilization was Elizabeth Jordon Carr, who was born December 28, 1981. This procedure has been very successful in the United States as well as in England, and it is now widely available (Colen 1982; Gorman 1982). If couples are not successful with the first attempt, repeated attempts have a success rate of about one in three (Halme 1985).

Researchers have found that the rate of pregnancy increases when more than one zygote is transferred. In one study the rate of pregnancy increased from 7.4 percent when only one zygote was transferred to 21.1 percent and 28.1 percent when two and three zygotes were transferred, respectively. Multiple pregnancies also increased with the number of zygotes transferred but the risk was far outweighed by the poorer result experienced from transferring only one zygote (Wood et al. 1984; Sondheimer et al. 1985; Wood et al. 1985).

Recombinant DNA

One of the most controversial issues surrounding genetic engineering is **recombinant DNA.** This process manipulates DNA by splitting and transferring genetic material from one species to another, creating life-forms unique to nature. The process involves isolating a DNA plasmid and separating it from a DNA ring. Researchers have developed techniques for removing plasmids from their host bacteria, splitting the plasmids open chemically, and inserting new genes into them. The fresh plasmids thus created can then be introduced into other bacteria, where the genes begin changing the hereditary characteristics of their new host bacteria (Gwynne 1976).

Many benefits, as well as possible mishaps, were predicted by scientists,

In vitro fertilization
A procedure in which an egg from a woman is fertilized in a petri dish by her husband's sperm, then implanted in her womb approximately four days after the fertilization.

Recombinant DNA
A form of genetic engineering that manipulates DNA by splitting and transferring genetic material from one species to another, creating life-forms unique to nature.

politicians, and the media concerning this procedure. To date, more benefits than mishaps have been realized. One definite benefit concerns a growth hormone produced through recombinant DNA. This hormone has made growth possible for children whose pituitary glands did not produce growth hormone. Prior to this, such children were injected with natural growth hormone extracted from pituitaries of cadavers—which were scarce and expensive. Genentech, a California-based genetic engineering firm, and the University of California at San Francisco simultaneously announced their success in engineering bacteria to produce human growth hormone (Angier 1982).

The development of recombinant DNA techniques has advanced the understanding of many other human genetic defects and diseases by permitting isolation and sequencing of specific defective genes. For example, it is now possible to identify the location of chromosomes of defective genes that cause nervous system disorders such as Huntington's disease. The discovery of a DNA marker connected to Huntington's opened new approaches in researching this disorder and characterization of the defective gene in the future (Gusella et al. 1984). Other benefits, many of which are still experimental, include manufacturing large cultures of antibodies and administering them to patients as soon as they catch a virus; manufacturing human insulin; creating cheaper and improved vaccines, antibiotics, and other drugs; instead of using oil to produce fertilizers, crossing plants that can fix their own nitrogen with established crop strains; creating plants that can more efficiently photosynthesize sunlight into nutrients, therefore increasing food production; helping the study of hereditary disorders or analyzing genetic cell growths that lead to cancer; exploring, through the genetic code, tumor viruses that cause cancer; producing human interferon to combat cancer.

● INTERACTION OF HEREDITY AND ENVIRONMENT

For centuries the argument has raged over whether our genes (nature) or our environment (nurture) determine who and what we are. Plato believed that the soul was incorporated into the body at birth. He believed the soul had a prior existence and that it provided the individual with preestablished ideas and knowledge about the world. Essentially Plato took the position that nature determined behavior. On the other hand, Aristotle argued that the mind was nothing until it had thought and that it was simply a writing tablet on which nothing was yet written (similar to Locke's theory that we are born with a *tabula rasa,* i.e., a blank slate). According to Aristotle, all of our knowledge, everything we become, is due to our experience or environmental stimulation, that is, nurture.

Whole societies have based their policies, educational systems, and politics on either nature or nurture. Conservative political philosophy tends toward the hereditary, or nature, side of the issue. Liberal philosophy supports the environmental, or nurture, view by holding that people are not predestined to develop in a particular manner and are not limited by their genes. Liberals believe that one is a product of his or her experiences.

The two beliefs are reflected at various levels of our society and in various geographical locations. They influence which social programs receive support, and they affect the priority in which government efforts are directed at developing large-scale humanitarian programs. As Anastasi (1958) stated, we must quit asking *which* influences behavior but rather *how* they interact to do so.

Following Anastasi's advice, most contemporary scientists tend to accept a more multifactorial approach to the argument and stress the interaction of nature and nurture. The most important human characteristics, especially the complex ones such as personality and intelligence, are not simply the result of heredity *or* environment, but rather heredity *and* environment. Every human quality is affected by genes, but experience, via the environment, is almost always crucial.

Hurlock (1980) listed three factors that sum up the interactionist concept of development:

1. Individual differences in ability, personality, and behavior patterns are the result of an interaction between heredity and environment and not of either factor acting in isolation.
2. Maturational variables set limits to development, regardless of even the best environmental conditions.
3. An individual's ability to respond to stimulation is dependent on his or her "readiness" to learn (i.e., developmental readiness is partially dependent on maturational forces interacting with environmental factors in influencing the timing of development).

The study of identical twins offers some of the most important clues to the degree to which human traits are due to heredity or environment. Since identical twins carry the same genes, any differences between them must be due to environment. This applies to differences in IQ, behavior, achievement, and personality, as well as differences in height, weight, body proportion, and health. The greater the difference in any trait between identical twins, the more likely environment influenced that trait. Different environmental influences may affect identical twins from the time they begin to develop in the womb (Neubauer and Neubauer 1990).

Impact on Intelligence

The impact of heredity and environment on intelligence has historically raised a great deal of controversy and stimulated the most heated arguments. Therefore, the reared-apart twin studies are especially useful. Most twin studies involve administering intelligence tests to identical twins who have been reared together and identical twins who have been reared apart.

Classic twin studies (Newman et al. 1937; Shields 1962) indicate that twins in general score similarly whether reared together or reared apart. The similarity is greater for identical twins reared apart than for fraternal twins reared together. (Note that fraternal twins are no more alike than nontwin siblings, but if raised together, they have a shared similar environment. Fraternal twins score more similarly than other siblings, so the differences must be due to the environment, since they are not genetically the same.)

The highest correlation between familial relationships and IQ is found in identical twins reared together, followed by identical twins reared apart, fraternal twins reared together, siblings reared together, and finally unrelated children reared together. Therefore, the closer the genetic relationship, the more similar the IQ scores. But this does not discount the environment, since there is a difference between the identical twins reared apart. Among fraternal twins, the IQs of same-sex twins are more similar than those of opposite-sex twins. This may reflect a social-environmental effect; that is, parents may treat same-sex twins more similarly than opposite-sex twins (Bouchard and McGue 1981).

In a fifteen-year longitudinal study, Wilson (1983) administered intelligence tests to identical twins and fraternal twins at three months. Each set of twins received similar scores on the tests. But as the twins got older, the identical twins' scores became more similar, and the fraternal twins' scores became less similar. Wilson also studied the twins' home environment, assessing the physical and emotional surroundings. He concluded that the principal link between parents' and children's intelligence is genetic, and that the environment intensifies the effects of heredity.

The most extensive study of identical twins reared apart is ongoing at the University of Minnesota. This study is being conducted by Thomas J. Bouchard, Jr., and his colleagues. Over fifty sets of identical twins have been found. The majority were separated early in life and spent their critical years in different homes. Many had not seen each other prior to becoming subjects in the study. The Minnesota research team conducted a complete battery of psychological tests, including tests of intelligence, information processing, memory, mechanical ability, and spatial processing. In almost all cases, the IQ scores of the twins were remarkably similar, and even the brain wave tracings were almost identical (Holden 1980). At least one exception was a set of twins whose IQs were 20 points apart. One twin, a tenth-grade dropout, was raised by a fisherman in Florida in a home with few books. His brother, who was adopted by a cosmopolitan family, became an electronics expert with the CIA and lived all over the world. The latter twin had the higher IQ (Holden 1980).

Because Bouchard's initial findings show a strong genetic component in intelligence, he and his colleagues are concerned about the political and moral implications of their work. Their results could conceivably be misused to support theories of inherent racial superiority. That is, if intelligence is largely inherited, then the conclusion would be that little can be done to improve people's abilities through education or any other interventionist programs (Farber 1981a).

The use of reared-apart twin studies to support a genetics viewpoint has been highly criticized. In reality, most twins are raised in a similar environment. They are often raised by relatives or friends who have a shared similar lifestyle. Also, adoption agencies traditionally make an effort to place all children with parents who will provide a reasonable environment, so the adoptive environments may not be radically different.

Studies of adopted children are also employed to try to explain the influence of heredity and environment on intelligence. Adopted children do not share any of the genes of their adopted families but do share the environment. Adopted children and their adoptive family members have the lowest correlation of IQ scores when compared with the other possible familial relationships. Nonetheless, when very young black children are adopted by white middle-class families, they show IQ levels higher than those of black children from the general population (110.4) and much higher than the national average of 100 (Scarr and Weinberg 1981, 1983). The Texas Adoption Project (Loehlin et al. 1989) found that the shared family environment has a decreasing influence on IQ as children grow older. Also, the Louisville Twin Study (Wilson 1983) found that the contribution of shared family environment to IQ decreased from 70 percent at age three to 30 and 40 percent in middle childhood to 20 percent at age fifteen.

In another study, Israeli children of European Jewish parents had a mean IQ of 105, while Israeli children of Middle Eastern Jews had IQ scores averaging 85. Children in the kibbutzim (an Israeli commune), with parents from both groups, had an average IQ of 115. This was a 10-point improvement for the European children and a 30-point improvement for the Middle Eastern children. The improvement was attributed to the twenty-two-hour-a-day stay in the kibbutzim nursery, which had an intensive learning environment (Bloom 1969).

The predominant theory regarding intelligence is that we inherit a collection of tendencies that influence such things as the speed with which our nervous system carries messages and the rate of body and brain growth, and these tendencies in turn may affect a person's rate of learning. Genetic instructions are inherited for synthesizing the materials from which the brain and nervous system are made and the biochemical processes involved in learning, memory, thinking, and perception. In addition, a variety of prenatal and environmental factors affect initial development and later functioning of the brain and nervous system. The extent and ways in which the brain is used and developed depends on the interaction between the individual and the stimulation and experience offered by the environment.

Impact on Personality

Personality is another characteristic that has received some notoriety in the nature versus nurture controversy. Again, the focus should not be on which factor influences the personality more powerfully but on how heredity and the environment interact. Research in personality development is complicated by the fact that there is no way to analyze the complete genetic endowment of any individual.

In a well-controlled adoption study, Scarr et al. (1981) found no significant correlation between the personality test scores of adolescents who had been adopted during infancy and the scores of their adoptive parents. However, the scores of adolescents and their biological parents were moderately correlated.

Twin studies have also been implemented in investigating the impact of heredity and the environment on personality development. Vandenberg (1967), in a review of the literature of twin studies, concluded that heredity plays a role in the general level of activity, the degree to which emotions are openly expressed in interpersonal relations, and the degree to which long-range goals rather than immediate stimuli influence interests and thoughts. Wilson and Harpring (1972) found identical twins more alike in behavior and motor abilities as young infants than fraternal twins but found that they became less so as they grew older. These data suggest an initially strong genetic influence on behavior but as individuals gain experience, environmental factors gain importance. In another study it was concluded that identical twins are more likely to have similar personality traits and interests than fraternal twins but that the correlation is substantially lower than for intelligence. Thus it appears that heredity influences personality development less directly than it does intellectual characteristics. The interaction of heredity and environment that shapes social behavior, values, interest, emotions, and other aspects of the personality is highly complex (Lindzey et al. 1971).

Juel-Nielson (1965) studied a group of identical twins who had been reared apart from infancy. Little similarity was found in the ways the twins behaved toward others, in their religious and political views, fields of interest, or choice of mates. It was also found that they differed in ambition, aggressiveness, emotional expression, and taste in clothes. However, marked similarities were noted in their walks, their smiles and laughter, and the tones in their voices.

Bouchard's preliminary findings are not necessarily consistent with Juel-Nielson's concerning personality traits. His findings suggest that subtle differences between and within families are not as important as once thought in determining interests, abilities, and personalities (Holden 1980). Bouchard and his colleagues uncovered spectacular similarities in personality patterns, behavior, quirks, attitudes, and tastes in his sample of twins reared apart (Bartlet 1981). For example, the "Jim" twins (both sets of adoptive parents named them James) did not meet each other until they were thirty-nine years old. When tested on such personality variables as tolerance, conformity, flexibility, self-control, and sociability, they were so close on their scores that they approximated the scores that result when the same person takes the test twice (Holden 1980).

Another set of twins from Bouchard's study were Jack Yufe, who had been raised as a Jew in the Caribbean by his biological father, and Oskar Stohr, who had been raised as a Catholic in Nazi Germany by his biological mother and grandmother. They shared many mannerisms and habits, and their profiles on the MMPI (Minnesota Multiphasic Personality Inventory) were very similar. Note that in this particular example, with one twin reared by a father and the other by a mother and grandmother, the sex of the parents did not necessarily mold the twins' personalities in different ways (Holden 1980).

Bouchard observed that twins reared apart have similar scores on measures of tolerance, conformity, flexibility, self-control, and sociability, as well as some of the same phobias.

The most interesting finding in the area of personality was probably the most paradoxical. Bouchard found that the twins reared apart were the most similar and they had had the least contact prior to the study, while the least similar twins were those who had had the most contact. The probable reason is only speculative, but it has been observed that families of identical twins treat them in subtly different ways, probably unconsciously, in an attempt to differentiate them. Twins themselves tend to vacillate between close identification

The "Jim" twins

with each other and exaggerated independence. Thus, it's possible that twins' being reared together overshadows probable genetic-based tendencies to grow up alike. But when twins are reared apart and interaction does not occur, then perhaps the genetic predispositions show themselves more forcefully (Farber 1981b).

A study that compared the personality characteristics of adopted children with those of their biological mothers found that extroverted mothers had extroverted babies and introverted mothers had introverted babies. The same study also found that unwed mothers who were especially poorly adjusted gave birth to infants who became especially well adjusted children in their adoptive families. It appears that some aspects of personality development may have a genetic component and other areas of personality development may be more environmently related (Loehlin et al. 1982). Bouchard and McGue (1981) found that adopted offspring are somewhat more similar to the same-sex adoptive parent than to the opposite-sex adoptive parent.

Twin studies, adoption studies, and family histories can indicate the existence of a particular trait or behavior that may have a genetic component. However, these studies do not tell us how particular genes might contribute to the complex behaviors seen in schizophrenics and manic-depressives. *Schizophrenia* appears to be a brain disease (or diseases), and the limbic system and its connections to the brain are involved (Torrey 1985; Wender and Klein 1981). Researchers have also found abnormal patterns in the levels of neurotransmitters in the arousal of the sympathetic nervous system, and in perceptual processes (Schuckit, Goodwin, and Winokur 1972).

Schizophrenia is generally characterized by highly inappropriate emotional and behavioral responses. Other symptoms include illogical, scrambled thinking and speech and apparent loss of touch with reality. When psychiatrists used a strict diagnosis of schizophrenia, 35 to 55 percent of monozygotic twins who had schizophrenia had a twin who also had the disorder, while the incidence for dizygotic twins was not substantially higher than would be expected for any siblings of schizophrenia patients (Fischer 1973; Gottesman and Shields 1982; Kendler 1983; McGuffin et al. 1984; Bertelsen 1985; Farmer et al. 1987). Twenty percent of the children born to schizophrenic parents but adopted by nonschizophrenic parents developed schizophrenia or schizoid tendencies. Five percent of the children born to nonschizophrenic parents developed schizophrenic or schizoid tendencies. Twenty-four percent of the natural children of schizophrenic parents who raised them developed schizophrenia (Farber 1981b; Kallman 1946, 1953; Gottesman and Shields 1982). In the case of fraternal twins, the likelihood of both twins' being institutionalized in fraternal pairs of the same sex is greater than in fraternal pairs of the opposite sex again, this suggests that the environment plays a part.

A classic case study of the identical Genain quadruplets indicated that all four girls were diagnosed as having various degrees of schizophrenia or schizoid tendencies. Their home life was very difficult. Their father was very domineering and controlling. When they were adolescents he would not allow them to have any privacy, even in the bathroom, and he would not allow them to date. His family had a history of mental illness. This longitudinal case study suggests an interaction of heredity and environment (Rosenthal 1963).

With another mental illness, *manic-depression,* a bipolar disorder, a person vacillates from extreme elation to deep depression. Studies of reared-apart twins support a genetic predisposition to the illness (Farber 1981b). Gottesman and

Shields (1973, 1982) suggest that what may be inherited is some threshold for responding to stress or tension with some kind of emotional disturbance. Identical twins would thus inherit the same threshold, and if they experienced similar above-threshold life stress, they both would be likely to develop schizophrenia or manic-depression. But if one twin experienced a much higher level of stress or tension or other triggering experience, then only that twin would develop the illness. It is, therefore, possible to inherit a whole series of tendencies that remain latent unless or until some particular experience or series of experiences trigger the behavior. In most cases, the origins of these personality disorders are multifactorial (that is a genetic predisposition and a variety of environmental factors interact causing abnormal behavior) (Farber 1981b; Kallman 1953).

Violent behavior has traditionally been blamed on external influences and the environment. However, more recent data indicate a genetic component as well. This position has created a great deal of controversy among social scientists. One proponent of this position is Sarnoff Mednick, from the University of Southern California. His theory is that the factor that may be genetic is the difference in the functioning of the autonomic nervous system. The *autonomic nervous system* controls unconscious effects of emotion, such as heart rate, blood pressure, muscle tension, respiration, and even the queasiness of fear. If the activity of the autonomic nervous system is reduced, then it makes it difficult for a child to inhibit antisocial behavior. This does not mean, however, that the child is automatically doomed to a life of crime. Mednick's theory suggests that the autonomic nervous system works in conjunction with social factors as a conscience. The same reduced response to fear that points some children toward crime may make others excel at highly respectable professions, such as test piloting. The environment is the determining factor (Gabrielli and Mednick 1984; Mednick and Finello 1983; Mednick et al. 1984).

Other studies support the possibility of a genetic factor that, when triggered in certain environments, may produce violent behavior. If a person's physiology is unbalanced because of brain damage, hormonal irregularities, or genetic abnormalities, then his or her ability to judge a threat is also off balance. What may seem to be a minor intrusion to a normal person becomes a major threat to a person with a low aggression threshold. The brain misperceives some incoming stimulus, such as a harmless gesture or joking remark, as extremely threatening or enraging (Ingber 1982).

Mednick et al. (1984) stress that the presumed genetic factor is significant for only 5 to 10 percent of the criminals who account for 50 percent of the crimes, and these are the more serious and disturbing crimes. This theory does not reject the influence of social and economic factors and says absolutely nothing about racial factors. There is a real concern in linking genes or biology to violence, especially during tough economic times and political conservatism. Such research might be used to justify deeper cuts in programs designed to combat crime by providing jobs or to improve scholarships with enrichment programs.

Hyperkinesis, now considered a dimension of Attention Deficit Disorder (ADD) and sometimes called hyperactivity, is influenced by genetic factors as well as the environment. A child with hyperkinesis is high in activity and impulsivity. Such a child is excessively active in contexts that require relative immobility, quiet, and focused attention. The problem is not so much excessive motion but lack of control. Hyperkinesis is a serious childhood problem that has been studied intensively. As these children mature, they slowly gain control. They learn to suppress their motility but can also organize their activity into socially acceptable channels. For many of these children, distractibility remains a serious problem into adolescence. Many hyperkinetic boys become delinquents when they reach adolescence (Buss and Plomin 1975; Ross and Ross 1976; Bohline 1985; Nichamin and Windell 1984; Wolkenberg 1987).

Impact on Physical Characteristics

Many physical characteristics, which in the past were considered the result of either the environment or heredity, are seen now as a result of interaction between the environment and heredity . Allergies, for example, were thought to be the result of environment. Data indicate that it is rare that an individual is born with an allergy. Rather, an individual may be born with an inherited predisposition to allergic diseases. That is, an individual may be allergic to something but may never know it because he or she is never exposed to it. Everyone produces protective antibodies called Immunoglobin G. Allergic persons also inherit the capacity to produce an antibody called immunoglobin E, which is chemically different from immunoglobin G. Thus nonallergic persons do not develop allergies because they do not have the capacity to produce Immunoglobin E (Joseph 1980). The reared-apart twin studies show a high concordance for twins with hay fever, asthma, and other allergies (Farber 1981a). For example, between Carolyn and Joan, a set of twins reunited in Bouchard's study, Carolyn was allergic to ragweed while Joan was not. However, when they were tested with a variety of other allergens, it was found that they shared some allergies (Miller 1981).

The actual cause of stuttering is unknown, but it is more common in boys than in girls. It is thought that perhaps boys inherit a threshold for stuttering and will develop it if given the right environment. Kidd, Kidd, and Record's (1978) data support such a gene-environment interaction theory concerning stuttering. Some of the reared-apart twins in Bouchard's study both stuttered. Four other sets of twins struggled with the same speech defects (Holden 1980).

Dyslexia, the inability to read with understanding, can be analyzed into partial brain functions. Apparently there is some genetic component that remains to be clarified. A single cause is unlikely. In four separate studies involving thirty-six pairs of identical twins, both twins in each set had the trait. In the case of sixty-six pairs of fraternal twins, less than one-third of the pairs were both dyslexic. Many environmental factors, such as an intense reading program, can modify the course of the disorder (Herschel 1978).

Maximum possible height is genetically determined but is dependent on environmental factors such as adequate nutrition and good health. During the eighteenth and nineteenth centuries, Americans were approximately six inches shorter than they are today. This phenomenon is known as the **secular trend,** the tendency for children to grow taller and mature at a faster rate over the past century. Now most Americans appear to have reached their optimum height, because today's adolescents are no taller than the adolescents of the 1960s.

Secular trend
The tendency for children to grow taller and mature at a faster rate over the past century.

Obesity appears to be due to a genetic predisposition with a definite environmental factor present. If one parent is obese, the children will have a 40 to 50 percent chance of also being obese. If both parents are obese, the children have a 70 to 80 percent chance of becoming obese. Even if their parents are of normal weight, 8 to 9 percent of the children are obese. Identical twins reared in the

● **FIGURE 2.7**
Fatness-Leanness Chart
Weight is often determined by an interaction of heredity and environment. Depending on the amount of food ingested, an individual who has a gene for "fatness" may weigh less than an individual with a gene for "leanness."

same environment show less difference in weight than fraternal twins do. No relationship has been found between the weights of adopted children and their adoptive parents, even though the children were adopted soon after birth (Milunsky 1977).

Handedness is familial, but it is not certain if a child imitates his or her parents or if he or she inherits a predisposition for it. There is more support that it is an inherited trait (Corballis 1983; Corballis and Morgan 1978). In one study, only 2 percent of the children with right-handed parents were left-handed. Forty-two percent of children who have a left-handed parent are left-handed themselves (Piazza 1980).

Menstruation, according to the reared-apart twin studies, begins at about the same time for both twins in a pair; nine months apart is the average difference. Reared-apart identical twins fall between identical twins and fraternal twins reared in the same home. This physical characteristic appears to be heavily influenced by the environment as well as heredity (Farber 1981a, 1981b).

Conclusion

In conclusion, it appears that the functioning of genes may be altered, depending on the process or progress of development. Most experts perceive that the characteristics displayed by human beings could not occur without heredity or the environment. Perhaps the environment affects some physiologic processes but not others. Although it is believed the every human quality is affected by genes, experience via the environment is almost always crucial. The degree to which each factor causes developmental change may never be fully known.

S U M M A R Y

- The study of genetics or heredity is not new. Early Greek philosophers, including Plato, Hippocrates, and Aristotle, made their own observations and developed their own philosophies on the topic.

- The invention of the compound microscope, in the seventeenth century, opened new avenues for discussion with the discovery of sperm and ova. Two preformationist theories emerged: the spermists and ovists, each arguing that a tiny preformed embryo existed in either the sperm or the ovum.

- Mendel, an Austrian monk, provided the world with the foundations of our modern-day understanding of genetics. His research was primarily concerned with genes and their recessive and dominant characteristics.

- Each parent contributes a gene for each human characteristic. If each parent contributes a dominant gene for a particular characteristic or if they each contribute a recessive gene, the genetic code is homozygous, or alike. If one parent contributes a recessive gene and the other a dominant gene, the genetic code is heterozygous, or different. In this case the dominant gene will cancel out the recessive gene and its characteristic will be expressed.

- Phenotype is the visible expression of an inherited trait, and genotype is the genetic makeup for a trait. For example, a person with brown eyes may be phenotypically brown-eyed but genotypically have a recessive gene for blue eyes and a dominant gene for brown eyes.

- Each individual inherits twenty-three chromosomes from each parent, thus carrying a complement of twenty-three pairs. Twenty-two pairs are called autosomes. The twenty-third pair are sex chromosomes, and they determine the sex of an individual. A female has two X chromosomes, and a male has one X and one Y chromosome.

- The human body has two kinds of cells. The somatic, or body, cells govern the formation of the human body, including the skin, bones, muscles, and organs. Gametes, or sex cells, are the sperm in the males and ova in the females. Mitosis is the process by which the somatic cells are developed. Meiosis is the means by which the gametes are developed.

- Monozygotic, or identical, twins develop from one fertilized ovum that splits, forming two identical embryos. On rare occasions such a split may form four or five identical offspring. (The Dionne quintuplets are the only known identical quintuplets.)

- Conjoined, or Siamese, twins are produced when a fertilized egg does not completely split. The most famous Siamese twins were Chang and Eng, from whom the name *Siamese* originated.

- Dizygotic, or fraternal, twins are the result of two ovum being fertilized during the same menstrual cycle. The genetic relationship between the twins is the same as between any other siblings.

Surrogate Parenting

Surrogate parenting has created new moral and legal issues. The most widely known approach to **surrogate parenting** involves the hiring of a fertile woman by a couple in which the wife is infertile. The surrogate mother is then artificially inseminated with the husband's sperm and carries the fetus to term. The reasons for using this alternative to normal reproduction include infertility and the desire to prevent potential genetic defects, inheritable diseases, or Rh factor incompatibility. The surrogate mother carries the baby for the full gestation period. One physician, who was one of the pioneers of the surrogate system, requires that the surrogate be married, have her own children, and be subjected to extensive physical and psychiatric examinations. A contract is drawn up in which she must agree to surrender the child at birth and abstain from tobacco, drugs, and alcohol during pregnancy (Seligmann 1980).

One of the issues that has arisen concerning this approach involves the payment to the surrogate mother. In many states, adoption laws against the sale of babies prevent surrogates from receiving any payment beyond medical expenses (Gorlin and Miley 1984; Seligmann 1980). Are the couple paying the surrogate to carry the baby, or are they paying her *for* the baby? What if the surrogate mother decides to keep the baby? After all, she is a biological parent. In such a situation, the New Jersey courts gave the biological father custody. How does this whole situation affect the surrogate mother morally when she gives up her baby? Does feel she is selling her child? How do her other children view her "disposal" of this baby? Are they concerned that she will give them away too? How will the couple, especially the wife, view this child later, since it is not the wife's biological child? What happens if the child is deformed and neither party wants to keep him or her?

What kind of woman would agree to be a surrogate mother? A psychological and motivational profile of women in surrogate mother programs was compiled from two studies. High femininity and social extroversion scores were found in 90 percent of the sample in one study (Franks 1981). Several complementary motivations were noted in the other study. The motivations included acquiring money, being pregnant, "giving" a baby, and resolving internal psychological conflicts over a previous voluntary abortion (Parker 1983). For the surrogate mother, a period of grief and mourning follows the birth for about four to six weeks. Many women have not been able to give up their babies. They broke their contracts and kept their children (Andrews 1984).

Another form of surrogate parenting is similar to embryo transfer, which was discussed earlier. In this approach an embryo is implanted in a surrogate mother, who carries the fetus to term and then gives the infant to the biological parents. The embryo may be removed from the biological mother because, for some reason, she cannot carry the baby to term. Or the embryo may be the result of in vitro fertilization. But in any case, the infant is the biological child of the couple. What happens to the surrogate mother? Does she experience bonding with the infant that her body nourishes and nurtures for nine months? What are her legal rights to the child? In 1990, a California surrogate mother was denied legal custody and visiting rights to the child she carried and to whom she gave birth.

As biological technology speeds ahead, laws and social customs remain appreciably behind (Mawdsley 1983). How can our society balance these issues and at the same time maintain the rights of each individual involved?

- *Superfecundity* is the term for fraternal twins who are fathered by two different men.
- Superfetation is the rare occurence of a second ovum being fertilized in the following reproductive cycle, producing fraternal twins with different gestation periods. It is, therefore, possible to have a twin a few weeks or a couple of months after the first twin's birth.
- Many factors contribute to the phenomenon of dizygotic twins, including race, age, family size, season, geography, hormones, and heredity.
- Abnormal patterns of inheritance can be the result of dominant, recessive, or sex-linked genes or chromosomal abnormalities.

- Genetic engineering is no longer science fiction. Broadly defined, it is a conscious manipulation that affects the frequency or expression of genes. Genetic counseling, artificial insemination, embryo transfer, in vitro fertilization, and recombinant DNA are some examples of genetic engineering.
- Nature versus nurture has been argued for centuries. Most contemporary scientists tend to accept a more multifactorial approach to the argument and stress the interaction of heredity and environment. Twin studies and adoption studies have contributed to our knowledge about this interaction. Human characteristics most commonly focused on in these studies are intelligence, personality, and physical characteristics.
- Surrogate parenting has raised some moral and legal issues. Surrogate parenting involves the agreement of a woman to maintain a pregnancy for another couple. In some cases the baby is biologically hers, and in other cases she has no biological connection to the infant.

R E A D I N G S

Butterworth, G., Rutkowska, J., and Scaife, M. (Eds.) (1985). *Evolution and developmental psychology.* London: The Harvester Press.
An edited collection concerning the current thinking of the relationship of behavior and biology.

Farber, S. (1981). *Identical twins reared apart: A reanalysis.* NY: Basic Books.
The author reviews the many reared apart twin studies and attempts to track genetic effects on intelligence and personality.

Gould, S. J. (1981). *The mismeasure of man.* NY: W. W. Norton.
The author presents a strong indictment concerning the beliefs concerning genetics and IQ. He also presents a history of mental measurement.

Neubauer, P. B. and Neubauer, A. (1990). *Nature's thumbprint,* Reading, MA: Addison-Wesley Publishing Co.
The authors attempt to balance the nature-nurture debate. They show how genes affect how we interact with the world and how they are related to the development of the human personality.

Walters, W. and Singer, P. (Eds.) (1982). *Test-tube babies.* NY: Oxford University Press.
The ethics of *in vitro* fertilization is discussed and debated.

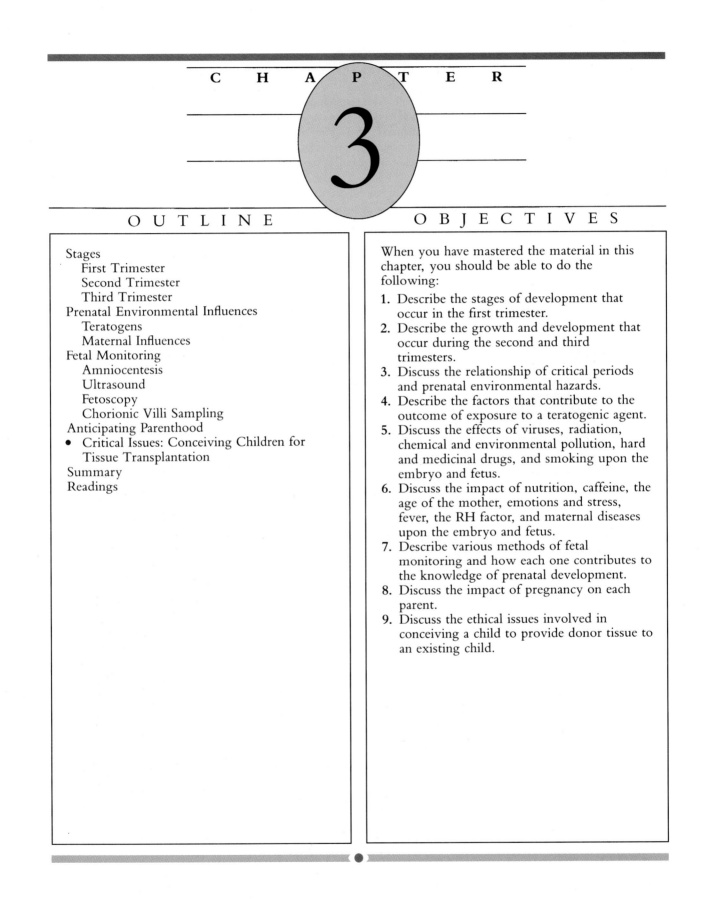

C H A P T E R

3

O B J E C T I V E S

When you have mastered the material in this chapter, you should be able to do the following:

1. Describe the stages of development that occur in the first trimester.
2. Describe the growth and development that occur during the second and third trimesters.
3. Discuss the relationship of critical periods and prenatal environmental hazards.
4. Describe the factors that contribute to the outcome of exposure to a teratogenic agent.
5. Discuss the effects of viruses, radiation, chemical and environmental pollution, hard and medicinal drugs, and smoking upon the embryo and fetus.
6. Discuss the impact of nutrition, caffeine, the age of the mother, emotions and stress, fever, the RH factor, and maternal diseases upon the embryo and fetus.
7. Describe various methods of fetal monitoring and how each one contributes to the knowledge of prenatal development.
8. Discuss the impact of pregnancy on each parent.
9. Discuss the ethical issues involved in conceiving a child to provide donor tissue to an existing child.

Inner Space:
Prenatal Development

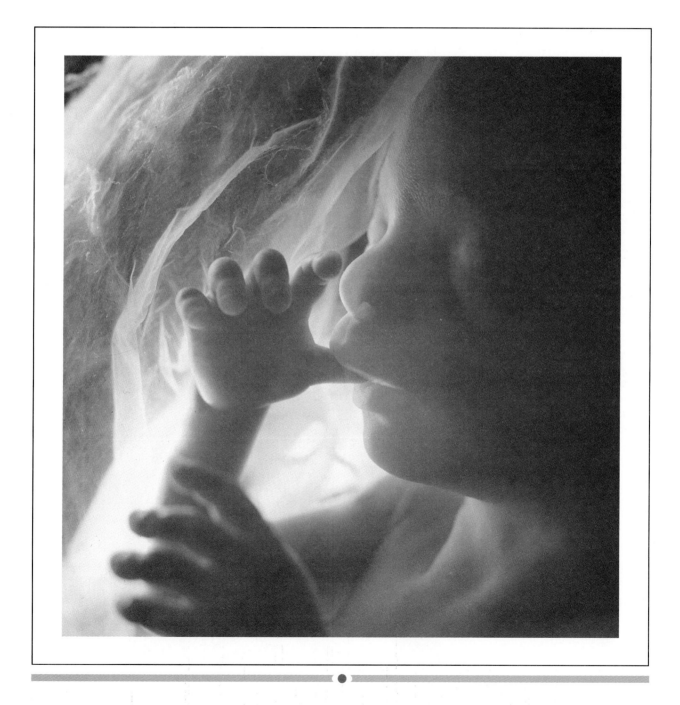

Conception is the first event in the development of a human being. It occurs at the moment a single sperm cell from the male penetrates the wall of the ovum of the female. The best opportunity for this penetration usually occurs in the middle of each menstrual cycle, when the ovum is in a position that is accessible to the sperm. A woman generally produces one ovum per month from one of two ovaries. Occasionally, however, some women, either naturally or because of fertility drugs, produce more than one ovum a month and therefore may produce multiple births.

The period of pregnancy is equally divided into three trimesters. The first trimester incorporates the *germinal stage, the embryonic stage,* and the beginning of the *fetal stage* of development. The second and third trimesters are marked by continued rapid growth and maturation of the fetus. The normal period of **gestation,** or prenatal development, for humans is nine and a half lunar months (about 266 days, since a lunar month is 28 days). The due date is calculated by counting back three calendar months from the first day of the last menstrual period and adding seven days. For example, if the last menstrual period began on August 20, we would count back three months to May 20, add seven days, and predict that May 27 of the following year would be the due date. Only 5 percent of women actually deliver exactly on that date; however 65 percent deliver within five days before or after the predicted due date (Reeder and Martin 1987).

First Trimester

Germinal Stage

The **germinal stage** begins at conception, when the ovum is fertilized, and ends when the fertilized ovum implants itself in the lining of the uterine wall, the *endometrium.* This process takes about two weeks after conception.

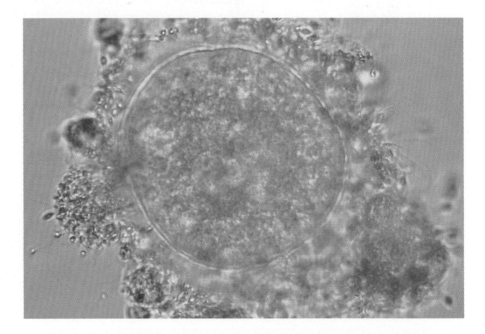

Gestation
The period of prenatal development. For humans it is nine and a half lunar months.

Germinal stage
The first stage of prenatal development. It begins at conception when the ovum is fertilized, and ends when the fertilized ovum implants itself in the lining of the uterine wall, which is about two weeks after conception.

Out of the millions of sperm that are released upon ejaculation, only several dozen are able to swim to the ovum, and only one can penetrate it.

Out of the millions of sperm that are released upon ejaculation, only several dozen are able to swim to the ovum, and only one can penetrate it. After initial penetration, the sperm releases digestive enzymes, eating its way into the ovum. This process alters the ovum's surface so that no other sperm can follow. Then the sperm merges its genetic material with that of the ovum (Parker and Bavosi 1979).

After the sperm and ovum merge and the chromosomes pair up, the organism becomes a zygote. Sometime during the first twenty-four to thirty-six hours after conception, as the zygote moves down the fallopian tube, it splits in two, a process call mitosis. Each of the new cells contain twenty-three pairs of chromosomes, one of each pair from each parent. Mitosis continues with increasing rapidity so that after several days there are several dozen cells. When this tiny cluster of cells reaches the uterus, it continues to subdivide and begins to absorb nutrients from the intrauterine environment (Tuchmann-Duplessis 1975).

The zygote then begins to send out a network of cells (*chorionic villi*), which root in the uterine wall. When the specialization of cells begins to take place, the organism is called a **blastocyst.** After the blastocyst has implanted itself in the uterine wall, it changes from a cluster of cells into an organized structure that differentiates into layers. The outside layer of the blastocyst is called the **ectoderm.** This layer later forms the skin, teeth, hair, nails, and nervous system of the fetus. The inner layer of the blastocyst, the **endoderm,** later develops into most of the body organs, including the liver, pancreas, and lungs. At a later time the **mesoderm,** the middle layer, will develop, creating future muscles, the skeletal system, and the circulatory system (Parker and Bavosi 1979; Reeder and Martin 1987).

The blastocyst secretes a hormone that signals the woman's pituitary gland to inhibit menstruation, allowing the blastocyst to continue to develop. This hormone, *chorionic gonadotropin,* can be isolated in the urine of a pregnant woman, thus making it possible to detect a pregnancy (Reeder and Martin 1987). Between one-half and two-thirds of fertilized human ova fail to implant themselves in the uterus and are washed away unnoticed. Approximately 69 percent of implanted embryos develop to term (Wilcox et al. 1988).

Embryonic Stage

The **embryonic stage** begins when the zygote attaches to the uterine wall and ends when the zygote's rudimentary organ systems and body parts take shape. The word *embryo* comes from the Greek word meaning "to swell" (Begley and Carey 1982). The period of time involved is from the end of the second week to the end of the eighth week of gestation. Rapid cell division and differentiation take place during this stage.

The **amniotic sac,** which contains fluid, surrounds the beginning embryo and continues to do so until birth. This sac protects the embryo by functioning as a shock absorber, plus it maintains a constant temperature and allows the embryo the opportunity to move its primitive limbs. The sac consists of two membranes: the outer membrane is called the **chorion,** and the inner layer is called the **amnion** (Noble 1980).

By the end of the fourth week, the embryo is about one-sixth to one-fourth of an inch long and has begun to develop a circulatory system, a nervous system, a skeletal system, and other organs. The yolk sac, a protective membrane, partly develops into the digestive tract, urinary system, and lungs. The

Blastocyst
During the germinal stage, the specialization of cells formed from the zygote that root in the uterine wall.

Ectoderm
During the germinal stage, the outside layer of the blastocyst. This later forms the skin, teeth, hair, nails, and nervous system of the fetus.

Endoderm
During the germinal stage, the inner layer of the blastocyst. This later develops into most of the body organs, including the liver, pancreas, and lungs.

Mesoderm
During the germinal stage, the middle layer of the blastocyst. This later develops into muscles, the skeletal system, and the circulatory system.

Embryonic stage
The second stage of prenatal development. It begins when the zygote attaches to the uterine wall and ends when the zygote's rudimentary organ systems and body parts take shape. The period of time involved is from the end of the second week to the end of the eighth week of gestation.

Amniotic sac
A bag or envelope of clear fluid that surrounds and protects the embryo by functioning as a shock absorber. It maintains a constant temperature and allows the embryo the opportunity to move its primitive limbs.

Chorion
The outer membrane of the amniotic sac.

Amnion
The inner membrane of the amniotic sac.

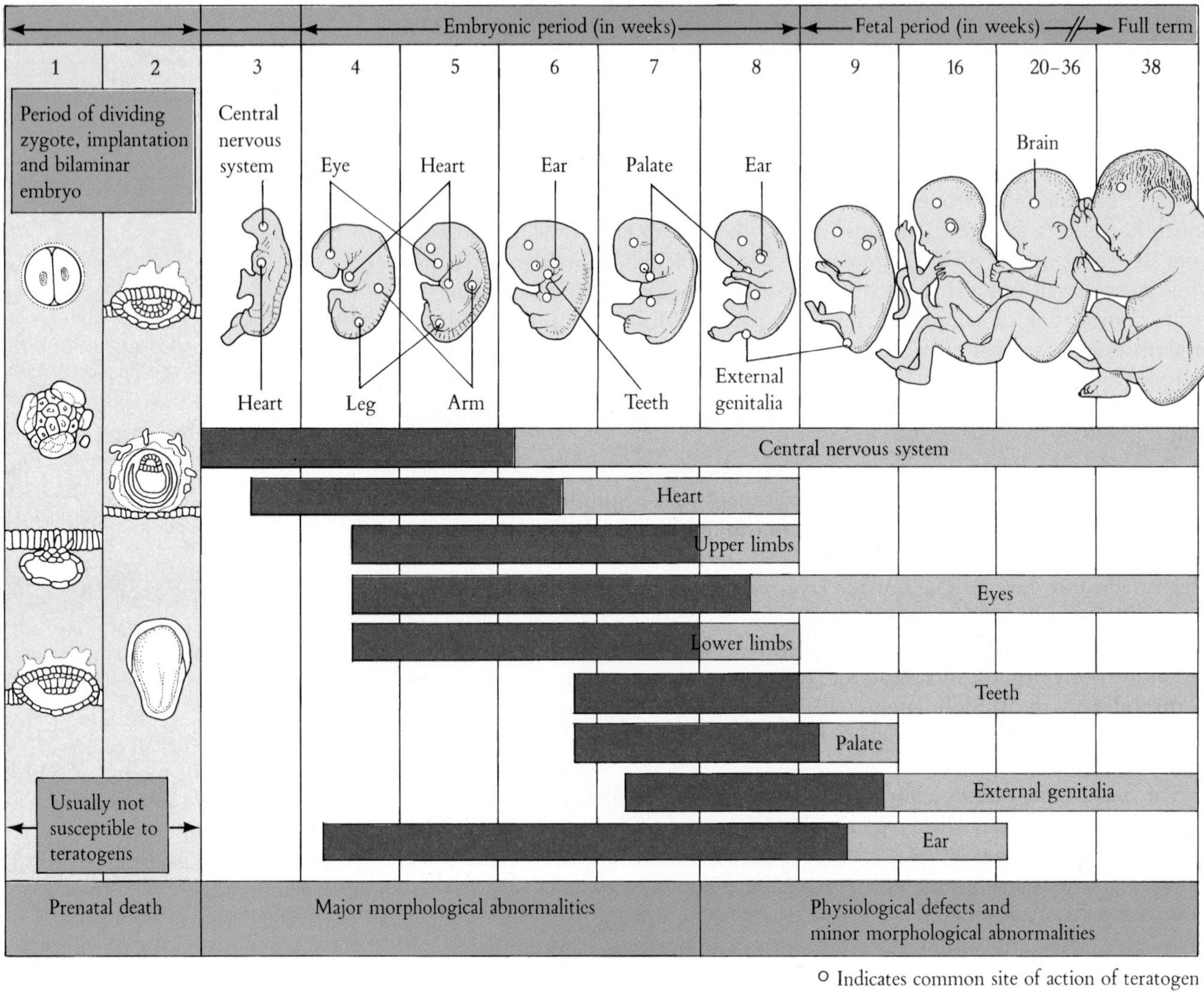

● FIGURE 3.1
Critical Periods in Pre-natal Development

Schematic illustration of the critical periods in human development. During the first two weeks of development, the embryo is usually not susceptible to teratogens. During these predifferentiation stages, a substance either damages all or most of the cells of the embryo, resulting in its death, or it damages only a few cells, allowing the embryo to recover without developing defects. Red denotes highly sensitive periods; yellow indicates stages that are less sensitive to teratogens.
Source: Moore, Keith L. *The Developing Human,* 3rd ed. (Philadelphia: W. B. Saunders Company), 152.

remainder of the yolk sac gradually disappears by the second month of pregnancy. One function of the yolk sac is to provide blood cells for the embryo until the liver, spleen, and bone marrow can operate by themselves.

The **placenta** develops on the outer side of the chorion. This is a critical organ that separates the infant's bloodstream from the mother's, as well as provides nourishment to the developing organism. It develops secretory and regulatory functions essential for maintaining the pregnancy. It also provides immunizing agents that combat certain diseases, acts as a filtering system, helps prepare the mother's mammary glands for lactation, and helps stimulate uterine contractions later on (Tuchmann-Duplessis 1975). The embryo is attached to the placenta by the **umbilical cord,** which contains two arteries and a vein. The

Placenta
A critical organ that separates the infant's bloodstream from the mother's, provides nourishment to the embryo and later the fetus, provides immunizing agents that combat certain diseases, and acts as a filtering system.

arteries remove waste products and carbon dioxide. The vein brings in oxygen and nutrients. This is the means by which blood is transported to and from the embryo. Membranes serve as screening devices between the mother's bloodstream and the embryo, preventing potentially harmful substances from crossing the placenta. Proteins, sugars, and vitamins found in the mother's bloodstream pass through the membranes to the embryo's bloodstream (Reeder and Martin 1987). Unfortunately, various drugs also get through.

The form of the embryo gradually takes shape. The head and the arm and leg buds are visible by the end of the first month. Also by this time the primitive heart has started to pulsate, and other organs are beginning to develop. The human embryo at this stage resembles the embryos of most animals.

The fifth and sixth weeks are important for the shaping of the face, eyes, and ears. The head and upper body develop somewhat earlier than the lower part, which gives the embryo a top-heavy appearance. It is about one-third of an inch long, with the head representing about 50 percent of the embryo's size. Simultaneously, the lungs, liver, kidneys, and other vital organs and glands are taking form.

By the end of the eighth week, the embryo is a little over one inch long and weighs less than one ounce. Its face looks human, the limbs hinge on joints, the hands spread out into fingers, and primitive genitals appear (gender is not recognizable until the end of the third month). At about this time the cells forming the penis have become differentiated from the cells forming the corresponding organ in the female, the clitoris. By now this little organism has all of its organ systems and body parts in at least a rudimentary form. This marks the beginning of the fetal stage (Parker and Bavosi 1979; Reeder and Martin 1987).

Fetal Stage

The term *fetus* is from the Latin word meaning "offspring" (Begley and Carey 1982). Formation of the major organs and body parts continues during the **fetal stage.** The eyelids develop and seal the eyes shut during the ninth week. The roof of the mouth, or palate, is formed about the tenth week. During the eleventh week the teeth buds appear inside the gums. By the end of the first

Umbilical cord
A cord that attaches the embryo and fetus to the placenta. It contains two arteries and a vein. The arteries remove waste products and carbon dioxide. The vein brings in oxygen and nutrients.

Fetal stage
The third stage of prenatal development, during which the formation of the major organs and body parts occurs.

Formation of the major organs and body parts continues during the fetal stage.

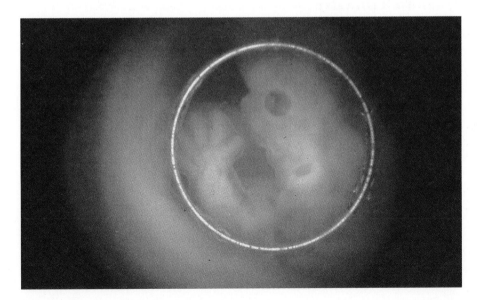

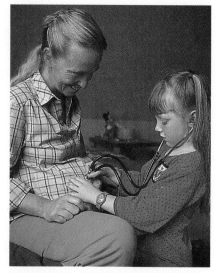

During the second trimester, the mother is aware of the life developing within her.

Organogenesis
The basic formation of the fetus's major organs, organ systems, and body parts.

Quickening
During the second trimester, a period of activity in the womb that makes the mother aware of the fetus's presence.

Lanugo
A soft hair that covers the body of the fetus during the fifth and sixth months.

Vernix caseosa
A whitish, waxy substance that covers the fetus and protects the skin.

trimester, the basic structure of the body's major organs, organ systems, and body parts have been completed. This is termed **organogenesis.** The central nervous system further develops and continues to do so until several months after birth (Tuchmann-Duplessis 1975). The fetus is only three inches long and weighs one ounce. The mother's uterus is just beginning to expand, while at the same time the tiny, primitive organs of the fetus have begun functioning. The fetus is capable of swallowing small amounts of amniotic fluid and excreting small amounts of urine. The sex of the fetus is now distinguishable. It looks human, although the head is still very large in proportion to the rest of the body (constituting one-third of the fetus's body). Although the fetus moves, it cannot be felt by the mother until the sixteenth week.

Second Trimester

During the second trimester, the mother is aware of the life developing within her. **Quickening,** a period of activity in the womb, makes the mother aware of the fetus's presence. It is first felt as a mild fluttering, but later it is more like good, solid kicks. During these periods of activity, it is possible to see and feel the bulge of an arm, foot, leg, or head. Most parents and future siblings find this an exciting experience. Quickening has traditionally been viewed as the beginning of life. The fetal heartbeat can be detected by a physician during the fourth month. The primitive skeleton is beginning to *ossify,* or harden, and the body and face appear more human.

Lanugo, a soft hair, grows and covers the body of the fetus during the fifth and sixth months. Most of the hair sheds before the birth. A whitish, waxy substance called **vernix caseosa** covers the fetus and protects the skin. Fingernails, eyelashes, and eyebrows materialize at this time. In the sixth month, the eyelids open. The fetus weighs a little more than two pounds and is approximately fourteen inches long. If a fetus were to be born at twenty-four to twenty-five weeks, it is unlikely that it could function on its own unless cared for by specialists in a modern facility. However, by twenty-six weeks, the fetus has a good chance of surviving (Reeder and Martin 1987).

Third Trimester

At the beginning of the third trimester, the nervous, circulatory, and respiratory systems are well enough developed to support life. (However, premature infants born at this time have poor sleep-wake cycles and irregular breathing.) During the last few weeks before birth, the fetus gains weight by developing fatty tissues under the skin, which will insulate it from the outer environment, where the temperature is much lower and no longer stable. With the development of the fatty tissues, the appearance of the fetus changes from thin and wrinkled to rounded. During these last few weeks the brain and central nervous system develop further, with a general finishing of the various body systems. Just before birth, the fetus has almost no room to move around. The uterus expands so much that it crowds the mother's other organs, putting additional strain on her heart, lungs, and kidneys. The placenta reaches its maximum size and working capacity. Full term has now been reached and the baby is ready to emerge into his or her new world. The newborn weighs, on the average, about seven pounds if a girl and about seven and one-half pounds if a boy. The average length of a newborn is twenty inches.

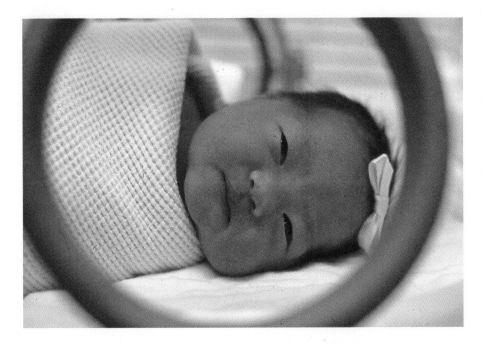

The newborn weighs, on the average, about seven pounds if a girl and about seven and one-half pounds if a boy. The average length of a newborn is twenty inches.

● PRENATAL ENVIRONMENTAL INFLUENCES

A major concern of prospective new parents is whether their baby will be free of congenital defects. An overwhelming majority of babies are born without serious abnormalities that cause a physical or mental handicap. About 20 percent of the handicaps are due to heredity, while 20 percent are caused by environmental factors such as drugs, medicine, vitamin deficiencies, and viral infections. The final 60 percent are due to the interaction of environmental factors and genetic predisposition (Korones 1981).

In the series of events involved in producing the human baby, each organ, organ system, and anatomical structure develops certain of its elements at fixed times. These fixed times are called **critical periods.** If an environmental factor interferes with the growth of an organ during its critical period, the organ does not develop properly. Permanent damage will result, because after the time for the organ's formation passes, there is no second chance. Critical periods for most of the organs and parts of the body are during the first trimester. After the first trimester, the basic structure of the fetus is established, and the fetus spends time primarily growing. Environmental factors during this period can interfere with growth, but not with the basic structure of the organs. The main exception is brain development (O'Brien and McManus 1978).

Critical periods
Fixed times in the development of an organ, organ system, or anatomical structure, which, if interfered with, will permanently hamper further development of the organ, system, or structure.

Teratogens

An environmental factor that interferes with the development of an embryo and is responsible for producing a physical defect in the embryo is called a **teratogenic agent.** *Teratology* is literally defined as "the study of monsters." Teratogens are those agents that "deleteriously affect an embryo that was otherwise differentiating normally." Teratogens can cause a malformation either chromosomally or genetically (Moore 1983). In Western countries, 2 to 3 per-

Teratogenic agent
An environmental factor that interferes with the development of an embryo and is responsible for producing a physical defect in the embryo.

TABLE 3.1 Prenatal Milestones Chart

FIRST TRIMESTER

First Lunar Month (first to fourth weeks)
Cells rapidly divide.
Spinal canal and brain are forming.
Heart has first pulsations.
Skeletal and digestive systems begin to form.
Small budlike nubbins form for future arms and legs.
No eyes, nose, or ears are visible.
Embryo is one-fourth to one-sixth of an inch long.
Head is one-third of entire embryo.

Second Lunar Month (fifth to eighth weeks)
Embryo is now called a fetus.
Genital organs are apparent, but sex cannot be distinguished.
Brain, spinal cord, and nervous system are developed and responsive.
Heart pumps some blood, irregularly.
Limbs begin to show distinct arms and webbed hands, legs and webbed feet.
Face and features are forming; eyelids are fused.
Distinct umbilical cord is formed.
Length is about 2.5 cm (1 in.) by eighth week.
Weight is about 18 g. (two-thirds of an ounce).

Third Lunar Month (ninth to twelfth weeks)
Arms, legs, and feet are formed.
Bone is replacing cartilage.
Sex can be distinguished.
Fetus begins to move but is too weak to be felt by mother.
External ears appear.
Tooth sockets and buds are forming.
Eyelids, fingernails, and toenails are forming.
Rudimentary kidney secretes small amount of urine.
Length is about 7.5 cm. (3 in.).
Weight is about 28 g. (1 oz.).

SECOND TRIMESTER

Fourth Lunar Month (thirteenth to sixteenth weeks)
Mouth opens and closes.
Eyes blink.
Hands can grip.
Toes and fingers are separated; fingerprints emerge.
Movements become stronger.
Length is about 15 cm. (6 to 6.5 in.).
Weight is about 112 g. (4 oz.).

Fifth Lunar Month (seventeenth to twentieth weeks)
Heartbeat is fairly regular.
Sweat glands develop.
External skin is no longer transparent.
Fetus sleeps and wakes at regular times.
Fetus may put thumb in mouth.
Length is about 20 to 30 cm. (8 to 12 in.).
Weight is about 224 g. (8 oz.).

Sixth Lunar Month (twenty-first to twenty-fourth weeks)
Taste buds develop on tongue.
Fetus is able to inhale and exhale and could make a crying sound.

TABLE 3.1 (Continued)

Whitish, waxy substance called vernix caseosa covers fetus and protects the skin.
Fine soft hair called lanugo begins to grow.
Outline of fetus can be felt.
Fingernails materialize.
Eyes are developed and eyelids may separate.
Fetuses have been born at this point and have survived.
Length is about 27.5 to 35 cm. (11 to 14 in.).
Weight is about 900 g. (2 lbs.).

THIRD TRIMESTER

Seventh Lunar Month (twenty-fifth to twenty-eighth weeks)
Fetus's body is filling out.
Fetus can differentiate basic tastes and odors.
Internal organs are formed and almost functional.
Fetuses born at this stage have good chance of survival but are immature.

Eighth Lunar Month (twenty-ninth to thirty-second weeks)
Fetus settles into favored position.
Fetus's fat deposits increase.
Fetus gains about .5 lb. per week.
Length is about 40 to 45 cm. (16 to 18 in.).
Weight is about 1,800 to 2,250 g. (4 to 5 lbs.).

Ninth Lunar Month (thirty-third to thirty-sixth weeks)
Fetus develops extra layer of fat and thickened, smooth, polished skin.
Bones of fetus's head are soft and flexible.
Antibodies pass from mother to fetus, which immunizes infant for several
    months after birth.
Fetus gains 225 g. (.5 lbs.) a week.
Length is about 45 cm. (18 in.).
Weight is about 3,000 g. (6 lbs.).

Middle Tenth Lunar Month (thirty-seventh to thirty-eighth weeks)
Fetus's skin becomes pinkish.
Contractions signal approach of labor and delivery.
Full term; end of gestation period; fetus is now prepared to live in outside world.
Length is about 50 cm. (20 in.).
Weight is about 3,100 to 3,600 g. (7 to 8 lbs.).

cent of children are found to have gross malformations at birth (Tuchmann-Duplessis 1975).

The outcome of an individual's exposure to a particular teratogen is determined by several factors:

- Some agents are more likely to be teratogenic than others.
- Each teratogen has a characteristic way of disrupting normal prenatal development. For example, mercury attacks only the central nervous system prenatally, resulting in cerebral palsy or similar syndromes.
- The amount or dose of a teratogen is related to the damage incurred and may range from causing no effects to causing lethal effects. At any given time the embryo can respond to the teratogen in one of three ways, depending on the dosage level: (1) a low level may produce no effect; (2) an intermediate level can result in specific organ malformation; and

(3) a high level may kill the embryo, with damage to a specific organ going undetected. The dosage effect depends on the developmental stage of the embryo when the drug is administered; for example, the agent may be teratogenic only at a higher or lower dose at a specific stage. Also, at one dose an agent might be lethal yet not teratogenic, and at another dose it could be either lethal or teratogenic. The administration of small doses of a teratogen over several days may produce a different effect than an equal amount administered at one time. For example, Vitamins A and D, in appropriate amounts, are necessary for normal development, whereas both a deficiency and an excess are teratogenic in experimental animals and in isolated cases in humans.

- The development stage of the organism at the time of the teratogenic exposure is significant in determining the *incidence* of damage as well as the type of damage. During the first two weeks, the embryo is relatively resistant to a teratogenic onslaught. A large onslaught might kill the embryo, but the surviving embryo expresses no anomalies in specific organs. However, between three and eight weeks, the susceptibility to teratogens is at its maximum. (This is the critical period when organogenesis occurs). A teratogen may affect one organ system at one time and another system at another time. Generally, a system that is undergoing rapid development, such as in organogenesis, is more susceptible to the influence of a teratogen.

- The genetic composition of the various animal species varies as to the susceptibility to teratogenic agents. For example, thalidomide, a nonprescription sleeping pill and nausea preventative, was not detrimental to mice but was to humans.

- The genetic composition of individual embryos, even those with the same parents, may provoke a different response to the same teratogens. The differences in teratogenic susceptibility can be explained by differences in the maternal ability to absorb and metabolize a teratogen, differences in the rate of placental transfer, and differences in fetal metabolism. Certain embryos may prove unusually susceptible to a teratogen, whereas others may be unusually resistant.

- The interaction of two or more teratogens when simultaneously administered may or may not produce the same effect as if they were administered separately. One agent might enhance the teratogenic potential of another. The enhancing agent does not necessarily have to be a drug; it might be some universal environmental factor such as a food preservative. For example, benzoic acid, a food preservative, enhances the aspirin teratogenicity in rats.

- The various responses to a teratogen may be related to environmental factors not traditionally considered genetic. Such factors include maternal or fetal weight, in utero position of the fetus, proximity to other affected litter mates, the uterine vascular system, and the diet and age of mother. Experimental and clinical data show that risks of malformation and fetal death are higher if the mother is very young and even more so if she is older. Pathological factors such as chronic and metabolic diseases, diabetes, obesity, hypertension, toxemia, and liver dysfunction in the mother may enhance the toxic action of drugs and increase the frequency of fetal damage (Streitfeld 1978; Simpson 1976; O'Brien and McManus 1978; Tuchmann-Duplessis 1975; Moore 1983).

A teratogen affects the development of the embryo through a variety of mechanisms, such as gene mutation, chromosome breakage, and/or depletion of energy sources. Regardless of what the specific teratogenic mechanisms are, the final result is usually an organ with too few cells. The critical mass necessary for the initiation or continuation of organ differentiation is lacking; thus, the particular organ system fails to develop properly. A few anomalies, such as polydactyly (one or more extra fingers), could result from increased cell proliferation. Nonetheless, scientists are still unaware of the causes of 70 percent of birth defects (Moore 1983).

Viruses

After the *rubella* epidemic in the United States between 1963 and 1965, twenty thousand pregnancies were lost and twenty-five thousand children with severe handicaps survived. These children were born deaf, blind, mentally retarded, with small head size, at low birth weight, and/or with malformed hearts. Yet the mothers' symptoms were so mild that many of them were unaware that they had the disease. Rubella, or German measles, is the most widely known lethal virus for embryos. Fifty percent of the embryos of pregnant women who contract rubella are affected. The disease is most detrimental during the first two months of gestation. Although abnormality rates decrease progressively after the first trimester, both fetal death and abnormalities are associated with rubella in the second trimester. Even after birth, infants with congenital rubella excrete the virus in their throats, stool, and urine for months. These infants can be a source of infection for susceptible individuals, so it is important that they be isolated from pregnant women. In fact, the infection may go unrecognized during the early weeks of life, so it is wise to prohibit susceptible women from working in hospital nurseries or pediatric wards (U.S. Centers for Disease Control 1989; Hardy 1973; Hardy 1969).

Recent data show a 5 percent risk of birth defects resulting from the inadvertent administration of the rubella vaccine close to the time of conception or during the first three months of embryonic and fetal life. The current recommendation is that conception not take place within three months of immunization (Nora et al. 1981).

A new viral illness that is spreading rapidly is *acquired immune deficiency syndrome* (AIDS). Infants born to mothers who have the disease are suffering severe consequences. Most of these infants show growth failure, with small heads and facial deformities. Within only a few months after birth, many of these infants contract repeated infections and show developmental delays. No cure for the disease has yet been found. Over half of the infants born with AIDS have died (Macklin and Needles 1987).

Other viruses that are implicated in congenital malformations or birth defects include pneumonia, rubeola (measles), hepatitis, influenza, smallpox, chicken pox, scarlet fever, toxoplasmosis (found in the feces of cats and in some uncooked ground beef), mumps, herpes simplex, and cytomegalovirus (a sexually transmitted disease that occurs in about 3 percent of pregnant women). The incidence of defects with these viruses is lower than with rubella (Fine 1985).

Radiation

The use of radiation is extremely serious early in pregnancy. X rays, radioactive materials used in some industries or research, and leaks from nuclear power plants are sources of radiation. Radiation has been implicated in changing the genetic patterns of chromosomes and causing central nervous system damage in the fetus that often results in stillbirth or miscarriage. The amount of damage is proportional to the dosage and the time of exposure to the radiation. After the 1945 bombings of Hiroshima and Nagasaki, Japan, of the surviving pregnant women who were within fallout range, 28 percent experienced miscarriages, 25 percent had neonatal deaths, and 25 percent experienced mutations in their offspring (Langman 1975).

The effects of radiation are cumulative, so repeated overexposure during childhood and adolescence can produce mutagens of genes in the ova and sperm stored in the ovaries or testes (before each one matures and is discharged for possible fertilization). One study compared 972 children who were conceived after their mothers were exposed to diagnostic radiation with the same number of children who were born of mothers without radiation exposure. Significantly more trisomic children (their chromosomes were matched in threes rather than in pairs) had mothers who had been exposed to abdominal radiation (Tuchmann-Duplessis 1975).

Another study was designed to investigate the relation between prenatal exposure to X rays and childhood cancer, including leukemia, in over thirty-two thousand twins who were born in Connecticut from 1930 to 1969. Twins in whom leukemia or other childhood cancer developed were twice as likely to have been exposed to X rays in utero as twins who were free from cancer. This study supports other evidence that low-dose prenatal irradiation may increase the risk of childhood cancer (Harvey 1985). Occasionally, however, the need for pelvic X rays to diagnose obstetrical problems outweighs the possible radiation risks to the unborn child.

Chemical and Environmental Pollution

Mercury that is ingested prenatally can cause central nervous system damage, blindness, and cerebral palsy. Mercury can be obtained from water polluted by industrial mercury waste or from the meat of animals who have been fed grain treated with organic mercury salts (to protect against insects and fungi).

In 1953, a new disease, Minimata syndrome, appeared in Japan. It originated from the consumption of great amounts of fish from the Minimata Bay area. The bay was polluted by methyl mercuric sulphide and methyl mercuric chloride from waste discharged into the Minimata River. The total number of victims was 134: 78 adults, 31 infants, and 25 fetal cases. The fetal Minimata disease was characterized by cerebral palsy, deformation of the skull, and sometimes microcephaly (smaller-than-normal head and brain) (Tuchmann-Duplessis 1975). Alkyl mercury has adverse effects upon mammals, including humans, in intrauterine life (Streitfeld 1978). Organic mercury impairs embryonic development and acts upon the brain during the fetal period. The fetal brain is much more susceptible to alkyl mercury than the adult brain (O'Brien and McManus 1978).

Neurological damage and growth retardation have been found in the offspring of industrial workers with excessive exposure to lead and vinyl chloride (Streitfeld 1978). Agent Orange, a chemical defoliant used in Vietnam, has also been implicated in birth defects.

Anesthetic gases have been identified as another teratogen. Higher rates of spontaneous abortion and congenital abnormality were found among the offspring of exposed females as well as nonexposed wives of exposed male operating-room personnel. Exposed personnel also had a higher proportion of female to male children than did comparable groups (Brackbill 1979).

Medicinal Drugs

Thalidomide was widely used in Europe in the late 1950s and early 1960s. It was manufactured in West Germany and banned in the United States by the Food and Drug Administration. Shortly after the drug was widely used by pregnant women to control nausea from morning sickness, there was a huge increase in the number of birth defects. These defects included deformities of the heart and digestive system, as well as phocomelia, a deformity in which the hands and feet grow directly from the body on short, stunted nubs. Because phocomelia is so rare, obstetricians realized that the large increase was due to an unusual factor and quickly isolated thalidomide as the agent. Women who took thalidomide in the first trimester of their pregnancies had deformed babies, but those who took it after the first trimester had normal babies. A later study revealed that among the women who took it during the critical period of pregnancy (the first trimester), less than 25 percent had deformed babies, with the remainder escaping the deleterious effects of the drug (Reeder and Martin 1987; Carlson 1984). Nonetheless, thousands of children were born with severe deformities.

Thalidomide baby.

Aspirin, which interferes with blood clotting, is also suspected of increasing the gestation period, lengthening labor, and causing greater blood loss at delivery (March of Dimes 1983). There is no clear evidence that aspirin by itself causes defects in human embryos and fetuses. Animal research suggests that it might represent some danger when certain other substances are present. For example, research on rats indicates that the toxic potential of aspirin is increased when given with benzoic acid, a common food preservative (Kimmel et al. 1971; Heinonen et al. 1977). Because research remains inconclusive, it is best not to take aspirin during pregnancy.

Tetracycline, an antibiotic, when taken in large doses intravenously, may cause a fatty liver in the mother and possibly a stillborn fetus. If it is taken after the fourth month, it will stain the deciduous (baby) teeth irreparably and cause defective enamel development. It may decrease fetal skeletal growth and inhibit long-bone growth (March of Dimes 1983).

Fetal iodide toxicity causes massive thyroid enlargement in the fetus, which leads to respiratory difficulties postnatally. No other drug or maternal disorder produces thyroid enlargement to such a degree. Excessive amniotic fluid production is a common accompanying feature. Fetal iodide toxicity is known to cause permanent hypothyroidism and cataracts. Cough suppressants and expectorants sold over the counter contain iodides. Such medication is normally not harmful but is potentially dangerous during pregnancy (O'Brien and McManus 1978).

Phenobarbital and other barbiturates can cross the placenta and are stored in the placenta and the fetal liver and brain. Because fetal kidneys are unable to eliminate barbiturates, the concentration in the fetus is greater than the maternal concentration. Barbiturates are known to cause minimal fetal depression, decreased neonatal responsiveness, and an inhibited ability to suck, and they are capable of causing reproductive disorders in both male and female offspring. In male offspring, they can cause a delay in the testicular descent, with subsequent infertility and decreased production of testosterone and gonadotropin throughout adulthood. Phenobarbital has also been implicated as a possible cause of congenital malformations such as cleft lip and palate (Gupta and Yaffe 1982; March of Dimes 1983).

Anticoagulants, when taken during the first trimester, have been associated with incomplete development of the nasal bones, spotted appearance in the growth areas of long bones, deformities of the bones of the hand, hemorrhage, death in utero, mental retardation, and eye and heart defects. The fetal organs that are affected are the ones that are being formed when the chemical takes effect (March of Dimes 1983; O'Brien and McManus 1978).

Diethylstilbestrol (DES), a synthetic estrogen, was used in the late 1940s in the United States for the treatment of pregnancy complications, particularly for patients with a history of previous early-pregnancy losses and for patients with threatened miscarriage. The success of saving the fetuses and the low cost of the drug led to its widespread use throughout the 1950s and 1960s (Carrington 1974). It is now well established that there is an association between maternal ingestion of DES during pregnancy and the occurrence of vaginal cancer years later in the female offspring. When DES daughters reach childbearing age, they appear to be more vulnerable than others to miscarriage, stillbirth, premature birth, and ectopic pregnancy. Among male offspring, a high incidence of urinary tract problems, genital abnormality, and infertility have been identified (Capsules 1980; Carrington 1974; Cosgrove 1977).

Other hormones, such as progesterone and androgens, have been implicated in the masculinization of female genitalia and in congenital heart disease. Oral contraceptives, which contain the hormones estrogen and progestin, are associated with congenital limb reduction, heart abnormalities, and other defects (Nora et al. 1981; O'Brien and McManus 1978).

Hard Drugs

Fetal alcohol syndrome, or FAS, has been identified as a pattern of mental, physical, and behavioral abnormalities in the infants of women who drink alcoholic beverages when they are pregnant. The belief that the parental consumption of alcohol can have adverse effects on the health of offspring has a long history. Potential danger was recognized in Sparta and Carthage with laws prohibiting the use of alcohol by newly married couples, in order to prevent conception during intoxication. Aristotle addressed the hazard in his *Problemata:* "Foolish, drunken or hair-brain women for the most part bring forth children like themselves. . . . " In 1726, Britain's College of Physicians petitioned Parliament to control the distilling trade, calling gin a "cause of weak, feeble and distempered children." Throughout the nineteenth century, the medical community observed that the offspring of alcoholics had a high frequency of mental retardation, epilepsy, stillbirth, and infant death. This information was used by the religious temperance leaders to prove that the sins of the parents were visited on their children for several generations.

In 1899, a physician to a Liverpool prison, William Sullivan, published a careful study of 600 offspring of 120 alcoholic women. He located 28 nondrinking female relatives of the alcoholic women and found that the infant mortality and stillborn rate was two and a half times higher in the alcoholics' children than in the comparison population. Dr. Sullivan also observed that several alcoholic women who had had infants with severe and often fatal complications, later bore healthy children while in prison. This was thought to be due to the forced abstention from alcohol during pregnancy while imprisoned. In American and

British literature, the interest in the effects of alcohol on offspring declined after 1920 (Rosett and Sander 1979).

In a more recent study of 417 pregnant women, the women who consumed over six ounces of alcohol per day were likely to give birth to infants with FAS. These children had smaller-than-average heads and brains, were unable to suck well, showed poor muscle tone, and showed a wide range of learning and behavioral problems. Over 17 percent of the children of heavy drinkers had serious birth defects, compared with 3 percent of the children of nondrinkers (Streissguth et al. 1983). In an economically high-risk maternal population, 35 percent of the newborns of light drinkers displayed some form of physiological or neurological problem, compared with 45 percent of the infants of moderate drinkers and 71 percent of the infants of heavy drinkers (Ashley 1981). In another study, congenital anomalies were three times more frequent among the children of heavy drinkers than among the children of abstinent or rare drinkers (Streissguth et al. 1983). These and other studies indicate there is a risk in light and moderate drinking as well.

The various studies concerning FAS noted similar symptoms, such as small heads, narrow eye openings, an extra eyelid fold, limited movement in the elbows and the joints of the hands, hip dislocation, prenatal and postnatal growth deficiency, congenital heart disease and delayed motor development. Follow-up studies of FAS children found that most abnormalities were in the area of mental function. Although not all of these children were retarded, it was rare that they had average or better-than-average mental ability. They were found to be impulsive and distractible, and they had attention deficits. "Safe" limits for alcohol consumption during pregnancy have not been determined, so for pregnant women, it is best to abstain totally (Clarren and Smith 1978; Abel 1981; Hanson et al. 1978; Kolata 1981; Begley and Carey 1982; Streitfeld 1978; Nora et al. 1981; Ouelette et al. 1977; Ashley 1981; Streissguth et al. 1983).

Cocaine and the highly potent smokable form of cocaine, called *crack,* have also been linked to birth defects. Chevez et al. (1989) reported that mothers who used cocaine in early pregnancy were four times more likely to have an infant with an urinary tract defect, and two times more likely to have an infant with a defect of the genital organs. Zuckerman et al. (1989) found that women who used cocaine in pregnancy had infants who weighed less, were shorter and had a smaller head size than the infants of women who did not use cocaine.

Heroin and *methadone* cross the placenta and addict the fetus in utero. Immediately after birth, such an infant suffers from withdrawal symptoms, including irritability, seizures, tremors, diarrhea, and vomiting (Householder et al. 1982; Hale 1978; Brazelton 1970). In a longitudinal study, the infants of twenty-five heroin addicts, twenty-six addicts receiving methadone therapy, and forty-one drug-free mothers in a comparison group were followed through the preschool years. An increased incidence of low-average and mildly retarded intellectual performance was noted in the drug-exposed children (Lifschitz et al. 1985).

Marijuana use during pregnancy is associated with prematurity; low birth weight; decreased maternal weight gain; complications of pregnancy; difficult labor; congenital abnormalities; increased change of stillbirth; perinatal problems; and poor Brazelton Scale scores, (which assess the way neonates adapt to their environment) (Fried 1982; Fried et al. 1987; Gibson et al. 1983; Greenland et al. 1982; Hingson et al. 1982). The marijuana usage of pregnant Jamaican

Smoking heavily during pregnancy has been linked to increased risk of premature delivery, low birth weight, and prenatal or postnatal infant death.

women affects the cries of their newborn infants, indicating neurophysiological damage (Lester and Dreher 1989). Fried (1982) has also documented high-pitched cries in the infants of marijuana users.

Smoking a pack or more of cigarettes a day is associated with premature delivery, low-birth-weight babies, and increased risk of the death of infants prenatally and postnatally (Lefkowitz 1981; Magnus et al. 1985; Heinonen et al. 1977). Smoking interacts with other factors, creating deleterious effects. It has been found that older women who have had previous premature births and are heavy smokers have a 70 percent risk of losing their fetus (Meyer and Comstock 1972). Paternal smoking has also been implicated in causing low-birth-weight babies, fetal deformities, and stillbirths. The exact relationship is not known (Yerushalmy 1972). Evidence of the deleterious effects of secondary smoke to nonsmokers has surfaced in recent years. Perhaps the secondary smoke from the father is related to the negative effects on the unborn child.

Maternal Influences

Nutrition

Nutritional requirements increase considerably during pregnancy, for energy and building material in the embryo and fetus. In humans, vitamin, calcium, and iron deficiencies are frequent. Although the precise role of vitamins in human reproduction has not been clearly established, we do know it is necessary to provide pregnant women with sufficient amounts of certain vitamins, since these compounds are involved in basic metabolic processes, including protein synthesis. Pregnant women should eat two hundred to one thousand more calories per day than they did before they were pregnant, as long as the extra calories consist mainly of carbohydrates and protein. The extra calories promote weight gain; which helps to ensure a healthy baby (Carter 1980).

Premature birth, stillbirth, prolonged labor, and greater susceptibility to disease are caused by poor nutrition. The effects of a poor diet are most serious in the first three months of pregnancy, when the cells of specific organs differentiate and increase rapidly. The heart is especially susceptible at the end of the first month. Brain and nerve development are also affected by a poor diet. Malnourished children may be born with brains that weigh up to 36 percent less than normal. Malnutrition also disrupts the growth of myelin sheaths around nerve cells. (Myelin sheaths are white fatty coverings that insulate nerve cells and aid in the transmission of nerve impulses.) The lack of myelination often causes mental retardation (Brozek and Schurch 1982).

If the fetus does not get adequate nourishment, especially in the form of proteins, the rate of brain cell development will slow down, so the newborn may have significantly fewer brain cells than an adequately nourished fetus. Not only will the infant have fewer brain cells, but he or she will be smaller in general and less likely to survive the first twenty-eight days.

A lack of a particular food can be more deleterious than an inadequate amount of food in general. Such a restriction can cause the death of the embryo, induce congenital malformation, or interfere with the differentiation of the cerebral cortex of the brain (Tuchmann-Duplessis 1975).

Fetally malnourished infants are usually born into a socially and economically deprived environment. These infants are the offspring of mothers who, as children, were themselves malnourished and were also exposed to a variety of conditions, such as chronic disease. The cumulative effect may be a lowered maternal intellectual status and an increased probability for obstetric risk, such as miscarriage, premature birth, and other obstetric health-related problems. These mothers are also more prone to make poor use of available stimulation of everyday household events and have deficient social interactive behaviors (Children's Defense Fund 1989, 1990).

Caffeine

Research has shown that caffeine crosses the human placenta, and it is known to penetrate the preimplantation blastocysts of mice, rats, and rabbits and cause teratogenic defects. Evidence indicates that the way humans metabolize caffeine may minimize its effects. Caffeine is rapidly and thoroughly broken down, with about one percent of it excreted unchanged. Although there is reason for caution in using caffeine during pregnancy, there is yet insufficient evidence to implicate it as a teratogen. Products that contain caffeine include coffee, tea, cola soft drinks, some decaffeinated drinks, over-the-counter headache and cold remedies, and chocolate (Linn et al. 1982; Streitfeld 1978; Heinonen et al. 1977).

Age of Mother

The age of the mother appears to be related to early fetal loss. The higher risk is apparent at maternal ages under twenty and over thirty-five years. The higher rate of fetal death occurs under twelve weeks' gestation. Mothers of the stated ages are more likely to have irregular ovulation, miscarriages, complications in pregnancy, stillborns, and infants with brain damage (Goodman 1986).

A woman's prior pregnancy history and the outcome of her current pregnancy are closely related. The loss or disability rate is twice as high in pregnant women with a history of either a premature birth or a fetal death as in those with a history of normal pregnancy. A history of gynecological disorders and bleeding in early pregnancy are associated with an increased risk of loss and disability in the current pregnancy (Tuchmann-Duplessis 1975).

Emotions and Stress

Severe, prolonged emotional stress is associated with lower birth weight, irritability, and digestive problems in the infant and aggressive behavior in later years. Any strong emotion can release certain hormones into our bloodstream. The hormones are useful in producing temporary mobilization of the body, so we are more alert and can run faster and are stronger. In a pregnant woman, these hormones can be transmitted through the placenta into the bloodstream of the fetus. The mother's emotional state is, therefore, directly communicated to her child. Fetal activity increases greatly according to the amount of maternal stress. If the stress is temporary, the fetal activity is temporary. If the stress is prolonged, then the increased fetal movement will last throughout the mother's stress period (Institute of Medicine 1985; Moliter et al. 1984).

Fever

Mothers with a high fever between the eighteenth and thirtieth days of pregnancy have a greater chance of bearing anencephalic children (children with a rudimentary brain or no brain at all). This fetal malformation occurs when the neural tube fails to close at the head end, perhaps because the heat from the fever kills the cells and prevents them from dividing (Begley and Carey 1982).

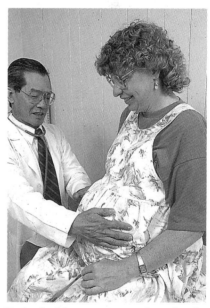

Early fetal loss appears to be related to the age of the mother. The higher risk is apparent at maternal ages under twenty and over thirty-five years.

Rh Factor

Rh disease is one of the complications of pregnancy in which there may be devastating fetal effects with virtually no maternal risks. When a father with an Rh-positive blood type and a mother with an Rh-negative blood type conceive, their child may have Rh-positive blood, which is incompatible with the mother's Rh-negative. The first pregnancy presents little difficulty because the mother's and child's blood supplies are separate. However, at birth or if a miscarriage occurs, some of the fetus's blood cells will pass to the mother. The mother's body will start producing antibodies to combat the foreign blood of the fetus. Antibodies that are formed as a result of this first exposure will persist throughout life.

When subsequent pregnancies occur, there is a good chance that the antibodies will enter the fetal bloodstream, because they can cross the placental barrier. These antibodies can produce anemia and fluid retention in the newborn, resulting in death. If the neonate survives, jaundice or brain damage often develops. If a physician finds that the antibody count in a fetus is high, and if the fetus is old enough to survive, labor can be induced and a blood transfusion can be given immediately. If the fetus is too young to be delivered, the physician may attempt a fetal transfusion every ten to fourteen days. This transfusion is given directly to the fetus through the uterus and replenishes the red blood cells. The treatment is very risky and is unsuccessful 50 to 60 percent of the time (March of Dimes, Rh Disease, 1984).

Preventive measures were introduced in 1969 with an anti-Rh immunoglobulin, or *Rhogam,* which is administered to the mother within seventy-two hours after the first delivery or miscarriage. Rhogam prevents the formation of Rh antibodies in the mother by combining with and destroying fetal red blood cells that enter the mother's circulation. Rhogam must then be readministered following every delivery or miscarriage to guarantee protection (Reeder and Martin 1987).

Diabetes

Diabetic pregnant women have many problems adjusting to new and increased needs for nutrients and insulin. Their sugar-insulin imbalances seriously affect the fetus. For example, the placenta ages prematurely. Fetal malformations, stillbirths, perinatal mortality, and some structural heart anomalies are approximately three times more frequent among children of diabetics than in the general population. Mills et al. (1988) found that diabetic mothers who had spontaneous abortions had higher, less well-controlled blood sugar in the first trimester of pregnancy.

The infants of diabetic mothers are usually much larger than the norm. Their lungs may be immature, and they may be born with too much or too little sugar in their bloodstream. Many diabetics have labor induced or deliver by cesarean section after thirty-five weeks of gestation, depending on the severity of the diabetes and the condition of the baby. The infants of diabetic mothers usually require immediate medical care after birth (Tuchmann-Duplessis 1975; Nora et al. 1981; Reeder and Martin 1987).

Toxemia

Toxemia is a disorder during pregnancy that is deleterious to both the mother and the fetus. The mother retains fluid, vomits, gains weight rapidly, and has high blood pressure. If toxemia is allowed to go unchecked, it could result in seizures, a coma, or even death for the mother. This disorder is responsible for the majority of maternal deaths, accounting for one thousand deaths in the United States per year. At least thirty thousand stillbirths and neonatal deaths in the United States each year are the result of toxemia. Acute toxemia is divided into two stages: *preeclampsia* and *eclampsia*. **Preeclampsia** occurs after the twenty-fourth week of pregnancy and is a condition in which the woman's blood pressure increases, she accumulates salt and water, and she develops swelling. Proteins are found in her urine during this time. **Eclampsia** is a more serious stage, in which convulsions develop. Convulsions may cause fetal oxygen deprivation as well as endanger the life of the mother. The hazards of this disorder can be prevented with good prenatal care. The three most common symptoms are an increase in blood pressure, sudden excessive weight gain, and swelling of the face or fingers. Other symptoms include severe continuous headaches, persistent vomiting, a decrease in the amount of urine, and pains over and above the stomach (Reeder and Martin 1987).

Preeclampsia
The first stage of toxemia, which occurs after the twenty-fourth week of pregnancy. A pregnant woman's blood pressure increases, she accumulates salt and water, and she develops swelling.

Eclampsia
The later, more serious stage of toxemia. Convulsions develop in the mother, which may cause fetal oxygen deprivation as well as endanger the life of the mother.

● FETAL MONITORING

Medical technology has made tremendous advances in recent years regarding the monitoring of the fetus while in the mother's womb. Most pregnancies are not at risk and do not need technological intervention. However, if there is evidence of a possible genetic disorder or abnormality, then technological intervention may be in order. The various fetal monitoring techniques make it possible to prenatally diagnose genetic diseases, identify developmental problems, monitor the fetal heart rate, determine the position of fetus, discover if the birth will be single or multiple, and so on. Fetal monitoring techniques give prospective parents the opportunity to make decisions concerning the well-being of their future offspring.

Amniocentesis

Amniocentesis is a procedure in which a three-inch needle is inserted through the abdominal and uterine walls of the mother and into the amniotic sac, and a small amount of the amniotic fluid is withdrawn. This procedure cannot be done until after the fifteenth week of pregnancy. The amniotic fluid contains cells that have been shed from the fetus. The removed cells are grown in cell cultures for about two to four weeks. They are then *karyotyped,* a procedure in which the chromosomes are made visible and sorted, and the fluid is analyzed. Over sixty types of birth defects can be detected through this procedure. It is especially effective with chromosomal abnormalities, including Down's syndrome. Facial clefts, Tay-Sachs, muscular dystrophy, and gross defects such as missing or deformed limbs and brains are examples of conditions that can be identified. The sex of the fetus can also be determined.

Amniocentesis is usually recommended for mothers who are over thirty-five years old, parents who are carriers of genetic diseases, parents who have a relative with a chromosomal abnormality, and any other parents who are at risk. The procedure is assumed to be relatively safe, although there is always some risk involved. It is usually undertaken only when there is a good chance of an abnormality. One percent of women who have amniocentesis suffer spontaneous abortions (Nora and Fraser 1974; Nora et al. 1981; Chedd 1981). Some

Amniocentesis
A fetal monitoring procedure in which a three-inch needle is inserted through the abdominal and uterine walls of the mother and into the amniotic sac, and a small amount of amniotic fluid is withdrawn. This procedure cannot be done until after the fifteenth week of pregnancy.

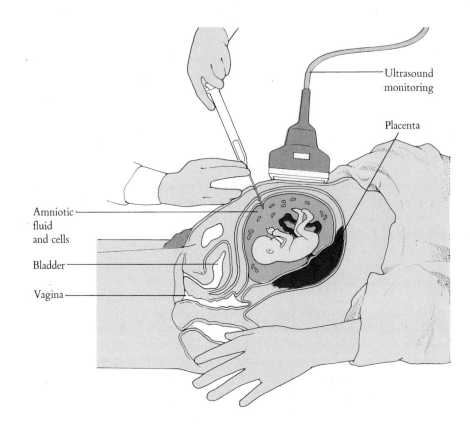

Ultrasound
monitoring

Placenta

Amniotic
fluid
and cells

Bladder

Vagina

physicians have found that they minimize the risk if they use ultrasound simultaneously with the amniocentesis. They can then ascertain the location of the placenta, fetal head, trunk, and collection of the largest pocket of amniotic fluid (Goldstein et al. 1977).

Ultrasound

Ultrasound is an important diagnostic tool used to detect abnormalities before birth. High-frequency sound waves are directed toward the fetus; they then bounce off the contours of the fetus's body, and a device transforms them into a fairly detailed picture called a **sonogram.** Ultrasound avoids the risk of X ray damage to the fetus, and unlike X rays, ultrasound depicts soft tissues. Organs such as the fetal heart, liver, kidneys, and bladder can be examined and checked for abnormalities. The gestational age can also be determined with great accuracy. It is also possible to ascertain if a pregnancy is inside the uterus or if it is a tubal pregnancy (Reeder and Martin 1987; Arehart-Treichel 1982).

Experts are not in complete agreement about the risk to the fetus. Most studies have found that ultrasound probably does not cause major birth defects, or grossly impair neurological development or growth, or cause childhood cancer. However, some researchers have found that it might cause some subtle and long-range health problems and possibly change some hereditary patterns, such as breaking genetic material on the chromosomes (Arehart-Treichel 1982).

Ultrasound
A diagnostic tool used to detect abnormalities before birth. High-frequency sound waves are directed toward the fetus; they then bounce off the contours of the fetus's body, and a device transforms them into a fairly detailed picture called a sonogram.

Sonogram
A picture from an ultrasound.

CHAPTER 3   *Inner Space: Prenatal Development*

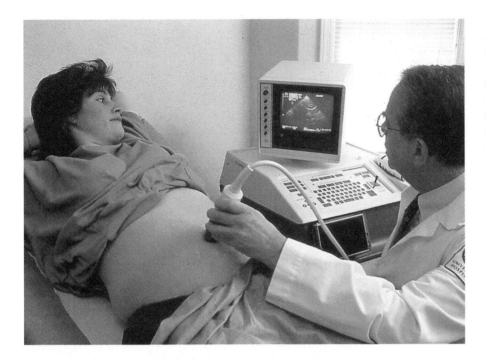

Ultrasound is an important diagnostic tool used to detect abnormalities before birth. High-frequency sound waves are directed toward the fetus. They then bounce off the contours of the fetus's body, and a device transforms them into a fairly detailed picture called a sonogram.

Fetoscopy

Fetoscopy is a delicate procedure in which a tiny telescope is used to view the inside of the uterus. This procedure is performed between fifteen and twenty weeks into the pregnancy under a local anesthetic. The doctor scans the mother with ultrasound to determine the outline of the fetus, the umbilical cord, and the placenta. After making a small incision in the mother's abdomen, a pencil-lead-thin tube containing an endoscope is inserted into the uterus. The endoscope permits direct visual examination of the tiny areas of the fetus. By inserting biopsy forceps into the tube, a skin sample can be taken from the fetus. To draw a blood sample, the doctor inserts a needle through the tube and draws blood from the fetal vein in the umbilical cord. From these samples, sickle-cell anemia, hemophilia, thalassemia, muscular dystrophy, cardiovascular disease, and possibly Tay-Sachs disease can be detected.

Fetoscopies are performed on women who are concerned that they may have defective children. In many cases the test can reassure patients that their babies will be normal. Fetoscopy carries a greater risk than amniocentesis. Miscarriages are induced in 5 percent of the cases (testing fetuses 1980; Nora 1981).

Fetoscopy
A fetal monitoring procedure in which a tiny telescope is used to view the inside of the uterus.

Chorionic Villi Sampling

Chorionic villi sampling (CVS) is a relatively new prenatal diagnostic procedure for obtaining fetal cells to check for genetic and chromosomal abnormalities. This procedure involves obtaining sample *villi,* which are hairlike projections of the membrane around the embryo, and then examining the embryo's chromosomes for signs of birth defects. This procedure provides earlier diagnosis than amniocentesis. It can be done at eight to twelve weeks' gestation. The rates of pregnancy loss following chorionic villi sampling are comparable with the rates of loss following amniocentesis (Jackson, Wapner, and Barr 1986; Herrmann and Thomas 1986; McGovern, Goldberg, and Desnick 1986).

Chorionic villi sampling
A prenatal diagnostic procedure that involves obtaining sample villi, which are hairlike projections in the chorion, and then examining the embryo's chromosomes for signs of birth defects. This procedure can be done eight to twelve weeks' gestation.

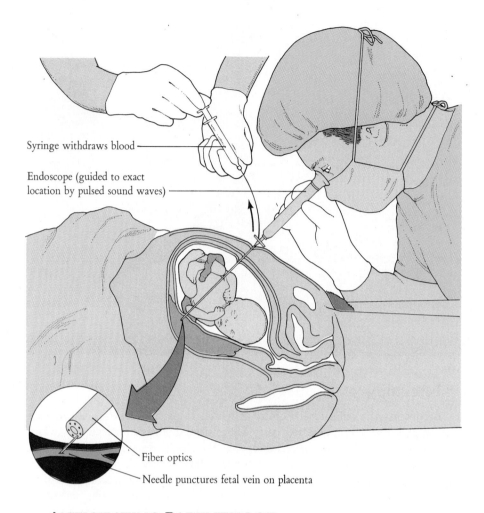

Syringe withdraws blood

Endoscope (guided to exact
location by pulsed sound waves)

Fiber optics

Needle punctures fetal vein on placenta

● ANTICIPATING PARENTHOOD

Adjustment to parenthood is a major developmental task for adults, especially for new parents facing the first pregnancy. Parenthood involves a great
psychological and financial investment. Sacrifices are often made: jobs and hobbies may be surrendered, freedom is curtailed, finances are often strained, and
the marital relationship reaches a new dimension.

Parenthood often brings a dramatic change in the life of a woman and is
considered by many to be the major transition in an adult female's life. She must
deal not only with psychological changes but with unique physical changes as
well. She must come to terms with a new body image and an altered self-
concept. She may experience a feeling of uniqueness or distance from old friends
and a desire for protection. Quite often pregnancy is regarded with uncertainty
because of modifying career goals or educational plans. A woman may worry
about her health and that of her baby, as well as about her appearance. She may
be unsure of her ability to mother and worry about the changes in her relationship with her husband. Her appearance and sexual readjustment after giving
birth may also be sources of concern (Jessner et al. 1970).

Until recently, the role of father was given little thought by the general
public. Now it is known that new fathers also may experience a major emotional upheaval during the pregnancy. The first child, especially, forces a sense

of responsibility and maturity on the father. Some fathers experience a great deal of anxiety over responsibilities and are unable to bear them. Gelles (1988) found that some men even physically assault their wife during pregnancy; the assaults either focus on their wife or on the unborn child. Other men may perceive their wife as needing or receiving a great deal of attention, and they may resent it. Some men may feel that the child is going to replace them in their wife's affection. Others may be concerned about changes in their wife's appearance and about sexual readjustment after the birth.

In some primitive societies, the father is allowed to show distress and neediness at childbirth through a custom called **couvade.** Couvade allows the father to go through the symptoms of childbirth with his wife. He may actually go to bed as if he were giving birth. In this way he too can receive emotional support.

Couvade
A practice of allowing the father to go through the symptoms of childbirth with his wife.

Redefined sex roles and the women's movement have opened the way for the contemporary father to become more of a part of the child's birth. Active involvement in prepared childbirth classes, such as coaching, promotes satisfaction and self-esteem in the father and turns the focus away from his perceived problems.

The anticipation of a new child signals subtle and overt changes in the sex roles of the husband and wife. The transition period to parenthood is an appropriate time frame to focus on changes in sex roles, since in most societies motherhood is central to the definition of the feminine role, and traditionally fatherhood has been viewed by childless men as a mark of masculinity. Feldman and Aschenbrenner (1983) found that both men and women increased in feminine role behavior, feminine identity, and instrumental personality traits (goal directed), and women decreased in masculine role behavior. These results implied that parenthood served to reduce the previously large gap between feminine and masculine role behaviors for both parents. Men appeared to be more personally fulfilled through parenthood than had been previously thought. Feldman and Aschenbrenner found that most fathers, in fact, are happy to have an active role in the childbirth.

Because the period of pregnancy is so significant in the lives of prospective parents, they need help and support from their families, their friends, and the medical profession. They must also acquire or improve the skills needed to communicate with each other and share their fears and concerns. Obtaining accurate information concerning the physical and psychological changes of pregnancy and the birth process is beneficial in comprehending and appreciating the whole process of parenthood.

SUMMARY

- The prenatal stage of development is equally divided into three trimesters. The first trimester includes the germinal stage, the embryonic stage, and the beginning of the fetal stage of development. The second and third trimesters are marked by continued rapid growth and maturation of the fetus.
- Prenatally, if an environmental factor interferes with the growth of an organ during its critical period, the organ does not develop properly. Permanent damage will result, because after the time for the organ's formation passes, there is no second chance.
- Teratogens are agents that deleteriously affect an embryo that was otherwise functioning normally. Teratogens can include viruses, radiation, chemical and environmental pollution, medicinal drugs, and hard drugs.

Conceiving Children for Tissue Transplantation

Why do people have children? To carry on the family name, to provide a playmate for an existing child, to prove a parent's femininity or masculinity, to have someone to love, to provide grandchildren, because society expects it, and so on. In the past two years, a new reason has emerged: *to provide a bone marrow donor for an existing child.* Two such cases have been featured in the media. One case involved the children of Abe and Mary Ayala.

Two years ago, Abe and Mary Ayala's sixteen-year-old daughter Anissa was diagnosed as suffering from chronic myelogenous leukemia. Unless a suitable donor could be found, Anissa's life expectancy was no more than three to five years (she is still alive at present). Neither the parents nor Anissa's brother are compatible, and the National Bone Marrow Donor Registry has been unsuccessful in locating a possible transplant candidate. With time running out, last year the Ayalas decided to have another baby in the hope that the new infant would be a successful match. Although the odds were only one in four, tissue typing of the baby born in April, Marissa Eve, indicate that she is a nearly identical match. With the bone marrow transplant, her sister now has a 70 percent chance of surviving her illness. (Tomlinson 1990, 3)

Is this a legitimate reason to have a baby—to save the life of another child? Is this baby seen as just a source of body parts? Are the other reasons that people have babies any less self-serving? Most infants are conceived out of a complex mixture of motives; most of them are self-interested, and few of them are as altruistic as the Ayalas' concern with saving Anissa's life. Was what the Ayalas' did wrong? If Marissa had already been born, would there even have been a discussion about it? Probably not, since this type of transplant is now somewhat commonplace. Although Marissa was used as a means to save her sister's life, there is no reason to suspect that her parents do not value her for other reasons as well. Tomlinson (1990) points out that "using Marissa as a means of obtaining bone marrow is not incompatible with respecting her as an end in herself."

When Marissa is older, how will she view the circumstances surrounding her conception? Do you think she will feel like a "means" or like an "end"? Why?

What about Anissa? Wouldn't it be wrong *not* to explore all possible means to save her life?

- Factors related to the mother can also negatively affect prenatal development. Such factors include poor nutrition, caffeine, the age of the mother, emotions and stress, fever, the Rh factor, diabetes, and toxemia.
- Fetal monitoring techniques make it possible to prenatally diagnose genetic diseases and developmental problems. Some fetal monitoring techniques are amniocentesis, ultrasound, and fetoscopy.
- Anticipating parenthood for the first time traumatically affects each parent in different, as well as similar, ways.
- Parents, in some unique situations, have made an ethical decision to conceive a child in order to provide a tissue donor for an existing child who is critically ill and who would not survive without the donor.

That Lynn Bremer is an attorney with a good job was not enough to keep her from developing a cocaine habit. The fact that she was pregnant was not enough to make her drop it. So when her daughter tested positive at birth for the presence of drugs in her urine, health officials in Muskegon County, Mich., took the child into temporary custody. But, to Bremer's astonishment, there was more. The county prosecutor stepped in to charge her with a felony: delivery of drugs to her newborn child. The means of delivery? Her umbilical cord.

After Bremer completed a drug treatment program, she regained her daughter, who is apparently healthy. But the criminal charges remain. "I could lose her," says Bremer. "I could go to prison, and she could grow up with who knows who." Prosecutor Tony Tague is unmoved. He says the threat of prison is sometimes the only way to get pregnant addicts to seek treatment: "Someone must stand up for the rights of the children."

Similar cases involving prenatal drug delivery have cropped up in nine states across the country. Like the abortion issue, they raise serious questions about a woman's right to privacy and the obligations of the state and the individual toward the unborn. At the center of these cases lies a controversial legal concept: fetal rights. This notion also underlies one of the most important cases before the Supreme Court during its current term. At issue are "fetal-protection policies" used by many companies to forbid fertile female employees from taking jobs that might expose them to substances that could harm an unborn child. Fetal-rights advocates say such policies are needed to protect the unborn. Critics say they are an intrusion into the lives of women and a false comfort for a society that fails to offer adequate prenatal care for all women or workplace safety for all workers.

Human Development in the News: Do the Unborn Have Rights?

RICHARD LACAYO

Courts in the U.S. have recognized that third parties—for instance, a drunk driver who injures a pregnant woman—can be sued for doing harm to a fetus. More recent is the notion that expectant mothers can be held criminally responsible for problems suffered by their fetuses. Even pregnant women who are resigned to the legalisms pervading American life might wince to learn that the child forming inside them is also a budding legal entity, possessing rights that may put it at odds with its mother even before it emerges into the world. But the idea has gathered support with the growing spectacle of drug-damaged newborns. Maternity wards around the country ring with the high-pitched "cat cries" of crack babies, who may face lifelong handicaps as a result of their mothers' drug use.

With some researchers estimating that each year as many as 375,000 newborns in the U.S. could suffer harm from their mothers' prenatal abuse of illegal drugs, district attorneys are tempted by what looks like the quick fix of pregnancy prosecution. "You have the right to an abortion. You have the right to have a baby," says Charles Molony Condon, prosecutor for the Charleston, N.C., area. "You don't have the right to have a baby deformed by cocaine." Courts have given a mostly skeptical reception to the attempt to apply existing drug laws in such a novel fashion, but eight states and Congress are considering legislation that would explicitly criminalize drug use and alcohol abuse

by pregnant women that results in harm to the child.

Critics of such measures say that a true effort on behalf of unborn children would focus on the needs of expectant mothers rather than punishing bad behavior after the fact. Few drug treatment programs, for instance, accept pregnant addicts. A study of New York City drug-abuse programs found that 87% turned away pregnant crack users. Says Sidney Schnoll, a Psychiatrist at the Medical College of Virginia: "We seem more willing to place the kid in a neonatal intensive-care unit for $1,500 or $2,000 a day, rather than put $1,500 into better prenatal care."

Some legal experts also warn that prenatal drug-use prosecutions could open the way to punishing women for many other kinds of behavior during pregnancy. What about drinking? Smoking? Taking prescription drugs? Or working too hard? "Are we going to be policing people's wine closets?" asks Stanford University law-school professor Deborah Rhode. Other legal scholars insist that such "slippery slope" arguments are exaggerated; laws commonly distinguish between reckless behavior and acceptable risk.

Still, the efforts to protect the rights of the fetus have far-reaching implications, and not just for pregnant women. The *UAW, et al. v. Johnson Controls* case, now facing the Supreme Court, provides a dramatic example. In 1982 Johnson Controls, a Milwaukee-based company that is one of the nation's largest car-battery manufacturers, decided to forbid its fertile women employees to hold jobs that would expose them to lead levels potentially damaging to a fetus. High doses of lead—higher than any permitted by law in the workplace—have been linked to miscarriages and fetal death. Even lower levels, however, can result in learning problems and diminished growth for exposed babies.

Continued

"This decision was not taken lightly," says Denise Zutz, director of corporate communications for Johnson Controls. "We were concerned about the risks to children." The company was also seeking to avoid later lawsuits by any children who might be harmed in the womb.

That was not much comfort to Shirley Jean Mackey, who worked at one of the company's plants in Atlanta. A mother of one who had no immediate plans to get pregnant, she was forced to move from a job she liked, bundling lead plates, to another she hated, punching holes in hundreds of battery containers. "Each hole I punched, it was somebody's head," says Mackey. "That's just the way I felt." Along with the United Auto Workers, which represents many of Johnson Controls' employees, she is one of eight workers bringing suit against the company. They charge that its policy violates the 1964 Civil Rights Act, which bars employment discrimination on the basis of sex, pregnancy or related medical conditions unless the practice in question directly relates to the worker's ability to do the job.

So far, two lower federal courts have ruled in favor of the company. But a California court went the other way, calling the policy "blatant" discrimination and adding, "A woman is not required to be a Victorian broodmare." If the Supreme Court rules for Johnson Controls, then by some estimates up to 20 million jobs, many of them well paid, could eventually be closed to women. Gulf Oil, B. F. Goodrich, Du Pont and Eastman Kodak are just some of the companies that have instituted fetal-protection policies since a federal court upheld such measures in 1984. Johnson Controls estimates that more than half its production jobs are barred to fertile women.

To some people, fetal-protection policies are merely a way to avoid making the workplace safe for men and women equally. Feminists also dismiss them as discrimination masquerading as compassion, a disguised way of keeping women out of more lucrative men's jobs. Critics of the fetal-protection policies also point out that toxic substances in the workplace may damage genes in male sperm. "A man or woman working in a plant should be told the dangers and make up their own minds," says Molly Yard, president of the National Organization for Women.

Ironically, it was the Supreme Court's decision creating a right to abortion in *Roe v. Wade* that also provided some of the legal underpinning for fetal rights. The same ruling recognized a government interest in protecting the fetus during the last trimester of pregnancy. But while judges had a hand in creating fetal rights, courts will never be able to ensure real protection to an unborn child. That will have to come from mothers who take responsibility for the lives they carry within them—and a nation willing to provide the fetus with real prenatal care. For now, it seems more willing to provide a lawyer.

Richard Lacayo, "Do the Unborn Have Rights?" *Time,* special issue, Fall 1990, pp. 22–23. Copyright 1990 The Time Inc. Magazine Company. Reprinted by permission.

R E A D I N G S

Falkner, F. and Macy, C. (1980). *Pregnancy and birth.* New York: Harper and Row.
  Easy-reading description of pregnancy experiences and childbearing.
Guttmacher, A. (1984). *Pregnancy, birth and family planning.* New York: Signet.
  Easy to comprehend informational book by medical authority geared to expectant parents.
Heinowitz, J. (1982). *Pregnant fathers.* Englewood Cliffs, NJ: Prentice-Hall.
  Helps fathers deal with emotions concerning a pregnancy and suggests ways to build a relationship between themselves, their wives, and their infants.
Kitzinger, S. (1985). *Birth over thirty.* New York: Penguin.
  Discussion of possible problems of being an older mother such as Downs' syndrome and cesarian sections. Also discussion of how to tell adolescent siblings about pregnancy and how to cope with being a middle-aged mother of an infant.

Nilsson, L. (1986). *A child is born.* New York: Delacourt.

A colorful photographic essay of the zygote, embryo, and fetus within the womb.

Shapiro, H. (1984). *The pregnancy book for today's woman.* New York: Consumers Union.

Practical advice concerning hazards to the pregnant woman and the importance of good nutrition.

O U T L I N E

O B J E C T I V E S

When you have mastered the material in this chapter, you should be able to do the following:

1. Describe the three stages of labor.
2. Describe the Apgar scoring system and the Brazelton Neonatal Assessment Scale and discuss their functions.
3. Describe prematurity and the factors that contribute to it and discuss the unique problems faced by premature infants.
4. Discuss possible complications of birth, including forceps delivery, breech delivery, oversized infants, cesarean section, obstetrical medication, and anoxia.
5. Discuss why new parents are dissatisfied with the traditional hospital delivery and describe the Dick-Read and Lamaze methods of natural childbirth.
6. Discuss the advantages and disadvantages of home birth, birthing rooms or centers, and the birthing chair.
7. Define *neonate* and discuss the various states and capabilities of neonates.
8. Discuss the advantages and disadvantages of breast-feeding and bottle-feeding.
9. Discuss the purpose of reflex testing and describe and discuss the following reflexes: Babinski, palmar, plantar, Moro, placing, stepping, and tonic neck.
10. Describe the impact of a neonate on each of the parents and the siblings.
11. Describe the profile of a SIDS infant and the possible causes of SIDS.

Facing a New World:
The Birth Process
and the Neonate

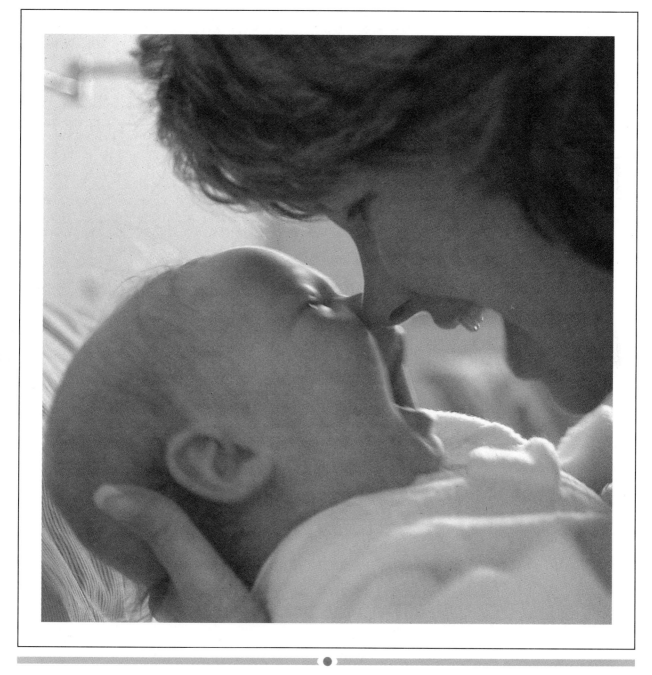

• INTRODUCTION

The birth of a child is an exciting event for all of the family members: mother, father, siblings, grandparents, aunts, uncles, cousins, and so on. A new human being is about to enter this unique family constellation. His or her presence will irrevocably change that family constellation, whether subtly or overtly, by just being there. After nine months of everyone's anticipation and waiting, this human being makes his or her "grand entrance."

• STAGES OF BIRTH

The onset of labor signals the upcoming birth. However, prior to the actual labor, about ten to fourteen days before delivery, **lightening** occurs. This alteration is brought about by the settling of the fetal head into the pelvis or *pelvic inlet,* which is the space between the bones of the pelvis through which the child must pass to be born. Lightening may take place suddenly. For example, the expectant mother arises one morning entirely relieved of abdominal tightness but with a feeling of greater pressure on the bladder. Lightening is more likely to occur before the first birth than before subsequent ones; in many later births the baby's head may not descend to the pelvic inlet until the mother is already in labor.

The most common indicator that birth is imminent is the beginning of contractions of the uterus. Many women are aware of some contractions, called **Braxton Hicks contractions,** several weeks before giving birth. This phenomenon is often called *false labor.* The difference between false labor and true labor is that true labor contractions produce a demonstrable degree of dilatation of the cervix in the course of a few hours, while false labor contractions do not affect the cervix. Contractions during false labor prepare the uterus for true labor later, but remain irregular and do not become stronger. True labor contractions are regular, increase in intensity, become more closely spaced, and generally do not stop once they have begun. They also are usually felt in the lower back and extend in a girdle-like fashion from the back to the front of the abdomen.

Another sign of impending labor is pink "show." After the discharge of a mucous plug that has filled the cervical canal during pregnancy, the pressure of the descending fetus causes the minute capillaries in the cervix to rupture. This blood is mixed with mucus, which therefore has a pink tinge. This "show" must be differentiated from a substantial discharge of blood, which would indicate a possible medical complication.

The average duration of labor for a first pregnancy is about fourteen hours, with approximately twelve and one-half hours for the first stage, one hour and twenty minutes for the second stage, and ten minutes for the third stage. The average duration of labor for succeeding pregnancies is approximately six hours shorter than for the first—for example, seven hours for the first stage, a half hour for the second stage, and ten minutes for the third stage (Reeder and Martin 1987).

First Stage: Dilatation

The **dilatation stage** begins with the first true labor contractions and ends with the complete dilatation of the cervix. The initial labor contractions may begin as far apart as thirty minutes or as close together as five minutes. At first

---

Lightening
Prior to the beginning of labor, the settling of the fetal head into the mother's pelvis or pelvic inlet, which is the space between the bones of the pelvis through which the child must pass to be born.

Braxton Hicks contractions
Contractions of the uterus that occur several weeks before giving birth. This phenomenon is often called false labor.

Dilatation stage
The first stage of the birth process, which begins with the first true labor contractions and ends with the complete dilatation of the cervix.

they last about thirty seconds, but gradually they become longer. They are mild at first and are similar to the Braxton Hicks contractions in intensity. Some women say they are similar to menstrual cramps.

The dilatation stage can be further divided into the latent phase and the active phase. The *latent phase* is from the onset of the uterine contractions. It takes many hours and accomplishes little cervical dilatation. The contractions recur at shortening intervals and become stronger and last longer. When labor progresses to the *active phase,* women usually prefer to remain in bed, because walking is no longer comfortable. They become intensely involved in the sensations within their body and tend to withdraw from the surrounding environment.

As a result of the uterine contractions, two important changes occur in the cervix during the first stage of labor: *effacement* and *dilatation.* **Effacement** is the shortening of the cervical canal from a structure that is one or two centimeters in length to one in which no canal at all exists. Effacement is measured during the pelvic exam by estimating the percentage by which the cervical canal has shortened. For example, if the cervix was two centimeters long before labor, 50 percent of effacement has occurred when the cervix measures one centimeter in length. **Dilatation** is the enlargement of the cervix to permit the passage of the fetus. The cervix usually reaches ten centimeters in diameter. The cervical dilatation proceeds at an accelerated rate and reaches a deceleration phase shortly before the second stage of labor.

Second Stage: Expulsion

Expulsion begins with the complete dilatation of the cervix. Contractions are now strong and long, lasting fifty to seventy seconds and occurring at intervals of two or three minutes. The rupture of the membranes usually occurs during the early part of this stage, with a gush of amniotic fluid from the vagina. (Sometimes the membranes rupture during the first stage, and occasionally before the labor begins.) The muscles of the abdomen as well as the uterine muscles aid in the birth of the baby. During this stage, the mother directs all of her energy toward expelling the fetus. The **crowning** of the head occurs when the widest diameter of the baby's head is at the mother's vulva (the outer entrance of her vagina). With the next contraction, the head usually appears. This portion of delivery is very slow in order to prevent damage to the baby's head. After the head emerges, the baby slowly turns so one shoulder at a time can emerge. In a normal delivery the neonate is born with the face downward. Finally, usually during the next contraction, the rest of the baby emerges.

Third Stage: Placental

The **placental stage** of the birth process has two phases: the *placental separation* and the *placental expulsion.* Immediately following the birth, the remainder of the amniotic fluid escapes with a slight flow of blood following it. Indicators that suggest the placenta has separated include a firmer and globular uterus that rises upward in the abdomen, the umbilical cord's descending three or more inches farther out of the vagina, and finally a sudden gush of blood. These indicators usually occur within five minutes after delivery. The actual placental expulsion may be brought about by bearing-down efforts on the part of the mother if she is not anesthetized. This process takes about twenty minutes and is virtually painless (Reeder and Martin 1987).

Effacement
The shortening of the cervical canal from a structure that is one or two centimeters in length to one in which no canal at all exists.

Dilatation
In childbirth, the enlargement of the cervix to permit the passage of the fetus. The cervix usually reaches ten centimeters in diameter.

Expulsion
The second stage of the birth process, which begins with the complete dilatation of the cervix and ends when the baby emerges.

Crowning
During the birth process, the point at which the widest diameter of the baby's head is at the mother's vulva.

Placental stage
The third stage of the birth process, which includes the placental separation and the placental expulsion.

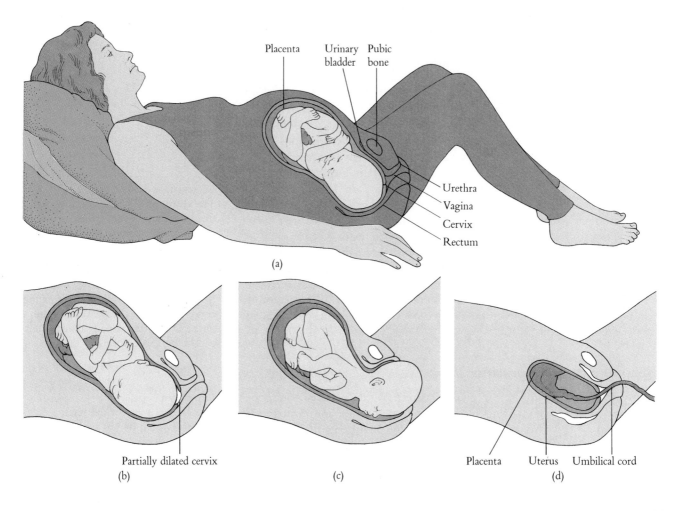

Placenta   Urinary   Pubic
           bladder   bone

Urethra
Vagina
Cervix
Rectum

(a)

Partially dilated cervix
(b)

(c)

Placenta   Uterus   Umbilical cord
(d)

● FIGURE 4.1
Labor and Delivery: Stages of the
Birth Process

In the days following delivery, a new mother may feel overwhelmed by sadness and burst into tears for no apparent reason. This condition is often called *postpartum blues* or *postpartum depression*. It affects more than half of all new mothers. Rubin (1984) suggests that it follows a roller coaster pattern, occurring on the third, fifth, and seventh days following delivery, with the fifth day postpartum as the peak day. Most doctors believe that the blues are brought on by the rapidly changing hormone levels taking place in a woman's body after delivery, combined with the stress and fatigue of the delivery itself and the feelings of responsibility for the newborn.

● **NEONATAL SCREENING**

Apgar Scale

The **Apgar scale** is a valuable index for evaluating and measuring a neonate's physical condition at birth. It is simple, accurate, and a safe means of quickly appraising the neonate's condition. The evaluation is generally made at one minute after birth and again at five minutes. Each sign is evaluated by the

Apgar scale
A scoring system used to evaluate and measure a neonate's physical condition at birth.

TABLE 4.1 Apgar Scoring System

FUNCTION*	0	1	2
HEART RATE	Absent; no heartbeat seen or felt.	Heartbeat less than 100 beats per minute.	Heartbeat of 100–140 beats per minute.
RESPIRATORY EFFORT	No breathing within 60 seconds of birth.	Slow, irregular breathing.	Good breathing with lusty crying.
MUSCLE TONE	Flaccid; completely limp.	Some flexion of extremities, moderate muscle tone, limbs flexed.	Good muscle tone, flexed limbs, active motion.
REFLEX IRRITABILITY (RESPONSE TO SKIN STIMULATION OF FEET)	No response.	Weak cry or grimace.	Facial grimace, sneezing, or coughing; vigorous cry.
COLOR	Pale gray or blue.	Pink body, blue hands and feet.	Completely pink.

*ranked in order of importance
Source: Reeder and Martin 1987.

degree to which it is present and is given a score of 0, 1, or 2. (See Table 4.1.) A score of 2 represents the best functioning, 1 shows marginal functioning, and 0 indicates a lack of any perceptible functioning. The scores of the signs are added to give a total score, with 10 as the maximum.

At the one-minute evaluation, 70 percent to 90 percent of newborns receive a score of 7 or above; at the five-minute evaluation, the score is about the same or better. An Apgar score of 7 to 10 indicates that the infant's condition is good. A score of 4 to 6 indicates a fair condition, with moderate central nervous system depression or some muscle flaccidity and cyanosis (imperfectly oxygenated blood, which causes the skin to turn blue). Respiration is not readily established. Infants in this condition must have their air passages cleared and must be given oxygen promptly. A score of 0 to 3 indicates a very poor condition. Resuscitation is needed immediately (Reeder and Martin 1987). Almost 97 percent of neonates who score below 3 at five minutes develop without noticeable aftereffects (Nelson and Broman 1977).

Brazelton Neonatal Behavioral Assessment Scale

The **Brazelton Neonatal Behavioral Assessment Scale** is relevant whenever there is any question of the neurological integrity in the neonate. It was devised to detect mild dysfunctions of the central nervous system and the development of behavioral responses during the neonatal period. The scale is given for the first time two or three days after birth, when the immediate stresses of delivery and some of the medication effects have begun to wear off. The scale is given again on the ninth or tenth day, when the baby has been home and has adjusted to the home environment. The intent is to determine the extent of recovery of the neurological system and the extent of the behavioral responses. This is accomplished by ascertaining the capacity of the neonate to

Brazelton Neonatal Behavioral Assessment Scale
A scale used to detect mild dysfunctions of the central nervous system and the development of behavioral responses during the neonatal period.

organize responses to social stimuli as he or she moves from sleep to crying and to alert states of consciousness.

The major part of the exam assesses the newborn's interactive behavior repertoire on twenty-six behavioral items, each scored on a nine-point scale. These twenty-six items can be grouped together into four behavioral dimensions of newborn organization. The first dimension, the *interactive capacities,* assesses the neonate's capacity to attend to and process simple and complex environmental events, such as a rattle, bell, or light. The second dimension, *motoric capacities,* assesses the ability of the neonate to maintain adequate tone, to control motor behavior, and to perform integrated motor activities. Examples would include the neonate's ability to bring hands to mouth, insert a thumb or finger, and maintain it there long enough for a good suck. The third dimension, *organizational capacities regarding state control,* detects how well the infant remains calm and alert despite increased stimulation; to what extent exhaustion plays a part; how much the environment makes an impact; and how vulnerable the infant is to continued stimulation. The final dimension, *organizational capacities regarding physiologic responses to stress,* assesses how well the infant is able to inhibit startles, tremors, and interfering movement as he or she becomes aroused or as he or she attends to social and inanimate stimuli (Brazelton 1986).

● AT-RISK NEONATES

The infant who is born prematurely is deprived of all the maternal, physiological, and regulatory influences that permit him or her to grow to the stage of maturity and allow him or her to function as a separate organism. Suddenly the infant is forced, before he or she is ready, to cope with temperature regulation, nutritional requirements, the task of using oxygen, and the impact of gravity—all of which the mother's body had either regulated, provided, or protected against. The premature infant is also deprived of all the sensory experiences that supported life in utero and that are important for normal growth and development of the individual (Korner 1980).

Seven percent of all births are premature (Kopp and Parmelee 1979). **Premature,**or **preterm,** babies are born before the thirty-seventh week of pregnancy (dated from the mother's last menstrual period) and weigh less than 2,500 grams (five and one-half pounds). There are several diagnostic groupings of infants who fall under this definition. Infants who are clearly below their expected weight for their gestational age are included in this group. These infants are further divided into two groups: infants who are born at term (that is, forty weeks' gestation) and preterm infants (thirty-seven weeks' or less gestation). Both groups of infants are labeled **small-for-dates.** They are often inadequately nourished in utero. Another group of infants are those born before their due date but at the appropriate weight for their gestational age. Recognizing the different groups of premature infants is important, since they differ greatly in the type of care they need (Olds et al. 1988).

Prematurity is more common among firstborns, boys, the lower socioeconomic class, and nonwhites. Of the babies who die within four weeks after birth, over half were premature. Prematurity is the greatest cause of neonatal death in the United States. Approximately seven thousand premature infants die of *hyaline membrane disease,* or respiratory distress syndrome, each year (Olds et al. 1988). This disease results from a deficiency of surfactant in the lungs.

Premature
Babies who are born before the thirty-seventh week of pregnancy and who weigh less than 2,500 grams (five and one-half pounds).

Preterm
See Premature

Small-for-dates
Neonates who are clearly below their expected weight for their gestational age.

(Surfactant keeps the lungs partially expanded at all times). Infants with this deficiency must completely reexpand their lungs with each breath, which greatly increases the work of breathing (Olds et al. 1988; Reeder and Martin 1987; Kopp and Parmelee 1979).

For years the prognosis for a substantial number of infants born preterm was pessimistic. Between 10 and 40 percent of these infants later showed intellectual and neurological problems, with most of them being the ones with the lowest birth weights (Kopp and Parmelee 1979). However, great progress in the medical care of premature infants and the development of new life-support systems have made the prognosis for these infants more optimistic. Good medical care has made it possible for approximately 85 percent of infants weighing 2.2 to 3.2 pounds, and approximately 55 percent of those weighing 1.6 to 2.2 pounds, to survive (Paneth et al. 1982). The bigger and more mature the infant, the better the chance for survival. Lower-birth-weight infants take more time to process information and have more immature visual systems than full-term infants at forty weeks' postconceptual age (Spungen et al. 1985).

Premature infants who seem vulnerable to later problems often are the most immature and the most physiologically distressed. Both males and females have shown evidence of having problems in school, although the percentage of males is generally greater than that of females. Areas of concern for children who were born prematurely include learning difficulties, negative interactions with teachers, and language problems (Kopp and Parmelee 1979; Korner 1980).

Although there are still developmental problems in the earlier years (the first three years), prematurity is no longer considered a factor in the later years (after they start to school). Instead, the social and economic environment is considered a factor (Rode et al. 1981). Children from relatively well off and stable homes tend to develop better. By the time they start school, they show good family relationships and few or no signs of learning impairment. Children

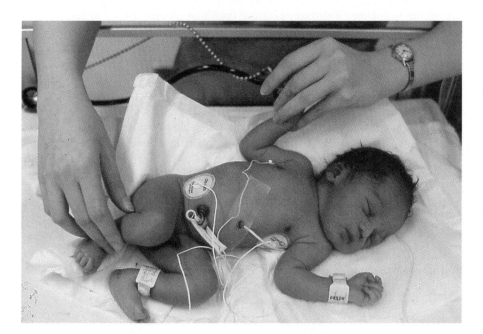

Seven percent of all births are premature. Premature, or preterm, babies are born before the thirty-seventh week of pregnancy and weigh less than 2500 grams (five and one-half pounds).

who come from homes with social or economic stress are more likely to show continued social and cognitive deficiencies (Cohen and Parmalee 1983).

Premature birth is the biggest single problem facing those caring for newborns. Most body organs function fairly adequately by the twenty-eighth week of gestation, with the brain still insufficiently developed to control behavior. The cerebral cortex has little control over behavior patterns of the seven- or eight-month-term infant. At birth, these infants require a great deal of special attention. They need three times as much oxygen as the full-term infant; often they are anemic, they may require a blood transfusion; they are more subject to infection; and they require careful medical supervision. The use of an isolette, or incubator, provides temperature and humidity control designed to duplicate the climate of the intrauterine environment (Olds et al. 1988; Kopp and Parmelee 1979). Computerized equipment in intensive-care nurseries continuously monitors the vital signs of the preterm neonate, including heart rate, temperature, blood pressure, and blood chemistry (Paneth et al. 1982).

Premature babies also need breast milk or a formula that contains protein with a whey/casein ratio of 60:40 (a similar proportion to that found in breast milk) and a caloric value of twenty-four calories per ounce (Olds et al. 1988). (If the mother did not plan to breast-feed, her milk may be pumped and given to the infant via a bottle. There are also breast milk banks in many larger hospitals, where breast milk is donated.) Breast milk is easier to digest than formula and carries antibodies to protect infants from many diseases, especially *necrotizing enterocolitis,* a disease that causes inflammation and death of tissues in the intestines and colon (Noble 1980). Although the changing pattern of care has led to the reduction of mortality and morbidity, the young and sick premature infants are still a vulnerable group.

Several factors contribute to a premature birth. Toxemia, accidental hemorrhage during pregnancy, placenta previa (the placenta is not in the proper place), hypertensive cardiovascular disease, diabetes, a multiple birth, glandular disturbance, nutritional deficiency, undue emotional stress, heavy smoking, age, height, weight, weight gain, the use of drugs, a lack of prenatal care, and overwork are some of the contributing maternal factors. Many of these conditions can be linked directly or indirectly to adverse social and economic conditions. Studies show higher rates of premature births among women who are disadvantaged. Disadvantaged women are more likely to lack prenatal care, have poorer nutrition, are more likely to overwork, and may use drugs during pregnancy (Olds et al. 1988; Kopp and Parmelee 1979).

Prematurely born children are in greater danger of being abused than children born at term. It is possible that certain characteristics of the newborn infants may contribute to the development of maladaptive mother-infant relationships, leading to abuse. Premature infants are more likely to cry and be irritable, are more difficult to feed, are typically separated from their mothers for the first critical few weeks necessary for forming a bonding relationship, and have unusual sleep patterns (Brown and Bakeman 1980; Stern and Hildebrandt 1984; Dierker et al. 1982). In studies, premature newborn infants at twenty-eight to thirty weeks' gestation demonstrated less well defined sleep patterns than those observed in full-term newborns. Also, they generally displayed restlessness and an indeterminate amount of sleep (Dierker et al. 1982).

So not only is prematurity a disturbance in the development of the infant, but it is also a crisis in the parenting process. Many parents encounter a dramatically different transition to parenthood than they had anticipated. They are deprived of the last few weeks of pregnancy, in which to complete their psychological preparation for the arrival of the infant (Noble 1980). They may not have finished their childbirth classes, prepared a nursery, or purchased a crib.

Many observers believe that later problems may be due to the way the infants are treated during the first few weeks of life. Premature infants have little normal contact of touching and closeness, because of life-sustaining incubators. The infants have no opportunity to enjoy early contact after delivery. Few premature infants are breast-fed; few are even held when bottle-fed. Some are not able to suck at all for the first few weeks. Thus, the social experiences of normal feeding, which establish early mutuality between the caregiver and full-term infant, are missing for the premature infant at the beginning of life.

The caregiver may be less responsive because the infant appears unattractive or sickly or has a high-pitched, grating cry. These are obstacles to effective bonding in the early weeks of life. The infant fails to develop a sense of power and competence and cannot elicit parental responses as often as desired. On the other hand, parents feel frustrated and incompetent in soothing distress since the infant often lacks the ability to clearly signal distress and then reward the parents with positive, detectable responses. Premature infants tend to be less responsive to sights and sounds (Goldberg 1979; Stern and Hildebrandt 1984).

However, Easterbrooks (1989) found no differences in the way parents, both mothers and fathers, bond and attach to their preterm infants and full-term infants. Preterm infants were no different in forming attachment relationships with their mothers and fathers than were full-term infants. These findings may reflect the growing understanding of new parents that preterm infants need as much or more stimulation than full-term infants do.

In more recent years some hospitals have encouraged parents to become more involved with the hospital care of premature infants. The parents put on masks and gowns, go into the intensive-care unit to help with feeding and diaper changing, as well as involve themselves with other care. Stroking and talking to the infant are thought to stimulate bonding prior to going home (Kennell and Klaus 1982).

● COMPLICATIONS OF BIRTH

Birth is usually a normal process with very few complications. The complications that do occur can be dealt with successfully by the obstetrician and the hospital personnel. Ninety-five percent of all babies are born in the *vertex presentation,* that is, with their heads emerging first. This type of birth is the normal spontaneous delivery.

Forceps Delivery

Occasionally **forceps** are necessary in delivery. Forceps are curved, tonglike instruments shaped to fit on each side of a baby's head. Some indicators that such a procedure is necessary include the malposition of the fetal head; toxemia; a threatened rupture of the uterus; and the inability of the mother to push after full dilatation of the cervix, because of anesthesia, exhaustion, or heart disease. The primary fetal indicator is fetal distress as suggested by a slow, irregular fetal

Forceps
Curved, tonglike instruments shaped to fit on each side of a baby's head and used in the delivery of a baby.

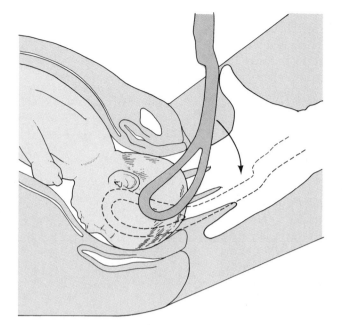 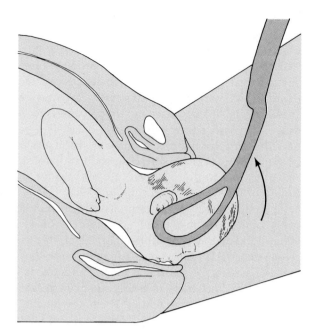

● FIGURE 4.2
Diagram of Forceps Delivery

Breech delivery
An infant born with the buttocks instead of the head delivered first. This is the case in about 3 to 4 percent of births.

heartbeat. Forceps operations are not attempted unless the cervix is completely dilated (Reeder and Martin 1987; Olds et al. 1988).

Breech Delivery

A **breech delivery** is the case in about 3 to 4 percent of births. In breech presentations, the buttocks instead of the head are delivered first. Such deliveries are more common when the baby is premature or there are multiple births. The reason for breech presentations is not always apparent, but they are associated with factors such as twinning, births closer together, hydrocephalus, and placenta previa. Although most breech babies are healthy, there is a considerable increased risk of death and injury. Infant death is three times higher in breech deliveries than in normal deliveries. The major cause of death is trauma (Reeder and Martin 1987).

Oversized Infants

Trauma associated with the passage of oversized infants (over ten pounds) through the birth canal causes a decided increase in fetal mortality. The death rate is 13 percent among oversized babies, in contrast with the usual death rate of 4 percent among normal-sized infants. Uterine dysfunction is frequent in labors with oversized infants because the head becomes not only larger but harder and less malleable with increasing weight. When these infants are born alive, they often do poorly in the first few days because of cerebral hemorrhage.

The excessive size of the fetus is usually due to maternal diabetes, the large size of one or both parents, or multiparity (when a mother has had several children). Tremendously large infants (over thirteen pounds) are extremely rare, and almost all are born dead. Most oversized babies are boys. Large women who are heavy tend to have excessive weight gain during pregnancy and also larger babies (Reeder and Martin 1987).

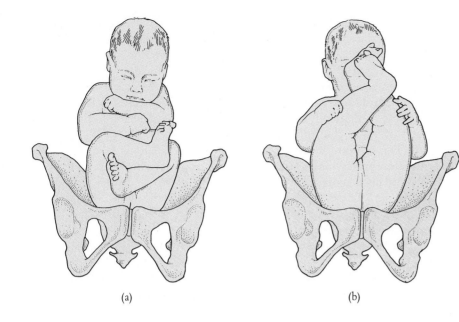

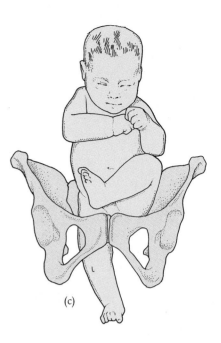

(a)   (b)   (c)

● FIGURE 4.3
Breech Deliveries

Cesarean Section

Cesarean section is the removal of an infant from the uterus through an incision made in the abdominal wall and the uterus. After the incision, the child is removed through the slits, and then both incisions are carefully sewn. The risks are minimal with modern medical techniques. Formerly it was believed that once a woman had a cesarean section, the uterus and abdominal wall were weakened. Now it is known that a woman may have several cesarean births satisfactorily and in some cases may have a vaginal birth after a cesarean.

A cesarean section may be used when there is a disproportion between the size of the fetus and that of the bony birth canal. This could be due to a contracted pelvis or a tumor blocking the birth canal. Also, in certain cases, a patient who has had a previous cesarean section may have the operation done again because of the fear that the uterus will rupture during labor. The procedure is also performed in certain cases of severe toxemia, placenta previa, and premature separation of a normally implanted placenta. Finally, it may be performed in a case of actual or impending fetal distress.

When a cesarean section is done prior to the onset of labor, as a result of a prearranged plan, it is called an elective cesarean section (Reeder and Martin 1987). Up to 15 percent of all babies are delivered through cesarean section (National Institutes of Health 1981). This has concerned many medical experts and parent advocates (Reeder and Martin 1987; Kliot and Silverstein 1980). Many cesarean sections are unnecessary and turn what should be a natural childbirth into an unnecessary medical emergency. Cesarean sections also rob parents of the opportunity to participate in their child's birth.

Cesarean section
Removal of an infant from the uterus through an incision made in the abdominal wall and the uterus.

Obstetrical Medication

Obstetrical medication has a history of controversy. Today it is an issue concerning the impact of the labor and delivery drugs on the child. When obstetrical medication was introduced, it was already controversial, but for different reasons. The issue was morality, not safety. According to the Christian-Judaic belief, Eve was to be punished with the pain of childbirth, which "was to be visited as well on all of her descendants." However, on January 19, 1847, all of this changed. James Young Simpson, a Scottish obstetrician, used ether on a woman to deliver her child. News of the success in the painless birth spread like wildfire. Within five months, etherized deliveries were also performed in England, Ireland, France, Germany, and the United States. By the end of 1847, chloroform was also used successfully as an obstetrical anesthetic. The obstetrical medication met strong objections from the clergy and the medical profession. The practice was seen as an act of heresy. God had apparently ordained women to suffer during childbirth as eternal punishment for ancestral sin. These pain killers, and the men who administered them, flaunted the divine will. The event that wiped out the criticisms and further objections was Queen Victoria's use of chloroform in two births, one in 1853 and the other in 1857. Queen Victoria was the secular head of the Church of England (Brackbill 1979).

It has been long known that drugs that reduce the mother's level of awareness and sensitivity also affect the infant's alertness and responsiveness at birth. Brackbill's studies (1979) found that the routine use of general anesthetics at birth have subsequent effects on infant behavior. The strongest effects are increases in the incidence of brain damage and the delay in the development of memory and gross motor coordination abilities in the child for at least one year after birth. Most obstetrical medications are dose-related, with the most substantial results observed in the infants of mothers who have received high-potency drugs or have had high total doses of drugs. Infants whose mothers received relatively large doses of obstetrical medication were atypical in several respects, including infrequent smiles, sluggishness, irritability, and difficulty with feeding or cuddling in the first few weeks of life. The larger dosages also prolonged labor.

Brackbill also found that obstetrical medication decreased the amount of food the neonates consumed and the amount of weight they gained. The medication was also related to decreased sucking rate and pressure, the number and vigor of sucks, responsiveness to feeding, and the alteration of feeding intervals.

Murray et al. (1981) found that the effects of obstetrical medication on neonatal behavior were the strongest on the first day. By the fifth day, there was evidence of behavioral recovery, but medicated babies continued to exhibit poor state organization. At one month, examiners observed few differences between groups, but unmedicated mothers reported that their babies were more sociable, rewarding, and easy to care for, and these mothers were more responsive to their infants' cries. Perhaps for first-time mothers, early interactions constitute important transactions that serve to shape the mothers' expectations concerning their infants' behavior. Although the direct biochemical drug effects may wear off during the first few days, the mother's early impressions may remain to influence how rewarding she finds her baby and the manner in which she responds to her infant's initiatives at one month of age. The results of this study emphasize the necessity of minimizing the elective use of medication. Also, mothers who, for whatever reason, receive medication during childbirth should have additional support in coming to terms with what may at first be perceived as a disorganized and difficult baby.

One study, however, found a benefit to obstetrical medication. Myers and Myers (1979) found that anesthetics actually facilitate certain high-risk deliveries. They concluded that maternal exposure to psychological or other stress, when sufficiently marked, may adversely affect the fetus. Therefore, reassuring the mother or administering sedative drugs may improve the fetal status. Barbiturates and possibly other sedatives offer the possibility of active therapeutic intervention in those cases in which fetal asphyxia has been identified.

Anoxia

Anoxia is a condition in which an insufficient amount of oxygen reaches the neonate's brain. The ease or difficulty with which the neonate starts to breathe is critical. If breathing is not established soon after birth, serious consequences occur. Any lack of oxygen can have serious, long-lasting effects on the child's later mental and motor development, including cerebral palsy. A significant number of children whose mothers were given a routine anesthetic during childbirth, and who suffered from anoxia as a result, were delayed in learning to sit up, stand, walk, and talk. If the oxygen deprivation is extremely severe, it could cause death. One cause of anoxia is the use of anesthetics. Another cause of anoxia is a prolonged or difficult birth, which, again, could be related to the use of anesthetics (Brackbill 1979).

Corah (1979) found that a group of anoxics who were studied at birth and again at three years and seven years still exhibited deficits at seven years but were much better than they had been earlier. They were slower in perceptual motor ability and perceptual attention and exhibited impairment in the area of social competence.

Anoxia
A condition in which an insufficient amount of oxygen reaches the neonate's brain.

● ALTERNATIVE CHILDBIRTH PROCEDURES

During the last few years, couples have investigated alternatives to birth in the traditional hospital setting. These couples have a desire for a more relaxed, personal atmosphere, togetherness, and more flexibility in the type of care offered. Traditionally, there has been a perceived in-hospital attitude that childbirth is an abnormal and pathological process. Therefore, these new parents want birth with less medical interference. They have expressed a need to have the newborn nearby and have been disappointed because of the lack of organization of rooming-in accommodations. Also, there is a real concern over the possible contact with hospital germs. Lack of rest and the high cost of hospitalization are other concerns cited (Olds et al. 1988; Ingalls and Salerno 1979).

In the past, removing childbirth from family and community resulted in the loss of rich social support. The new mother, who may be separated from her husband except during visiting hours, may feel alone and vulnerable. In-hospital childbirth is considered mysterious and often an unhappy isolation from family members who have no part of it. Children grow up without any knowledge of the birth process, except for the bits and pieces they pick up. Even new parents are surprised at the appearance of a small, wrinkled newborn with a misshappen head. New parents are more likely to have a feeling of satisfaction if they are involved in choosing the various birthing procedures and can be surrounded by loved ones if they so desire.

Natural, or Prepared, Childbirth

Natural, or prepared, childbirth is preparation of the mother and father for labor and delivery, and it allows for their active involvement in the birth.

Natural childbirth
Preparation of the mother and father for labor and delivery, which allows for their active involvement in the childbirth process.

Prepared childbirth
See Natural childbirth

The whole process implies the avoidance or minimal use of drugs or anesthetics. Prepared childbirth provides the mother an opportunity to be alert and actively engaged with the infant in the first few hours of life. Parents who share childbirth together often describe a deepening relationship and a strong sense of elation in their marriage. Prepared childbirth often involves a program of exercises to strengthen the appropriate muscles, breathing techniques to aid during labor and delivery, and psychological mind-set, imagery, or relaxation procedures that lessen birth pains and permit spontaneous birth. Two prepared childbirth programs, Grantly Dick-Read's program and the Lamaze program, are widely used today.

Dick-Read

Dick-Read method
A natural childbirth method in which the key to childbirth is preparation, limited medication, and participation.

The term **natural childbirth** was probably made popular by the late English obstetrician Dr. Grantly Dick-Read (1972) in his book *Childbirth Without Fear.* Dick-Read believed the key to childbirth was preparation, limited medication, and participation. He felt that the mother should be awake, aware, and undrugged and the father should share the experience and provide support to his wife. In Western society, children were anticipated with exaggerated fear, which he felt created tension. Tension causes the tightening of muscles, making labor more painful than necessary. In the 1930s and 1940s, Dick-Read expounded the view that pain and fear could be reduced if mothers understood the birth process and learned to relax properly. His training program included prenatal health care, a childbearing and birth education program, and a series of techniques for proper breathing, physical fitness, and relaxation. He proposed that if the mother knew about the birth process and knew how to help herself at each stage, she would be more relaxed during labor. Pain would be less, so she would not need medication and she would be prepared for delivery. The emphasis was placed on positive thinking, passive relaxation, and the performance of the

Natural childbirth is a team effort that includes the mother, father, and a family-centered maternity hospital health-care unit.

woman. This made natural childbirth a team effort that included the mother, the father, and a family-centered maternity hospital health-care unit (Dick-Read 1972; Ingalls and Salerno 1979).

Lamaze

While visiting the Soviet Union in 1952, Dr. Fernand Lamaze, a French obstetrician, became intrigued with the labor and delivery techniques based on Pavlov's theory of conditioned response. Upon his return, he introduced *psychoprophylactic* concepts into his practice to better prepare his patients for their maternity experiences and assist them in a rewarding, conscious participation in the childbirth process.

The **Lamaze** program involves the education of both parents in various techniques of breathing and relaxation that ease the birth process. They are taught how to respond with the effective type of breathing during each phase of labor. (If the father is unable or unwilling to participate, a close friend can be trained as a labor coach.) Relaxation and breathing exercises are taught and practiced during a class period. The parents are taught as a team how each can aid in the expulsion of the baby. Lamaze believed, as did Dick-Read, that fear and helplessness are caused by a lack of knowledge and that fears lead to tension, which leads to pain. Lamaze's relaxation techniques to control pain are based on the principle that the brain can efficiently process only one stimulus at a time. Concentrating on one focal point allows the woman to increase her tolerance to pain and thus decrease her perception of the intensity of the contraction. Since she knows what to expect from labor and delivery and has learned the relaxation techniques, her discomfort is generally eased during labor. Women who employ the Lamaze method use less medication than other women. They feel more in control, generally remain calmer, and are more able to cooperate with physicians or midwives in the birth process (Ingalls and Salerno 1979; Lamaze 1970).

Lamaze method
Natural childbirth in which the mother uses various techniques of breathing and relaxation that ease the birth process and the father functions as a coach to help the mother's breathing techniques.

Home Birth

Home births, which are still occurring in some rural areas, have begun to reappear in urban areas. The major reason for home birth is the dissatisfaction with hospital procedures. Many parents feel that childbirth is an emotional, deeply personal experience that should not take place in the cold, impersonal, sterile environment of a hospital. Some physicians and certified nurse-midwives are now consenting to assist at home deliveries, provided no problems or abnormalities are indicated. Other possible attendants are lay-midwives, a friend, or the father. Legality and the proficiency of the attendant differs depending on the location and the circumstances (Olds et al. 1988).

Most physicians feel that the health-care system in the United States is not organized to render home births safe—especially since 5 to 10 percent of the mothers and infants who are not considered high risk develop problems during the labor-birth period. They are also concerned about professional backup in case they cannot attend the birth and the threat of malpractice suits (Zimmerman 1980). However, home birth may be the only feasible alternative for those who live too far from the hospital or birthing center.

In 1979, the vast majority, 99.1 percent, of American babies were born in hospitals. Throughout the world, however, 80 percent of all babies are delivered by midwives. The home-birth movement has made quite an impact on the policies of hospitals. Their rules have eased in the last ten to twenty years regarding who may be present at birth and afterwards. Many have opened birthing centers on their premises (Lubic 1981).

Birthing Centers or Rooms

Birthing rooms or the **alternative birth center (ABC)** offer another alternative to the traditional hospital birth. Usually it is part of or near a hospital or clinic, with emergency equipment and staff available on call. The birthing rooms are especially designed to care for uncomplicated births in a home-type setting. These rooms combine the privacy, serenity, and intimacy of a home birth with the safety and medical backup of a hospital. The birthing rooms accommodate the entire process, from labor through delivery and recovery. Often soft music, colored bedspreads, and rocking chairs create a warm, homelike atmosphere. Visitation policies are usually rather liberal for family members. Nurse-midwives or physicians monitor the labor and assist in the birth. The mother and baby are usually discharged several hours after birth. Follow-up nursing visits to the home are usually made a few days after the discharge (Butnarescu and Tillotson 1983; Ingalls and Salerno 1979).

Birthing Chair

In the past, women delivered their babies from a squatting position. The structure of the human pelvis lends itself to delivering a baby from that position. Gravity increases the woman's natural uterine contractions, usually reducing the time needed for delivery. A *birthing chair* allows a woman to sit or squat while giving birth. Its molded contours give her something to push against, which takes the pressure off of her back while reducing the pains that often follow conventional birth. Recent studies show that women laboring in an upright position have shorter and more efficient labor as well as less painful contractions. Women using birthing chairs average only thirty minutes in second-stage labor, compared with ninety minutes for women delivering horizontally. Also, it has been found that birthing chairs decrease the risk of blood clots in the woman's legs. Some women enjoy the psychological benefits of delivering from a seated position. One woman's reaction: "When you're supine, you feel vulnerable. In the chair you feel more in control" (Clark and Gosnell 1981; "Squatting helps" 1985).

● THE NEONATE

Professionals usually refer to a newborn infant as a *neonate* for the first two weeks after birth, and some apply the term to an infant for the first four weeks. The neonate is viewed by most people as totally dependent, capable of only eating, sleeping, crying, and dirtying diapers. But those who know neonates better know that they are responsive, quick to learn, and interesting to observe because they develop so rapidly. And they do have individual personalities. In recent years, the neonate has proven to be a very exciting subject for psychological study. Neonates have been observed to possess important perceptual, motor, and social abilities. They can also take more responsibility for their own development than once thought. Every infant from the beginning is an active, perceiving, learning individual who is capable of organizing information (Brazelton 1986).

Alternative Birth Center (ABC) Birthing rooms that are usually a part of or near a hospital or clinic, with emergency equipment and staff available on call. The birthing rooms are especially designed to care for uncomplicated births in a home-type setting.

Physical Characteristics

Most American neonates range from eighteen to twenty-one inches long and weigh between six and eight and one-half pounds. They appear blotchy and wrinkled because they have not developed the full layer of fat that makes older infants pudgy. The neonate's head may look misshapen and elongated as a result of the process during birth called **molding.** In molding, the soft bony plates of the skull (connected by cartilage) are squeezed together in the birth canal. Later the head will return to its proper shape. It is overly large in proportion to the rest of the body, constituting one-fourth of the total length. The cranium has six **fontanels,** or soft spots, where the skull has not yet closed. These allow the skull and brain to continue to grow. (At about one and a half years, the skull will have filled the gaps, and the soft spots will disappear.)

The neonate usually has a broad, flat nose, a tiny chin and jaw, a prominent forehead, disproportionately large eyeballs, and practically no neck. The stomach may protrude, and the genitals seem overly large. The legs may appear bent and are often pulled up close to the body. Often neonates of either sex are born with some breast enlargement and may even secrete a small amount of fluid, sometimes called "witches' milk." This does not last long and is due to hormones present during prenatal development. The majority of neonates are toothless. Teeth are not necessary anyway, since neonates are not ready for solid foods. The eye color is usually a dark gray-blue for all racial groups.

Physiological Functions

Many internal changes must take place as the neonate's body adjusts to living outside the uterus. Right after birth the arteries leading to the placenta by the way of the umbilical cord close off, and blood begins to flow through the lungs to pick up oxygen as the infant begins to breathe on his or her own. After a few days, the digestive and excretory systems will also start working, which usually results in the loss of a pound or so before the infant begins to gain. For the first couple of weeks, the mechanisms that regulate the body's temperature do not fully function; therefore the infant needs to be kept from becoming too warm or too cold.

States

The behavior and responses of the neonate vary with and depend upon the **state** he or she happens to be in. The term *state* refers to the level of arousal, such as asleep, drowsy, or alert. It was only within the last twenty years that researchers began considering the infant's state. Behavior that had previously appeared random and chaotic became recognized as predictable and often sequential. Wolff (1966) and Prechtl and Beintema (1965) developed classification systems describing these states. *Regular sleep* occurs when the infant is completely relaxed. No muscle or eye activity occurs, and the respiration rate is constant. In *irregular sleep* some limb movements and gentle stirring occur, along with facial grimaces, smiles, mouthing, and puckering. Eye movements may be observed although the eyes are closed. Respiration tends to be irregular and faster than during regular sleep. *Drowsiness* usually occurs when an infant is waking up or falling asleep. The eyelids may open and close. If the lids are open, the eyes have a dull, glazed appearance and are not focused. Drowsiness involves less activity than irregular sleep but more than regular sleep. In *alert inactivity* the eyes are bright and shining. The important aspect of this state is the infant's apparent stimulation. After about three to four weeks, the infants will also display

Molding
A process during which soft bony plates of the skull (connected by cartilage) are squeezed together in the birth canal, causing the neonate's head to look misshapen and elongated.

Fontanels
Six soft spots on the head of a neonate, where the skull has not yet closed.

States
The level of arousal of an infant, such as asleep, drowsy, or alert.

Circumcision

Circumcision, the removal of the foreskin from the penis of a neonate boy, has been an emotional issue and now is a health issue. In 1975 the American Academy of Pediatrics (AAP) stated that it saw no medical reason for the routine circumcision of neonate boys. Few pediatricians continued to perform circumcisions after that statement was released. Since then, urinary infections have increased among infant boys. (Wiswell et al. 1988). The Report of the American Academy of Pediatrics Task Force on Circumcision (1989) states that boys who have not been circumcised have ten to twenty times more urinary tract infections in the first few months of life than boys who have been circumcised. The task force also points out that "a properly performed circumcision" prevents constriction of the foreskin around the penis and a rare condition of penis and foreskin inflammation. There is also evidence that circumcision decreases the incidence of cancer of the penis and may reduce cervical cancer in women who are sexual partners of uncircumcised men infected with a recently identified virus, human papillomavirus.

The AAP points out that circumcision is "a rapid and generally safe procedure by an experienced operator. It is an elective procedure to be performed only if the infant is stable and healthy" (p. 7). When done early and well, the procedure is quick and relatively painless (Wiswell et al. 1988). Some infants sleep through most of the procedure when given extra attention, cuddling, and a pacifier. Although there appears to be no elevated physiological response to pain during circumcision (Waters et al. 1982), the neonate's sensitivity to pain increases with neurological maturity (D'apolito 1984). Therefore, it would be less traumatic for a one-day-old infant compared with a one-week-old infant.

a state of alert activity, which is the same as alert inactivity except that the infant is motorically active. *Waking activity* occurs when the infant exhibits frequent bursts of general motor activity and the eyes are open. The infant does not cry but may moan, grunt, or whimper. Respiration is irregular. *Crying* needs no description. This state makes the strongest impression on anyone who spends much time with babies. The infant may grimace and flush with the eyelids tightly closed. The crying is usually accompanied by general motor activity.

Function of Crying

Crying among neonates is unlearned and involuntary. However, at the same time, it incites the parent to caregiving activities. Most crying, within hours after birth, will quiet down when the neonate is held and carried. Studies by Mary Ainsworth and Sylvia Bell (Bell and Ainsworth 1972; Ainsworth and Bell 1977) revealed that a responsive mother provides not only the conditions that stop the crying but also a setting that prevents the crying in the first place. They also found that ignoring babies' cries increases the likelihood that they will cry more as they approach the end of their first year. Mothers who respond to their neonates when they cry have babies who cry little and whose crying decreases during the first year. Ainsworth and Bell also found that the infants of responsive mothers, when compared with the infants of unresponsive mothers, are more likely later on to develop communication channels other than crying, such as motioning for what they want or holding their arms out to be picked up.

A great deal can be determined about neonates from their cry. Parents usually can differentiate between types of infant crying, a feat most nonparents cannot do. Three distinct patterns of crying have been identified. The first is a cry that begins irregularly at low intensity but gradually becomes louder and more rhythmical. The second cry is a mad or angry cry, which is also rhyth-

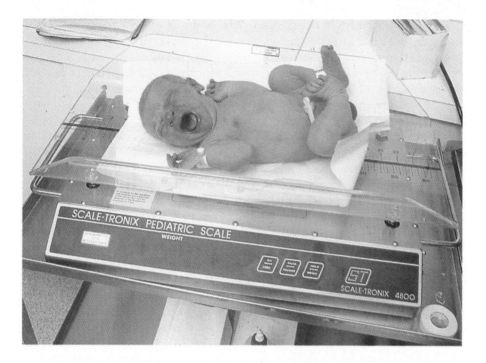

Crying among neonates is unlearned and involuntary. Nevertheless, it incites the parent to caregiving activities.

mical but more energetic. The third cry is a pain cry, which begins with a sudden shriek, followed by several seconds of silence as the infant regains its breath, then episodes of energetic, gasping cries (Schaffer 1971).

The neonate's cry has proven to be helpful in detecting certain abnormalities and diseases. Infants with more complications require higher levels of stimulation to elicit the cry. They take longer before they start to cry, have a shorter first cry expiration, cry less, and have higher-pitched cries than infants with little or no complications (Fogel 1984). For example, research since the 1960s has shown that brain-damaged and Down's syndrome babies, when compared with normal babies, produce a less sustained cry with less rhythmic flow in the crying (Fisichelli and Karelitz 1963; Lind et al. 1970). A malnourished infant's cry has an initial longer sound, higher pitch, and lower amplitude than a well-nourished baby's (Lester 1976, 1984, 1987). Crying can thus be used to determine an infant's internal state or diagnose potential abnormalities.

Function of Sleeping

Neonates may sleep almost continuously for the first twenty-four to forty-eight hours. They usually do not require total silence when they sleep but usually are disturbed by an abrupt change in noise level or an abrupt lack of noise.

Rapid eye movement (REM) sleep and nonrapid eye movement (NREM) sleep have attracted the attention of psychologists in recent years. Both sleep patterns occur in infants and adults. NREM sleep is a deeper sleep with a regular heartbeat, rhythmical respiration, low levels of metabolic activity, and moderate to high muscle tone. Although dreaming is more strongly associated with REM sleep, 15 percent of people awakened from NREM sleep report dreams. These dreams lack the clear imagery, emotional tone, and structure of REM sleep dreams. Large fluctuations in the heart rate, lowered muscular activity, and a substantial increase in brain activity are some of the characteristics of REM sleep. It is thought that REM sleep clears the brain of neurochemicals accumulated during the awake hours, and dreaming provides a release or "safety valve." This makes it possible for intense daytime impulses to be relieved at night (Olds et al. 1988). Depriving an adult of REM sleep can increase tension, anxiety, irritability, and hostility. Evidence supported by recording brain activity indicates that almost half of a newborn's sleep time is REM sleep. By two years of age, 25 percent of the sleep time is REM sleep, and by five years it is 10 percent, the same as for an adult (Berg and Berg 1979).

REM sleep in infants stimulates the development of the brain by the activity it generates. Neonates have little opportunity to respond to environmental events because they spend so much time in sleep. They may then require the neurological self-stimulation provided by REM sleep (Coons and Guilleminault 1982).

Feeding Patterns

Neonates' hunger and sleep patterns are closely linked. In fact, they spend a great deal of their awake time eating. On the average they may eat eight to fourteen times during the day, with intervals between feedings from one and a half hours up to four hours, and four- or five-hour intervals at night. As babies get older, they require fewer feedings. By twelve months they eat three to five meals a day.

Each neonate is remarkably different from others. Parents are encouraged to feed their babies when they are hungry, which means the infant chooses his or her own twenty-four-hour cycle in which to eat and sleep. This is called **self-demand feeding.** The parents must then choose whether to feed the baby with breast milk or a commercially prepared formula.

Approximately one-half of the mothers of neonates in this country breast-feed their babies. Breast-feeding provides many advantages. Besides the psychological and emotional rewards, it is also practical. During the first seven to ten days after a birth, the breast produces a substance called **colostrum,** a high-protein mixture loaded with protective antibodies. Colostrum provides immunities for the neonate until his or her immune system is developed (Olds et al. 1988). Human milk is always ready and at the correct temperature. Also, human milk is easier for an infant to digest than cow's milk and contains antibodies that protect against ear infections, respiratory infections, colds, bronchitis, meningitis, pneumonia, German measles, viral infections, scarlet fever, polio, and diarrhea (Goldman and Goldblum 1982; Pipes 1981; Addy 1976; Endres and Rockwell 1980).

It has also been found that breast-fed babies are more likely to have healthy teeth. The muscle action of breast feeding is associated with the development of the baby's jaw and mouth in a way that reduces crowded teeth later (Guthrie 1979). Breast-fed babies are less likely to be obese and less likely to suffer from premature arteriosclerosis (Olds et al. 1988). A reduction in allergic problems such as eczema has also been found (Olds et al. 1988; Eastham and Walker 1977).

Within a few days after birth, breast-fed babies respond to either breast or breast-milk odors from their own mothers as compared to other breast-feeding mothers (Cernoch and Porter 1985; Schaal 1986). On the other hand, bottle-fed babies do *not* recognize their own mothers by smell (Cernoch and Porter 1985). Makin and Porter (1989) found that female neonates were attracted to the odor

Self-demand feeding
The practice of feeding infants when they are hungry rather than on a particular schedule determined by the parent and/or doctor.

Colostrum
A high-protein substance loaded with protective antibodies that is produced by the mother's breast shortly after a birth.

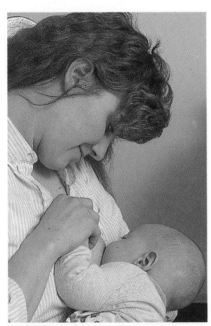

Approximately one-half of the mothers of neonates in this country breastfeed their babies. Breastfeeding offers physiological, emotional, psychological, and practical advantages.

of a breast-feeding woman even though they had had no prior breast-feeding experience. Male neonates, however, did not show such an attraction. It could be that the male neonate's olfactory capabilities are not as mature as those of the female neonate.

When a mother chooses to breast-feed, it is important for her to remember that breast-fed babies are susceptible to the harmful effects of certain drugs and toxins taken by the mother. Medicines (such as anticoagulants, most laxatives, radioactive drugs, and tetracyclines), tobacco, alcohol, marijuana, cocaine, plus other hard drugs can be transmitted to the child in the mother's milk and constitute a health hazard (Fried et al. 1987; Streissguth et al. 1983; Foman 1974; Chaney and Wadlington 1988; Reeder and Martin, 1987).

The main disadvantage of breast-feeding is the limiting of the mother's physical freedom. Another disadvantage is that the father cannot participate in breast-feeding. Commercial formulas or preparations tend to fill the baby up more, so they do not eat as often (Endres and Rockwell 1980). Also, bottle-fed infants sleep through the night earlier than breast-fed infants do (Elias 1984; Tynan 1986).

Capabilities

The neonate has a functioning sensory system, a repertoire of motor reflexes and skills, and an array of social behaviors. The neonate is also capable of discriminating between stimuli and can learn very efficiently.

Senses

It is now accepted that all of the senses are functioning at birth for normal full-term neonates. Neonates are equipped with a functional and intact *visual* apparatus. The eye is capable of responding differentially to most aspects of its visual field. Neonates can see well enough to imitate other people. For example,

---

TABLE 4.2 Advantages and Disadvantages of Breast-feeding

ADVANTAGES

Breast-feeding provides colostrum the first five to seven days after birth.
Breast milk is nutritionally superior, with the proper proportion of nutrients.
Breast milk is pure, clean, and free of bacteria.
Breast milk is easily digested for fewer disturbances such as colic, diarrhea, constipation.
Breast milk provides better resistance to a number of infectious diseases.
The infant is less likely to develop allergies.
Breast milk is immediately available and convenient and is always at the correct temperature.
Breast-feeding is more economical.
Breast-fed infants are less likely to be obese and have better teeth.
Breast-feeding provides the mother more time to rest, since there is no formula to measure, mix, and heat.
Breast-feeding is an emotionally and psychologically satisfying experience for both the mother and the child.

DISADVANTAGES

Breast-feeding limits the mother's physical freedom, especially if she works.
Breast milk does not fill the infant up as much as formula does (bottle-fed infants go longer between feedings).
The diet of the mother is limited; it must contain adequate fluids, nutrients, and calories.
The mother must be cautious about medications and drugs that may pass to her milk.
The father cannot participate.

A neonate can see well enough to imitate his mother sticking out her tongue.

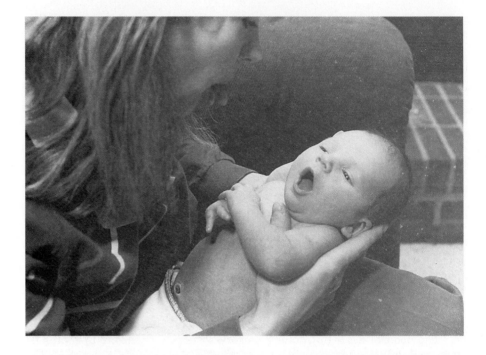

if an infant's mother sticks her tongue out at the baby, within a short time the baby will begin to stick his or her tongue out at the mother. Neonates will also imitate fluttering eyelashes and an opening and closing mouth. This phenomenon not only indicates that neonates can see but also indicates that they can interact and are already social beings (Bower 1977).

The *hearing* apparatus is also remarkably well developed in the neonate. Of all the senses, hearing is the least functional at birth, due to amniotic fluid in the middle ear. After the fluid drains out, which may take several hours to several days, then hearing is normal. Ockleford et al. (1988) found that sounds that were repeatedly experienced before birth, especially the mother's voice, became so familiar to the fetus that he or she responded to the mother's voice during the first few hours after birth. They also found that neonates can differentiate between the mother's and father's voices as well as strangers' voices. Neonates can also localize sound. For example, a researcher sounded a clicker on a neonate's right side, then on her left side. The neonate turned her eyes to the side on which the clicker sounded. This not only indicated that she was able to localize the sound in space, but because she turned her eyes toward the sound source, she apparently expected to see something at the source of the sound. This indicates that at a minimal level, intersensory coordination occurs (Wertheimer 1961).

Interactional synchrony
The synchronization of neonates' body movements with the sound patterns of adult speech.

Neonates also engage in **interactional synchrony,** that is, their body movements are synchronized with the sound patterns of adult speech. When they are spoken to by an adult, they move their bodies in rhythms that coordinate perfectly with the basic units of adult speech. Not only does this phenomenon support the neonates' ability to hear, but it also indicates their truly social nature. Neonates react only to the human voice in this manner, not to any other sounds (Condon and Sander 1974; Condon 1975).

Other senses present at birth are *taste* and *smell*. Neonates relax and suck contentedly when provided with sweet solutions. They can differentiate milk from water, sugar, and salt, and they respond differently to different concentrations of sweet, salty, and bitter solutions (Ganchrow, Steiner, and Daher 1983).

Neonates also respond to different odors, and the vigor of the response corresponds to the intensity and quality of the stimulant. Cernoch and Porter (1985) found that two-week-old breast-fed neonates recognized their mothers by smell but did not recognize their fathers. Bottle-fed babies were unable to recognize their mothers by smell. Montagner (1985) found that from the third day after birth, neonates could discriminate the odor of their mothers' necks and breasts. Interestingly, from the second and third days after birth, the mothers could also recognize their infants' odor.

Pain, heat, cold, and pressure are *cutaneous sensations* present at birth. For the first few days, little pain is experienced. At the time of birth, sensitivity to pain is lessened so that the baby will not feel its effects while passing through the birth canal. However, sensitivity to pain increases within a matter of days (Waters et al. 1982). Neonates react to differences in temperature, as shown by different sucking reactions to changes of temperature in milk. Neonates also show discomfort when the air temperature moves above or below normal.

Motor Development

Motor development is extremely important in the early stages. Babies are born with a general ability to move parts of the body and with a remarkable range of built-in behavioral responses called **reflexes.** Some reflexes appear during the fetal stage. A reflex constitutes a specific, automatic reaction to a particular kind of stimulus. Reflex testing involves applying a stimulus, which in turn produces a motor activity. Such testing is one component of a neurological exam that does not require the active cooperation of the infant, since a reflex is an involuntary response. The reflex is dependent not only on the structure of the central nervous system, but also on the physiological state of the infant at the time of the exam. Internal factors that can affect reflex responses include whether the infant is asleep or awake, hungry or satisfied, irritable or contented, and also body temperature. Some external factors that can make an impact on an infant's reflex responses include variations of head and limb positions, a cold or warm environment, and the type of clothing worn by the infant.

Reflex testing has several important clinical applications. First, it makes it possible to localize a central nervous system abnormality. Second, it makes it possible to assess the maturation and development of the nervous system. Finally, it determines the quality of peripheral nerves.

Reflexes may be divided into four general categories: those needed for survival, those that are regarded as the primitive beginnings of conceptual and exploratory skills, those that serve little function now but may have filled some purpose in humanity's distant past, and finally, general activities that express discomfort or arousal and that communicate various emotional states to the caregiver.

Some of the survival reflexes include blinking, sucking, rooting, crying, breathing, coughing, sneezing, and yawning. *Blinking* appears around the sixth or seventh fetal month and increases throughout life. This reflex may be elicited by a puff of air in the face, a loud noise, a strong odor, a bitter taste, a bright light, or by touching the eyelashes, the eyebrow, or the bridge of the nose.

Sucking appears around the second or third fetal month. It can be elicited by placing a finger or nipple in the infant's mouth. The *rooting* reflex appears in the

Reflexes
A range of built-in behavioral responses to particular kinds of stimuli.

Yawning is a reflex that gives a quick gulp of air when it is needed.

second or third fetal month and lasts to about the fourth month after birth. This reflex can be elicited by stroking the corner of the mouth or cheek, which causes the infant to move the tongue, mouth, and head towards the stimulated side.

The *cry* is thought to reflect the neurophysiological development of the infant and can be used to detect any neurological adversities (Golub and Corwin 1984; Lester 1984, 1987). The acoustical level of the cry appears to be related to the development of the brain stem (Rapisardi et al. 1989).

The *breathing* reflexes are coordinated with and activated by an oxygen and carbon dioxide balance. *Coughing* and *sneezing* clear the air passages and lungs. *Yawning* gives a quick gulp of air when it is needed suddenly.

Those abilities that indicate the primitive beginnings of conceptual and exploratory skills include *tracking moving objects* with coordinated eye and head movements and *turning the head toward the source of sound.*

Other types of reflexes are those that serve little function today but may have filled some function in humanity's distant past. The absence of these reflexes may be an indication of immaturity or brain damage. The *Babinski* is one such reflex. This reflex is elicited by lightly stroking the sole of the foot. The response consists of flexing the foot and fanning the toes. Normal full-term infants have a complete positive response, which persists to a varying degree up to twelve or eighteen months. It is absent in infants with lower spinal cord defects. If it persists in older infants (past eighteen months), it may indicate the presence of spinal cord injuries, meningitis, and other central nervous system disorders.

The grasp reflexes, the *Palmar* and *plantar,* appear around the fourth or sixth fetal month. The Palmar grasp is elicited by putting pressure on the palm of the hand with an object. The infant then grasps the object with his or her fingers. The Palmar grasp disappears between the fourth and sixth month, with a voluntary grasp superseding it. The plantar grasp is elicited by placing an object on the sole of the foot just behind the toes, which causes a plantar flexion of the toes (that is, the infant's toes curl under). It disappears between nine and twelve months.

The *Moro* reflex appears at about seven fetal months and disappears between four and six months after birth. It can be elicited when infants suddenly lose support of their neck and head. Infants throw their head backwards, arch their back, throw open their arms and legs, and then quickly bring them back against their body. It is related to the fear of falling and self-preservation. In the Moro reflex, the hands curl slightly, as if preparing to grasp something. The response looks much like the startle of children and adults and may be a precursor to it. An absence of the Moro reflex may indicate a malfunctioning of the central nervous system and other brain stem problems that would result in mental retardation due to brain damage.

The *placing* reflex persists throughout the first year. It can be elicited by placing the top of the foot under a tabletop or another edge, causing the infant to place the foot on top of the table or surface. This reflex is absent in children with spinal cord injuries.

The *stepping* reflex is elicited by placing the baby's foot on top of a surface, causing what appears to be stepping movements. This reflex lasts until around the third or fourth month. It has little value in judging maturation or an abnormal central nervous system.

The *tonic neck* reflex often manifests itself in infants who are lying on their back. They turn their head to the side, extend the arm on the side they are facing

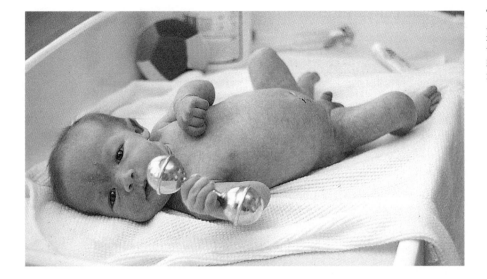

The Palmar grasp is elicited by putting pressure on the palm of the hand with an object. The infant then grasps the object with his or her fingers.

and bend the other, while arching their body away from the direction they face. The need for this reflex is not obvious, but it is thought that perhaps it allows the fetus in the womb to assist in the birth process and later helps with learning to use one side of the body separately from the other. This particular reflex is quite often difficult to elicit in full-term neonates, but is easier with two- to three-month-old babies. By six to seven months it is usually unobtainable. Past this age, the reflex signifies a lack of motor organization, but it is not necessarily associated with a mental deficiency (Butnarescu and Tillotson 1983; Reeder and Martin 1987; Taft and Cohen 1967; DiLeo 1967).

The neonate uses some of these reflexes to assimilate stimuli from the environment in an attempt to know what is going on. Some of these reflexes become learned and are then voluntary. Reflexes are controlled in the midbrain

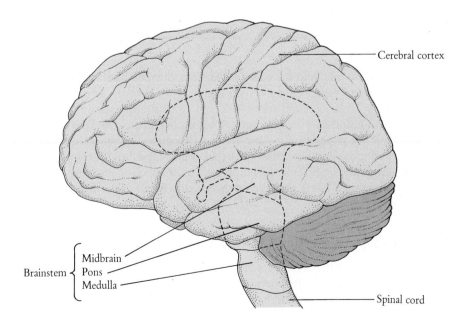

● FIGURE 4.4
Diagram of the Brain
Reflexes are controlled in the midbrain and spinal cord, while voluntary responses are controlled by the cerebral cortex.

TABLE 4.3 Reflexes

REFLEX	DESCRIPTION	DEVELOPMENTAL COURSE
SURVIVAL REFLEXES		
Blinking	Closes both eyes.	Appears around sixth or seventh fetal month and increases throughout life.
Sucking	Makes strong sucking motions with throat, mouth, and tongue.	Appears around second or third fetal month.
Rooting	Turns cheek in direction of touch.	Appears in second or third fetal month and lasts to about fourth month after birth.
Breathing	Alternates and exhales.	Is permanent but becomes partially voluntary.
INDICATORS OF NORMAL CENTRAL NERVOUS SYSTEM		
Babinski	Flexes big toe; fans out other toes; twists foot inward.	Appears in fourth to sixth fetal month Disappears at end of first year.
Moro	When support of head and neck is lost, throws head back, arches back, throws open arms and legs, and then quickly brings them back against body.	Appears at seventh fetal month and disappears between fourth and sixth months after birth.
GRASPING		
Palmar	Grasps object with fingers; can suspend own weight for brief period of time.	Appears between fourth and sixth fetal months and disappears between fourth and sixth months after birth.
Plantar	Curls toes under when object is pressed under toes.	Appears between fourth and sixth fetal months and disappears between ninth and twelfth months after birth.
Stepping	When foot is placed on top of surface, begins stepping.	Appears eighth to ninth fetal month. Disappears around third or fourth month after birth.
Placing	When top of foot is placed under surface, places foot on top of surface.	Appears in eighth or ninth fetal month. Persists throughout first year. (Absent in children with spinal cord injuries.)

and spinal cord, while voluntary responses are controlled by the cerebral cortex. The midbrain and spinal cord evolved earlier and are more primitive than the comparatively large cerebral cortex. They control, for example, digestion, sweating, and blood pressure changes. The cerebral cortex, on the other hand, is responsible for control over such things as complex information processing, memory, and most intelligent behavior that is considered uniquely human. The development and use of the cerebral cortex results from continuing interaction between the human being and the environment (Emde 1985; Yakolev and Lecours 1967).

The Impact of the Neonate on the Family

Neonates alter the lives of those around them, especially their parents. These little beings come into the world with their own unique personalities and capabilities. The firstborn child, probably because of the novelty, usually receives more caregiving interaction than subsequent children.

Bonding is a term used widely in the popular literature as well as the professional literature. It has become synonymous with good mothering. Kennell et al. (1979) perceive bonding as occurring during a sensitive or critical period and occurring between mother and infant. Bonding is thought to occur immediately after delivery. This is a period of heightened sensitivity for the mother, during which she interacts with the neonate and begins to form a special attachment to him or her. What if, because of a medical emergency, the mother and infant are not allowed to see each other during this sensitive period? Will this impair their relationship? Not necessarily, according to Lamb and Hwang (1982), as long as there are other forces that exist to encourage a good relationship as the infant gets older.

Klaus et al. (1970) noted a common interaction pattern among new mothers, which included holding the naked infant immediately after birth. The mothers would first begin touching the neonates' fingers and toes, a phase that lasted about four to eight minutes. After this they began to move inward, touching limbs and then making massaging movements on the abdomen. The original mother-infant bond is viewed as the wellspring for the infant's subsequent attachments, and this relationship is how the child eventually develops a sense of self. Throughout the child's lifetime, the strength and character of the mother-infant attachment will influence the quality of all bonds to other individuals (Kennell et al. 1979; Reeder and Martin 1987).

So many studies have focused on the attachment and bonding between the mother and infant that the father has gone relatively unnoticed. Studies by Weaver and Cranley (1983), Bowen and Miller (1980), Jones (1981), Peterson et al. (1979), and Greenberg and Morris (1974) found that fathers are not only profoundly impacted by the birth of their children, but they establish a strong attachment to them as well. Fathers may develop attachment bonds to their infants by three days after the birth and sometimes earlier. Fathers that were present at the birth of their infants were better able to distinguish their infants from others. They were also more comfortable holding their infants. Early

Bonding
A period of heightened sensitivity of the new mother, during which she interacts with the neonate and begins to form a special attachment to him or her.

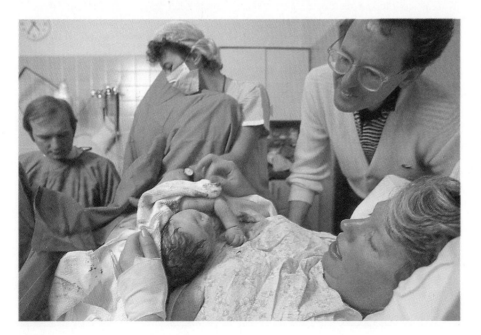

Neonates alter the lives of their parents. Bonding occurs in a period of heightened sensitivity for the mother, during which she interacts with the neonate and begins to form a special attachment to him or her. The father experiences engrossment which includes a feeling of preoccupation, absorption, interest, and the desire to touch, hold, and interact with the infant.

Three Case Studies

CASE 1

One couple well illustrated how the birth experience could alter the father's perceptions.

Prenatally the wife expressed confidence in her ability to give birth, mother, and raise a child. The husband, however, was not savoring the prospect of living with and raising a child. He seemed disinterested in the pregnancy and child-to-be, and his general affective state during all the prenatal visits ranged from apathy to sarcastic cynicism. His prenatal attitude was very low.

His wife expressed a firm commitment to giving birth at home, feeling that it was the best place for her and the baby. The husband's reasons for having the birth take place at home were that his wife had already decided upon that course anyway and that it was inexpensive. He was uncertain about being present but felt he had no choice since it was occurring in his home. He stated that he definitely would not be present were the birth to occur in the hospital.

Two of us attended the delivery as observers. The husband's behavior was the opposite of what we had expected, based on his prenatal attitude. After an initial period of severe discomfort for his wife, he became very concerned about her and supported her both physically and emotionally by massaging her back and engaging in frequent touching and reassuring talking. At times he seemed overwhelmed and occasionally withdrew from the room, but he always returned. His disinterest and apathy were replaced by concern, amazement, and involvement. Following the birth of the baby he proceeded to cry and within 30 minutes held, rocked, and talked to his new son.

After the birth, he reported feeling very close to his son and very involved in the caretaking. This was corroborated by direct observation and by his wife's report of his behavior. He attributed his confidence, feelings of closeness, and (unexpected to him) high degree of involvement with his son to the positive nature of the birth experience. His birth-experience score was above average, as was his father-attachment score.

CASE 2

Another couple illustrated the effects that disappointment and a negative emotional experience of birth could have for fathers.

Prenatally, the husband was very involved in the pregnancy. He planned to share some of the caretaking and was interested in maintaining close emotional and physical contact with the infant. He anticipated being able to relate easily to the baby and very much wanted a baby at that time in his life. He wanted an equal role with the mother in deciding on philosophy and practice of child rearing. During prenatal interviews, he seemed to be interested, concerned, and involved. He scored high on the prenatal attitude score. Both parents were looking forward to a home delivery. Due to uterine inertia, however, the couple went to the hospital.

Because of hostile feelings of the hospital staff toward home birth, the husband was not permitted to join his wife in the labor room for quite some time after she was ad-

mitted. Hospital rules also prohibited friends from joining them in the labor room. By the time he was allowed in, his wife had requested epidural anesthesia, and he became uninvolved in the labor from that point on. He disinterestedly (and angrily) attended the delivery, which was by forceps, and left soon afterward for home without having contact with his infant. He came to the hospital daily but spent only one hour each day. His first physical contact with the baby was on the fourth day and was brief.

Both the husband and wife, during their post-delivery interview, expressed high levels of anger and frustration regarding their delivery experience. She felt that the epidural and the resulting forceps had been forced onto her at a time when she needed emotional support and was very angry that her friends were not allowed to be present (as had been planned) since she felt capable of delivering without anesthesia with their help. She was also angry that her husband had been kept out of the labor room as long as he had. She felt his absence had been a strong contributing factor toward her requesting anesthesia. She was angry at the hostile treatment she felt she had received; when her infant's separation from her was mentioned, she cried for quite some time. It was clear that the separation had depressed her.

Postnatally, this father was very uninvolved. He participated in virtually none of the caretaking, expressed dissatisfaction with his infant's behavior, and, even at three months, felt that he did not know his infant very well. His father-attachment score was very low, as

Continued

was his birth-experience score. Postnatally, he very much resembled those fathers who had planned, along with their wives, anesthetized deliveries. Several other cases corroborated these observations.

CASE 3

A third case showed how unexpectedly positive birth experience could alter a father's prenatal perceptions.

The father had not been present at the delivery of his first child. Prenatally, he had expectations for involvement similar to his experience with his first child. He was somewhat uneasy about being present for the delivery but was attending childbirth preparation classes and planned to attend. His prenatal attitude score was average.

He was present at the labor and delivery and was very uninvolved in giving his wife physical and emotional support. He held and talked to his infant soon after delivery and frequently during the two days of hospital rooming-in. He expressed wonder and amazement at the birth itself. Afterwards, he reported feeling a much stronger bond to the new infant than he had to his first-born son at the same age. He was surprised at how much he had enjoyed the labor and delivery and the feeling of knowing his newborn baby only a week after birth.

Comparing his two experiences with childbirth, he felt he had missed out on much of the early interaction with his first child because he had neither been present at the birth nor been given the opportunity for contact soon after birth. Postnatally, he scored high on attachment. He did more caretaking with this baby and felt more enjoyment from his second newborn than he had with his first. This was the reverse of the general trend we found for father attachment to decrease with increasing parity.

Gail Peterson, Lewis Mehl, Peter Leiderman, "The Role of Some Birth-Related Variables in Father Attachment," *American Journal of Orthopsychiatry* 49(2), April 1979. Reprinted, with permission, from the American Journal of Orthopsychiatry. Copyright 1979 by the American Orthopsychiatric Association, Inc.

contact with their infants was significant in releasing **engrossment,** a term describing the father-infant bond, which includes a feeling of preoccupation, absorption, interest, and the desire to touch, hold, and interact with the infant. Not only did these fathers experience a strong attraction to their infants and extreme elation, but they also experienced an increased level of self-esteem (Greenberg and Morris 1974).

Peterson et al. (1979) found that a more positive birth experience led to greater levels of father attachment. They also found that longer labor and the home environment, as compared to the hospital environment, were associated with greater attachment. Further findings indicated that the father's experience of the birth and his behavior towards his spouse and baby during delivery were more important than his prenatal attitude in determining his involvement with the newborn. This supports other studies that claim the birth experience itself acts as a powerful catalyst for nurturing behavior from any observer (Bowen and Miller 1980; Jones 1981).

For young siblings, the introduction of a new baby could be traumatic. It is especially difficult for children of three years and younger to adjust. The arrival of a new sibling may overburden the capabilities of the young child who is already struggling with intellectual development, learning a language, and building a self-concept. The new infant represents a need for additional complex adjustments. However, the older child quite often asks for a new sibling.

Studies by Dunn and Kendrick show that firstborn two- to three-year-old siblings of neonates show increases in disturbance and negative behavior toward the mother after the new baby arrives. An increase in deliberate naughtiness during feedings and caring for the new baby was found among the older first-

Engrossment
The father-infant bond, which includes a feeling of preoccupation, absorption, interest, and the desire to touch, hold, and interact with the infant.

borns (Kendrick and Dunn 1980; Dunn et al. 1982; Dunn and Kendrick 1982). It is normal for these children to regress by wetting the bed, acting babyish, talking baby talk, or throwing temper tantrums (Field and Reite 1984).

How well prepared the older siblings are for the new sibling will determine if their reaction is positive or negative. While the mother is pregnant, the older child or children should be realistically prepared. The role of the big sister or big brother should be emphasized so he or she can take pride in this new status. Older children should be involved in the preparation for the new baby. They should be told the good and the bad so that their expectations are realistic and they are not disappointed. Parents should also give quality individual time to the older siblings.

SUMMARY

- Birth occurs in three stages. The first stage, dilatation, begins with the first true labor contractions and ends with the complete dilatation of the cervix. Expulsion, the second stage, begins with the complete dilatation of the cervix and ends when the baby emerges. The third stage, or the placental stage, is the expulsion of the placenta.
- Two widely used neonatal screening procedures are the Apgar scale, a scoring system used to evaluate and measure a neonate's physical condition at birth, and the Brazelton Neonatal Behavioral Assessment Scale, used to detect mild dysfunctions of the central nervous system and the development of behavioral responses during the neonatal period.
- *Premature* refers to infants who are born before the thirty-seventh week of pregnancy and who weigh less than 2,500 grams (five and one-half pounds) at birth.
- Many factors contribute to a premature birth. Children born prematurely face unusual problems not only at birth but in later years as well.
- Birth is usually a normal process, but occasionally complications do arise. Such complications include forceps delivery, breech delivery, oversized babies, cesarean section, obstetrical medication, and anoxia.
- Many couples are disillusioned with traditional hospital births and have sought alternative means of having their babies. The alternatives include natural, or prepared, childbirth (usually the Dick-Read or the Lamaze method), home birth, birthing centers, and the birthing chair.
- The newborn infant is called a neonate for the first two to four weeks after birth. Neonates have their own unique physical characteristics. Many internal changes must take place as their bodies adjust to living outside the uterus.
- Six states, or levels of arousal, have been identified in the neonate. They include regular sleep, irregular sleep, drowsiness, alert inactivity, waking activity, and crying.
- Crying has many functions, including communication of the neonate's needs and the signaling of certain abnormalities and diseases.
- The sleep patterns of neonates, such as REM, are thought to be related to stimulating the development of the brain.
- Breast-feeding has many advantages and disadvantages. Parents must choose what is best for their own individual situation.
- The neonate has many capabilities, including the use of all five senses.
- Reflex testing makes it possible to localize a central nervous system abnormality, assess the maturation and development of the nervous system, and determine the quality of the peripheral nerves.
- *Bonding* is the term used to describe attachment between mother and child immediately after birth. The bonding phenomenon experienced by new fathers after birth is called engrossment.

- Siblings should be prepared for the neonate. Young siblings, under three years, quite often regress to bed wetting, acting babyish, talking baby talk, or throwing temper tantrums.
- SIDS is the quiet, unexpected killer of ten thousand to twenty thousand infants each year. Contrary to past beliefs, SIDS infants may not be normal. Recent data have established a profile of SIDS infants. The death of these infants has a devastating impact on the surviving family members.

R E A D I N G S

Goldberg, S. and DiVitto, B. A. (1983). *Born too soon: Preterm birth and early development.* San Francisco: W. H. Freeman.
Contemporary view of preterm infants that includes significant aspects of their development and methods of caring for them that will encourage their optimal development.
Klaus, M. and Klaus, P. (1985). *The amazing newborn.* Reading, MA: Addison-Wesley.
Well illustrated discussion of the capabilities and capacities of the newborn.
Leboyer, F. (1975). *Birth without violence.* New York: Alfred A. Knopf.
A French physician's unusual system of delivering infants that emphasizes the feelings of the newborn.

C R I T I C A L   I S S U E S

Sudden Infant Death Syndrome

One of the greatest fears of new parents is **sudden infant death syndrome (SIDS).** SIDS is the quiet, unexpected killer of ten thousand to twenty thousand infants in the United States each year. It is commonly called "crib death" and is the unexpected and painless death of a seemingly healthy infant, usually under four months of age. But contrary to past beliefs, SIDS infants may not have been normal infants.

In a review of the SIDS literature, Valdes-Dapena (1980) concluded that SIDS infants as a group are significantly different from normal infants. More and more investigators are convinced that infants who die in this manner were subtly physiologically handicapped from before birth. As neonates, they seemed to have a variety of abnormalities, including brain stem dysfunction, upper respiratory infections, feeding problems, difficulty with temperature regulation, larger right heart ventricles, unusual lung tissue, abnormal reflexes (especially an abnormal Moro reflex), and low Apgar scores (Duffty and Bryan 1982; Kahn and Blum 1982; Lipsitt et al. 1981). Some SIDS babies had to be resuscitated at birth. Some showed signs of a chronic lack of oxygen. Their overall length,

head circumference, and weight were less than normal. Some of the infants showed jittering movements and had high-pitched cries, while others were less active, tired easily, and were weaker.

A recent study (Sparks and Hunsaker 1991) found that SIDS is a disorder of the central nervous system that develops during pregnancy. Their study found that in SIDS infants, the brain's hippocampal region contained more than twice as many dead nerve cells on the average as the same region in other infants who died under other circumstances. Some nerve cells die in normal infants as part of development, but SIDS infants had more dead cells, and the dead cells were more widespread.

Males are more likely to be victims than females; more African-Americans than whites; and more Native Americans than African-Americans and whites combined (Lipsitt 1979; Valdes-Dapena 1980; Blok 1978). The risk is slightly greater for multiple-birth infants, and it is ten times greater for infants who weigh three and one-half pounds to four pounds at birth than for those who weigh seven and one-half pounds to eight and one-half pounds.

Continued

Sudden Infant Death Syndrome
(Continued)

The risk is twice as high for infants of unwed mothers and times as high when there is no prenatal care. Mothers under twenty years of age and those who smoke are also more likely to have SIDS infants (Valdes-Dapena 1980). Also at risk are subsequent siblings of SIDS victims. They are three to four times more likely to succumb to SIDS than infants in the general population (Duffty & Bryan 1982; Irgens et al. 1988). Also, infants of mothers who use cocaine are more susceptible to SIDS (Bauchner et al. 1988).

Death usually occurs at night, with the victims found in all positions (that is, lying on their back, side, or stomach). It is more likely to occur in the winter, during periods of low temperature and low humidity. Quite often the infant had a mild cold or stuffy nose. Viral infections, although probably not the cause of SIDS, may well serve as a trigger mechanism in the infant at risk (Lipsitt 1979; Valdes-Dapena 1980).

Ongoing investigations of breathing mechanisms, abnormalities of the central nervous system, and sleep disturbances in SIDS victims may reveal more clues to the causes of SIDS. Most infants have short interruptions in their breathing during sleep, a phenomenon called **apnea,** which is defined as a period of nonbreathing that lasts for more than ten seconds. Perhaps with certain SIDS infants, some neurological mechanism that controls breathing did not mature properly.

With a profile such as this, do you think it is possible to prevent SIDS? What evidence indicates that SIDS may be genetic? What evidence indicates that it may be due to environmental causes? What about the possibility of an interaction of both?

Hospitals, as well as concerned parents, now monitor infants who appear at risk. Some hospitals and private foundations provide monitors for those families who have an at-risk infant.

SIDS has a devastating impact on the surviving family members. Grief reactions include shock, disbelief, and denial; negativism, hostility, and anger; self-reproach and guilt (Halpern 1983). In helping families to deal with this crisis, it is important to talk sympathetically with the parents and allow them free expression of their grief, no matter how it is manifested. A professional should be available to answer accurately whatever questions they may have about the death of their baby. Surviving siblings should not be excluded from the mourning process and should be reassured about their own good health and blamelessness. Parents should also defer from having other children until their grief has subsided and the psychological environment in their home becomes healthier (Nicol 1989; Valdes-Dapena 1980). Support groups have proven to be extremely beneficial for the parents in dealing with their grief. It helps the parents to know that their feelings and reactions to this situation are normal (Nicol 1989).

5

O B J E C T I V E S

When you have mastered the material in this chapter, you should be able to do the following:

1. Describe the predictable physical growth patterns of the first two years of life.
2. Describe the factors that contribute to the development of motor skills.
3. Describe the two basic types of motor skills and outline the sequences of each.
4. Describe digestive disorders common among infants and discuss their possible causes.
5. Discuss the nutritional benefits of breast milk.
6. Explain the cause of kwashiorkor and its long-term effects.
7. Describe bottle mouth and discuss its cause.
8. Discuss the impact of overfeeding an infant.
9. Describe the factors that contribute to successful toilet training.
10. List and describe the two major functional processes necessary to produce cognitive growth and alter the structure of the intellect, according to Piaget.
11. Describe the six substages of Piaget's sensorimotor stage and discuss the importance of the concept of object permanence.
12. Discuss the three major theories of language acquisition.
13. Outline the stages of prelinguistic and linguistic speech.
14. Discuss the mental activities necessary for an infant to appreciate humor.
15. Discuss the causes of the high infant mortality rate and the impact of high infant mortality on our society.

The Emerging Human:
Infants' and Toddlers' Physical and Cognitive Development

● INTRODUCTION

The word *infant* literally means "without language." Infancy is the period of life that begins at birth and ends with the beginning of language use. The normal duration of infancy, in the strict sense, is the first eighteen to twenty-four months. During these initial months, the skills that separate human beings from other animals are acquired. By the end of infancy, babies are sociable and cooperative, and they have learned what is necessary for language. Not only can they walk on their own two feet, but they have the refined manual skills that humans share with no other animal. They can use tools to a limited extent, but still to a greater extent than any nonhuman. They have acquired some very basic and important concepts, such as space, causality, and number.

● PHYSICAL DEVELOPMENT

Predictable Patterns

The physical growth patterns of children are especially dramatic during the first two years of life. It takes approximately six hundred days for a child to change from a newborn to a walking, talking, socially functioning child. The physical growth generally takes place in orderly, predictable patterns.

Height

One predictable pattern is height. Differences in or changes in height are noticeable early in the first year. Infants destined to be tall adults grow faster than those destined to be short. By two years, there are already indications of how tall a child will eventually become. Height at that age correlates with .80 height at maturity. A rough estimate of the eventual adult height can be made by multiplying the height at two years by 2.0 for a boy and 1.9 for a girl (Tanner 1978b).

Body Proportion

Another predictable pattern of growth is the change in body proportion. At birth an infant's head is one-fourth of his or her height. A neonate's arms and legs are relatively short but begin to grow faster than the head and torso.

Motor Coordination

Change in motor response is another predictable pattern. Infants may respond to stimulation with undifferentiated gross movements. For example, their whole body reacts if the bottom of their foot is touched with an ice cube. Or once infants begin a particular behavior, they have trouble inhibiting it. They may continue to cry long after the stimulation that caused the crying in the first place is gone. Neurological, or nervous system, development determines how quickly the infant goes from one state to another. As the infant gets older, motor activity is more differentiated and specific; that is, it develops into a set of precise movements, each adapted to a precise function. When an ice cube is placed on the infant's foot, only the foot moves, not the whole body. The infant is now more capable of inhibiting and changing behavior.

Direction of Development

Another predictable pattern of growth is the direction of development. Infants develop vertically from head to feet. This is called **cephalocaudal de-**

Cephalocaudal development
A principle governing physical growth in which an individual develops from head to feet.

velopment. For example, infants can control their eye and head movement before they can sit by themselves. They control their back and arms well enough to sit long before they can use their legs for walking. Infants also develop horizontally, that is, from the midline, or center of the body, out to the extremities. This is called **proximodistal development**. For example, they can control their shoulders and arms before their hands. They can grasp objects with their hands long before they can do so with their fingers.

Sex Differences

Sex differences can affect the growth rate. Neonatal girls have more fat and less muscle tissue than boys and are usually shorter and lighter. Neonatal boys tend to have larger heads and larger faces than girls and are able to hold their heads up earlier. At birth, girls are somewhat more advanced in physical development than boys. They develop faster and at a more constant rate than boys. Girls are also more sensitive to various kinds of stimuli, especially touch, cold, pain, and taste. Boys' activity levels are usually more vigorous. They tend to cry more than girls and are a little harder to soothe, and they tend to startle more easily.

Motor Skills

The most obvious change during the course of infancy is the acquiring of new motor skills. The word *motor* refers to muscular movements. In a very brief span of time, the infant progresses from helplessness to the point of walking alone. The neonate's general mass activity and reflex actions gradually change to specific muscle control such as voluntary, coordinated motor responses. Changes in motor skills occur at a fairly consistent rate, indicating that maturation is a primary factor in their development. Motor development follows a broad general pattern in which postural control precedes efforts at locomotion, efforts at locomotion precede success at locomotion, and some form of locomotion precedes walking. With rare exception, all babies go through each stage, but there are minor differences in the sequence of stages from baby to baby. Environmental factors, such as the lack of opportunity to practice the motor skills, the attitude of the child toward learning the skills, and the child's physiological and psychological inhibitions to learning, can influence the development of motor skills. Therefore, the process of development is sequential unless there is interference from unusual conditions within or external to the infant (Bremner 1988).

Many theorists now believe that the neonatal reflexes are related to voluntary motor development (Twitchell 1970; Zelazo 1976; Thelen 1981; Thelen and Fisher 1982; Thelen and Fisher 1983). It is thought that **rhythmical stereotypies** provide the link (Thelen 1981). Rhythmical stereotypies are inborn behavior patterns that involve fairly rapid bursts of repetitious movements of the arms, legs, head, or torso. Forty-seven different stereotypies—including variations of kicking, scratching, bouncing, and rubbing—have been identified in normal human infants. These rhythmicities occur in a predictable manner before voluntary behavior. For example, kicking occurs more frequently just prior to the onset of locomotion. When locomotion does appear, then kicking declines. So when voluntary behavior is well established, the respective rhythmicity disappears. These rhythmicities actually appear to predict motor development. Thelen (1981) suggests they represent an intermediary stage between spontane-

Proximodistal development
A principle governing physical growth in which an individual develops from the midline out to the extremities.

Rhythmical stereotypies
Inborn behavior patterns that involve fairly rapid bursts of repetitious movements of the arms, legs, head, or torso. These rhythmicities occur in a predictable manner before voluntary behavior.

Gross motor skills
Large-muscle skills that include upright postural body control and locomotion.

Fine motor skills
Small-muscle skills that include the ability to reach with the hand, to grasp, and to manipulate objects.

Crawling
The progression made by an infant in which he or she does not lift the abdomen from the floor while moving all four limbs.

Hitching
A situation in which the infant may move about in a sitting position, using one leg to push the body along.

Scooting
See Hitching.

By two months, as the neck muscles develop strength and control, the infant can hold his or her head face up. By four months of age, most infants can lift their head and upper trunk when placed prone on a table.

ous, random gross movements and voluntary behavior. The infant can formulate and practice muscle coordinations that will be used in intentional movements.

Two basic types of motor skills emerge during infancy: *gross* and *fine*. **Gross motor skills** include upright postural body control and locomotion. **Fine motor skills** include the ability to reach with the hand, to grasp, and to manipulate objects.

Gross Motor Skills

In developing the gross motor skills, there is a basic sequence that leads to walking. This sequence also illustrates the cephalocaudal and proximodistal patterns of development. The neonate normally is unable to hold his or her head erect when lying prone or when being held in a sitting position. At one month, the infant can hold his or her head straight out in a horizontal plane when lying on his or her stomach. By two months, as the neck muscles develop strength and control, the infant can hold his or her head face up. By four months of age, most infants can lift their head and upper trunk when placed prone on a table. They no longer are content to lie on their back.

Rolling Over   Between four and seven months, as an infant gains control and coordination of voluntary muscles, he or she can roll over. Rolling over constitutes the infant's first maneuver with his or her whole body. In order to accomplish this feat, the infant must have control over his or her head, torso, and legs. To roll from front to back, the infant raises his or her head and one shoulder, arches his or her back, and twists, giving a shove with his or her legs. An infant will practice for the pure pleasure of the movement itself, and later he or she may roll over to reach a toy or with some other purpose in mind. This skill leads to more complex maneuvers such as pulling up and standing.

Sitting Up   At about seven months the spine becomes more rigid and the back muscles strengthen, making it possible for the infant to sit up unsupported. Prewalking motions appear about the seventh month.

Crawling and Creeping   Crawling refers to the progression made by an infant in which he or she does not lift the abdomen from the floor while moving all four limbs. **Hitching,** or **scooting,** is a situation in which the infant may move about in a sitting position, using one leg to push the body along. He or she may go backwards, sideways, or in circles. No matter how the infant maneuvers, he or she usually ends up where he or she wants to go. This is also the time when heads and hands get stuck in openings big enough to get into but not out of.

By the eighth month, the infant may be able to pull himself or herself up with support. This ability usually occurs just before *creeping* begins, at around ten months. From this time until around twelve months an infant is proficient in getting around on his or her hands and knees. When a ten- or eleven-month-old infant explores independently, he or she comprehends spatial relationships much better than an infant who is carried most of the time (Benson and Uzgiris 1985). An infant during this stage delights in getting into everything. He or she may be able to walk when led. As the leg muscles strengthen, he or she can cruise along stepping sideways, holding on for support and balance. Finally, the infant sets out on his or her own. With arms held out and feet wide apart for balance, he or she takes the first jerky steps. The infant is now a *toddler*!

Walking   By fourteen months of age, two-thirds of American babies can walk without support, and by the age of eighteen months, the toddler walks more like an adult. Once the walking ability is refined, he or she begins to run. Maneuvering turns is difficult, so the toddler usually stops before changing direction.

Around the twenty-first and twenty-second months, the toddler will squat while playing, walk upstairs while holding the railing, and kick a large ball. There is the urge to carry objects, as well as push, pull, haul, or drag all sorts of things—the larger the better.

By twenty-five months the toddler can run without falling and can walk up and down the steps alone, putting both feet on each step. Between twenty-four and thirty months, children can jump with both feet and stand on one leg (Bayley 1973b; Neilon 1973; Shirley 1973; Smolak 1986).

Racial Differences   Beginning in the 1970s, racial differences were noted in several studies concerning the rate of gross motor development in white and African-American infants during the first year (Ainsworth 1973; Williams and Scott 1973; Bayley 1973b). Williams and Scott (1973) found that African-American infants scored well above the norm on Gesell developmental schedules as compared with American white infants. They also found that African-American infants of lower socioeconomic status scored well above African-American infants of upper socioeconomic status. Ainsworth (1973) reported a similar finding when comparing Uganda village infants with infants from highly acculturated Uganda homes. The village infants were more precocious in motor skills during the first year of life, with the greatest difference in the first six months. The gap began closing after the first year, and by the end of the second year, it completely closed. These studies present a clear example of the nature-nurture debate, indicating that motor development in infants may be due to the interaction of heredity and environment.

Fine Motor Skills

In developing fine motor skills, the infant's grasping reflex and uncoordinated arm movements mark the beginning for a sequence that eventually leads to the more skilled manual activities. As an infant matures, simple strategies such as mouthing are replaced by more complex strategies such as fingering objects, transfering objects from one hand to the other, and rotating objects with both hands. Preterm at-risk infants are delayed in acquiring these skills when compared with full-term infants (McCune and Ruff 1985).

Reaching and Grasping   The reflex grasp, present at birth, is different from the voluntary grasp developed later. The reflex grasp is a palm grasp and not a thumb-and-finger grasp. About the second month, the reflex grasp begins to decline and the voluntary grasp begins to develop. Between one and four months, with their hands usually open, infants spend a great deal of time looking at their hands and swiping at objects within reach. Late in this stage they can raise their hands close to an object and will look back and forth from the object to the hand many times. This is the beginning of visually directed reaching. By about five months of age, infants can successfully reach out and grasp an object (*prehensile reaching*). The grasp is crude, using both hands. If an infant uses one hand, he or she will often hold the object without using the thumb and will fumble it. Between four to eight months, the infant reaches more often with one hand than with both hands. Finally, between nine and fourteen months, the thumb and forefinger are used together in the form of a pincer grasp (Smolak 1986).

Once the infant can reach and grasp, everything goes into the mouth. This

When infants and toddlers explore independently, they comprehend spatial relationships much better than infants who are carried most of the time.

African-American infants develop at a faster rate in gross motor skills than white American infants during the first year. By the end of the second year the gap closes.

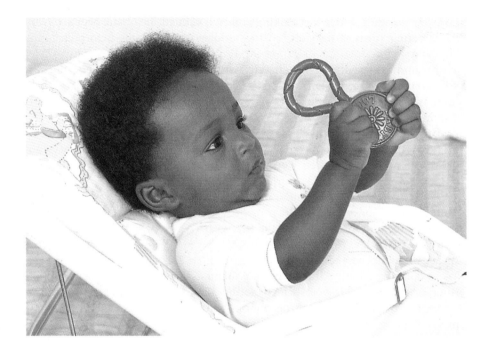

type of exploration exercises the tongue and mouth muscles, which are important for future speech development. Freud saw this activity as part of the oral stage, in which chewing, sucking, and biting are the infant's chief sources of pleasure and means of reducing tension (Freud 1924). The thumb-and-finger grasp, evident by seven months of age, is a position in which the thumb and fingers cooperate in picking up and holding a cube against the palm of the hand.

Hand Transfer   Between six and ten months, babies gain the ability to transfer objects from on hand to the other.

Skill Accomplishments   Between ten and twelve months, infants can take things apart but cannot put them back together. Fine motor control continues to increase between twelve and eighteen months. Infants at this stage can hold a cup and begin to use a spoon, which rarely makes it to the mouth right side up. Voluntary release is developing now. The infant enjoys practicing this new ability by continuously dropping things. As a more accurate release develops, this ability is used in play, such as in building a two-block tower.

By twenty-four to thirty months, skills become more and more refined. For instance, the infant can hold a cup with one hand and no longer overturns the spoon. He or she can build a tall tower with blocks and put things together.

Digestive Disorders

Digestive disorders are common among infants. "Spitting up" is caused by an undeveloped muscle valve at the upper end of the stomach that cannot hold down all of the contents when a full baby is jostled.

Colic

Infants occasionally have mild indigestion or gas. **Colic** is the most notorious of indigestion problems. The term *colic* is a catchall word that describes the symptoms of infants who have apparent extreme intestinal discomfort and cry

Colic
A catchall term that describes the symptoms of infants who have apparent extreme intestinal discomfort and cry a great deal because of it.

a great deal because of it. It is thought that the abdomen becomes distended with gas, causing severe pain. For the infant who suffers from colic, the problem usually begins a few weeks after birth and usually subsides around three months. The distress seems to be relieved by feeding, so colicky babies usually gain weight faster than other infants. There is no known cause of colic. X-rays taken of colicky babies do not show any structural irregularities of the digestive tract. To date, no reliable remedies are known (Maksimak et al. 1984). However, a Swedish study (Jakobsson and Lindberg 1983) found that eliminating cow's milk from the diet of the breast-feeding mother eliminated colic in over 50 percent of the infants.

Allergies

Allergies are another cause of digestive disorders. Some of the most common foods infants are allergic to are eggs, citrus fruits, honey, and cow's milk. Honey should not be given to infants who are under a year old, because they are unable to neutralize the botulism toxins that are naturally present in honey (Arnon et al. 1979). The symptoms of allergies include digestive upsets such as vomiting and diarrhea or skin rashes such as eczema or hives. If the infant is allergic to milk, then soybean substitutes may be used. Pediatricians usually recommend that eggs and citrus fruits not be introduced until the end of the first year. In the meantime, vitamin C supplements should be given to these infants, especially the bottle-fed infants (Endres and Rockwell 1980).

Nutritional Needs

Nutrition is vitally important to an infant's physical and intellectual development. Mother's milk, formula, or a combination of both sufficiently meets all of a baby's needs for the first six months of life.

Breast-feeding

Breast-feeding is encouraged because the mother's milk has many nutritional advantages (see also the earlier discussion in Chapter 4). It contains higher levels of lactose (milk sugar), vitamin C, and cholesterol than cow's milk. The protein in infant formulas comes from cow's milk and is fundamentally different from the protein in human milk. The human protein is easier to digest and richer in certain amino acids. Breast milk does not contain great amounts of iron, but its iron is remarkably easy to absorb. Adults usually absorb about 30 percent of the iron in meat and about 5 percent of the iron in vegetables, while an infant can absorb as much as 50 percent of the iron in breast milk. Breast-fed babies rarely become iron deficient. Iron deficiency can affect brain development and can ultimately hurt intellectual performance (Maksimak et al. 1984). The additional cholesterol from breast milk in early infancy may induce the production of enzymes required for cholesterol breakdown in adulthood (Rohr and Lothian 1984).

Another advantage of breast milk is that it contains antibodies against several bacterial and viral organisms. Breast-fed babies have respiratory and gastrointestinal illnesses two or three times less frequently than bottle-fed babies (Popkin, Bilsborrow, and Akin 1982; Maksimak et al. 1984).

A benefit particularly for the mother is that the process of lactation (the secretion of milk by the mammary glands) stimulates the uterus to shrink more rapidly to its normal nonpregnant size (Rohr and Lothian 1984).

By twenty-four months to thirty months, skills become more and more refined.

Breast-feeding may be discouraged if the mother is in poor health, malnourished, or taking medicines that may diffuse into the breast milk. Breast-feeding may also be discouraged if the infant is very small, weak, or premature, or if he or she suffers from a cleft lip or palate. Sometimes the mother's milk may be pumped, or expressed, and fed to these infants until they are capable of sucking (Marx 1984; Rohr and Lothian 1984).

Bottle-feeding

Many commercial formulas are available for bottle-feeding infants. These are fortified with vitamins and are modified in protein content. Since many infants have adverse reactions to cow's milk, these formulas are particularly advisable. Care must be taken when bottle-feeding to assure cleanliness and psychological stimulation such as touching and fondling (Rohr and Lothian 1984).

Either breast- or bottle-feeding can be satisfying if accompanied by tender loving care. Infants should not, however, be fed by propping bottles in their cribs. In addition to emotional deprivation, this may cause obstruction of the short auditory tube and lead to repeated ear infections (Rohr and Lothian 1984). Severe malnutrition problems can arise if infants are weaned too early from milk and are not given other foods equally rich in proteins. The effects of malnutrition on brain cell development are profound (Grant 1982).

Malnutrition

Infancy is a critical period for the growth of brain tissue. Infants acquiring *kwashiorkor* (a disease caused by protein deficiency in early infancy) suffer irreparable brain damage. Infants who are affected by kwashiorkor in later infancy (from fifteen to twenty-nine months) have a milder residual mental retardation. Children who get the disease after age three can recover normal intelligence if they are no longer malnourished (Grant 1982). Children who are chronically malnourished from infancy through early childhood tend to be shorter and cognitively slower in middle childhood (Bogin and MacVean 1983).

Bottle Mouth

Often a bottle containing sweetened liquid is used as a pacifier for comforting an infant or controlling behavior. This can lead to **bottle mouth,** a condition found in a two-, three-, or four-year-old child whose teeth have been destroyed by tooth decay. The cause of bottle mouth is prolonged exposure to sweetened liquids. As soon as the infant's teeth appear in his or her mouth, they are susceptible to decay.

The sugar found in formulas, some juices, sweetened gelatin, soft drinks, honey-coated pacifiers, and so on, mix with plaque, a thin, sticky, colorless film of bacteria that constantly forms in the mouth. This interaction forms an acid that attacks tooth enamel, and decay begins. If the teeth are not cleaned immediately each time sugar is eaten, whether in a solid or liquid form, acid will attack the teeth for twenty minutes. Using a sweetened liquid as a pacifier during the daytime is harmful because the teeth have prolonged direct contact with sugar. But it is even more detrimental when infants are allowed to fall asleep with the bottle in their mouth. During the day, saliva helps to wash some of the liquid out of the mouth. However, at naptime or bedtime the saliva flow decreases, allowing the sugary liquid to pool around the teeth. When this pooled liquid remains for a prolonged period, the teeth are constantly attacked by acids. Obviously it is important to avoid sweet liquids. However, even milk, which normally does not support tooth decay, can be harmful when it is allowed to remain in the mouth for long periods.

Since frequent contact with sweetened liquids is damaging to infants' teeth, parents should wipe the teeth and gums after each feeding, using a damp washcloth or gauze pad to remove plaque. This practice should be continued until all of the primary teeth have erupted, between two and two and one-half years. Then parents should begin brushing and flossing their child's teeth (Paige and Owen 1988).

Solid Foods

Solid foods are generally started at about five to six months, depending on the advice of a physician. There is no advantage to starting solid foods earlier. There are no data to support the common claim that solid foods will cause an infant to sleep through the night. Solid food does, however, provide the nutrients that are necessary for the second six months of life. Infants physiologically are ready for solid foods at about four to six months of age. Their kidneys, pancreas, and intestines are mature enough to tolerate the increased nutrients. The musculature in their mouth, as well as in their head and neck, make it easier for them to chew and swallow (Rohr and Lothian 1984).

Rice cereal is usually introduced first, followed by strained fruits, vegetables, and meats. Foods with soy or wheat flour and egg products are usually postponed until the infant is older. Only a few teaspoons of any new food should be introduced at a time. This should be continued for a day or two to ensure no allergic reactions or other intolerances (such as diarrhea) before starting another new food (Rohr and Lothian 1984; Endres and Rockwell 1980).

In the past, baby foods were made with excessive salt and flavorings to please mothers who tasted them. Baby food manufacturers no longer follow

Bottle mouth
A condition found in a two-, three-, or four-year-old child whose teeth have been destroyed by tooth decay. The cause of bottle mouth is prolonged exposure to sweetened liquids.

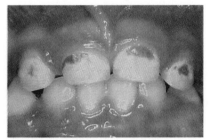

The cause of bottle mouth is prolonged exposure to sweetened liquids. As soon as the infant's teeth appear in his or her mouth, they are susceptible to decay.

this practice, but some mothers still flavor the food for themselves. They do not realize that young children are satisfied with bland food, and that it is better for youngsters than highly flavored food.

Overfeeding

Overfeeding during infancy can evolve into a lifelong problem. For the first twelve months, infants who are fed more calories than they can utilize from day to day experience an increase in fat-cell size. On the other hand, infants from twelve to eighteen months old develop additional fat cells to store the unused energy sources. Evidence indicates that these fat cells, which proliferate in infancy, will continue to replace themselves as children grow. If this theory is correct, fat infants will have excess fat cells to fill throughout their lives and will either be obese or have difficulty holding their weight down to their normal range. However, this theory remains controversial (Dietz 1984). An alternate theory of the effect of infant overfeeding on adult obesity is that eating patterns become habits that are difficult to change. Whatever the explanation, fat babies do tend to become overweight adults.

Adequate Diet

Infants gain an average of twenty-four to thirty-nine grams per day during the first three months of life and fifteen to twenty-one grams per day during the second three months. Since this is the most rapid weight gain of any period of life, the infant needs high energy intakes of nutrients. It is recommended that a distribution of 35 to 65 percent carbohydrate, 7 to 16 percent protein, and 30 to 55 percent fat be included in an infant's diet (Rohr and Lothian 1984).

Infants generally show a decrease in appetite at about twelve to eighteen months. They are no longer growing as rapidly and therefore do not need as many calories. Adequate nutrition consists of a diet balanced with proteins, carbohydrates, and fats plus sufficient vitamins and minerals. This can be achieved by giving children two or more servings every day from each of the four basic food groups: (1) milk, (2) vegetables and fruits, (3) bread-cereal, and (4) meat. Empty calories, found in soda pop and candy, should be avoided. If, from early on, infants are offered what is good for them, they will be off to a positive nutritional start (Endres and Rockwell 1980).

Toilet Training

In young infants, the sphincter muscles of the rectum and bladder relax reflexively, allowing the contents to be discharged. As infants mature, they can learn to inhibit these reflex actions. This ability requires motor control and awareness of the sensations indicating a full rectum or bladder. Both the control and the awareness depend on the maturation of the cerebral cortex (Tanner 1978a). Bowel control comes first, beginning around the middle of the second year. The infant later begins to gain bladder control, first during the day and then during the night.

Boys achieve control later than girls do because they are physically less mature. Girls are usually toilet trained between two and two and one-half years of age. Boys are sometimes not reliable until three years of age. Most children learn control over a period of several months and sometimes longer. The process of acquiring night control may span several years.

Lapses of control will occur occasionally, especially when the child is ill, tired, in a strange place, absorbed in play, or if he or she has a new sibling. Also, the child who has been dry for several months may occasionally have an episode of *enuresis,* or bed wetting. Because toddlers have difficulty holding urine for a period of time, they should be dressed in clothes that are easy to remove. In 1972, Chess, Thomas, and Birch reported a longitudinal study involving 231 children from birth through adolescence. Ninety-five percent of the group showed no sign of disturbance related to toilet training. The few who were disturbed also had problems in other areas of behavior. Most infants want to be trained and are proud of the fact that this is something they can learn to do by themselves.

Toilet training requires not only physical readiness but also language development. The child must be familiar with social expectations and be able to understand what he or she should do (Azrin and Fox 1981). A classic study by Sears, Maccoby, and Lewin (1957) found that toilet training was accomplished faster and easier when not started until twenty months of age. Erikson points out that toddlers exercise autonomy when they control their bowels and bladders. A nurturing relationship, proper instructions, and a child mature enough to understand what he or she is supposed to do lead to successful toilet training.

● COGNITIVE DEVELOPMENT

Cognitive development begins in infancy. Piaget (1952), a widely known cognitive theorist and researcher, suggested that the structures of an individual's intellect change and develop as a result of action upon the environment. Two major functional processes occur and interact in the child in order to produce cognitive growth and alter the structure of the intellect. They are *adaptation* and *organization.*

Adaptation of the organism to the new environment is one process. The infant's acts or behaviors are gradually altered from the initial reflexes to more complex acquired activities. This process entails two separate, different, and yet complementary processes: *assimilation* and *accommodation.* **Assimilation** occurs when information is assimilated, or incorporated, into existing categories, habits, and preferences by integrating the new experience into what the individual already knows; that is, new information is taken in and adapted to conform to the individual's already existing mental or intellectual structures or schemes. **Accommodation** occurs when children notice something new (a new sound, color, or contour) and then must adjust existing schemes to understand the new information; that is, they modify previous experiences to conform to new information, new environmental input, and/or new interactions and add new categories.

Assimilation and accommodation are universal modes of functioning that operate to modify sensorimotor structures called **schemes**. Schemes are the infant's way of knowing and acting upon the world. These schemes begin as reflex actions, but through the processes of assimilation and accommodation, they become modified and provide the underlying patterns required in adapting to the world. It is through these processes that infants can construct more intricate and elaborate structures for interpreting sensory input.

Organization is the second functional process. This process enables expe-

Adaptation
The inherent tendency to cognitively adjust to the environment through the processes of assimilation and accommodation.

Assimilation
In Piaget's theory, a process in which information is incorporated and adapted to conform to the individual's already existing mental or intellectual structures or schemes.

Accommodation
In Piaget's theory, a process in which previous experiences are modified to conform to new information, new environmental input, and/or new interactions. New categories are added.

Schemes
In Piaget's theory, structures for interpreting sensory input from the environment. Schemes begin as reflex actions, but through the processes of assimilation and accommodation, they become modified and provide the underlying patterns required in adapting to the environment.

Organization
In Piaget's theory, the process that enables experience and knowledge to be categorized and sorted out into meaningful segments or wholes that become more complex.

rience and knowledge to be categorized and sorted out into meaningful segments or wholes that become more complex. They are the individual's interpretation of reality based on action (Piaget 1952). In organizing experiences, the individual integrates two or more schemes into a more complex, higher-order scheme. For example, the young infant will see a rattle if it is placed in front of him or her, and he or she will reach for and grasp it if it is put in his or her hand. As the infant gets older, he or she will integrate the schemes of looking, reaching, and grasping so that when a rattle is placed in his or her view, he or she will not only see it but will reach for it and grasp it as well. Then eventually he or she will see it, reach for it, grasp it, and put it in his or her mouth to suck it. But initially, as a neonate, he or she can perform only one of these schemes.

Sensorimotor Stage

According to Piaget (1952), the sensorimotor stage of development encompasses the period in a child's life from birth to about two years of age, and it is essentially a preverbal stage. The infant's knowledge of the world is limited to what he or she knows through perceptual awareness and motor acts, hence the term *sensorimotor*. Piaget believed that the interaction between perceptual and motor skills provided the opportunity for cognitive growth.

Reflexive Substage

Reflexive substage
In Piaget's theory, the first substage of the sensorimotor stage. It begins at birth and continues through the first month of life. Neonates assimilate all stimuli through their reflex system.

The first substage of the sensorimotor stage of development, **reflexive,** begins at birth and continues to the end of the first month. At this point neonates assimilate all stimuli through their reflex system, including the innate reflexes of sucking, rooting, and grasping. Piaget's theory regards these reflexes as building blocks of cognitive growth. These reflexes are the infant's first sensorimotor schemes, and they gradually become more efficient as well as more voluntary. Infants during this substage cannot differentiate the self from the environment. However, within a few weeks, simple accommodations are observable. For example, at birth infants suck on anything that touches their mouths. Later they search for the nipple, thereby accommodating themselves to the environment. When searching occurs, it cannot be attributed to the reflex system, and the infant is ready to move to the next substage, which is *primary circular*.

Primary Circular Reactions

Primary circular reactions
In Piaget's theory, the substage of the sensorimotor stage that begins after the first month and continues through fourth month. The infant's behavior is centered on his or her body rather than on external objects, and the behavior is endlessly repeated.

The second substage, **primary circular reactions,** begins after the first month and continues through the fourth month. *Primary* refers to the fact that the infant's behavior is centered on his or her body rather than on external objects. *Circular* refers to the fact that the behavior is endlessly repeated. When an infant stumbles onto an act that produces a new experience, he or she will repeat the act in order to reproduce the experience. For example, Piaget (1952) described this phenomenon when his son Laurent learned to suck his thumb when he was two months old. "Laurent's hands flailed about wildly at first, but one day his left hand landed on his face, eliciting the rooting reflex and making it possible for him to get his thumb in his mouth." Before the thumb escaped again, he sucked it "with greed and passion." The next day Laurent's hands no longer seemed to move randomly, and they approached his mouth more often. The following day, Piaget noted, "There is no longer any doubt that coordination exists. The mouth may be seen opening and the hand directing itself toward it simultaneously." A month and a half later, Laurent comforted himself with his thumb when he was hungry or tired.

The infant is capable of coordinating functional relationships, like hearing and looking at some object, or seeing and reaching for, as well as grasping, an object. At around two months, coordination and convergence occur in both eyes. At four months, the infant can imitate and respond to smiling people and can laugh out loud. Also, he or she can focus on objects at any distance as well as an adult can. He or she can turn his or her head in response to things heard and seen. His or her hands are usually open, and he or she spends quite a bit of time looking at them. The infant also swipes at objects within reach. He or she can raise his or her hands close to an object and will look back and forth from the object to the hands many times. This is the beginning of visually directed reaching.

Secondary Circular Reactions

The behavior patterns of the third substage, **secondary circular reactions,** from four to eight months, consist of repetitive actions that are no longer centered around the infant's body but instead around the environmental consequences of those actions. That is, the infant now realizes that his or her actions produce interesting consequences, so the actions are repeated not just for their own sake, but for the consequences they produce.

An infant can now reach and grasp and anticipate listening to a noise. This is the beginning of goal-directed intentional behavior. For example, an infant will kick his or her legs to shake the crib and make a hanging mobile or toy move, or he or she will shake a rattle to produce a noise. The infant shows a greater awareness of his or her world. He or she also begins to recognize objects and people who are familiar to him or her. The concept of a stable world has begun. The infant's understanding of **object permanence** (an object exists even when it is out of sight) is not established as yet, but there are indications that it is developing. If a favorite rattle is partially visible, the infant will kick or scream for it; however, if it is completely out of sight, he or she will forget about it and act as if it no longer exists.

Coordination of Secondary Schemes

Between the eighth and twelfth months, the fourth substage, **coordination of secondary schemes,** emerges. Two principal areas of intelligence are accomplished during this period. First, behaviors are now unquestionably intentional, and the infant can anticipate coming events. For example, he or she will remove a lid from a box to find an object inside it. Second, the infant is capable of using new schemes in different situations to solve problems. These behavior patterns constitute the first clear acts of intelligence.

At around nine to ten months, object permanency is not completely established. The infant will look for an object under a blanket if he or she saw it being hidden. However, if the object is moved from one hiding place to another while the baby watches, he or she will look for it in the first hiding place. Some researchers interpret this continued search behavior as demonstrating that the infant knows the object is permanent and somewhere (Siegler 1986). Piaget's view is that he or she must still connect the reappearance of the object to his or her own motor activities. He or she perceives the object as not yet having a permanence independent of his or her own activity.

Constancy of size and shape is also established during this substage. For

Secondary circular reactions
In Piaget's theory, the substage of the sensorimotor stage that lasts from four to eight months of age. It consists of repetitive actions that center around the environmental consequences of those actions.

Object permanence
In Piaget's theory, the cognitive capacity to realize that an object exists even when it is out of sight.

Coordination of secondary schemes
In Piaget's theory, the fourth substage in the sensorimotor stage. It occurs between the eighth and twelfth months of age. Behaviors are now unquestionably intentional, and the infant can anticipate coming events. The infant is also capable of using new schemes in different situations to solve problems.

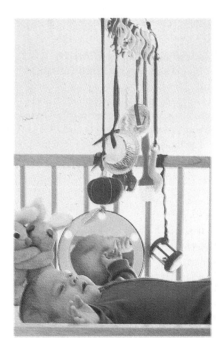

During the substage of secondary circular reactions, the four to eight month old will kick his or her legs to shake the crib and make a hanging mobile move.

During the substage of tertiary circular reactions, the twelve to eighteen month old will explore by trial and error, pursue new experiences, and try to produce new actions that create a pleasing effect for himself or herself.

example, if a bottle is presented upside down to an infant, he or she will turn it right side up, a feat he or she would not have been able to do in the earlier substages.

Tertiary Circular Reactions

The fifth substage, **tertiary circular reactions,** occurs between twelve and eighteen months. An infant will experiment to discover new properties of objects and events. It is similar to hypothesis testing. Object permanency is more stable. The infant will search and find an object through a series of displacements and will explore by trial and error. For example, when trying to insert nesting cups of descending size, he or she will experiment to see if a larger cup fits in the smaller cups. He or she pursues new experiences and tries to produce new actions that create a pleasing effect for himself or herself. The infant sees every situation as having new possibilities that need further exploration, explanation, or modification—an indication of developing intelligence.

Tertiary circular reactions
In Piaget's theory, the fifth substage of the sensorimotor stage. It occurs between twelve and eighteen months of age. Infants experiment to discover new properties of objects and events and learn about the consequences their actions have on objects.

Internalization of Sensorimotor Schemes

The final substage, **internalization of sensorimotor schemes,** occurs between eighteen and twenty-four months. The infant can now solve problems without having to physically explore their possibilities or solutions. For example, when playing with nesting cups, he or she knows which cups fit into the others. He can symbolically represent or visually imagine solutions. Not only can he or she solve simple problems, but he or she can remember and plan. For example, a twenty-two-month-old girl announced to her parents, "I'm going to bug grandpa when he comes over." They are also capable of recognizing a familiar picture even if it is upside down.

Researchers have replicated Piaget's original studies and have found that infants do move sequentially in the patterns of behavior outlined by Piaget.

Internalization of sensorimotor schemes
In Piaget's theory, the sixth substage of the sensorimotor stage. It occurs between eighteen and twenty-four months of age. The infant can now solve problems without having to physically explore their possibilities or solutions.

However, they found that many infants reach the various milestones at earlier ages (Corman and Escalona 1969; Kramer, Hill, and Cohen 1975; Uzgiris and Hunt 1975). Some researchers question Piaget's interpretation of his findings (Bower 1977; Harris 1974, 1983). They believe that infants younger than stage four understand the concept of object and understand that an object is permanent. However, they lack the ability to determine where an object is or the ability to carry out an effective search. Different researchers, using various techniques that do not require the infant to search for and locate something, found that infants as young as two months may understand that objects are permanent (Bower 1967), while others found that infants five to seven months understood that objects were permanent (Baillargeon, Spelke, and Wasserman 1985). Although not all developmentalists agree with Piaget's description or explanation of cognitive skills during the sensorimotor stage, they do agree on the general character of the limitations during this stage (Fischer 1980; Case 1985).

Language Beginnings

How do children learn to speak? Do they need to be taught a language, or are they genetically programmed to speak? Observers have been surprised at how easily infants learn to talk. Although cross-cultural studies indicate that all children progress through a series of milestones at the same age, there are some disagreements as to how language is acquired. Some researchers support environmental influences while others support a genetic basis for language acquisition. Most current theorists support more of an interactionist model that takes a middle-of-the-road approach to this nature-nurture issue. Language development is perceived as being influenced by both environmental and biological factors. These theorists note that each human being is programmed to learn language, but his or her experience with language is necessary in order to develop language.

Language is a form of communication that uses symbols. It provides a link between parents and their child and opens a door of communication to the child's inner world.

Prior to using language, infants have the capacity to use strategies to categorize information, making it possible to discriminate between objects and events (Sherman 1985). The beginning of the understanding of speech occurs well before the infant can actually begin speaking.

Infants can discriminate one consonant or vowel from another, as indicated by measured cardiac response to a novel utterance. Infants as young as one month can dependably make fine auditory discriminations, such as the voiced *b* from the unvoiced *p* sound, even when the stimuli are presented without context and in synthesized speech. These findings establish the young infant's phenomenal ability to discriminate auditory events, especially speech sounds, long before he or she can produce them (Eisenberg 1976, 1979; Kuhl 1983; Stone, Smith, and Murphy 1973).

Combinations of gestures by infants function as a means of communication before language. The child then progressively uses words to replace gestures such as pointing. Language reflects a complex communication system that previously existed between people before the acquisition of words and grammar (Bremner 1988).

Beckwith (1973) and Moerk (1985) found that maternal behaviors influence the vocalization of infants. During the first four months, the infant responds to speech with vocalizing. During the next six months, the infant does not respond but listens. After ten months, the infant responds by imitating the sounds and intonations he or she hears. Between eighteen and twenty-seven months, the infant not only learns language rules but also employs abstracting, analytical, and synthetic methodology.

Theories

Three major theories of language acquisition have emerged. The **behaviorist theory** claims that language is the product of environment and experience. The **nativist theory** views language acquisition as a product controlled by biology. The **cognitive-developmental theory** occupies the middle ground between the other two theories and views language development as growing out of intellectual development that is controlled by heredity and environment.

Behaviorist Theory Behaviorists believe that, like any other behavior, language can be explained as conditioned responses and/or imitation. Parents reinforce babbling sounds that resemble a word, such as "ma-ma" or "ba-ba," through smiles, hugs, and other positive reactions. Having speech models to copy is also important. This may explain how infants learn words or phrases, but not how they form sentences that they are not imitating.

Nativist Theory Nativists view language acquisition as being closely linked to the maturation of the brain. It is predictable and similar in humans. Support for this theory is reflected in the fact that children normally pass through a series of milestones at about the same age regardless of their language or culture. Also, progress in language development appears to be synchronized with progress in motor development. Language and motor development appear to be controlled by the central nervous system. Added support to this theory is the fact that verbal functions in humans are controlled by specific speech centers in the brain (Ramsey 1985; Gesell and Ilg 1946; Gesell and Ames 1947).

Noam Chomsky (1975), a noted nativist theorist, proposed that the central nervous system contains a mental structure called a **language acquisition device (LAD).** The LAD is similar to a computer that is prewired or programmed to acquire language. This enables the infant to listen carefully to speech patterns and sounds and then process these sounds. Each child, therefore, has an innate ability to process information about language. Every utterance he or she hears registers on the brain. The LAD then collects a body of these utterances. This includes grammatical sentences as well as nongrammatical utterances such as interrupted sentences, fragments, and mistakes. This body of utterances is examined or analyzed by the LAD, which searches for and finds order in the chaos of utterances. From this examination and search for order, the child discovers on a nonconscious level the rules that govern the structure of the language that has been heard. The LAD helps explain the innate ability of the human brain to not only process words but understand the structure of language and the fundamental relationship between words.

Chomsky theorizes that there are two levels of structure to language: *surface structure* and *deep structure*. **Surface structure** involves the grammatical rules of language such as the order of words in a sentence. **Deep structure** involves the syntactical relationship between words. For example, "Joe shoveled the driveway" and "The driveway was shoveled by Joe" have a different surface structures but the same deep structure. Children are able to recognize that even

---

Behaviorist theory of language development
The theory that that language is a product of environment and experience and can be explained as conditioned responses and/or imitation.

Nativist theory of language development
The theory that views language acquisition as a product controlled by biology and closely linked to the maturation of the brain.

Cognitive-developmental theory of language development
The theory that views language development as growing out of intellectual development, which is controlled by heredity and environment.

Language acquisition device (LAD)
According to Chomsky, a mental structure that enables an infant to process sounds and speech patterns and that triggers milestones of speech. It helps explain the innate ability of the human brain to not only process words but understand the structure of language and the fundamental relationship between words.

Surface structure
According to Chomsky, the structure of language that involves the grammatical rules of language such as the order of words in a sentence.

Deep structure
According to Chomsky, the structure of language that involves the syntactical relationship between words.

though the two sentences are different in surface structure, they still have the same meaning.

The LAD, according to Chomsky, also triggers various milestones of speech so that infants babble at about six months, produce single words at about one year, and speak in short sentences at about two years.

Cognitive-Developmental Theory The cognitive-developmental theory views language development as being rooted in cognitive development, with cognitive development occurring first and language second. According to Piaget, language is dependent on cognitive development. Therefore, language does not structure thought but is the vehicle for expressing it. Piaget points out that before an infant acquires language skills, he or she can solve problems and acquire basic concepts. For example, the infant must understand the concept of object permanence before speech can begin. Language acquisition is dependent on acquiring knowledge through touching, tasting, manipulation, and other experiences with people and objects. As the cognitive capacities become more complex, acquiring language becomes more sophisticated and complete. Thought is, therefore, seen as preceding language (Piaget 1959).

The Russian psychologist and cognitive theorist Lev Vygotzky (1962) views language and thought as developing at the same time and eventually becoming interdependent. He contends that with the beginning of symbolic thought, at about age two, language regulates the child's thoughts and behaviors. "Inner speech," according to Vygotzky, controls the child's behavior. Language and thought are related to the same underlying cognitive ability. Thought is then facilitated by language, and the two processes become interdependent.

Many psychologists agree with Piaget that thinking occurs first and is then expressed in words, while others agree with Vygotzky that language facilitates thinking.

Stages

Crying Crying is more than likely the first sound that a baby makes. It is the first stage of prelinguistic speech. The crying of the newborn or very young infant is involuntary and serves no intentional communicative purpose. As the baby gets older, however, the cry is a signal or a means of communicating that he or she has some needs to be met. In order to understand the meaning of these cries, caregivers must consider the context in which they occur. The young infant may cry when overaroused due to hunger, pain, wetness, and so on. However, pain cries can usually be differentiated from other cries.

Cooing Sometime between the first and third month, the prelinguistic sound of *cooing* emerges. Cooing consists of primarily vowel and some consonant sounds and is usually sounds of contentment and happiness. Cross-cultural studies indicate that babies everywhere cry and coo alike. Generally adults respond favorably to cooing and coo back to the infant. This situation creates a two-way communication cycle.

Babbling Babbling appears just before six months of age. Babbling consists of combining the vowel and consonant sounds. It more closely resembles the sounds of syllables of words. All infants produce early babbling sounds that are much alike. Often infants can babble a sound that they may have trouble learning later as part of a foreign language.

Hearing-impaired infants begin to babble at the same time and in the same way as normal-hearing infants. After six months, however, they begin to differ.

Normal babies increase the amount of babbling and the number of sounds, while the amount of babbling and the number of sounds decrease in hearing-impaired infants. Thus, in order to produce early vocalizations, children do not have to have feedback provided by sounds of their own voices or those of others. However, after six months such feedback becomes crucial for further language development. Hearing-impaired infants appear to babble for the sake of communication, while the normal-hearing infants babble for pleasure as well as for communication (Barclay 1985; Oller 1980).

Echolalic Babbling **Echolalic babbling,** or **jargonese,** begins at around nine months. Infants begin to repeat or echo sounds and produce the intonational qualities of true speech. Adults can quite often guess the intent of the child's communication because of the intonation. The thirteen-month-old is in a transitional period of echolalic babbling that includes syllables, vowel-like and consonant-like productions, periodic intonated utterances, and complex babbling sequences, as well as the actual production of his or her first word (Kent and Bauer 1985).

First Words At the end of the first year, the infant makes a transition from the prelinguistic stage to the linguistic stage. The first word is typically considered to be a significant milestone in speech development. Elbers and Ton (1985) explored the interplay of words and babbles after the child's first spoken

Echolalic babbling
Babbling in which infants, at around nine months, begin to repeat or echo sounds and produce the intonational qualities of true speech.

Jargonese
See Echolalic babbling.

TABLE 5.1 Stages of Prelinguistic and Linguistic Speech

PRELINGUISTIC STATE

NEWBORN TO FOUR WEEKS	Cries of displeasure, reflexive movements, and facial expressions.
ONE TO THREE MONTHS	Cooing, squealing, gurgling, fussing, crying, occasional vowel sounds.
THREE MONTHS	First signs of babbling, with mostly vowel sounds but only rarely consonant sounds.
SIX MONTHS	Babbling with both consonant and vowel sounds.
NINE MONTHS	Echolalic babbling, or jargonese, in which infant begins to repeat or echo sounds and produce the intonational qualities of true speech.
TWELVE MONTHS	Echolalic babbling that includes syllables, vowel-like and consonantlike productions, periodic intonated utterances, and complex babbling sequences. Production of first word.

LINGUISTIC STAGE

TWELVE TO EIGHTEEN MONTHS	Holophrastic speech. Slow growth of vocabulary, up to fifty words.
TWENTY-ONE TO TWENTY-FOUR MONTHS	Telegraphic speech. Combination of words into two-word sentences. Expressive vocabulary between thirty and fifty words.
TWENTY-FOUR MONTHS	Vocabulary between fifty and three hundred words, with not all used accurately. Child understands most simple language intended for him or her.

word. They found that new words may influence the character and the course of babbling, while babbling encourages phonological preferences for selecting other new words. This interplay may provide the key to understanding the highly variable phenomenon of early word production. Usually the first word is a reduplicated syllable such as *ma-ma* or *da-da,* which is associated with a certain person. First words are mostly nouns and references to things that can be acted upon or objects that hold particular interest to the child, for example, *bottle, ball, cat,* or *car.* First words are usually acquired by direct imitation of adult speech.

After the first word is learned, other words follow in close succession, until the one-year-old has a vocabulary of three to eight words. Each word is used singly as an utterance.

Baldwin and Markham (1989) found that with ten- to twenty-month-old infants, an adult's verbally labeling objects instead of just pointing to them increased the infants' attention to those objects. That is, it is important for parents to verbally label objects for their infant in order for the infant to remember or recall the objects.

Holophrastic Speech   A **holophrase** is a one-word sentence or phrase that conveys meaning. Verbal understanding is necessary in order to use and respond to true speech. The single words of holophrastic speech are thought to be equivalent to the full sentences of adult grammar. For example, when an infant says "cookie," he or she may mean "I want a cookie," "I see a cookie," or "The dog took my cookie." Holophrastic speech reveals that children are limited phonologically to uttering single words at the beginning of language acquisition, even though they are capable of understanding and conceiving of full sentences (McNeill 1970).

Holophrase
A one-word sentence or phrase that conveys meaning.

On the average, children begin to use true speech between twelve and eighteen months of age, although their first spoken word may have been said at ten or eleven months of age. They usually speak ten intelligible words by fifteen months of age, while being capable of understanding more than fifty words. By eighteen months the average speaking vocabulary is about fifty words (Nelson et al. 1978).

Telegraphic Speech   By two years of age, children not only use more than fifty words, but they can put two distinct words together into a sentence. When children begin putting two or more words together to represent a larger sentence, they are involved in **telegraphic speech**. Children's telegraphic speech resembles a telegram. It is a patterned speech in which small, unstressed parts of speech such as articles, auxiliary verbs, connecting verbs, and inflections of every sort are left out and content words that carry the meaning of the sentence are retained. This speech indicates more than holophrases do, that the child is learning **syntax,** that is, the rules that govern the development of sentence structure (McNeill 1970).

Telegraphic speech
The speech of toddlers, in which they put two or more words together to represent a larger sentence. It resembles a telegram. It is a patterned speech in which articles, auxiliary verbs, connecting verbs, and inflections are left out and content words are retained.

Syntax
The rules that govern the development of sentence structure.

Humor

Humor is seen as a key element in the human repertoire, so much so that many consider it a defining human attribute. However, it has often been overlooked when discussing human development.

Humor has been described as "a form of intellectual play" that is founded in incongruity (McGhee 1979). The development of humor has been linked to Piaget's stages of cognitive development (Piaget 1962; McGhee 1979, 1986;

Courtruier, Mansfield, and Gallenger 1981). Some humor researchers believe humor is essentially a "construction" that requires a certain level of cognitive development and linguistic understanding of incongruity. Age-related changes in humor do appear to have a strong link to maturation. General developmental changes in children's humor reflect cognitive developmental changes. Therefore, as new levels of cognitive skill are achieved, new forms of humor comprehension, production, and appreciation emerge.

Smiling and Laughing: The Precursors to Humor

Smiles and grins appear at around two months of age, and laughter appears at around three months of age (Honig 1988). Piaget (1962) characterized the grin and chuckle of the four-month-old baby as an indicator of the first experience of cognitive success. However, laughter may not be a response to humor, but instead a physical reaction to a buildup of anxiety and then a release of tension (Shaeffer and Hopkins 1988). Various cognitive developmental processes, such as symbolic representation (with images), must occur before an infant is capable of truly comprehending and/or experiencing humor.

Although smiling and humor have traditionally been associated with each other, smiling and the comprehension of humor are not correlated in the early months of life. However, smiling is a prerequisite to the comprehension of humor. It is an indicator of proper brain development, the recognition of significant others, the ability to note discrepancies, and a sign of pleasure at problem solving (Barclay 1985).

Early infant smiling can be categorized into two types: **Endogenous smiling,** which is due to internal stimulation only, is present at birth and occurs in the neonate during REM sleep and during those waking states in which rapid eye movements are present. **Exogenous smiling,** which is due to external stimulation, develops in the first and second month after birth (Barclay 1985; Stone, Smith, and Murphy 1973).

The endogenous smiles appear to the observer as false smiles. The smiles involve the mouth and cheeks, but they do not seem to involve the eyes or forehead. They do not seem to have the general affective, emotional tone of the true baby smile. At this time they appear spontaneously, such as during sleep. Preterm babies produce more REM smiles than do full-term babies do. This is one indicator that endogenous smiling is probably based on brain stem activity. As the cortex of the brain matures, this activity is inhibited. Endogenous smiling occurs only rarely at three to four months, and by six months it usually has completely disappeared (Stone, Smith, and Murphy 1973).

By the third week, real smiles, or exogenous smiles, begin to appear. They do not last as long as true social smiles, but they are recognizably real smiles. Exogenous smiles are elicited by stimulation from the outside world rather than being spontaneous. The human female voice is the most effective stimulus to elicit them. Around the fifth and sixth weeks, a human face appears to be the most effective stimulus to elicit a smile. This indicates a developmental progression that is determined by the process of growth and heredity. At least two studies have shown that babies start to smile at human faces at the *conceptual age* of forty-six weeks. The chronological age of the baby might be six weeks, eighteen weeks, or only two weeks. In other words, in predicting when a particular baby will smile at a human face, his or her chronological age can be disregarded. Babies smile at a conceptual age of forty-six weeks, regardless of how long they have actually been in the world (Bower 1977; Barclay 1985).

Endogenous smiling
Early infant smiling that is due to internal stimulation only, is present at birth, and occurs in the neonate during REM sleep and during those waking states in which rapid eye movements are present.

Exogenous smiling
Smiling that develops in the first and second month after birth and is due to external stimulation.

When infants smile at the high-contrast pattern of a human face, they elicit such loving attention from their caregivers that they associate the human face with pleasure, that is, the pleasure they get from the attention given them. They therefore begin to smile with pleasure whenever they see a human face (Bower 1977).

The Experience of Pleasure

There is clear evidence that babies derive great pleasure from problem solving, from intellectual mastery of some bit of their environment, and from comprehension of some aspect of the causal structure of the world around them. It has also been observed that once infants detected a contingency, they stop performing in the situation and start again only if the contingency is changed (McGhee 1972, 1974, 1976, 1979). A good example of this process was related by Bower (1977):

> . . . When a baby learned that by turning his head to the right he could switch on a light, he would no longer make rightward head turns with any particular frequency. However, when the contingency was changed, so that he had to turn his head to the left to make the light come on, he would sooner or later notice that his turn to the right didn't make the light come on, and there would be a rapid burst of activity until the baby figured out what movement was necessary to switch on the light. Then again, there would be vigorous smiling and cooing and a diminution of activity. If the problem was then made more complicated still—for example, a turn to the left and then to the right—the process would repeat itself. The baby would notice that a left turn by itself no longer had any effect. There would be a burst of activity. The baby would eventually discover the proper combination of movements, and then activity would subside.

Uzgiris and Hunt (1975) also found that infants derived pleasure from problem solving. In their study, two groups of infants were given identical mobiles in their cribs. For one group of infants, the mobiles were set in motion and the infants had no control over them. For the other group, the mobiles were attached to the cribs so that the infants could set them in motion by moving their crib. These infants showed clear smiling and cooing behavior while they were controlling the mobiles. The infants in the other group attended to the mobiles, but they did not coo or smile significantly.

Smiling is not only a response to the pleasures resulting from problem solving, but it implies the working of memory. This smiling may turn to laughter by four months. Laughter, at first, occurs mainly as a result of physical stimuli such as tickling. Later, by the second half of the first year, the baby laughs at interesting or incongruous events. Sustained joy or elation can be observed in infants by the end of the first year and during the second, particularly in anticipating events that will occur and in planning such events (Sroufe 1979).

Humor: Stage One

The first stage of humor coincides with the end of Piaget's stage of sensorimotor development. It is during the second year that the toddler acquires the cognitive ability to represent things symbolically with images, thus enabling the infant to experience humor.

Humor appreciation involves two distinct mental activities: identifying the nature of the incongruous event and then setting out to resolve or make sense of it. This earliest form of humor, stage one, centers on pretend activity toward

When an infant receives loving attention after smiling at a caregiver, he or she learns to associate pleasure with smiling when seeing a human face.

objects, and it commonly has as its basis the child's doing something to produce an incongruous event or relationship.

Eighteen-month-olds treat the image of a toy as if it were that toy, fully aware of the difference between the two. It is the very knowledge of the inappropriateness of the action that leads to humor and its accompanying laughter when the child is in a playful frame of mind. Laughter reflects the pleasure of creating, in fantasy play, a set of conditions that are known to be at odds with reality. For example, Piaget's daughter Jacqueline saw a piece of fabric whose fringed edges resembled those on her pillow, so she took it, held a fold of it in her right hand, sucked the thumb of the same hand, and lay down on her side, as she did with her "real" pillow. Then she laughed hard. She kept her eyes open but blinked as if pretending to sleep (McGhee 1979, 1974).

The nature and intensity of reactions to incongruous events may depend on the context in which the events occur. Infants sometimes cry and sometimes laugh at the same event, depending on the circumstances. For example, an infant may laugh at his or her mother wearing a mask if she is seen putting it on, but cry if she walks into the room already wearing it (McGhee 1979).

Humor: Stage Two

The second stage of humor is very similar to the first stage of humor. The two stages overlap considerably because each one relies on the manipulation of images and events. However, where in stage one an action toward an object can elicit humor, in stage two a verbal statement can create the incongruity that a child finds funny.

Eighteen-month-olds to two year olds (still in stage-one humor) will direct incongruous actions toward objects that have some similarity to an appropriate object. For example, they may use a block for a pretend piece of food. From the second year on, however, there is a decreasing reliance on such resemblances in make-believe play, regardless of whether the play is of an exploratory or humorous nature. The second stage of humor is characterized by the use of words to create incongruities. The inconsistency between the verbal label, the real object (or action initiated toward the object), and the image brought to bear on that object combine to supply the source of humor (McGhee 1972, 1979).

Toward the end of the second year, the child thinks mere misnaming is funny. He or she might either identify one object as another or identify his or her own body as another person or thing. For example, a little girl might call herself by her brother's name or call a foot a "hand" or a dog a "cat." The absence of action toward objects epitomizes humor at the second stage (McGhee 1972, 1979).

The first stage of humor does not simply disappear as the capacity for the second stage forms. Everyday humor experiences are composed of various combinations of stage-one and stage-two incongruities. Some may be purely one or the other, but most are likely to consist of both discrepant actions toward objects and inaccurate descriptions of those actions or objects (McGhee 1979).

Verbal labels that are understood by other children or adults mark the beginning of social influence on the production as well as the enjoyment of humor for the stage-two child. Most children prefer to share humorous fantasy play with others once they discover that enjoyment can be mutual. Others prefer to restrict their humorous creations to their own imagination. Children who share their earliest verbal humor have already developed a close social bond with the people with whom it is shared. A child who has already developed a

When parents are delighted by play creations and react with affection and attention, the child will share humorous creations with the parents, siblings, peers, and others.

pattern of maintaining a close proximity to his or her parent(s) for affection and other forms of positive contact may be especially likely to use such simple jokes as a means of gaining positive reactions.

Another means by which humor becomes primarily social is related to the reactions of the parents and significant others to the child's early name-changing and other pretend games. Some parents pay little attention to children's fantasy play or call it "childish" or "a waste of time." If the child is prone to fantasy play, whether with objects or words, the parents and other adults may tell the child to stop being silly or foolish. The child will then get the message that humor and other forms of fantasy play are not viewed positively. The child will react either by reducing the amount of time spent in such play or by developing a pattern of avoiding others when engaged in it. On the other hand, the parents may be delighted by play creations and react with affection and attention. When such reactions are typical, the child will share humorous creations with the parents, siblings, peers, and others (McGhee 1979).

Play signals or clues are important in humor within a social context. Although two-year-olds have made considerable progress in understanding their world, their confidence about the nature of objects and word labels given to objects is easily shaken. For example, in name-changing humor, the toddler's reaction depends on who issues the statement and how it is done. With the limited mastery of language between two and three years of age, play signals from others are essential if incongruities are to be perceived as funny. However, there is no need for play signals when a toddler originates his or her own fantasy play. The majority of a toddler's humor is self-generated. Only in the midst of a clearly playful interaction will the name-changing games of others be experienced as humorous (McGhee 1979).

Infant Mortality

Although the United States considers itself a world leader in many areas, infant health is not one of them. Maternal and infant health care made steady progress during the late 1960s and the 1970s but declined in the 1980s (Children's Defense Fund 1989). In 1987 there were more than thirty-eight thousand infant deaths in the United States. For every 1,000 live births, 10.1 babies die in the first year, and 13 die before their fifth birthday.

Between 1950 and 1985, the U.S. infant mortality rate fell in ranking from sixth to last place among the other industrialized nations. It ranked nineteenth worldwide in 1988. When just the African-American infant mortality rate was compared with other nations' overall rates, the ranking went down to twenty-eighth. The Children's Defense Fund notes that an African-American infant born in Boston is more likely to die than an infant born in Panama or North or South Korea (Children's Defense Fund 1990).

Why are so many babies dying in the United States?

- HIV infection (AIDS) was the ninth leading cause of death among one- to four-year-olds in 1987. In 1989 approximately 1.4 pregnant women per 1,000 gave birth to live infants infected with HIV. Since 1981, 1,500 of the nearly 2,000 pediatric AIDS cases have been among African American or Latino children, and 855 of the African American and Latino cases have been related to intravenous drug use. About half of all children who have had AIDS have died.

- Low-birth-weight infants are twenty times more likely to die than other infants. During the 1980s, there was no progress in the United States in reducing low-birth-weight births. The United States ranks twenty-ninth worldwide.

- Prenatal care during the critical first three months of pregnancy can dramatically improve infant health. An infant whose mother had no prenatal care is three times more likely to die in the first year of life than other infants.

- Infants born to adolescent mothers are more likely to have poor health than infants born to adult mothers. In 1987, 12 percent of all births were to mothers under twenty years of age. Adolescent mothers between fifteen and seventeen years old increased 4 percent between 1986 and 1987. These young mothers tend to have inadequate prenatal care, births too closely spaced (adolescent mothers account for one out of five repeat births within eighteen months), and lower educational attainment than adult mothers.

The Children's Defense Fund (1990) points out that there are three reasons why the United States as a nation needs to improve the health of its infants and children. First, we need every child to become a productive member of society in order to achieve and maintain our competitive edge internationally. Second, prevention strategies and early diagnosis cut down on the health costs to not only the families involved but the state and federal governmental agencies as well. Third, good health care is a basic and equitable right for every citizen in any civilized society. Many American infants and children face the risk

Continued

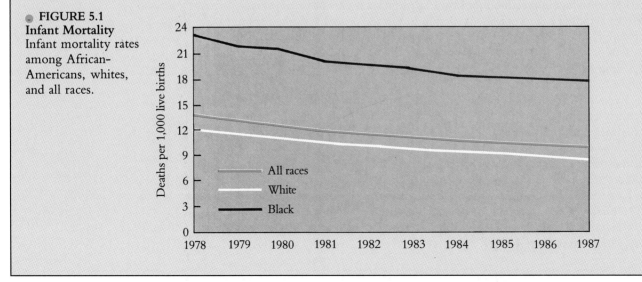

● **FIGURE 5.1**
Infant Mortality
Infant mortality rates among African-Americans, whites, and all races.

Infant Mortality (continued)

of death or poor health care because they are from poor families, because their parents are employed in certain types of industry, or because they live in certain geographical areas.

How can the high infant mortality rate affect you individually? How does it affect us as a society? What can be done at the local, state, and national levels to change this trend in the infant mortality rate?

● **FIGURE 5.2**
Infant Mortality
Thermometer

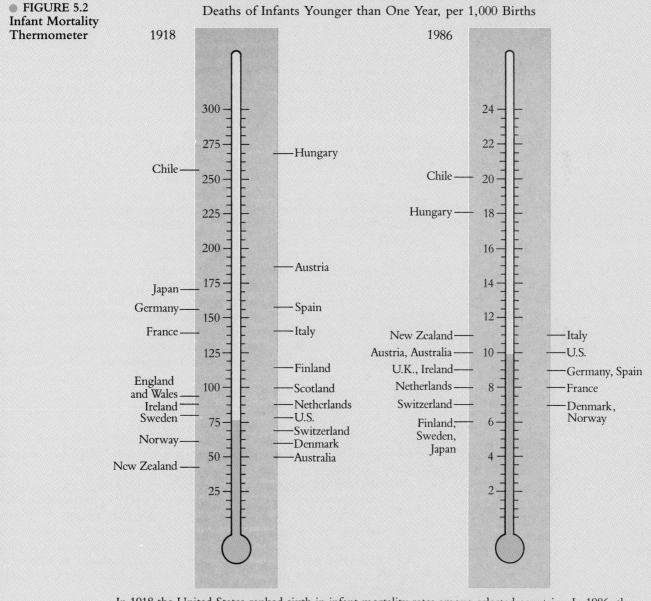

Deaths of Infants Younger than One Year, per 1,000 Births

1918

300
275 — Hungary
Chile — 250
225
200
175 — Austria
Japan — — Spain
Germany — 150
France — — Italy
125
— Finland
England and Wales — 100 — Scotland
Ireland — — Netherlands
Sweden — 75 — U.S.
— Switzerland
Norway — — Denmark
50 — Australia
New Zealand —
25

1986

24
22
Chile — 20
Hungary — 18
16
14
12
New Zealand — — Italy
Austria, Australia — 10 — U.S.
U.K., Ireland — — Germany, Spain
Netherlands — 8 — France
Switzerland — — Denmark, Norway
Finland, Sweden, Japan — 6
4
2

In 1918 the United States ranked sixth in infant mortality rates among selected countries. In 1986, the U.S. rank was thirteenth, behind such countries as Spain, Ireland, Japan, Germany, and France.
Source: Left, Children's Bureau, U.S. Department of Labor, 1921. Right, UNICEF.

S U M M A R Y

- Physical development in infants occurs in predictable patterns. These patterns are found in height, body proportion, motor coordination, direction of development (cephalocaudal and proximodistal), and sex differences.

- Changes in motor skills occur at a fairly consistent rate, indicating that maturation is a primary factor in their development. Environmental factors can also influence the development of motor skills. Therefore, the process of motor development is sequential unless it is interfered with by unusual conditions within, or external to, the infant.

- Two basic types of motor skills emerge during infancy: *gross,* which includes upright postural body control and locomotion, and *fine,* which includes the ability to reach with the hand, to grasp, and to manipulate objects.

- Digestive disorders are common among infants. "Spitting up" and colic are the two most common digestive disorders. Allergies are often considered the cause.

- Proper nutrition is vitally important to an infant's physical development. Human breast milk is nutritionally superior to formula or cow's milk, with some exceptions.

- Nutritional deficiencies, especially protein deficiencies, in an infant's diet can cause irreparable brain damage.

- Bottle mouth, a condition in which a young child's teeth have been destroyed by tooth decay, has been traced to the practice of allowing infants to sleep with a bottle in their mouth for long periods of time.

- Overfeeding during infancy can lead to a lifelong problem with obesity.

- Toilet training is accomplished faster and easier when it is not begun until after twenty months of age. Girls tend to achieve bladder control before boys. Not only does toilet training require physical readiness on the part of the child, but he or she should be familiar with social expectations and be able to understand what he or she should do.

- Piaget theorized that three major functional processes occur and interact in the child in order to produce cognitive growth and alter the structure of the intellect: *adaptation,* which includes assimilation and accommodation; *schemes,* which are psychological structures based on the individual's interaction with external reality; and *organization,* which enables experience and knowledge to be categorized in increasingly more complex segments.

- Sensorimotor is the first stage of cognitive development according to Piaget. It includes six substages: reflexive, primary circular reactions, secondary circular reactions, coordination of secondary schemes, tertiary circular reactions, and internalization of sensorimotor schemes.

- Three major theories of language acquisition have emerged: behaviorist, nativist, and cognitive-developmental.

- The stages of prelinguistic speech include crying, cooing, babbling, and echolalia, or jargonese. The stages of linguistic speech include holophrases and telegraphic speech.

- Although smiling and humor have traditionally been linked, they are not related in the early months of life. Both are related to the cognitive development of the infant. Endogenous smiling and exogenous smiling are present in the very young infant. Smiling is an indicator of brain development, recognition of significant others, the ability to perceive discrepancies, and pleasure at problem solving. Various cognitive developmental processes, such as symbolic representation with images, must occur before an infant is capable of truly comprehending humor.

- The infant mortality rate is climbing in this country. HIV infection, poor or no prenatal care, adolescent mothers, and low birth weight are just some of the reasons why. We as a society need to find creative ideas to stop this rise. The Children's Defense Fund has outlined some strategies.

Beck, J. (1984). *How to raise a brighter child.* New York: Pocket Books.
   Geared for the middle class parent with ideas of how to encourage cognitive development.
Bruner, J. (1983). *Child talk.* New York: Norton.
   View of children's development of language.
Lamb, M. E. and Bornstein, M. C. (1987). *Development in infancy.* New York: Random House.
   Well researched portrayal of infant development.
White, B. (1985). *The first three years of life.* (2nd ed. Englewood Cliffs, NJ: Prentice-Hall.
   Using research as a basis, White presents practical suggestions in encouraging the cognitive development of infants.

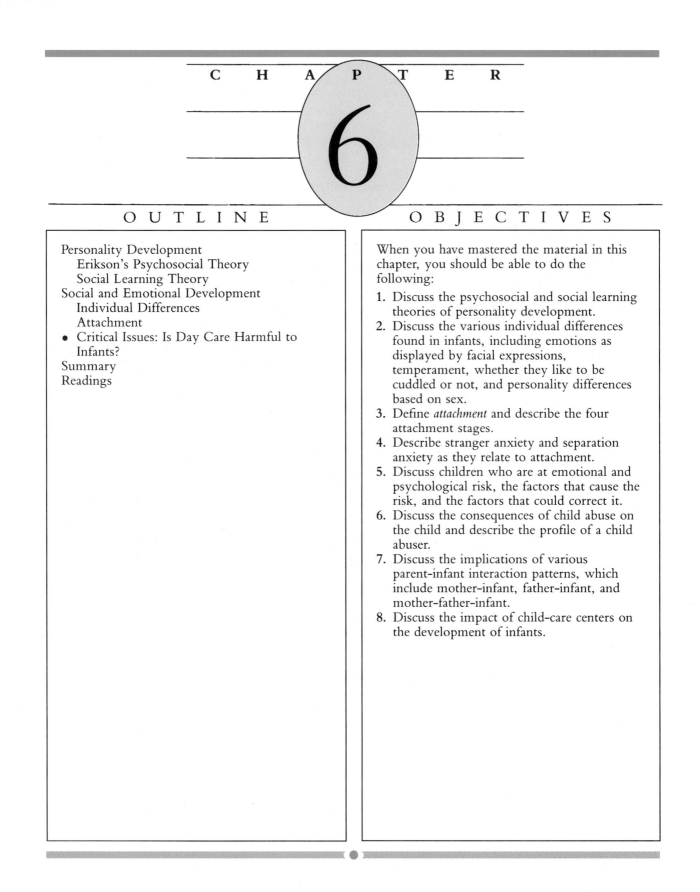

C H A P T E R

6

O B J E C T I V E S

When you have mastered the material in this chapter, you should be able to do the following:

1. Discuss the psychosocial and social learning theories of personality development.
2. Discuss the various individual differences found in infants, including emotions as displayed by facial expressions, temperament, whether they like to be cuddled or not, and personality differences based on sex.
3. Define *attachment* and describe the four attachment stages.
4. Describe stranger anxiety and separation anxiety as they relate to attachment.
5. Discuss children who are at emotional and psychological risk, the factors that cause the risk, and the factors that could correct it.
6. Discuss the consequences of child abuse on the child and describe the profile of a child abuser.
7. Discuss the implications of various parent-infant interaction patterns, which include mother-infant, father-infant, and mother-father-infant.
8. Discuss the impact of child-care centers on the development of infants.

The Emerging Human:
Infants' and Toddlers' Psychosocial Development

● PERSONALITY DEVELOPMENT

Personality development is related to the social and emotional development of the infant. According to Freud, the emotional relationships that
infants develop with people close to them may well affect the ways in
which they relate to other people later in life. Because early social experiences
are important experiences, infancy is truly a sensitive period for personality
development.

Erikson's Psychosocial Theory

One widely accepted theory of personality development is Erikson's (1963,
1968) psychosocial theory. In the first of his eight stages, trust versus mistrust,
Erikson noted that the creation of trust is accomplished by caring for an
infant's basic physical and emotional needs. As the infant is cared for in a
predictable, warm, and sensitive manner, his or her sense of trust and the
knowledge that he or she is loved will develop. However, if the infant's world
is chaotic and unpredictable and he or she cannot count on the parents' or
caregivers' affection, a sense of mistrust will develop and he or she will feel
inadequate and insecure in interactions with others in his or her life. Basic trust
or mistrust does not develop all at once but is acquired throughout the first
year of life.

Infants who are trusting show their secure feelings concerning their world
by sleeping deeply, eating well, and enjoying bowel relaxation. The main determinant of establishing trust in an infant is the mother-child bond, with the
quality of the relationship more important than the quantity. Trust makes it
possible for an infant to let the mother or primary caregiver out of sight, because
he or she develops an inner certainty that the person will return. If left to cry for
long periods, the infant concludes that any effort he or she makes to communicate will be neglected, thus establishing a sense of mistrust.

Once mistrust is established, a cycle of mistrust is reinforced. For example,
parents may assume that a baby cannot always be attended to just because he or
she is cranky and crying. Then when the infant is held, it is usually by someone
who wants the infant to be quiet rather than to just cuddle him or her. Basic
mistrust leads to self-defeating behavior, low self-esteem, and the inability to
interact appropriately with others. Erikson sees this as one of the most serious
forms of emotional illness, because such a child does not know how to relate to
others and withdraws into his or her own world.

Basic trust corresponds with a sense of self-confidence and control. A
child's trust in his or her primary caregivers and his or her world makes the child
aware of his or her own sense of self. He or she begins developing a will, which
in turn makes it possible to assert himself or herself. This is the beginning of
Erikson's second stage: autonomy versus shame and doubt.

In the stage of autonomy versus shame and doubt, the toddler learns a
degree of independence from his or her caregivers. The process of getting up
and walking clumsily is a means of asserting his or her independence from
someone having to pick up and carry him or her. This autonomy represents the
will of the child to be himself or herself.

A toddler also exercises autonomy when he or she controls his or her
bowels and bladder. According to Erikson, by controlling himself or herself, the
toddler is more comfortable out of diapers and can be proud of his or her
newfound maturity. The parents' demands serve as a gentle external aid that

helps their child initiate his or her own desire to be toilet trained. The self-control learned at this stage can provide a long-term sense of personal pride and goodwill.

The parents must be firmly reassuring and help their toddler make the proper choices without causing him or her to lose self-esteem. If the parents are overcontrolling or nonsupportive, the toddler may become upset and feel a loss of self-control. When a well-guided autonomy cannot be achieved, the toddler will develop a sense of shame and a compulsive doubt about himself or herself and his or her ability to be independent. For example, a two-and-one-half-year-old who does not feed himself because his mother is afraid he will get his clothes dirty will not only doubt his ability to feed himself but will also doubt his ability to do other things for himself.

The parents must monitor their toddler's activities and set limits on his or her behavior so he or she can acquire an understanding of what he or she can and cannot do.

Social Learning Theory

The social learning theory of infant personality development does not make a distinction between behavior and personality and suggests that infants learn from the environment around them. It is thought that infants imitate significant models and are reinforced when those models approve of their actions. Thus imitation is seen as the primary factor behind personality development. Bandura (1985) theorizes that people learn by observing others and that reinforcement helps to determine whether we will do what we have learned. Observation and imitation are, therefore, starting points in the process of learning.

The social learning theory views the mother as the logical attachment object for the infant. Mothers take on the responsibility of feeding their infants, changing them when they are wet and soiled, and providing warmth, tender touches, and soft, reassuring vocalizations when their infants are upset or afraid. An infant, therefore, associates his or her mother with pleasant feelings and pleasurable sensations, so the mother becomes a conditioned stimulus for positive outcomes, that is, a *secondary reinforcer*. When the mother reaches the status of a conditioned or secondary reinforcer, the infant is attached and will do anything (smile, babble, etc.) to attract her attention or remain near her.

Feeding is seen as playing an important role in determining the character or quality of the infant's attachment to the primary caregiver. Feeding elicits positive responses from the infant that are likely to increase the caregiver's affection for the child. Therefore, feeding is thought to be important because it provides positive reinforcement for the infant *and* the caregiver, which will strengthen their affection for one another.

● SOCIAL AND EMOTIONAL DEVELOPMENT

Individual Differences

Infants appear not to be the blank slates described by John Locke (see Chapter 1). Even at birth differences are obvious between individual infants. Infants differ not only in size, shape, and physical maturity but also in personality. Such personality differences include emotions as displayed by facial expressions (Izard et al. 1980), temperament (Thomas and Chess 1977), whether the infant likes to be cuddled or not (Schaffer and Emerson 1973), and differences based on the sex of the infant. Because of the differences among infants, parents should adjust their child-rearing practices to the individual infant. The same given environment does not provide identical consequences for all children, even those from the same family. Each infant will react to the environment in his or her own individual way.

Emotions and Facial Expressions

Infants can disclose their emotions through their facial expressions. Izard et al. (1980) support the theory that infants' facial expressions reveal a number of distinct emotions, including general excitement, joy, surprise, anger, fear, shame, and guilt. However, it is sometimes difficult to differentiate between closely related emotions such as joy and surprise or distress and anger. Campos et al. (1983) claim that basic emotions such as anger, joy, disgust, and sadness are innate, and that these "core" emotional states are present throughout life. They also believe that infants may have difficulty expressing some emotions because of neurological immaturity; that is, they may express a different emotion than they are actually feeling. On the other hand, infants can differentiate between facial expressions. LaBarbera, Izard, Vietze, and Parisi (1976) found that four- and six-month-old infants recognized facial expressions of joy. Young-Browne, Rosenfield, and Horowitz (1977) found that three-month-old infants could differentiate between expressions of happiness and surprise, and sometimes between sadness and surprise. Legerstee, Pomerleau, Malcuit, and Feider (1987) have shown that when two-month-old infants are faced with a communicative adult, they will smile, vocalize, and alternate their gaze. But when confronted with a nonresponsive adult, they will cry and turn their head. These findings suggest links between emotional and cognitive development.

Temperament

Temperament is a broad term that refers to an individual's pattern of responding to the environment, and it is seen as the foundation upon which the personality is developed. Various studies (Chess and Thomas 1982; Kagan 1984) have found individual differences in activity level and temperament from birth, before the environment had time to affect the infants. These differences appear to be the result of genetics, prenatal factors (such as exposure to alcohol), or perinatal influences (such as exposure to anesthetics or anoxia) (Goldsmith 1983; Abel 1984).

Three unique temperaments, or dominant reaction patterns, have been identified (Thomas, Chess, and Birch 1970; Chess and Thomas 1986; Hubert and Wachs 1985; Rothbart and Derryberry 1981). Some infants are *difficult,* some are *easy,* and some are quiet and *slow to warm up.*

The **difficult** infant has irregular biological cycles such as eating and sleeping patterns and tends to respond negatively and with withdrawal to new stimulation such as new people or new situations. This infant is slow to adapt to change, is rather intense, and is often irritable and unhappy.

The **easy** infant is a good or happy infant who reacts with moderation rather than intensity, adapts easily to new situations, exhibits a positive mood, and enjoys being handled.

The **slow-to-warm-up** infant is characterized by a combination of mildly negative responses and slow adaptability to new stimuli. With repeated exposure to a new or changed situation, the slow-to-warm-up child can adapt in a positive manner.

Difficult infant
A temperament in which the infant tends to respond negatively, is slow to adapt to change, is rather intense, and is often irritable and unhappy.

Easy infant
A temperament in which the infant reacts with moderation, adapts easily to new situations, exhibits a positive mood, and enjoys being handled.

Slow-to-warm-up infant
A temperament in which the infant reacts with a combination of mildly negative responses and slowadaptability to new stimuli.

It is possible to identify an infant's dominant reaction by his or her initial reaction to new situations such as the first bath, the first solid food, or the first day of nursery school.

Thomas and Chess (1986) and Green et al. (1989) assert that not only are temperament differences genetically related because they are apparent at birth, but they are also stable over time. Easy babies tend to continue to show positive personality traits, while difficult babies tend to continue to show negative personality traits. Thomas and Chess (1986) also found that 70 percent of difficult infants entered psychiatric counseling or treatment later in life, while only 18 percent of former easy babies did.

An infant's temperament will either negatively or positively affect interactions with the people who care for him or her. For example, an easy infant gives his or her parents a feeling of confidence and reassurance concerning their parenting abilities. A cycle is established in which the parents display a relaxed, happy attitude, and the child, in turn, continues to respond positively. At the other extreme, a difficult child provokes parental anxiety because the parents believe that it is their ineptness and inadequacies that cause their child's extreme behavior. A negative cycle is therefore established. Uncertain parents often act inconsistently in response to their child's unpleasant behavior. This in turn contributes to the child's negative behavior.

The slow-to-warm-up child is less intense than the difficult child and therefore shows less negativism. Subsequently, the parents of a slow-to-warm-up child tend to be as positive and self-assured as the parents of an easy child. Only when exposed to new situations does the slow-to-warm-up child show some problem behaviors. However, rarely are the problem behaviors as severe as those of a difficult child, and the problem behaviors tend to resolve themselves over time. The long-term stability of personality traits can, therefore, be influenced by the **interaction** patterns and caregiving approaches of the parents in response to the temperament of the child.

In a study of infant temperament in three African societies, deVries and Sameroff (1984) found that each culture's maternal orientation and child-rearing

The difficult infant is slow to adapt to change, is rather intense, and is often irritable and unhappy.

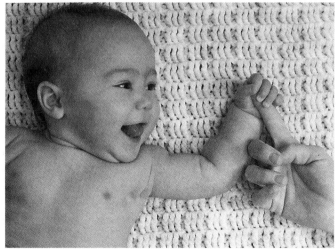

The easy infant reacts with moderation rather than intensity, adapts easily to new situations, exhibits a positive mood, and enjoys being handled.

The slow-to-warm-up child can adapt in a positive manner with repeated exposure to a new or changed situation.

Infants exhibit their individuality by being either cuddlers or noncuddlers. Cuddlers love to cuddle and snuggle. Noncuddlers love to be bounced and swung and they resist restraint. They also tend to develop gross motor skills earlier than cuddlers.

patterns contributed to infants' temperament. Other studies also indicate that temperament is not necessarily inherited. Prenatal care, early infant experiences, and parental expectations and perceptions may be contributors as well. Moliter et al. (1984) noted that maternal anxiety during pregnancy can contribute to difficulties during the newborn period. Also, mothers who expect their newborns to be difficult do, in fact, have difficult babies. Parents' perceptions and "imaginings" of what their baby will be like, prior to the baby's birth or even before fetal movements begin, are remarkably consistent with the actual temperament of the child (Zeanah et al. 1986). Bates (1987) found a link between a child's difficult temperament and negative or deficient mother-child interactions in toddlerhood and later years.

Temperament, therefore, is more of a complex dimension than previously thought. Temperament, whether innate or due to the environment, can directly influence parent and child interaction patterns.

Cuddlers and Noncuddlers

Infants also exhibit their individuality by being either cuddlers or noncuddlers. Even as neonates, babies can be classified in either of these two ways. Although noncuddlers do not like close physical contact such as cuddling, they do not resist all forms of physical contact. For example, the child will not avoid being kissed or having his or her face stroked. Noncuddlers actively enjoy being swung, bounced, danced around, or romped with in any way that involves contact but not restraint. As soon as restraint is applied, they will struggle and resist.

Descriptors of noncuddlers by their mothers include "gets restless when cuddled," "turns face away and begins to struggle," "will not allow it, fights to get away," "gets restless, pushes you away," "wriggles and arches back, and only stops when put down again," "will kick and thrash with his arms, and if you persist will begin to cry." Cuddlers, on the other hand, are described by their mothers in ways such as "cuddles you back," "snuggles into you," "loves it," "would let me cuddle him for hours on end."

Noncuddling is not related to a negative interaction with the caregiver or to the social situation. It appears to be congenital. Apparently the active conduct with the noncuddlers enhances their motor development, since the motor development of noncuddlers is well ahead of cuddlers. For example, milestones such as the ability to sit unsupported, to stand holding on, and to crawl develop considerably sooner in noncuddlers than in cuddlers (Schaffer and Emerson 1973; Greenspan and Greenspan 1985).

Sex Differences

At birth girls are physiologically more mature than boys, and they continue to mature more quickly through puberty. Parents treat their infant girls differently than they do their infant boys. Mothers appear to respond differently to boys and girls at as early as three weeks. Moss (1973) states that these differences are not based on sex-role expectations but on probable physiological differences in maturity; that is, infant boys fuss and cry more and induce their mothers to respond to them more. However, by the time the boys are three months old, the mothers respond less often than before and are less casual or easygoing when they do so.

Moss also found that mothers respond vocally more to their girls' vocalizations than to their boys'. Fathers reverse the pattern; that is, at three to four weeks they verbalize more to girls, and at three months they respond more to boys. Mothers respond more often to their daughters' expressions of pain but tend to ignore similar expressions in their sons (Haviland 1977).

Infant girls and boys differ in other areas as well. For example, at fourteen weeks, girls are more responsive to auditory stimulation (as reinforcement) and boys are more responsive to visual stimulation (Watson 1973). Girls cling more to their mothers, vocalize more, respond less actively to barriers and to toys, and prefer more fine-muscle activities (Goldberg and Lewis 1973). Very nurturing mothers tend to encourage increased dependence in toddler boys and decreased dependence in toddler girls (Frankel and Bates 1990).

Attachment

Attachment to a primary caregiver is essential to the optimal development of an infant. Bowlby (1958, 1973) describes **attachment** as strong affectional ties that bind a person to his or her most intimate companions. Someone who is attached will interact often with, and attempt to maintain proximity to, the person to whom he or she is attached. For example, when an infant is attached to his or her mother, he or she may show the attachment by crying, clinging, following, and so on, to maintain or establish contact with her. The bond established between a mother and father and their infant is a very special attachment. Perhaps the strongest bond in the human species is the parents' attachment to a child. Through this attachment the child develops a sense of himself or herself. The strength and character of this attachment will influence the quality of his or her future bonds to other individuals (Kennell, Voos, and Klaus 1979). Secure toddlers are more enthusiastic, compliant, positive in affect, persistent, and attentive to suggestions from their mothers (Frankel and Bates 1990). Lewis, Feiring, McGuffog, and Jaskir (1984) found that twelve-month-old boys who were insecurely attached had more internal emotional problems than boys who were securely attached. They found that twelve-month-old girls who were insecurely attached had more external emotional problems.

A classic longitudinal study by Schaffer and Emerson (1964) identified four attachment steps and stages. The **asocial state** occurs during the first six weeks of life, when the very young infant lacks the capacity for social interaction. However, favorable reactions can be elicited by social and nonsocial stimuli. At the end of this period, the infant shows a distinct preference for social stimuli, such as a smiling face. The second stage is that of **indiscriminate attachment,** which occurs between six weeks and six to seven months. Infants prefer human company and are likely to protest when an adult puts them down or leaves them alone. Their protests are indiscriminate, that is, they dislike being separated from anyone, whether the person is a stranger or a regular companion. The third stage is that of **specific attachments,** and it occurs at about seven months. The infant protests only when separated from a particular individual, usually the mother. Also, the infant begins to fear strangers at this time, an indication that he or she has formed his or her first genuine attachment. Finally, the infants move into a state of **multiple attachment.** Within weeks after forming their initial attachment, about half of the infants in Schaffer and Emerson's study started becoming attached to other people, such as their father, siblings, grandparents, and consistent babysitters. By eighteen months, very few infants were attached to only one person, while some were attached to five or more close companions.

Attachment
Strong affectional ties that bind a person to his or her most intimate companions.

Asocial state
The stage of attachment that occurs during the first six weeks of life, when the very young infant lacks the capacity for social interaction.

Indiscriminate attachment
The second stage of attachment, which occurs between six weeks and six to seven months of age. Infants prefer human company and are likely to protest when an adult puts them down or leaves them alone.

Specific attachment
The third stage of attachment, which occurs at about seven months of age. The infant protests when separated from a particular individual, usually the mother.

Multiple attachment
The final stage of attachment, when the infant starts becoming attached to people other than the mother, including the father, siblings, grandparents, and consistent babysitters.

The objects of an infant's attachment may serve different functions, so that the infant's preference may depend on the situation and the function. The quality of attachment to the mother is usually independent of the quality of attachment to the father. This independence is thought to be related to differences in interactional style provided by these attachment figures (Bretherton 1985). For example, most infants prefer their fathers for playmates, but prefer their mothers for comfort if they are upset or frightened (Lamb and Stevenson 1978).

Children who were securely attached as infants have more positive interactions with others when they become preschoolers. Waters et al. (1979) found a correlation between children who were securely attached as infants and nursery school success. Toddlers at three and one-half years who had been securely attached at fifteen months were social leaders in the nursery school setting. They often initiated play activities, were generally sensitive to the needs and feelings of other children, and were popular with their peers. They were also described as curious, self-directed, and eager to learn.

Three and one-half year olds who had been insecurely attached at fifteen months were socially and emotionally withdrawn and hesitated to engage other children in play activities. They were also less curious, less interested in learning, and much less forceful in pursuing goals. Matas et al. (1978) and Gove (1983) found that competent functioning in twenty-four-month-olds was related to secure attachment as eighteen-month-olds. Fagot and Kavanaugh (1990) found that insecurely attached eighteen-month-old girls, while involved in play groups, were more difficult to deal with and had poorer relationships with their peers. Sroufe (1983) found that preschoolers who had behavior problems had been classified as insecure during infancy.

These findings support Erikson's theory concerning the importance of developing an early sense of trust in other people. Perhaps securely attached infants become curious problem solvers because they feel comfortable at venturing away from their parents to explore. This enables them to learn how to answer questions and solve problems on their own. On the other hand, the insecure child, who cannot trust his or her caregivers, will have difficulty trusting other people. The insecure child may be less interested in the novel aspects of his or her environment, making it difficult for him or her to explore and preventing him or her from developing the initiative necessary to answer questions and solve problems.

Ainsworth et al. (1978), Belsky et al. (1984), and Cohn and Tronick (1983) found that mothers who respond consistently and appropriately to their infant's social bids and who initiate interactions geared to the capacities, intentions, moods, goals, and developmental level of the child are more likely to have children with secure maternal attachments. Tronick and Gianino (1986) suggest that when mothers are unable to respond to, or miss, their infant's social bid, the infant will feel frustrated and will attempt to restore the interaction. If the infant is successful in restoring the interaction, then he or she will begin to develop interactive skills. However, if the parent consistently fails to respond, the infant will turn to more internal regulatory behaviors for comfort and will develop limited means of soliciting external support. Girls are more likely to show distress if their mother or caregiver does not respond to their social interaction bids and vocalizations (Stoller and Field 1982; Mayes and Carter 1990).

Stranger Anxiety

At around six months an infant realizes that those people who are familiar, such as the mother, are different from others. This infant displays a distressful behavior called **stranger anxiety,** which is a negative reaction to strangers. Symptoms may include wary looks followed by turning away, pulling away, or occasional whimpering and crying. Between six months and three years, a child develops attachment behavior to those he or she interacts with most often, such as the mother or primary caregiver.

Separation Anxiety

Separation anxiety may occur between six months and three years when a child is separated from his or her mother or a primary caregiver over a length of time, such as during a long hospital stay. Periodically it is also manifested in temporary or short-term separations.

Bowlby (1969) identified three stages a child experiences in coping with the absence of the primary caregiver. Take, for example, a hospitalized child who is necessarily separated from his mother. First comes the *protest* stage, which may last from a few hours to a few days. The child cries, shakes the crib, expects the mother to return, exhibits grieving and confusion, and tries to follow the mother if possible. The second stage is *despair.* The crying and the attempt to find the mother stop, which can be dangerously deceptive. In fact, the child's hopelessness increases, and he goes into deep mourning, even though appearing to be happier, easier to manage, and seemingly resigned to the situation. If the mother returns, the protest starts over. The danger here is that some doctors and nurses feel a parent's presence, not absence, causes the problem. Therefore, they think the parent should not visit the child. If the absence of the mother is for several months, the third stage, *denial,* or *detachment,* may occur. At this time the child accepts care from a succession of nurses and is willing to eat and to play with toys. When the mother visits, the child remains apathetic and even turns away, completely ignoring her.

Kennell, Voos, and Klaus (1979) found that children whose primary caregivers remained with them during a long hospital stay showed none of the three stages exhibited by children who were separated. Under normal conditions, children who stay in their own home, and other nonthreatening environments, will gradually learn to separate from the primary caregiver, which is the beginning of establishing independence. Erikson (1963) noted that an infant's first social achievement is to willingly let his or her mother out of sight without being anxious, upset, or angry, because she has become "an inner certainty as well as an outer predictability."

Separation anxiety occurs almost simultaneously with object permanency as described by Piaget. Bell (1970) showed that the development of "person permanence" preceded that of object permanence in the majority of her subjects who had strong maternal attachment, but it lagged in infants with low or ambivalent interest in their mothers.

Children at Risk

Infants who do not develop attachment feelings for a primary caregiver are at risk for not developing normally emotionally and psychologically. Many studies support the developing infant's need for nurturance (Fagot and Kavanaugh 1990; Sroufe 1983; Lewis et al. 1984). In fact, it is critical for optimal development.

A now classic, longitudinal study conducted by Skeels (1966) in Iowa in the 1930s compared two groups of toddlers. One group of thirteen toddlers were placed in an institution for mentally retarded young women. Their IQs were

Stranger anxiety
A distressful behavior in which an infant reacts negatively to strangers.

Separation anxiety
A distressful behavior that occurs when a child is separated from a parent or significant caregiver. Separation anxiety is prominent between six months and three years of age.

If children are raised in institutional environments that provide little nurturing, their intellectual and psychological development can be impaired. This picture shows a child care center in Germany during the 1920s.

assessed at between 35 and 85 and their average age was 19.4 months. Twelve children functioned as a contrast group and were left in an orphanage. Their IQs were assessed between 81 and 103 and their average age was 16.6 months. At the end of the first two and one-half years, the children in the institution for mentally retarded women had gained an average of 28.5 IQ points; all were considered adoptable. Those children who had been left in the orphanage lost an average of 26.2 IQ points by the end of the first two and one-half years.

Twenty-one years later, all of the original subjects were located. All of those who had been in the institution for the mentally retarded were self-supporting; all had graduated from high school; four had gone to college, and one had a bachelor's degree and was doing graduate work; eleven were married; nine had children; all had incomes comparable with the national average. Of those who had been left in the orphanage, one had died as an adolescent in a public institution for the mentally retarded; three were in wards for the mentally retarded; one was in a mental institution; two were married, one with a mentally retarded child and the other with four children; the median completed educational level was third grade. The man who had the four children had consistently been an exceptional case when compared with the others in the contrast group. Because he had a hearing loss, the orphanage officials had felt that he should receive more individual attention and appropriate instruction at a school for the deaf. He was transferred there when he was eight years old. While there he had the added advantage that the matron in his cottage took a special interest in him because he was one of the youngest children and had no family. As an adult he not only had a good job but had a salary above the national average (as well as above the mean of the experimental group) (Skeels 1966).

In another now classic study, in the 1940s, Spitz (1949) compared two groups of institutionalized children. He gave both groups tests that measured perceptual ability, body mastery, social relations, memory, relations to inanimate objects, and intelligence. One group of children were from a foundling home and had an average IQ of 124. The second group of children were from a jail nursery and had an average IQ of 101.5. By the end of the first year, the

TABLE 6.1 EXPERIMENTAL AND CONTRAST GROUPS: OCCUPATIONS OF SUBJECTS AND SPOUSES

CASE NO.	SUBJECT'S OCCUPATION	SPOUSE'S OCCUPATION	FEMALE SUBJECT'S OCCUPATION PREVIOUS TO MARRIAGE
EXPERIMENTAL GROUP			
1.[a]	Staff sergeant	Dental technician	
2	Housewife	Laborer	Nurses' aide
3	Housewife	Mechanic	Elementary school teacher
4	Nursing instructor	Unemployed	Registered nurse
5	Housewife	Semiskilled laborer	No work history
6	Waitress	Mechanic, semiskilled	Beauty operator
7	Housewife	Flight engineer	Dining room hostess
8	Housewife	Foreman, construction	No work history
9	Domestic service	Unmarried	
10[a]	Real estate sales	Housewife	
11[a,b]	Vocational counselor	Advertising copy writer	
12[c]	Gift shop sales	Unmarried	
13	Housewife	Pressman-printer	Office-clerical
CONTRAST GROUP			
14	Institutional inmate	Unmarried	
15	Dishwasher	Unmarried	
16	Deceased		
17[a]	Dishwasher	Unmarried	
18[a]	Institutional inmate	Unmarried	
19[a]	Compositor and typesetter	Housewife	
20[a]	Institutional inmate	Unmarried	
21[a]	Dishwasher	Unmarried	
22[a]	Floater	Divorced	
23	Cafeteria (part-time)	Unmarried	
24[a]	Institutional gardener's assistant	Unmarried	
25[a]	Institutional inmate	Unmarried	

[a]Male.
[b]B.A. degree.
[c]Previously had worked as a licensed practical nurse
Source: Skeels 1966.

children in the foundling home had an IQ drop to an average of 72. One-fourth of the infants had died. Of those eighteen months to two and one-half years old, only two out of twenty-six could walk, and hardly any could eat by themselves or say a few words. However, those infants in the jail nursery had a rise in IQ to an average of 105. None of them had died. At eight to twelve months they could not be held down. Because of their active climbing and walking, their cribs had to be built higher, and they had to be given more floor space. Their mothers were allowed to care for them and, in turn, provided the essential nurturing the children needed to thrive.

Both of these studies illustrate the necessity of providing nurturing care to young children for their survival. The mentally retarded women provided an excessive amount of nurturing to the babies in the Skeels study, while the children in the orphanage received only the minimal necessities of food, clothing, medical care, and shelter. The children in the foundling home in Spitz's study also received only the basic necessities, whereas the children in the jail nursery thrived under their own mothers' nurturing care.

Clearly, prolonged social and sensory deprivation can have a number of adverse effects on the developing child. However, many studies present evidence that socially deprived infants can recover from their handicaps if they are placed in homes where they receive individualized attention from affectionate and responsive caregivers. For example, a study by Dennis (1973) compared the development of two groups of children who lived in an understaffed Lebanese institution. One group of children were adopted into good homes prior to their second birthdays. Although their developmental quotients were in the mentally retarded range at the time of the adoptions, they attained average IQ scores after spending several years in stimulating home environments. The children who remained in the institution until adulthood continued to score in the mentally retarded range on all intelligence tests.

Clark and Hanisee's (1982) study of a group of Asian children also illustrates the potential of recovery from adverse circumstances. As preschoolers the Asian children were adopted by highly educated and relatively affluent American parents. The adoptees had been separated from their biological parents as infants and had lived in institutions, foster homes, or hospital settings during their infancy and part of their preschool years, prior to coming to the United States. Many were war orphans who had early histories of malnutrition or serious illness. They made remarkable progress. The Asian adoptees scored significantly above average on standardized intelligence tests and assessments of social maturity after only two to three years in their stimulating adoptive homes.

Children adopted from impoverished environments by American families scored significantly above average on standardized intelligence tests and assessments of social maturity after only two or three years in their adoptive homes.

It is rather clear that the longer infants suffer from social and sensory deprivation, the more their development is hampered. However, humans have shown a strong capacity for recovery and may overcome many of their initial difficulties if placed in settings where they can receive ample amounts of individualized attention from concerned and attentive caregivers.

Child Abuse

Child abuse is defined differently in the various parts of the country. However, traditionally a broad definition of child abuse is *a child under eighteen years of age who suffers nonaccidental serious physical or mental injury, sexual abuse or exploitation, and/or serious physical or emotional neglect caused by the acts or omissions of the child's parents or guardians or others responsible for his or her care or welfare.* Child abuse crosses all socioeconomic levels, ages, and religious and ethnic lines. It is a very complex problem that cannot be reduced to a single cause. Abuse is not a single isolated event but instead represents an overall pattern of care.

Although children can be neglected or abused at any age, abused children are more likely to be toddlers under three years of age, with an equal number being boys and girls (Garbarino and Gilliam 1980).

Child neglect and abuse can have some very negative long-term consequences. When physical neglect occurs—that is, when the basic needs of food, warmth, cleanliness, and so on, are not met—it produces a lack of competence in dealing with the world (Egeland and Sroufe 1981; Schneider-Rosen and Cicchetti 1984). Emotional unavailability of the parent (often connected with depression in the parent) is related to a marked decline in the functioning of the child, leading to apathetic behavior, a lack of joy or pleasure, and to being easily frustrated and upset (Egeland and Sroufe 1981). Physical abuse and emotional unavailability promote behavioral and emotional problems such as avoidant attachment relationships (Egeland and Sroufe 1981; Schneider-Rosen and Cicchetti 1984), aggressiveness (George and Main 1979), and blunted emotions (Schneider-Rosen and Cicchetti 1984). Low self-esteem, a sense of apathy, or antisocial behavior may eventually result in criminal acts because abuse prevented the child from developing controls on his or her aggression, anger, and tension (Wolfe 1985).

Main and George (George and Main 1979; Main and Goldwyn 1984; Main and George 1985) compared a group of abused toddlers (one and two years old) and their mothers with a matched group of nonabused children and their mothers. The abused children imitated the destructive behavior of their mothers; that is, they hit, slapped, kicked, and assaulted their playmates more often than the nonabused children. They also assaulted and threatened their caregivers more often than the other children did. They acted aggressively without provocation. Seven out of the ten abused children harassed their caregivers, compared to two out of the ten nonabused children. The abused children avoided friendly overtures from other people by moving away or turning away as another child or caregiver approached them. They would also crawl with head averted toward someone and then suddenly turn away. None of the nonabused children displayed ambivalent behavior in this way. Several of the nonabused toddlers responded to another child's distress by showing sadness, concern, or empathy, while none of the abused children did so. In fact, all but one of the abused children, more than half of the time, responded to another child's crying with fear, anger, or physical abuse.

Children who are likely to be abused are those who, for some reason or another, are difficult to care for. For example, infants who are premature, irritable and fussy, and who have physical defects may add to pressures already faced by an overstressed parent, which in turn may lead to mistreatment (Frodi 1984). There is also a modest relationship between complications of pregnancy or birth and later mistreatment of a child (Brunnquell, Crichton, and Egeland 1981). This is not necessarily a cause-and-effect relationship. Often, mothers who are abusive have received inadequate prenatal care that can result in childbearing complications. Factors that lead to a woman's neglecting her health during pregnancy could also encourage her to neglect her baby later.

Only one in ten abusing parents is seriously mentally disturbed (Kempe and Kempe 1978). One large-scale study (Brunnquell, Crichton, and Egeland 1981; Egeland and Brunnquell 1979) found that first-time mothers who later became abusers differed in two ways from nonabusing women. First, they were less able to cope effectively with the ambivalent and stressful emotions that accompany a first pregnancy. Second, they had significantly less understanding of what is involved in caring for an infant. That is, they had negative reactions to pregnancy and lacked knowledge concerning parent-child relationships. Also, their anxiety and fear increased after the birth of their baby.

Often abusive parents themselves were parented in an environment with models of hostile ways to deal with stress, leaving them with feelings of low self-esteem. Not all people who are abused as children become child abusers, but a strong link exists between being abused as a child and becoming a child abuser (Parke and Collmer 1985; Egeland, Jacobvitz, and Papatola 1987). In other words, at an early age children learn maladaptive responses to pressures involved in child rearing. Thus, child abusers are victims of unusual pressures and stress linked with the lack of opportunity to learn effective coping mechanisms.

Egeland and Brunnquell (1979 and Brunnquell, Crichton, and Egeland (1981) profiled abusive mothers from their study:

	ABUSIVE MOTHERS	NONABUSIVE MOTHERS
PLANNED PREGNANCY	17%	48%
ATTENDED CHILDBIRTH CLASSES	30%	100%
PREPARED LIVING QUARTERS (e.g., ARRANGED FOR INFANT'S PLACE TO SLEEP)	29%	88%
HAD REALISTIC EXPECTATIONS ABOUT RAISING AN INFANT	18%	90%

Mothers who are young, poor, and have problems feeding their babies are at risk of abusing or neglecting them. These mothers have difficulty interpreting their infants' emotional expressions. Butterfield (1986) found that at-risk mothers were more likely to see their infants as expressing fear and interest.

Azar et al. (1984) found that mothers who abused their children had unrealistic expectations of how their children should behave and expected them to do more than they were capable of doing. The mothers also had poor problem-solving skills in child-rearing situations; that is, they were unable to find alternative solutions in dealing with child-rearing problems. Pruitt and Erickson (1983) found that child abusers were reactive and emotional, had personal problems, and had ineffective coping and problem-solving skills. Other characteristics of child abusers include higher levels of apprehension, tension, and anxiety, plus a lower level of stability (Robertson, Gold, and Milner 1984).

Social support is a good preventative for child abuse and neglect. The principal caregiver needs support from other adults. Less than half of the mothers who are abusers have adequate support from others, while virtually all of the mothers who are nonabusers have support (Brunnquell, Crichton, and Egeland 1981; Egeland and Brunnquell 1979). Also, mothers who themselves were abused are less likely to abuse their children if they have social support (Crockenberg 1986; Egeland, Jacobvitz, and Papatola 1987).

Intervention programs that work provide at-risk parents with educational and emotional support that helps them cope with rearing a child in a stressful environment. Parents Anonymous groups have been successful in providing support networks.

Parent-infant Interaction Patterns

The way parents interact with their infants can determine the degree of self-esteem found in their infants. In Coopersmith's (1967) classic study on self-esteem, he found that mothers who were emotionally stable and had high self-esteem tended to have children with high self-esteem. He speculates that such women tend to marry men with high self-esteem. These parents are comfortable with age-appropriate independence in their children. They enforce well-defined limits of behavior. They are affectionate, approving, and accepting of their children for who they are, but they do not hesitate to disapprove of unacceptable behavior. They tend to use positive techniques of behavior modification; that is, acceptable behavior is rewarded by praise and approval, whereas unacceptable behavior is punished by such techniques as restraining the child, denying activities or privileges, or separating the child from others. (On the other hand, children with low self-esteem are often disciplined with negative methods of control, which emphasize force and withdrawal of love. Children with low self-esteem usually harbor feelings of guilt, shame, and defensiveness, and they have difficulty in giving or receiving love.)

The interaction of the infant with his or her parents can contribute to the cognitive development of the infant. Infants of mentally retarded women are at risk in developing full cognitive potential. Feldman et al. (1986) found that two-year-old children of mentally retarded mothers (IQ of 69) were at risk for developmental delay, particularly in language. In the study, a child's cognitive development significantly correlated with whether the mother had previously had a child removed from the home by child protection authorities. A mother who had previously had a child taken away was less likely to foster cognitive development in her present child. The children of mothers who were involved, responsive, restrictive, and punishing had higher Bayley Mental Development Index scores than the children of mothers who showed less overall interest.

KANSAS CITY, Mo.—The boy said his parents had burned him with cigarettes; his mother said he had done it himself and made up a story of child abuse to tell his counselors at school.

Human Development in the News: Program Aids Families in Abuse Crisis

KENDALL J. WILLS

KANSAS CITY, Mo.—The boy said his parents had burned him with cigarettes; his mother said he had done it himself and made up a story of child abuse to tell his counselors at school.

In the past, a social worker would have put the boy in a foster home immediately, then tried to figure out who was to blame later.

But under a pioneering state program, the first-grader stayed with his parents while social workers began monitoring his family 24 hours a day for six weeks.

"In six weeks, you can reverse the risk to the child, stabilize the situation and get the family back on the right track," said Gary Stangler, director of the state Department of Social Services. "Our priority is, first, the preservation of the family."

More than 13,000 children in Missouri, and 330,000 nationwide, are removed from their homes each year because of abuse, neglect or abandonment.

Family preservation programs are under review in more than 20 states, but only two—Missouri and Michigan—are close to implementing them statewide.

Experts said the program does have its risks, particularly when children are left in potentially violent situations.

"There will come a time that a child will die when the kid is receiving family preservation services. But we always want to err on the side of safety for the child," said Phyllis Rozansky, executive director of Citizens for Missouri's Children, a non-profit organization that supports and monitors the family preservation program.

Its advocates argue that separation itself causes psychological problems and does not get to the root of the problems that led to the abuse.

"You cannot underestimate the trauma a child suffers from being separated from the family," Stangler said.

Officials said the program, started two years ago with seed money from the New York-based Edna McConnell Clark Foundation, could divert one-third of all foster care cases in Missouri when it is in place statewide by the end of next year.

Kendall J. Wills, "Program aids families in abuse crisis," *Lansing State Journal*, June 23, 1991.

Turner (1980) noted that an infant gains a sense of mastery and competence by accomplishing something as simple as shaking a rattle and creating a noise. When the infant has the opportunity to feel competent in this way, he or she is motivated to interact with the people and objects he or she encounters, thus acquiring knowledge. When an infant is not allowed these opportunities to exert influence over the environment, he or she develops a sense of helplessness rather than a sense of competence. The infant will also believe that he or she cannot do much to change his or her circumstances. When an infant feels this helpless he or she will no longer attempt to interact with the environment and will lose his or her motivation to learn.

Mothers' interactions with their infants can be influenced by the gender of their infants (Carter, Mayes, and Pajer 1990). Malatesta (1982) found sex differences in maternal affective responses to infants' affective displays. Mothers tend to respond more positively to their sons' positive bids during play interactions than to similar displays by their daughters. Tronick and Cohn (1989) found that mothers are more likely to be in synchrony with their infant sons' moods than with their infant daughters'. Bayley (1973a) found, in her longitudinal study, that boys' scores on behavior and intelligence throughout an eighteen-year span correlated with the quality of maternal behavior in the first three years. Boys were more permanently affected by the emotional climate in infancy, whether it was one of warmth and understanding or of punitive rejection. Girls were more resilient and were not as affected by the emotional climate generated by maternal behavior.

An interest in the role of the father and his relationship with his infant has surfaced in recent years. Parke and O'Leary (1976) found that fathers are as interested in caring for their infants as mothers are, and fathers are as competent in providing care if given the opportunity to do so. However, if a man does not feel skilled in child care, he will become less involved with his infant (McHale and Huston 1984).

Fathers are more likely to participate in the care of their infants if their wives are employed outside of the home. However, they are more likely to be involved in play activities with their infants than in providing direct care for them (Pleck 1985; Darling-Fisher and Tiedje 1990). The spouses of professional women who work full-time are more involved in child-care activities than the spouses of women who work part-time and the spouses of full-time homemakers. Women are still the primary caregivers regardless of their employment status (Darling-Fisher and Tiedje 1990).

The gender of the infant can influence the amount of caregiving by the father. Fathers of boys are more involved in caregiving with their infants than are fathers of girls (Hawkins and Belsky 1989). Snow, Jacklin, and Maccoby (1983) found that interactions between the fathers and their infant sons and between fathers and their infant daughters were different in tone. Fathers of sons used more verbal and physical prohibitions than fathers of daughters. Also, sons were more likely to evoke their fathers' prohibitions by their behavior. Perhaps fathers expect their sons to be more difficult to care for, so their expectations influence their perceptions.

Parke and Sawin (1980, 1981) found that fathers were more likely to be affectionate toward their daughters than toward their sons. For mothers, the reverse was true. However, parents were more likely to attend to and stimulate newborns of the same sex as themselves. For example, mothers showed toys to their daughters more often than to sons, while fathers did the reverse. The fact that there are different interaction patterns emphasizes the idea that mothers and fathers play different roles in child development. The roles become complementary rather than redundant, suggesting that the absence of one parent during any period of development may be detrimental to the child.

The father not only influences the infant directly through interactions with the infant but also indirectly influences the behavior of the mother with the infant (Parke 1979). The presence of the father seems to affect the behavior of the mother toward the infant. When the father is present, the mother shows more interest in the infant and does more smiling and cuddling than when the father is not there.

Stylistic differences have been found in mothers' and fathers' play with infants. Lamb (1977a) studied a group of infants at seven and eight months and again at twelve and thirteen months. He found that fathers engage in more physical, rough-and-tumble play and unusual play activities than mothers do. Lamb (1977b) found similar results in home observations of a different group of infants at fifteen, eighteen, twenty-one, and twenty-four months of age. Fathers played more physical games and engaged in more parallel play (play with similar toys) with their infants. Mothers engaged in more conventional play activities (for example, peekaboo and pat-a-cake), stimulus toy play (jiggling or operating a toy to stimulate the child directly), and reading (Lamb 1977b). Fathers, therefore, are tactile and physical, while mothers tend to be verbal. Infants do not experience simply more stimulation from their fathers but a qualitatively different stimulatory pattern (Lamb 1984).

Infants in Child-care Centers

Two trends have necessitated the contemporary interest in infant day care: the need for both parents to work full-time and the increase in single-parent households. More women are, therefore, in the work place, and they must find suitable care for their infants. If present trends continue, by the year 2000, four out of five infants under one year will have a mother working outside of the home (Children's Defense Fund 1989).

Two major aspects of infant caregiving influence the quality of care: the social environment and the physical environment. In view of the research that emphasizes how extremely important human interactions are in infant development, it follows that caregivers must be highly competent in interpersonal skills in order to provide quality care. Infants need to form a satisfying and secure relationship with a few consistent caregivers before they can cope with or benefit from a large number of children and adults. Most studies concerning infant day care have concentrated on infants' intellectual, emotional, and social development. High-quality day care appears to have a positive effect on cognitive development, especially for those infants who are at risk (Breitmayer and Ramey 1986).

Most of the research on emotional development focuses on attachment between the mother and the infant or toddler. Findings in this area are not clear-cut. Owen et al. (1984) found no differences in the attachment of day-care and mother-care infants. However, recent evidence indicates that in some instances, day care during the first year of life may negatively affect the infant-mother attachment and subsequent social development. Belsky (1988) found that infants involved with day care extensively (more than twenty hours per week) were more likely to show insecure attachment as infants and heightened aggressiveness and noncompliance during the preschool and early school-age years. Such risk can be moderated by above average day-care quality; the child's age, sex, and temperament; fewer hours of separation from the mother; overstimulation by the mother; and a positive attitude by the mother toward her work status. Clarke-Stewart (1988), on the other hand, states that the most promising factors to be used in accounting for differences in day-care infants' emotional development are the mother's expressing a positive attitude toward the infant, her emotional accessibility, and her desire for independence (her own and her infant's).

Although more time away from the parents may increase the risk of an insecure relationship with the mother (Belsky 1988), more time in the day-care center appears to promote a secure relationship between the infant and the caregiver. Infant-caregiver attachments appear to be independent of infant-mother and infant-father attachments (Goossens and vanIJzendoorn 1990). Strayer and Moss (1987) and Weinraub, Jaeger, and Hoffman (1988) found no differences in the attachment security of infants of employed and nonemployed mothers.

Consistent, nurturant caregivers are the most important variables in a high-quality infant-care facility. Positive relationships between infants and their caregivers may even compensate for insecure maternal attachments (Howes et al. 1988; Oppenheim et al. 1988; vanIJzendoorn and Tavecchio 1987; Goossens and vanIJzendoorn 1990). Trust and attachment can be established only if contact with the same caregivers is frequent and regular and there is predictability in the caregiving arrangement. Daily routines, such as feeding, diapering, nap time, and so on, can aid in developing intimate relationships with the infants. Social and learning skills can come out of these daily routines when the infants are encouraged to initiate interactions as well as to be responsive to people and things in the environment. Infants and toddlers with responsive and sensitive caregivers have higher cognitive and language scores and are more socially competent (Carew 1980; Rubenstein and Howes 1983).

Although the social environment is key to the development of infants, the physical environment can also be of importance by influencing the social interactions between infants and adults. The physical environment should include variety, complexity, and responsiveness of play materials. Also within this environment, the amount of time for exploratory play must be considered. The optimal play environment should include an open playroom equipped with a variety of play areas and toys. The toys should be visible and accessible to the children and should be placed on low, open shelves. Toys should be matched with the infants' developmental levels in order to encourage and extend play. Play materials should be responsive to the infants' actions, with the response being perceptible to the infants. For example, toys that make a sound when they move should have the sound-making parts visible. A baby's banging two pots together has more exploratory significance than an electronic toy that flashes bright lights when the baby pushes a button.

If infants are provided with nurturant, high-quality daycare, they will not suffer from emotional or social deficits.

Stability and order in the infants' physical environment allow them to build up experiences and make sense out of those experiences. Having the same toys, cribs, and basic routines each day allows infants the opportunity for mastery and for building new competencies on ones they have already established. Infants will feel more significant in their world if their caregivers believe learning is important and if the caregivers support efforts by the infants to make sense out of their world (Honig 1981; Caruso 1984).

The fact that infants are in group settings is not an issue; rather, the conditions that exist in these settings and within the infants' families are the issue. Howes and her colleagues (Howes and Olenick 1986; Howes and Stewart 1987) found that infants and toddlers who were enrolled in high-quality child-care arrangements and had families who were low in stress and high in social support and used developmentally appropriate child-rearing practices were more socially competent than home-care infants and infants with poor child-care environments. These same children were better able to adjust to the first grade than their counterparts (Howes 1988). A Swedish study by Andersson (1989) found that eight-year-old children who started in day care during their first year of life rated more favorably and performed better on aptitude tests, school performance, and social and personal development than children who entered day care later or were home-care children.

In short, as long as infants are cared for in high-quality day-care environments, where they receive nurturant and appropriate care, they will not suffer from emotional and social deficits.

The infant and toddler years are important for social and emotional development. It is during this period of time that children form their first attachments to their caregivers. These attachments form a base for the children's self-worth and social relationships. The security of an attachment is related to the caregiver's ability to be responsive and sensitive to the child, whether the caregiver is the child's parent or a child-care worker.

Is Day Care Harmful to Infants?

In 1989 there were five million infants and toddlers who needed day care (Children's Defense Fund 1989). Many parents who would like to stay home with their infants are unable to do so. The economic risk is too high. As yet the United States does not have a parental leave policy that guarantees a leave of absence and job security when the parent returns to work. Because there is no protection, parents are in need of quality care for their infants and toddlers.

Infant day care has been a controversial issue in the United States for several years. Parents and child development experts agree that quality infant day care is a necessity for the optimum development of the child. How can quality be determined? Who is responsible to make sure infant day-care centers are of good quality? Parents, teachers, the state, or the federal government?

Should the United States have a national policy for infant day care? If so, what should it be? What do you think of unpaid parental leave (after the birth or adoption of a baby, a parent stays home with the baby for six months to one year, without fear of losing his or her job)?

If single parents or dual-earner families need day care for their infants, what should they do? How is day care beneficial to the infant? When is it detrimental? What would you do if you had an infant and were a single parent or if both you and your spouse had to work outside the home?

SUMMARY

• Two theories of personality development were presented in this chapter: (1) Erikson's psychosocial theory, including the first two stages, trust versus mistrust and autonomy versus shame and doubt, and (2) social learning theory, which stresses the impact and interaction of environment on behavior and personality.

• Individual differences in the personalities of infants are related to temperament (which includes easy, difficult, and slow-to-warm-up babies), whether an infant likes to be cuddled or not, and the sex of the infant.

• An infant's attachment to a primary caregiver is essential for the infant's optimal development. The four attachment stages are the asocial state, indiscriminate attachment, specific attachment, and multiple attachment. Stranger anxiety and separation anxiety are indicators that an infant has established an attachment relationship. Children who are not given the opportunity to establish an attachment relationship with nurturing human beings are at risk in their personality development.

• Child abuse crosses all socioeconomic levels, ages, and religious and ethnic lines. Abused children are more likely to be toddlers under three years of age. Also, children who are difficult to care for may add to pressures already faced by overstressed parents, and thus these children may become the subjects of abuse. Child abuse is a very complex problem that cannot be reduced to one single cause. Abuse is not a single isolated event but instead represents an overall pattern of care. The consequences of child abuse can be devastating and long-reaching. Also, children who are difficult to care for may add to pressures already faced by overstressed parents, and thus these children may become the subjects of abuse. Social support is a good preventative to child abuse. Parents Anonymous groups have been successful in providing support networks.

• The self-esteem of parents can influence how they interact with their infants. Mothers and fathers interact differently with their male infants and female infants. Fathers' play with infants tends to be more tactile and physical, while mothers' play tends to be more verbal.

- Infant child care has become a major focus in contemporary society due to more dual-earner families and the increase in the number of single parents. Most studies concerning infant day care concentrate on the infants' intellectual, social, and emotional development.

READINGS

Adams, P. L., Milner, J. R., and Schrepf, N A. (1984). *Fatherless children*. New York: John Wiley.
The impact of father absence on children.

Bowlby, J. (1982). *Attachment and loss (Vol. 1)*. New York: Basic Books.
Discussion of mother-infant interaction with an emphasis on attachment.

Kaye, K. (1982). *The mental and social life of babies: How parents create persons*. Chicago: University of Chicago Press.
Original theory of roles of mothers and infants in their face-to-face interactions.

Kemp, R. S. and Kempe, C. H. (1985). *Child abuse*. 8th ed., Cambridge, Mass.: Harvard University Press.
Focus on treatment and prevention of child abuse with discussions on neglect and sexual abuse.

Klaus, M. H. and Kennell, J. H. (1983). *Bonding: The beginnings of parent-infant attachment* (revised edition). St. Louis: C. V. Mosby.
Views and supports the critical period explanation of mother-infant bonding.

Scarr, S. (1985). *Mother care/Other care*. New York: Warner Books.
Examines historical and contemporary view of motherhood and advantages and disadvantages of day care. Correlates the developmental needs of infants and young children and the choice of child care.

Stern, D. (1985). *The first relationship*. 4th ed., Cambridge, Mass.: Harvard University Press.
Research and practical application of mother-infant interaction. Appraisal of what is known and not known about parent-child relationships.

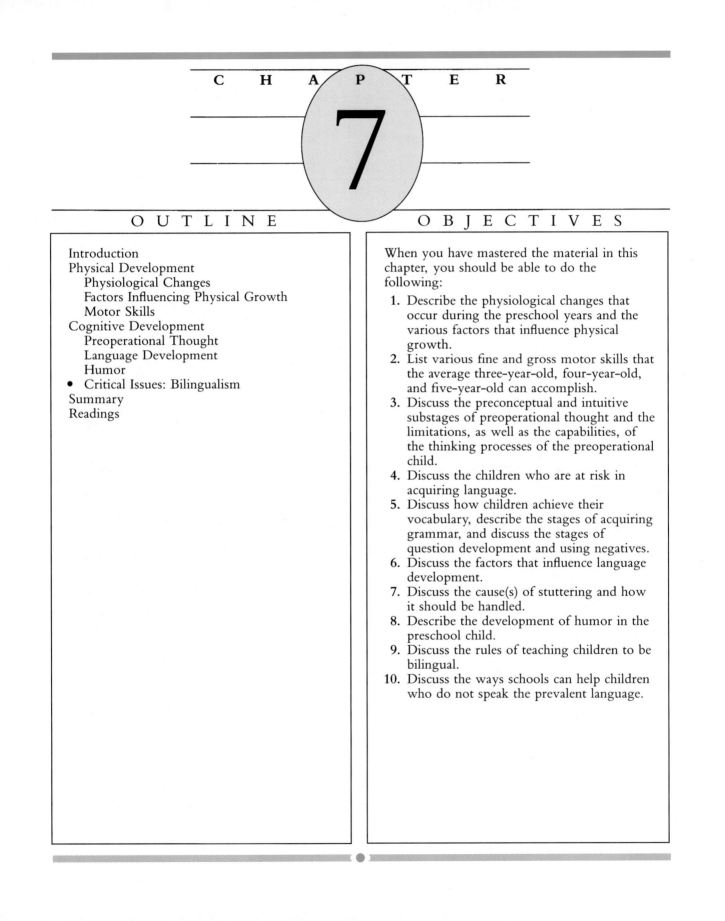

C H A P T E R

7

O B J E C T I V E S

When you have mastered the material in this chapter, you should be able to do the following:

1. Describe the physiological changes that occur during the preschool years and the various factors that influence physical growth.
2. List various fine and gross motor skills that the average three-year-old, four-year-old, and five-year-old can accomplish.
3. Discuss the preconceptual and intuitive substages of preoperational thought and the limitations, as well as the capabilities, of the thinking processes of the preoperational child.
4. Discuss the children who are at risk in acquiring language.
5. Discuss how children achieve their vocabulary, describe the stages of acquiring grammar, and discuss the stages of question development and using negatives.
6. Discuss the factors that influence language development.
7. Discuss the cause(s) of stuttering and how it should be handled.
8. Describe the development of humor in the preschool child.
9. Discuss the rules of teaching children to be bilingual.
10. Discuss the ways schools can help children who do not speak the prevalent language.

The Exploring Years: Preschoolers' Physical and Cognitive Development

• INTRODUCTION

The preschool years, approximately ages two and one-half to five years, are probably the most charming in human development. It is during these years that children change from rounded, fat infants to well-proportioned children. Their language and cognitive skills accelerate rapidly. The limitations in their thinking processes allow them to perceive the world from a dimension different from that of adults, which makes them even more endearing. They are curious about their world and amaze adults by their questions. Their motor skills advance from awkwardly attempting to maneuver a three-wheeler to becoming a sophisticated jockey on a two-wheeler. They become socialized into the larger world. Their personality development and language development expand immensely. Their conception of themselves becomes stronger, and they identify themselves now in terms of gender. All aspects of development—physical, cognitive, social, and emotional—intertwine to make these youngsters unique individuals.

• PHYSICAL DEVELOPMENT

Physical development during the preschool years slows down markedly compared with physical development during infancy. But preschoolers' bodies still grow steadily taller and stronger, making it possible for them to run faster and reach higher with each passing year. Specifically, from ages two through six, children gain about four and a half pounds and add almost three inches per year (Johnston 1986). A growing child's bodily structure partially determines or influences his or her skills and aptitudes. Muscle and brain cell development that occurs during this time is crucial to learning. **Body image,** that is, the way individuals see themselves and how they feel about their own bodies, influences preschoolers' social interactions.

Body image
How individuals perceive themselves, especially their bodies.

Preschoolers' motor skills advance from being able to awkwardly maneuver a three-wheeler to becoming a sophisticated jockey on a two-wheeler.

Physiological Changes

Physical changes proceed in a predictable pattern during the early childhood years if the environmental conditions are adequate and no congenital problems are present.

Body Proportion

The most noticeable physiological change is in body proportion, which is brought about by different rates of growth in different parts of the body. Head growth is the slowest, followed by trunk growth. The limbs grow most rapidly. The top-heavy two-year-old, whose head is one-fourth of his or her total height, will become the five-year-old, whose head is one-sixth of his or her total height, a proportion which is much more adultlike. The change in body proportion influences a child's performance of motor tasks, because as children become less top-heavy, they can better balance their body. Also, longer limbs lead to greater proficiency in a wide variety of activities. Most preschoolers have an abdomen that is large compared with the rest of their body. This is because a relatively short trunk has to accommodate internal organs that are close to adult size (Johnston 1986).

Bones

The preschool child still has a fair amount of cartilage in the skeletal system, and there is less density of minerals in the bones than in those of older children and adults. The joints are more flexible. The ligaments and muscles are not as strongly attached as in the older child. Thus, it is easier to damage young bones, joints, and muscles by pressure and pulling and by infection (Roche 1986).

Height and Weight

The growth in height and weight during early childhood is not as fast as during infancy, and it approaches a nearly linear rate of increase throughout the preschool years. Boys and girls of this age differ little in their height and weight (Seidel et al. 1987; Johnston 1986).

Brain

The brain is more nearly complete in early childhood than the rest of the child's body, attaining approximately 75 percent of its adult weight by the age of three and approximately 90 percent of its adult weight by the age of six. During this time, connections between brain cells increase steadily in size, num-

Most preschoolers have a "potbelly," that is, their abdomens are large compared to the rest of their bodies. This is because a relatively short trunk has to accommodate internal organs that are close to adult size.

TABLE 7.1 Height and Weight Chart (inches and pounds)

| AGE | BOYS | | GIRLS | |
	HEIGHT	WEIGHT	HEIGHT	WEIGHT
3	38	32¼	37¾	31¾
4	40¼	36½	40½	36¼
5	43¼	41½	43	41
6	46	48	46	47

Source: (Lowrey, 1986)

ber, and complexity (Tanner 1978; Trevarthen 1986). Brain-wave rhythms also change. The slower delta waves of infancy decrease and the faster theta waves dominate during the preschool years. Theta waves are associated with emotions, particularly with frustration, and they coincide with the onset of temper tantrums. Still faster waves called alpha waves begin to emerge at age five (Dreyfus-Brisac 1986).

Digestive System

From four to six years, a child's stomach has less than half the capacity of an adult's. Because the rate of growth during early childhood is slower than during infancy, the child has a smaller appetite. The gastrointestinal difficulties common during infancy are no longer a problem during the preschool years (Endres and Rockwell 1980).

Taste buds are more generously distributed in the young child than in the adult. They are scattered on the insides of the cheeks and throat as well as on the tongue, which makes preschoolers more sensitive to taste (Korslund 1962).

Ears

The preschooler's ears are more susceptible to infection than an older child's. The eustachian tube, which connects the throat and middle ear, is wider, shorter, and more horizontal, thus providing an easier route for organisms to travel from throat to ear. When a preschooler is ill, his or her temperature does not usually go as high as it did in infancy, because he or she is physiologically more stable (Behrman and Vaughn 1982).

Teeth

Between six months and thirty months, most children gain a full set of twenty primary, or deciduous, teeth (Demirjian 1986). A study with French Canadian children (Tanguay et al. 1984) found that boys had a full set of de-

From four to six years, a child's stomach has less than half the capacity of an adult's. Because the rate of growth during early childhood is slower than during infancy, the child has a smaller appetite.

ciduous teeth one month before girls. However, there was no difference between boys and girls in when the first primary molar erupted. There are a variety of differences between different racial and ethnic groups concerning the emergence of various deciduous teeth; however, almost all children have completed the eruption of their deciduous teeth by the time they are thirty months old (Demirjian 1986). Between six and seven years, these teeth begin coming out, starting with the lower central incisors. Then the first permanent tooth—the six-year, or first, molar—erupts (Tanner 1978; Demirjian 1986).

Eyes

The retina in the eyes is not completely developed until six years, and the eyeballs do not reach adult size until twelve or fourteen years. The young child is often farsighted because of the shape of the eyeballs (Trevarthen 1986).

The normal visual acuity in young children is as follows:

AGE	VISUAL ACUITY
3	20/50
4	20/40
5	20/30
6	20/20

Source: Sprague 1983.

Physical Characteristics and Personality Development

Physique, or body build, can influence the personality of the child directly and indirectly. As a direct influence, physique determines what a child can and cannot do. Indirectly, it determines how a child feels about his or her own body. This, in turn, is influenced by how significant others view the child's body. Children who are markedly overweight may not be affected by their obesity until they are made aware that other people may think overweight is ugly. If respect and prestige are associated with being tall, it favorably affects the self-concepts of those who are taller. Every cultural group has developed standards of what is considered appropriate for boys and girls. Extremes are regarded as undesirable.

Early in life children are made aware of any marked deviation from the group norm, because of the effect on social relationships. Being different makes children feel inferior, which in turn affects their personalities. Children who are obviously different in physique from their peers often develop some compensatory behavior such as showing off or clowning, which leads to unfavorable reactions from their peers.

Sleep

Sleep is important for preschoolers because of its protective function, allowing for repair and recovery of tissues after activity. Sleep enables cognition to be more adequate and emotional life to be more positive. As children mature, they sleep less. The average total hours of sleep at two to three years is almost twelve hours; and at ages three to five, about eleven hours. During the second year, a common pattern is two naps a day and an all-night sleep. One nap is more common between two and five years. And after that, no nap. A practical way to judge whether children are getting enough sleep is to use criteria such as

Sleep is important for preschoolers because of its protective function, allowing for repair and recovery of tissues after activity. Sleep enables cognition to be more adequate and emotional life to be more positive.

readiness to get up in the morning, good appetite, emotional relaxation, cheerfulness, warm skin with good color, bright eyes, good posture, activeness in play, curiosity, and enthusiasm.

Hand Preference

Hand preference is an area in which sex differences, heredity, and cultural factors play a part. Fifteen percent of preschoolers are left-handed, while only 5 to 10 percent of adults are left-handed. Boys are more often left-handed or ambidextrous than girls in our culture. Only 2 percent of children with right-handed parents are left-handed. Forty-two percent of children who have a left-handed parent are left-handed themselves (Piazza 1980). Heredity controls handedness to a considerable degree, but the training of brain-injured children has shown that hand preference can be changed (Trevarthen 1986). Therefore, hand preference can be the result of both heredity and training.

Several theories have emerged as to when and how hand preference emerges. Some theorize that handedness is evident in the tonic neck reflex position of the newborn. This asymmetrical position supposedly predicts which hand the child will later prefer, because the arm he or she extends reflexively is likely to be on the dominant side. Or some feel that hand preference can be observed when the infant begins to swipe at objects. Yet many studies have found that a child will change hand preference many times and will use both hands during certain periods in infancy and early childhood. Lateral and hand preference develop with age (Coren et al. 1981; Kinsbourne and Hiscock 1983). However, between four and six years, hand preference is rather well established.

Children who do not establish a hand preference are at a disadvantage. Tan (1985) found that four-year-olds who lacked a definite hand preference obtained significantly lower scores on tests for fine motor skills. Tan also found that children who establish handedness early are better coordinated than those children who might establish it later or not at all. Girls are more likely than boys to have a definite hand preference. Gottfried and Bathhurst (1983) found that consistency of hand preference was indicative of higher intellectual capabilities in girls under four years but not in males of the same age.

Factors Influencing Physical Growth

Normal physical development covers a wide range. Several factors that influence physical growth help to explain individual differences.

Gender

Girls are closer to final physical maturity even at birth and are more resistant to stress than boys. Although boys tend to weigh slightly more than girls, boys have less fat on their bodies than do girls, and boys lose their body fat more quickly (Holiday 1986). Boys are more vulnerable to infections and noninfectious diseases (Tanner 1970). Girls lose their baby teeth earlier than boys do (Demirjian 1986). They continue to develop ahead of boys until they reach physical maturity.

Heredity

Stature, weight, and rate of growth are more alike among identical twins, fraternal twins, and siblings than nonsiblings (Johnston 1986). For example, in one family, rapid growth and early maturation may be predominant, while in another family, growth may be slow and maturation comes later.

Socioeconomic Levels

Living conditions reflect socioeconomic levels. Children from middle and upper socioeconomic groups tend to be larger at all ages. Factors such as sufficient and regular exercise and sleep, proper nutrition, regular eating habits, and periodic checkups are all conducive to optimal physical growth. On the other hand, environmental hazards can prevent a child from achieving his or her genetically determined potential growth. For example, poor nutrition can affect the rate and speed of growth as well as the child's final height (Johnston 1986; Bailey et al. 1986).

Secular Trend

A combination of environmental forces seems to be the cause of the phenomenon known as the **secular trend.** This is the tendency, noted over the past hundred years or more, for children to be larger and heavier at all ages (Van Wieringen 1978). This trend of increased body size, which can be noted right at birth, is probably the greatest between ages two and five. Since 1900, five-year-olds have grown about one to two centimeters (one-half inch) each decade. This is particularly evident in Western Europe and the United States, where environmental conditions have most improved over the years. Even in Japan, five-year-olds have gained three centimeters per decade since 1950. The secular trend generally reflects rapid maturation. In the past, a person's final height was reached at about 25 years; now it is reached at about 18 or 20 years. Adult height has also increased somewhat during the last hundred years.

The secular trend can be attributed to a number of factors, such as greater knowledge about nutrition; fewer vitamin deficiencies; higher protein intake during infancy; immunizations and the use of antibiotics to prevent and control

Secular trend
The tendency, noted over the past hundred years or more, for children to be larger and heavier at all ages.

childhood diseases; and the greater emphasis on outdoor exercise and physical fitness (Roche 1979; Byard and Roche 1984).

Motor Skills

Motor development, motor skills, and body control play significant roles in the overall development of children from two and one-half to five years. A child's motor development, like his or her physical growth, partially determines all of the youngster's skills, aptitudes, and emotions. Parental expectations and attitudes can affect motor development. A positive parental attitude builds self-confidence in the child. On the other hand, an overprotective parental attitude can cause the child to become fearful of many motor activities. A child who pursues activities that are too difficult will become totally discouraged. A child faced with activities in which he or she cannot succeed will eventually become discouraged from trying new things and exploring the environment.

For optimal development, it is necessary for children to have time and space to exercise their motor skills and to build self-confidence about their motor abilities. Motor exploration, activities, and skills are also important for the development of language skills, expressive abilities, independence, social behavior, and concept formation, all of which will encourage cognitive growth.

The development of large muscles, called **gross motor development,** predominantly involves muscles of the neck, back, shoulders, legs, and arms. One reason that preschool children become more fluid in their gross motor activities is that they are losing much of their baby fat, including their protruding tummies. As a result, their center of gravity gradually moves downward, and they become capable of coordinated actions requiring a degree of balance that is impossible for a top-heavy infant or toddler. Gross motor skills include walking, running, jumping, hopping, climbing, throwing, and catching.

The preschool years are a critical time for the development of gross motor skills. If this area is not developed, there is a proficiency barrier during the

Gross motor development
The development of large muscles, which predominantly involves muscles of the neck, back, shoulders, legs, and arms.

The development of large muscles, called gross motor development, predominantly involves muscles of the neck, back, shoulders, legs, and arms. Gross motor skills include climbing, walking, running, jumping, hopping, throwing, and catching.

TABLE 7.2 Motor Skills of Preschool Children

FINE MOTOR

THREE YEARS	FOUR YEARS	FIVE YEARS
• Adept at eating and pouring without spilling.	• Dresses, buttons own clothes, and laces shoes.	• Pencil hold is mature.
• Folds paper vertically and horizontally, but not diagonally, even when shown.	• Holds pencil in adultlike manner.	• Drawings are more easily recognizable.
• Grasp on a pencil is immature, but can copy a circle and draw a straight line.	• Can print letters and draw designs.	• Draws recognizable man and can copy a square or triangle.
• Dressing is still difficult, but can unbutton clothes and put on shoes (though not necessarily on the correct feet).	• Art begins to be representational, and adults can recognize the objects drawn.	• No longer has difficulty with diagonal lines and folds paper into double triangles.
• Builds tower of blocks or makes bridge of three blocks.	• Adept with scissors and can follow cutting line.	• Ties shoes.
	• Folds paper three times, the last making a diagonal fold.	
	• Can saw with a saw.	

GROSS MOTOR

THREE YEARS	FOUR YEARS	FIVE YEARS
• No longer watches feet to avoid obstacles.	• Has a well-developed sense of balance.	• Moves with ease, grace, and abandon due to longer legs and better coordination and balance.
• Balances on one foot for several seconds.	• Gait is very steady, run is smooth, and can make sharp turns and quick stops.	• Skips with both feet and can jump over objects.
• Hops on one foot for several steps.	• Carries a cup without spilling, follows a circular path, and goes down steps with alternating feet.	• Handles a small two-wheeler and may learn to roller-skate.
• Jumps down from low heights.	• Skipping is not perfected; skips on one foot and walks on the other.	• Catching ability is mature; moves to catch a ball and cups hands to receive it.
• Walks and runs on tiptoe.	• Coordinates movements of different parts of the body, making it possible to somersault and swing.	• Throwing shows marked improvement; involves the whole body by taking a step and turning with the throw.
• Throws a ball without losing balance.	• Throws ball overhead with strength.	• Hops on one foot for ten or more steps.
• Runs fairly smoothly, but does not have enough control to stop or turn quickly.		
• Proficient at propelling and steering a wagon or maneuvering a tricycle.		
• Cannot throw a ball precisely because of throwing with the shoulders and elbows rather than the whole body. Faces front rather than turning sideways and does not take a step during the throw.		
• Can roll a ball.		

Source: Cratty 1970; Espenschade and Eckert 1967; Gesell et al. 1940; Smart and Smart 1977.

elementary years in learning complex motor skills. The development of gross motor skills also provides a basis for social skills, which are related to self-esteem and self-confidence.

The development of small muscles, called **fine motor development,** predominantly involves muscles of the fingers, wrists, and ankles. Fine motor skills require the coordination of small movements but not strength. They include

Fine motor development
The development of small muscles, which predominantly involves muscles of the fingers, wrists, and ankles.

The development of small muscles, called fine motor development, predominantly involves muscles of the fingers, wrists, and ankles. Such skills include drawing, buttoning, tying shoelaces, washing hands, eating with silverware, turning a doorknob, and using a zipper.

Expressive movement
The movement of preschoolers that expresses emotions and needs through motor activities, and curiosity by direct involvement.

Instrumental movement
The movement of preschoolers in which they learn to use instruments or tools and thus are capable of increasing the range of motor activities available to them.

Preconceptual thinking
The first substage of preoperational thinking, in which the two- to four-year-old uses symbolic thinking to a limited degree and tends to confuse his or her own thoughts with the thoughts of other people. He or she creates simple classifications that are necessary for identifying major objects and events.

such skills as tying shoelaces, washing hands, buttoning, eating with silverware, turning a doorknob, using a zipper, and drawing.

Some motor activities require the coordination of both large and small muscles. The child develops large-muscle control earlier than small-muscle control. As a child matures, he or she develops basic motor skills, such as running and jumping, without any special training. But more complex activities, such as throwing a ball, can be improved with training and encouragement.

Different types of movement emerge as a child develops. Much of the movement of preschoolers is **expressive.** They express emotions and needs through motor activities, and curiosity by direct involvement. But as their eye-hand coordination becomes more precise and their fine muscles become more developed, young children begin to practice a new type of movement called **instrumental** movement. They learn to use instruments or tools and thus are capable of increasing the range of motor activities available to them. The ability to master instrumental movement tends to progress in stages. For example, in learning to use a hammer, a child will first handle it simply as a heavy object. Next, it is used as an extension of the hand; that is, the hammer will follow the same path as the hand. Finally, the child begins to take advantage of the properties of the tool, such as the weight, shape, and momentum, to regulate its movement. The hammer is used as a lever and the child's hand acts as a fulcrum on which the lever turns Zaporozhets and Elkonin 1971). A child must be able to inhibit general body activity before he or she can develop instrumental movement. In order to learn to do any fine motor activity well, the child must hold still.

Most children develop motor skills in definite sequences, but each child develops at his or her own rate and in his or her own style. In these early years, the child makes tremendous strides in both physical growth and motor development. Development reflects both innate characteristics and environmental conditions.

COGNITIVE DEVELOPMENT

Preoperational Thought

The budding cognitive development, or mental ability, observed in infants blossoms between two and seven years of age, as imagination and language open up new ways of thinking and playing. Although preschool children can think symbolically, they cannot perform what Piaget calls logical "operations." For example, they cannot transform information and form an organized network of knowledge that is necessary to perform addition, multiplication, subtraction, or division. Thus, they are preoperational. There are two substages of preoperational thinking: *preconceptual* and *intuitive*. The **preconceptual** substage spans approximately ages two to four. Children use symbolic thinking to a limited degree, in which they make one object or action stand for another. They tend to confuse their own thoughts with the thoughts of other people and believe that objects and events are developed for their benefit. Preconceptual thinking makes it possible to create simple classifications that are necessary for identifying major objects and events.

The second, or **intuitive,** substage of preoperational thinking extends approximately from ages four to seven. Children in this group are capable of some mental operations that involve classifying, quantifying, and relating of objects.

However, they cannot comprehend the underlying principles of these operations. This stage is labeled "intuitive" because children cannot explain the reasons for solving problems in given ways.

How young children interpret messages illustrates the differences between the preconceptual and the intuitive child. The younger preschooler, or preconceptual child, overestimates the informativeness of ambiguous and ineffectual messages, while the older preschooler, or intuitive child, evaluates message quality accurately and knows the intended meaning. The preconceptual child tends to overestimate the message quality because he or she offers his or her interpretation of the message rather than the literal meaning. In other words, the preconceptual child tends to focus on what he or she thinks the speaker intends rather than on the literal meaning of the message (Beal and Belgrad 1990; Ackerman 1981; Robinson and Whittaker 1986; Torrance and Olson 1989). When communications fail, the preconceptual child assumes that the listener is at fault for not knowing what was meant, rather than blaming the speaker for not providing enough information (Robinson 1981).

In recent years there has been some controversy as to how much young children know about mental states and how readily they attribute them to others (Astington et al. 1988). Traditionally preschoolers have been viewed as behaviorists who either misconstrue mental events as behaviors or do not recognize the existence of mental processes at all. For example, Piaget (1929) noted that young children sometimes described thinking as talking and dreams as pictures that everyone could see. Selman (1980), similarly, found that children claimed they thought with their mouths and that emotions are always expressed by external features. Harris (1985) described a young child who explained that you cannot be happy and sad at once because your mouth cannot go up and down at the same time. Thus, sometimes preschoolers appear to equate mental states with concurrent external events and behaviors.

Lillard and Flavell (1990) found that preschoolers, specifically three-year-olds, do have a fundamentally correct understanding of mental life. Perhaps young children have seemed to focus on the external because in test situations the external has been more cognitively available to them, not because they are unaware of the internal. Lillard and Flavell found that three-year-olds prefer to describe human action in mentalistic terms rather than behavioral terms. Thus, given equally available options, preschoolers may prefer to describe people in terms of their mental states rather than their behaviors. For example, one child in the study showed an understanding of the interplay between emotions and desires when he described a boy who was sad about wiping up his spilled milk: "He's very sad and he wants to tell his sister about the spilled milk." Another child, when responding to the experimenter's words "wants to get a cupcake," said, "He wants some cupcakes so he's on his tiptoes, but he can't reach it cause it's far away." In this last sentence, the term *want* refers to a mental state, because the tiptoe behavior is stated as caused by, not analogous to, the "want."

Capabilities

During the preoperational stage, children have difficulty understanding various concepts. *Egocentrism* refers to the lack of awareness that there are viewpoints other than one's own. Children at this stage are so absorbed in their own impressions, they fail to recognize that their thoughts and feelings may be different from other people's and vice versa. They simply assume that everyone thinks the same thoughts they do at the same time. For example, a three-year-

Intuitive thinking
The second substage of preoperational thinking, in which the four- to seven-year-old is capable of some mental operations that involve classifying, quantifying, and relating of objects. However, the child cannot comprehend the underlying principles of these operations.

Animism
A view, common in preschoolers, that nonliving objects are alive and human.

Artificialism
A view, common in preschoolers, that everything, including living things, can be made or built the same way.

old boy, hearing his mother crying, might bring a teddy bear or blanket or Band-Aid to comfort her. Obviously this child is not selfish, because he is willing to give up something of his own. But he is egocentric because he assumes that his mom can be comforted by the same things that comfort him.

A preschool child often expresses **animism,** a view that nonliving objects are alive and human. For example, a four-year-old boy got very upset when his father accidentally stepped on his plastic Ninja Turtle figure. The boy talked to the smashed toy as if it were mortally wounded. Piaget (1968) conducted some comprehensive studies concerning children's animistic thinking and arrived at four states. In stage one the child believes that all objects are alive, whether they are animate or inanimate. The stage-two child believes that everything that moves has life, including things like cars, wagons, clocks, and so on. The stage-three child believes that objects that can move on their own accord, such as the wind and the sun, are alive. Finally, the stage-four child realizes that both plants and animals, or maybe only animals, possess life.

Bullock (1985) found that three-year-olds had an animistic attitude and fit Piaget's description. However, she found that four- and five-year-olds performed near adult levels in perceiving animate and inanimate objects. Bullock (1985) believes that Piaget erred in suggesting that an animistic attitude pervades much of early childhood thought.

Children also egocentrically reason that because they can build things from blocks, sand, water, and so on, then everything, including living things, can also be made the same way. This type of thinking is called **artificialism.** For example, a child might think that babies can be constructed out of bones and blood from the butcher shop. It is interesting to note that the preoperational child's concepts are very similar to early legends, myths, religious beliefs, and philosophies.

The preschool child's thinking is **irreversible,** which means he or she cannot mentally retrace operations. For example, when a three-year-old boy was asked if he had a brother, he said, "Yes," but when asked if his brother had a brother, he said, "No." Also, when looking at a family album, children find it difficult to believe that infant pictures of parents, grandparents, or older siblings could really be them. They cannot mentally retrace the fact that these individuals were once infants.

Centration restricts a child's focus. A preoperational child will focus, or center, on one feature or dimension of a situation at a time, to the exclusion of all others. For example, when looking at three sticks of graduated length, the child cannot see that one stick, while larger than another, is simultaneously smaller than another. He or she can only center on the relation of one stick to one other stick. Children also center on the relationships that family members have to them. For example, the three-year-old cannot understand that his grandmother can also be his dad's mother. The ability to understand two conflicting or complementary facts does not seem to appear until age seven or so.

Transductive reasoning is also common among preoperational children. Preschool children reason from one specific event to another, unrelated specific event. They simply associate one unrelated situation with another. For example, a little girl who had just had her ears pierced thought that as long as she had her earrings in, she was a girl (because girls wear earrings), but if she took them out, she would be a boy (because she had been taught that boys do not wear earrings). (This situation occurred, of course, before men and boys wore earrings in our society.) Or a more disturbing example is the child who thought he was responsible for his grandfather's death because he had had negative thoughts about him and had kicked him in the shins a week before.

These limitations make it difficult for the child to fully comprehend the various events and concepts they are confronted with daily. One concept they have difficulty with is what Piaget calls **conservation.** This is the idea that a

Irreversible thinking
A limited form of thinking in which children have difficulty mentally retracing operations.

Centration
Focusing, or centering, on only one feature or dimension of a situation at a time, to the exclusion of all others.

Transductive reasoning
Reasoning from one specific event to another, unrelated specific event.

Conservation
The idea that a quantity or amount of something remains the same regardless of changes in its shape or position.

quantity or amount of something remains the same regardless of changes in its shape or position. Conservation of liquid presents one area of difficulty. A preoperational child cannot understand that when water is poured out of a full glass into a wider glass, the amount of water is unchanged. Quite often the child perceives that the new wider glass is half empty and concludes that there is less water than before. Preschool children also have the same problem with conservation of matter. When a preschooler is asked to make two balls of clay of equal amount and then asked to roll one of them into a long skinny rope, the child will perceive that the two pieces of clay now have different amounts. Not until the stage of concrete operations, at six, seven, or eight years of age, does the average child realize that the amount of matter remains the same despite any change of shape.

Preoperational children also have difficulty comprehending the concept of **classification,** that is, sorting objects into categories and classes. Although they can tell the difference between two objects, such as an orange and a banana, and can place them in their appropriate class, their understanding of classification is still in the process of being acquired. They will not completely grasp it until the end of the preoperational stage. If presented with a basket of a variety of buttons and asked to put the buttons that are alike together, the preoperational child would see only one way of categorizing or classifying them. For example, he or she might sort them according to color.

Time is another concept that preschoolers have difficulty comprehending. The earliest experiences of time are most likely those of bodily rhythms, that is, states that recur in regular patterns, such as hunger, eating, and fullness. Interactions with the environment (breakfast, nap times, bath time, bedtime, etc.) also impose some patterns on bodily rhythms. Time is seen as a concrete event, embedded in activity. Time and space are not differentiated from each other. The child judges duration in terms of content, forgetting speed. Children from two through four years of age were questioned concerning their understanding of *yesterday* and *tomorrow.* The youngest had little comprehension of either term. At three years, children understood *yesterday* in two ways: the correct way and also as a time other than today. *Tomorrow* was understood only as some time in the future. At four years, children understood both terms correctly (Gesell et al. 1974).

Spatial relations is another concept that is sometimes difficult for a preschool child. The meaning of words such as *in, out, to, from, near, far, over, under, up, down, inside,* and *outside* are first learned very directly, with the active involvement of the child's body (such as crawling under a table). The child eventually identifies the concept in pictures, such as seeing a ship go under a bridge. Finally, the child is able to verbalize the concept.

Sequence, or *seriation,* is also a difficult concept for preschoolers. For example, when presented with six sticks of graduated length, a child can usually pick out the shortest or longest, or may even be able to divide the sticks into piles, putting the shorter sticks in one pile and the longer sticks in another. But the preoperational child has difficulty lining up the sticks in the correct order, like a staircase, because this operation requires the simultaneous judgment that each stick is longer than another one but at the same time shorter than still another. When trying to identify the sequence of real-life events, the very young preschooler, two and one-half to three years, may have some difficulty in recalling the events. As the child gets older, four to five years, he or she is able to properly sequence the events and develop a "script" as to the order in which these events

Classification
Sorting objects into categories and classes.

Language Development

Language expands rapidly for most children after infancy. The search for the answer to language acquisition is not an entirely new issue. In the thirteenth century, Frederick II, of Prussia, conducted a rather drastic experiment to find out whether there was a universal language that babies would speak if they did not hear the language of their own culture. He had foster mothers and nurses feed, bathe, and wash the children involved in the experiment, but in no way were they to play with them or talk to them. In this way he hoped to learn whether they would speak Hebrew (which was thought to be the oldest language), Greek, Latin, Arabic, or perhaps the language of the parents. Unfortunately, all of the children died (Ross and McLaughlin 1949).

Eric Lennenberg (1967), a noted linguist, believed there is a critical period for people to develop language. He maintained that the preschool years are an especially critical period. At that age, the ears, brain, and voice are primed, ready to absorb language like a sponge, if someone provides the proper input. Support for Lennenberg's hypothesis comes from the fact that child victims who suffer damage to the speech area of the brain can relearn language much better than adults who suffer the same damage. Other support is evidenced in situations where families move to an area in which a different language is spoken. The children usually learn the second language with much greater ease than their parents. Normal children, then, acquire language in certain stages, providing they have linguistic experiences and they hear the language of the adults around them. Adult-child communication, necessary for children to acquire language, helps children learn the particular language they hear spoken.

Children at Risk

Most deaf children are severely handicapped in language development because they do not understand or develop speech. They usually experience difficulty with grammar and with written vocabulary all of their lives. Children who are congenitally deaf, or who become deaf as infants or in early childhood, are quite often taught American Sign Language as their first language. Deaf children of deaf parents have a distinct advantage in many areas of cognitive and psychological functioning as compared with deaf children of hearing parents. Possibly one reason for this difference is early parent-child communication using sign language in the first situation (Schlesinger and Meadow 1972). Sign language is the use of gestures and signs made with the fingers to represent words. Deaf children have been known to learn signing before their first birthday. There are even indications that deaf babies may babble in sign, similar to hearing babies who babble orally (Dale 1976). At the one-word-sentence, or holophrase stage, deaf children use signs in the same way as hearing children use words; that is, one sign can have a range of meanings. Therefore, deaf children learn sign language at about the same rate that hearing children learn oral language, thus indicating that the processes are similar (Goldin-Meadow and Mylander 1985).

One little girl named Ann signed her first two words, *father* and *stupid,* at ten months. At twelve months she signed *pretty* and *wrong.* She used 117 signs and 5 letters of the manual alphabet at nineteen months (compared with more

Most deaf children are severely handicapped in language development because they do not understand or develop speech. Deaf children are often taught American Sign Language as their first language.

than 3 but less than 50 words, which is the typical range for hearing children). Because her parents were deaf, Ann was tested for deafness within a few days after her birth. Testing a child this young is rather unusual, since most parents just assume their infant hears normally (Schlesinger and Meadow 1972).

If deafness is not detected in a child, secondary problems may arise; for example, a two-year-old who has not begun to talk or a five-year-old who cannot be understood. Because the first few years of language development are critical, an undetected hearing problem could become a permanent handicap. Hearing problems need to be detected early so appropriate language input can be provided through training in sign language, the introduction of hearing aids, surgery, and/or special education that will prevent the hearing difficulty from becoming a major handicap.

Neglect and deprivation can also make an impact on the acquisition of language and its development. An extreme example of this is the case involving Genie. Genie was born in California in 1957. Her father hated children, and her mother, who was blind, was terrified of him. During Genie's first twenty months, she was underfed and ignored most of the time. After that her life got worse. Susan Curtiss (1977), the psycholinguist who worked with Genie after she was rescued, described her situation as this:

> Genie was confined to a small bedroom, harnessed to an infant potty seat. Unclad, except for the harness, Genie was left to sit, tied up, hour after hour, often into the night, day after day, month after month, year after year. At night when Genie was not forgotten, she was removed from her harness only to be placed in another restraining garment—a sleeping bag which her father fashioned to hold Genie's arms stationary. Therein constrained, Genie was put into an infant's crib with wire mesh sides and a wire mesh cover overhead. Caged by night, harnessed by day, Genie was left to somehow endure the hours and years of her life. (Curtiss 1977)

Genie's isolation encompassed an eleven-year time period. She was totally cut off from language because she never overheard a conversation and was never spoken to. The only way her father "communicated" with her was to bark and growl like a wild dog. If she made a sound, she was beaten. After she was finally rescued, she was completely unsocialized and could not talk. (Before the authorities could talk to her father, he committed suicide.) Most psychologists predicted a grim future for Genie because she had already experienced what was considered a critical period for socialization and language development. However, after six years of intensive therapy and language lessons with psychologists and a foster family, she could talk in primitive sentences and expressed normal feelings, such as showing affection to her foster family. She was also able to discuss some of her memories of her terrible childhood. This progress indicated that language can develop after puberty.

Genie's speech, however, was still not normal. She had difficulty with some aspects of language. For example, she could not use words like *what, that,* and *which*. She could not ask questions with an inverted auxiliary verb and would not use the passive voice. She could not put more than one simple idea in a sentence. She rarely used auxiliary words. She said "I eaten" rather than "I have eaten," or "I jumping" rather than "I was jumping". In her progress of language development, she followed many of the same sequences and made some of the same errors typical of preschoolers. For example, she dropped the *s* at the beginning of words like *spoon* and *stop,* and she used the word *no* at the beginning of a sentence in order to make a negative sentence out of a positive one, as in "No take me home," and "No want to eat breakfast." She also had articulation problems. Because these errors continued to persist, it was felt that her early language deprivation, plus her abuse and malnutrition, may have permanently restricted her language-learning capacity. Despite her great progress in language and social behavior, she never used more than the telegraphic speech that is typical in a two- to three-year-old child.

This tragic example leads researchers to believe that there are few truly critical periods (intervals during which specific areas of development are either permanently vulnerable to pertinent harmful events or open to beneficial effects) in normal human development. But there is evidence that there are many sensitive periods, when certain types of development are temporarily vulnerable to a negative environment. The period from one to five years is considered a sensitive period for language development.

Vocabulary

Between three and four years of age, children use three- to four-word sentences. They ask many questions, can give and follow simple commands, and can name familiar things like pets, body parts, or significant people. They can use plurals and past tenses, and their vocabulary includes about nine hundred to twelve hundred words. Between four and five years, sentences average between four and five words, and the child's vocabulary includes fifteen hundred to two thousand words. Between five and six years, sentences average six to eight words. Everyday speech includes conjunctions, prepositions, and articles (Dale 1976). By age six, the child's vocabulary ranges from eight thousand to fourteen thousand words (Carey 1977). The large number of vocabulary words may be the result of the exposure to television.

Preschoolers use verbs more than nouns. Three types of verbs used by preschoolers include instrument verbs, action verbs, and result verbs. An *instrument* verb explicitly labels an instrument being used in an event: "He *hammers* and *saws* wood." *Action* verbs have been defined as verbs that explicitly label the physical movement of an agent without specifying the result of the movement:

"She *pounds* and *squeezes* lemons." *Result* verbs explicitly label a change of state or the result of a movement without specifying what that movement was: "They *flatten* tires or *break* windows." Behrend (1990) found that three-year-olds use action verbs more often than five- and seven-year-olds and adults.

In using nouns, preschoolers use *basic-level* terms (for example, *dog*) earlier and more frequently than either *superordinate* (for example, *animal*) or *subordinate* (for example, *poodle*) terms (Anglin 1977). Using basic-level terms corresponds with the preschooler's level of conceptualization, which is best suited for him to learn word meanings.

Grammar

Vocabulary can be acquired through understanding and imitation, but the acquisition of grammar is more complicated. Imitative speech generally is not grammatically better than nonimitative or spontaneous speech, which is the sentences formed by children themselves. Also, imitative speech is not longer than spontaneous speech. If a three-year-old's spontaneous speech consists of only three or four words, his or her imitative speech will also be only three or four words long. This is called telegraphic speech because of its similarity to a telegram, in that it contains only the most important words and leaves out most articles, prepositions, and conjunctions (Dale 1976). Some researchers believe that a child's telegraphic speech is the result of a natural inability to program longer sentences. As the child matures, neurological development and practice create an ability to program longer and longer sentences (Brown and Bellugi 1964).

Direct instruction through correction and imitation is not always an efficient way to help young children acquire grammar. The interchange between a three-year-old and her mother illustrates this: A little girl was looking at the picture book *The Three Billy Goats Gruff*. She carefully pointed to each goat and said, "Look! Three billy goats eated." Her mother, busily working near her, corrected her and said, "Ate." The girl once again counted the figures in the picture and said, "Three billy goats eated." Her mother mechanically responded again saying, "Ate." At that point the little girl shrugged her shoulders and said "OKay! Eight billy goats eated." (Source unknown.)

Research by Brown and Bellugi (1964) found that mothers tend to use simplified speech called *motherese* with their children. They tend to speak in short, simple, grammatical sentences and adapt their speech to their children's level of development. Simple sentences may be repeated in different forms for emphasis. For example: "Don't fall, Jeff. Don't fall. Watch out. You'll fall." In contrast to speech to adults, motherese has shorter sentences separated by longer pauses, more commands and questions, more present tenses and references to the here and now, and fewer pronouns, modifiers, and conjunctions. Mothers use basic, simple words that their children will understand. They also overextend terms just as their children do. For example, a mother will label tigers, panthers, lions, and so on, as cats for her child. As children mature and learn more language, adults speak to them in longer and more complicated sentences. Declarative forms replace questions and commands (Maratsos 1983; Kavanaugh and Jirkovsky 1982). When adults speak to other adults, their speech contains long, complex, and often ungrammatical sentences.

Motherese is not an attempt to teach children language but is mainly an attempt to speak so that the child can understand. Shorter utterances make it easier for children to comprehend because their memory is limited. Pauses between sentences enable children to pick out syntactic units (Hirsh-Pasek et al. 1986).

Children imitate adult speech by **reduction;** that is, they reduce adult sentences to the number of words and the grammatical forms that they can manage at their particular stage of language development. For example, when imitating "I want to go home," the child may say, "Go home." Adults do the opposite. They imitate children's sentences with **expansion,** by adding words or parts of words to the children's sentences to make them grammatically correct. For example, a child may say, "Red ball," and the adult will imitate by saying, "There's your red ball" (Brown and Bellugi 1964). Nelson et al. (1983) found that when mothers of two-year-olds made simple explanations of what the children said, they spoke in longer sentences and used more auxiliary verbs at younger ages. However, two-year-olds who heard complex expansions progressed more slowly. Thus, simple expansions help children notice and analyze new syntactical structures, which holds their attention and apparently helps them acquire language.

Nelson (1981) had adults expand children's sentences by either restating the statement as a question, such as

CHILD: "Dog run."

ADULT: "Did the dog run?"

or by fixing the verb:

CHILD: "It go here."

ADULT: "Yes, it goes here."

The children's language was assessed after five one-hour sessions. Children who had heard restated questions advanced in their use of questions but not verbs. Children who had heard expanded verbs advanced in their use of verbs but not questions. Apparently children notice extensions of their language and learn from them. Hoff-Ginsberg (1986) found that mothers' whose language contained more complex utterances, more repetitions, and more questions that required more than yes/no answers, encouraged their children's language to develop more quickly.

Noam Chomsky (1975) noted that there are basic aspects of language that are universal and exist in all languages. He also proposed that children have an innate ability to process information about language through the language acquisition device (LAD). (See Chapter 5 for an earlier discussion of the LAD)

Once a child has acquired the rules of language, it is possible for him or her to distinguish between the grammatical and the ungrammatical. And the rules of grammar can be applied to an infinite number of word combinations. This ability enables children and adults to generate an infinite number of original sentences. The development and knowledge of language are nonconscious. Children cannot express what they know about the basic structure of language, and neither can most adults. This would seem to indicate an intuitive nature of language (Chomsky 1975).

Chomsky's theory has much support. For example, at every stage of development, a child's language is systematic and organized. Sentences are grammatical and arranged within some age-associated system, even when deviating from adult standards. It is possible, by observing a child's errors, to see that he or she is applying rules when constructing sentences (McNeill 1970; Mussen et al. 1974; Whitehurst 1982).

Reduction
A means children use to imitate adult speech. Adult sentences are reduced to the number of words and the grammatical forms that the children can manage at their particular stage of language development.

Expansion
A means adults use to imitate children's speech. They add words or parts of words to children's sentences to make the sentences grammatically correct.

A child who has discovered the rule for forming the past tense by adding *ed* will add *ed* to all verbs in the past tense. Using *rided* rather than *rode,* or *goed* rather than *gone,* may be incorrect, but it follows the rule the child has learned. Similarly, when a child incorporates the rule that says plurals are created by adding *s,* then all plural nouns will end in *s.* Thus we hear such words as *tooths, foots, gooses,* and so on. Even if the child knows the irregular plural, the *s* may be added anyway, and we get *teeths, feets, and geeses.* This phenomenon is known as **overregularization;** that is, when a child acquires a rule, he or she tends to apply it to situations that do not fit. Also, a child in the process of learning the rule about substituting pronouns for nouns may actually say both the pronoun and the noun it should have replaced, as in "Mommy she gave me a cookie."

The development of questions is another area in which rule discovery and the stages of language acquisition are apparent. A child's first questions are extremely simple and usually differ from statements only by inflection or intonation. Most early questions are yes/no questions. For example, "We go now?" "I go too?" "I have another one?" But in the first stage a child may also form questions in a telegraphic speech format using a *wh*-word, like "What man doing?" or "Where mommy going?" (McNeill 1970).

In the second stage of question development, a child definitely forms questions by using a *wh*-word in front of a statement. At this stage we might hear "What you do?" or "Why the dog can't come?" or "What this is for?" Children begin asking *why* questions at age three, usually in conversations with adults. The child simply adds *why* or *why not* to the adult's statements. *Why* questions are one of the characteristics of young children that can be charming and exasperating at the same time. This is because they ask *why* questions one after another. For example:

CHILD: "Why you shoveling?"

Overregularization
The tendency of a child, when acquiring a grammatical rule, to apply the rule to situations that do not fit.

ADULT: "To dig up the rocks."

CHILD: "Why?"

ADULT: "So I can plant my flowers."

CHILD: "Why?"

ADULT: "So they will have room to grow."

CHILD: "Why?" And so on. And so on.

Up to this point, in the first two stages of question development, a child's yes/no questions are simply statements spoken with a rising inflection to indicate questioning.

The third stage of question development is marked by the child's discovery of the rule to invert word order in yes/no questions. "Can I go too?" or "Is this the right one?" At this stage, children usually are not yet able to invert the order of subjects and auxiliary verbs in *wh*-questions, even though they can do so in yes/no questions. So it's still "Why the dog can't come?" instead of "Why can't the dog come?" In the fourth and final stage of question development, the order more closely resembles the adult form (McNeill 1970). Children seem to use *what, where, whose,* and *who* before they learn *"how", "why",* or *"when"* (Ervin-Tripp 1970).

Children use negatives in three distinct stages. At first children simply attach *no* or *not* to the beginning or end of a sentence. For example, they say, "No see Jeff," or "No like eggs." In the second stage they move the negative inside the sentence, as in "I no want bath," or "He not nice." Finally, they change the sentence structure so that it is similar to the adult negative (Bellugi 1967).

By five years, almost all children have acquired the basic syntactic structure of their language, but language development is not complete at that age. According to linguist Carol Chomsky (1969), some structures of language acquisition are not achieved until nine years of age, and others not even by ten years.

Egocentric Speech

Piaget (1955) refers to a final aspect of early language development as **egocentric speech.** Children can concentrate on one thing at a time, and they have difficulty seeing things from another person's perceptive. Egocentric speech is similar to parallel play, in which children play side by side but are concerned only with the self. They speak to themselves. It is thinking out loud, and it is not directed at anything or anyone. It may be spoken in the presence of others, but it contains what is on the child's mind, with no intention of communicating. Little or no relationship seems to exist between what is said and what is done. Quite often preschool children will engage in what Piaget calls a **collective monologue.** In a collective monologue, a couple of children may give the impression of being engaged in a conversation, pausing after having said something to listen to the partner. However, their statements and responses have little or no relationship to each other. Each child's utterances follow a particular line of thought, but there is little reciprocal interchange, where something said by one child elicits an appropriate response from the other. They talk about themselves and their own concerns while rarely speaking from the point of view of someone else or listening to the other child.

A conversation witnessed by the author illustrates this.

JOHN: "My brother got a new water pistol."

CURT: "We went to the fire station yesterday."

Egocentric speech
Speech in which children can concentrate on only one thing at a time, and they have difficulty seeing things from another person's perspective.

Collective monologue
Egocentric speech among two or more children in which they give the impression of being engaged in a conversation but their statements and responses have little or no relationship to each other.

JOHN: "He said I could use it sometime."

CURT: "There were big fire trucks there, and they let us get in them."

Cognitive structures that are established during the early stages of sensorimotor development make learning language possible and allow language to be used later for communication. Piaget observed that a high percentage of speech between three and five years is egocentric and a high percentage between seven and eight years is social (that is, the child makes an effort to make his or her thoughts known and attempts to understand what others are saying).

Occasionally, in specific situations, preschool children do engage in genuine conversation, when one child asks another a question or when a mutually interesting point comes up. Usually, however, such socialized speech will not appear with any consistency until around seven years of age.

It has been found that preschoolers, in conducting a conversation, begin to differentiate mental terms with respect to certainty and uncertainty, such as *know* and *think*. Moore et al. (1989) presented children from three to eight years of age with a task in which they had to find an object hidden in one of two places. The only clues were two statements that contrasted a pair of mental terms. The statements were presented by two puppets: one puppet would say, "I know it is in the red box," while the other puppet would say, "I think it is in the blue box." It was not until the children were four years old that they were able to locate the object by using such information. Therefore, at four years children were beginning to recognize the degrees of certainty in speakers' utterances.

Factors in Developing Language

Ordinal Position Generally, firstborn children develop language more rapidly, as do only children. Twins and other multiple-birth groups show slower language development when compared with firstborns and with singletons

Twins, especially identical twins, often develop a private jargon and a gesture vocabulary. Because of this, they have less incentive to invent syntax or learn a spoken vocabulary.

(Noble 1980). One reason twins and other multiple-birth children have slower language development is because they do not receive as much individual attention from their mother as would a single child. Also, twins, especially identical twins, seem to develop a private jargon and a gesture vocabulary, so they have less incentive to invent syntax or learn a spoken vocabulary.

Gender   Girls appear to have a slight edge in learning language. Not only do they learn to speak at an earlier age than boys, but frequently they articulate better and have fewer speech defects.

Stuttering

Stuttering in young children is not abnormal. Stuttering appears between two and one-half and four years, that is, about the time words become increasingly important in the lives of children. It is generally accepted that throughout most of the early years of language acquisition, young children's brains are working faster than their ability to coordinate their vocal muscles and articulate the words they are attempting to use. Thus, they frequently want to say things that they cannot quite articulate or find that their words come more slowly than they wish. This is particularly true when a child becomes tense or excited.

Adults' expressions of overconcern or constant attempts to correct the child may lead to feelings of frustration, self-consciousness, or nervousness on the part of the child. If children feel that their attempts are inadequate, inner tension may develop, and this pattern may in turn result in the beginning stages of long-term stuttering (Smith 1986).

Long-term stuttering is not the same as the temporary stuttering common among preschoolers. The incidence of long-term stuttering in males is four times higher than that found in females. Stuttering is, therefore, considered to be biologically based, because of the numerous ways in which males and females differ in neurological development (Kidd et al. 1978).

Humor

Preschool children's humor is related to their stage of cognitive development. Three- to six-year-old children, in stage-three humor, are in Piaget's stage of preoperational thought. Their thinking is limited by perception, and they are heavily influenced by appearances and less influenced by what they may know is true. For example, they might laugh at a picture of a bicycle with square wheels without having a well-developed sense of the effect this would have on trying to ride it (McGhee 1979). When their knowledge conflicts with appearance, they will rely on appearance. This centeredness accounts for the preschool child's emphasis on perceptual features of events in their humor. Their thought is intuitive, so there is no need for the logical necessity for events or objects to be related to one another in a particular way (McGhee 1972, 1979).

Only by *stage four* can a child step beyond the appearance of things and begin to think in a logical manner about what could and could not happen and why. When asked to explain why an event is funny, the stage-three preschooler cannot go beyond a purely descriptive account and indicate what about the described situation makes it funny (McGhee 1979).

All jokes contain two distinct structural dimensions: **incongruity** and **resolution.** Four- and five-year-old children can resolve incongruities, which play an increasingly important role in the humor process (Pien and Rothbart 1976). For very young, less cognitively advanced children, the mere identification or

Incongruity
The dimension of humor in which the expectation of reality is not met.

Resolution
The dimension of humor in which an individual can cognitively resolve a joke or riddle.

invention of incongruities may be sufficient enough to create a humor reaction (Winchell 1977; McGhee 1972). The child must know what is normal before being able to perceive an incongruity. A child can appreciate incongruities of size and space only after he or she is familiar with the normal relationships between objects (Kappas 1967).

Play signals, such as a smiling or playful facial expression, are important for preschoolers. A cue is needed from a person telling a joke to indicate that the statement is meant as a joke. Because of preschoolers' very limited level of cognitive mastery over their world, they need such cues more than older children and adults do. An older child is more likely to assume that a joking interpretation is called for because of his or her absolute certainty of the impossibility of the event (McGhee 1979).

Precocious language development is consistent with heightened humor development. The comprehension and expression of verbal humor follows the mastery of language and grows only at the rate that language does (Kappas 1967). Between three and five years of age, children are intrigued that objects have particular names and can be called some names but not others. Once the child is confident of the correct name of something, it is funny to either misname it or distort the correct name in some way. For example, a three-year-old might call a shoe a "floo," or a "poo," or a "shoop" (McGhee 1979).

Once they find humor in misnaming objects and activities, preschool children begin to enjoy simple riddle-type questions and guessing games. It is especially funny to preschoolers when adults enter into the fun and give inept answers. Non-name words, such as *Mrs. Fool-around, Johnny-out-in-the-grass,* and *Uncle Funny-bunny,* are frequently made up by preschoolers. Not only do they play with simple name substitutions, but they become involved in the repetitious rhyming of words and the creation of nonsense words such as *itsy-bitsy* and *happy-sappy.* This behavior is consistent with the strong perceptual orientation of the period; it is the sound change that is funny, not the altered meaning of the word. Nonsense words such as *squidzel, zwimpy,* and *glorkel* are funny because they do not sound like any word the child has heard before (McGhee 1979).

Another form of altering familiar words is found in the systematic distortion of a whole communication, such as trying to speak with the lips spread wide and rigid or talking in a squeaky or gruff voice. Nonlanguage sounds may be imitated by the child in a distorted fashion too. For example, the child may find it funny to make a "moo" sound in a low voice with odd variations in pitch, or in a stuttering fashion. In both cases the child is introducing elements known to be incongruous or inappropriate, and it is the acknowledgment of the inappropriateness that makes it funny (McGhee 1979).

A common source of preschool children's laughter is socially unacceptable behavior. A simple depiction of a child engaging in a forbidden act or engaging in an activity incompatible with traditional sex-role behavior is sufficient to produce laughter in a three- to five-year-old (McGhee 1979). Preschool children also laugh at jokes or other communication in which some taboo content is verbalized (McGhee 1972). Dirty, sexual, and other taboo words have probably been sources of humor for young children for as long as adults have shown signs of concern about their expression. The content of "taboo" jokes depends on the child's concerns at the time and on the prohibitions or concerns expressed by his or her parents (Fry 1974). Elimination jokes are popular among preschoolers because of special taboos related to defecation and urination at the time. By the time sexual matters become a strong source of curiosity for the child, considerable progress has been made in his or her awareness of the development of the "joke facade." Most children learn to use the playful context of a joke to express sexual or aggressive ideas, always having at their disposal the claim "I was only joking" (McGhee 1979, 1972; Kappas 1967).

Creative thinkers are better at creating humor spontaneously, and at quickly understanding humor initiated by others (McGhee 1979). From the second year on, it may be possible to see early precursors of creativity in children's make-believe play. Creative children tend to be more playful. During childhood, the more creative individuals are viewed by their peers as having a better sense of humor. Producing humorous incongruities in fantasy probably fosters the development of creative thinking as well, because the child must continually look for new ways to alter or distort familiar ideas (McGhee 1979).

Findings from a longitudinal study with preschoolers indicate that fat children have a better sense of humor than skinny children do. Overweight children initiated humor more often than their peers, but did not laugh more. Generally it was the taller and heavier children who showed the greatest humor development. However, at the elementary level, the measures of height and weight were not predictive (McGhee 1979).

Children who were unusually persistent in efforts to master gross motor skills showed increased humor development, while those persistent in efforts to master fine motor skills showed reduced levels of humor development. In a preschool sample, children who were highly persistent at intellectual achievement tasks clowned, joked, and laughed less frequently during nursery school free-play sessions. A child is more likely to be serious when doing intellectual and fine motor tasks. Gross motor activities, which are usually physically vigorous and are undertaken in the midst of social play, are more likely to be accompanied by a more playful frame of mind (McGhee 1979).

Preschool humorists, those youngsters who make others laugh, are likely to be energetic and aggressive both verbally and physically. The critical factor in developing a sense of humor seems to be a lot of opportunities for social play. An audience and an ever-changing play situation stimulate verbal inventiveness

and physical clowning. Other children's responses play a central role in building up the habit of being funny and laughing at others' humor. Preschool children also seem to be funny purely for the fun of it (McGhee and Lloyd 1982).

Sex is a factor in determining humorous attitudes. Boys and girls on the whole fail to find the same things funny to the same degree. The sex difference increases with age (Kappas 1967). Groch (1974) found that girls most frequently show evidence of the appreciation of humor in incongruous or surprising events, the amusing behavior of others, verbal jokes, stories or songs, or the antics of animals. Very little hostility or aggression is present in their humor situations. However, for boys, some form of hostile joking is typical. Boys use humor to attack or threaten others, to ridicule through name calling, or to defy adults.

In an early study, McGhee (1976) found no sex differences apparent in the amounts of laughter, verbal attempts to initiate humor, or hostility in children's humor. But in a later study, McGhee and Duffey (1983) found that preschool middle-income boys and girls and preschool low-income African-American, white, and Mexican-American boys found humor victimizing a parent funnier than victimizing a child, and humor victimizing the opposite sex funnier than humor victimizing their own sex. However, low-income girls found humor vicitimizing their own sex funnier than humor victimizing the opposite sex. (Among adult women, this pattern appears only among women with more traditional sex-role values. Women who identify more strongly with the feminist movement show the male pattern of preferring jokes in which the opposite sex is disparaged [McGhee 1983].)

A positive self-concept seems to facilitate humor development. Children with positive self-concepts tell more jokes or humorous stories on request, which suggests they spend a great deal of time listening to and telling jokes generally. On the other hand, children with poor self-concepts relate fewer

Bilingualism

Historically in our country, children with a principal language other than English have been at a disadvantage. The children have difficulty when entering school because they cannot speak the language being used, and thus they become socially isolated from their peer group.

Many linguists have expressed interest in how children can learn more than one language simultaneously. By four years of age, bilingual children appear to move through three stages before they can speak their two languages fluently. First, they learn each word in one language at a time, not both. Second, they apply one set of syntactic rules to each set of words. Finally, they associate each language with the person who speaks it and/or the place they hear it.

Bilingual children see the world from two different perspectives and can try out two different approaches to situations. They seem to better understand the difference between symbols and objects and the functions of language (Diaz 1985). Oren (1981) found that bilingual preschoolers were better than monolingual preschoolers in understanding that names are only labels for things and that changing labels does not change the content or properties of the things. Diaz (1985) found that when a child learns two languages simultaneously in a parallel manner, his or her cognitive functioning increases.

Wallace Lambert and G. Richard Tucker (1972), of McGill University, have identified several rules parents should follow if they wish to teach their child to be bilingual. First, the teaching should begin as early as possible, definitely before the child starts school. Second, each language should be spoken only at specific times or in specific places. Third, there should be no pressure for the child to use words in only one language. That is, the child should feel free to use words from both languages. Finally, the child should know enough English to avoid ridicule, thus encouraging peer acceptance. Teaching and encouraging bilingualism will enhance a child's appreciation of other cultures and perhaps prevent prejudice and discrimination in the long run.

Several studies indicate that minority children who are monolingual learn a second language more readily and more effectively if they are taught to read and write in their own language first (Gudschinsky 1977; d'Anglejan and Tucker 1970; Lambert and Tucker 1977). For example, a bilingual study involving Spanish-speaking American children of Cuban descent found that it was easier for children to learn to read two languages at the same time (provided one was the language spoken at home) than to learn one language that was alien to them. In fact, these children became better readers than the control group, who had been taught to read English only (Friedenberg 1983).

What do you see as the implications of teaching languages other than English in our schools and preschools? Should state school systems mandate that foreign-speaking monolingual children be taught in their own language? If such children are taught in their own language, will they ever have the opportunity to learn English and function within our society as adults?

jokes or funny incidents when asked to do so; also, they include more hostility in the few jokes they do tell. Their humor may reveal underlying hostility that they feel about themselves and their interaction with others (McGhee 1979).

- The preschool child's physical growth patterns proceed in a predictable pattern, with several physiological changes occurring in the following areas: body proportion, bones, height and weight, brain, digestive system, ears, teeth, eyes, sleep, physical characteristics, and handedness. These changes affect the behavior and personality of the child.
- Factors that influence physical growth include gender, heredity, socioeconomic levels, and the secular trend.

- The motor skills, both fine and gross, develop at a steady rate between three and five years of age.
- The preoperational child's thinking processes occur in two substages: preconceptual and intuitive.
- The preoperational child's thinking is limited by egocentrism (which includes animism and artificialism), irreversible thinking, centration, and transductive reasoning.
- The limitations in a preschool child's thinking make it difficult for him or her to understand concepts such as conservation, classification, time, spatial relations, and sequencing.
- Children who are at risk in learning language are deaf children and children who are neglected and deprived of language experiences.
- Vocabulary development increases many times over during the preschool period and is closely related to cognitive development.
- Grammar development is more complicated than vocabulary acquisition. Grammar develops in stages and is related to language experiences such as expansion and modeling. Children go through stages in developing questions and using negatives.
- Egocentric speech has been observed in preschool children. They engage in collective monologues, in which the statements between two children have little or no relationship to one another.
- Firstborn children, only children, and girls develop language more rapidly. Multiple-birth children are slower at developing language.
- Stuttering is common among children between two and one-half and four years. Their brains are working faster than their ability to coordinate their vocal muscles and articulate the words they are attempting to use. Boys are four times more likely than girls to have a long-term stuttering problem. Parents should be patient and not draw undue attention to it.
- Preschool children's humor is related to their stage of cognitive development. At this stage (stage-three humor) children enjoy language play; that is, they change or distort the names of people and objects. They like nonsense words and distort nonlanguage sounds.
- Common sources of a preschooler's humor are socially unacceptable behavior and the use of dirty, sexual, and taboo words.
- Preschool children who have the best sense of humor are creative, somewhat overweight, tall, persistent in gross motor skills, and of a positive self-concept. Boys' and girls' humor differs somewhat at this age and becomes more diverse as they get older.
- Bilingual children have traditionally been at a disadvantage in our society. If the children are taught to read and write in their own language first, they more readily learn a second language.

R E A D I N G S

Daehler, M. W. and Bukatko, D. (1985). *Cognitive development*. Random House.
Overview of cognitive development in children.

DeVilliers, P. A. and DeVilliers, J. G. (1979). *Early language*. Cambridge, Mass.: Harvard University Press.
Use examples of deaf, retarded, and autistic children to explain language development in normal children. Explains the process of learning language between birth and six years.

Piaget, J. (1987). *Possibility and necessity*. (translated by Helga Feider). Minneapolis, MN: University of Minnesota Press.

Description of children's understanding of possibilities and how they choose between alternatives.

Singer, D. G. and Revenson, T. A. (1978). *How a child thinks: A Piaget primer.* New American Library. Summary of Piaget's ideas.

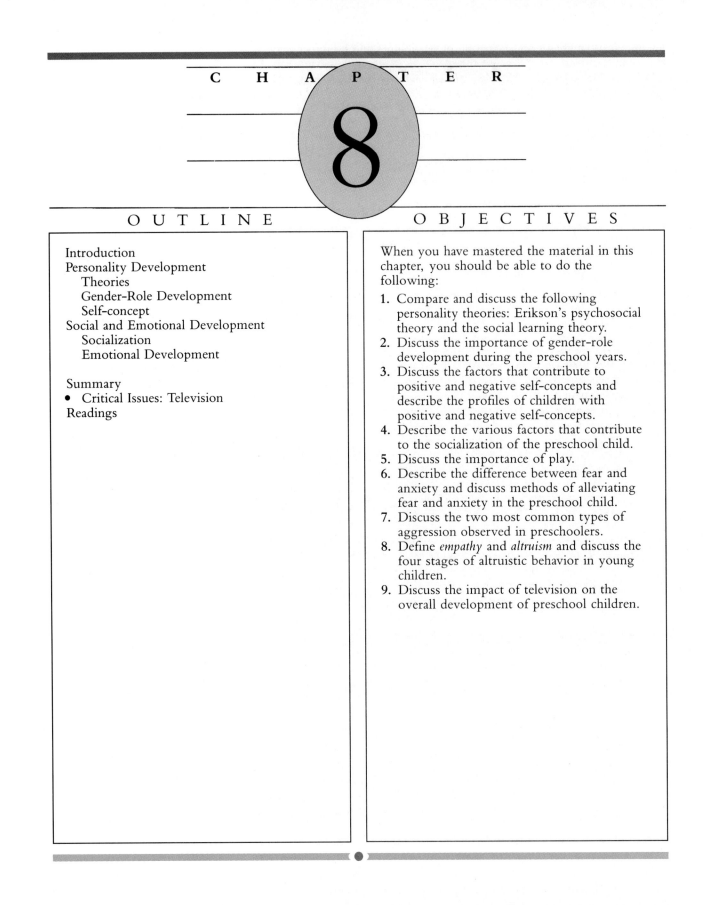

C   H   A   P   T   E   R

8

OUTLINE

Introduction
Personality Development
    Theories
    Gender-Role Development
    Self-concept
Social and Emotional Development
    Socialization
    Emotional Development

Summary
• Critical Issues: Television
Readings

OBJECTIVES

When you have mastered the material in this chapter, you should be able to do the following:

1. Compare and discuss the following personality theories: Erikson's psychosocial theory and the social learning theory.
2. Discuss the importance of gender-role development during the preschool years.
3. Discuss the factors that contribute to positive and negative self-concepts and describe the profiles of children with positive and negative self-concepts.
4. Describe the various factors that contribute to the socialization of the preschool child.
5. Discuss the importance of play.
6. Describe the difference between fear and anxiety and discuss methods of alleviating fear and anxiety in the preschool child.
7. Discuss the two most common types of aggression observed in preschoolers.
8. Define *empathy* and *altruism* and discuss the four stages of altruistic behavior in young children.
9. Discuss the impact of television on the overall development of preschool children.

The Exploring Years: Preschoolers' Psychosocial Development

INTRODUCTION

A preschooler's social skills and unique personality are primarily a result of experiences within and outside of his or her family as well as a function of his or her gender and social circumstances. Various theorists perceive the interaction of these variables in different ways.

PERSONALITY DEVELOPMENT

Theories

Erikson's Psychosocial Theory

The resolution of the crises in Erikson's first two stages has social significance and long-term consequences in the child's personality development. During the first two stages, a time of total dependency, the child comes to trust or mistrust and to experience autonomy or doubt. Cuddling, comfort, and sensory stimulation contribute to the achievement of trust and autonomy during these critical first three years.

Erikson's third stage, initiative versus guilt, occurs around age four or five. With the resolution of the previous crises, the child has not only developed a sense of trust and autonomy but also discovered that he or she is "somebody." The child's language development is more flexible, and he or she is ready to participate in many physical activities. These conditions set the stage for initiative. With a sense of initiative, the child explores curious occurrences and asks many questions. He or she is also more likely to wander into strange places. This increased exploratory behavior and mastery of some of the environment may also lead to a sense of guilt if the parents withhold permission to do certain things. Also, the parents are often too demanding of the child during this time, by expecting him or her to perform tasks well and by belittling the child if he or she is not successful. When this occurs, the child may become overwhelmed with a sense of guilt, which may inhibit further attempts to pursue activities of his or her own initiative. These feelings of guilt and doubt may also occur when the child's own aggressive coercion or manipulation is allowed to go too far. The child realizes that he or she has too much power and does not know how to handle it.

According to Elkind (1970), the concern is that children who experience too many no's and feelings of guilt and doubt may not achieve a fully developed conscience. Exploration and initiative are encouraged when parents answer children's questions and give them freedom to initiate their own activities. When children's activities and questions are restricted, they may feel guilty about doing things on their own.

Social Learning Theory

The social learning theory claims that children develop their personality through observing others, through seeing how other people behave and the consequences of their behavior. Often, children simply imitate the behavior of other people; that is, they model what they observe. A little boy might watch his father shaving, cutting the grass, and playing basketball and might then perform some of these same actions himself. But little boys do not imitate only their fathers, and little girls do not imitate only their mothers. Young children of both sexes learn from parents of both sexes. Children also imitate other children, people they see on television, and people they see on the street. Words, actions, gestures, facial expressions, and subtle voice intonations are imitated. Children imitate behaviors we want them to acquire as well as behaviors we do not want them to acquire (for example, when a child brings home a new four-letter word from nursery school or the child-care center) (Bandura 1973).

Gender-Role Development

Gender-role development has a major effect on children's personality development during the preschool years. The behaviors appropriate for boys and girls are generally established by the parents and the culture. Gender-role attributes are passed on to children in subtle, as well as direct, ways by the home, the school, the mass media, and other social forces (Eccles and Hoffman 1984).

Children also learn gender roles by putting together bits and pieces of behavior that they are learning. Biological processes and socialization processes interact to lead to the development of gender roles. By age two, most children know whether they are a boy or girl. However, they may not be clear about what is meant by the terms *boy* and *girl*. They may believe that if a boy puts on a dress he becomes a girl, or that if a girl takes out her earrings she becomes a boy. But by the time children are three years old, they start to get a clearer idea about gender roles. They learn the social roles of being boys and girls, and they may develop strong "moral" feelings about what girls or boys should do or should not do. Such feelings are reinforced when children are praised for sex-appropriate behavior (Eisenberg 1982).

At about age six, children achieve **gender conservation,** or *gender constancy.* According to Kohlberg (1966), children now understand that their biological sex is irreversible. That is, they now realize that they will always remain male or female.

Gender conservation
The ability of preschoolers to understand that their biological sex is irreversible.

Culturally determined standards—in which girls are frequently encouraged and expected to be nurturant, obedient, and responsible and boys are expected to be self-reliant and independent—seem to be fairly consistent and persistent. In all probability, little boys and girls would like to achieve the best attributes of both sets of standards (Block 1982). Most parents are aware of the sex-appropriate behavior of their children and agree with the stereotypes established by our culture. For example, boys have been encouraged to hit back and girls have not. Dependency behaviors are accepted in girls more than in boys. Girls are expected to play with certain toys and boys are expected to play with others (Huston 1983). So by age five, children are very aware of sex-appropriate interests and behaviors and tend to prefer activities, clothes, and toys appropriate to their own gender. However, boys show more consistency in choosing sex-appropriate toys than girls do (Greenberg 1984; Sears 1957; Carper 1978; Thompson 1975). In a study involving preschool girls, it was found that girls associate dresses with traditionally feminine activities and pants with traditionally masculine activities (Kaiser, Rudy, and Byfield 1985).

In a review of literature concerning differences between males and females, Maccoby and Jacklin (1974) revealed that some of our traditional stereotypes are unfounded and others are real.

Unfounded beliefs:

1. Girls are more socially oriented.
2. Girls are more receptive to suggestions.

3. Boys and girls differ in learning ability.
4. Boys are more analytical.

Real differences:

1. Girls are more proficient at verbal skills.
2. Boys are more capable at making visual-spatial judgments.
3. Boys are better in mathematical areas.
4. Boys have higher activity levels.

Debatable areas:

1. Are girls more anxious than boys?
2. Is one sex more competitive and dominant than the other?
3. Are girls more nurturant and compliant than boys?

Self-concept

Self-concept
One's representation of one's own personality.

The **self-concept** has been described as one's representation of one's own personality (Kihlstrom et al. 1988). The self-concept differs between individuals. By eight years of age children differ from one another in perceived self-competence, that is, the extent to which they view themselves as competent in a variety of areas. Children also perceive themselves differently in their global self-worth, that is, the degree to which they feel themselves to be worthwhile persons (Harter 1982).

As long as children are helped to recognize, value, and accept themselves and their feelings, they can develop a positive self-concept. Children with a positive self-concept are confident of their ability to meet everyday problems and demands and are at ease in their relationships with other people. They compare themselves favorably with their peers and feel that authority figures are supportive and interested in them as individuals. These children tend to be comparatively independent and reliable and are relatively free from anxiety, nervousness, excessive worry, tiredness, and loneliness. They are seldom considered behavior problems (Curry and Johnson 1990; McCandless and Evans 1973).

Children with a poor self-concept are insecure and pessimistic about their ability to meet everyday problems and demands and are unsure in their relationships with others. They compare themselves unfavorably with their peers and see authority figures as a threat. They are insecure about new experiences. They also appear to be tired, anxious, and nervous (Block and Block 1980; Curry and Johnson 1990; McCandless and Evans 1973). The extreme of a low self-concept is the lack of a self-concept. A child may not even realize that he or she is a person, with a name, distinguished from all others (Curry and Johnson 1990).

Conditions leading to high self-esteem are acceptance of the child, well-defined limits and values, and respect for the child's decision making within those limits (Curry and Johnson 1990). In very poor families, parents tend to be indecisive, disorganized, apathetic, and rejecting. Low in self-esteem themselves, they do not believe that they can control their own lives, let alone their children's. Though they may be warm and nurturant, they are more likely to try to give their children immediate pleasure, through candy, money, toys, and clothes, than to guide them to develop competency (Coopersmith 1967).

Another component related to the development of a self-concept and self-esteem is body image. A child's body image grows clearer and stronger as he or she gains control and expands his or her sensory experiences. The growth of body image may be limited by all sorts of restrictions, such as illness, handicaps, lack of play space, lack of equipment, and lack of guidance and stimulation.

Another aspect of body image is evaluation in terms of beauty or attractiveness. Children get many clues from parents and siblings as to whether they are attractive or unattractive. These cues are nonverbal as well as verbal. Clothing and grooming may express what the mother or primary caregiver thinks of the child's worth and beauty. Clothing and grooming may also determine other people's reactions, including the teacher's, to the child's appearance. A child who has a runny nose and dirty face gets fewer smiles and hugs than a child who is well-scrubbed. Thus the dirty child gets the message of not being very attractive. Such messages are incorporated into one's body image.

By three years of age children take an interest in how they are like other people and how they differ from them. For example, they notice racial differences in appearance, such as skin color and hair. When children ask their parents about the differences, the parents' answers show the children how to think of themselves as members of particular ethnic groups (Stevenson 1971).

Differences in the self-concepts of three- and five-year-old children parallel age differences in memory (Eder, Gerlach, and Perlmutter 1987). Eder (1990) found that by three and one-half years of age, children have a rudimentary dispositional concept of themselves. These children possess an elaborate self-concept that enables them to recognize behaviors and emotions as being consistent or inconsistent with their self-concept. For example, a five and one-half year old in Eder's study seemed to match some puppets' statements with herself.

By three years of age, children take an interest in how they are like other people and how they differ from them. They notice racial differences in appearance, such as skin color and hair.

PUPPET 1: "My friends tell me what to do."

CHILD: "Mine don't."

PUPPET 2: "I tell my friends what to do."

CHILD: "I do too. I like to boss them around."

● SOCIAL AND EMOTIONAL DEVELOPMENT

Socialization

Socialization is the process by which we transmit our culture to our children, making them properly participating members of our society. Social development relies on interaction with other people and is closely related to emotional, physical, cognitive, and language development. Family groups and peer groups provide children with opportunities for face-to-face encounters, which play a crucial role in acquiring new social knowledge and transmitting that knowledge already gained. Most early social experiences are with family members, and experiences in the home are more important than experiences with outsiders.

Family

Relationships with family members, including parents, siblings, and grandparents, affect children's attitudes toward those people outside the home. The more positive the interactions with family members, the more positive the interactions with other people.

The most significant people in a child's life are family members, especially the parents. The family is the first social group with which the child is identified. More time is spent with the family than with any other social group.

Patterns of Parenting   The family's influence has many components. The parents' interaction with the child and the method of discipline can have a tremendous impact on the child. In a study focusing on preschoolers, Baumrind (1967, 1975) identified three major patterns of child rearing. One style was labeled **authoritarian,** which is comparable to old-fashioned strictness. This viewpoint is that obedience is a virtue, and if a conflict arises between the child and the parent, it is met with punishment and force. The child does what the parent expects without argument. Children with authoritarian parents are not given much freedom or independence and are more apt to be discontent, withdrawn, and distrustful.

The second style has been labeled **authoritative**. These parents also believe in firm enforcement of family rules, but there is a difference. Authoritative parents give their children reasons behind their decisions and permit verbal exchange. They take their children's objections into consideration, but the final decision belongs to the parents. The children are encouraged to be independent. These parents tend to respect their children's interests, opinions, and unique personalities. They are more loving, consistent, demanding, and respectful of their children's independent decisions.

The third parenting style is called **permissive**. Parents behave in a kind, accepting, indifferent way toward their children and demand very little. The children are given as much freedom as possible. These parents see their role as helping or serving their children.

When assessing children from families of these various parenting styles, Baumrind made rather surprising discoveries. She found few differences between the children of authoritarian parents and the children of permissive par-

Authoritarian child rearing
A parenting style in which the parent expects strict obedience from the child, and punishment and force are used.

Authoritative child rearing
A parenting style in which parents give children reasons behind their decisions and permit verbal exchange, but the parents have the final say in the decisions.

Permissive child rearing
A parenting style in which parents behave in a kind, accepting, indifferent way toward their children and demand very little. The parents see their role as helping or serving their children.

Authoritative parents give reasons behind their decisions and permit verbal exchange.

ents. Both groups were less motivated to achieve and less independent than children of authoritative parents. Also, the children of authoritarian and permissive parents tended to be discontented, distrustful, self-centered, and the boys were hostile. The most successful children came from authoritative parents. These children were responsible, assertive, self-reliant, and friendly. Because of these findings, Baumrind strongly favors firm but reasonable parental control enforced by punishment when necessary. She believes parents should listen to a child's point of view, but they should not have to accept it. Reasons should be given for rules, and when rules are not needed, they should not be used.

Ordinal Position The birth of each child in a family affects the family system. The **ordinal position** of the child will not only make an impact on the family but will also make an impact on the personality development of that child. Numerous studies have focused on the personality of the child in various ordinal positions. Most of the literature centers around the firstborn child. For example, a study in 1896 showed that the majority of Great Britain's eminent scientists were firstborns (Galton 1896). Forer (1976) found that firstborn girls are more likely to be shy than later-born girls. This difference appears to continue into adolescence. Firstborn boys are shyer through preschool and the early elementary school years, but by the time they reach adolescence there is no difference between them and later-born boys. Whiting and Whiting (1975) found that firstborn children have more helping experience and tend to be more prosocial than last-born or only children. Koch (1955) found that firstborns are more competitive and have an advantage in several areas of development. Other studies support the notions that firstborn children have a high need to achieve and tend to be more curious than younger siblings (Sampson 1962; Altus 1967). Hoopes and Harper (1987), Pfouts (1980), and Zajonc (1975) found firstborn and only children to be independent, ambitious, self-sufficient, and achievement oriented. Also, birth-order and IQ differences among siblings indicate that

Ordinal position
The order in which a child is born into a family.

family social interaction patterns are the most important variable in shaping firstborns' overachievement in comparison with secondborns, even when the secondborns are more intellectually gifted.

Hoopes and Harper (1987) found that secondborns adopt the responsibility for the affective state of each family member by supporting the family members' emotional needs. Secondborns feel others' feelings and absorb those feelings as if they were their own. The third-born sibling needs to feel connected with both the mother and the father. As an adult the thirdborn has difficulty in making a commitment to a relationship, but once committed, it is very difficult for him or her to get out. The fourthborn feels responsible for family unity and connects with each family member to assure harmony. He or she takes the blame for anything that goes wrong in relationships within the family. He or she needs a lot of approval and forms relationships easily (Hoopes and Harper 1987).

The Changing Family   The family has changed drastically in recent years. Couples are having fewer children. Many households have only one parent. Other households have two parents, both of whom are working outside of the home. Whatever the situation, it is the family that meets most social, economic, sexual, and child-rearing needs (Glick 1989; Glick 1990).

The *single-parent family* is the fastest growing type of family in the United States. The single-parent family may be the result of divorce, separation, death, or the parent's never being married. The most common situation is divorce. Approximately one in five American children lives in a single-parent home. Most single-parent homes are headed by mothers. However, there has been a recent increase in single-parent households headed by fathers, many of whom assumed some of the more traditional female roles in the family prior to divorce. Parenting roles seem to be changing for both men and women (Amato 1987).

In assessing the impact of divorce on children, it is important to consider the timing of the divorce, the sex and age of the child, and the attitude of the divorced parents toward each other. The greatest impact of divorce is immediately after the disruption. The relationship between children and their custodial mothers deteriorates immediately after the separation. One to two years later, their relationship stabilizes. Problems occasionally arise between mothers and sons (Hetherington et al. 1982).

Preschoolers, who are still limited by egocentric thinking, have difficulty evaluating the impact of divorce and cannot comprehend their parents' needs, emotions, and behavior. Because of the limitations in their thinking, they may have fears of abandonment or may believe that something they did hampered their parents' reconciliation, such as, "If I'd kept my room clean, maybe Dad would have come back."

Children actually are better off if conflict between their parents is not an everyday occurrence. In fact, children from single-parent homes function better than children from nuclear families that are in constant conflict. Overall, research strongly suggests that the quality of children's relationships with their parents matters much more than the fact of divorce (Lowery and Settle 1985; Amato 1986; Hanson 1986).

Research appears to support that boys have more difficulty adjusting to divorce than girls. The most accepted explanation is that the father's leaving home deprives the boy of a male model. It is especially difficult for the boy if the mother is hostile and critical of the father. The boy may fail to develop masculine traits, make exaggerated attempts to prove his masculinity, be immature, and/or have problems relating to peers. On the other hand, divorced

Human Development in the News: Only the Lonely

mothers who have a positive attitude toward ex-husbands and men in general encourage their sons to be independent and mature. These boys are not different from boys who are reared in father-present homes (Hetherington et al. 1982; Kurdek and Siesky 1980; Biller 1971). Santrock and Warshak (1979) found that boys show more maturity, more competent behavior, and are less demanding when their fathers have custody.

For girls, if the father's absence occurs before they are five years old and if there are no males in the home, the effects manifest themselves during adolescence. The girls are more dependent and seek adult supervision more. They also show an inability to interact appropriately with male peers and adult males. For example, daughters of divorcées display inappropriate seductive patterns of behavior toward males. They tend to be involved in dating earlier and engage in more sexual activities at earlier ages than other girls do. Daughters of widows, however, show anxieties, tensions, shyness, and discomfort around male peers (Hetherington 1973; Wallerstein and Kelly 1980). Block et al. (1981) found that these girls were less aggressive than boys. They also found that daughters of widows tend to worry more about schoolwork and often take on more household responsibilities.

Levy-Shiff (1982) found that children from mother-headed families in which the father died just prior to the children's birth (there were no other siblings in the families) were emotionally more dependent, showed more separation anxiety, and showed more developmental and behavioral disturbances than children from intact families. The most significant differences were centered around the boys from father-absent homes. When compared with boys from intact families, these boys were less instrumentally independent and showed less autonomous achievement-striving. They were more aggressive and noncompliant, and they were observed to be less emotionally and cognitively adjusted. It was also found that these boys were less socially adjusted and had more difficulty in peer interaction. On the other hand, girls from father-absent homes were more independent and socially assertive when compared with the girls from intact homes. Perhaps their mothers modeled independence and coping skills.

In a review of the father-absence literature, Coonrad (1981) noted that the influence of the ineffective, passive father and the overrestrictive and rejecting father are, occasionally, more damaging to healthy personality formation than the effects of the absent father. Coonrad notes that in children's sex-role adjustment, fathers and mothers play a vital role, with the father being a particularly powerful influence on the son's masculine orientation. The emotional scars created by absent fathers, rejecting fathers, and weak, passive fathers devalue children's feelings of self-worth and adequacy both in their sexuality and in their general competency.

The greatest negative impact on cognitive development occurs when the onset of the paternal absence begins in the first two years of the child's life. The absence of the father, and the effect of a passive or overrestrictive, rejecting father, contribute greatly to antisocial behavior and a higher crime rate in youngsters. An ineffective father seems to invoke contempt and disregard for the male image. The way the father treats the mother, the amount and quality of the time he spends interacting with his daughter, the limits he sets and his expectations for behavior, and the continuity of his presence seem to greatly influence feminine development. A girl's heterosexual relationships are related to the kind of fathering she experiences. Coonrad also emphasizes the need for children to see both parents appreciating compliments from one another. This interaction pattern is very important to a child's total development.

Working mothers, single or married, are commonplace in our society. The overall development of the preschool child does not seem to suffer if the mother works (Hoffman 1984). A study comparing the behavior of the children of working and nonworking mothers reported that boys who received full-time mothering during the preschool years were more advanced cognitively; however, they were rated as more conforming, fearful, and inhibited as adolescents (Moore 1975).

Maternal employment has several benefits. First, working mothers report more satisfaction with their lives than nonworking mothers do (Dubnoff et al. 1978). A mother's satisfaction with her professional role increases her effectiveness as a parent (Gold and Andres 1978b). Married mothers who enjoy their profession outside of the home and do not see their roles as conflicting enjoy their children and their parenting role more than married mothers who see their roles as conflicting (Tiedje et al. 1990). Married mothers and fathers and single working mothers who are concerned about the well-being of their children while they work experience more stress and have negative feelings about their work 'Greenberger and O'Neil 1990).

Second, working mothers may serve as more appropriate models for their children. Children of such women are more responsible, become more independent, and develop self-esteem. Research also indicates that daughters of working mothers admire their mothers more than do daughters of nonworking mothers. Daughters of working mothers are also more likely to become higher achievers later in life. For boys, some studies indicate that sons of working mothers are above average in social and personality adjustment (Gold and Andres 1978a, 1978b). As boys and girls approach adolescence, they are more likely to support women's employment generally (Scarr 1984).

Friends

Friends are those people with whom an individual chooses to interact most frequently. Friends like to be with each other. It takes more time for preschool children to acquire friends than it does for older children and adults. The degree of intimacy between any two children fluctuates quite a lot during the early stages of friendship. After having been friends for a long time, however, the children tend to be more stable in their relationships with each other than with newer members of the group. Friendships become more stable as children grow older.

Imaginary Friends   An early sign that a child has acquired the concept of "friend" is the appearance of one or more imaginary companions in the absence of, or in addition to, real companions. Between 15 and 30 percent of children three to four years old have imaginary friends. By the time they enter school and have children for playmates, they usually abandon their imaginary playmates. The imagined persons or animals seem real to the children, who talk to them, talk about them, and play with them. Firstborn and only children have imaginary companions more often than later-born children. Bright and creative children are also more likely to have them (Schaefer 1969).

An important function of an imaginary companion is that it provides an opportunity for the child to practice and develop social and language skills. The imaginary companion can be an outlet for the child's aggression and hostility. Such a companion also illustrates the importance of play and fantasy for the preschool child's development of skills necessary in interpersonal relationships. High school students who produce more-creative literary works are more likely to have had imaginary companions in childhood (McGhee 1979).

A. A. Milne (1927), creator of Winnie-the-Pooh, wrote a wonderful description of a child's invisible friend in an ode to "Binker":

> Binker—what I call him—is a secret of my own,
> And Binker is the reason why I never feel alone.
> Playing in the nursery, sitting on the stair,
> Whatever I am busy at, Binker will be there. . . .
> Binker's always talking 'cos I'm teaching him to speak:
> He sometimes likes to do it in a funny sort of squeak,
> And he sometimes likes to do it in a hoodling sort of roar. . . .
> And I have to do it for him 'cos his throat is rather sore. . . .
> Binker's brave as lions when we're running in the park;
> Binker's brave as tigers when we're lying in the dark;
> Binker's brave as elephants. He never, never cries . . .
> Except (like other people) when the soap gets in his eyes. . . .
> Binker isn't greedy, but he does like things to eat,
> So I have to say to people when they're giving me a sweet,
> "Oh, Binker wants a chocolate, so could you give me two?"
> And then I eat it for him, 'cos his teeth are rather new. . . .
> Well, I'm very fond of Daddy, but he hasn't time to play,
> And I'm very fond of Mummy, but she sometimes goes away,
> And I'm often cross with Nanny when she wants to brush my hair. . . .
> But Binker's always Binker, and is certain to be there."

Friends and peers make a tremendous impact on the socialization process of preschool children. By three years, children have acquired some specific techniques for initiating and maintaining social encounters. As children grow older, peer play changes.

Parten's Stages   Mildred Parten (1932), in her classic study, identified six stages or ways in which two- to five-year-olds behave in group situations. The first is **unoccupied behavior**. In this situation, the child does not appear to be playing but watches whatever is taking place nearby. When nothing is going on, the child may play with his or her own body, sit in one spot glancing around the room, or just stand around.

Unoccupied behavior
According to Parten, a situation in which the child does not appear to be playing but watches whatever is taking place nearby.

Onlooker
According to Parten, a child interested in watching other children play. He or she often talks to, asks questions of, or gives suggestions to the other children, but does not actually enter into the play.

Solitary play
According to Parten, a situation in which the child plays alone with a separate group of toys, without trying to get close to other children and without paying attention to what they are doing.

Parallel activity
According to Parten, a situation in which a child plays independently, but with the same toys other children are using. The child is playing beside other children rather than with them.

Associative play
According to Parten, a situation in which the child plays with other children.

Cooperative play
According to Parten, a situation in which a group of children are organized around a goal or theme. One or two children direct the activities of the others.

Onlooker is the next stage. The child is interested in watching other children play. He or she often talks to, asks questions of, or gives suggestions to the other children, but does not actually enter into the play.

During **solitary play** the child plays alone with a separate group of toys, without trying to get close to other children and without paying attention to what they are doing.

In **parallel activity** the child plays independently, but with the same toys other children are using and in close proximity to them. The child is playing beside other children rather than with them.

In **associative play** the child can be said to be playing with other children. They talk about what they are doing, borrow toys from each other, follow one another around, and sometimes try to control the membership of the group. All are engaged in similar activities (Parten 1932).

Finally, in **cooperative play** a group of children are organized around a goal or theme. One or two children direct the activities of the others. In this type of play, the efforts of one child are supplemented by those of another. Various group members take on different roles with a division of labor.

Parten's stages of interaction are increasingly sophisticated. The more sophisticated forms are observed in older children. Between the ages of two and three, play is predominantly parallel, with relatively little time spent in cooperative interaction. By age five, associative play and cooperative play increase in frequency. Bakeman and Brownlee (1980) found that often a preschooler's play includes several of the types described by Parten. They found that parallel play serves as a transitional or warm-up strategy that enables a child to move into associative and cooperative play, allowing him or her to get involved and play with others.

Peers   Close relations with parents provide skills that optimize children's peer contacts. This, in turn, seems to lead to successful peer relations as the child grows older. The quality of peer behavior acquired at an early age may be more important for social development than the number of opportunities for social interaction.

It is also possible that peers can provide social nurturance and protection that might otherwise be lacking. This was found to be true in the case of six children whose parents were killed in concentration camps during World War II and who subsequently lived together for several years. The children were flown to England after the war. They were then between three and four years old. Since they were so young, it was decided that they should be given some time to adjust to the change in their circumstances before being placed among larger groups of children. Arrangements were made for them to live in a country house for a year. While there, they showed no interest in forming attachments with adult caregivers. In fact, they showed active hostility toward the caregivers. When angry, the children would hit and bite, shout and scream, and spit at the adults. In contrast, the children were strongly attached to one another. The children's positive feelings were centered exclusively in their own group. It was evident that they cared greatly for each other and not at all for anybody or anything else. They had no other wish than to be together and became upset when they were separated from each other, even for short periods of time. No child would consent to remain upstairs while the others were downstairs, or vice versa, and no child would be taken for a walk or an errand without the others. If anything of the kind happened, the single child would ask for the other children, while the group would fret for the missing child (Freud and Dann

1954). In short, the children had suffered greatly from the loss of their parents and from the upheaval of their lives. They were hypersensitive, restless, aggressive, and difficult to handle. But the children had developed positive social attitudes toward one another. Envy, jealousy, rivalry, and competition were not observed within the group.

When children begin to interact with peers, they are influenced for the first time by individuals other than their parents and siblings. When children enter a social group, their personalities and behaviors are influenced by that group. They become eager to win the group's approval and affection. Thus the hypotheses accounting for the way parents influence their children's socialization also apply to the way children influence each other.

Preschool children who are eager for the approval of their peers tend to imitate their peers. In one study, when children observed a peer generously sharing things, their own sharing behavior increased. Thus peers can serve as models and as important reinforcing agents, which supports the claims of social learning theory. The preschool child who asks for help from peers and is eager for their approval tends to be more popular than the child who seems primarily interested in attracting attention (Hartrup and Coates 1967).

In a study by Hazen and Black (1989) preschool children who were liked by their peers were better able to initiate and maintain coherent discourse than disliked children were. They directed communications to specific other children and responded appropriately to the initiation of others. Liked children were also able to split their initiations more evenly between two playmates. This ability reflects a type of "decentration" applied to social interaction, since the child can attend to more than one interaction partner simultaneously.

Responding to the initiations of others is important to the social acceptance of preschoolers. Hazen and Black also found that socially accepted children are likely to provide responses that are related to the preceding initiations, can acknowledge the initiations of others, and can reject initiations by offering a reason or alternative idea. Well-liked children also use what Hazen and Black call *back-channel listener responses*. For example, the following dialog was taken from an actual transcript:

DIANE: "The baby wants to drink her bottle."

ALLISON: "Okay."

DIANE: (after feeding the doll) "Now, that's done."

ALLISON: "Uh-humm."

DIANE: "Now I've got to dust the walls, of course."

ALLISON: "Good."

Allison acknowledged each of Diane's communications even though they were not directed at anyone in particular and so did not require a response.

Liked preschoolers are also better able to adapt their communication style to different social situations. They use a lower proportion of expressives and a higher proportion of informative statements when entering a group than when they are already a part of the group. For example, expressives are nonpropositional expressions of feelings and attitudes. They include exclamations (such as "Oh, no!" and "Yahoo!") as well as word play (such as "mop, mop, mop, moppity, mop" and "Su-per-man! Ta-ta-ta!"). Informative statements are propositions that report facts, conditions, opinions, and feelings. They include identifications ("I'm Batman"), descriptions ("That hat is too big"), explanations

("Here's how it works"), and statements of feelings or opinions ("That's yucky," or "I like your dress").

Preschool children seem to like to have peers seek their approval or help, but it bothers them to be pestered by someone. Some evidence indicates that brighter children are more popular than those with below-average intelligence (Hartrup 1970).

Pets Pets can function as friends. Preschool children include their pets in their physical, imaginative, and free play. Pets can serve as sources for learning, as well as help minimize emotional trauma and alleviate some emotional problems. It has been suggested that a pet can serve as a major factor in a normal child's ability to maintain psychological equilibrium when faced with unusual negative circumstances (Heiman 1965). Pets also generally promote good mental health. Levinson (1962, 1964, 1967, 1969a, 1969b, 1972) categorized the importance of pets as companions, friends, teammates, admirers, confidants, mirrors, trustees, defenders, toys, servants, slaves, and scapegoats.

Children's Play

The content and quality of children's play is a good index to every phase of development. Play can be simple and unstructured or it can be complex and very structured. Therefore, no matter how it is defined, play and playful interaction with peers is important for the overall development of preschool children (Deutsch 1983). Play is also useful in instilling the appreciation of the role of play in adult life. A child who does not learn to play well grows up to be an adult who cannot work well (Erickson 1985).

Active play is essential for children's physical and motor development. It not only develops muscles and exercises all parts of the body, but it also acts as an outlet for surplus energy. If this surplus energy remains pent up, it makes children tense. Play also encourages communication. In order to play successfully with others, children must learn to communicate in terms the other children can understand. They must also learn to understand what others are trying to communicate to them. By playing with other children, they learn how to establish social relationships and how to meet and solve problems that these relationships present.

Play allows children to prepare for life. Play provides an opportunity for children to be acting agents as well as reacting agents in their environment. Children are expected to follow set patterns at home and at school, but at play they can be the decision makers. Play permits the child to trim the world down to manageable size and manipulate it (Caplan and Caplan 1973). Play allows a child to experience reality and fantasy simultaneously. Through imaginary episodes, a child can harmlessly confront creatures such as witches, ghosts, robbers, lions, dogs, and other villains and maybe even triumph over them. Play enables a child to achieve needs and desires that cannot be met in other ways. For example, when a child cannot achieve a leadership role in real life, he or she may accomplish this desire through being a leader of space people or giants.

Through experimentation in play, children can discover the satisfaction of creating something new and different. James Johnson (1975) found a correlation between fantasy play, creativity, and intelligence in three- to five-year-olds. He found a cycle in which cognitive skill and play feed into one another. In order for children to pretend to be something else, they need to reach a certain minimal level of cognitive development. They need to know the difference between being something and pretending to be something. They need to have some idea of what a tiger is and does before they can roar like one. As the cycle continues, the more children fantasize with each other, the more they develop cognitively.

Certain factors aid children in their pretend play. They must have some familiarity with adult roles in order to use them to structure their play, although quite often their notions are skimpy and inaccurate. Props such as cast-off clothes, large cardboard boxes, blocks, and so on, will enhance pretend play. Frost and Sunderlin (1985) found that children who do not have space to play in or materials to play with do not play as much as children who do have space and materials. They do not need expensive toys, however. Children usually need other children with whom they can fantasize. This is probably the most important factor in creative fantasy, because children stimulate each other with new ideas and interests. Fantasy, or dramatic, play peaks between three and six years of age.

Many authorities believe that pretending and make-believe activities lay the foundations for the development of well-adjusted and fulfilled adults. Research shows that when children are involved in pretend play, they are more likely to smile and show other signs of contentment and elation. On the other hand, children who are limited in their capacity for fantasy seem to be sad and more physically violent. They are also more likely to disrupt the play of others and get into trouble more often (Singer and Singer 1977; McGhee 1979). Biblow (1973) studied children who were high and low in fantasy level. He found that low-fantasy-level children not only were more aggressive but were more likely to become hostile when stimulated by an aggressive film. An implication of the study was that fantasy training would be beneficial in helping an aggressive child cope with hostile impulses.

Make-believe play exposes children to originality and makes it possible for them to try original themes of their own.

Other studies have shown that children with a rich fantasy life tend to have better-developed cognitive skills. One study found that children who were given training in acting out fairy tales were better able to recognize causal sequences and showed more skill in making up stories. Fantasy may be very important to vocabulary growth, and children with a rich fantasy life are better able to plan ahead and anticipate everyday situations (Saltz and Johnson 1974; Saltz and Brodie 1982; Singer and Singer 1977; Saltz, Dixon, and Johnson 1977).

The most obvious benefit of fantasy play is the creativity it encourages in children. Make-believe play exposes children to originality and makes it possible for them to try out novel themes of their own. Such activity also allows children to recognize the creativity of others. It has been found that creative adults engaged in a great deal of fantasy play as children (Vandenberg 1980; Singer and Singer 1977; McGhee 1979).

Piaget (1952) stresses that cognitive stimulation can be achieved through children's exploratory and play behavior. Children can make motor and sensory discoveries concerning sizes and shapes, up and down, hard and soft, smooth and rough, and so on, through play. The properties of things and the conceptions of weight, height, volume, and texture can be understood through tearing down and building up, handling, measuring, manipulating, matching, and patterning.

Through play, children are helped in building their own individual sense of identity. They can get outside themselves and view themselves from other perspectives. Children learn what their abilities are and how they compare with their peers. This helps them to shape and mold their self-image and to develop a more definite and realistic concept of themselves.

Studies have shown that children who participate in make-believe situations seem to develop more social awareness and emotional sensitivity toward others. Pretending makes it possible for young children to imagine themselves in many different roles and to become familiar with the point of view of others. Pretending also makes it possible to try on the emotions and attitudes of others. The kind of play children are involved in, the variety of their play activities, and the amount of time they spend in play are indicators of personal and social adjustments (Crum et al. 1983; Rubin et al. 1983).

The number of playmates decreases with age. Preschool children will play with anyone who is willing to play with them. If they find someone playing in a more interesting way, they shift from the children they are playing with to the other child or children. All neighborhood children or preschool-group children are seen as potential playmates. When children are older they become members of a gang. They play with a small select group whose members have common interests and whose play gives them particular satisfaction. Thus older children limit the number of their playmates and spend most of their playtime with those playmates (Hurlock 1978).

Early Childhood Programs

Good-quality early childhood programs, whether they are day-care centers, nursery schools, or Head Start programs, provide opportunities for preschool children to develop socially as well as physically, emotionally, and cognitively. A variety of programs are available to meet the individual needs of the family and the child. Day-care centers serve parents who are employed outside of the home. Nursery schools and cooperative preschools offer enrichment and social interaction opportunities for three- to five-year-old children. Head Start was developed to give the preschoolers of low-income families a boost both cognitively and socially before they enter the public school system.

Quality varies from program to program. In evaluating a program, parents should look at the child/teacher ratio. The number of children per class should not exceed twelve for three-year-olds and sixteen for older preschoolers (Zigler and Turner 1982). Children have better experiences in smaller groups and in smaller centers or schools (Stith and Davis 1984). Children in small groups are more sociable with their peers (Clarke-Stewart 1987; Kontos and Fiene 1987). In centers where there are too many children per adult, caregivers are less positive and more prohibitive (Smith and Connolly 1986).

The caregivers should have training and/or education in child development (Clarke-Stewart 1987). One of the best predictors of a positive experience for the preschool child in day care is the quality of caregiver-child interactions. Preschool children who have responsive and involved caregivers display more exploratory behaviors (Anderson et al. 1981) and are more intelligent and responsive (McCartney et al. 1982; Phllips et al. 1987) when compared with children who have less responsive caregivers.

Parents should examine the facility's objectives, aims, and philosophy. Research shows that programs that have a high degree of parental involvement are usually high-quality programs (Laser and Darlington 1982).

Studies concerning the impact of day care on the developing child, in which home-reared children were compared with day-care children, indicate that quality centers encourage various areas of development. A concern of child development authorities and parents is that children in day care will not develop critical attachment behaviors for their parents. Kagan et al. (1978) and Rutter (1982) found that day-care children were just as attached to their parents as home-reared children were.

Quality day care seems to have neither harmful nor beneficial effects on the cognitive development of middle-class children. However, quality day care can be beneficial in upgrading the development of deprived children (Norman 1978).

The Montessori (1964) preschool program was originally designed for poor and deprived children. It emphasizes the perceptual and cognitive development of the preschool child. This program organizes activities around highly structured materials that illustrate particular geometrical and mathematical relationships. For example, a set of cylinders may be graded by size and each cylinder designed to fit snugly into size-graded holes in a board. When a child chooses this toy, he or she experiments with the cylinders and holes to find the best fit. Verbalization is de-emphasized, while the chief purpose is the experimenting with the materials. This program has been found to be effective in promoting overall cognitive development (Consortium for Longitudinal Studies 1983).

Social development is one of the most common goals in the curriculum of day-care centers and nursery schools. Studies concerning the social development of day-care children have had mixed results. Some studies have found that day-care youngsters are less apprehensive in new situations. Children reared at home are somewhat more distressed than day-care children when an unfamiliar child and his or her mother enters the room to play. Day-care children play at a higher developmental level and interact more with peers (in both positive and negative ways) than home-care children do. They share more, but they also fight more. Aggressiveness, impulsivity, egocentrism, and intolerance for frus-

Social development is one of the most common goals in the curriculum of day care centers and nursery schools.

tration, failure, and interruption are more frequently encountered in full-time day-care children (Clarke-Stewart 1982; Kagan et al. 1978; Belsky and Steinberg 1978).

Robertson (1982) found that first-grade boys who had had day-care experience were more disobedient, quarrelsome, and uncooperative than children with no day-care experience. They also had problems interacting with adults. On the other hand, other studies have found that day-care children are, on the average, more self-confident, more outgoing, more socially competent with both peers and adults, as well as less timid than home-care children (Clarke-Stewart and Fein 1983; Clarke-Stewart 1986).

Day-care children get sick more often than home-care children do. This is true in day-care centers as well as in day-care homes (usually more than four children and less than twelve are on the latter premises). Day-care children under two years old have twice as many sieges of diarrhea and have more respiratory infections. Young children and adults they come in contact with are more susceptible to influenza type B (H-flu). This virus may result in middle-ear infections and one type of meningitis. Day-care children may also be symptom-free carriers of viral A hepatitis, which they pass on to adults. However, children get sick less often after the first year in group care (Belsky and Steinberg 1978).

Head Start, a federal program for three-, four-, and five-year-olds, has served more than 10.9 million children since 1965. Studies concerning Head Start show that well-designed preschool programs have impressive and lasting benefits. Graduates of Head Start scored higher on IQ tests, got better grades, dropped out of school less, and were much more likely to meet school standards. The children who benefited the most were those who were the most needy, such as children whose mothers did not finish high school, children from single-parent families, or children with low IQ scores when they began Head Start. Speech-impaired, learning-disabled, and emotionally disturbed Head Start pupils did better on some measures of intellectual achievement than similarly handicapped children who were not enrolled in Head Start (Lazer and Darlington 1982; Palmer 1978).

Studies have found that Head Start children are sociable and assertive, as well as more attention-seeking, attention-getting, and aggressive than non–Head Start children. The children's physical development and motor control are positively influenced by Head Start. The children are more apt to attain normal height and weight and are more proficient on physical tests than non–Head Start children. Their school attendance records are better too. Head Start's stress on parental involvement made a positive impact on pupils' families and the community (Lazer and Darlington 1982; Palmer 1978).

Studies of intervention programs like Head Start found that their graduates, when they reached nineteen years of age and older, had higher rates of employment and vocational and college training after high school than individuals who had not attended preschool. They were also involved in fewer arrests, and fewer dropped out of high school as compared with those who had not been involved in preschool programs (Berreuta-Clement et al. 1984).

Emotional Development

Emotions are states of feeling that arise when we psychologically process certain kinds of external stimuli. Fear and anxiety are two real emotions faced by preschoolers. Attempting to control aggression is also an area of emotional development that preschool children face. These problems of emotional development are not settled in early childhood. They are dealt with throughout life in varying circumstances. But the manner in which the problems are met early in life tends to establish a pattern for later behavior. Prosocial behavior, such as altruism and empathy, emerges during this time and helps the young child interact with other children, as well as establish a sense of self.

Fear and Anxiety

Ninety percent of the preschoolers interviewed in one study feared some specific thing (Macfarlane et al. 1954), and 5 percent had extreme phobias and fears (Miller 1983). Physiologically, fear differs from anxiety in that fear dries the mouth and anxiety increases both salivation and gastric secretion (Cattell 1963). **Fear** is an emotional state in anticipation of a dangerous or unpleasant stimulus. **Anxiety** is a generalized, nonspecifiable fear. Fear is a reaction to imminent danger, while anxiety is reaction to an anticipated or imagined danger.

Jersild and Holmes (1935a) conducted a series of classic studies of fear in young children. These researchers found that from two to five years, children showed a decrease in fear of noise, strange objects and persons, pain, falling, sudden loss of support, and sudden movement. During the same age span, there was an increase in fear of imaginary creatures, the dark, animals, ridicule, getting lost, and the threat of harm, such as from traffic, deep water, and fire. Miller (1983) found that most three-year-olds fear dogs and four-year-olds may fear the dark. These fears develop as the children gain greater awareness of their environment and become capable of understanding potential danger.

Jersild and Holmes (1935b) also studied a variety of ways of dealing with children's fear. They found that ignoring, ridiculing, or punishing a child's fear or forcing the child into the feared situation did more harm than good. On the other hand, they found several positive ways of handling fear, such as explaining the situation to the child. For example, when explaining thunder to a child who is afraid of it, one might say that it is caused by hot and cold clouds bumping together. Another way would be to set an example. It was found that if a child sees another child the same age who is not afraid of a particular situation, he or she will lose the fear or at least not be as fearful (Bandura, Grusec, and Menlove 1967).

Positive conditioning is another method of alleviating fear. The fear situation might be matched with a positive experience; the child will then associate the fear with something positive. Or it may help to give the child confidence in dealing with the feared object or situation. For example, children who are afraid of the dark might have a light switch by the bed so they can control the dark.

Parents should learn to share and accept children's emotions and feelings as the children confront fear. They should also learn the idiosyncrasies of the children. Individual children may be affected differently by the same fear. Fear should never be used as a disciplinary tactic. Threatening a child with "if you don't quit crying I'm going to have the policeman arrest you" will only increase his or her fear of police officers. Fantasy play should be encouraged so children can retreat from the real world into a world where they not only can be master but can control and reduce their fears (Jersild et al. 1975).

In order to prevent children's fear, it is important to give a warning when an element of pain may be involved. A common example is a visit to the doctor

Fear
An emotional state in anticipation of a dangerous or unpleasant stimulus; a reaction to imminent danger.

Anxiety
Generalized, nonspecifiable fear; a reaction to an anticipated or imagined danger.

or dentist. If children are told "it won't hurt" and it does hurt, they may lose faith in the parents and doctor and may generalize all medical treatment as something to fear. Conversely, if the parents go too far in describing how much it is going to hurt, the child may become so tense that the pain will be magnified.

For children who are going to be hospitalized, it is now a common procedure to take them through a rehearsal of their stay a day or two before they are admitted. They are usually informed about what will be done, where they will go, how they will feel when it is over, and what can be done to control pain.

Another way to prevent fear is to allow children to approach a potentially frightening situation in their own way and at their own pace. For example, in a classic study by Schramm (1935) children were placed in a chair so that their movements were restricted. Then one at a time a frog, a rabbit, a rat, and a parakeet were placed on a tray and moved slowly toward the children. In almost every case the children were frightened, and in some cases they were terrified. A different group of children who were the same age were allowed to roam freely around a room in which these same animals were placed on the middle of a table. The children were allowed to approach or ignore the animals as they wished. None of the children showed any fear. If children feel trapped and cannot avoid a frightening situation that is forced on them, they may have a panic reaction. Today, this study would be considered unethical.

In general, it is believed that the best fear preventative is developing a sense of security, and a way to define *security* is "the absence of anxiety" (Jersild and Holmes 1935a, 1935b). Fear and anxiety are similar in that they represent unpleasant states of mind and both are responses to perceived or real dangers and threats. The main difference between fear and anxiety is the perception or awareness of the cause of distress. Fear usually focuses on a particular object or situation or something tangible with a specific origin, such as a dentist or doctor who has caused painful experiences. Anxiety may be the result of unsuccessful attempts to cope with fear.

In order for children to experience anxiety, they must possess the ability to imagine something not present. Thus anxiety develops later than fear. It often develops after a period of frequent and intense worry that undermines a child's self-confidence, causing generalized feelings of inadequacy. Anxiety can be contagious; that is, if children are closely associated with anxious people, they may imitate anxiety. And if they are already suffering from anxiety, associating with anxious people will probably increase it.

Children may respond in a variety of ways when anxiety occurs. They may regress to earlier patterns of behavior. For example, they may sleep more than they need to, they may withdraw, and/or they may either overeat or undereat. Although their anxiety responses are internal, chronic uneasiness can make them more nervous than other children, as can be seen when they bite their lips or fingernails. Other recognizable ways in which anxiety can be expressed are through depression, irritability, mood swings, quick anger, and extreme sensitivity to what others say or do. These children are unhappy because they feel insecure. Their self-dissatisfaction is generalized rather than limited to a specific situation (Burch 1973).

It is not always obvious when children are suffering from anxiety. They can cloak their anxiety in several ways. By being boisterous and showing off, anxious children try to convince themselves and others that they are competent. Anxiety makes it difficult to concentrate, so the child becomes bored and restless. These children will also avoid threatening situations by going to sleep even when they are not tired, or by keeping themselves so busy that they do not have time to think. Or they might withdraw into a fantasy world. Another characteristic is out-of-character behavior. For example, a normally friendly child might show a streak of cruelty, or a child who is usually kind may commit a brutal act. Anxious children tend to watch television or use other mass media more than their peers. Thus they can escape temporarily from anxiety-producing situations. These defense mechanisms are unconscious, so they keep the child and others from recognizing the anxiety (Hurlock 1978).

Using the withholding of love as a means of punishment for misbehaving can cause anxiety in preschoolers. Parents should continue to provide support and protection even when punishing their child for misbehavior. The child should be helped to cope with the conflict between desires and restrictions. For example, if a child steals something from a store, the parents need to explain firmly, but gently, why the object must be paid for or returned, and the child should not be punished or berated.

Parents need to help their child set realistic goals and then avoid criticizing the child if he or she cannot accomplish them. When a child initiates doing things on his or her own, the parents should be patient, and they need to refrain from providing help unless it is asked for or it is absolutely essential. If a child does something wrong, he or she should not be made to feel excessively ashamed. The parents' responsibility is to be always available to provide love and support so that the child feels secure. It is also important for the parents to be especially supportive and reassuring when the child encounters negative or belittling experiences with peers.

Aggression

Because preschoolers' behavior is so complex, it is not always easy to distinguish between acts that may be aggressive or acts that are outgoing and healthy. Some aggressive behaviors may really be attempts at social interaction or normal assertions of self-interest.

Two types of aggression have been identified: *instrumental* and *hostile*. **Instrumental aggression** aims at the retrieval of an object, territory, or privilege. Because this negative peer interaction is object centered, the behavior lacks the negative personal intent needed to qualify as true aggression (Bronson 1981). **Hostile aggression** is oriented towards another person following some sort of threat or the belief that another person has behaved intentionally.

Some studies indicate that instrumental aggression is far more common in young children. The very young have more disputes over possessions. By the end of the preschool years children learn alternative ways to settle disputes over objects. As they get older, their aggression is more person-directed, with retaliation and hostile outbursts more common (Hay 1984; Cummings et al. 1986).

Aggression has been the topic of many studies in this country as well as cross-culturally (Hay 1984; Cummings et al. 1986). The findings of these studies indicate that boys around age three show more open aggressive behavior than girls of the same age do. Preschool boys do more pushing and hitting, have more aggressive contact with peers, and participate in more rough-and-tumble play than girls do. Boys also more frequently display negative means to gain attention, such as hitting or pushing another child even if they are not angry with that child. Around age five, boys choose other boys, rather than girls, as targets of physical aggression.

Differences between boys and girls could be attributed to cultural expecta-

Instrumental aggression
Aggression that aims at the retrieval of an object, territory, or privilege.

Hostile aggression
Aggression oriented towards another person following some sort of threat or the belief that another person has behaved intentionally.

Hostile aggression is oriented toward another person following some sort of threat or in the belief that another person has behaved intentionally.

tions and stereotyping. Girls are capable of expressing physical aggression. Cummings et al. (1989) found that for girls, greater aggressiveness at age two was related to less frequent bodily aggression at age five. Expressing anger is less acceptable to parents in girls than in boys (Malatesta and Haviland 1982) and girls are socialized not to be aggressive (Cummings et al. 1986). There appear to be stable differences in aggression among preschool girls and boys (Olweus 1979; Parke and Slaby 1983; Cummings et al. 1989).

Childhood aggression may be due to biological factors, environmental factors, or an interaction of psychobiosocial factors. In a study that compared preschool settings, aggressive actions were more frequent in crowded and dense conditions than in settings that were not as crowded (Szegal 1981). Adult behavior can also affect childhood aggression. Weintraub et al. (1978) found that children of depressed mothers were more impatient, defiant, and aggressive. Patterson (1980) also found that children of depressed mothers were more aggressive. The emotional unavailability and irritability that often characterizes depression may provide a model for the expression of anger and produce conditions in which it is difficult for parents to help children learn how to regulate their emotions (Belle 1982; Tronick and Field 1986). Also, prolonged exposure to high levels of aggression will increase aggression in preschool children (Zillman 1982). Angry behavior between adults will lead to aggressiveness in children (Cummings 1987; Cummings et al. 1985).

Another study found that physical punishment inhibited direct aggression but increased displaced aggression (Sears et al. 1957). Obviously, physical punishment is not the answer in helping children control aggressive behavior. The adult who uses physical punishment to deal with physical aggression is not only modeling aggression but is also demonstrating a belief that aggression is a viable solution to problems.

Authorities have offered some suggestions to curb aggressive behavior. One study found that a verbal rebuke just as a child initiated an aggressive act rather than after the behavior had been completed was more effective in preventing future aggressive behavior. Another way to prevent aggression is to strengthen altruism. Helpfulness and cooperation should be emphasized as highly valued behaviors (Feshbach 1970).

Another type of aggression displayed by children might be manifested through jealousy or rivalry. **Jealousy** results from frustration over the desire to be loved best; **rivalry,** from the desire to do best. A young child is likely to feel jealous of the new baby who displaces him or her as the youngest or the only child in the family. He or she is likely to feel rivalrous with an older child who is stronger and abler. This is called *sibling rivalry*. It is more likely to occur if parents practice inconsistent discipline or if they are overindulgent toward a particular child. Children who experience feelings of jealousy and rivalry may become aggressive or regress to earlier behavior such as bed-wetting, thumb-sucking, or other infantile behavior.

Prosocial Behavior

Prosocial behavior comes in two forms: *empathy* and *altruism*. **Empathy** is the ability to experience the thoughts and feelings of others, and **altruism** is the practice of acting unselfishly to help others. In order to fully understand these prosocial behaviors, a child must first realize that he or she is an independent agent who is responsible for his or her own actions.

Most parents and teachers agree that prosocial behavior is a goal they want for young children. However, many people believe that children are totally selfish and cruel. Research does not support this belief. In fact, some studies show that children as young as one year old show signs of altruism. An early altruistic reaction is crying as an expression of sadness at another's distress.

Dr. Martin Hoffman (1975a, 1975b, 1978) states that altruism in children develops in four stages. In the first stage, which is the first few months of life, infants react to someone else's distress as their own because they have no clear sense of self. During the second stage, starting at around ten months, the child will help others by giving them what the child himself or herself would want if in distress.

Stage three starts at about three years. Children will help by offering what others want or need. Radke-Yarrow et al. (1983) found that the capacity for altruism is widespread among preschoolers. However, Iannotti (1985) found that although a preschool child can experience others' distress, he or she will not necessarily act on it to offer comfort or assistance. Sometimes preschoolers will not offer help because they assume an adult will help.

Finally, the stage-four child, beginning at age six, is able to put another's distress into a larger context. For example, this child can feel empathy for another child who has lost a parent. Thus preschool children not only are aware that other people have feelings, but also make an effort to understand those feelings. As children grow older, they become less egocentric. Perhaps they are increasingly able to "center" on the feelings of others.

Two factors appear to play major roles in the acquisition of altruistic behavior: cognitive development and adult modeling and nurturance. Increased altruism is associated with certain aspects of cognitive development. If children are generous or helpful to others, they must be able to perceive the other persons' state or condition. They also must know something about how the conditions of trouble or sorrow can be relieved, and they must be willing to give themselves to others.

When a child watches someone else helping or giving, he or she is likely to

Jealousy
A result of frustration over the desire to be loved best.

Rivalry
A result of frustration over the desire to do best.

Empathy
The ability to experience the thoughts and feelings of others.

Altruism
The practice of acting unselfishly to help others.

engage in similar behavior. Radke-Yarrow et al. (1983) found that when a caregiver is nurturant and models empathy and helpfulness toward others, then the child will show empathy. When adults demonstrate altruistic behavior, and especially when they accompany such actions with expressions of pleasure in what they are doing, children are more likely to follow suit. Children's evaluations of altruistic people are more favorable than their judgments of people who behave selfishly. Thus, they are more likely to imitate helpful, charitable people (Hoffman 1970; Radke-Yarrow et al. 1983).

By the age of four, generosity involves a rather diverse set of behaviors. One form of generosity is the giving of help to those who need it. Helpful children are helpful in a number of ways. Children who offer to help others are generally more nurturant than less helpful children. They tend to give positive attention to their peers and are emotionally expressive. The giving of aid requires a general quality of outgoingness, which exposes the child's own vulnerability.

Helpful children will try to resolve their problems by themselves whenever possible. However, because they are trustful, they freely show their distress and ask for help, having confidence they will get it. They are, in turn, *more* likely to help others who are in need (Bryan 1975). Another characteristic related to generosity is a lack of competitiveness. Children who are generous tend to be less competitive in situations in which competition is possible but not encouraged.

S U M M A R Y

- According to Erikson's theory, the personality development of the preschool child depends on resolving the crises of autonomy versus shame and doubt and initiative versus guilt.
- The social learning theorists claim that children develop their personality through seeing how others behave and observing the consequences of their behavior.
- Gender-role development has a major effect on preschool children's personality development. The culture determines the appropriate behavior for girls and boys.
- Children with a positive self-concept are confident; have a good body image; see authority figures as supportive and interested; are independent, reliable; are relatively free from anxiety, nervousness, excessive worry, tiredness, and loneliness; and are seldom behavior problems.
- Children with a negative self-concept have a poor body image, are insecure and pessimistic, see authority figures as a threat, and appear to be tired, anxious, and nervous.
- The primary socializing agent of preschool children is still the family. Baumrind identified three parenting styles: authoritarian, authoritative, and permissive. The ordinal position of the child makes an impact on the family as well as affects the personality of the child. The family is changing drastically, with more single-parent families and mothers working outside of the home.
- Imaginary friends help preschoolers acquire the concept of "friend." Parten identified six stages in which children interact with peers. When children begin to interact with peers, they are influenced for the first time by individuals other than their parents and siblings.
- The content and quality of children's play is a good index to every phase of development. Play and playful interaction with peers is important for the overall development of preschool children.

Television

Long before children in our culture walk or talk, they have been exposed to television. Television is in over 98 percent of all American homes. Most homes have at least two television sets. Television sets are on for approximately seven hours per day (Ellis 1983). Three- to four-year-olds watch two or more hours of television each day (Williams 1986). Before a child enters school, he or she watches sixty-five hundred hours of television. By the time a child is five years old, he or she has watched television for as many hours as it takes to earn a bachelor's degree (Cohen 1974). The average elementary-age child watches fifteen to twenty-five hours of television a week (Murray 1980). The average family member will watch approximately ten years of television over his or her life span (Ellis 1983).

In general, television does not teach prosocial behavior or cognitive or language skills to young children, with the exception of such shows as "Sesame Street," "Mr. Rogers' Neighborhood," and "Electric Company" (Rice 1983). "Sesame Street" and "Mr. Rogers' Neighborhood" illustrate two completely different types of programming, but both are still beneficial to children. Using a slow-paced and often repetitive style, Mr. Rogers attempts to instill in children a sense of security and personal worth. He also represents an adult male model who listens to them and allows them to express their feelings. Singer and Singer (1979) note that "children seem to benefit enormously from [Rogers'] relaxed rhythm, the way he follows a subject over a period of days, his reassuring attitude, and his willingness to ask a question and then, in defiance of most television conventions, to say nothing for seconds—while children answer for themselves."

One study of children who viewed "Sesame Street" found a greater gain in simple facts and basic preschool know-how such as body parts, letters, numbers, forms, matching, relationships, sorting, and classification than for those children who did not watch. Disadvantaged children who were heavy viewers of "Sesame Street" surpassed advantaged children who were not viewers or who viewed very little. Heavy viewers were rated by teachers as being better prepared for school than low viewers, and they adapted better to the school situation (Who Wants to Live on Sesame Street? 1973; Collins and Getz 1974; Ahammer and Murray 1979; Gorn et al., 1976) However, Singer and Singer (1982) found that the fast pace of "Sesame Street" often induces inattentiveness in children after they enter elementary school.

Pinon et al. (1989) investigated the characteristics that influence the viewing of "Sesame Street" by preschoolers. The children watched less "Sesame Street" if their mothers were employed outside of the home and if they attended day care or preschool. If they had older siblings, they watched it less, but if they had younger siblings, they watched it more. Viewing was unrelated to parent education or occupational status, the gender of the child, or the child's vocabulary level, involvement in television, or interest in print and other media. Children were also more likely to view the show if their parents encouraged it.

Parents, educators, and psychologists have been concerned for some time about the possible effects of television violence on children. Numerous studies compiled in *Television and Behavior: Ten Years of Scientific Progress and Implications for the 1980s* (Pearl et al. 1982) provide evidence that *heavy* viewing of television is associated with aggression in children and adults.

Several studies concerning the impact of aggressive and violent television on children show a definite correlation with aggressive behavior in preschool children (Singer and Singer 1980a, 1980b; Pearl et al. 1982; Gadow and Sprafkin 1986; Zuckerman et al. 1980). Much of what a preschooler views on television is far from the real world. Crime is portrayed ten times more often than it occurs in real life (Gerbner 1980). According to the report of the surgeon general on television violence (Pearl et al. 1982) 80 percent of television programs contain at least one overt act of aggression or a violent act. Even music video channels present segments that contain violence, including sadistic violence (National Coalition on Television Violence 1984).

Another study found a correlation between how much television children watched at home and how aggressive they were with their nursery school classmates. Watching action and adventure shows, in particular, tended to increase aggressiveness, while watching "Sesame Street" and "Mr. Rogers' Neighborhood" did not. The three- and four-year-olds in this study spent an average of twenty-three hours per week watching television, with one child watching seventy-two hours per week (Singer and Singer 1981).

Eron et al. (1983) and Huesman et al. (1984) found that children will behave more aggressively if they

- are objects of aggression,
- identify strongly with aggressive characters on TV shows,

Continued

Television (continued)

- watch many violent TV shows,
- believe these shows are real and not fiction,
- are reinforced for their own aggressive behavior,
- have parents, particularly mothers, who act aggressively towards them,
- observe their parents, friends, and heroes commit aggressive acts,
- prefer physically active and rough activities, and/or
- have aggressive fantasies.

Gadow and Sprafkin (1987) exposed a class of six-year-old emotionally disturbed (ED) children and ten-year-old ED children to high- and low-aggression cartoons. The older children showed an increase in physical and nonphysical aggression after viewing high-aggression cartoons. The younger children's level of physical and nonphysical aggression decreased following the low-aggression cartoons. They did, however, become more nonphysically aggressive after viewing the high-aggression cartoons.

Bronfenbrenner (1970) feels that the real threat of television is the behavior that it prevents, such as the games, family festivities, conversation, and even arguments.

Before a child enters school, he or she watches sixty-five hundred hours of television.

These behaviors allow the child to learn, and help him or her in character development. Bronfenbrenner feels viewing television is a means of turning off the process that transforms children into people. Condry and Keith (1983) demonstrated that time spent watching television interferes with time spent in other, more active recreational pursuits. Parents often use television as a babysitter, which removes some of the burden of interacting with their child while providing entertainment or special educational experiences (Parke 1978).

If a child is going to benefit from watching television, the parent or caregiver needs to watch television with him or her in order to offer explanations about what he or she is watching (Bryce and Leichter 1983; Messaris 1983; Christopher et al. 1989). Young children do not know how to interpret the relationship between camera shots, and they do not understand many of the visual signals used on television (Greenfield 1984). Also, the social portrayals children see on television are complex, and children are likely to misinterpret them (Collins 1983). Preschoolers lack the skill to figure out the motive of actors and the subtleties involved in plots. The murder of someone on television will, to a preschooler, look the same as a killing in self-defense or to protect innocent people (Collins et al. 1981).

Children have an endless capacity to ask questions, but television cannot provide the direct question-and-answer communication young children seek. Television is only one-way communication. In fact, children who spend more time watching television develop more slowly intellectually than other children (Carew 1980). Children who are restricted from watching television spend more time reading, are more careful and reflective on tests, and improve their IQ scores (Gadberry 1980).

Television may prevent children from developing skills in interpersonal relationships and from practicing behaviors that are necessary for successful living with family and peers. Watching television rarely encourages social interaction, even though the people watching it are in proximity to one another. Television has been labeled an "insistent communicator" because it is the only "family member" that does any talking (Singer and Singer 1977; Dorr 1985).

Television can shape children's conceptualization of family life. The most common family structure portrayed on television consists of a family headed by one or two

Television (continued)

parents plus children. Television families are more likely to be middle class than working class (Greenberg et al. 1980). Middle-class parents are portrayed as mature, intelligent "superpeople" who can deal with any problem. Working-class parents and children, however, are portrayed as more inept, especially the father (NIMH 1982). Therefore, middle-class families are portrayed as more glamorous and successful than they are in real life. Families portrayed on television seldom have problems making ends meet (NIMH 1982). Such unrealistic portrayals may present unattainable and unrealistic goals for children and may lead them to question the quality and adequacy of their own families (Fabes et al. 1989).

- Good-quality early childhood programs, whether they are day-care centers, nursery schools, or Head Start programs, provide opportunities for the preschool child to develop socially, as well as physically, emotionally, and cognitively.
- Although fear and anxiety are similar, they have different physiological symptoms. Preschoolers usually fear imaginary creatures, the dark, animals, ridicule, and the threat of harm, such as from traffic, deep water, and fire. Children who suffer from anxiety cloak their feelings in a variety of ways. Parents can follow several guidelines in preventing children's fear and anxiety, as well as in alleviating their fear and anxiety.
- Two types of aggression have been observed in preschoolers: instrumental and hostile. Instrumental aggression aims at the retrieval of an object, territory, or privilege. Hostile aggression is oriented towards another person following some sort of threat or the belief that another person has behaved intentionally.
- Preschool children are more altruistic than many adults believe. Cognitive development and adult modeling and nurturance play major roles in preschoolers' acquiring altruistic behaviors.
- Television makes an impact on the overall development of the child, including cognitive and language development, prosocial behavior, social interaction, aggressive behavior, and family interaction.

READINGS

Clarke-Stewart, A. (1982). *Daycare*. Cambridge, Mass.: Harvard University Press.
Complete history and analysis of day care. Practical suggestions on selecting day care.

Dunn, J. (1985). *Sisters and brothers*. Cambridge, Mass.: Harvard University Press.
View of how siblings influence each other.

Garvey, C. (1977). *Play*. Cambridge, Mass.: Harvard University Press.
Thorough discussion of play and its importance.

Reit, S. (1985). *Sibling rivalry*. New York: Ballantine Books.
Sibling rivalry is portrayed as normal and as important in establishing and maintaining other social relationships. Also presents description of each ordinal position.

Rubin, K. H., Gein, G. G., and Vandenberg, B. (1983). "Play." In P. H. Mussen (ed.), *Handbook of child psychology (4th ed.)* Vol. 4. New York: Wiley.
Thorough analysis of play and the direction research is taking regarding children's play.

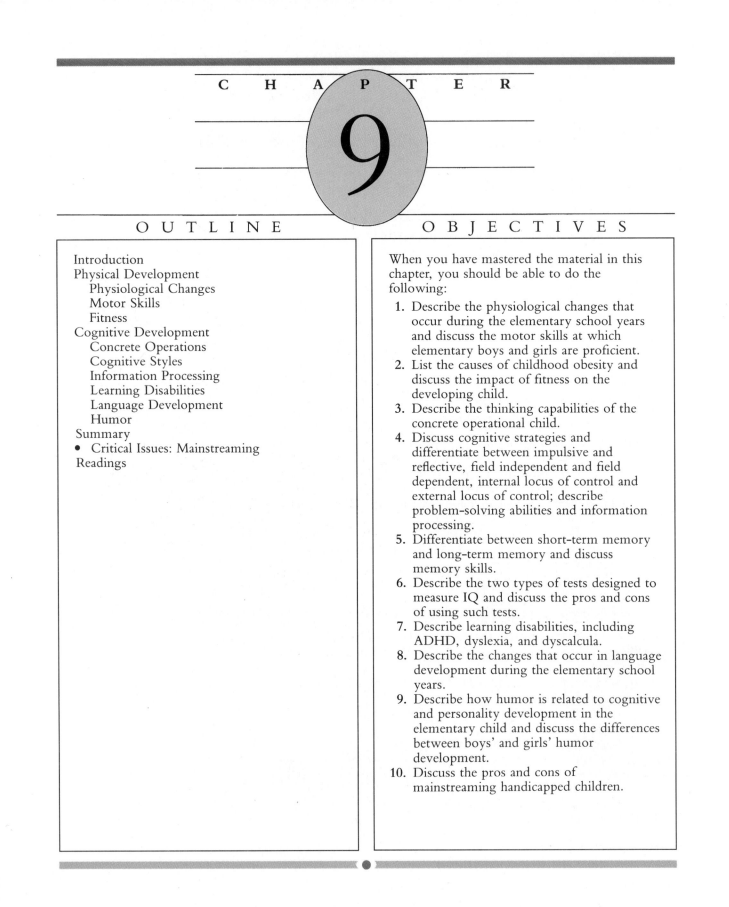

C H A P T E R

9

O B J E C T I V E S

When you have mastered the material in this chapter, you should be able to do the following:

1. Describe the physiological changes that occur during the elementary school years and discuss the motor skills at which elementary boys and girls are proficient.
2. List the causes of childhood obesity and discuss the impact of fitness on the developing child.
3. Describe the thinking capabilities of the concrete operational child.
4. Discuss cognitive strategies and differentiate between impulsive and reflective, field independent and field dependent, internal locus of control and external locus of control; describe problem-solving abilities and information processing.
5. Differentiate between short-term memory and long-term memory and discuss memory skills.
6. Describe the two types of tests designed to measure IQ and discuss the pros and cons of using such tests.
7. Describe learning disabilities, including ADHD, dyslexia, and dyscalcula.
8. Describe the changes that occur in language development during the elementary school years.
9. Describe how humor is related to cognitive and personality development in the elementary child and discuss the differences between boys' and girls' humor development.
10. Discuss the pros and cons of mainstreaming handicapped children.

The Wonder Years:
Middle Childhood's Physical and Cognitive Development

• INTRODUCTION

When children enter the elementary school years, or middle childhood, they are dependent on parents and other adults for emotional support and companionship. By the end of middle childhood, or at preadolescence, adults are much less central in their lives. Social and emotional needs are filled to a large extent by friends or peers. Differences in children's size, shape, facial features, intellectual ability, and talents are not as evident in the early years of middle childhood as in the later years of middle childhood.

• PHYSICAL DEVELOPMENT

Physiological Changes

For the elementary school child, the rate of growth is slower but steadier than it was during infancy and the preschool years. The rate is less than two and one-half inches and eight pounds per year. Weight gain is mostly muscle rather than fat, which increases the child's strength considerably. Muscle development is partly responsible for the disappearance of the bulging stomach that is characteristic of the preschooler. The flatter stomach contour is also due to a larger trunk that can better accommodate the internal organs. By six years of age, the child's trunk is almost twice as long and twice as wide as it was at birth. The ribs shift from a horizontal position to a more oblique one as the chest broadens and flattens. The rapid growth spurt of the arms and legs contributes to a leaner appearance. Because overall physical size increases slowly during middle childhood, it is possible for the child to gain control of and perfect motor skills he or she was unable to accomplish earlier (Tanner 1978).

The activity level of elementary school boys is much higher than that of elementary school girls. Eaton and Yu (1989) note that the girls are less active because they are farther along on the developmental path.

Height and Weight

At age six, gender differences in height and weight are negligible. The average six-year-old boy is slightly taller and heavier than the average six-year-old girl. By the end of the elementary school years, however, this will change. Girls begin the adolescent growth spurt about two years earlier than boys. At eleven or twelve years of age, the average girl is taller and heavier than the average boy (Tanner 1978).

Muscle Development

During the elementary school years, a boy's body has a higher proportion of muscle and a lower proportion of fat than a girl's body, and the difference increases as the children get older. With a proper amount of physical exercise, the muscles of elementary school children grow rapidly, change composition, and become more firmly attached to the bones (Bailey et al. 1986). In some children, however, the muscles continue to remain immature in function. This is reflected in frequent awkwardness and inefficient movement, erratic changes of tempo, an inability to sit still for long periods, and quick fatigue.

The muscles of elementary school children as compared to those of adolescents are more easily injured by strain. For example, elementary school children who pitch baseball are more prone than adolescents to "Little League elbow," a

CHAPTER 9   *The Wonder Years: Middle Childhood's Physical and Cognitive Development*

The muscles of elementary school children are easily injured by strain. Elementary children who pitch baseball are prone to "Little League elbow," a muscular injury caused by overuse of the arm.

muscular injury caused by overuse. The fitness and development of muscles depend on the muscles' structure, good physical care, rest, and activity. Proper muscle and nerve development provides steadiness of movement, speed, strength, and endurance (Tanner 1978).

Heart

Between ages four and ten, the heart grows slowly. As the child nears maturity, between six and twelve years, the heartbeat slows and the blood pressure rises. The average adult heart rate of seventy to eighty beats per minute is reached, but the blood pressure remains below the adult norm. Boys' hearts are larger than girls' and their circulatory systems are more efficient (Tanner 1978).

Skeleton

In middle childhood the skeleton is still producing centers of *ossification*. This is the process through which minerals, particularly calcium and phosphorus, are deposited in cartilage. The soft and spongy bones of young children consist mostly of cartilage, but they are given hardness and rigidity by these mineral salts. This process continues into the twenties. Because the growth of the skeleton often is more rapid than the growth of muscles and ligaments, loose-jointed, gangling, and swaybacked postures are not uncommon among children during the elementary years. Growth spurts are accompanied by muscle aches, particularly at night. These growing pains, which are very real for many children, occur as developing muscles try to catch up with the increased skeleton size (Waechter and Blake 1976; Marshall and Tanner 1986).

Teeth

The facial structure undergoes a noticeable change during middle childhood. As permanent teeth replace baby teeth, the jaw lengthens, and the face increases in size. The first two teeth, the bottom front, usually fall out at around six years of age. On average, girls lose their baby teeth earlier than do boys. They are usually one to six months ahead of boys in the emergence of permanent teeth (Demirjian 1986).

Health

During middle childhood the most frequent threat to life is accidents, especially car accidents. The most frequent health threat is the common cold. Most childhood diseases, with the exception of chicken pox, are preventable.

Motor Skills

Children in middle childhood are more proficient than preschoolers in strenuous activities that require large-muscle movement (Bailey et al. 1986). By six years of age children can roller-skate, skip rope, and begin to ride a bicycle. Most seven-year-olds have begun to perfect movements necessary for catching, throwing, and hitting a baseball. The factors necessary for success in motor skill activities include physical maturity, opportunities to engage in physical activity, and a degree of self-confidence. Improvement is gradual in the process of refining coordination abilities and mastering grace of movement. Clumsiness and awkwardness are still to be expected at this time. The degree to which a motor skill is mastered may affect a child's sense of competence, achievement, peer acceptance, and self-acceptance. A positive correlation has been found between the motor skill proficiency of third graders and such behavior as calmness, cooperation, and attentiveness (Havighurst 1963; Zion 1965).

The motor skills that are developed during middle childhood include speed, power, coordination, agility, and balance (Gallahue 1982). Motor skills that rely on strength and size improve 25 to 35 percent in proportion to overall body growth. Six-year-olds can run faster than twelve feet per second, and by age ten children can run about fifteen feet per second. A child can broad-jump about three feet at six years and more than four and one-half feet at ten years (Roche and Malina 1983). Activities that require coordination and timing include throwing and catching. The typical six-year-old can throw a ball about fifteen feet, compared to thirty feet at age ten or twelve. Six-year-olds can catch an eight-inch rubber ball bounced to them from fifteen feet. Ten- or twelve-year-olds can catch a ball thrown from thirty to forty feet without its bouncing (Cratty 1979). Improvements in these basic motor skills enable children to participate in team sports such as soccer, softball, basketball, and football. They are also more capable of mastering such complex skills as skateboarding, roller-skating, dancing, gymnastics, swimming, and tennis.

Although both girls and boys are capable of performing many motor skills, Weisfeld, Weisfeld, and Callaghan (1982) found that in mixed-sex situations, girls are unwilling to compete with boys. Their study compared twelve-year-old girls and boys playing dodgeball, which they had previously played only in school. The scientists divided the children into four groups: high-skill girls, high-skill boys, low-skill girls, and low-skill boys. In general, the boys were better at the game, but the high-skill girls were noticeably better than the low-skill boys in same-sex competition. Nevertheless, in mixed-sex competition the boys always won, even when the low-skill boys played against the high-skill girls, and even though the girls were heavier and taller than the boys. One explanation is that twelve-year-old girls want to attract boys and have been socialized not to excel against boys even when they can.

Fitness

The National Children and Youth Fitness Study conducted in 1984 found that children were less physically active and were fatter than in the 1960s. They were not physically fit, which means the heart, lungs, muscles, and blood vessels did not function optimally. Elementary school children in the 1980s tended to watch television a lot, play Nintendo, or spend time on a computer rather than engage in active outdoor sports or games (Dorr and Kunkel 1990; Kubey and Larson 1990; Greenfield et al. 1987). The study also found that the fitness of these children lagged behind that of most middle-aged joggers. More than half the children did not participate in any activity during the winter months, and most did not learn in school about activities that could improve their fitness. Many health practitioners point out that physical fitness habits should be formed in childhood and maintained through adulthood.

Obesity leads to physical and medical problems at any stage of life. The overweight person usually exercises less and runs a greater risk of having a serious illness. Psychological problems often are present as well. Fat children are teased, picked on, and rejected. They have fewer friends, and if they are accepted into a peer group, they frequently pay a high price. They must endure such nicknames as Tubby and Fatty as well as suffer jokes about their shape (Shonkoff 1984). Since obesity occurs more often among low-income children than among middle-income children, many overweight youngsters must cope with both liabilities (Eveleth and Tanner 1976).

The point at which an overweight child qualifies as obese depends partly on body type, partly on proportion of fat to muscle, and partly on culture. At least 5 percent of North American elementary school children are classified as obese. At a height of fifty-three inches, obese children weigh more than eighty-five pounds, as compared to the average weight of sixty-six pounds (National Center for Health Statistics 1985). Reif (1985) found that American children ages seven to twelve had body fat levels 2 to 5 percent above what is considered normal for optimal health. Reif's study also revealed that 41 percent of the children had high levels of cholesterol, 28 percent had higher-than-normal blood pressure, and 98 percent had at least one symptom indicating they were at risk of developing coronary heart disease later.

Increased physical activity can help curb childhood obesity. Such individual sports as aerobics, swimming, and gymnastics, which use the whole body, are better physical activities than group sports like baseball or football, which call for specialized movement, tend to be sporadic (on and off the bench), and frequently cause bone and tendon injuries. Most individual sports also can be pursued throughout life.

Less active than their peers, obese children burn fewer calories and add pounds even when they eat less than other children. For most obese children the problem is not too much food but too little activity (National Children and Youth Fitness Study 1984). Nutritionists caution against strenuous dieting during childhood, since inadequate calcium or protein could hinder bone or brain growth. The general recommendation is to stabilize the weight of obese children to allow them to "grow out of" their fat (Winick 1975).

Overweight children need emotional support to overcome a negative self-concept and lose weight. Reducing is difficult. Obesity is usually fostered by family attitudes and habits, which are hard to break. Crash diets not only make children irritable, listless, and sick but also add to the psychological problems associated with obesity, without accomplishing a long-term weight loss.

At least 5 percent of North American elementary children are classified as obese.

The factors causing obesity begin in infancy and continue throughout adulthood.

Heredity influences one's body type, distribution of fat, height, and bone structure. Overweight children tend to have overweight parents, and underweight children tend to have underweight parents (LeBow 1984). For children adopted at birth, no correlation has been found with the weight of the adoptive parents (Weil 1975; Mayer 1975).

Activity level, as mentioned above, is another factor. Inactive children burn fewer calories and are more likely to be overweight than active children. The greatest weight gain seems to take place in fall and winter, when there are fewer opportunities for activity (White 1986).

Types of food eaten also can contribute to obesity. Many common foods that children like, such as cornflakes and catsup, have sugar as a main ingredient. Junk food, like doughnuts and cookies, and fast food have become staples in the diet of many of today's hurried families. These foods are high in fat, sugar, and/or salt.

The attitude toward food can be a factor. Food is seen as a symbol of love and comfort, so individuals often eat whenever they are upset. The pattern begins when parents feed a crying infant rather than try to discover the real problem. Reinforcement occurs throughout childhood if adults use sweets to console the sad or upset child.

The quantity of food eaten is another factor. In some families, parents take satisfaction in watching children eat, urging them to take extra helpings. Even with infants, the caloric intake should be adjusted to the individual's needs (White 1986).

Obesity can protect *family boundaries* by delaying children's development. When family members are overinvolved with one another but socially isolated, they perceive the outside world as a foreign, dangerous, and hostile place. Children with strong feelings of loyalty toward their parents are torn between that loyalty and their interest in getting involved with peers. Obesity "solves" this dilemma by isolating the child from his or her peers and then becoming the rationale for staying close to home. Obesity relieves the family of the difficulties associated with developmental transitions.

In many cases, obesity onset occurs during a major family crisis, such as death, divorce, or relocation. An intensified focus on obesity functions as a distraction from more serious or painful issues and offers a way to organize or unite family members during the transition (Harkaway 1987).

Whatever its cause, obesity is a major health problem in the United States. One adult in five is 30 percent or more over his or her ideal weight. Obese children need support in changing eating and exercise habits in order to make childhood more enjoyable and adult obesity less likely.

● COGNITIVE DEVELOPMENT

Children during the elementary school years are maturing not only physically but also cognitively. They mature from preschoolers who use their senses to understand their world into children who can plan, reason, calculate, read, and memorize. A first grader can read a few simple words and perhaps can add pairs of numbers. A sixth grader can read and understand complex stories and can do multiplication tables and manipulate fractions.

Concrete Operations

According to Piaget, concrete operational thinking usually occurs between seven and eleven years of age. That is, children can reason about *concrete,* tangible things, as well as ideas and concepts that are beyond the ability of younger children. Their thinking is *operational* because they can perform mental actions in an organized and systematic way. Concrete operational children begin to think and reason logically about objects. A growing objectivity becomes apparent. They become capable of dealing with many variables simultaneously, such as time and space (as in geography and history) and speed and distance (as in math). This capability does not develop evenly in all content areas, and there are rather important differences between the younger and older children in the concrete operational stage. These differences relate to abstract thinking, judgment, and perspective.

Elementary school children increase their understanding of the physical world, and their perceptions are more accurate. They still have intellectual limitations, such as not being prepared to deal with abstract problems. Nor can they analyze their own thoughts or think about problems that might occur in the future. They can reason about what is, but they cannot construct what may be. For elementary school children, concepts deepen, but learning is extended in only one concept at a particular time. For example, the challenge of learning the

Some elementary children can logically manipulate several ideas at once. They are able to learn laws and rules, such as those that govern games.

number of hours in a day in relation to the number of minutes in an hour is more appropriate to their capacity than figuring out the distance a car travels when going a certain number of miles per hour for a given number of hours.

Children in middle childhood find it difficult to consider several logical operations at once. Not until adolescence (and sometimes not even then) do young people develop the systematic use of several logical ideas that is characteristic of formal operational thought. Some elementary school children can logically manipulate several *ideas* at once, as is apparent to anyone who has been beaten in chess by a fifth grader. These children learn laws and rules, such as those that govern games, which are made by mutual agreement and can be changed by mutual agreement (Piaget 1965). Between eight and ten years, a child can usually understand logical principles if they can be applied to specific, or concrete, examples.

Many preschoolers think a dream is actually visible to everyone in the room. By age seven or eight, most children realize that another person cannot see their dream, but they still localize the dream as being "in the room." By age nine or ten, they localize their dreams as being "in the head" (Piaget 1929).

Mental Operations

With the onset of concrete operations, children are capable of performing four basic operations that will affect their understanding of various concepts. These operations are *combinativity, or class inclusion, reversibility, associativity,* and *nullifiability*.

Combinativity, or class inclusion, is the ability to reason simultaneously about the whole and the part, to group elementary classes into an encompassing class, and to reverse the process by reducing the broader class into its subordinate components. That is, two or more classes can be combined into one larger and more comprehensive class, or a general class of items can be divided into

Combinativity
The ability to reason simultaneously about the whole and the part, to group elementary classes into an encompassing class, and to reverse the process by reducing the broader class into its subordinate components.

Class inclusion
See Combinativity.

subclasses. For example, a child can now understand that white wooden beads and brown wooden beads belong to the whole class of wooden beads.

Reversibility is the understanding that for any operation there exists an opposite operation that can cancel it. Thus, children can mentally retrace the steps of a problem. For example, $2 + 3 = 5$ is the reverse of $5 - 3 = 2$; or $2 \times 5 = 10$ is the reverse of $10 \div 5 = 2$.

Associativity is the understanding that when three structures are combined, it does not matter what the order of the combination is. That is, combining A with the result of combining B and C is the same as combining C with the result of combining A and B. For example, $(5 + 3) + 2$ is the same as $(2 + 3) + 5$.

Nullifiability is the awareness that structures can exist that leave others unchanged. That is, in every system there is one element that, when combined with other elements in the system, leaves the result unchanged. That one element is called the *identity element*. Where the I is the identity element, $A \cdot I = A$ and $I \cdot A = A$. For example, if the operation were multiplication, the I would be 1; if the operation were addition, the I would be 0. Thus, $4 \times 1 = 4$ and $4 + 0 = 4$.

Once children are capable of these basic operations, they can understand a variety of concepts that eluded them during the preschool years (Piaget and Inhelder 1969).

Conservation

The elementary school child can comprehend the law of conservation. This law dictates that the properties of substances will remain the same despite changes in shape or physical arrangement, provided that nothing is added or taken away during the transformation. That is, a substance will tend to "conserve" its mass, weight, and volume even though its appearance has been altered. Younger children presented with the same substance in different shapes or arrangements are confused about its properties. Not only is this confusion due to centering, but the child does not realize that the substance can change in one respect without changing in others.

So the elementary school child is capable of reasoning that objects remain the same although outside appearances have been altered. Having learned the principle of reversibility, he or she can understand that objects can be restored to their original condition after changes are made in the physical shape. With an understanding of reversibility, the child can reason that the flattened ball of clay can be remolded into the original ball, and liquid can be poured back into an original container to restore its original level. The child knows the substance has been conserved despite transformations. When the law of conservation is understood, an important step is made toward higher-order mental processes. Judgment is now based upon reason rather than upon perception.

Number conservation appears between the fourth and sixth year. Previous difficulties in counting were due to the inability to conserve and reverse number quantities. As Piaget pointed out, although younger children may know the names of numbers, they have not grasped the true concept, which is that the number of objects in a group remains the same, or is conserved, no matter how the objects are arranged. Prior to attaining number conservation, children may be able to count yet know little about what the numbers actually represent. Instead of having conceptual understanding, the prelogical child merely memorizes.

Reversibility
The understanding that for any operation there exists an opposite operation that can cancel it.

Associativity
The understanding that when three structures are combined, it does not matter what the order of the combination is.

Nullifiability
The awareness that structures can exist that leave others unchanged. That is, in every system there is one element that, when combined with other elements in the system, leaves the result unchanged.

During the elementary school years, children can come to understand *conservation of quantity*. Most ten-year-olds can add, subtract, multiply, divide, and deal with simple fractions. They can also grasp the durability and abstractness of numbers, which begin to be understood, manipulated, and recognized as parts, wholes, and units. This is accomplished through the ability to differentiate number from such irrelevant perceptual cues as space and size. As they become more capable, children can establish meaningful number concepts, whether applied to such forms of measurement as weight, height, length, or volume (Cohen 1972).

Decentration

A child who can **decenter** no longer "centers," as does the preschooler, on only one aspect or dimension of a problem, excluding all others. The child can now consider two or more aspects of a problem simultaneously. Decentering can be applied to classification in that the parts can be compared with the whole. For example, when children are given a box of brown and white wooden beads and asked whether there are more brown beads or wooden beads, they are capable of realizing that brown beads are a subclass of the class of wooden beads. They can simultaneously see that the brown and white beads are "parts" to the "whole" of wooden beads.

With the capability of decentering, children can consider things that occur over time. Preschoolers tend to focus primarily on the present. They may see juice in one glass, then another, and compare the appearances directly. Elementary school children will note that "all you did is pour," a reference to the past. They may also anticipate the future: "If you pour it back into the other glass it will be the same again." With the ability to decenter and to consider changes that occur over time, elementary school children are not as likely as preschoolers to be misled by appearances. They understand that things are not always what they seem to be at first. These children's judgments are based not just on what they perceive but also on what they know (Flavell 1977).

Seriation, or the ability to arrange objects in a series, starts to be understood toward the end of the preoperational period, but it is not firmly established until age seven or eight. When asked to arrange a series of ten sticks according to length, the typical six-year-old might first put together three sticks—short, medium, and long—and then insert others, rearranging several times before getting the correct order. The typical eight-year-old would look at the whole jumble, pick out the shortest, then the next shortest, and systematically and quickly arrange the series. A practical example of seriation is number sequence. Many preschoolers can say numbers but are not aware of the one-to-one correspondence necessary to count objects or things; that is, they do not understand that numbers are arranged in a series and that they correspond to specific quantities. In elementary school, children can understand that correspondence. Children in transition between the preoperational and concrete operational stages may count objects correctly but not grasp other aspects of the number system, such as "Which is greater, 5 or 7?" or "What number is one less than 5?" These concepts take a long time to develop. Many first graders need to do much object counting and hard thinking in order to add simple sums.

Time, Speed, and Distance

Combining the concepts of time, speed, and distance is much harder than understanding any one of these ideas separately. When watching two toy trains that move along a track, one stopping farther along than the other, preopera-

Decenter
The capability of considering two or more aspects of a problem simultaneously.

● FIGURE 9.1
Conservation Chart
Ages at which U.S. children tend to achieve the various conservation tasks.

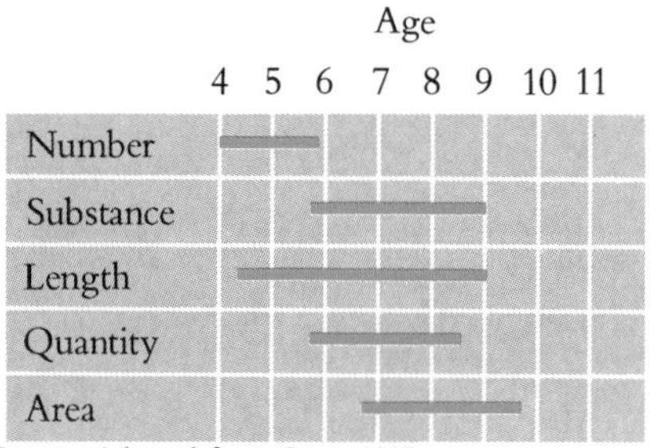

Source: Adapted from Gross 1985.

tional children always say that the one in the front is faster, regardless of when or where the trains started or how fast they actually went (Piaget 1970b). The ability to judge the relationship of time, speed, and distance develops gradually throughout middle childhood, and by age twelve most children have grasped the general principles. Even some adults may have trouble applying these principles in specific situations, however. For example, one study found that college undergraduates had difficulty when presented with more difficult versions of the two trains problem (Siegler and Richards 1979).

Soon after a child enters elementary school, calendar time is learned. First the days of the week are mastered, then months of the year. Around the second or third grade, children acquire the ability to master clock time. In about the fourth grade, they can exhibit striking improvement in estimating adults' ages, an excellent indication of understanding time.

The basic processes of concrete operational thought enable children to understand the passage of time. A six-year-old might ask his or her parents if they were alive before cars were invented and what it was like traveling in covered wagons. One six-year-old made the opposite mistake. He decided he was born before his father. He also believed that he would grow older with time but his father would remain the same age and that his mother would not grow older "because she is old already." Such mistakes are rare with eight-year-olds. Perhaps this is why movies and TV dramas that show life in earlier times ("Guns of Paradise") and future times ("Star Trek II") are popular with eight-year-olds (Piaget 1970a).

Understanding time as it relates to movement is a difficult concept for the younger elementary school child, but older children in this group can comprehend it when provided with instruction. When children of ten and eleven years were asked to find out what determines the length of time it takes for a pendulum to complete its swing, fewer than 10 percent succeeded. A second group of the same age was given the same problem but first went through an instructional procedure that trained them in the use of scientific methods. Seventy percent solved the pendulum problem (Siegler, Liebert, and Liebert 1973).

The concept of distance is poorly understood before middle childhood. A six-year-old, after looking at a map, might talk about taking a walk from California to New York or from Detroit to Michigan. The lack of a sense of distance and lack of classification skills make it frustrating to try to teach first graders the geographical distinctions between cities, states, and countries. Such information is not appropriate to first graders. Once concrete operational thought is attained, however, children can understand that some places are much farther away than they can see or walk and that one geographical area can contain smaller areas. Their delight in comprehending geographical locations sometimes results in their giving not only their name, street, city, and state in their address but also "United States, North America, the Western Hemisphere, the World, the Solar System, the Milky Way Galaxy, the Universe."

Cognitive Styles

Although Piaget's theory recognizes that children from all over the world go through stages of sensorimotor, preoperational, and concrete operational thought in essentially the same sequence, they may differ in **cognitive style.** This refers to the manner in which an individual takes in and responds to information. New subject matter may be acquired quickly or slowly, attention

Cognitive styles
The manner in which an individual takes in and responds to information.

may be distracted or focused, and so forth. A child's cognitive style can play an important role in his or her performance in school.

Impulsive and Reflective Attitudes

The tendency to react impulsively or to react reflectively is especially noticeable in situations that offer a choice among several alternatives. **Impulsive** children respond quickly, without thinking and without checking carefully to see whether their response is correct. As a result, they tend to make errors. They usually accept and report the first idea they generate, not giving much consideration or thought to its accuracy.

Reflective children respond much more slowly than impulsive children do and make fewer errors. They devote longer periods to considering various aspects of a hypothesis (Kogan 1983; Kagan et al. 1964; Kagan 1971; Ross and Ross 1976). Reflective, attentive children are more likely to be analytic.

Impulsive and reflective children do not differ consistently in IQ but do differ in many other ways. Reflective children tend to do better in school (Kagan 1965). They devise better strategies for solving problems and follow them more consistently (Cameron 1984). They make fewer mistakes in reading text material (Lawry et al. 1983; Kagan 1971; Ross and Ross 1976). Impulsive children are more likely to jump to conclusions and to identify words incorrectly based on one or two letters. When given a list of words to memorize, both groups forget approximately the same number of words, but an impulsive child is more likely to name words not on the original list (Kagan 1965).

A reflective attitude appears to be the result of anxiousness to do well on intellectual tasks. Reflective children believe they can do well if they try. Usually they want to be correct and will try to avoid mistakes. Impulsive children seem to be less upset over mistakes and, therefore, respond quickly. They have less confidence in their intellectual abilities, and they are more motivated by the desire to escape the difficult situation. With age, American children become more reflective than do children from other cultures (Kogan 1983; Kagan 1971; Kagan and Kogan 1970).

Impulsive children are likely to do things that involve risk, such as walking a narrow plank or joining children they do not know well. In comparison, reflective children are more cautious. Reflective children are more likely to choose difficult problems to work on and are less likely to give up easily (Kogan 1983). When younger elementary school children are given Piagetian conservation problems, the reflective ones are more likely to understand the concept of conservation, and the impulsive ones are more likely to respond at the preoperational level (Cohen, Schleser, and Meyers 1981).

Field Independence and Field Dependence

Field Independence versus *Field Dependence* assesses the ability of a child to separate a figure from the field in which it is embedded. The **field-independent** child can isolate a figure and can analyze pictures into their distinct parts. The **field-dependent** child has trouble separating parts from the whole and responds globally to the most attention-directing features of the task (Ross and Ross 1976).

Field-independent individuals tend to be active, self-motivated, and willing to assume a participant role. They prefer physical science subjects. Field-dependent individuals assume a spectator role, are more sensitive to social situations, and prefer social science projects (Witkin and Goodenough 1976).

Impulsive
A cognitive style in which an individual responds quickly, without thinking and without checking carefully to see if the response is correct.

Reflective
A cognitive style in which the individual responds slowly and devotes a longer period of time to considering various aspects of a hypothesis.

Field independence
The capability of isolating a figure from the field in which it is imbedded.

Field dependence
To respond globally to the most attention-directing features of the task of separating a figure from the field in which it is embedded.

Field independence or dependence and reflectivity or impulsivity seem to be quite enduring characteristics of individuals. Even so, some training procedures can promote reflectivity (Neimark 1975), and field-dependent children perform as well as field-independent children if they are trained to look for hidden cues (Globerson et al. 1985).

External and Internal Locus of Control

As children develop, a sense of control and autonomy becomes very important. *Locus of control* refers to the degree to which they perceive they control their own fate. Children who have an *internal locus of control* are called **internalizers**. They believe they are responsible for their own successes and failures. If they do well at something, it is because they have worked hard or have the ability. Children with an *external locus of control,* the **externalizers,** feel they have little control over events. They attribute their successes and failures to luck or to the attitudes and actions of other people. Many children fall between the two extremes. Children who are high in achievement motivation tend to be internalizers. They tend to come from the social classes and ethnic groups that produce high-achievement motivation. They are more successful students than externalizers (Hrncir 1985; Crandall, Katkovsky, and Crandall 1962, 1965).

An internal locus of control evolves gradually. Parents who warmly praise achievement are likely to foster their child's belief in an internal locus of control. Granting or encouraging independence seems to be particularly important. Children who are allowed at an early age to do independent things, such as spend the night at the home of a friend, tend to become internalizers. Children who are not granted these privileges often become externalizers (Crandall 1973; Wichern and Nowicki 1976).

Cognitive style, which appears to be determined largely by social and family context and the behavioral development of the child, is a vital factor in understanding how an individual learns. Equally important is an understanding of how the human brain functions.

Information Processing

The human brain has been compared to the computer in its capacity to process information (Kuhn 1984). **Information processing** occurs when the brain receives a stimulus, registers or identifies it, stores that information, and later retrieves it and applies it to new experiences.

The identification or registration process is called **encoding**. It is the encoded version of what a person sees or hears that is stored in the short-term memory. Encoding and storing seem to be done with greater and greater efficiency as children grow older, perhaps because this ability improves with practice. The biological reason for this improvement is that **myelination,** the process that facilitates the transmission of neural signals by coating the nerve fibers with a protective fatty sheath called myelin, is still going on during middle childhood, and myelination speeds neural functioning (Case, Kurland, and Goldberg 1982; Wilkinson 1980).

Memory

Short-term memory, the immediate or working memory, has limited storage capacity. It is the current, active repository of information. An adult can

---

Internalizer
An individual who believes that he or she is responsible for his or her own successes and failures.

Externalizer
An individual who feels he or she has little control over events and attributes his or her successes and failures to luck or to the attitudes and actions of other people.

Information processing
The process in which the brain receives a stimulus, registers or identifies it, stores that information, and later retrieves it and applies it to new experiences.

Encoding
The identification or registration process involved in information processing.

Myelination
The process that facilitates the transmission of neural signals by coating the nerve fibers with a protective fatty sheath called myelin.

Short-term memory
The immediate or working memory, with limited storage capacity.

Memory span
The number of individual items held in short-term memory.

Long-term memory
Memory that retains information for the long run and contains more information than we can retrieve at any given time.

generally hold six or seven items in short-term memory. More than seven words are likely to be remembered if they form a meaningful sentence, because the sentence provides a structure for remembering the words, just as words provide a structure for remembering letters. The number of individual items held in short-term memory, called the **memory span,** increases during childhood from three items at age three, to four or five items at age six, to five or six items at ages eight to twelve (Case, Kurland, and Goldberg 1982; Linton 1980). Things stored in short-term memory are lost almost at once unless they are rehearsed. In order to retain something for the long run, it must be put in **long-term memory.** Everything stored in long-term memory has first been in short-term memory. Our long-term memory contains much more than we can retrieve at any given time, and this stored memory is not necessarily readily accessed. The ability to retrieve information from long-term memory depends on how well it was perceived, organized, and stored initially.

Four aspects of memory listed by Flavell (1985) help us understand how memory skills change during middle childhood. The four aspects are basic processes, knowledge, mnemonic strategies, and metamemory.

Basic processes refers to the fundamental aspects of remembering, such as the routine acts of storing and retrieving information. These processes enable infants to recognize familiar objects or people they see repeatedly. Basic processes develop from infancy through the preschool years. During middle childhood they undergo minor refinements but no dramatic improvements.

Knowledge refers to information people store in memory throughout their lives. It affects what is currently learned and remembered. In middle childhood, new information is integrated into meaningful data already stored in memory. Elementary school children are capable of making inferences from information they are given because of previously learned knowledge. In short, what is known influences what is learned.

Mnemonic strategies are cognitive ways of facilitating memory. As children get older they develop better strategies for meeting the need to remember specific things. Younger elementary children, around five and six years, do not often spontaneously use mnemonic strategies, but by age ten these strategies are used maturely (Kail and Hagen 1982; Justice 1985; Kunzinger 1985). Rehearsal, which is repeating information over and over again, is one mnemonic strategy. Organizing information in a way that encourages later recall is another mnemonic strategy. Preoperational children have difficulty developing the latter strategy because they are egocentric and they center, which prevents them from developing classification skills. When children develop classification skills, they are capable of organization. The greatest increase in using this method is around age nine or ten.

Metamemory refers to an intuitive understanding of how memory works. The metamemory is used when there is a need to remember and a need to know how to go about remembering. It also entails monitoring memory performance in a given situation and knowing when information committed to memory is sufficiently memorized. These skills develop rapidly during middle childhood (Waters and Andreassen 1983; Wellman 1986; Howard and Polich 1985).

Measuring Intelligence

Humphreys (1971, 1980) defines intelligence as the repertoire of intellectual information, knowledge, and skills available at a particular time. Because intelligence changes during growth and maturation, it cannot be isolated into one valid measure (Humphreys et al. 1985). Piaget focused on how intelligence develops, how the mind operates in various stages of the early years, and how the structure of a child's mind changes with maturation.

Standardized tests to measure intelligence fall into two major groups: achievement tests and aptitude, or ability, tests. Achievement tests measure academic knowledge that a child has already learned. Examples are tests on reading, arithmetic, or other curriculum content. Aptitude tests try to measure ability or estimate future performance by sampling present skills and knowledge (Anastasi 1985).

One well-known test of intelligence, the Stanford-Binet Intelligence Scale, emphasizes verbal skill and abstract reasoning. It was designed in 1905 by Binet and Simon and has undergone several revisions. At one time it gave one score (the IQ, or intelligence quotient) that supposedly reflected overall intelligence. The score was based on a child's performance compared with that of other children the same age. It was determined by a formula:

$$\frac{\text{Mental Age}}{\text{Chronological Age}} \times 100 = \text{IQ}$$

Today, children's IQs are computed so that the mean score for each age is adjusted to 100 with a standard deviation of 15 points. Approximately 66 percent of the population falls within the "normal" IQ range, between 85 and 115 points, and 95 percent falls within the 70- to 130-point range.

The Wechsler Intelligence Scale for Children, Revised Form, or WISC-R, is divided into verbal and performance subtests that yield twelve separate subscores. The verbal subtests tap the child's knowledge and information, vocabulary, comprehension of everyday skills, mathematical ability, recall, and interpretation. The performance subtests tap intelligence through a child's ability to copy designs made with blocks, code numbers into symbols, put pictures into logical order, assemble a cut-up picture of an object, and complete a picture. The subscores help diagnose special learning needs of individual children. Humphreys et al. (1985) found that the results of these subscores correlate with the mental operational capabilities and tasks outlined by Piaget. Therefore, a Piagetian test can be formed that is an excellent measure of general intelligence.

A major problem with intelligence tests is the cultural bias under which they were developed. Most tests reflect white, middle-class values and experiences from Western Europe and North America. It is difficult to design one test that can be used in various cultures and to screen for values and attitudes that reflect a cultural bias.

Results of IQ tests have been widely misinterpreted in the past. They tend to measure only academic skills and disregard other talents a child may possess. Also, because there is a numerical test score, parents and many teachers assume that the tests are very precise, which is not true.

Intelligence tests can help parents and teachers understand children. These tests add to information already known about a certain child but do not replace that information. They also help in understanding a child who is at either extreme, that is, highly intelligent or extremely slow. They do not contribute much information or help in planning personal educational goals for the vast majority of children, who are in the middle.

Although present intelligence tests measure only certain aspects of cognition, they are the only objective measures available.

Standardized tests to measure intelligence fall into two major groups: achievement tests and aptitude, or ability, tests.

Learning Disabilities

Learning disabilities is a label attached to the problems some children experience in one or more of the basic processes necessary for understanding numbers or language. Many of these children can process certain information but have difficulty functioning on other tasks. A profile of the learning-disabled child shows a middle-class boy, age eight to eleven, with relatively well-educated parents. All reports indicate that a higher percentage of boys than girls are affected. The gender difference, therefore, is apparently great. In one public school system the ratio of learning-disabled boys to learning-disabled girls was approximately 25 to 1; in another system it was 15 to 1.

The IQ scores of learning-disabled children fall within normal limits, but reading, writing, drawing, and/or spelling abilities are at least two years behind those of normal children of the same age (Cruickshank 1977; Farnham-Diggory 1978). Learning disabilities negatively affect the self-worth and self-concept of elementary-age children. Not only do they perceive themselves negatively, but their peers also perceive them negatively (Bear et al. 1991; Cooley and Ayres 1988; Kistner and Osborne 1987; Renick and Harer 1988; Rogers and Saklofske 1985).

Attention Deficit–Hyperactive Disorder

Attention deficit–hyperactivity disorder (ADHD)
A disorder in which a child has a high level of activity and is unable to inhibit it on command.

Hyperactivity
See Attentive deficit–hyperactivity disorder

A child who has been diagnosed with **attention deficit–hyperactivity disorder (ADHD),** traditionally called hyperactivity or hyperkinetic syndrome, has a high level of activity and is unable to inhibit it on command. Children with ADHD cannot stay in their seats, finish their work in a reasonable period, keep their mind on their work, stay at one task, refrain from calling out in class, or inhibit aggression. They make errors in oral and written work and do not stop to think. The disorder affects approximately five million children and is more common among boys than girls. It has been classified as largely a physical disorder that is often inherited. ADHD can appear early in infancy and persist through adulthood. Clinical descriptions and research have shown that hyperactivity can affect all major facets of a child's life in the middle childhood years (Wolkenberg 1987).

Learning difficulties may develop in ADHD children because they cannot adapt, lose learning opportunities, and fall behind. Eventually the lag will be reflected in achievement tests and IQ. For example, in one study the mean IQ scores of hyperactive boys and girls in the first and second grade did not differ from the scores of the control group. By the fifth and sixth grades, however, the IQ scores of the hyperactive children were significantly lower than those of the controls. For this reason the hyperactive child may be classified as learning disabled even if no other difficulties (such as dyslexia) are present (Farnham-Diggory 1978; Ross and Ross 1976).

The cognitive style of ADHD children appears to be impulsive and field dependent. They seldom follow oral directions accurately, and their behavior and academic performance are unpredictable. The hyperactive child is unable to inhibit touching, which is seen as cognitive immaturity (younger children manipulate objects in order to develop representations of them). Hyperactive children may grab, manipulate, poke, and push to an intolerable degree (Brown 1982; Farnham-Diggory 1978; Ross and Ross 1976). It is possible that they lack sophisticated symbolic representational systems and learn about their world by manipulating it, almost like blind children.

A study conducted by Siegel and Ryan (1989) found that ADHD children have a working memory similar to normal achieving children and higher than children who are reading disabled and/or arithmetic disabled. Similar to short-term memory, working memory is the temporary storage of information while other tasks are being performed. Working memory requires both the simultaneous processing of information and the retrieval of other information.

Often ADHD children are light sleepers, with their sleep patterns quantitatively different from those of normal subjects. They spend less time (of total sleep) dreaming, have fewer dreams per sleep period, and frequently disrupt their dream periods by awakening (Nichamin and Windell 1984).

In one study, ADHD boys who were antisocial were more likely to be involved in family adversity and to have lower verbal intelligence and reading skills. ADHD boys who were not antisocial had normal family lives and normal intelligence and reading scores (Moffitt 1990).

The frustration felt by hyperactive children is illustrated by the following excerpts:

Boy, 8 years, 4 months: "I just wish I could be just an *ordinary boy,* like I mean OK in school but not all A's and have the other kids ask me to play ball, and most of all I wish I could not cry when I get mad. It's really terrible when you can't stop crying and everyone's looking."

Boy, 6 years, 11 months: ". . . I am very tired of everything always being wrong and having to go for tests and my mom and dad look awful worried and soon I might have to go to another school. And what I would like a lot would be if I could just sit still and be the way the other kids are and not have all these things happen. And most of all I wish I did not break that mirror at Teddy Work's birthday party."

Boy, 8 years, 6 months: "What I would like best of all would be to be like Jimmy Markhall. When *he* says the wrong answer the other kids all laugh but not mean laughs and when *he* drops something or knocks things down our teacher says, 'Oh Jimmy,' but not real cross and I would like that most of all."

Boy, 6 years, 11 months: ". . . I would like it a lot if Mrs. Miller [teacher] would just once in a while, even once in the whole of second grade, say, 'Here's a boy who's really moving up fast' to me like she did to Stu and Jackie. . . . And I also would like to do something good like Elliot [older brother] does right from the start. Elliot hit a baseball right off, and he just catches good, and my dad says, 'That boy is a natural,' and I would like it if I was natural at something" (Farnham-Diggory 1978, 79–80).

The stimulant drug Ritalin has been used successfully to treat hyperactive children, as have other medications. The first reported study using psychostimulants in children was done by Charles Bradley in 1937. He was seeking a drug that would raise the blood pressure of institutionalized problem children. When they were placed on Benzedrine, an amphetamine, fourteen of the thirty showed remarkable scholastic improvement. They showed greater interest in and the ability to do schoolwork, as well as increased feelings of well-being. The drug seemingly calmed the overactive children without having a subduing effect (Sroufe 1975; Paluszny 1977).

Amphetamines decrease a child's hyperactivity and impulsivity, enhancing the child's feelings of being in control. They help hyperactive children calm down, be cooperative, sit still, and focus their attention (Paluszny 1977). Amphetamines enhance performance on tasks requiring attentiveness, such as typing with speed and accuracy. The positive effect of stimulant drug therapy is that it breaks the vicious cycle of failure, reprimand, and unhappiness. The children begin to have successful experiences, parents and teachers like them better and believe in them more, and school becomes a positive rather than a dreaded situation. Both attitude and performance appear to be enhanced by the short-term administration of stimulant drugs.

Medication for hyperactivity may suppress physical growth, at least temporarily. Since mental growth has been shown to correlate with physical growth, it is possible that the medication may temporarily suppress mental growth as well. Ingestion of amphetamines may be linked to Hodgkin's disease, a form of cancer involving the bone marrow (Farnham-Diggory 1978). Other side effects include speech impairment, eating problems, and decreased alertness (Sprague and Ullman 1981).

Drug therapy does not work with every hyperactive child, and in some cases behavior modification techniques are used. One study showed that when parents and teachers gave praise and rewards for desirable behavior, the symptoms of hyperactivity declined (Ross and Ross 1984).

Adults who were hyperactive as children often are restless, lively, energetic extroverts, and very successful in their careers despite poor school records. Jobs that require endless energy, an outgoing manner, quick decisions, and physical risk and that allow some flexibility and individual freedom are well suited to hyperactive individuals (Ross and Ross 1976).

Dyslexia

Dyslexia The inability to read with understanding.

Dyslexia is the inability to read with understanding (Herschel 1978). Children with dyslexia make their letters backward, such as *b* for *d,* and may read *saw* as *was* (Stanovich 1982). Perhaps 5 percent of all children have some degree of dyslexia, for no obvious cause, and normal intelligence. Some may reverse the order of letters and words or may show bizarre spelling. Some cannot recognize sounds. Some have an unreliable visual memory combined with difficulty of vocal expression (American Association of Ophthalmology 1970).

As early as 1905, evidence suggested that dyslexia tended to occur within families, and studies indicate that it is transmitted as a dominant disorder. In the case of identical twins, if one has dyslexia, both have it. With fraternal twins, in only one pair in three do both have the disorder (Herschel 1978; Milunsky 1977). Although there appears to be more than one hereditary type of dyslexia, the most important and common one is the dominant form. One type is gender-linked; that is, the mother's X chromosome transmits it to her sons only (Milunsky 1977). Siblings of dyslexics, even when not dyslexic themselves, score behind peers in reading and spelling. One or both of the parents are likely to have had learning difficulties in school (Farnham-Diggory 1978; 1984).

Scientists have learned that each hemisphere of the brain specializes in certain types of cognition. The left side handles language and serial processing. The right side specializes in spatial and pictorial perception and wholistic processing. In fluent reading and writing, the two hemispheres coordinate their functions in intricate, high-speed sequential programs. Words and letters, whether printed on a page or written by one's own hand, have spatial characteristics, for which the right hemisphere is specialized. Reading and writing also involve serial and language functions, for which the left hemisphere is specialized (Farnham-Diggory 1978, 1984).

One possible cause of dyslexia is the lack of clear-cut dominance of the left hemisphere of the brain. Reading problems are associated with left-handedness or with mixed dominance (for example, when a right-handed child is left-eyed or left-footed) (Hynd, Obrzut, and Obrzut 1981; Watson and Engle 1982).

Males and females with learning disabilities show deficient left-hemispheric processing. For dyslexic females, this appears to be the sole deficiency. For dyslexic males, the left hemisphere not only is deficient in its own skills but also is burdened with extra right-hemispheric skills. This may explain why dyslexia is more frequent and often more severe in males than in females (Farnham-Diggory 1978, 1984).

Dyscalcula

Dyscalcula is the inability to perform operations of arithmetic. It is not clear, as in dyslexia, that a brain dysfunction might be inborn in children who cannot learn arithmetic. Four types of arithmetic disorders have been identified. *Defects of logic* involve the inability to understand phrases like "triangle below a cross." The problem is with spatial relationships, holding two or more elements in mind simultaneously, and comparing them along some dimension. Logical defects can also appear in handling numbers, such as the failure to grasp the logic of 0 as a place holder and difficulty in understanding clocks and calendars. *Defects in planning* involve the failure to perform a preliminary analysis of the conditions of a problem. As a result, the individual is never able to formulate a plan for solving the problem. He or she jumps into impulsive arithmetic operations and loses all connection with the original problem, then fails to verify the answers. The third type of dyscalcula involves the *preservation of inappropriate procedures.* The fourth type is the *inability to perform simple calculations,* although the individual may still retain the ability to analyze problems and may even invent new strategies for circumventing the calculation defect (Farnham-Diggory 1978).

Arithmetic disabilities observed in schoolchildren can also be found in adults who have suffered brain injuries. It should not be concluded, however, that children with dyscalcula have injured brains. Rather, it appears that some

Dyscalcula
The inability to perform operations of arithmetic.

forms of arithmetic disability, like some forms of reading disability, may have a basis in brain dysfunction (Farnham-Diggory 1978).

Language Development

The grammar of a five-year-old differs in a number of significant respects from the grammar of an adult, and the gradual disappearance of these discrepancies can be traced as the child exhibits increased knowledge over the next four or five years of development. A major discrepancy is the child's interpretation of constructions. Consider, for example, two sentences:

1. John promised Mary to shovel the driveway. 2. John told Mary to shovel the driveway.

Adults know that in sentence 1 it is John who intends to do the shoveling and in sentence 2 it is Mary who is supposed to do it. Many children of age five or six interpret both sentences as meaning Mary will do the shoveling. The word *promise,* in the first construction, appears to be an exception to the general pattern of the language, and most six-year-olds have not yet learned the exception or are not mature enough to comprehend it. They know what a promise is, and they are able to use and correctly interpret sentences containing *promise* in other syntactic environments. By eight years of age, most children have internalized this special grammatical concept about *promise* and can interpret sentences such as number 1 correctly.

As they mature, children learn more about sentence structure and, in turn, acquire more devices to convey different functions. As they learn more about functions, they extend the uses to which different sentence structures can be put. This is difficult to do and illustrates the complicated dynamics behind learning language (Clark and Clark 1977).

The use of compound and complex sentences increases during the elementary school years, and the use of incomplete syntactic structures declines. The basic syntactic structure of most children's sentences appears to be similar to adult grammar. As they get older, children show a substantial increase in the number of adjectives, adverbs, and conjunctions they use, plus the ability to use abstract and unfamiliar language rules. This is especially pronounced when the child has appropriate models to imitate and caretakers who reward correct responses. The ability to understand and use proper nouns, pronouns, and prepositions also increases (Goodglass, Gleason, Hyde 1970).

Elementary school children increase their accuracy with word definitions and are able to understand abstract relationships between words. Other capabilities include naming the agent when an action has been given and understanding word pairs, many of which eluded them earlier (such as "before–after," "big–little," "wide–narrow"), including knowledge of the meaning that distinguishes the words in each pair from one another (Donaldson and Wales 1970; Moskowitz 1978).

Elementary school children shift from egocentric speech to more socialized styles of communication. **Socialized speech** enables the child to exchange thoughts with others, show a genuine interest in what others are thinking and saying, and use the interchange of ideas or collaborations to pursue common goals. The child can adapt information when he or she adopts the point of view of another speaker. *Social speech* is taught by rote, involves societal expectations of politeness, and includes such expressions as "please," "thank you," and "I'm

Socialized speech
Conversation that enables the child to exchange thoughts with others, showing a genuine interest in what others are thinking and saying, and use the interchange of ideas or collaborations to pursue common goals.

sorry." Social speech puts no obligations on the speaker or listener but is often considered essential to the smooth running of society. It may or may not express the speaker's feelings, but it conveys the feeling expected by society in a particular situation (Clark and Clark 1977).

Both socialized speech and social speech involve questions and answers. Younger children ask questions but rarely listen to answers, whereas elementary school children use questions as a means of obtaining information. Their questions usually concern aspects of human life, causality, or classification.

Listening, a primary way that elementary children obtain knowledge and acquire beliefs, is especially important when one considers the amount of time that children spend listening in educational settings. It is estimated that teachers expect children to be engaged in listening 50 percent of the time they are in the classroom (Wolvin and Coakley 1988). Children are very poor at evaluating and regulating their comprehension of what they hear. They often do not detect glaring message violations, such as ambiguities and inconsistencies, and they often fail to ask questions or let anyone know they are confused (Markman and Gorin 1981). One study has shown that elementary children do know how to listen more effectively. Miller and Bigi (1979) found that seventy-seven of the seventy-nine children in their sample realized that they could listen more carefully to the teacher if they looked at the teacher, did not talk to anyone else, were interested in what the teacher was saying, and did not "fool around."

McDevitt et al. (1990) found that first, third, and fifth graders had considerable understanding about the nature of listening. The children realized that they should address questions to the speaker when they were confused. When they were confused by their mothers, they would ask questions directly of their mothers. But if they were confused by their teachers, they believed it was best to listen more carefully. When dealing with younger siblings, they sidestepped them and went to their mothers for clarification. The children in the study seemed to combine their perception of the speaker's ability and status with the norms of the situation.

Although, overall, the children showed a great deal of understanding about listening, their responses did vary by age. For example, the older children, more than the younger children, appreciated that good listening means something other than quiet and nondisruptive behavior and that vigorous attempts to comprehend are essential. First graders may believe that comprehension is possible only if the listener remains quiet. As they get older and have more experiences, children begin to value inferential activity and to integrate incoming information with existing knowledge. They also see more value in listening carefully and asking the speaker a question when confused.

Humor

For children, humor not only is a means of developing cognitive mastery but also is used to communicate and socialize with other children. Humorous situations teach a child socially acceptable behavior and what is perceived as humorous by the culture (Simons et al. 1986). Children who are socially accepted are more likely to be exposed to effective social problem solving and to have experiences that reinforce their social skills and enhance their sense of humor (Pellegrini et al. 1987). Social factors play a strong supporting role in a child's perception of humor, and a child might never develop a sense of humor without the reactions of others. Playful moods or attitudes are maintained largely through interaction with others, and without playfulness humor cannot occur (Simons et al. 1986).

A sense of humor does not become a staple of personality until the early elementary school years. This period is pivotal in determining whether laughter will become a permanent resource for meeting, or coping with, life (McGhee and Lloyd 1982). Humor development is strongly associated with a history of attempts to seek attention, affection, and emotional support. Humor development also corresponds with the child's frequent requests for help on tasks related to recognition and achievement. A budding clown or joker with a history of being sensitive to adult reactions will gear much of his or her behavior to obtaining some form of positive reaction from adults. When humor is modeled and reinforced with laughter, attention, affection, and so forth, the child learns that humor is not only enjoyable but also useful in eliciting favorable reactions. Children with a particularly great need for affection or recognition are especially likely to adopt humor as a predominant component of their interaction with others (McGhee 1979).

By acquiring concrete operational thinking skills, children can simultaneously keep two ideas in mind at the same time (decentering), and this makes it possible for them to understand jokes and riddles based on double meanings (McGhee 1986). This marks the beginning of Stage 4 of Humor, which is also the first step toward adult humor. Much of adult humor is based on the fact that two or more meanings can be applied to a particular key word in a joke or story. Puns are a classic example of this type of humor. For the child or adult to appreciate the humor in puns, he or she must be simultaneously aware of the two meanings; one meaning provides for a normal set of circumstances while the less probable meaning creates an incongruous situation. For example, the classic joke: "Hey, did you take a bath?" "No. Why, is one missing?" The Stage 3 (preschool) child would understand both usages of the word "take" but would not be able to keep both in mind simultaneously. Thus, there is no sense of incongruity for the child and the joke does not make sense (McGhee, 1979).

As children master language skills, they appreciate word play and take pleasure in the evolving thought processes required to understand what is funny. In a study of children between the ages of six and eleven, it was found that their appreciation of riddles increased with age and cognitive maturity (Whitt and Prentice 1977). Humor about who has knowledge and who does not is sharpest at about age six, which suggests that the emphasis placed on learning in school may be a major motivating force behind such joking. Given the children's intense preoccupation with the issue of smartness and dumbness, telling riddles demonstrates that they are smart and the other fellow (who does not know the answer) is dumb (Wolfenstein 1954; Whitt and Prentice 1977).

Yalisove (1978) found an interaction between a child's cognitive level and the comprehension of riddles. Three categories of riddles were identified. **Reality riddles,** popular in first grade and decreasing in popularity thereafter, require that the child have a notion of what is real. They are based on a conceptual trick that remains within the context of reality. Word play and absurdity are not involved. An example is, "How many balls of string would it take to reach the moon? One, but it would have to be a big one." To appreciate this riddle the child would have to be able to comprehend relative size and distance.

Most popular between the third and fifth grades are **language ambiguity riddles.** The ambiguity can be in either the question or the answer. These riddles are based on a play on words. Examples include, "What state can you write

Reality riddles
Riddles based on a conceptual trick that remains within the context of reality.

Language ambiguity riddles
Riddles in which a play on words can be located in either the question or the answer.

Boys and girls show similar levels of comprehension and appreciation of most forms of humor.

with? *Pencil*-vania"; "What goes into an astronaut sandwich? "*Launch*meat"; "How many skunks does it take to smell up a neighborhood?" "Just a *phew*." To be able to comprehend riddles like these, children must know that certain words that sound the same have different meanings, as well as realize that some words can have two meanings. Their thinking processes must be flexible enough to switch quickly from one meaning to another. Children at this stage focus on the reasonableness of the answer and are unable to tolerate the idea of something absurd, fantastic, or illogical and unexplainable.

Absurdity riddles first appear in the sixth grade and continue through the high school years. The absurdity is positioned either in the question or in the answer. The question contains a blatant impossibility that, if mentally negated, allows the riddle to be answered logically. For example, "How can you fit six elephants into a VW? Three in the back and three in the front." The thinking required for this type of riddle is related to Piaget's formal operational thinking in that it implies the ability to consider the hypothetical within a logical framework.

A child's cognitive style can influence his or her humor appreciation. Reflective children tend to demonstrate better spontaneous comprehension but seem to appreciate humor less than impulsive children do. Thus, impulsive children laugh more at humor but do not understand "the point" as well as reflective children do (McGhee 1986; Simons et al. 1986).

Numerous studies have documented the fact that boys and girls show similar levels of comprehension and appreciation of most forms of humor (Simons et al. 1986; McGhee 1976; Groch 1974; Chapman 1975). The exception is that boys generally enjoy hostile forms of humor more than girls do. When given a choice between nonsensical incongruity and aggressive cartoons, boys choose the latter. Girls are more likely than boys to show exaggerated laughter, but boys laugh more frequently than girls do. Boys also try more often to make others laugh by clowning around, acting silly, and saying funny things (McGhee 1976).

Absurdity riddles
Riddles in which an absurdity is positioned either in the question or in the answer. The question contains a blatant impossibility that, if mentally negated, allows the riddle to be answered logically.

Jokes help children vent aggression in a socially acceptable way. In a preschool and elementary sample, boys and girls with more pronounced humor development had a long history of verbal and physical aggressiveness in interactions with peers. Humor may have been a means of expressing hostility while claiming it was only meant to be a joke. A sense of humor can also be predicted by other forms of dominance in interaction with peers. Children who later become clowns or jokers are highly assertive at as early as three years of age. They are used to having social power in dealings with other children, and humor enables them to continue this pattern. The child or adult who is constantly joking or clowning maintains control of most ongoing social interaction by creating circumstances to which others are obliged to react. Through the use of humor they can dominate others in a manner that is not only socially acceptable but also lavishly rewarded. They realize that they can get away with an awful lot if their antics leave everyone laughing (McGhee and Lloyd 1982; McGhee 1979; Simons et al. 1986).

Preadolescents often disarm irate adults by making them laugh. Humor becomes a favored form of self-defense. When children discover they can vent a lot of hostility under cover of kidding, humor may become a thinly veiled attack. Most youngsters have ambivalent feelings toward authority figures and, therefore, use humor as a way to take potshots at adults from a protected position, while at the same time gaining a reputation as a wit. Some youngsters indulge in borderline kidding as a means of dealing with hostile feelings without hurting anyone. They are using cleverness and intellect to handle difficult feelings, and this is less harmful to all than overt expressions of aggression. Parents, in particular, may be targets of a steady barrage of sarcastic one-liners. Once parents understand the mechanism underlying the attack-humor, they usually develop the forbearance to laugh at their live-in comic's funny quips and disregard the others. Banning these remarks would bring into question the adults' own sense of humor. Children outgrow the need to exercise power over authority figures as they get older and gain more control over their own lives (McGhee 1979; Wolfenstein 1954).

Nevertheless, parents do a child no favor by allowing him or her to become chronically unpleasant. If a preadolescent's humor is consistently cruel and people inside and outside the family are left "bleeding" instead of laughing, it may be that the child is struggling with problems that are no joke. The need to hurt others knowingly should be investigated. When children learn to leash their tongues, their sense of humor becomes a social resource for themselves and everyone who knows them (McGhee 1979).

S U M M A R Y

- The rate of growth during middle childhood is slower but steadier than during infancy or the preschool years. The rate is less than two and one-half inches and eight pounds per year.
- Muscle growth in the elementary school child is rapid; the heartbeat slows down and the blood pressure goes up; the growth of the skeleton is more rapid than that of the muscles and ligaments, causing "growing pains"; and the facial structure changes noticeably with the loss of baby teeth and the introduction of permanent teeth.
- Elementary school children are proficient in strenuous activities that require large-muscle movement. Fine motor skills lag behind large motor skills, but

Mainstreaming

The Education for All Handicapped Children Act of 1975 (Public Law 94–142) is an excellent example of translating social policy into practical changes in public school procedures at the local level. At one time children who were physically and mentally handicapped were isolated from other children and taught in special classes. Public Law 94–142 guarantees every handicapped youngster an education that is tailored to meet the individual needs of the child. It mandates that each handicapped child will have an individualized plan for educational goals formulated by both parents and teachers and that the child will be educated in the "least restrictive environment," which most often has been interpreted to mean that he or she will be mainstreamed into the regular classroom. Each child, however, has a different "least restrictive environment." For one this may be integration into a regular classroom. For another this may be integration only during field trips. A child who is severely handicapped will not be placed in a regular classroom.

Legislation, of course, does not necessarily ensure success. Public Law 94–142 has been vigorously debated (Sarason 1983; Corrigan 1978; Vernon 1980). While most people support the intentions of the act, many consider the expense disproportionate and the federal mandate unnecessary and heavy-handed.

The benefits of Public Law 94–142 are numerous. Handicapped children now have access to their local public school system, whereas before they had none. State and local educational authorities are now accountable for providing the services necessary to rear and educate a handicapped child. Another innovation is the requirement for parental involvement in the development of an individualized educational program for a handicapped child. Of primary importance is the act's intention to benefit handicapped children and expand educational opportunities for them. The chance to socialize with "normal" children and adults helps the handicapped child learn more social and academic skills than would be the case in special education classes with other handicapped children (Salend 1984). Also, being a part of the normal education mainstream reduces the stigma of being taught in a segregated educational setting. Society benefits by a reduction in negative attitudes toward the handicapped. An unexpected benefit of mainstreaming is that mainstreamed mentally retarded students hold more positive attitudes toward their retarded and nonretarded peers than do nonmainstreamed,

or segregated, mentally retarded students (Altman and Lewis 1990).

The opposition to Public Law 94–142 centers around (1) the question of the actual benefit of mainstreaming to handicapped children and (2) the disproportionate expense of mainstreaming as compared with that of educating other children in the public school system. The first concern listed above is that mainstreaming does not expand but *reduces* educational opportunities for handicapped children. Most regular classroom teachers are not prepared to teach handicapped youngsters. (Many school systems, however, are addressing this issue by providing seminars and in-service training for their faculty [Sarason 1983].) In addition, depending upon the handicap, the children need to learn specific skills that will help them live and work in society.

In a period of economic restrictions, how much money can be allocated for the needs of just a few students? Vernon (1980) points out three major issues related to the costs of this law.

1. Can we continue to make our biggest per capita educational investment in those least able to return a dividend to society? If we can, is it appropriate? The question makes us all uncomfortable. For this reason, neither Congress nor education has confronted the facts directly and realistically. Attempts to do this cause one to be perceived as against handicapped children, hardly a position with which a politician or teacher wants to be identified.

2. Can the federal government tell local school districts how to spend their own educational dollars and remain consistent with the Constitution?

3. PL 94–142 places tremendous emphasis on a local program for the child. Theoretically this can benefit young children in particular. Is it feasible economically, however, and in terms of other resources? To illustrate, let's take a deaf child living in a small town in Illinois. For this child to acquire a good education requires a specifically trained teacher who understands his communication and language learning problems, a speech pathologist who can work with this aspect of education, an audiologist to measure hearing, sound treated classrooms, a sign language interpreter, special textbooks, a loop induction amplification system in all classrooms, in-

Continued

Mainstreaming (continued)

service education of all teachers and administrators, *ad infinitum*. To provide these services locally for only one child is inordinately expensive, costing in the range of $25,000 to $50,000 annually. Even then, I seriously doubt the wisdom of keeping a deaf child isolated from other deaf children. Furthermore, when you start requiring several professionals to work individually in a small locality with a single handicapped child, the supply of professionals, as well as the supply of money, soon runs out. In a purely economic sense, PL 94–142 is analogous to the federal government directing Chrysler Motor

Company to build each car in the locale where they will sell it. Picture the cost of this kind of decentralization. Remember PL 94–142 states that the optimal program is to be provided and that we cannot raise costs as a relevant issue.

To what extent should we consider the financial issue? Public Law 94–142 presents both moral and practical issues. On what basis should one value be given priority over another? What about the children? How do segregation and mainstreaming affect the self-esteem of the children?

they mature at a gradual and steady pace. Boys and girls differ on skills at which they are proficient.

- Self-esteem and peer acceptance of the elementary child are related to the degree that motor skills are mastered.
- Obesity can make a negative impact on an elementary child's self-esteem. Several factors cause obesity. The obese child needs emotional support to overcome a negative self-concept as well as to lose weight. Childhood obesity correlates with adult obesity.
- Concrete operational thinking occurs approximately between seven and eleven years. Four mental operations accompany this ability: combinativity, or class inclusion, reversibility, associativity, and nullifiability. These operations make it possible for a child to comprehend conservation.
- With the onset of new thinking capabilities, various cognitive styles—such as an impulsive or reflective attitude, field independence or field dependence, internal locus of control or external locus of control—become possible.
- Information processing by the human brain is similar to the very complex operation of a computer. Short-term and long-term memory involve basic processes, knowledge, mnemonic strategies, and metamemory.
- Learning disabilities take on many forms and are difficult to define. Hyperactivity can appear to cause a learning disability or it can be one. Psychoactive drugs enable a hyperactive child to function in society; however, there are many pros and cons surrounding the drugs' use. Children with dyslexia are unable to read with understanding. Children with dyscalcula are unable to perform operations of arithmetic.
- Language development continues to occur throughout the elementary school years. By the end of this period the basic syntactic structure of most children's sentences appears to be the same as adult grammar. The children shift from egocentric speech to socialized speech.
- Social factors influence a child's perception of humor. A sense of humor becomes a staple of personality during the early elementary years. A correlation has been found between a child's cognitive level and the comprehension of

riddles. Three categories of riddles are reality riddles, language ambiguity riddles, and absurdity riddles. Girls and boys differ in their expression of humor. Jokes help children vent aggression in a socially acceptable manner.

- The Education for All Handicapped Children Act of 1975 (Public Law 94–142) provides that all handicapped children shall have access to an education that is tailored to their individual needs. This includes mainstreaming the majority of handicapped students into the public school systems. Although the intention of the act is widely accepted, the actual implementation has caused much disagreement among educators.

R E A D I N G S

Bryant, P., and Bradley, L. (1985). *Children's reading problems.* Oxford: Basil Blackwell.
An account of why children have trouble learning to read and what can be done to improve their reading skills.

Davis, G. A., and Scott, J. A. (1981). *Training creative thinking.* New York: Holt, Rinehart, and Winston.
Contributions from several psychologists who study creativity, with suggestions on how to stimulate creativity in a classroom setting.

Featherstone, H. (1981). *A difference in the family: Living with a disabled child.* New York: Penguin.
A description of life with a disabled child and the accompanying emotional and practical strains.

Ross, D. M., and Ross, S. A. (1982). *Hyperactivity: Current issues, research, and theory.* (2nd ed.) New York: Wiley.
A description of the hyperactive individual from infancy through early adulthood that includes drug therapies, special school programs, and the child's viewpoint.

Zimbardo, P. G., and Radl, S. L. (1982). *The shy child.*
A view of the shy child with an explanation of how the child's thinking processes can be used to help him or her become more outgoing.

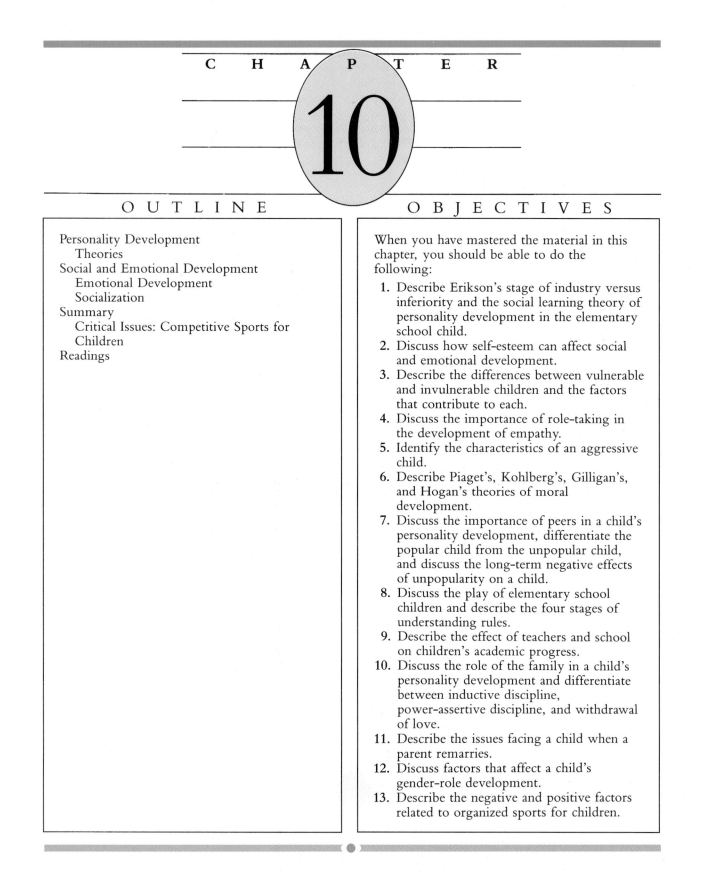

C H A P T E R

10

O U T L I N E

Personality Development
    Theories
Social and Emotional Development
    Emotional Development
    Socialization
Summary
    Critical Issues: Competitive Sports for
    Children
Readings

O B J E C T I V E S

When you have mastered the material in this chapter, you should be able to do the following:

1. Describe Erikson's stage of industry versus inferiority and the social learning theory of personality development in the elementary school child.
2. Discuss how self-esteem can affect social and emotional development.
3. Describe the differences between vulnerable and invulnerable children and the factors that contribute to each.
4. Discuss the importance of role-taking in the development of empathy.
5. Identify the characteristics of an aggressive child.
6. Describe Piaget's, Kohlberg's, Gilligan's, and Hogan's theories of moral development.
7. Discuss the importance of peers in a child's personality development, differentiate the popular child from the unpopular child, and discuss the long-term negative effects of unpopularity on a child.
8. Discuss the play of elementary school children and describe the four stages of understanding rules.
9. Describe the effect of teachers and school on children's academic progress.
10. Discuss the role of the family in a child's personality development and differentiate between inductive discipline, power-assertive discipline, and withdrawal of love.
11. Describe the issues facing a child when a parent remarries.
12. Discuss factors that affect a child's gender-role development.
13. Describe the negative and positive factors related to organized sports for children.

The Wonder Years: Middle Childhood's Psychosocial Development

PERSONALITY DEVELOPMENT

Theories

Two theories of personality development are widely accepted and provide different perspectives on the changes that occur during the elementary school years. These perspectives are generally complementary rather than competitive, and when viewed together they provide a balanced view of personality development.

Erikson's Psychosocial Theory

Erikson (1963) calls the elementary years the stage of industry versus inferiority. He describes the elementary school child as an industrious individual pursuing a sense of accomplishment and learning to win recognition by using tools and producing things. Play intermingles with work and becomes productive. The product becomes all-important to the child's self-esteem (Erikson 1963).

In this "Robinson Crusoe" stage, the ingenuity, attention to detail, and enthusiasm of that fictional character appeal to children's budding sense of industry.

All cultures provide some sort of systematic instruction at this stage. In the United States it is provided in the classroom, while in other societies it may occur in the field, by tying fish nets, by throwing spears, or by learning other forms of competency necessary within the culture. The industrious child takes pleasure in accomplishing new and different goals. Each attainment motivates both more and new industrious behavior (Erikson 1963).

The danger at this stage is that children will feel inadequate in their ability to use utensils and tools within their learning environment. If this happens, their self-worth diminishes. They can develop a sense of inferiority, of being doomed to mediocrity or inadequacy. A child may feel less able than peers to carry out work assigned to him or her by society. The child may also feel less able to win the respect and friendship of peers. Such feelings of inferiority interfere with the ability of children to apply themselves to their work (Erikson 1963). School experiences can profoundly affect the industry–inferiority balance. On the one hand, school can be traumatic for marginal children with an IQ of 80 to 90 even if their sense of industry is rewarded at home. "Too bright" for special classes but "too slow" for the conventional classroom, they may experience repeated academic failures that reinforce a sense of inferiority. On the other hand, children who are belittled and put down at home can have their self-concept revitalized at school by a sensitive and committed teacher. Thus, personality and school achievement are closely related (Elkind 1977).

This is a socially decisive stage, since industry involves doing things beside and with others. Children accept the fact that their future lies not within the family but in a larger world outside the home. They take on the task of acquiring skills that will equip them for that future, and they learn to apply themselves to work rather than play. It becomes crucial to get along with people outside the immediate family. As this locus shifts, the caretaking efforts of the parents no longer are determinate in shaping the child's sense of industry or inferiority. Other adults as well as peers can make a positive or negative contribution to the development of the elementary school child (Erikson 1963; Elkind 1977).

Social Learning Theory

In formulating the social learning theory, Bandura and Walters assumed that human functioning cannot be independent of cognitive functioning. Because of this emphasis, Mischel (1973) renamed it the cognitive social theory. Both versions recognize the role played by mental constructs, such as encoding strategies, incentives, and competencies. Behavior is seen as the result of a cognitive process. Thought *and* behavior are considered equally important. Bandura viewed behavior as originating from direct learning and from reinforcement and observation. Thus, the ability to trust others, behave morally, inhibit aggression, and so forth, is acquired through being taught, through observation of those behaviors, and through having those behaviors in oneself be reinforced. Bandura saw direct learning as a more rudimentary process than observational learning.

Direct learning occurs when actions are repeated or not repeated as a result of their positive or negative outcomes. When children observe the results of their actions, they can develop hypotheses about what behavior is appropriate in given settings. For example, a fifth grader who is caught cheating on a spelling test is unlikely to do so again if the teacher and peers show disappointment with this behavior. But not all direct learning is efficient, and it can even be hazardous. For example, a child using a ramp to do a bike stunt can be hurt if he or she has not seen or practiced the stunt before. He or she can be severely injured in testing an incorrect hypothesis.

Observational learning, which accounts for much of human behavior, occurs by watching others in order to understand how to act and what to anticipate in the future from certain actions. Observational learning can be acquired from live models or symbolic models (such as television characters). Many needless and dangerous mistakes can be avoided by *attending* to the model's behavior. Attention can be determined by the attractiveness or power of the model and/or the conditions under which the model is viewed. Because television is so powerful

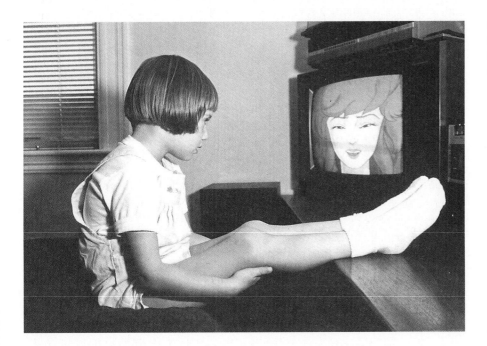

Observational learning can be acquired from live models or symbolic models such as television characters.

in attracting the attention of a child, it can easily promote antisocial and aggressive behavior if that is what it models. In order for a child to model a certain behavior, however, he or she must have some *incentive* to do so (Bandura 1985). For example, a three-year-old who had watched the "911" television program summoned help for his unconscious mother by dialing 911.

In summary, the social learning theory emphasizes that learning experiences are more important than maturational processes in forming character. Significant learning experiences depend on social class attitudes and learning conditions, cultural and traditional behavior, parental emphasis and attitudes, and the type of disciplinary measures used.

By middle childhood a variety of socializing forces and sociocultural factors can influence the developing child. Socializing forces can include parents, siblings, other children, teachers, and other adults. Children learn by observing the behavior of these adults and children. Each child develops a unique personality pattern because each child's social learning experiences are different (Bandura 1977).

● SOCIAL AND EMOTIONAL DEVELOPMENT
Emotional Development

It is during middle childhood that a child becomes increasingly aware of himself or herself as a unique individual. It is also during this stage that a child is able to consider others' views and take them into consideration. Parents can play an important role in shaping the child's self-esteem and self-concept (Maccoby 1984). Experience in elementary school also has significant implications for personal and social growth. Adjusting successfully to the school setting and to widening peer contacts is helpful in the child's developing self-concept. Other factors that contribute to children's evaluation of themselves include reinforcement of their self-image, a level of self-esteem, continuing gender-role identification, developing moral understanding, and emotional growth.

The Self

Parents and peers are largely responsible for the self-concept of children during the middle childhood years. Parents can help by showing their children how much they love them through hugging, stroking, and putting their arms around them—that is, through positive touching (Maccoby 1984).

Coopersmith's (1967) classic study of fifth- and sixth-grade boys found that those with a high degree of self-esteem were generally expressive and successful in a school setting and social situations. They were also verbally active in discussions, expressed their opinions, and were able to handle criticism effectively. They exhibited low levels of anxiety and destructiveness. Boys who ranked in the middle range of self-esteem shared many traits with the first group but tended to be more dependent on acceptance, showed some uncertainty in self-ratings, and exhibited more conventional behavior patterns and values. The boys with low self-esteem were fairly well convinced of their inferiority, showing discouragement, timidity, and sometimes depression. They could not engage in effective social interaction with peers and lacked the social skills to make new friends. They were virtually unable to engage in and contribute to group discussions. The factors Coopersmith identified as influencing self-esteem included parents' interest, concern, and availability. In a study with fifth- and sixth-grade

Parents can play an important role in shaping the child's self-esteem and self-concept.

girls and boys, Sears (1970) found results similar to those of Coopersmith, particularly that parental warmth and affection contribute to self-esteem.

Compared with boys, girls register a higher correlation between their real and their ideal self (Maccoby 1984). One possible explanation is that the average girl is more mature than the average boy. Older children are more realistic in projecting a self-image because of greater maturity and experience. A study of grades three through six found that the self-image of sixth graders corresponded more closely to reality than did the self-image of third graders (Harter 1982). Intelligence also affects differences between real and ideal self-images. Research by Katz and Zigler (1961) showed that fifth, eighth, and eleventh graders with high IQs had greater disparity levels (differences between the real and the ideal self) than those with low IQs. The result seems surprising since children with low IQs might be expected to show greater dissatisfaction with themselves, but more-intelligent children are more critical of themselves as they age and are more conscious of their ideal self.

Emotional Maturity

One characteristic of emotional maturity is a change from helplessness to independence and self-sufficiency. Maturity implies progressive stages of growth and the overall acquisition of emotional flexibility. Emotional maturity is evidenced by the ability to make successful life adjustments (Harter and Miner 1979; Wolman 1978).

Certain fears diminish during middle childhood, particularly those related to bodily safety (such as sickness and injury) as well as the fear of dogs, noises, darkness, and storms. No significant decline is apparent in fears of supernatural forces, such as ghosts and witches. Most new fears are related to school and

A sense of *social competence* in a child effects total personality growth. This sense of competence is a highly important ingredient of self and self-esteem. High self-esteem makes it possible to feel confident in doing things that matter, which allows the individual to influence the course of his or her life. On the other hand, a low degree of social competence in children seems to be related to psychopathology. These children need to acquire enough of a sense of competence to encourage social interaction. Competence plays an instrumental part in social development. In the past the emphasis of socialization was on getting children together without considering what would be the most conducive to the growth of real social competence (White 1979).

Three general patterns of social incompetence have been identified by White (1979): *social anesthesia, social isolation,* and *social enslavement.* A child with **social anesthesia** is unaware of the consequences of his or her behavior, and some of his or her behavior is a blind expression of feeling. Many of the child's expressions, like crying, hitting, and tantrums, are vaguely directed at the environment. These actions are forced out by strong feelings almost regardless of who is there. A child who, venting anger and perhaps getting some inner relief, tears down party decorations as fast as the other children put them up will not increase social competence. Individuals who are impulsive have difficulty recognizing the social consequences of their acts. They are slower to develop social competence even though initiatives come easily. To help a child who has social anesthesia, it might be wise to verbalize the effects of his or her behavior. For example, "Look, Michael, if you push Karen so hard that she falls down, it hurts her." That is, clarifying the consequences might be beneficial when a child seems not to be registering what those consequences are.

Social isolation more commonly takes the form not of being away from other people, but of being with people while wanting to be away from them. If a child feels uneasy in human company, the desire to be away may take precedence over the inclination to interact. Being with others while wanting to be elsewhere has highly damaging effects on social competence. If a child perceives other people as intruders and has no sense of competence to deal with them, he or she may soon see them as annoying. A child with a pattern of social isolation becomes adept at withdrawing when with others, averting eye contact, remaining expressionless, and answering questions reluctantly with monosyllables. Such isolation serves the short-term purpose of allowing privacy, but it does not permit the child to develop healthy patterns of social interaction.

A pattern of social isolation sets a trap for social development. Children with this pattern make no attempt to become interested and involved, and do not put forth the effort to have an

---

Invulnerable children
Children who appear to be stress-resistant and retain mastery and control over their lives even when coping with poverty and emotional and social stress.

family. Fears of ridicule by parents, teachers, and friends increase, as do fears of parental disapproval and rejection (Wolman 1978).

Vulnerable and Invulnerable Children   Some children seem to find ways to cope with poverty and emotional and social stress, retaining a degree of mastery and control over their lives. Garmezy (1976, 1983) refers to these children as **invulnerables** because they seem so stress-resistant.

Early studies of invulnerable children indicated that adversity can be overcome (Garmezy 1976; Rutter 1979; Baldwin et al. 1983). Factors that increase vulnerability include difficult temperament, problems related to birth, and biogenetic problems. Events that trigger stress include hospitalization, separation from parents, and war. Protective factors include adult models who maintain some control amid chaos, emotional security, happy or flexible temperament on the part of the child, the gender of the child (girls suffer less than boys), and/or a supportive environment, such as an encouraging school atmosphere (Garmezy 1983). It was found that children who were institutionalized, hospitalized, separated from their parents, or reared in poverty or other chaotic conditions did not necessarily suffer long-term deficits in development.

For example, a paranoid schizophrenic woman insisted on eating at restaurants because she thought someone was poisoning the food at home. Her

effect on other people even an effect as mild as pleasing someone or entertaining them. The company of several other children is not helpful in getting over the anxiety. A compromise may develop when superficial social amenities are learned and physical mingling is not wholly avoided. However, relations with others will tend to remain formal, distant, and lacking in warmth. Those who are not able to compromise continue to feel tension in human company. This lack of interaction may lead to a pathological outcome. The extreme form of social isolation is autism.

In summary, social isolation is a defensive maneuver preventing initiative toward others. The experience of social competence is blocked at the source, and change depends on conditions that will overcome the basic fear of initiative.

Social enslavement involves a person who wants to be in the company of others and is afraid of being thrown out of it. The desire to be accepted is combined with the lively fear

of being rejected. Fear dictates doing nothing that could possibly give offense. The range of safe actions include being pleasant, agreeing, helping, and going along with whatever seems to be expected. It leaves little room to express wants of one's own. Initiatives are risky and may lead to ridicule, rejection, and even punishment. This situation has two possible connections with psychopathology. In the first possibility, the child is so dependent on acceptance and so fearful of losing it that he or she is vulnerable. The second possibility is that the pattern of social enslavement inflicts grave damage on other aspects of personal growth. Too great a dependence on the company of others may seriously interfere with the child's independent sense of self. This pattern often backlashes such that this child is often the least interesting and, there-

fore, the most expendable member of the group (White 1979).

Historically we have clamored too loud for social adjustment. We have not been sensitive to the dangers of throwing children together regardless of their anxieties and their own social needs. We have been enchanted with peer groups, as if the highest form of social behavior were getting along with age-equals, the relation where competition is most salient. We take it as bad adjustment, for instance, when someone gets along well only with younger and older people and is uncomfortable with peers. As most of the people in our adult lives are either older or younger, we might better judge this person as showing fine promise, certainly more promise than one who thrives only with peers and treats older and younger people as if they did not exist. (White 1979, 21)

twelve-year-old daughter had the same phobic attitude. Her ten-year-old daughter would eat at home when the father was there but otherwise would go along to a restaurant. The father was not dysfunctional. The seven-year-old son, who always ate at home, was asked by the psychiatrist why he did not accompany his mother. He simply shrugged and said, "Well, I'm not dead yet." The older girl eventually became ill like her mother. The younger girl went to college and did reasonably well. The boy performed brilliantly all through school and afterward. His mother's illness apparently challenged him to overcome all sorts of problems (Segal and Yahraes 1979).

Genetic factors, which play a significant role in determining individual differences in personality and intelligence, affect how a child responds to environmental stresses (Rutter 1979). Even in quarrelsome and discordant homes, a temperamentally easy child tends to avoid much of the negative interchange. When parents are depressed and irritable, they do not take it out on all of their children to the same extent. The targeted child tends to be the temperamentally difficult one and is twice as likely as the other siblings to be subjected to parental criticism. Thus, a child's personal characteristics can partly determine the social environment, and in this sense genetic variables help shape environments (Rutter 1979).

Highly intelligent children are less likely to show behavioral deviance than are children of average intelligence (Pellegrini et al. 1987). Children of average intelligence but with specific reading retardation have a greater rate of conduct disorders. Rutter (1979) suggests that perhaps these children lose confidence in themselves due to reading failures, which diminishes self-esteem, and react with antagonism and sometimes delinquency.

Young children who experience numerous hospitalizations that result in long separations from their parents are more likely to suffer psychiatric disorders during their adolescent and adult years (Garmezy 1983). Compared with children from advantaged homes, children from deprived and disadvantaged families are more likely to have multiple admissions to the hospital and are also more likely to suffer such long-term adverse effects as psychiatric disorders. No long-term effects are associated with a single admission to the hospital, regardless of the age at which it occurred (Rutter 1979).

Boys are more likely than girls to be negatively affected by family discord and disruption. Males are more vulnerable to physical stress, and they also appear to be more susceptible in some respects to psychosocial trauma. Both genders are equally likely to suffer ill effects from an institutional upbringing (Rutter 1979).

Six family variables have been strongly and significantly associated with childhood psychiatric disorders:

1. severe marital discord of the parents
2. low social status
3. overcrowding or large family size
4. paternal criminality
5. maternal psychiatric disorder
6. admission into the care of the local authority

Children with just one of these risk factors, however, are no more likely to have a psychiatric disorder than are children with none at all. The presence of any two of the stresses quadruples the risk (Rutter 1979; Garmezy 1983).

Rutter (1979) found that children who experience brief separations from their parents (such as staying overnight with friends or relatives, having babysitters, attending nursery school, or being left all day with a familiar person) are less likely than other children to show behavioral disturbance when separated for longer periods, such as during an extended hospital stay. It appears that short separations in happy circumstances can protect children from the stress of later unhappy separations.

In a longitudinal study reported by Murphy and Moriarty (1976), all the children in the sample experienced unexpected stress, and almost all coped quite well. For example, one girl compensated for her chronically ill mother's unavailability by spending most of her time with a neighbor who functioned as a surrogate mother. A boy overcame his mother's efforts to keep him a baby by devoting all of his energy to sports. The researchers concluded that most children are much more resilient than previous clinical studies of emotionally disturbed children had indicated. Youngsters who have trouble coping tend to be those with chronic or very serious stresses and without steady support and encouragement from adults.

Coping strategies typical of middle childhood are sometimes thoughtful, conscious responses. For example, a tomboy "decided to be a girl" when she was seven; another girl "decided to stop being shy" at ten; a boy whose parents had separated during his preschool years decided to begin another life, forgetting the first one. Coping skills can also be unconscious, such as in seriously ill children who use defense mechanisms of fantasy and regression to help endure pain.

Garmezy (1983) found that African-American children who survive in the inner city may develop remarkable social skills. They are typically well liked, sensitive, and socially responsive. They have a positive self-image and feel they have control over their environment. Their homes are ordered and neat, in contrast with the disorganization of the inner city. Their mothers encourage them to achieve in school. As with children in other stressful situations, the personal characteristics of these children, combined with a supportive adult, provide a reasonable environment for growth.

The way children respond to the stress of war depends largely on the behavior of their parents or guardians and other significant adults. Even with daily life punctuated by gunfire and death, the majority of children in war zones seem to cope. The best protective factor is adults who model ways to maintain some control amid chaos. Another protective factor is emotional security. Children also gain strength by identifying with the community and its goals (Garmezy 1983).

> In Belfast . . . the way in which each child reacted to riot stress seemed to depend on three main factors. There was, first, the degree of emotional security enjoyed by the child both before and during the period of acute stress. This related not only to his own psychological resources, but also to those of his immediate family. Secondly, there was the role of the stressful experience itself. Thirdly, each child's response was idiosyncratic, or unique, depending on his own usual way of responding to new experiences. (Garmezy 1983, 77)

Children subjected to poverty, war, or psychotic parents are able to cope with stress if the environment includes sufficient protection. Pain and suffering can have a steeling or hardening effect on some children, rendering them capable of mastering life despite the obstacles (Garmezy 1983; Garmezy et al. 1979).

In summing up his work and that of others, Garmezy (1983) identified several protective factors possessed by coping children.

- They have social skills. They are seen by peers and adults as friendly and are well liked; they are interpersonally sensitive; and they are not sullen and restless. They are low in defensiveness and aggressiveness and high in cooperation, participation, and emotional stability.
- They have a positive sense of self. They manifest self-regard rather than self-derogation and a sense of personal power rather than a sense of powerlessness.
- They have an internal locus of control and believe they can exercise a degree of control over their environment.
- The dominant cognitive style appears to be reflectiveness and impulse control (Pellegrini et al. 1987).
- The intact family is *not* an identifiably consistent variable, but in nonintact families the mother's style of coping with and compensating for the absence of the father appears to be a powerful redemptive variable.
- The physical and psychological environment of the home is important. The households of coping children tend to be less cluttered, less crowded, neater, cleaner, and marked by the presence of more books. The family environment is warm, praising, protective, and supportive. (A study reported by Rutter [1979], however, found that in conditions of chronic

Children who survive in the inner city may develop remarkable social skills.

stress and poverty, strict parental attention to children's activities was more effective in preventing delinquency than was a happy family atmosphere. Some of the supervision was simply good parenting—that is, setting sensible limits and reasonable expectations—whereas some appeared intrusive and restrictive, but it seemed to help prevent delinquency. Strict supervision, *not* extreme punitiveness, was what seemed of value.)

The parents are concerned about the child's education, assist willingly with homework, and participate in school-related activities.

The parents carefully define their own role in the family as well as the child's. (The mothers of underachieving youngsters use their children to meet their own needs and play the role of pseudo-sibling rather than parent. They practice a permissive or laissez-faire parenting style. The role relationships for competent children are more structured and orderly.)

The parents accord their child self-direction in everyday tasks and are aware of the child's interests and goals, but they adopt an authoritative style of parenting.

Coping children seem to have at least one adequate model among the significant adults who touch their lives. Achieving youngsters have a positive attitude toward adults and authority in general.

Garmezy does not want to give the impression that some children are impervious to all stressors. There *are* differences in vulnerability, and unless adults are careful, they may tax the resources of even the most invulnerable child (Honig 1986).

Empathy and Role-taking   Empathy is the ability to recognize and share the feelings of others. Related to empathy is the ability to take another person's role or perceptual perspective. The way children react to the emotions of others and their understanding of others' emotional states affect the development of their social behavior and interpersonal relations. The increasing capacity to empathize, to take on another person's role, and to cooperate is related to the child's age. Hughes et al. (1981) found that kindergarten children develop an understanding of others' emotions from situational cues and obvious causal events. Second graders, in contrast, place themselves cognitively in another person's place and transfer their own emotional reaction. For example, when asked, "What makes the girl feel sad?" the kindergarten children were more likely to report the most obvious situational event, such as "the dog ran away," whereas the second graders were more likely to say, "Her dog is lost and she *lost someone she loved*." Hughes et al. (1981) found no gender difference in empathic feelings.

Selman (1976) and his colleagues (Selman and Bryne 1974) have outlined a developmental sequence of role-taking ability. They define four levels in the child's acquisition of this skill, occurring at less than four years and through age twelve.

In *level 0, egocentric role-taking,* children under four years assume that others have thoughts and feelings similar to their own. They cannot distinguish between their own perspective and that of others.

In *level 1, subjective role-taking,* children of approximately four years realize that others think and feel differently because they are in a different situation, have different information, or interpret the same event differently. At this level, however, children have difficulty thinking about their own and others' perspectives simultaneously, and they have trouble putting themselves in the position of the other person when it comes to judging what the other person thinks.

In *level 2, self-reflective role-taking,* children of approximately six years realize that others may have their own particular values and interests. The children can put themselves in the other person's place, and they realize that the other person can do the same. They realize that their perspective is not necessarily the right or valid one.

In *level 3, mutual role-taking,* children of approximately ten years are not only able to distinguish their perspective from that of other people, but they can also think about their own point of view simultaneously with that of another person.

Role-taking stages seem to be related to maturation and social experience. A given child's ability to take roles may fluctuate from one occasion to another (Maccoby 1984).

Aggression   Aggression appears to be a stable behavior. For example, infant boys identified as having a "difficult" temperament were later reported to be aggressive as adolescents (Olweus 1980). In reporting a longitudinal study of six hundred subjects from ages eight to thirty, Huesmann et al. (1984) estimated the stability of aggression at about .50 for boys and .35 for girls. They also found that early aggressiveness is a good predictor of severe antisocial behavior—such as criminality, physical aggression, child abuse, spouse abuse, and delinquent driving—in the young adult.

Cross-cultural studies indicate that boys are more aggressive than girls (Omark et al. 1975; Williams et al. 1985; Hyde 1984). Cummings et al. (1986) note that levels of aggression are higher in boys than in girls and that boys may experience greater hostility. Because boys tend to interact more with other boys, they are involved in more aggressive interchanges (Tieger 1980). Boys are more aggressive not only physically but also verbally (Williams et al. 1985). Their aggression decreases, however, when they are involved in caregiving activities, such as taking care of a younger sibling (Maccoby and Jacklin 1980). Unfortunately, our society is more likely to reward girls for altruistic behavior than boys. Hostility combined with minimal reinforcement for altruism can lead to a negative self-image, which is related to a lessened concern for others.

Aggressive parents tend to have aggressive children. These parents tend to be inconsistent in their use of punishment and are likely to label neutral events as antisocial rather than prosocial. They provide models of aggressive behavior and also arouse hostility in their children. They create an environment that is not conducive to developing empathic concern for others (Patterson 1986). In a longitudinal study of aggressive and nonaggressive boys, it was found that 95 percent of the aggressive boys were reared in homes where one or both parents were rejecting and restrictive. The nonaggressive boys were from warm and affectionate familial settings (McCord, McCord, and Howard 1961).

Aggressive children see interactions with others, even in neutral situations, from a different perspective than do nonaggressive children. Aggressive children are likely to attribute hostility to a provocative act of a peer and are likely to respond with retaliatory aggression (Dodge 1980). These children also are more likely to be victims or targets of aggression from their peers. In a study of seven-year-old boys, Dodge (1986) found a significant correlation between the frequency with which boys initiated and were targets of aggression.

Moral Development

Piaget (1932) and Kohlberg (1969) describe moral development from the perspective of cognition, viewing it as a function of cognitive development. According to Piaget, morality consists of a system of rules handed down from adults to children. Through training, practice, and the development of con-

Heteronomous morality
According to Piaget, a stage of morality in which children ages six to nine regard rules as unchangeable, even when they are lax in following the rules themselves. An infraction of the rules is judged according to the amount of damage done, regardless of whether it is accidental or intentional.

Autonomous morality
According to Piaget, a stage of morality in which children between nine and twelve years take their peers' intentions into consideration in evaluating their actions.

sciousness, children learn to nurture respect for these standards of conduct. Piaget found that children's ethics and views of the world progress through a number of stages. His observations of play revealed differences in how younger and older children perceive the rules for simple games, such as marbles (Piaget 1932; Piaget and Inhelder 1969).

Piaget noted that children ages six to nine use **heteronomous morality,** or a "morality of constraint." They regard the rules of a game as unchangeable, even when they are lax in following the rules themselves. An infraction is judged according to the amount of damage done, regardless of whether it is accidental or intentional.

At nine to twelve years of age, children shift to **autonomous morality,** or a "morality of cooperation." Intentions are taken into consideration in evaluating actions. Children no longer see rules as fixed and unchangeable, and they feel they can change them if the group agrees. Piaget stressed that play and social interactions are responsible for the shift from heteronomous to autonomous morality. Through the disagreements and compromise common in play, children learn to be more democratic and become more mature in creating, changing, and following rules.

Building on Piaget's observations, Kohlberg outlined a series of stages based on cognitive reasoning. When moral dilemmas were presented to children in various cultures it was found that stages of moral development are universal. Six stages are encompassed within three major levels: *preconventional* (approximately zero to nine years), *conventional* (approximately nine to fifteen years), and *postconventional* (approximately sixteen years and older). The sequence does not vary (Kohlberg et al., 1984).

Preconventional (Stages 1 and 2)   Children at the preconventional level have little concept of socially acceptable moral behavior but begin to display signs of it. The emphasis is on avoiding punishment and getting a reward.

Stage 1 is the *punishment and obedience orientation*. Children conform to rules imposed on them by authority figures. They follow the rules in order to avoid punishment. Moral conduct is based largely on fear associated with the consequences of rule violation. The seriousness of the violation depends on the magnitude of the wrongdoing. For example, if a child broke ten cups accidentally, he was more at fault than if he broke one cup intentionally.

Stage 2 is the *instrumental relativist orientation*. The child maximizes mainly tangible rewards and minimizes punishment. He or she will do something for someone else with the intent of receiving something back. Children will do the right thing to satisfy not only others' needs but also their own (you scratch my back, and I will scratch yours).

Conventional (Stages 3 and 4)   At the conventional level, the child perceives the expectations of his or her family, group, or nation as valuable in their own right, regardless of immediate and obvious consequences. Conformity to the social order as well as loyalty to it is expected of the child. He or she will actively maintain, support, and justify that order as well as identify with the persons or group involved in it.

Stage 3 is *interpersonal concordance,* or the *"good boy–nice girl"* orientation. Children perceive good behavior as right if it meets the approval of significant and important others. Approval is more important than other specific rewards. An individual at this stage conforms to what the majority believes or to what is considered normal by society. Children (and sometimes adults) judge behavior by perceived intention, and one earns approval by being nice or good.

Stage 4 is the *"law-and-order" orientation*. Maintenance and emphasis of the social order are of utmost importance. Authority and fixed rules are valued. Doing one's duty, showing respect for authority, and maintaining the social order for its own sake are indicators of the "right behavior."

Postconventional (Stages 5 and 6) A clear effort to reach a personal definition of moral values occurs at this level. The goal is to define principles that have validity and application apart from the individual's own identity.

Stage 5 is the *social contract orientation*. The individual perceives that the concept of individual rights, values, and standards has been critically evaluated and agreed upon by society. There is a clear awareness of the importance of personal values and opinions and an emphasis on procedural rules for reaching consensus. With the exception of rights that have been constitutionally and democratically agreed upon, rights are a matter of personal values and opinion. The emphasis, therefore, is on the legal point of view and on the possibility of making rational and socially desirable changes in the law, rather than on its immutability (as in the law-and-order orientation).

Stage 6 is the *universal ethical-principle orientation*. The conscience defines what is right according to self-chosen principles. These are abstract and ethical, not concrete moral rules like the Ten Commandments. At the heart of this stage is the equality of human rights and the dignity of human beings as individuals (Kohlberg 1969).

Kohlberg's framework describes only the form of thinking, not its content. The moral opinions of children are relatively independent of their moral development. The form of ethics develops, but the content does not. Several individuals may display the same behavior, but their reasons for doing so may differ. For example, three adults may drive at the legal speed limit of fifty-five miles per hour. One may do so to avoid getting a speeding ticket (stage 1); one may do so because the *law* says so (stage 4); and one may do so because research has shown that going this speed has saved lives (stages 5 and 6).

Not all researchers agree with Kohlberg. Youniss (1980) argues that children construct a moral code socially through discussion with others rather than in keeping with cognitive capabilities.

Carol Gilligan (1982) disputes Kohlberg's findings because much of his theory was based on research with only men. In her study of women considering an abortion, Gilligan found that females base their moral decisions on different types of reasoning than males do. Men subscribe to a morality of rights and organize social relationships in a hierarchy. They are more interested in legal issues and rules. Women think in more mature ways about ethical problems of special concern to women, such as abortion issues. They are more interested in relationships and social responsibilities and weigh these in their moral reasoning. Gilligan notes that women develop through a sequence of three levels and two transitions, each level representing a more complex understanding of the relationship between self and others and each transition involving a critical reinterpretation of a moral conflict between responsibility and selfishness. Women's moral judgment appears to proceed from an initial concern with survival to a view that principled nonviolence is the most appropriate guide to resolving moral conflicts. Gilligan argues that an expanded developmental theory is needed to provide an "understanding in both sexes of the characteristics and precursors of an adult moral conception" (Gilligan 1979, 87). She does not claim that one theory is better than the other; both are equally valid.

Gilligan's Stages of Moral Development

Level 1: The Orientation toward Self-Interest

At the simplest level of moral reasoning, women are solely preoccupied with the self and survival. Constrained by a lack of power, females perceive morality as a matter of obeying restrictions imposed upon helpless subjects by society. At this level a woman would consider what is best for her without much consideration for anyone else.

The First Transition: From Selfishness to Responsibility

During the transitional period, the individual becomes aware of the terms *selfishness* and *responsibility*. She is conscious of the difference between what she wants (selfishness) and what she ought to do (responsibility). The implication is that she has more moral maturity and a more differentiated self-concept than in level 1. The growth from self-centeredness to an emerging concern for others is the first major step toward a more mature level of moral reasoning.

Level 2: Goodness as Self-Sacrifice

The transition from selfishness to responsibility is a move toward social participation. Consensus is paramount. Self-interest recedes to the background as the need to please others surfaces. Thus the woman moves from selfishness to self-sacrifice and an overriding sense of responsibility for others. At this level the woman's underlying assumption is that she is responsible for the actions of others, while holding others responsible for the choices she makes. This confusion is comparable to Kohlberg's stage 3, which combines the need for approval with the wish to care for and help others.

The Second Transition: From Goodness to Truth

The second transition is marked by a reconsideration of the relationship between self and others and a questioning of one's values. The woman begins to ask whether concern for the self is really selfish, whether considering one's own values and needs along with those of others might be responsible judgment. She questions whether it is possible to be responsible for herself as well as others, but her sense of self-worth is still too uncertain to claim full equality with others.

Level 3: The Morality of Nonviolence

The individual develops a universal perspective at this level. She is able to assert a moral equality between self and others. She asserts her independent rights and gives equal consideration to her responsibilities to others. She no longer sees herself as powerless and becomes actively involved in her own decision-making process. She now considers what action would minimize hurt for others as well as for herself. The moral basis of this level is the commitment to nonviolence and the duty to minimize pain for all concerned.

Walker (1984), who disagrees with Gilligan's assessment of Kohlberg's theory, found that moral reasoning for males and females is more similar than different.

Kohlberg's theory does not fully distinguish between the concepts of morality and social convention. The latter refers to the customs and agreements within society that are deemed acceptable, such as table manners and forms of greeting. Morality refers to the more weighty matters of justice, right, and wrong. Whereas social conventions usually are widely supported, the definition of what is moral may not have broad agreement. Kohlberg glosses over these differences, defining some stages in terms of social convention and others in terms of morality (Nucci 1982, 1985; Davidson et al. 1983; Turiel 1978). Nucci (1981) found that by distinguishing between social convention and morality, a less stagelike picture appeared. Children between the ages of six and seventeen were asked such questions as, "Is it wrong to steal?" (morality-related) and "Is it wrong for a group to change the rules of a game?" (convention-related). At *every* age the children felt stealing was wrong but that changing the rules of a game was acceptable. Therefore, if morality had developed at all, it had done so before the school years began. By age six the children already had learned to distinguish between moral and conventional behavior.

Prosocial moral reasoning involves conflicts in which an individual must choose between satisfying personal wants and those of others (Eisenberg-Berg and Neal 1981; Eisenberg and Miller 1987). Among children this skill increases with age, at least during the elementary school years, and this may be related to the role of hedonistic reasoning in the prosocial moral judgment of children. The major change in a child's moral development during the elementary years is the shift from self-orientation to other-orientation (Eisenberg et al. 1983; Eisenberg 1987).

Hogan's framework (1975) addresses the difference between moral reasoning and action, between theory and practice. Moral behavior depends not only on cognitive functioning but also on affect, or feeling. Hogan sees moral development as governed by five independent dimensions that gradually emerge as the individual progresses through cognitive stages. As individuals grow from infancy to adulthood, their social world expands and presents them with new situations to be mastered. To build a sense of trust, infants need to be nurtured and protected. Once mobile, they must learn to obey caregivers for their own protection and survival. At this point Hogan's first dimension emerges; the individual becomes aware of rules. That knowledge enables self-control to develop. The child must learn to take others' viewpoints into consideration in order to function socially.

The second dimension of moral development, according to Hogan, is *role-taking ability,* or empathy. At this stage the child learns to comply with group expectations and to interact more flexibly with others. Role-taking skills enable individuals to consider the implications of their actions on others.

The third dimension is the *awareness of the changeability of rules.* While the younger child believes that rules are unbreakable, the older child realizes that rules are made by people and can be changed. The older child attaches importance to some or most of the rules within society and chooses which will be obeyed and under what circumstances.

The fourth dimension Hogan delineates is the *freedom to deviate from the standards established by others.* The adolescent or young adult is in the process of establishing an identity and a personal life-style. He or she is often caught between family expectations and the demands of peers and the larger culture.

In the fifth dimension, individuals fall along a continuum between complete acceptance of moral behavior as defined by society and making *moral decisions based on intuition and a personal ethical code.* Expressed another way, at one end of the continuum is the ethic of social responsibility, and at the other is personal conscience.

The theories of Kohlberg, Gilligan, and Hogan are useful in highlighting developmental changes in moral judgment. Each takes a different perspective, focusing on stages of cognitive development, gender, and affect, respectively, but each offers insight. The process of moral development both affects and is affected by social development.

Social Development

Peers

Peer groups are a major socializer of the elementary school child, rivaled in importance only by the family. Through preadolescence the child will spend progressively more time with peers rather than adults, a trend that began during the preschool years. Peer groups are highly selective and accept newcomers primarily on the basis of similarities in age, gender, race, and social status; gender appears to be the most important criterion. Children at this age wear similar modes of dress, use the same language, wear the same hairstyles, pursue similar activities, and adopt the same mannerisms. Each peer group represents a separate and unique sociological phenomenon.

Girls appear to display higher degrees of conformity to peer groups than do boys. Status in the group and such personality factors as dependency affect the degree of conformity (Hartup 1970; Shaffer 1979). Conformity peaks between the ages of twelve and fourteen, then decreases gradually in adolescence.

Boys are more likely to play in groups than are girls, who are more likely to pair off. Since closeness and the sharing of personal concerns are more apt to occur in a one-to-one relationship, girls' friendships tend to be more intimate than boys'. Girls are likely to reveal more of themselves to their friends (Rubin 1980; Dweck 1981). Girls are more exclusive than boys and are less likely to expand their two-person friendships to include a third person. Girls are more acutely aware of the fragility of intimate relationships and of the ways in which one friendship may sometimes threaten another. Boys are usually less sensitive to dilemmas involving intimacy. Because girls tend to have more intimate relationships, jealousy occurs more often among them than among boys (Rubin 1980). Girls, however, perform more prosocial acts, such as sharing and helping, than boys do. In a study of fourth through sixth graders, children had opportunities in five situations to help, share, or cooperate with others. Girls behaved more prosocially than boys in four of these situations, and in the fifth situation there was no gender difference (Payne 1980).

Peer relationships can provide a staging area for interaction, a cultural institution for transmitting knowledge and performance techniques, and a trial

Unpopular children are more likely to be low achievers in school, to have lower self-esteem, to experience learning difficulties, and to drop out of school.

CHAPTER 10   *The Wonder Years: Middle Childhood's Psychosocial Development*

context for the shaping of the self. These aspects of peer relationships have implications for interaction within and outside the friendship bond.

Peer groups as staging areas for interaction allow the performance of actions that otherwise would be improper. For example, close friendships can provide a context for testing pranks. Some scholars believe this socializes children by allowing them to explore the boundaries of allowable behavior and enabling them to gain poise in stressful situations. The actions of a friend are less likely to be defined as inappropriate than are the same behaviors from others. Male friendship groups also provide support in initiating boy-girl contacts (Fine 1981).

Friendships also facilitate the transmission of cultural information. They provide the child with a stock of knowledge and a repertoire of behavior useful for encounters with other peers.

Friendship also helps socialize the preadolescent through its positive effect on self-image, and it provides a context for learning the appropriate self-image to project in social situations (Fine 1981).

Friendship is a crucial factor in the social development of popular as well as unpopular children. Many variables influence a child's popularity or interpersonal success, including acceptance of the ideology of the school he or she attends, the attractiveness of his or her first name (social risk seems to accompany uncommon names), role-playing skills, intelligence, adjustment to parents and teachers, physical appeal, and positive attitude toward learning and school. Children also appear to use race and gender as criteria for selecting friends, since there is a tendency for them to establish same-race and same-sex friendships. Acceptance or rejection by peers is a multidimensional phenomenon (Fine 1981; Putallaz and Gottman 1981b).

Children who do not form friendships are not a homogeneous group and can be divided into two subsets: neglected and rejected. Neglected children are perceived by their peers neither positively nor negatively. They are quiet and nontalkative. Rejected children are perceived negatively and behave aversively toward their peers (Parker and Asher 1987; Asher and Renshaw 1981).

Measures of peer acceptance are good indices of psychological risk. Unpopular children are more likely to be low achievers in school, to have lower self-esteem, to experience learning difficulties, and to drop out of school (Dishion et al. 1984; Patterson 1982; Forehand et al. 1986). Studies indicate that rejected unpopular children act in a way that maximizes the probability that they will be ignored, whereas the behavior of popular children maximizes the probability that they will be accepted. Rejected unpopular children also tend to disagree more than popular children do. They attempt to call attention to themselves by stating their feelings and opinions, making self-statements, and asking informational questions not relevant to the group's activity, all of which results in their being ignored (Putallaz and Gottman 1981b; Horowitz 1962). They are likely to be less physically attractive than popular children and are likely to be firstborn or only children (Shaffer 1979). Unpopular children lack knowledge of their peers' norms and values and do not know how to make friends. They display aggressive and disruptive behavior (Coie and Dodge 1988; Dodge 1983; Putallaz and Gottman 1981a).

Children's interaction with their peers is related to their relationship with their parents. Putallaz (1987) found that mothers who behave aversively toward their children (for example, exhibit controlling and negative behavior) are likely to have children who display aversive and disagreeable behavior with unfamiliar

Group play is important to social development because it provides the opportunity to share common interests and to assume different roles.

peers. This type of mother correlates with her child's sociometric status at school, that is, how the child is viewed by classmates. In another study (MacDonald and Parke 1984), children's abrasiveness with peers was correlated with parental directiveness, especially from the father. Forehand et al. (1986) found that parent-child conflict was related to poor grades.

Dishion (1990) found that rejected boys had poor self-monitoring and self-discipline skills. They also showed more family stress, were from a lower socioeconomic level, and displayed more academic and behavioral problems than their average peers did.

Rejected or unpopular children frequently face a negative future. Antisocial behavior in children often translates to social failure in adulthood. Negative repercussions include a downward social drift, academic underachievement, and difficulty in marriage and family relationships (Caspi, Elder, and Bem 1987). Other maladjustments that may appear in adulthood are bad-conduct discharges from the military, emotional and mental health problems, adult schizophrenia, and psychosis (Putallaz and Gottman 1981a).

Play

Group play is important to social development because it provides the opportunity to share common interests and assume different roles. The group creates security in bonds of loyalty, which encourages friendship and cooperation. Games of approach and avoidance, such as hide-and-seek, incorporate withdrawal and escape and test the emotion of fear. Games of attack, such as dodgeball, test anger and destruction. Games of observation, such as "twenty questions," test expectancy, sensory functions, and exploration. Games of impulse control, such as "kick the can," exercise surprise, stopping, and orientation (Sutton-Smith 1975).

Preadolescent children generally prefer to form their own formal, organized, play groups. These groups structure their activities under the authority of a leader, who is usually physically stronger and older, extroverted, and above average in intelligence (Strayer and Strayer 1975).

Organized games such as marbles, hide-and-seek, and tag bring children into social contact while teaching them that rules and various codes of conduct are expected to be upheld. Children learn to follow rules in four stages, related to their stages of cognitive development. During *toddlerhood,* there is no concept of rules, and children react in any fashion they desire. In the *individual stage,* before five years of age, a child's conception of rules is largely personal. Although some imitation of codified rules is present, most often a game will be played without any attempt to win. In the *incipient cooperation stage,* at around seven or eight years, the child attempts to unify and obey the rules of the game. Winning becomes important. The child realizes that in order to win, he or she must follow the rules. During the fourth stage, *rule codification,* children accept a system of conduct. Cheaters are ostracized, and those who do well are recognized (Piaget 1932). According to Fine, as children "argue about rules, add new ones, agree to exceptions, and censure a playmate who is cheating, they are exploring how necessary rules are, how they are made, and what degree of consensus is needed to make them effective. They are also learning something about the relationship of personality to power, and of fairness to order" (Fine 1981, 17). Rules are topics for negotiation. It is the process of negotiation that is central to interaction, rather than the rules themselves (Fine 1981).

School

School can influence a child's popularity level. When a child moves from school to school, his or her popularity does not seem to be affected. However, if a sizable number of children move in and out of a given school, then the popularity of those students is negatively affected. For example, schools near military bases and headquarters for large major corporations, such as I.B.M., have a large turnover of children.

School size appears to affect peer acceptance, as students who attend smaller schools have more opportunity to participate in school activities and social interaction. Class size also determines the number of opportunities for social interaction. Encouragement from teachers or peers to engage in friendship-making behavior also seems to influence popularity (Putallaz and Gottman 1981b).

Because nutrition, or the lack of it, has been linked to poor performance in school, researchers (Meyers et al. 1989) from Boston studied the effect of the U.S. School Breakfast Program (SBP) on achievement. They found that the group of third through sixth graders on the breakfast program had better scores in math, reading, and language skills than the control group.

In a review of the literature concerning the effect of schools on the progress of students, Rutter (1983) found three ways in which teachers have an important influence. The first is *classroom management.* A high proportion of lesson time is spent on the subject matter (as opposed to setting up equipment, handing out papers, dealing with disciplinary problems, and so forth). A high proportion of the teacher's time is spent interacting with the class as a whole, rather than with individuals. Disciplinary interventions are at a minimum. Lessons begin and end on schedule. Feedback to pupils is clear and unambiguous on performance and what is expected of them, and praise for good performance is consistent and generous.

The second way that teachers affect achievement is through *role-modeling.* To some extent the children imitate their teacher's behavior. If he or she frequently is late, attendance is poor. If he or she is careless about school property, the rate of vandalism is likely to be high. Pupil outcomes are better in schools that are kept in good order and condition, with graffiti quickly removed and

Elementary children on a breakfast program had better scores in math, reading, and language skills than children in the control group.

broken furniture rapidly repaired. (Several studies have shown that people's morale and behavior generally tend to improve when the environment is upgraded and that neglected buildings are particularly prone to vandalism.) Pupil behavior is worse in schools where teachers respond to provocation and disruption by hitting students or pushing them around (thus providing an adverse model of behavior).

The third important influence is teachers' *attitudes and expectations*. Individual teachers and the composition of a particular class can be important determinants in the progress of students. In a study that assessed the effect of teacher support on children's valuing of math, Midgley et al. (1989) found that when students moved from elementary teachers who were low in their perceived support to junior high teachers who were supportive, the intrinsic value of math was enhanced. In the reverse case, there was a sharp decline in the intrinsic value students attributed to math as well in its perceived usefulness and importance. Furthermore, the decline was greater for low-achieving students than for high-achieving students. Thus, teachers who expect their students to do well tend to motivate their students, who in fact do well (Shaffer 1979).

Seaver (1973) found that children with older siblings who were good students tended to do better in the first grade if they were taught by the same teacher who had taught the sibling. They performed better academically than the control group with bright older siblings but a different first-grade teacher. Children with older siblings who had done poorly also tended to do poorly if taught by the same first-grade teacher of their sibling. They did less poorly if they had a different teacher. In the classic study by Rosenthal and Jacobson (1968), teachers of the first through sixth grades were told that certain of their pupils were likely to show sudden rapid growth in intellectual ability. In actuality, the "bloomers" were simply chosen at random. By the end of the school year, in the first and second grades in particular, these children showed significantly larger gains in IQ scores than did other children in the class. The researchers attributed the gains to the fact that the teachers expected these children

Teachers who expect their students to do well tend to motivate their students, who, in fact, do well.

to perform, and this expectation led the teachers to treat the "bloomers" in subtly positive ways.

Pedersen et al. (1978) found a positive correlation between one first-grade teacher in a disadvantaged urban neighborhood, Miss A, and the adult success of children she taught. Their findings suggest that an effective first-grade teacher can influence social status and that a good teacher can shape both the academic self-concept and achievement of pupils so that an initial foundation yields benefits in later life. A former student stated "it did not matter what background or abilities the beginning pupil had; there was no way that the pupil was not going to read by the end of grade one." One reported that Miss A left her pupils with a "profound impression of the importance of schooling, and how one should stick to it," and "she gave extra hours to the children who were slow learners." "When children forgot their lunches," another said, "she would give them some of her own, and she invariably stayed after hours to help children." Not only did her pupils remember her, but apparently she could remember each former pupil by name even after an interval of twenty years. She adjusted to new math and reading methods, but her secret for success was summarized by a former colleague this way: "How did she teach? With a lot of love!" One would add, "with a lot of confidence in children and hard work."

Rutter (1983) found in his literature review that some factors previously considered important to academic achievement were no longer regarded as such. These included the following:

1. the amount of money per pupil allocated to a school
2. the number of books in the school library
3. the size and luxuriousness of the school building and classrooms
4. the proportion of teachers with advanced degrees
5. gender segregation (In England, where some schools are coed and some are not, no differences were found.)
6. class size (In the first few years of school, when beginning reading and math are taught, small class size does provide a real advantage.)

Family

Ideally, the family protects the child from the rest of the world and also provides opportunities for the child to learn to cope with the rest of the world. Parents and older siblings interpret the expectations of society for the child and may insist that he or she behave in socially acceptable ways at least in public. The child may learn that family members put on their best behavior among strangers but express themselves more freely when at home.

Children realize that different rules govern interaction with their parents and their peers. Parents and children recognize that parents have the right and obligation to direct children's behavior and that children have the obligation to obey. Relations change as the inequality decreases.

In their study on social support among elementary school children, Reid et al. (1989) found that youngsters perceive their mother as the best multipurpose provider of social support available, better than friends and teachers. Friends are perceived as the best source of companionship support and as second only to parents in providing emotional support. Friends are also perceived as less able than parents to provide direct help or information. Teachers are viewed as providers of informational but are not considered good sources of emotional support or companionship. Fathers receive high ratings for informational support and are second only to mothers as providers of emotional support. Fathers are rated as less satisfactory than mothers in their availability for and provision of direct help or instrumental support, such as in doing schoolwork, lessons, or chores; locating things; or trying new or difficult activities, like building a fort or making a model.

Furman and Buhrmester (1985) found that preadolescents rated friends as the most satisfactory source of companionship but parents as the best source of instrumental help. Fathers were rated higher than mothers, contrary to the findings of Reid et al. (1989) among the younger age-group.

According to Hunter and Youniss (1982) intimacy or emotional support from parents is relatively consistent across ages, while intimacy with friends increases with age.

Parental disciplinary methods affect a child's behavior, which in turn affects the method of discipline. One method, **inductive discipline,** consists of explaining reasons and justifications for the child to behave in a particular way. Through **love withdrawal** techniques, the parent gives direct but nonphysical expression of anger or disapproval at the child's undesirable behavior. For example, the parent may ignore the child, refuse to speak or listen, state a dislike for the behavior or the child, and/or isolate or threaten to leave him or her. **Power-assertive discipline** consists of enforcing standards of behavior with threats and punishment (Hoffman 1977).

Most parents use a combination of methods. Many begin by explaining why they do not want the child to do something; if the child persists, they punish him or her. Children probably realize that the threat of punishment is present even when parents reason with them (Kuczynski 1983). Love withdrawal does not foster internalization of parental values and standards. It does contribute to the inhibition of anger, and it is related to the expression of hostility toward peers and to aggression in adolescent boys (Hoffman 1977). When parents rely more on inductive techniques, children tend to be more advanced in moral development, to internalize their parents' moral standards, and to feel guilty if they deviate from them. Children of parents who use more power-assertive techniques seem to be motivated by a desire to avoid punish-

Inductive discipline
A method of discipline that consists of explaining reasons and justifications for the child to behave in a particular way.

Love withdrawal
A method of discipline in which the parent gives direct but nonphysical expression of anger or disapproval at the child's undesirable behavior.

Power-assertive discipline
A method of discipline that consists of enforcing standards of behavior with threats and punishment.

Parents and children recognize that parents have the right and obligation to direct children's behavior and that children have the obligation to obey. Relations change as the inequality decreases.

ment. They have a tendency to break the rules if they think they can get away with it. In relation to Kohlberg's theory, their behavior and reasoning are at a lower level of moral development than those of children disciplined inductively (Hoffman 1975, 1977; Brody and Shaffer 1982; Olejnik 1980).

Since elementary school children are more able than preschoolers to imagine and sympathize with the feelings of others, they find it easier to consider future consequences of current actions. Because of this more advanced reasoning ability, inductive discipline is likely to be successful with elementary school children but not with preschoolers (Brody and Shaffer 1982; Johnson and McGillicuddy-Delisi 1983).

Stepfamilies

Thirty-five million U.S. adults are stepparents, and one in six children under age eighteen (approximately 9.6 million) is a stepchild. Among divorced adults, 80 percent will remarry, and 60 percent of the remarriages will involve at least one child from a previous marriage (Pink and Wampler 1985; Lagoni and Cook 1985; Coleman, Ganong, and Gingrich 1985).

Remarriage and the creation of stepfamilies has been part of the American family system since the beginning of our history. Until this century, however, most remarriages followed widowhood or widowerhood. The issues and problems characteristic of a second family add to the complexity of the adjustment process in remarriage. The most prevalent problem revolves around the relationship between the stepparent and stepchild. Stepparents must battle myths and fairy-tale stereotypes as well as search for appropriate models on which to base their role. In our society the role of stepparent is poorly defined, has no definitive legal status, and contains contradictory elements of both parental and nonparental roles. Most stepparents learn through trial and error. There also are no role prescriptions to guide interaction between the nonresident biological parent and the stepparent. It has been found, however, that remarried persons who maintain moderate frequency of contact with a former spouse exhibit better marital quality than those who maintain either high or low frequency of contact (Pasley and Ihinger-Tallman 1985; Lagoni and Cook 1985; Pink and Wampler 1985; Clingempeel and Brand 1985; Mills 1984).

Coleman, Ganong, and Gingrich (1985) found that stepchildren have no more problems than other children, although they are still viewed as having more problems than children from an intact nuclear family. Elementary school youngsters adjust to stepfamilies better than adolescents do but have more difficulty than preschoolers do.

Children entering a new family formed by the remarriage of a divorced parent face many significant issues.

1. *Dealing with the loss of a parent.* Children may experience unresolved grief over the loss of the first family as well as guilt feelings. They often feel responsible for the divorce. Parents must be frank about their own responsibility for the breakup and reassure their children that they are not responsible. A quick remarriage may not give a child enough time to mourn the departed parent (this is also true in separations due to death). The child needs time to recognize and deal with the loss and needs support from adults in coping with feelings.

2. *Coping with divided loyalties.* Loyalty conflicts are especially prevalent when the stepparent has children from a previous marriage. If it is perceived that the personal resources of the stepparent (not only money but also time and affection) are meted out disproportionately to stepchildren and biological children, the quality of the marriage may be adversely affected. A child also feels loyal to his or her noncustodial parent. Parents, stepparents, grandparents, and other relatives can help by not forcing the child to take sides and by recognizing the child's desire to maintain relations with the noncustodial parent.

3. *Shifting positions and roles.* When stepsiblings are involved, the child's ordinal position may shift. The formerly oldest child may become the middle one, or an only child may become the oldest and have to share the responsibility of caring for younger children. New extended families may emerge, with new sets of grandparents, aunts, and uncles. Building new relationships takes time, especially when there are no guidelines about what is expected in these new roles.

4. *Living in new homes.* In many cases children divide their time between two remarried parents, which usually means two physical settings and two sets of interacting members, especially when stepsiblings are involved. If the child does not also have to cope with change in schools and peers, he or she can have more stable, ongoing experiences.

5. *Meeting new expectations.* The child as well as the parent and/or stepparent may expect too much. Not all remarried families are like the Brady Bunch. It takes time to develop a relationship between the child and the stepparent, and it will not be the same as the relationship between the child and the absent parent.

6. *Hoping for the reunion of the natural parents.* Children often fantasize that their natural parents will remarry. It is beneficial for all concerned if the divorced parents can separate their parental roles from their spousal roles. They still must cooperate in caring for their children, but at the same time they should make it clear that they have stopped being husband and wife. When the custodial parent supports the stepparent's decisions and actions, the child is more able to recognize the permanence of

the new marriage (Carter and McGoldrick 1980; Pink and Wampler 1985; Clingempeel and Brand 1985; Pasley and Ihinger-Tallman 1985).

In general, children are better off in stepfamilies than in single-parent families, as measured by school behavior, achievement, social development, and personality. Stepchildren can learn problem solving, negotiation, and coping skills as well as flexibility and adaptability. The presence of another adult in the family offers support, exposure to a wider variety of people, and a potentially good model of marital interaction. The literature indicates that stepchildren derive strengths from their families, just as do children from first-marriage families (Pink and Wampler 1985; Coleman, Ganong, and Gingrich 1985).

Gender-role Development

By the time children enter school, boys realize they are male and are destined to remain so, and it is equally clear to girls that they are female and will remain so. They have absorbed many of society's stereotypes; they believe that males are strong, aggressive, and independent and that females are emotional, gentle, and somewhat foolish (Williams, Bennett, and Best 1975).

Elementary children identify readily with gender-typed play activities and state preferences for these as well. Boys are typically involved in physical types of play, while girls are less physical. Toys for boys usually require more physical types of expression, while girls' toys do not (Fagot 1974; Rheingold and Cook 1975). Boys are more aware of gender differences than girls are, and they avoid playing with objects that might be labeled "sissy" or feminine. Boys seem to hold more rigidly stereotyped beliefs than do girls. Parents encourage children to engage in gender-typed forms of play (Flerx, Fidler, and Rogers 1976; Fling and Manosevitz 1972).

Generally, elementary school children segregate themselves into all-girl and all-boy groups. This phenomenon is called **sex cleavage**. Gender stereotypes are rather well established by the second grade, after which there is no increase in their intensity. In fact, eleven-year-old girls' sex-role attitudes have been shown to be less stereotyped than those of seven-year-old girls (Meyer 1980). If girls find boys' play exciting and attractive, the boys usually reject their overtures. If girls try to enter boys' groups, they are usually unsuccessful (Pitcher and Schultz 1984).

Sex cleavage
The phenomenon of elementary school children segregating themselves into all-girl and all-boy groups.

Girls' play and boys' play are different in character. Boys form large groups and play more physical games in larger spaces. Their games are competitive and contain explicit rules. In these activities boys demand attention and give orders, learn how to form long-range goals, engage in rough-and-tumble play, and experience a feeling of group solidarity. Their peer relations are *extensive*. Girls form smaller groups and play in smaller spaces. They refine social rules and roles. From their groups they learn about personal relationships, subtle social cues, and unspoken rules of social contact. They practice responding to others' needs. Because they play with only one or two other girls, their interactions become intimate and *intensive* (Pitcher and Schultz 1984; Hartup 1983; Hallinan 1981).

Between eight and eleven years of age, children perceive gender roles in much the same way adults do. When tested on what they would like to do when they grow up, most children reject items traditionally related to the opposite sex. Children with working mothers are less likely to engage in gender-typed activities than are children whose mothers are not employed outside the home (Etaugh 1974; Flerx, Fidler, and Rogers 1976). Children from lower-class families hold more sex-typed attitudes than do middle-class children (Nadelman 1974).

Parents allow boys more freedom to explore and encourage them to do more on their own (Huston et al. 1986). Girls are encouraged to stay closer to home, to be more docile and dependent, and to be more involved in domestic activities (Block 1979).

Intelligence is a factor in gender-role development. Brighter children exhibit less gender-typed role attitudes than do children with average intelligence. Thus, gender-role identity, like morality and some other facets of growth, appears to follow cognitive-developmental principles (Maccoby 1980; Kohlberg and Zigler 1967).

Parents and teachers reinforce same-sex groupings and activities. Teachers, for example, complement girls but not boys or a mixed group when they play with dolls (Fagot 1982). The parent who is the same sex as the child tends to encourage more gender-typing than does the parent of the opposite sex (Fling and Manosevitz 1972). In a study of third graders, the behavior of child-parent pairs was observed in a playroom furnished with an assortment of toys. No difference was noted between boys and girls in the tendency to engage in active, physical play. The mothers did not differ in their behavior according to whether the child was male or female. The fathers did differ. When a boy engaged in active, physical play, his father tended to be supportive and to talk to him a great deal. When a girl played that way, her father tended to withdraw from her. Boys were under more pressure to be "masculine" than girls were to be "feminine." The fathers were much more stereotyped in their gender-role attitudes than were the mothers. In general, the fathers were more concerned that sons be tough and active and daughters be sweet and ladylike. Thus the fathers acted differently with sons than with daughters (Tauber 1979). Such behaviors and experiences help create conscious gender stereotypes in the minds of children.

S U M M A R Y

- Erikson's psychosocial stage for elementary-age children is industry versus inferiority. The personality develops through a sense of accomplishment and is sought by intermingling play with work.
- The social learning theory points out that a variety of socializing forces and sociocultural factors influence the personality development of the child.
- Parents and peers are largely responsible for the self-concept of elementary-age children. Children with a positive self-concept differ in many ways from children with a poor self-concept.
- Social competency effects personality growth as a whole. Three general patterns of social incompetence have been identified: social anesthesia, social isolation, and social enslavement.
- Emotional maturity is related to a change from helplessness to independence and self-sufficiency. Fears change during this time.
- Invulnerable children find ways to cope with severe financial, emotional, and social stress. Vulnerable children exhibit recurrent destructive, antisocial behavior. Various factors contribute to why a child may become either invulnerable or vulnerable.
- Empathy and role-taking increase with age. Selman and his colleagues have outlined a developmental sequence of role-taking ability. They identify four levels of role-taking that occur between four and twelve years of age, including

Competitive Sports for Children

If a child wishes to participate in organized sports, good instruction and practice are important. A good instructor instills confidence and encourages the child to use the body as well as the mind. Practice helps develop skills and corrects faults. Good instruction and supervision help the child understand the value of team play and sportsmanship (Hartley and Goldenson 1963).

The concern about physical injuries among children who participate in competitive sports has received mixed reviews. Some studies point out that child baseball players ages eight and up develop enlarged bones in their pitching arms (Bailey et al. 1986); child gymnasts have chronic stiffness in their backs and some have recurrent back pain (Cratty 1979); and almost all children who play football, flag or tackle, are injured at least once (DiStefano 1982). Other studies are more optimistic and point out that children who participate in regular athletics are in better shape physically because their hearts and large muscles function more efficiently. They also develop coordination and strength earlier (Bailey 1982).

Most naturalistic studies indicate that children who participate in organized competitive sports programs are more competent socially than those who do not. This does not necessarily mean that the participation causes the difference, but it may partly account for why some children try out for teams and others do not.

Burchard (1979) compiled some positive and negative factors related to competitive sports for preadolescent children:

Positive Factors

1. Sports can be powerful in teaching habits, attitudes, and characteristics of good citizenship.
2. Boys who participate in athletics are better adjusted socially and emotionally than boys who do not.
3. Boys who participate in competitive sports are more socially accepted and have broader interests.
4. Competitive athletics provide a socially desirable environment for the teenage child.
5. Athletics provide a setting for a good social experience.
6. Athletic competition brings about improved sportsmanship and a worthy use of leisure time, and it is an integrative factor in the community.
7. Organized citywide competitive sports in the upper elementary school grades go far in reducing delinquency and enhancing physical and emotional fitness.

Negative Factors

1. Athletic competition among children produces strong emotional reactions in adults: parents, teachers, leaders, coaches, and even spectators. These reactions (undue emphasis on winning the game, undue adulation of the skilled athlete, coercing the child to perform beyond his or her ability or interests) may all be reflected in children.
2. Competitive athletics tend to develop tensions to an undesirable level in the preteen group.
3. Stresses and strains put on children before they are ready to cope with them can lead to extreme cases of emotionalism.
4. Extreme undesirable behavior can result from the competitive environment, as during one Little League play-off series in which the Little Leaguers cried like babies, wrecked the hotel lobby, had no appetite, had upset stomachs, and could not sleep.
5. Too often the only object of the game is to win. This puts too much pressure on the young athlete.
6. Elementary school children should be developing skills and interests in a great variety of activities. Their participation should be broad rather than specialized.

Whether or not competitive youth sports programs promote social competence is probably a function of the behavior of parents, coaches, and other adults who organize such programs. A win-at-all-cost approach (adults yell at players, coaches, and officials after a defeat or threat of a defeat) is apt to produce incompetence. The literature indicates that when adults set up very competitive games and then allow children to fend for themselves, the result is increased hostility rather than friendship among the children. This does not imply that competitive sports programs cannot be made to promote social competence. In many ways sports provide excellent opportunities for children to learn constructive social skills. Some children in youth sports programs do learn to relate more effectively with others under varying degrees of frustration and emotion. If this is the case, and if we could develop these

Continued

Competitive Sports for Children (continued)

aspects of the youth sports programs, it would be beneficial if this experience were available to all children. *It is becoming clear that the character that competitive sports build depends on the character of those who bring their children to the programs and the character of those who teach these children* (Burchard 1979).

Another dimension of competition among children is the interest in video games. Ascione and Chambers (1985) divided their sample into two groups: one playing an aggressive video boxing match; and the other, a prosocial video adventure in which the players were to rescue a fantasy creature from danger. After the games the children were each given a dollar in change and told they could donate some or all of the money to a fund for local needy children. Those who played the rescue game donated, on the average, forty-one cents each, while the children who played the boxing game donated, on the average, twenty-eight cents each. The researchers interpreted the results to mean that the overtly aggressive and competitive nature of the boxing game encouraged a self-centered attitude in children so they were less inclined to help others when they had the opportunity. It should also be noted that playing the role of rescuer apparently encouraged greater sensitivity.

The character that competitive sports build depends on the character of those who bring their children to the programs and the character of those who teach these children.

egocentric role-taking, subjective role-taking, self-reflective role-taking, and mutual role-taking.

- Piaget's and Kohlberg's theories of moral development are related to stages of cognitive development. Gilligan disagrees with Kohlberg's findings because she feels he failed to look at possible gender differences in children's responses to moral dilemmas. Hogan's theory of moral development is similar to Kohlberg's

- and Piaget's and is governed by five independent dimensions that gradually emerge as the individual progresses through cognitive stages.
- Friendships are central to the preadolescent's social world. Friendships take on many social facets and responsibilities. Acceptance or rejection by peers is a multidimensional phenomenon. Popular and unpopular children differ in many ways. Unpopular children frequently face future negative consequences.
- Preadolescents prefer to form their own formal, organized play groups. Rules and various codes of conduct are expected to be upheld. According to Piaget, children learn to follow rules in four stages.
- Teachers can make an impact on children through classroom management, role-modeling, and attitudes and expectations.
- The family functions as a socializer for the elementary child. Parent-child relationships go through many phases as the child matures. A parent's method of discipline affects a child's behavior, and a child's behavior affects a parent's method of discipline.
- Stepfamilies have unique problems and issues that are not characteristic of first families. Several significant issues are faced by the children in stepfamilies.
- By the time children enter school, boys are clear that they are male and will remain so, and girls are equally clear that they are female and will remain so. Generally, elementary school children segregate themselves into all-girl and all-boy groups, a phenomenon called sex cleavage.
- Competitive sports for children have negative and positive factors. Nonetheless, it appears that the character that competitive sports build depends on the character of those who bring their children to the programs and the character of those who teach these children.

READINGS

Asher, S., and Gottman, J. (Eds.) (1981). *The development of children's friendships.* Cambridge: Cambridge University Press.
Collection of research concerning peer relations and their effect on children's development.

Development during middle childhood (1984). Washington, D.C.: National Academy Press.
A collection of essays by well-known authorities concerning current knowledge of the development of the elementary aged child including chapters on peers, families, schools, self, and psychopathology.

Hyde, J. S. (1985). *Half the human experience* (3rd ed.). Lexington, MA: D. C. Heath.
An overview of sex roles for females.

Minuchin, P. P. and Shapiro, E. K. (1983). The school as a context for social development. In P. H. Mussen (Ed.) *Handbook of child psychology* (4th ed.), Vol. 4. New York: Wiley.
A contemporary, authoritative review of how the school contributes to the development of the child.

Paris, E. (1984). *Stepfamilies: Making them work.* New York: Avon.
A discussion of problems facing stepfamilies and includes issues such as school failure, sexual attractions among step-siblings, and rebellion.

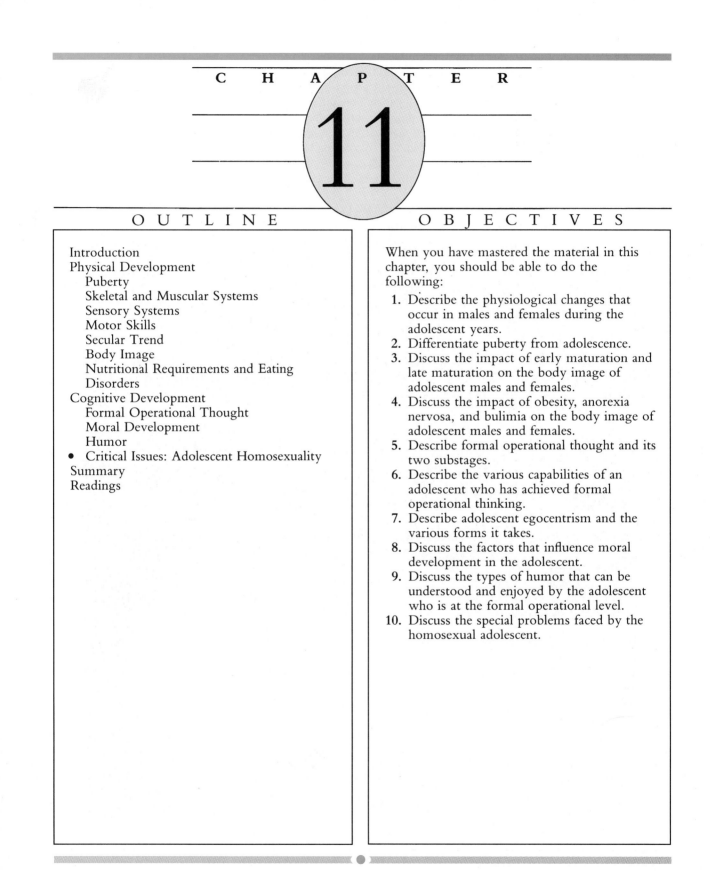

C H A P T E R

11

O U T L I N E

Introduction
Physical Development
    Puberty
    Skeletal and Muscular Systems
    Sensory Systems
    Motor Skills
    Secular Trend
    Body Image
    Nutritional Requirements and Eating
    Disorders
Cognitive Development
    Formal Operational Thought
    Moral Development
    Humor
 • Critical Issues: Adolescent Homosexuality
Summary
Readings

O B J E C T I V E S

When you have mastered the material in this chapter, you should be able to do the following:

1. Describe the physiological changes that occur in males and females during the adolescent years.
2. Differentiate puberty from adolescence.
3. Discuss the impact of early maturation and late maturation on the body image of adolescent males and females.
4. Discuss the impact of obesity, anorexia nervosa, and bulimia on the body image of adolescent males and females.
5. Describe formal operational thought and its two substages.
6. Describe the various capabilities of an adolescent who has achieved formal operational thinking.
7. Describe adolescent egocentrism and the various forms it takes.
8. Discuss the factors that influence moral development in the adolescent.
9. Discuss the types of humor that can be understood and enjoyed by the adolescent who is at the formal operational level.
10. Discuss the special problems faced by the homosexual adolescent.

The Transition Years: Adolescence—Physical and Cognitive Development

Adolescence
The psychosocial aspects of development in the years of life beginning with puberty and ending with the completion of general physical growth and maturation.

Adolescence refers to the psychosocial aspects of development in the years of life beginning with puberty and ending with the completion of general physical growth and maturation (Chumlea 1982; Katchadourian 1977). Adolescence is characterized by a wide variability in the norms of growth, increasingly independent behavior, and testing of adult roles. It lasts nearly a decade and traditionally is considered to begin around twelve or thirteen and end around nineteen or twenty.

The velocity of physical growth in adolescence is second only to the rate of growth during the prenatal period. Considering the biology of adolescence in isolation, though, is misleading. The changes of puberty are only one aspect of an integrated process of development. The repercussions of puberty affect the developing individual psychologically and socially, while the physical and human environments influence the biological processes. Therefore, there is no such thing as "the biology of adolescence" or "the psychology of adolescence"; they are intricately linked. But in order to study these phenomena, it is sometimes useful to examine them separately.

● PHYSICAL DEVELOPMENT

Adolescence marks a great and sudden increase in body size and strength as well as a change in many physiological functions, including reproductive capabilities. These changes all take place in a coordinated manner, and the child who is early with respect to one aspect of physical development is early with respect to all physical aspects. Changes take place approximately two years later in boys than in girls (Tanner 1978; Marshall and Tanner 1986). The second decade is an important transitional period for the developing individual because of the rapidity and magnitude of change and the fact that both biological and psychosocial changes occur simultaneously. The body changes elicit psychological reactions and a certain amount of self-consciousness in the adolescent (Katchadourian 1977).

Puberty
The morphological and physiological changes that occur in the growing child as the sex organs change from the infantile to the adult stage.

The term *adolescence,* defined above, must be differentiated from **puberty,** which refers collectively to the morphological and physiological changes that occur in the growing child as the sex organs change from the infantile to the adult stage. The reproductive system becomes mature, and sexual reproduction becomes possible. According to Marshall and Tanner (1986), "puberty is not complete until the individual has the physical capacity to conceive and successfully bear children" (p. 171). There are five principal manifestations of puberty:

1. Growth spurts alternate. An acceleration of growth is followed by a deceleration of growth in most skeletal dimensions and internal organs.
2. The gonads or sex glands develop.
3. Secondary reproductive organs and secondary sex charactersitics develop.
4. The body composition alters. The quantity and distribution of fat changes in association with the growth of the skeleton and musculature.
5. As the circulatory and respiratory systems develop, strength and endurance increase, especially in boys.

(Marshall and Tanner 1986)

Adolescence refers to the psychosocial aspects of development in the years of life beginning with puberty and ending with the completion of general physical growth and maturation.

Puberty

During the first decade of life, boys and girls seem to grow steadily and quite similarly. Before age ten there are no marked gender differences in height, weight, strength, or body composition. Shortly after age ten both sexes have attained about 84 percent of their adult height and 59 percent of their adult weight (Ahlstrom 1990). Shortly after age 10, pubertal changes become outwardly apparent, but by this time internal alterations related to puberty have long been in progress. By eight or nine years of age, certain hormones have already increased in amount, although neither the child nor others are aware of it. Other events have taken place in the brain even earlier, to trigger hormonal changes. Under these circumstances, we do not know precisely when puberty begins, but it becomes evident in most present-day Western youth at about ten or eleven years for girls and about eleven or twelve years for boys. The onset *range* is from eight and one-half to thirteen years for girls and from nine and one-half to fifteen years for boys. Most children enter puberty within this age range, and 95 percent of girls show at least one sign of puberty by age thirteen and one-half (Marshall and Tanner 1986).

During puberty most tissues in the body are affected. As noted earlier, there are alternate spurts in skeletal growth. The body composition is altered as a result of skeletal and muscular growth, together with changes in the quantity and distribution of fat. The developing circulatory and respiratory systems lead to increased strength and endurance, particularly in boys (Ahlstrom 1990). The gonads, reproductive organs, and secondary sex characteristics (such as breast buds and pubic hair) develop during this time. A combination of factors control the activity of the central nervous system and the endocrine system, which initiate and coordinate these changes. Two major biolgical outcomes that have profound psychosocial consequences occur at this time. First, a child attains the physique and physiological capabilities of an adult. Second, most of the major adult physical sex differences become established. Although these changes are universal, there are important differences between individuals with respect to the onset, order, and rate of growth at puberty (Marshall and Tanner 1986).

Sexual Maturation

In boys, growth of the testes occurs during a four-year period starting as early as nine and one-half years. In girls, breast development occurs as early as eight years or as late as thirteen and one-half years. The variability in the sequence of pubertal events is not as great as the variation in age at the onset of puberty. The stages of puberty differ in their order of appearance, and the variation in the sequence of these stages is as large between the genders as within a gender. The age range for the onset of events is large enough that the child may progress, for example, from stage-3 to stage-4 genital development and still be in stage-3 pubic hair development. On the average, boys attain stage-5 genital development before girls reach the average of stage-5 breast development (see Figure 11.3) (Lucas et al. 1985; Chumlea 1982).

Menarche, the first menstrual period, occurs at the end of a girl's **growth spurt,** approximately nine to twelve months after her *peak height velocity,* or full height, is attained. Menarche marks the definitive and mature stage of uterine growth, but it usually does not signify the attainment of full reproductive function. An infertility period of a year or eighteen months follows in most cases.

Exactly when and why a girl begins menstruation is unknown. Several of the body's dimensions and functions that change during adolescence may affect its onset. Body weight or total body fat has been hypothesized as a possible cause or indicator of a girl's physiological readiness for first menstruation (Tanner 1978; Lucas et al. 1985; Chumlea 1982). Supposedly, 17 percent of body weight must be fat in order to trigger menarche; 22 percent of body weight

Menarche
The first menstrual period, occurring at the end of a girl's growth spurt. Menarche marks the definitive and mature stage of uterine growth, but it does not usually signify the attainment of full reproductive function.

Growth spurt
The most rapid phase of adolescent growth.

● FIGURE 11.1
Stages of Sexual Development.

Breast Development

Stage 1 prepuberty, under 9 years
Stage 2 approximately 9 to 13½ years
Stage 3 approximately 10 to 14½ years
Stage 4 approximately 11 to 15½ years
Stage 5 approximately 12 to 19 years

Pubic Hair Development—Females
Stage 1 prepuberty, under 9 years
Stage 2 9½ to 14 years
Stage 3 10 to 14½ years
Stage 4 10½ to 15 years
Stage 5 12 to 16 ½ years

Genital Development—Males

Stage 1 prepuberty under 9½ years
Stage 2 approximately 9½ to 14 years
Stage 3 approximately 11 to 15 years
Stage 4 11½ to 16 years
Stage 5 12½ to 17½ years

Pubic Hair Development—Males
Stage 1 Under 11 years
Stage 2 approximately 11 years to 15½ years
Stage 3 approximately 11½ years to 16 years
Stage 4 approximately 12 years to 16½ years
Stage 5 approximately 13 years to 17 years

Adapted from Marshall and Tanner, 1969, 1970, 1986.

● FIGURE 11.2
Typical Progression of Female Pubertal Development
Pubertal development in size of female breasts

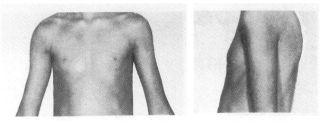

Stage 1. The breasts are preadolescent. There is elevation of the papilla only.

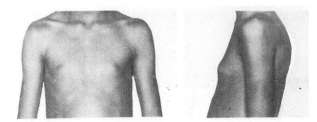

Stage 2. Breast bud stage. A small mound is formed by the elevation of the breast and papilla. The areolar diameter enlarges.

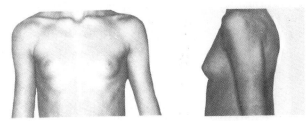

Stage 3. There is further enlargement of breasts and areola with no separation of their contours.

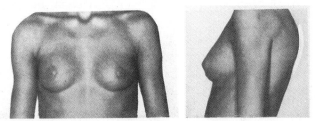

Stage 4. There is a projection of the areola and papilla to form a secondary mound above the level of the breast.

Pubertal development of female pubic hair
Stage 1. There is no pubic hair.

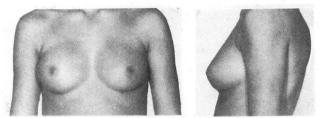

Stage 5. The breasts resemble those of a mature female as the areola has recessed to the general contour of the breast.

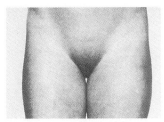

Stage 2. There is sparse growth of long, slightly pigmented, downy hair, straight or only slightly curled, primarily along the labia.

Stage 3. The hair is considerably darker, coarser, and more curled. The hair spreads sparsely over the junction of the pubes.

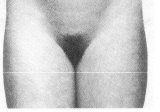

Stage 4. The hair, now adult in type, covers a smaller area than in the adult and does not extend onto the thighs.

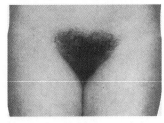

Stage 5. The hair is adult in quantity and type, with extension onto the thighs.

Source: Adapted from Tanner JM: *Growth at Adolescence,* ed 2. Oxford: Blackwell Scientific Publications, 1962.

Typical Progression of Male Pubertal Development
Pubertal development in size of male genitalia

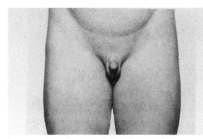

Stage 1. The penis, testes, and scrotum are of childhood size.

Stage 2. There is enlargement of the scrotum and testes, but the penis usually does not enlarge. The scrotal skin reddens.

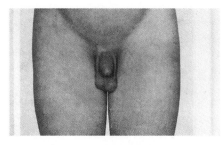

Stage 3. There is further growth of the testes and scrotum and enlargement of the penis, mainly in length.

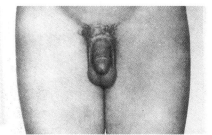

Stage 4. There is still further growth of the testes and scrotum and increased size of the penis, especially in breadth.

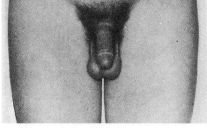

Stage 5. The genitalia are adult in size and shape.

Pubertal development of male pubic hair

Stage 1. There is no pubic hair.

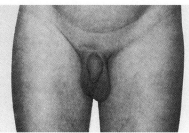

Stage 2. There is sparse growth of long, slightly pigmented, downy hair, straight or only slightly curled, primarily at the base of the penis.

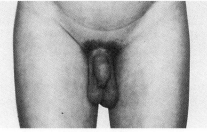

Stage 3. The hair is considerably darker, coarser, and more curled. The hair spreads sparsely over the junction of the pubes.

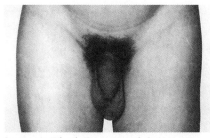

Stage 4. The hair, now adult in type, covers a smaller area than in the adult and does not extend onto the thighs.

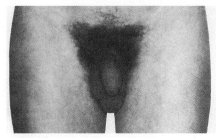

Stage 5. The hair is adult in quantity and type, with extension onto the thighs.

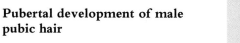

must be fat in order to maintain regular ovulatory cycles. Other factors that may affect menarche include skeletal development, strenuous physical activity, malnutrition, and stress (Lucas et al. 1985).

For boys, the first indication of approaching puberty is the enlargement of the testes and scrotum. (The age at which boys start to produce sperm is unknown, but production was present in approximately half of a select group of boys after 14.9 years of age.) Pubic hair may begin to grow at the same time but proceeds slowly. The penis begins to lengthen. There is an increased rate of growth in height about a year or more after the testes and scrotum enlarge. Axillary hair usually first appears about two years after pubic hair begins to grow. At about the same time that axillary hair appears, there is an increase in the length and pigmentation of hairs at the corners of the upper lip, which then spreads to complete the mustache. Next, hair appears on the upper part of the cheeks and just below the lower lip. Finally, it appears along the sides and border of the chin. This last development seldom occurs until genital and pubic hair development is far advanced. The amount and distribution of body hair in males is influenced by heredity.

A few boys undergo slight breast enlargement at puberty, which is temporary for the majority of them. In boys, enlargement of the larynx occurs a little after the height spurt and causes the voice to deepen perceptibly during the period when penis development is approaching completion (Marshall and Tanner 1986; Tanner 1963, 1978; Chumlea 1982; Lucas et al. 1985; Katchadourian 1977). In J. S. Bach's choir in Leipzig from 1727 to 1749, the average age for "breaking of the voice" was estimated at about 18 years. This is three to four years later than the age at which boys today begin to change voice in London (13.3 years), in Stockholm (13.9 years) (Malina 1979), and in the United States (14 years) (Marshall and Tanner 1986).

In summary, the onset of puberty is consistently two years earlier in girls than in boys. The magnitude of this difference depends on which aspects are being compared, for example, breast budding in girls precedes testicular enlargement in boys by six months; girls grow pubic hair a year earlier than boys do; and girls reach full height about two years before boys do (Marshall and Tanner 1986). In general, children who start pubescent development early reach maturity quickly; children starting at older ages may take a longer time to reach physical maturation (Chumlea 1982).

Skeletal and Muscular Systems

The adolescent's growth in skeletal and muscular dimensions is closely related to the development of the reproductive system. Both boys and girls produce testosterone and estrogen, but in significantly different amounts. Since testosterone stimulates muscle growth, the higher level in boys mean that more muscle is deposited in them. Estrogen stimulates maturation in the bones and increases deposits of fat. These hormones together with several hormones produced by the adrenal gland are responsible for the development of secondary sex characteristics (Marshall and Tanner 1986; Chumlea 1982).

The factors that control growth before adolescence are not completely understood, but it is clear that another pituitary product, called the **growth hormone** controls, to a great extent, the speed of growth from conception through adolescence. External stimuli such as stress, exercise, and sleep can affect growth hormone levels (Chumlea 1982).

Growth hormone
A pituitary product that controls, to a great extent, the speed of growth.

Peak height velocity (PHV)
The peak of linear growth.

The growth spurt is the most rapid phase of adolescent development, and the highest point is called *peak*. The child's growth velocity decelerates from birth until puberty, at which time the increased growth velocity of a fourteen-year-old boy is comparable to that of a two-year-old child. Although the peak velocity age occurs later in males than in females, it is more intense in boys and results in more tissue accumulation. (Tanner, 1981) American adolescents attain **peak height velocity (PHV)** earlier than, for example, English adolescents; nine months earlier for boys and three months earlier for girls (Marshall and Tanner 1986).

Virtually all aspects of skeletal and muscular growth are affected by the adolescent spurt and accelerate in a fairly regular order. Leg length usually peaks first, followed a few months later by body breadth and a year later by trunk length. Most of the height spurt is due to growth in the trunk rather than the legs. Muscles appear to have their spurt a little after the skeletal peak (Marshall and Tanner 1986).

Because their spurt occurs earlier, girls are bigger than boys from about ten and one-half to thirteen years. Boys are only 1 to 3 percent larger than girls in most body measurements before puberty, so the girls' adolescent spurt soon carries them ahead of the boys. Boys surpass girls when the greater and more sustained male adolescent spurt begins to take effect, and they finish about 10 percent larger in most dimensions. (Marshall and Tanner 1986).

The rapid growth of the skeleton during adolescence is not simultaneous with, but is coordinated to, muscular development. Differential skeletal growth between the genders produces differences in the size of male and female body segments; for example, males have longer arms and broader shoulders than females do. A bone's growth depends upon its type, but even those of the same type grow at different rates and start or stop growing at different times depending on their location (Chumlea 1982). Growth in stature ceases at the median ages of 21.2 years for boys and 17.3 years for girls (Roche and Davila 1972; Marshall and Tanner 1986).

Many bones of the skull do not experience rapid growth during adolescence (the skull vault reaches approximately 96 percent of its adult size by ten years of age), but a change occurs in head length and breadth due to the thickening of bones. The base of the skull and the mandible do have a growth spurt during adolescence. In the timing and intensity of growth spurts in the base of the skull, girls start and finish first, but boys have larger growth increments.

The rate of muscle and bone growth generally coincides with the adolescent's growth in height. Weight, which is the sum of various body components, is attributable to bone, muscle, and fat (Tanner 1963, 1978; Ahlstrom 1990). Though the main change at puberty is in body size, there is also considerable change in body shape, which differs between the two genders. Boys acquire the wide shoulders and muscular neck of a man, and girls acquire the relatively wide hips of a woman. Before puberty, it is difficult to distinguish gender from body proportions or amounts of bone, muscle, and fat alone. After puberty, using these aspects to distinguish between the two sexes is easier in a majority of cases (Marshall and Tanner 1986).

Quantifiable alterations occur in the amount of fatty tissue during adolescence, primarily in the subcutaneous, or storage, fat of the body (Ahlstrom 1990). The variability in deposition and patterning of subcutaneous fat on the arms, legs, and trunk is greater between boys and girls during adolescence than during any other period of childhood. Both boys and girls form deposits on the torso throughout adolescence, but in girls additional subcutaneous fat is added to the breasts, buttocks, lateral and medial thighs, and back of the arms. This additional fat accentuates sex differences in the body form (Chumlea 1982).

Sensory Systems

The eyes accelerate slightly in growth during adolescence, which explains the increased frequency of nearsightedness in children at puberty. The degree of myopia rises continuously from about age six to maturity, but a rapid rate of change occurs at about eleven to twelve years in girls and thirteen to fourteen years in boys (Chumlea 1982).

Internal Organs

Several changes help explain why athletic ability increases more in boys than in girls at adolescence. Not only do boys' muscles increase more in size and strength compared with girls', but boys alone show a profound increase in the vital capacity of the lungs (the amount of air the lungs will hold on maximum inspiration less the amount retained after maximum expiration). The number of red blood cells also rises sharply in boys but not in girls. This raises the amount of hemoglobin in the boys' blood and the quantity of oxygen that can be carried from their lungs to their tissues (Marshall and Tanner 1986).

Lymphoid tissue reaches maximum value by the beginning of adolescence and then actually decreases in value under the influence of sex hormones. (Lymphoid tissue is responsible for the production of white blood cells and antibodies.) Accordingly, children with large tonsils and adenoids may become less susceptible to many respiratory ailments when adolescence begins (Ahlstrom 1986).

Motor Skills

Muscle growth during adolescence produces differences between and within genders in terms of strength and motor performance. The strength of the average girl, with a small spurt between ten and thirteen years, increases linearly through adolescence and levels off between sixteen and eighteen years.

Boys, on the average, possess greater strength than girls throughout childhood. The increase in strength in normal boys is similar to that of girls until about age thirteen, when a marked rise begins and continues through eighteen years. This rise begins at about the same time that lean body mass (LBM) starts to increase, which is about when boys' grip strength increases. Larger muscles in boys account for their greater strength (Chumlea 1982).

Athletic ability undergoes a marked change during adolescence, particularly in boys. Girls' performance on the motor tasks of speed, agility, and balance peaks at about age fourteen, while that of boys improves steadily and noticeably throughout adolescence. Due to early maturation, girls briefly surpass boys in motor performance. After sixteen years of age, few girls perform as well as the average boy, and only a few boys perform at the level of an average girl (Marshall and Tanner 1986; Bailey et al. 1986; Chumlea 1982). Early maturation in boys is positively related to strength and motor performance.

Secular Trend

Adolescents today in all socioeconomic groups in the United States, Western Europe, and Japan are taller, heavier, and more physically mature than were their parents, grandparents, and particularly great-grandparents during adolescence. These differences are known as the secular trend. Evidence also indicates that adolescents achieve sexual maturation earlier, but this trend has stabilized in recent decades. (Bailey et al. 1986; Chumlea 1982; Lucas et al. 1985; Malina 1979). The largest secular differences in height and weight are apparent during the pubertal years. The secular trend in body size appears early in life and becomes greater during puberty (Malina 1979; Bailey et al. 1986).

The underlying causes of the secular trend are not known with certainty. Improved nutrition and environmental quality are most often offered as explanations. More specific factors include more fat and sugar consumption; changing patterns of infant nutrition; improved health conditions as reflected in reduced infant and childhood mortality and increased life expectancy; urbanization and industrialization; restrictions in child labor; reduction in family size; natural selection; and outbreeding (Malina 1979).

Differences between racial groups in body size and shape influence the growth of bone, muscle, and fat during adolescence. The adult body results from a complex interaction of genetic composition and environment. If living conditions are optimal, African-Americans are taller and heavier than whites during adolescence, while Asians are smaller and lighter than whites and African-Americans. Adverse environmental or socioeconomic conditions can delay sexual and skeletal maturity and thus permanently reduce adult stature and body size (Chumlea 1982; Marshall and Tanner 1986).

Body Image

No other age-group is as concerned with and sensitive about their bodies, or as devastated by criticism and comparison, as are adolescents. This is particularly true of early and late maturers and the obese adolescent. Those who mature early are not only vulnerable because they must contend with a host of bodily changes, but suffer psychological consequences because they experience these major changes earlier than their peers. Body image is the core of the overall self-image. Among the many adjustments adolescents must make, the most difficult is learning about their "new" body. Virtually any and all physical characteristics receive extraordinary attention during this phase. Being different is to be avoided at almost any cost, and undesirable physical characteristics can expose the adolescent to teasing, ridicule, or exclusion. Most early adolescents are more concerned about their physical appearance than about any other aspect of themselves. Early-adolescent girls report a greater dissatisfaction with their bodies and appearance than do boys of the same age. Approximately one-third of early-adolescent boys and one-half of early-adolescent girls report distress and dissatisfaction with some aspect of their physical development or appearance. A positive relationship has been noted between physical attractiveness and social acceptance during adolescence. Socially desirable personality traits tend to be attributed more often to the physically attractive than to the physically unattractive, which underscores the powerful effect of physical appearance on how early adolescents are viewed by others (Siegel 1982; Lucas et al. 1985).

Body image is influenced by advertising and the mass media, which dictate the "in" look, clothing styles, and other elements of being accepted. In attempt-

In general, the psychological differences between early and late maturers are less striking in females than in males.

ing to conform to cultural ideals, adolescents may compromise their own well-being, including proper nutrient intake. Other strong influences on body image are the desire to fit in and peer pressure, which may come from the immediate peer group or may include respected adults and national idols (Lucas et al. 1985).

Early and Late Maturers

The timing of puberty in the adolescent can influence the interactions between the adolescent and his or her family and peers. The impact is different for adolescent boys and girls. Early-maturing males enjoy more permissive family relationships, while late-maturing males experience what they perceive as excessive parental control (Clausen 1975). However, Steinberg (1987) found that early-maturing boys did experience conflict with their mothers.

Early-maturing girls experience increased parental restrictiveness and vigilance and greater conflict with their parents (Hill et al. 1985; Peterson 1985; Steinberg 1987). Hauser et al. (1985), on the other hand, found more strained relations in families with on-time girls and boys.

In peer relations, early-maturing males are at an advantage physically, athletically, and socially. They tend to be more popular with peers and more likely to be school leaders. They are also portrayed by researchers as being more concerned with making a good impression as well as having a higher degree of social responsibility. Other attributes include being less impulsive and more concerned with self-control, and an early-maturing boy may begin to appear somewhat less flexible and perhaps overcontrolled (Siegel 1982; Mussen and Jones 1963; Weatherley 1964).

The late-maturing adolescent male is more tense, restless, talkative, attention-seeking—and less popular. He has a negative self-concept and expresses more feelings of inadequacy, rejection, and parental domination. He is also less likely to lead and more inclined to seek encouragement from others. He is portrayed as anxious and lacking in self-confidence. While late maturers often reveal high motivation for social affiliation and a great deal of social activity,

Initially, early maturing girls are likely to be big and physically conspicuous, and may have a more difficult time psychologically. These difficulties and differences diminish over time and early maturing girls make better adjustments as adults.

their social techniques are often childish and attention-getting. The high social drive may be based on a general insecurity and basic feelings of dependency. Therefore, while early maturation offers certain psychological advantages, late maturation interferes with optimal personality development (Siegel 1982; Mussen and Jones 1963; Weatherley 1964).

Yet longitudinal studies indicate that to view an early-maturing boy as psychologically healthier than a late maturer is an oversimplification based upon an equation of social adjustment and psychological adjustment. The early maturer seems to pay a certain price for social advantages in terms of emotional constraint (that is, being cautious, rigid, bound by rules and routines), while the late maturer seems somewhat freer and more tolerant of his own impulses and inner life. Another more positive way to view the late maturer, is that a longer latency period provides an opportunity for developing, practicing, and expanding motor and intellectual skills in a relatively conflict-free setting. (Siegel, 1982)

The psychological consequences of maturational timing are less clear-cut for girls. In general, the psychological differences between early and late maturers are less striking in females than in males. Weatherley (1964) noted that late-maturing girls were rated by adult judges as significantly higher than early-maturing girls on a number of socially desirable traits, such as sociability, leadership, cheerfulness, poise, and expressiveness. Peers also rated late maturers in more positive terms than they did early maturers. Late-maturing girls were especially likely to participate in extracurricular activities in high school and hold positions of prestige in school clubs.

Initially early-maturing girls played a much less prominent role in school activities. Siegel (1982) also notes that an early maturer is likely to be big and physically conspicuous, more introverted, and shy. She generally experiences greater stress and may have a more difficult time psychologically. These difficulties and differences seem to diminish over time, however, and early-maturing girls apparently make better adjustments as adults. "The early maturer has developed from a quite unpromising adolescent to a quite integrated woman" (Siegel 1982, 7).

Adolescents of either gender who mature early are more likely to become sexually active sooner than their later-maturing peers (Dreyer 1982). The older early-maturing girls are also more likely to be at risk for excessive immersion in peer activities and early involvement in deviant behavior (Magnusson, Statin, and Allen 1985).

Nutritional Requirements and Eating Disorders

The rapid development of body image during adolescence accounts for much of the psychological component of eating disorders in some teenagers. Nutritional needs parallel the rate of growth that accompanies the onset of puberty. Adolescents consume more food in response to growth spurts, but psychological and social factors also influence eating patterns significantly. Many adolescents consume large quantities of high-calorie foods in addition to regular meals at home, becoming prone to excessive weight gain. Others may subsist on select foods, and the lack of a balanced diet leads to a deficiency in proteins and vitamins. Most adolescents complete their development without serious eating disturbances, but a significant number suffer from an eating disorder, most commonly obesity (Katchadourian 1977).

Eighty percent of adolescent females consume at least one snack per day, some as many as seven. Snacks provide between one-fourth to one-third of the daily energy intake for adolescents (Bigler-Doughten and Jenkins 1987). Snacks contribute 52 percent of the recommended daily allowance (RDA) for riboflavin, 43 percent of the RDA for vitamin C, and 39 percent of the RDA for thiamin (Bigler-Doughten and Jenkins 1987; McCoy et al. 1986).

A study of 140 adolescent girls found that those who scored high on family relations had better diets than those who scored low. Also, the girls who ate with their families regularly ate better and had more adequate diets than those who did not. Those whose families were critical of their eating habits skipped more meals. When parents are authoritarian and rigid, adolescents often use food to express rebellion against parental authority. This can lead to erratic and bizarre food practices, such as binges, strong food aversions, food refusals, odd diets, fasting, and missed meals. When parents are very permissive, the same behavior can be exhibited by teens, who are attempting to force their parents to set some limits on their behavior (Lucas et al. 1985).

Adolescents are generally unable to view themselves without distortion. (The fact that the image is distorted does not make the image any less important to the adolescent.) One study found that 70 percent of the female adolescent subjects wanted to lose weight, but only approximately 15 percent were actually obese; 59 percent of the male subjects wanted to gain weight, although only 25 percent were lower than average in fatness. Other body image studies also indicate that adolescents are dissatisfied with their body dimensions. Males want larger biceps, shoulders, chests, and forearms. Females want smaller hips, thighs, and waists. (Lucas, et al., 1985)

Obesity

The criteria for defining obesity vary and are culturally determined; the most widely accepted definition in the United States is that those who are 20 percent above the mean weight for their height are obese (those who are 10 percent above the mean are considered overweight). Obesity is the most prevalent eating disorder at all ages. In developed countries, about 10 percent of grade school children and 10 to 15 percent (some estimates are as high as 30 percent) of high school students are obese. This represents more than ten million adolescents in the United States. Eighty percent of them will remain obese as adults and be opposed to treatment. Obesity is seldom an isolated problem but is combined with social and psychological difficulties (Katchadourian 1977; Lucas et al. 1985).

Generally Western society views obesity with disapproval and contempt, while slenderness is favored. There are no typical obese adolescents, but certain physiological characteristics are common: rapid weight gain in the first year of life, earlier maturation, earlier menarche, a highly endomorphic physique, and advanced bone development. This is especially true for those who have been obese through the growing years (Lucas et al. 1985). The psychological tasks of the adolescent may become hampered by obesity and, in turn, interfere with efforts to control the disorder. It is necessary to differentiate the psychological factors that lead to overeating from the psychological effects of being overweight and the added effects of attempts at dieting. The problem of being obese has causes that go beyond caloric intake and expenditure. Eventually the issue has to be resolved in the context of the adolescent's overall relationship to self and to others in his or her world (Katchadourian 1977; Harkaway 1987).

Obese teenagers are especially affected by social rejection and derogatory attitudes in our culture. They are under constant pressure to change their bodies to conform with social norms. Obese girls have traits in common with other minority groups, such as obsessive concern (with food and being overweight), passivity, withdrawal, and self-contempt. They also experience actual discrimination; in reality, obesity affects attractiveness, popularity with the opposite sex, ability to obtain a job, acceptance into college, and other practical life situations. The youngsters may experience so much humiliating rejection and poor self-esteem that they become socially isolated. Their consistently low level of activity requires little energy. This combination of emotional and environmental factors often leads to more severe obesity. A vicious cycle follows whereby food and eating may be the only outlets for frustration and depression (Lucas et al. 1985).

The caloric intake of some obese adolescents is actually equal to or lower than that of nonobese adolescents. A tendency for obese teenagers to eat less frequently and to skip more meals, especially breakfast, is often accompanied by a pattern of continuous eating from after school until late in the evening (Lucas et al. 1985).

Inactivity is a major factor in obesity. It is a strong indicator of a poor-quality diet in terms of a reduced intake of energy foods. Obese adolescents decline to participate in sports and activities that make them feel awkward, embarrassed, and exhausted. They are also eliminated from participation in organized sports because of poor performance. Because they expend less energy than adolescents of normal weight, even if they eat less they may still gain or at least maintain their weight. This seeming self-denial without results often causes feelings of frustration and hopelessness. (The odds against an overweight adolescent becoming an average weight adult are 28 to 1) (Lucas et al. 1985).

Anorexia Nervosa

Anorexia nervosa literally means "lack of appetite due to nerves." This eating disorder was first described in the second half of the sixteenth century. It is characterized by an extreme reduction in food intake leading to a loss of at least 25 percent of original body weight. The exact etiology is still unknown, but current data suggest that anorexia nervosa is probably the result of a complex biological and psychological dysfunction. No matter what the cause, it has a 10 to 15 percent mortality rate. It is predominantly an illness of females (about 95 percent of all victims), with an incidence of about 4.6 per 1,000 in affluent Western countries. Anorexia nervosa almost always has its onset in the adolescent years, and in rare cases during preadolescence. When it occurs in early adulthood, it may be triggered by a major developmental milestone such as marriage and especially pregnancy (Katchadourian 1977; Milner et al. 1985; Muuss 1985; Mogul 1980).

In most cases of anorexia nervosa there is initially a strong urge to eat, which, as the condition progresses, may be displaced onto a mental preoccupation with food and acts of feeding or even stuffing others. A recent finding is that during the later stage there is a true sustained loss of appetite that may be the physiological result of starvation. Aggressive tendencies are expressed against one's self and body and against others in the form of puritanical moralizing. A sense of powerlessness is a fundamental developmental defect in anorexics and is the key to understanding their condition. They also have a sense of not owning themselves, of not even knowing clearly their own bodies' indicators of needs and wishes; in short, there is not a secure sense of identity as

Anorexia nervosa
An eating disorder characterized by an extreme reduction in food intake leading to a loss of at least 25 percent of original body weight.

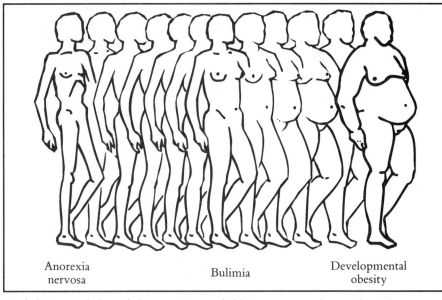

Anorexia
nervosa

Bulimia

Developmental
obesity

Underlying psychological characteristics are held in common, whereas physical
conditions vary across the spectrum. (From J. M. Rees, "Eating disorders," in Nutrition
in adolescence, ed. L. K. Mahan and J. M. Rees [St. Louis: The C. V. Mosby Co., 1984].)
Source. Lucas et al. 1985, 240.

these individuals separate from their mothers. Anorexics do not respond to
encouragement to go ahead on their own, but instead seem terrified of any
progress toward independence. They retreat, then, back to infantile feelings of
helpless impotence (Mogul 1980; Muuss 1985).

Initial symptoms of anorexia nervosa include **amenorrhea,** the cessation of
menstruation (often an early sign before significant weight loss sets in); weight
loss; compulsive physical activity; a distorted body image; and dietary restrictions. Anorexics are often highly intelligent overachievers and are described by
their parents as "perfect children." Everyday events or remarks critical of their
bodies appear to precipitate weight loss. The weight loss may be a response to
real or imagined obesity. Initially, anorexics' weight goals may be reasonable, but
with success these individuals are reinforced both externally and internally to
continue to lose weight. When weight loss goals are reached, even lower ones
may be established. Dieting becomes the primary focus in the life of an anorexic.

Alertness, restlessness, and lively activity are pursued to the point of fierce
regimens that belie the emaciated state of the body. There is dramatic increase
in hyperactive behavior and compulsive exercise patterns. It is significant that
this physical activity is done alone. Cognitive functioning (or reality testing) is
impaired. There is a distortion of body image and of the true body signals for
example, she may not actually feel hungry, or she may feel satiated.

Anorexics maintain a staunch denial of illness. Although they may not be
consciously aware of the condition in themselves, they can spot even subtle
signs of it in others (Lucas et al. 1985; Milner et al. 1985; Mogul 1980). Important sociocultural components in anorexia nervosa are thought to be dieting as
a normative upper-class female behavior, the fashion industry's idealized female
figure as thin and tubular, and greater expectations for women to be independent and successful (Kiecolt-Glaser and Dixon 1984). Diagnosis is difficult be-

Amenorrhea
The cessation of menstruation.

cause anorexics deny they have a problem, rationalize their behavior, and are not frank about their real feelings on the matter. Although anorexia nervosa is not a deliberately chosen way of coping with stresses and the uncertainties of adolescence, it is a compensatory attempt to suppress pubertal changes (Muuss 1985).

A high probability exists that sisters or the mother of the anorexic have also had the disorder or that the parents are excessively thin or obese. Family histories commonly reveal such conditions as depression, obesity, diabetes, or alcoholism. Frequently the family is preoccupied with food and eating. Even though the family may appear to be intact, there may be marital discord. Anorexic families are likely to be overprotective, rigid, and unable or unwilling to resolve conflicts. No single family pattern, however, has been identified as always or usually associated with anorexia.

A stressful life situation or crisis often seems to trigger the onset of anorexia nervosa. Examples are divorce of the parents, death in the family, family fights, breaking up with a boyfriend, weight loss after an illness, leaving home to go to college, and failing in courses or in important projects. Anorexics are also fearful of change. As children they may have experienced a strong dislike for change. Even positive change seems to be stressful for them and may exacerbate their condition. Because anorexics are secretive about their behavior, later it may be impossible to determine the point at which the exaggerated dieting ended and the anorexic eating pattern began (Muuss 1985).

Poor social interaction, such as isolation from meaningful peer relationships, has been identified as an essential feature in the beginning of the illness. Because they have not developed a network of peers, they are limited to relationships within the family. They spend more time alone and experience less affect than do other single women. They keep to themselves, lack self-esteem, and suffer from confusion over professional aspirations. They are ambivalent about their roles as women and about their vocational identity. Anorexia nervosa is completely absent from societies that have clearly prescribed roles for women (Muuss 1985).

As a group, anorexics have significantly more internal locus of control. In one study, the more internal anorexics evidenced more rapid weight gain during treatment (Strober 1982). Those who scored in the more external direction showed greater denial of illness, fear of weight change, rigidity of self-imposed controls, use of purgatives and diuretics, and body image distortion.

No single therapeutic approach for anorexia has proved satisfactory, perhaps because the condition is still incompletely understood. Evidently anorexia involves an interaction of biological and psychological factors, and a truly successful treatment cannot be accomplished until this interaction is clarified. The onset of anorexia in early adolescence is usually considered less serious than onset at a later age, but the prognosis may be no better. Long-term follow-up of treated anorexics of all ages reveals adequate weight in two-thirds of the patients but substantial continuing psychological impairment (Hodgman 1983). The earlier the diagnosis is made and treatment is begun, the better the chances for recovery and the less likely the need for hospitalization. The longer the symptoms persist, the more difficult the treatment becomes. The most severe outcome of untreated anorexia is death through starvation or cardiac arrest. The highly publicized 1983 death of Karen Carpenter, a popular singer, was the outcome of her twelve-year losing battle with anorexia nervosa (Muuss 1985).

Long-range follow-up studies indicate that anorexic adolescents, as compared with healthy non-anorexic adolescents, have a higher mortality rate, more frequent hospitalization, greater likelihood of psychological impairment (phobias and depression), and greater risk for marital and social maladjustment.

Treatment and management of anorexia are varied. Most programs include nutritional, medical, and psychiatric support. Several methods of treatment have been proposed (Muuss 1985). *Cognitive therapy* concentrates on eliminating the anorexic's incorrect, irrational, and self-defeating cognitions, attitudes, and beliefs about food, health, body image, and self-concept. *Family therapy* is indicated if the anorexic is less than sixteen years old and lives with her parents. Family therapy often starts with a brief hospital stay for the anorexic. *Behavior modification therapy* usually involves establishing an agreement (often a contract) about desirable conduct on the anorexic's part (for example, maintaining a certain body weight, eating three meals a day, consuming the basic food groups daily, and limiting exercise) in exchange for specific reinforcements (such as money, privileges, or other rewards). *Hospitalization,* including intravenous feeding, is another treatment method and may be used in combination with psychotherapy or family therapy.

Approximately 5 to 10 percent of anorexics are male. Some male cases are not manifested until later adulthood, while others do not involve dramatic weight loss or all the common psychological behaviors (Lucas et al. 1985). Explanations suggested for the low incidence of male anorexia include an emphasis on muscle development rather than slimness, a later entry into adolescence, and a greater propensity for acting out rather than internalizing. The etiology of male anorexia nervosa is related to major gender-identity problems and/or extreme obesity. The symptoms of preadolescent- and adolescent-onset anorexic males are similar to those of preadolescent- and adolescent-onset females, but the postadolescent-onset male deviates significantly. In cases of late onset, males are characterized by low educational and occupational achievement, apparent sexual disinterest, and failure to attain adult automony. This pattern of failure in work and educational endeavors is particularly striking when compared with the characteristics of female anorexics. Female anorexics seem to cope with their feelings of inadequacy by diligent effort and overachievement, while postadolescent-onset males seem to withdraw from any competition, even the challenge of everyday living. Whereas women in our society are allowed to assume a more dependent and passive role than men and have less pressure for achievement, the postadolescent-onset male's withdrawal from an active pursuit of achievement and autonomy deviates from the cultural sex-role norms. The poorer prognosis for later onset may reflect relatively greater immaturity and regression than that of their peers (Kiecolt-Glaser and Dixon 1984).

Bulimia

Bulimia is uncontrollable binge eating often associated with self-induced vomiting, abuse of diuretics and laxatives, and a depressive mood after eating. Killeen et al. (1986) found that 13 percent of fifteen-year-old females employed some form of purging—such as vomiting, laxatives, or diuretics—to lose weight. Of this group, 9 percent reported vomiting monthly or less, 2 percent reported vomiting at least once a week, and 8 percent reported using diet pills. Although long reported in conjunction with anorexia nervosa, bulimia has recently been recognized to exist also as a separate disorder (Hudson et al. 1982). Pope et al. (1984) estimate that 7.6 million American girls and women have a

Karen Carpenter

Bulimia
Uncontrollable binge eating often associated with self-induced vomiting, abuse of diuretics and laxatives, and a depressive mood after eating.

lifetime history of bulimia. It appears to be on the rise, especially on college campuses (Hodgman 1983), where it affects approximately 19 percent of women students (and is suspected to affect even more) (Lucas et al. 1985).

Among normal teenagers the use of vomiting as a form of weight control has become a growing practice. It may be socially reinforced on athletic squads or when groups of adolescents or college students live together. At the present time, bulimia and anorexia nervosa are thought to arise under similar patterns of familial disturbance. Bulimics may have previously been obese or may have experienced classic anorexia nervosa. They are often older than the average anorexic when seen for treatment (Lucas et al. 1985).

The psychological characteristics most prominently encountered in bulimics are an overriding sense of guilt and a linkage between self-worth and the ability to maintain a body size close to the "ideal." The preoccupation with these issues and the physical activities of eating and purging interfere with the ability to succeed in an educational or professional setting. Compared with peers, bulimics appear to be very attractive and lead a busy and successful life. They are prone to the problems of impulse control, including abuse of drugs and alcohol, shoplifting, and outbursts of anger. Bouts of binging and vomiting are often attempts to deal with unwanted feelings.

The bulimic is physically near normal weight for height. Sufficient nourishment is retained to sustain the body despite frequent vomiting and purging. Bulimics differ in the practices they follow. Some will define eating one cookie as a binge because of their distorted attitudes about food and physiological needs. They experience dental problems and irritation of the throat as a result of exposure to the acid accompanying the vomit. Rectal bleeding may be caused by excessive use of laxatives. More rare are electrolyte imbalances and the development of fistulas in the esophagus, and these may have serious consequences requiring hospitalization (Lucas et al. 1985).

In treating bulimia, the primary goal is to stop the vomiting. Once bulimics realize they can control vomiting, they are gradually able to control eating. As mentioned earlier, the behavior of the bulimic is commonly based on faulty ideas about physiological needs. The chance to learn within a trusting relationship allows the bulimic to formulate new concepts about food (Lucas et al. 1985).

● COGNITIVE DEVELOPMENT

The onset of puberty and the accompanying biological changes transform the child into an adult, both physically and sexually. But these changes are only one aspect of the transformation. Alterations in the thought processes are directly related to maturational changes that occur in the cortex during puberty. Intellectual maturity and brain development coincide, enabling adolescents to think about abstract ideas and events. Adolescents are also capable of speculating about the future and their role in life. They can reason logically about how the world is and how the world might be.

Formal Operational Thought

Around eleven or twelve years of age children begin to develop new mental abilities called formal operations, the final stage of cognitive development according to Piaget. During this period their capacity to acquire and utilize knowledge reaches its peak efficiency. Not all adolescents are capable of reaching this final level. Those who do, change from thinking like a child to thinking like an adult. They are no longer tied to thinking in rigid, concrete terms; they are now open to dealing with problems from a variety of perspectives and can systematically apply complex logical operations to solving problems. Some of the operations include abstract thinking, propositional logic, combinational logic, contrary-to-fact propositions, reflective thinking, and using a second symbol system.

While the concrete operational child is able to reason on the basis of objects, the formal operational adolescent is able to reason on the basis of verbal propositions (Muuss 1975). Practically all available research shows a clear change in the quality and power of thought during the age range of eleven to fifteen years, (Inhelder and Piaget 1958; Elkind 1978, 1981).

Stages III–A and III–B

Formal operational thinking has been divided into two substages: III–A (eleven to fifteen years) and III–B (fourteen years and onward). (Originally Piaget had three stages of cognitive development: sensorimotor, operational, and formal operational. Hence the substages III–A and III–B [Inhelder and Piaget 1958].) **Substage III–A** appears to be preparatory. Adolescents at this substage are capable of making correct discoveries and may handle certain formal operations. Their approach is cumbersome, however, and they are unable to provide systematic and rigorous proof. Adolescents at **substage III–B** are capable of advancing more inclusive laws and formulating more exquisite generalizations. They are also capable of spontaneously providing more systematic proof because they can use methods of control such as following a definite or specific procedure. The difference in approach and reasoning in substages III–A and III–B may be illustrated by actual responses. For example, if asked, "What number is thirty less than three times itself?" The III–A adolescent would substitute numbers until he or she arrived at a feasible result. The III–B student would convert the problem to an algebraic equation ($3x - 30 = x$). Most adolescents at substage III–B develop or follow social and political theories, while some follow and develop religious, philosophical, and scientific theories (Muuss 1975; Elkind 1981; Inhelder and Piaget 1958).

Abstract Thinking

Adolescents can think abstractly at the formal operational level. In order to do so, they must be able to think logically not only about things but also about statements and ideas. The concrete operational child is tied to concrete reality—he or she can think logically with real things in an immediate, physical world. For example, assume that a concrete operational child is told that "a concealed small ball is either red or not red" *and* "the small ball is red and not red." If then asked whether the statements are true, false, or impossible to judge, the concrete operational child will answer on the basis of what he or she sees. At the time the ball is concealed, he or she will say it is impossible to judge; when the ball is in view, the child's answer will reflect the color that the ball actually is. The response of an adolescent at the formal operational stage will focus on the *statements* rather than on the ball. The formal operational adolescent will realize that it is possible that the statement "a concealed small ball is either red or not red" is true, while the statement "the ball is red and not red" can never

Substage III–A
The first substage of formal operational thinking. III–A is preparatory. Adolescents at this substage are capable of making correct discoveries and may handle certain formal operations.

Substage III–B
The second substage of formal operational thinking. Adolescents at this substage are capable of advancing more inclusive laws and formulating more exquisite generalizations.

be true. It is not necessary for him or her to have the concrete, physical evidence to arrive at a response (Keating 1980).

Propositional Logic

Propositional logic enables the adolescent to test hypotheses, that is, evaluate logical relationships between propositions. A person who is capable of formal operations can manipulate the logic of propositions without regard to the propositions' content. Thus, he or she can consider all actual and possible solutions to a problem. His or her thinking is flexible. For example, consider the following statements:

It is raining and cold.	p	q
It is raining and not cold.	p	*q*
It is not raining and cold.	*p*	q
It is not raining and not cold.	*p*	*q*

These statements can be combined in various ways in order to look at their possible relationships. For example, the combination *p*q versus p*q* suggests that rain and cold are mutually exclusive or disjunctive. Also, the combination pq versus *p*q versus p*q* versus *pq* suggests that rain and cold are independent. Therefore, the four propositions can be combined in sixteen different ways to yield sixteen possible relationships between propositions (Elkind 1978).

Combinatorial Logic

The formal operational individual is also capable of thinking ahead and planning. **Combinational logic** is a formal operation in which the adolescent can deal with problems in which many factions operate at the same time. Problem solving can be approached in a systematic and efficient way. The individual can integrate what he or she has learned in the past while he or she considers all the possible combinations of pertinent factors. A classic experiment conducted by Inhelder and Piaget (1958) illustrates this capability. Each individual (a child or an adolescent) was shown five colorless, odorless liquids in test tubes. The test tubes were labeled 1, 2, 3, 4, and *g*. The information given to the individual was that adding *g* to some combination of the other four liquids would produce a yellow mixture. What was that combination? The child who was at the concrete operational stage would try to solve the problem through trial and error—for example, by adding a few drops of *g* to each tube and then giving up. Or he or she would haphazardly combine the liquids in various ways without keeping track of which combinations he or she used. The formal operational individual, in contrast, would develop a preconceived plan of action. He or she would anticipate what information was needed to solve the problem, realizing that all possible combinations had to be tried. First the formal operational individual would add *g* to each tube. Next he or she would combine liquid 1 with 2, then liquid 1 with 3, and so forth. He or she would usually keep notes in order to explain in detail what worked and what did not.

Another example of combinatorial logic is the problem of arranging four differently colored poker chips into all possible combinations, which is sixteen combinations. If the colors are red (R), blue (B), yellow (Y), and green (G), then the combinations are R, B, Y, G, RB, RY, RG, BY, BG, YG, RBY, RBG, BYG, RYG, RBYG, and none. Most adolescents can easily form all of these combinations, but most younger children cannot. It is in this sense that the combinatorial reasoning of adolescence goes beyond the more elementary syllogistic reasoning of the child (Elkind 1981).

Propositional logic
Logic that permits testing of hypotheses on purely a formal basis; that is, the kind of thinking required in scientific experimentation.

Combinatorial logic
A formal operation in which the adolescent can deal with problems in which many factors operate at the same time.

The formal operational individual is capable of thinking ahead and planning. Problem solving can be approached in a systematic and efficient way.

The capacity for combinatorial logic lays the groundwork for some characteristic adolescent reactions. Adolescents can now see a host of alternatives, which makes decision making a problem. They can now see many alternatives to parental directives, which makes it difficult to accept parental alternatives without question. Adolescents want to know not only where their parents stand on an issue but also why, and they are ready to debate the virtues of the parental alternative over that chosen by themselves and their peers. Adolescents' quarrels with parental decisions are part of the adolescents' own indecisiveness. Although they have trouble deciding for themselves, they do not want others making decisions for them. Adolescents demand that their parents take a stand, if only so they can rebel against it. If adolescents were not capable of grasping alternatives to parental directives, and if they were not in turmoil over their own decisions, at least some of the "storm and stress" of this period would never appear, or it would appear in a different form. The presence of structures that enable adolescents to construct multiple alternatives sets the stage for conflict between young people and their parents as well as for increased dependence upon the peer group for final decision making (Elkind 1981).

Contrary-to-fact Situations

The capacity to construct ideals, or **contrary-to-fact situations,** is another capability of adolescents. They can accept a contrary-to-fact premise and pro-

Contrary-to-fact situations
A contrary-to-fact premise constructed by an adolescent and proceeded with in argument as if the premise were correct. That is, the adolescent deals with the possible as well as the actual.

ceed with an argument as if the premise were correct. The capacity to deal with the possible, as well as the actual, frees the adolescent's thought to deal with many problem situations with which the younger child would be stymied. This also means that the future is now as much of a reality as the present, and it is a reality that can and must be dealt with. This capacity to construct ideals plays an important role in the adolescent experience and behavior. Adolescents can conceive of ideal families, religions, and societies. The problem arises when they compare these ideals with their own family, religion, and society. Much of the adolescent rebellion against adult society is derived from this new capacity to construct ideal situations. The ideals are almost entirely intellectual because the young person has little conception of how they might be made into reality and has even less interest in working toward their fulfillment. The same adolescent who professes to be concerned for the poor will spend money on records and clothes, not on charity. The fact that ideals can be conceived of by the adolescent does not mean they will be realized.

The adolescent can also construct ideal persons. A case in point is the adolescent crush, which is short-lived because no human can match the ideal created by adolescent thought. A lack of compassion for human failings—their own or those of others—is prevalent among adolescents. They criticize adults for ethical hypocrisy and at the same time belittle themselves for personal short-comings, such as academic failures, athletic failures, or social blunders. Perhaps adolescents feel superior to adults because they are relatively so uninvolved with the serious issues of justice, integrity, and obedience to the law (Elkind 1981).

Thinking about Thinking

Metacognition
A structural feature of adolescent thought that enables the individual to think about thinking.

Another structural feature of adolescent thought, the capacity to think about thinking, is called *introspection* and is commonly labeled **metacognition.** For the first time, adolescents can see themselves as objects, and can evaluate themselves from the perspectives of other people with respect to personality, intelligence, and appearance. Self-consciousness is a manifestation of this new capacity for introspection. Now that they can look at themselves from the outside, they become concerned about others' reactions to them. A regime of physical or intellectual exercise begins at about this time because, in examining themselves, they find a discrepancy between what they are and what they wish to be—that is, between the real and the ideal self.

Introspection leads adolescents to be more secretive about their thoughts. They realize now that thoughts are private and that they can say things that are diametrically opposed to their thoughts (Elkind 1981). When children fabricate, they tend to believe the fabrication, so once it is constructed they defend it as truth. Adolescents do not believe their own fabrication, but they can make it sound quite convincing. Adolescents can, therefore, create social disguises, common in adults and rare in children, behind which they conceal thoughts and wishes that are at variance with their verbal assertions. At one extreme these disguises are tact and politeness, while at the other extreme they are deceit and exploitation. The potential for both is present as soon as adolescents can say one thing and think another and be aware that they are doing so (Elkind 1981).

Second Symbol System

Second symbol system
A set of symbols for symbols.

The adolescent is capable of using a **second symbol system,** that is, a set of symbols for symbols. The capability of symbolizing symbols makes the adolescent's thought more flexible than that of the child. Words carry much more

An adolescent who is responsible for the maintenance of his car may use abstract mental skills in considering all possible reasons for the car's not starting, but may not apply the same skills in solving a physics or algebra problem.

meaning because they can now take on double meanings. The adolescent can understand metaphor and double entendre.

He or she can also produce many more concepts in response to verbal stimuli, as compared with what was possible during childhood. This ability allows the adolescent to make his or her own thought an object; that is, he or she can now introspect and reflect upon his or her own mental and personality traits (Elkind 1981).

Formal Operational Thinking

Piaget (1972) acknowledged that an individual may not reach formal operational thinking if he or she does not interact with individuals who engage in abstract and logical thinking, or if he or she is not part of a school experience in which formal operational thinking is required. Concrete operational reasoning persists even in mature adults. Not all normal adults attain formal operational reasoning. But the fact that individuals do not perform at a higher level does not mean they are incapable of doing so (Neimark, 1982)

An adolescent who purchases a "clunker" automobile and is required to assume the maintenance responsibilities may learn about the various functions of each part of the car in order to repair it. If the car breaks down, he or she uses abstract mental skills to consider all possible reasons for the car's not starting. But the same adolescent may not use the same capabilities in solving a physics or algebra problem. Much depends on individual interest and depth of knowledge in these areas. A particular person may or may not be able to think abstractly in given areas.

Adolescent Egocentrism

Egocentrism is a developmental term. It suggests that the individual has not yet made some differentiations that he or she will eventually make. Basically,

Adolescent egocentrism
Adolescent's failure to differentiate between their own mental preoccupations and what others are thinking.

adolescent egocentrism centers around thought and thinking. For the first time, adolescents can think about their own thinking and that of others. But their lack of experience in reflective thinking leads them into some characteristic egocentric errors (Elkind 1978). They fail to differentiate between objects that are the focus of other people's thoughts and objects that are the focus of their own concern. That is, they fail to differentiate between their own mental preoccupations and what others are thinking. Due to their physiological changes, they are primarily concerned with themselves. They assume that others are as obsessed as they are with their behavior and appearance (Elkind 1967, 1978, 1981).

According to Elkind (1978) the adolescent commits three egocentric errors. He or she has difficulty distinguishing between transient and abiding thoughts, the objective and the subjective, and the unique and the universal. The *inability to distinguish between transient and abiding thoughts* is illustrated when adopted children, during adolescence, make a great effort to find their biological parents. The search has many dynamic and intellectual components. The adolescent's curiosity about his or her biological parents is heightened by formal operational thinking, which makes an understanding of biological inheritance possible. However, it also makes the biological parents' emotional commitment appear to be *abiding* and the adoptive parents' emotional commitment to be more *transient*. Therefore, adopted adolescents sometimes fail to differentiate between biological and psychological parentage, although most emerge from this period with a fuller appreciation of the commitment of the adoptive parents.

Another example of the inability to distinguish between transient and abiding thoughts is the youngster who has been embarrassed among friends or acquaintances and is heard to say, "I can't see them ever again! My life is destroyed!" He or she assumes that a momentary embarrassment will live on permanently in other people's consciousness. Such an embarrassing experience that lives on in an adolescent's memory is called an "abiding moment." When the adolescent encounters the same people again under other circumstances, he or she is sure that the experience is as vivid in their memory as it is in his or her own. Usually this is not the case (Elkind 1978). The embarrassment is abiding to the young person but is usually transient to everyone else.

The second egocentric error committed by adolescents is the *inability to differentiate between the objective and the subjective*. An example is a well-known phenomenon of early adolescence: self-consciousness. Self-consciousness is derived from the failure to differentiate between the objective and the subjective in the realm of thought. Youngsters of this age are acutely aware of other people around them. Although they can think about other people's thinking, they do not differentiate between their personal concerns and preoccupations and those of other people. They are obsessed with their own bodies and minds. Because they cannot yet differentiate between the subjective content of their own thoughts and the objective content of the others' thoughts, they assume that others are as interested in and observant of them as they are of themselves (Elkind 1978).

The self-consciousness prevalent in a young adolescent encourages the construction of an **imaginary audience.** This audience of interested onlookers, the adolescent imagines, constantly monitors his or her appearance and behavior. In public, adolescents see themselves on stage, playing before a critical audience, which explains some of the boorish behavior of adolescents in public places. The imagined audience reflects the failure to distinguish between the objective and

Imaginary audience
An audience imagined by adolescents because they are self-conscious and feel they are the focus of attention.

Vandalism is a negative consequence motivated by an imaginary audience.

the subjective and has consequences other than self-consciousness as it becomes the motive for a variety of behaviors. Sports, music, and hobbies are taken up with these onlookers in mind. Many adolescents fantasize about performing before an audience as a concert pianist, pop singer, or star football player. The audience for these performances is important because young people need affirmation from the outside, since they cannot yet draw from past achievements for self-approval and support (Elkind 1978, 1981).

Often self-critical, adolescents are frequently self-admiring as well. To their way of thinking, the imaginary audience admires their loudness and faddish dress, which they themselves see as attractive. This explains why adolescents fail to understand adult disapproval of the way they dress or behave. The boy who stands in front of the mirror for two hours combing his hair is probably imagining reactions he will produce in girls. The girl who stands in front of the mirror applying makeup is probably imagining admiring glances that will come her way. When the two youngsters actually meet, each one is more concerned with being the observed than with being the observer. Gatherings of adolescents are unique because each individual is simultaneously the actor and the audience (Elkind 1981).

Vandalism is a negative consequence motivated by an imaginary audience. To adults, such behavior appears senseless and fruitless. The perpetrator, however, extracts an emotional gain from the reaction of the imaginary audience. Vandals are angry young people, and their anger is somewhat appeased when they imagine the anger of the adults who will witness the damage in the morning (Elkind 1981).

The third egocentric error of adolescents is the *inability to differentiate the unique from the universal,* the one from the many. The young adolescent experiencing feelings and ideas for the first time believes he or she is the first person on earth to do so. Elkind (1978, 1981) calls the belief in the uniqueness of one's

Personal fable

A belief in the uniqueness of one's feelings, thoughts, and experiences.

feelings, thoughts, and experiences the **personal fable.** It is a story that one tells oneself, and it is not true. For example, the young woman who falls in love for the first time is enraptured with her experience, which is new and thrilling. She fails to differentiate between what is new and thrilling to herself and what is new and thrilling to others. It is not surprising that she says something like, "But Mother, you don't know how it feels to be in love." Evidence of personal fables is found in adolescents' diaries, which often are written for posterity in the conviction that the young person's experiences, crushes, and frustrations are of universal significance.

The other side of the fable is the belief that what is unique to the individual is common to everyone. For example, an adolescent boy who has a slight blemish on his cheek may regard it as ugly and be convinced that everyone else shares his opinion. He has assumed that his personal evaluation is common to everyone and, consequently, feels negatively about himself.

The personal fable can have negative consequences if the sense of uniqueness contributes to reckless behavior. For example, it is not uncommon for adolescents to play "chicken" with cars ("others will get hurt and die, but not me") or experiment with drugs ("others will get hooked, but not me"). Similarly, adolescent girls who know about birth control may not take precautions because they are convinced that conception will happen to others but not to them. In each case the personal fable combines with other factors to produce the resulting behavior. In dealing with young people, one needs to take into account the personal fable as well as the other dynamics (Elkind 1978, 1981).

The personal fable can be a positive motivational force. The adolescent who feels unique may strive to excel in music, literature, sports, or other areas of endeavor. The sense of specialness can be a source of personal strength and comfort in the face of the many social and academic trials and tribulations of this period. Another result can be the tendency to confide in a personal God. The search for privacy and the belief in one's uniqueness can lead to establishing an I-Thou relationship with God as a personal confidant to whom one no longer looks for gifts but rather for guidance and support (Elkind 1979, 1981).

It is possible that the personal fable of adolescents differs according to socioeconomic class. There is evidence of differences in the aspiration level and other values held by different socioeconomic and subcultural groups (Looft 1971).

As adolescents discuss their personal "theories" with friends, inherent weaknesses in those theories are recognized by them. This is particularly true if they encounter other adolescents with personal theories quite different from their own. The realization dawns that others are more concerned with themselves and their own problems than they are with the adolescent and his or her problems. The adolescent's imaginary audience is gradually dispelled (Looft 1971). Elkind (1981) proposes that the personal fable is probably overcome by the progressive establishment of Erikson's "intimacy." Once they see themselves more realistically, as a function of having adjusted their imaginary audience to the real audience, adolescents can establish true rather than self-interested interpersonal relations. They then can discover that others have feelings similar to their own and have also been enraptured and have suffered in the same way.

Formal operational thought, in conjunction with the individual's interaction in the social world, leads to the dissolution of adolescent egocentrism (Looft 1971). The egocentrism tends to decrease by the age of fifteen or sixteen, when formal operations become firmly established. The adolescent gradually comes to recognize the difference between his or her own preoccupations and interests and the concerns of others (Elkind 1981).

Moral Development

Cognitive advancement is a major determinant in the advancement of moral judgment. Kohlberg and Piaget claim that development in Piaget's stages of cognitive development and in role-taking is a necessary prerequisite to moral thinking; that is, an individual cannot reach higher stages of moral judgment without being able to perform certain Piagetian logical operations and certain role-taking operations.

Eisenberg and her colleagues (Eisenberg et al. 1983; Eisenberg 1987; Eisenberg and Miller 1987) also found that as children mature they develop a greater capacity for abstract thinking and role-taking. These abilities result in qualitative changes in the children's reasoning about moral issues, including the ability to understand abstract moral principles related to the perspectives of others and society. High school students can verbalize abstract moral principles, and they reflect affective reactions (such as guilt or positive affect) related to living up to one's principles. They are also capable of self-reflective empathic reasoning (Eisenberg 1982).

The processes of cognitive and moral development are intertwined with those of identity. Principled moral reasoning (see Chapter 10 for an explanation of Kohlberg's levels and stages of moral development), formal operational thought, and identity achievement are positively related. Those whose identity status is diffuse tend to show preconventional moral thought. Moral functioning suggests adjustment of the individual to the social world. This adjustment serves the dual purpose of fitting a person to his or her society and contributing to the maintenance and perpetuation of that society. Moral development appears to be the core component of human adaptation and societal survival (Lerner and Shea 1982).

A phenomenon related to adolescent development involves the individual's attempt to find a role in society. This search requires the ability to try to see the world from the perspective of alternative roles. Perspective-taking seems to be as much involved in the search for adolescent identity as it is in overcoming egocentrism and hence moving to higher levels of formal thinking and principled morality (Lerner and Shea 1982).

Gilligan (1982), as discussed in Chapter 10, has pointed out that males and females differ psychologically in ways that affect their moral reasoning. According to Gilligan, women are more attuned to relationships between people, they take much of their personal identity from their personal relationships, and they are more likely to be morally concerned with how people are connected, interdependent, and obligated to one another. Gilligan sees men as being more attuned to individual achievement. Their personal identity is taken from their work, and they are likely to be morally concerned with justice and individual rights.

Gibbs, Arnold, and Burkhart (1984) found no sex differences in the stages of moral reasoning of adolescents around age eleven or twelve, but girls were twice as likely as boys to justify their stage-3 moral judgments and to show empathy in taking another person's position. In a sample of college students, Lifton (1985) found no sex differences in Kohlberg's stages of moral development, although there were differences between students who were judged as masculine or feminine on a scale of traditional gender-role attitudes. Masculine students reasoned at higher levels on Kohlberg's dilemmas than did feminine students. It appears that gender is subtly related to moral reasoning in a complex way.

Piaget emphasizes that the stage of moral development is influenced by the environment, including family and peers, as well as by the stage of cognitive development. Family interaction patterns have been found to be an influence. Haan et al. (1968) found that in young men (college students) intense family conflict, especially with the father, is associated with preconventional thinking. The least conflict was found with conventional thinkers. A moderate level of conflict existed for those with principled reasoning. In young women, increased conflict with the mother was associated with higher moral reasoning. Other studies have found that younger adolescents (ages eleven and twelve), especially girls, show higher levels of moral reasoning when they have a warm relationship with their same-sex parent. Girls who were honest and had a high level of altruism also had warm, intimate interaction with their mother and high self-esteem (Mussen et al. 1970). Hoffman (1970, 1975) found that differences in moral orientation in this age-group were related not to the parents' moral orientation but to their discipline and affection patterns.

Social interactions with peers may advance moral development. Whereas power differences between parents and children may hinder the reciprocal and mutual interactions involved in decentered, morally principled thinking, adolescents' interactions with their peers, who are equal to them, may provide the context necessary to facilitate moral development (Lerner and Shea 1982).

What role does religion play in the moral development of the adolescent? Many denominations regard this period as a time of "awakening," when the young person is ripe for religious conversion. The rites of confirmation, bar mitzvah and bas mitzvah, and other forms of introduction into adult religious privileges represent an acknowledgment of the adolescent's transition from childhood to responsible adulthood.

Religion may prevent the adolescent from feeling alienated and may inhibit deviant behavior by censuring unconventional conduct. Adolescents who report greater church attendance and stronger religious beliefs appear to make more rigid moral judgments than do their less religious peers (Frazier 1969; Lee and Clyde 1974). One study suggests that involvement in religion places adolescents in a conventional atmosphere that insulates them from problem behavior by reinforcing their existing personal controls. It has been found that adolescents who report more political activism, premarital sexual behavior, marijuana use, or general deviant behavior are less likely to be religious (Rohrbaugh and Jessor 1975).

James W. Fowler (1976) has examined stages of religious faith and finds that at around eighteen or nineteen years, many persons enter the *individuating-reflexive* stage. For the first time, they must take responsibility for their own commitments, life-style, beliefs, and attitudes. Certain polar tensions previously avoided must now be faced: individuality versus belonging to a community, subjectivity versus objectivity, self-fulfillment versus service to others, the relative versus the absolute. This stage often develops under the sponsorship of charismatic leadership or ideologies of other kinds that tend to collapse the polar tensions in one direction or another. It also brings a qualitatively new kind of self-awareness and responsibility for one's choices. This stage corresponds closely with Kohlberg's postconventional level of morality. It appears that the same developmental, experiential, and situational factors underlie both stages. The transitions to postconventional morality and individuating-reflexive faith occur at roughly the same age, and in both cases there is an advance from conventionality to individual responsibility. (Many people do not make this transition at all.)

Humor

During the adolescent years, humor is both an index of growth and a source of change. Adolescents employ humor to master the developmental tasks induced by the onset of puberty and the expectations of society. The three predominant developmental tasks include coming to terms with physical-sexual maturation, making identity decisions, and making vocational choices. Humor during adolescence may have adaptive and developmental significance. It provides a process whereby physical-sexual changes that produce anxiety can be dealt with according to the adolescent's own timetable. The humor of young adolescents (thirteen-year-olds) reflects reality testing of new cognitive abilities. Middle adolescents (age sixteen), who are in the midst of or near the completion of accepting sexual maturity, appreciate sexual humor more than do younger and older adolescents (Prerost 1980). Jokes and cartoons that match their developmental maturity are seen as funny, whereas those that are too advanced are seen as threatening. Older adolescents (nineteen-year-olds) are concerned about identity decisions that involve vocation, education, and companionship. Their humor preferences relate to these areas (Simons et al. 1986).

During late childhood and early adolescence, predilections for particular types of humor begin to be firmly established. After stage 4 (see Chapter 9), individual differences in patterns of humor appreciation become more prominent than any other changes related to the child's age or developmental level. Greater intellectual challenge is offered by more sophisticated jokes, whose true nature is somewhat disguised. The child's general progress in cognitive development determines how sexual and hostile ideas are expressed through humor (McGhee 1979).

Irony, a more abstract form of reality-based incongruity, cannot be appreciated until early adolescence and the beginning of formal operational thought. It is not uncommon for events in everyday living to turn out the opposite of what is expected, and adolescents see such situations as incongruous. As in earlier forms of humor related to real incongruities, the humor of irony results from the fact that something that should not have occurred (although its occurrence was possible) has happened. The humor of irony is usually further fueled by related embarrassments or awkward situations accompanying the unexpected reversal of events. Of course, humor will be seen in such situations only if the person is able to see the light side, that is, to approach the situations in a playful frame of mind (McGhee 1979 1986).

Compared with children, adolescents develop more sophisticated forms of humor and tend to favor anecdotes and spontaneous wit rather than memorized jokes, but the characteristics of stage-4 humor remain to some extent into adulthood (McGhee 1979). For adolescents, anecdotes replace riddles, and comic mimicry becomes a major component of joke telling (Wolfenstein 1954).

By adolescence, individual differences in a sense of humor, which are so evident among adults, are already well formed. The critical analysis and sensitivity with which adolescents approach friends and themselves have counterparts in their humorous attitude. There is a growing tendency of the majority to "reflect on why they laugh, and of a minority (especially among the girls) to deprecate laughter that is unfeeling" (Kappas 1967). Sometimes a sense of humor is directed toward parents or teachers, sometimes toward peers. Adolescents are just as likely, however, to be able to express mild, good-natured sarcasm or to turn their humor against themselves in a kidding way. They have achieved enough objectivity to be able to laugh at themselves occasionally (Kappas 1967).

Among peers, adolescents' humorous behavior consists primarily of joking insults, ridicule, and a considerable amount of loud, corny humor in public places. Practical jokes, previously very popular, now begin to lose appeal. Although humor dealing with forbidden ideas and subjects is prevalent, particularly among boys, it is not as common as it was earlier in group situations or mixed company.

Adolescents generally have definite preferences for certain forms of humorous literature. They rank the literature of absurdity first, slapstick second, satire third, and whimsy fourth. As they grow older, there is evidence of an increasing appreciation of satire and whimsy and a slight decrease in the enjoyment of absurdity. The level of maturity seen in the adolescent's capacity for logical thinking, verbal comprehension, and word fluency finds an outlet in greater appreciation for verbal wit. From this age on, verbal wit and humor will become increasingly dominant (Kappas 1967).

During childhood, the more creative individuals are viewed by their peers as having a better sense of humor. Fabrizi and Pollio (1987) found, however, that although older adolescents (eleventh graders) with a good sense of humor were more creative than their peers, younger adolescents (seventh graders) who had a sense of humor were neither the most creative nor the most self-satisfied among their peers (they had low self-concepts). Humorous eleventh graders were creative and self-assured. Fisher and Fisher (1981) reported similar findings. By adolescence, the more creative individuals attach greater importance to having a sense of humor than do their less creative peers. Creative individuals generally are more appreciative of humor, can understand it better, initiate it more often, and can produce funnier material than their peers (McGhee 1979).

Adolescents are poised on the edge of the adult world, and the level of development of their humor reflects this precarious balance.

S U M M A R Y

- Adolescence marks a great increase in body size and strength as well as a change in many physiological functions, including new reproductive capabilities. Definite differences are observable in males and females.
- The difference between puberty and adolescence is that the former is an event and the latter is a period of time.
- Many changes constitute puberty, including a growth spurt due to skeletal, fat, and muscle growth; development of the circulatory and respiratory systems; and development of the gonads, reproductive organs, and secondary sex characteristics.
- Motor skills undergo a change during adolescence, widening the athletic differences between the girls and boys.
- Due to the secular trend, today's adolescents are taller, heavier, and more sexually mature than their ancestors were during adolescence. Various environmental and hereditary factors account for this trend.

Adolescent Homosexuality

Although the majority of adolescents are attracted to individuals of the opposite sex, some wish for sexual relations with those of the same sex. Only 15 percent of adolescent boys and 10 percent of adolescent girls report ever having had a homosexual experience, and only 3 percent of adolescent boys and 2 percent of adolescent girls report on ongoing homosexual preference. Homosexual contacts are most frequent before age fifteen and are more likely to occur between boys than between girls (Dreyer 1982). Boys typically have their first homosexual relationship with an older boy or man at age eleven or twelve. Girls are more likely to have their first homosexual experience with another girl between the ages of six and ten (Bell et al. 1981). About 66 percent of adolescents interviewed in one study approved, in principle, of homosexual contacts (defined as petting, including touching and fondling of genitals and kissing in various forms) (Haas 1979). In another study, 75 percent indicated that homosexuality was all right for someone else but not for them (Bell et al. 1981).

It appears that that rate of homosexuality among adolescents has not changed since the early 1950s (Dreyer 1982). As a result of the AIDS epidemic, however, older homosexual adolescents have changed their behavior; either they no longer are sexually active, or they lessen the risk by using condoms (Morin et al. 1984; Carroll 1988).

There is little agreement about what factors lead to homosexuality. The psychoanalytic theory implicates the parent-child relationship and focuses on the inability of the adolescent to resolve the Oedipal dilemma with the opposite-sex parent. Other theories blame an overly protective and domineering mother and an ineffectual father. All of the above theories appear to be inaccurate as well as simplistic, since many heterosexuals come from similar family patterns. The social learning view argues that homosexuality reflects a rewarding and satisfying sexual experience between two people of the same sex, so the preference for same-sex sex partners is a conditioned behavior (Dreyer 1982).

The reality is probably a complex interaction of biological, psychological, and sociological factors. Biological factors, such as early hormonal events, may predispose a child to behave in a certain way that elicits certain reactions from parents and others. For example, a boy might behave in a feminine way that elicits hostility and rejection from his father, which in turn makes the child not wish to identify with this masculine model.

Whatever their sexual orientation, adolescents need to realize that healthy sexuality is not shameful but is an integral part of life, related to a person's role as student, worker, mate, friend, and family member. This is true for the heterosexual adolescent as well as the homosexual adolescent (Chilman 1990). Chilman (1990) states that the definition of healthy sexuality does *not* include the concept of "complete freedom to behave as one wishes so long as contraceptives, including condoms, are used and so long as this behavior is in private with consenting partners" (p. 124). She challenges the notion that "recreational sex" is permissible as long as it does not become "procreational sex." Her objection is that recreational sex, whether homosexual or heterosexual, trivializes the depth and meaning of intimacy and the involvement of the total self through intercourse.

Seeking a healthy sexual identity can be difficult for any adolescent, but it is especially traumatic for the homosexual youth. The most serious problem homosexual young people face is isolation, which can take three forms: cognitive, social, and emotional. *Cognitive isolation* reflects the lack of information available to the gay or lesbian adolescent. It leads to a lack of preparation for managing social identity. The gay or lesbian has no opportunity to discover what it means to be homosexual and cannot plan or even conceive of a future for himself or herself (Hetrick and Martin 1985). This kind of isolation also results from misinformation and stigmatization. Through society gay and lesbian adolescents receive information stating that homosexuals are predatory, cannot form stable intimate relationships, are criminals, hate the opposite sex, are immature, are pathological, and so forth. Such charges can be devastating to the naive, developing adolescent's sense of self (Martin and Hetrick 1988).

Social isolation is the result of self-loathing and the disdain of others. A social identity involves a set of expectations about what a person should do. A social identity as a homosexual is so stigmatized that it can lead the adolescent to deny other social roles for which he or she has been socialized. For example, a young Christian is told that one cannot be homosexual and a Christian (Baker 1985). A gay adolescent who has been discovered or who is clearly effeminate faces reactions ranging from public humiliation to violent attack. Youngsters handle this mistreatment through truancy, withdrawal from church and school activities and from family and friends, and/or exaggeration

Continued

Adolescent Homosexuality
(continued)

of stigmatized behavior, such as inappropriate mannerisms for their sex, cross-dressing, and inappropriate acting out (Martin and Hetrick 1988). Social isolation also may lead to promiscuity, especially among gay males (Martin 1982). Adolescents who are discovered are pushed by parents, counselors, health professionals, and religious zealots to change or deny their orientation.

Emotional isolation is so traumatic that approximately 20 percent of adolescent gay males attempt suicide (Martin and Hetrick 1988; Bell and Weinberg 1978; Saghir and Robins 1973). In the client population of one social service agency for homosexual adolescents (Hetrick and Martin 1988), 95 percent of the clients experienced feelings of being alone, of being "the only one who feels that way," and of "having no one to share feelings with." They all indicated they would like to have someone gay to talk to, especially an adult gay person. Clinical depression is an indicator of emotional isolation. The signs include feelings of sadness, loss of pleasure, sleep disturbance, slowing of thought, low self-esteem, increased self-criticism and self-blame, and strong feelings of guilt and failure (Martin and Hetrick 1988).

- Body image is the core of the adolescent's overall self-image. The adolescent who is an early or late maturer, is obese, or has anorexia nervosa or bulimia has a unique perception of his or her body and, consequently, a unique self-image.

- The final stage of cognitive development, according to Piaget, is formal operational thought. The stage is divided into two sub-stages: III–A and III–B. The former is preparatory and the latter is more abstract. Some of the capabilities of formal operational thought include abstract thinking, combinatorial logic, contrary-to-fact propositions, thinking about thinking, and a second symbol system. Not every adolescent or adult functions at a formal operational level.

- Adolescent egocentrism is based on the capacity to take account of other people's thought. The adolescent commits three egocentric errors: the inability to distinguish between transient and abiding thoughts, the objective and subjective, and the unique and the universal. These errors lead to the construction of the imaginary audience and the personal fable.

- The adolescent who is capable of formal operational thought is also capable of being at the principled level of moral reasoning. These capacities correlate with identity formation. Moral development is also related to family interaction patterns and religious beliefs.

- Humor is essentially a cognitive event. Because of the ability to think at a formal operational level, adolescents can appreciate irony. They also develop more sophisticated forms of humor and tend to favor anecdotes and spontaneous wit rather than memorized jokes.

- Although the majority of adolescents are attracted to individuals of the opposite sex, some wish for sexual relations with those of the same sex. There is little agreement about what pattern of factors leads to homosexuality. Recreational sex, whether among heterosexuals or homosexuals, is not considered healthy sex. Homosexual adolescents are isolated from peers, family, and other support systems. Both homosexual adolescents and heterosexual adolescents need support from others in helping them with their sexuality.

Brooks-Gunn, J., and Petersen, A. (Eds.) (1983). *Girls at puberty.* New York: Plenum.

Collection of writings concerning the role of puberty in the psychological life of girls by authorities in adolescent development.

Coles, R., and Stokes, G. (1985). *Sex and the American teenager.*

Explanation by teens on how they feel about their sexuality and sexual behavior.

Early adolescent sexuality: Resources for parents, professionals, and young people. (1983) Chapel Hill, NC: Center for Early Adolescence, University of North Carolina.

Annotated bibliography of variety of subjects related to sexuality in early adolescence.

C H A P T E R

12

O U T L I N E

Introduction
Personality Development
   Theories
Emotional and Social Development
   Emotional Development
   Socialization
● Critical Issues: The Transition to Junior
  High
Summary
● Critical Issues: Teen Employment
Readings

O B J E C T I V E S

When you have mastered the material in this chapter, you should be able to do the following:

1. Describe the three major routes through the adolescent period.
2. Describe Erikson's stage of identity versus role confusion; discuss identity diffusion, negative identity, foreclosure, and moratorium.
3. Describe social learning theory's perception of adolescence.
4. Describe the factors that make an impact on adolescents' self-esteem.
5. Describe the factors that influence the use of drugs among adolescents.
6. Describe the two types of delinquency.
7. Describe the factors that contribute to an adolescent suicide.
8. Discuss the sexual behavior of adolescents and the factors that have contributed to the increase in adolescent pregnancy.
9. Discuss reasons why adolescents run away.
10. Discuss the influence of peers and parents on the adolescent's socialization process.
11. Discuss how the community can help adolescents, especially those at risk, to develop life skills.

The Transition Years: Adolescence-Psychosocial Development

The psychological move from childhood to adulthood is long and complicated. The major goal is to attain meaningful independence, which involves going through variable degrees and kinds of rebellion. Painful states and even depression may be expected parts of the adolescent experience, but so are the perception of life at new levels and the anticipation of new challenges. The adolescent is interested in changing in order to take advantage of the opportunities of the adult world.

Three major models of "growth" development for the adolescent have been identified (Lerner and Shea 1982; Offer 1969): *Continuous growth* is a series of smooth and nonabrupt changes in behavior. Adolescents with continuous growth are not in any major conflict with their parents, do not feel that parental rearing practices are inappropriate, and do not see parental values as different from their own. Most adolescents fall into this category. *Surgent growth* implies an abrupt spurt, similar to the distinct transition in cultures that have puberty or fertility rites. This type of change does not necessarily involve turmoil. Crisis, stress, and problems characterize the *tumultuous growth* model of adolescent development. Only some adolescents experience this type of growth, and for a short period. The greatest amount of turmoil occurs between ages twelve and fourteen.

Personality development can be divided between early and late adolescence because of the differences between the central tasks of each phase. The physiological and bodily changes associated with puberty are major factors in understanding the personality of the early adolescent. This is when "storm and stress" are more obvious (Berzonsky 1982). After they adjust to the bodily and physiological changes, they then must contend with the critical developmental task of late adolescence: the consolidation of identity. The early adolescent, therefore, begins to experience the self in ways vastly different from during the childhood years. The late adolescent focuses on the issues related specifically to finding himself or herself socially, morally, politically, occupationally, sexually, and personally (Siegel 1982).

● PERSONALITY DEVELOPMENT

Theories

Erikson's Psychosocial Theory

Adolescence has been characterized by Erikson as a period when the individual must establish a sense of personal identity and avoid the dangers of role confusion. Adolescents begin defining themselves in terms of social, sexual, and occupational identities. As they struggle to do so, they may have an ill-defined concept of their role. **Identity,** which is a sense of sameness and continuity, must be searched for and acquired through sustained individual efforts. It involves a quest for personal discovery of "who I am" and a growing understanding of the meaning of one's existence. If the adolescent fails in the search for an identity, then self-doubt and role confusion will result. **Role confusion** is the bewilderment adolescents feel in wondering who they are, where they belong, and where they are going. Many of today's youth feel incapable of assuming the socially accepted role expected of American adolescents. They may run away literally or in other ways, such as by dropping out of school,

Identity
A sense of sameness and continuity that is sought after by adolescents. It involves a quest for personal discovery of "who I am" and a growing understanding of one's existence.

Role confusion
The bewilderment adolescents feel in wondering who they are, where they belong, and where they are going.

leaving their job, staying out all night, or withdrawing into bizarre and inaccessible moods. Erikson proposes that a certain amount of bewilderment is necessary because finding oneself too soon might limit the exploration of alternative roles and foreclose potential life experiences.

Adolescents are sometimes morbidly preoccupied with what they appear to be in the eyes of others (adolescent egocentrism) compared with what they feel they are. In searching for a new sense of continuity and sameness, some adolescents have to come to grips again with the crises of earlier years. The earliest stage of an identity crisis involves the need to trust in oneself and others. Adolescents look for people and ideas in which to have faith. At the same time, they are afraid of looking foolish and making too trusting a commitment, and consequently they may express a loud and cynical mistrust.

The adolescent is seeking avenues of duty and service but at the same time feels self-doubt and fears ridicule. He or she would rather act shamelessly in the eyes of elders, out of free choice, than be forced into activities that would be shameful in his or her own eyes or in those of peers (Erikson 1968).

Achieving identity also means learning where one stands in relationship to others. This is **social identity,** and it can be found only through interaction with other people. The adolescent goes through a period of compulsive peer group conformity to test various roles and see whether and how they fit. The peer group, the clique, and the gang help the individual by providing both role models and direct feedback. Adolescents can be remarkably cruel, clannish, and intolerant in excluding those who are "different" in social class, skin color, cultural background, tastes, and even petty aspects of dress and gesture. Such intolerance may be a temporary necessity to defend against a sense of identity loss or identity confusion. Adolescents temporarily help one another through discomfort by forming cliques and by stereotyping themselves, their ideals, and their enemies. They also test one another's capacity for sustaining loyalty and pledging fidelity in the midst of an inevitable conflict of values (Erikson 1963, 1968).

Some of the activities common to adolescents, such as telephoning, dancing, "hanging out," and driving around, share several important elements. The

Adolescents begin defining themselves in terms of social, sexual, and occupational identities.

Social identity
Where one stands in relationship to others; an identity found through interaction with other people.

telephone is a bridge between the adolescent and the world outside of the family, between the adolescent and an identity other than that of a child. "Hanging out" is a favored pastime of adolescents in places they discover and can claim as their own. Telephoning, dancing, and driving around provide a means of discharging sexual and aggressive feelings and tensions in a rather safe setting. The activities also serve as important self-esteem regulating functions; they provide socially acceptable means of obtaining narcissistic gratification, of feeling important, and of being the master of inner drives as well as external reality (Siegel 1982).

Sexuality is a cornerstone of identity, and adolescent sexual exploration is the means by which this aspect develops and crystallizes (Siegel 1982). The development of **sexual identity** proceeds from self-centered sexual preoccupations in early adolescence to mutual sexual relationships in late adolescence. Younger adolescents are absorbed with the bodily changes of puberty and with accompanying sexual excitement and curiosity. Their investigations of sexuality tend to be focused on their own body but can take many forms, including exploration of books and magazines, sexually explicit and exciting conversations with peers, mutual masturbation with a friend of the same sex, and heterosexual experimentation. Masturbation is rather common during early adolescence, and it is estimated that 50 to 80 percent of boys and 33 percent of girls have masturbated by age fifteen (Siegel 1982).

Adolescents must establish ego-identity and accept their pubescent bodily changes and sexual changes as part of themselves. They experience psychological strain when seeking intimacy, whether in friendships, competition, sex play, arguments, or gossip. Friendships take on an exploitative nature in that the choice of friends appears to be founded on an egocentric need for self-definition and self-interest rather than on a mutuality of concerns and interests.

During adolescence, falling in love is an attempt to define one's identity by projecting one's self-image onto the self-image of the other person. Those who are not sure of their identity shy away from interpersonal intimacy or throw themselves into acts of intimacy that are promiscuous. "The increment of identity is based on the formula 'we are what we love' " (Erikson 1968, 138). When maturing in their physical capacity for procreation, young people are unable to love in the binding manner that only two persons with reasonably formed identities can love each other, and they are unable to care consistently enough to take on the role of parenthood (Erikson 1968). Intimacy, mutuality, and love in a sustaining relationship are developmental tasks for later years (Erikson 1968; Siegel 1982).

One primary concern of adolescents is the unsettled question of *occupational, or vocational, identity*. They hold glamorized and idealized conceptions of their vocational goals, and it is not uncommon for goal aspirations to be higher than the individual's ability warrants. Goals frequently chosen—such as being a movie hero, a rock musician, an athletic champion, or a car racer—are attainable for only a select few. Adolescents temporarily overidentify with the heroes of cliques and crowds to the point of apparent loss of individuality (Erikson 1968).

Adolescence is least difficult or "stormy" for youth who are gifted and well-trained in today's technological trends, such as computers. These adolescents are more able to identify with new roles of competency and invention that are necessary in our contemporary technological and informational age (Siegel 1982).

Role Diffusion   When one is unwilling to work on one's own identity formation, the danger of **role diffusion** arises, and the result may be alienation

Sexual identity
Identity that proceeds from self-centered sexual preoccupations in early adolescence to mutual sexual relationships in late adolescence.

Role diffusion
Alienation and a lasting sense of isolation and confusion.

Adolescence is least difficult or "stormy" for youth who are gifted and well-trained in today's technological skills, such as using computers.

and a lasting sense of isolation and confusion. Role diffusion can be expressed in various forms, including *identity diffusion* and *negative identity*. The adolescent with a **diffused identity** has no apparent personal commitment to occupation, religion, or politics. An identity crisis has not been experienced related to these issues, which means that an active struggle has not occurred in terms of reevaluating, searching, and considering alternatives. Erikson points out that this is not a diagnostic problem but a developmental one. Nevertheless, it is easy for the public to label such a youngster as a delinquent. Once this occurs, it is imperative that significant others (such as older friends, advisers, and judiciary personnel) refuse to typecast him or her by using pat diagnoses and social judgments that do not recognize the changes and conditions unique to the stages of adolescence. Prolonged stagnation in the stage of identity diffusion may lead to personality disintegration, which in turn may lead to schizophrenia or suicide (Erikson 1968; Marcia 1980).

Diffused identity
No apparent personal commitment to occupation, religion, or politics.

Another danger is that the adolescent will make a **negative identity** choice. In a sense, the adolescent chooses to resolve matters by a premature closure of adolescence. Erikson describes a negative identity as one "perversely based on all those identifications and roles which, at critical stages of development, had been presented . . . as most undesirable or dangerous" (Erikson 1968, 174). For some adolescents, being "nobody" or totally bad, or even dead—as long as it is felt that the decision is one's own—is preferable to having no identity at all, that is, to being "not quite somebody" (Marcia 1966, 1980).

Negative identity
A premature closure of adolescence; undesirable and dangerous.

Foreclosure Some adolescents adopt a premature identity and do not explore all those available. This is called **foreclosure.** Adolescents who experience foreclosure do not undergo a crisis. Although they have made commitments to

Foreclosure
An adolescent's choosing a premature identity, not exploring all of the identities that are available.

Moratorium
A state in which the adolescent is exploring and actively searching for alternatives and struggling to find an identity.

Identity-achieved adolescent
The adolescent who has experienced a psychological moratorium and resolved crises on his or her own terms.

goals and values, an occupation, and a personal ideology, these commitments are not of their own choosing and are not a result of their own searching and exploring. They are determined by others, usually parents or peers. The personality structure shows a certain rigidity. If preprogrammed assumptions and values are not challenged, then foreclosure may become a permanent part of the adolescent's personality structure and he or she may remain dependent on others throughout life (Marcia 1966, 1980).

Moratorium The word *moratorium* means "a period of delay granted to somebody who is not yet ready to meet an obligation or make a commitment" (Erikson 1968, 157). The adolescent **moratorium** represents a state in which the adolescent is exploring and actively searching for alternatives and struggling to find an identity (Marcia 1966). Erikson (1963) believes the adolescent mind is essentially in a state of moratorium. If the adolescent actively searches, experiments, plays the field, and tries on different roles, he or she has a good chance of developing an identity and emerging with commitments to politics, religion, and a vocational career. Moratorium is seen by Erikson as prerequisite for identity achievement (Marcia 1966).

The **identity-achieved adolescent** has experienced a psychological moratorium and resolved crises on his or her own terms. Advanced cognitive performance is associated with advanced identity status. This relation suggests that generally a greater level of adaptive functioning is associated with achieving an identity. Identity achievers have a higher internal locus of control (Marcia 1980). As a result of resolving their crises, identity-achieved adolescents have made personal commitments to an occupation, a religious belief, and a personal value system, and they have resolved their attitudes toward sexuality. Individuals who have attained an identity feel in harmony with themselves. They accept their capacities, limitations, and opportunities (Erikson 1968).

Social Learning Theory

The social learning theory, or sociobehavioristic approach of Bandura (1977, 1985), does not view adolescence as a separate stage with unique characteristics and requiring theoretical explanations. The sociobehavioristic approach implies that the principles of learning that help explain child development are also applicable to adolescent development. The differences that do exist at the various age levels are due to sociocultural expectations, and adolescents choose different models than children do. Bandura and Walters (1959) found that adolescent boys imitate one another in making sexual advances and are more likely to engage in sexual intercourse when double- and multiple-dating. It appears that when behavior patterns are inhibited, observing a model perform that behavior removes personal inhibitions. Drug use by adolescents can be predicted by whether or not friends use drugs.

During the adolescent years, parents and teachers become less important models with regard to issues and choices that are of immediate consequence. Instead, the peer group and selected entertainment heroes assume more importance, especially if the parent-adolescent communication system breaks down. The peer group is especially influential in such areas as verbal expressions, hairstyle, clothing, food, music, and decisions related to the adolescent's changing social values. Problems that arise during adolescence may result from the individual imitating peers who are no more mature, knowledgeable, intelligent, or wise than he or she is.

Social learning theory perceives behavior within the context of social situations. The interrelationships between environmental and social changes are seen as causes, and behavioral changes are viewed as consequences rather than as a function of age. Descriptions and statements about adolescence are not of an all-encompassing nature. Unlike Erikson's theory of adolescents' resolving an identity crisis or Piaget's theory that adolescent thought processes begin to follow formal and abstract logic, social learning theory predicts relationships between external factors and behavior. Generally, the changes that occur during adolescence are not due to maturation but to sudden changes in social expectations, family structure, peer group interaction, or other environmental situations.

EMOTIONAL AND SOCIAL DEVELOPMENT

Emotional Development

Self-esteem

A positive self-concept is the cornerstone of emotional development. A sense of self is relatively stable over a period of time and refers to the whole person, that is, the ideas and feelings one has about one's own thoughts, body, appearance, and personal characteristics (Siegel 1982). The adolescent's over-evaluation of self is partially determined by efforts to gain emotional independence and a personal identity. Judgments of self influence one's view of others, and others may be defined in similar ways. For example, when boys have a positive attitude toward their father, they also have competent and warm relationships with their peers (Curtis 1975).

A temporary disturbance in self-esteem occurs during early adolescence, and girls have more difficulty at this time than boys do. This is consistent with findings that girls are generally more dissatisfied with their bodies and physical appearance than boys are. Older adolescents of both sexes have better self-images than do younger adolescents. They are less anxious and confused, more secure and comfortable with themselves than are younger adolescents (Siegel 1982). Gecas and Schwalbe (1986) found that adolescent boys' self-esteem was more strongly affected by self-attribution and by parental control through the granting of autonomy, while girls' self-esteem was more strongly affected by parental support, nurturance, and participation. They also found that fathers have a stronger influence on adolescents' self-esteem than do mothers.

Adolescents face the challenge of relinquishing parental ties and childhood identifications in order to establish a separate identity outside the family while still maintaining continuity of parental and familial relationships. To achieve identity, adolescents must find an orientation to life that fulfills the attributes of the self and is consistent with what society expects of a person (Lerner and Shea 1982; Siegel 1982).

Issues Associated with Adolescence

Due to their susceptibility to low self-esteem, their need to seek their own identity, and their egocentricity, adolescents quite often find themselves in many unfavorable situations that are linked to their stage of development.

Drug Abuse   A 1985 survey by the National Institute on Drug Abuse showed that 30 percent of sixteen thousand seniors had used illicit drugs and 65.9 percent had used alcohol in the month preceding the survey. The use of

● FIGURE 12.1

Age at Which Adolescents Began
Selected Behaviors
Age at which adolescent boys began
having sex and using alcohol and
marijuana.

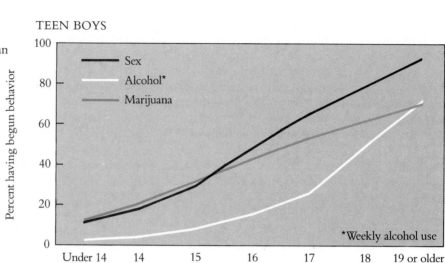

TEEN BOYS

Age at which adolescent girls began
having sex, became pregnant, and
began using alcohol and marijuana.

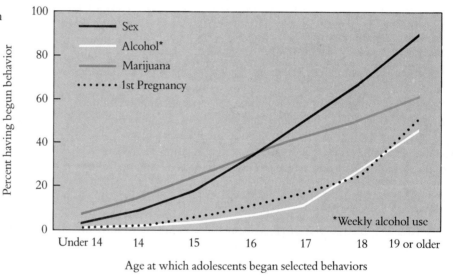

TEEN GIRLS

S.O.S. America! Children's Defense Budget. Washington, D.C.: Children's Defense Fund, 1990.

marijuana by students has steadily declined since 1978, when 10 percent of *all* high school seniors smoked marijuana. By 1986 the percentage had dropped by half (Matthews 1986; Thomas 1986).

Adolescents' ignorance of the effects of substance abuse is considerable, but providing information to them may inadvertently contribute to the problem; television publicity in particular has been found to increase such behavior as glue-sniffing (Dusek and Girdano 1987). One study (Hodgman 1983) found that peer disapproval contributed most, and parental disapproval contributed least, to the control of adolescent drinking behavior. Role models appropriate to the setting are essential in dealing effectively with the problem.

Recent findings suggest that American adolescents are not exceeding, or are decreasing, previous levels of substance abuse, with the exception of cocaine abuse. The use of opiates, inhalants, and hallucinogenic compounds by adolescents has dropped over the past decade, and there has been a corresponding decrease in drug-related hospitalizations (Dusek and Girdano 1987).

Many studies have established that adolescents who become involved in drugs hold less conventional values than nonusers do. Those who use marijuana, cocaine, or other illicit drugs are less religious, more delinquent, more liberal in political attitudes, more depressed, and lower in self-esteem than nonusers. They also are more likely to be involved in antisocial activities (Bachman et al. 1981; Brook et al. 1986; Dishion and Loeber 1985; Harlow et al. 1986; Huba and Bentler 1984; Johnston et al. 1986; Kaplan et al. 1984; Newcomb et al. 1986).

A growing body of literature dealing with adolescents demonstrates the importance of personality, peer, and family factors and their relation to adolescents' use of tobacco, alcohol, marijuana, and other illicit drugs. Mijuskovic (1988) found that feelings of separation anxiety, depression, and loneliness are contributing factors in teenage drinking disorders. He implies that drinking serves as an excuse to socialize with peers in a forbidden and romantic activity. It releases anxiety and social inhibitions. It permits the adolescent to experience the illusion of adult freedom by indulging in behavior that is falsely assumed to be free of insecurity in the adult.

According to Brook et al. (1983), drug use moves in stages: (1) nonuse; (2) use of legal drugs, such as tobacco and/or alcohol; (3) use of marijuana; and (4) use of illicit drugs other than marijuana. Drug use develops sequentially; that is, the drugs used later in the sequence depend on the drugs used earlier. The study also found that a general psychosocial propensity for drug use exists regardless of the adolescent's ethnic background or sex. Socialization experiences of adolescents as well as certain personality attributes are predisposing factors that contribute to the potency of drug models and imitation of those models. For example, there is a higher stage of drug use when both a lack of maternal positive reinforcement is present and the adolescent has friends who use drugs. In addition, the study found a correlation of adolescent unconventionality with lack of maternal warmth, which also results in a higher stage of drug use. Barnes et al. (1986) found that adolescent drinking can be explained in part by parental models. Parents who drink heavily are more likely to have adolescents who are heavy drinkers, whereas abstaining parents are more likely to have children who abstain.

Some adolescent athletes have the mistaken notion that moderate alcohol consumption improves their performance. To the contrary, alcohol is a depressant to the central nervous system, accentuates fatigue by increasing the production of lactate, slows reaction time, interferes with reflexes, and destroys coordination. The effect of alcohol on physical performance appears to be negative on all counts. Decreased performance has been reported thus far in tests of dynamic balance, visual tracking, arm steadiness, body sway, and various psychomotor tasks. The sensation related to alcohol is deceptively positive, as noted by one high school alcoholic: "I would drink before going to school, and I'd get to physical education class rarin' to go. But the coordination wasn't there. I *felt* I could perform better, but it was all in my head. In reality, I really performed worse" (Worthington-Roberts 1985).

Television has been criticized for sending mixed messages about alcohol and youth by either glamorizing or trivializing its use. DeFoe and Breed (1988) found that one of the most powerful ways television can teach about alcohol and youth is to use a young person as the intervention agent. Television can offer role models who are knowing, loved, and believable.

Cigarette smoking is reported to be the single largest preventable cause of death in the United States. Antismoking campaigns have significantly decreased adult smoking, but their success with adolescents has been questionable. Adolescents fail to personalize the long-term health hazards of smoking because these consequences are associated with adulthood and old age (Dusek and Girdano 1987).

Barton et al. (1982) found that early adolescents, especially sixth-grade girls, perceived smoking negatively. They saw smoking as unhealthy and foolish. This did not hold true for tenth graders. In this group the only significant correlations were found for social factors that represented positive incentives to smoke, such as interest in the opposite sex, wanting to be with the group, and relaxing. The most notable was interest in the opposite sex, which was significant for both boys and girls.

Barton et al. (1982) also found that sixth graders view drinking as very undesirable (less than 10 percent rated it as ideal), while tenth graders saw it as more desirable (about half rated it as ideal). Alcohol use, then, is regarded as a social liability in early adolescence but as a social asset in middle adolescence.

Family disruption can influence adolescent substance abuse. Flewelling and Bauman (1990), in a study of more than two thousand early adolescents, found that children of disrupted families are at a higher risk of *initiating* the use of controlled substances (including cigarettes, alcohol, and marijuana) and engaging in sexual intercourse than are children from nondisrupted families. This does not mean that these behaviors necessarily continue throughout life. Needle, Su, and Doherty (1990) found that adolescents who experienced parental divorce had greater overall drug involvement than did younger children who experienced parental divorce or adolescents who came from continuously married families. It also was found that the divorce had negative effects on boys but not on girls but that the custodial parent's remarriage led to increased substance abuse among girls and decreased use among boys. Substance abuse appears to be a strategy used by adolescents to cope with adverse circumstances associated with inadequate family structure or a lack of positive family relationships.

Delinquency Delinquency is more likely to occur during adolescence if there is a history of antisocial behavior during childhood. Approximately two-thirds of adolescent delinquents began their careers during preadolescence (Olweus 1979). Individuals age eighteen and younger account for about 20 percent of all violent crimes, 44 percent of all serious property crime arrests, and 39 percent of all overall serious crimes (Shannon 1982). Although the rate of juvenile crime is high, it has not risen since the mid-1970s (Chambers 1981).

Delinquency can be separated into two types: socialized and undersocialized. *Socialized delinquents* are psychologically intact but vulnerable to environmental influences. *Undersocialized delinquents* are exposed to more genetic, traumatic, and pervasive developmental hazards. The latter account for the largest proportion of delinquents. This group is particularly subject to problems with drugs and alcohol abuse, and there is likely to be a family history of depression or alcoholism. These adolescents have trouble thinking abstractly, concentrating, and putting things in temporal order. This pattern of abnormalities led investigators (Brickman et al. 1984) to conclude that delinquent adolescents have not developed the cognitive control to manage their feelings and moods. When combined with learning problems, it may be difficult for them to pay attention, deal with their feelings, or control their behavior and actions. Delinquents also have difficulty with role-taking or social perspective-taking. When they are trained in the latter, they are less likely to commit further crimes (Hains and Ryan 1983).

Patterson and Stouthamer-Loeber (1984) found that parents who supervised their sons, knew where they were, who their friends were, and what they were doing were less likely to have delinquent sons. Of the inadequately supervised boys, 80 percent were delinquent.

Boys and girls differ in age of onset, etiology, and kind of delinquency practiced. Four to seven times as many boys as girls become delinquent, but the ratio has shown a steady decline over the past fifty years (Quay 1982). Boys become delinquent at an earlier age than girls, probably because younger adolescent girls are more closely supervised. Also, sex offenses are the most frequent category of delinquency among girls and do not occur until an older age. The kinds of offenses committed differ by gender. The major misdemeanors committed by boys include stealing, mischief, traffic violations, truancy, and auto thefts. Both boys and girls are charged with running away from home (Gold and Reimer 1975).

Suicide   Closely connected with affective disturbances is suicidal behavior. Jacobs (1971, 3) says "the term suicide is applied to all cases of death resulting directly or indirectly from a positive or negative act of the victim himself, *which he knows will produce this result.*" Although most recent statistics suggest that trends toward higher adolescent suicide rates may not continue, overall rates, especially for older adolescent males, have shown a discouraging increase in recent years. Hodgman (1983) asserts that youngsters who attempt suicide are seriously deviant, but Ellis and Range (1989) point out that in many cases the suicidal act is a sudden impulsive reaction to a precipitating stressful situation. This impulsive quality is particularly characteristic of adolescents.

Feelings of separation anxiety, depression, and loneliness are contributing factors in teenage drinking disorders.

Suicide ranks as the third leading cause of death among adolescents and is exceeded only by accidents and homicide. In the United States, estimates are that more than 200,000 persons attempt suicide each year, and about 25,000 succeed; that is, the rate is 12 per 100,000 persons for the general population. More than 4,000 of the people who commit suicide each year in the United States are in the age-group fifteen to twenty-four years. Among adolescents, suicide rates vary considerably with age. The figure for early adolescents is less than .6 per 100,000; for middle adolescents, 4 per 100,000; and for late adolescents, 8.4 per 100,000. The greatest increase has been in the middle- and late-adolescent age-groups, for which the rate has almost doubled (U.S. Department of Commerce 1981).

Adolescents make more attempts per successful suicide than do adults. The ratio for adolescents has been estimated as high as 120:1 (more conservative estimates are 20:1), compared with an adult ratio of approximately 8:1. The college population has a ratio of 10:1. The significant number of attempts in the adolescent population is interpreted as a "cry for help" (Cantor 1985; Tishler et al. 1981).

Erikson (1968) points out that death and suicide can become a preoccupation with adolescents. They may not intend to commit suicide but may impulsively decide to do so. Social isolation is felt keenly by young people, and Ellis and Range (1989) note that the isolation from meaningful social relationships can lead to adolescent suicide attempts. They also point out that a chain reaction of dissolving meaningful social relationships often occurs in the days and weeks preceding an attempt, leading to the adolescent's feeling that he or she has

Suicide Note

ANONYMOUS

He always wanted to say things. But no one understood.
He always wanted to explain things. But no one cared.
So he drew.

Sometimes he would just draw and it wasn't anything.
He wanted to carve it in stone or write it in the sky.
He would lie out on the grass and look up in the sky and it would be only him and the sky and the things inside that needed saying.

And it was after that, that he drew the picture. It was a beautiful picture. He kept it under the pillow and would let no one see it.
And he would look at it every night and think about it. And when it was dark, and his eyes were closed he could still see it.
And it was all of him. And he loved it.

When he started to school he brought it with him. Not to show anyone but just to have with him like a friend.

It was funny about school.
He sat in a square, brown desk like all the other square brown desks and he thought it should be red.
And his room was a square, brown room. Like all the other rooms. And it was tight and close. And stiff.

He hated to hold the pencil and the chalk, with his arm stiff and his feet flat on the floor, stiff, with the teacher watching and watching.
And then he had to write numbers. And they weren't anything. They were worse than the letters that could be something if you put them together.
And the numbers were tight and square and he hated the whole thing.

The teacher came and spoke to him. She told him to wear a tie like all the other boys. He said he didn't like them and she said it didn't matter.
After that they drew. And he drew all yellow and it was the way he felt about morning. And it was beautiful.

The teacher came and smiled at him. "What's this?" she said. "Why don't you draw something like Ken's drawing? Isn't that beautiful?"
It was all questions.

After that his mother bought him a tie and he always drew airplanes and rocket ships like everyone else. And he threw the old picture away.
And when he lay out alone looking at the sky, it was big and blue and all of everything, but he wasn't anymore.

He was square inside and brown, and his hands were stiff, and he was like anyone else. And the thing inside him that needed saying didn't need saying anymore.

It had stopped pushing. It was crushed. Stiff.
Like everything else.

(This poem was written by a twelfth-grade boy shortly before he committed suicide.)

---

reached "the end of hope." The internal process by which people justify suicide to themselves enables them to bridge the gap between thought and action.

According to Rosenkrantz (1978) and Tishler, McKenry, and Morgan (1981), the most significant precipitating event in adolescent suicide seems to be the element of loss: for example, death of, desertion by, or separation from a significant other; loss of love and intimacy; or an adolescent's interpretation of loss in terms of his or her identity and self-worth. Most studies have found that the death or loss of one or more significant persons in an adolescent's life produces the predisposition toward suicide. Of those committing suicide, 50 percent come from dysfunctional homes, characterized by disorganization, parental disharmony, cruelty, and abandonment. Such conditions breed feelings of inadequacy and poor self-worth. Not being understood, appreciated, or cared for by the family is a consistently common factor in the case histories of suicidal youth. Such a home environment is not likely to provide the ego development, identity formation, and intimacy necessary to resolve the adjustment problems of adolescence. Destructive parental attitudes, such as rejection, can contribute to negative identity. At least half of the parents of suicidal adolescents convey the attitude that their children are burdensome and they wish the youngsters had not been born.

Less serious suicidal behaviors, such as threats and gestures, occur more frequently when loss is not permanent, such as in separation. In contrast, parental death is the most closely related factor to a completed suicide. In one study, a significantly high proportion of seriously suicidal college students had lost a parent (Kastenbaum 1986).

It is estimated that as many as half of all suicides are disguised as accidents; therefore, adolescent suicide attempts and completions are likely to be underestimated for this age-group.

Most studies show that suicidal behavior increases in the spring. For the college population, the greatest incidence is at the beginning or end of a school semester (Rosenkrantz 1978).

A study by Phillips (1977) reported that the number of U.S. suicides increases after a suicide is publicized. This increase occurs only after the suicide story is published, and the more publicity given to the story, the greater the increase in suicides. There is a suicidal component in motor vehicle fatalities, and these increase, on average, 9.12 percent in the week after a suicide story. The more publicity given to the story, the greater the rise in motor vehicle deaths thereafter.

In a study that compared the attitudes of twelfth graders with those of their parents, the adolescents consistently viewed suicide in less judgmental terms and as less stigmatized and less calamitous. They also placed more emphasis on the individual's right to commit suicide (Boldt 1982). Adolescents, in contrast to their parents, do not see suicide as an indicator of psychological disturbance (Gordon, Range, and Evans 1987). Therefore, the rising suicide rate may be attributed to adolescents' greater tolerance of suicide, their being less fearful of its consequences, and their view that it is a reasonable alternative.

Sexual Attitudes Premarital intercourse has psychological implications that are related to the gap between physical and social maturity. There is an attitude among adolescents that the physical capability implies social maturity. One of the most important psychological events in an adolescent's history is the first sexual intercourse experience. It is a psychological declaration of independence and autonomy from his or her parents, affirms his or her sexual identity, and makes a statement about being capable of interpersonal intimacy (Hopkins 1977).

The role and meaning of sex in the development of the adolescent have undergone a dramatic shift in the last thirty years. Today, sex for unmarried adolescents is no longer taboo, and sexual intimacy is seen as an important part of the identity formation process (Dreyer 1982). The rate of adolescent intercourse, particularly among younger adolescent whites, appears to be increasing, although this trend may have leveled off recently. Apparently, the incidence of both contraception and abortion is increasing even faster, so the rate of adolescent childbearing is falling (Hodgman 1983).

The changes in adolescent sexual behavior are due to a combination of factors. First, the lower age of sexual maturity (that is, the secular trend) indicates that the adolescent today is physiologically ready for sexual intercourse at an earlier age. Second, advances in contraception technology, especially the birth control pill, have opened the possibility that adolescents may engage in premarital sex without becoming pregnant. (The problem is that data clearly indicate that adolescents are much more ignorant about reproduction and contraception than might be expected, considering sex education classes and the widespread availability of contraceptives and family planning information.) Third, adult society in the United States is undergoing a change in norms about sexual behavior of all types. Overall, adults seem to be more accepting of premarital sexual intercourse and have reduced negative sanctions and punishments for such behavior, creating, more or less, a normless environment where sex is neither encouraged nor discouraged. At the same time, specific subgroups of adults (depending on ethnicity, educational level, income, age, and religiosity) present very strong values and norms for the young with regard to sex. Thus the young person is faced with a conflict of norms among various reference groups with whom he or she interacts. The meaning of sexual activity for a particular adolescent depends on the ways in which the subgroup values and norms are perceived. Fourth, the formation of an "adolescent society," or "youth culture," seems to have led to a normative structure within the peer group, accepting or encouraging full sexual relations between a boy and a girl who feel affection for each other or who are "in love." The norm in this case is that sex is part of a caring and affectionate relationship, although casual and exploitative or abusive sex are considered unacceptable.

The contradictory norms within the larger society and the "sex with affection" norm of peers tend to leave adolescents with little guidance in dealing with their sexual feelings and their fundamental need to understand themselves and their place in society. The result is that most adolescents seem to be highly ambivalent about their sexual activity, going along with a generally permissive culture yet feeling quite uncertain about the appropriateness or meaning of their own sexual activity (Dreyer 1982).

African-American adolescents of both genders tend to be more sexually active at an earlier age than their white counterparts. The latter, however, tend to have more sex partners and to have sex more frequently. Even among sexually active adolescents, intercourse is not frequent and generally confined to a single partner; that is, a pattern of serial monogamy seems to prevail (Wallis 1985; Siegel 1982). Koyle et al. (1989) found that females who had early sexual experiences were, at age nineteen, more likely to have older sexual partners, to have a greater number of partners, and have sexual intercourse regularly. The pattern in terms of number of partners and frequency also was true for males, although males in all age-groups tended to have intercourse with females from their own age-group.

The incidence of *sexually transmitted diseases* (STDs) among adolescents is skyrocketing (Blake 1990). STDs are passed from one person to another during sexual encounters. They include gonorrhea, genital herpes, syphilis, and acquired immune deficiency syndrome (AIDS). Adolescents are especially vulnerable because they are sexually active and often do not use birth control methods that create a physical barrier between sexual partners, such as condoms or spermicides. Most STDs can be cured or controlled by medical treatment. AIDS is an exception. There is no cure. Between 1988 and 1990, the number of AIDS cases among adolescents in the United States increased about 40 percent (Blake 1990). It is feared that the next crisis in the AIDS epidemic will be among adolescents. The major problem is in persuading them of the danger in their behavior. Some reports indicate that adolescents do not believe they are susceptible and continue to engage in indiscriminate and impulsive sexual behavior (Smilgis 1987). A study with freshmen and sophomore college students, however, found that more than half of the sexually active students claim to have altered their behavior in some way because of their concern about AIDS, and 15 percent of the nonactive students claim their concern has prevented them from becoming sexually active (Carroll 1988). Perhaps younger adolescents are still at risk, but the older ones seem to be heeding the warnings.

Teen Pregnancy   Every year more than a million adolescents become pregnant, and 64 percent are unmarried (Children's Defense Fund 1990). In 1950, fewer than 15 percent of the teen births were illegitimate; by 1983, the figure exceeded 50 percent, and in some regions of the country it was more than 75 percent. Roughly 25 percent of adolescent females are sexually active, and in a given year 30,000 become pregnant by age fifteen. About 40 percent of adolescent males have had intercourse by age fifteen. Researchers estimate that if the present trend continues, 40 percent of today's fourteen-year-old girls will be pregnant at least once before age twenty (Wallis 1985; Siegel 1982).

Pregnant adolescents under age twenty account for 12 percent of all births in the United States (Children's Defense Fund 1990), and 93 percent of these mothers keep their children (Coll et al. 1985), compared with about 65 percent in the early 1960s (Wallis 1985; Dreyer 1982).

Sexual activity for adolescent girls is often part of a larger pattern of low self-esteem, fueled by feelings of rejection, deprivation, and being unloved. They are passively dependent, long for nurturance, are disinterested in school, and associate with an older boyfriend who provides assurance and affection. The pregnancy is a perverse attempt to obtain some security and have nurturing needs met, not unlike a child's desire for a puppy. Girls who adopt a "feminine" gender role are thus often as sexually active as girls who appear more "modern" or "liberated." The latter females see their identity and life satisfaction as due to their own efforts rather than owing to a future husband. They are less likely to give in to an ardent suitor simply because he is an affectionate man, although they may participate in intercourse because it satisfies their own sexual needs or because they feel that form of intimacy is an acceptable part of a close relationship with a mutually caring partner. They are also more likely to use contraceptives (Dreyer 1982; Wallis 1985).

A study by Landy et al. (1983) found that pregnant teens were no more promiscuous than their nonpregnant peers. They were found, however, to be clinging and to need protection, as well as to be naive and open. They were vulnerable to suggestions by males that they should become intimate with them. All of the girls reported they knew about birth control methods, but for several reasons they failed to use these methods. For example, they wanted to show their "love," or they experienced anxiety about using contraceptive pills. There seemed to be a tendency for most of these single girls to view their pregnancy as fitting into their life plan.

Rogel et al. (1980) found that girls in their study were generally poor contraceptive users; viewed the costs of contraception (in terms of safety) to be high; and positively valued physical intimacy, opportunities for which come up unexpectedly and sporadically. These factors, along with their ambivalent views toward pregnancy and childbearing, seemed to encourage their risk-taking behavior. Once pregnant, they carried to term because of strong internal and external pressures to have and keep the baby.

Although nearly one-third of all abortions are performed on females under twenty years of age, abortion does not appear to be a solution to the teen pregnancy epidemic; adolescents who solve one pregnancy with abortion often

TABLE 12.1 Births to Women Younger than 20, 1987

	NUMBER OF BIRTHS TO WOMEN				PERCENT OF TEEN BIRTHS TO 18- TO 19-YEAR-OLDS	PERCENT OF BIRTHS TO ALL WOMEN THAT WERE TO WOMEN YOUNGER THAN 20	NUMBER OF BIRTHS TO ALL WOMEN
	YOUNGER THAN 20	YOUNGER THAN 15	15–17	18–19			
ALL							
Total Births	472,623	10,311	172,591	289,721	61.3%	12.4%	3,809,394
Married	170,082	728	41,851	127,503	75.0%	5.9%	2,876,381
Unmarried	302,541	9,583	130,740	162,218	53.6%	32.4%	933,013
% Unmarried	64.0%	92.9%	75.8%	56.0%			24.5%
WHITE							
Total Births	312,108	4,009	105,995	202,104	64.8%	10.4%	2,992,488
Married	151,193	617	37,760	112,816	74.6%	6.1%	2,493,843
Unmarried	160,915	3,392	68,235	89,288	55.5%	32.3%	498,645
% Unmarried	51.6%	84.6%	64.4%	44.2%			16.7%
BLACK							
Total Births	144,853	5,981	61,093	77,779	53.7%	22.6%	641,567
Married	13,050	64	2,659	10,327	79.1%	5.4%	242,423
Unmarried	131,803	5,917	58,434	67,452	51.2%	33.0%	399,144
% Unmarried	91.0%	98.9%	95.6%	86.7%			62.2%
LATINO[1]							
Total Births	66,150	1,402	25,347	39,401	59.6%	9.3%	406,153
Married	28,450	251	8,555	19,644	69.0%	10.4%	273,760
Unmarried	37,700	1,151	16,792	19,757	52.4%	28.5%	132,393
% Unmarried	57.0%	82.1%	66.2%	50.1%			32.6%

[1]Latinos include persons with ancestral lines to Spain and other Spanish-speaking countries. Latinos are an ethnic group, not a race, and therefore the white, black, and Latino percentages and numbers do not equal the total for all races. Latinos can be counted in any racial group, although the majority are counted as white. Only 23 states report births to Latino parents.

Source: National Center for Health Statistics, calculations by the Children's Defense Fund.

become pregnant again and in some cases repeatedly (Melton and Pliner 1986).

Pregnant teens usually do not receive early prenatal care. Four out of five pregnant teens under age fifteen receive no prenatal care during the vital first three months of pregnancy, thus increasing the risk for a poor outcome. Teen mothers are 92 percent more likely to have anemia and 23 percent more likely to give premature birth than are mothers aged twenty to twenty-four. Females are particularly at nutritional risk if pregnancy occurs before their own growth is completed, mainly before seventeen years. For the early-maturing female, pregnancy makes extra demands on a body that is still growing and has not reached skeletal maturation. Most pregnant adolescents receive inadequate amounts of nutrients (primarily iron, calcium, calories, and vitamin A). Also, nutrient stores may be minimal at the time of conception because of poor eating habits and dieting attempts. The multiple nutrient demands of adolescent growth and pregnancy combined with poor food intake add up to twice the normal risk of delivering low-birthweight babies. These infants are in danger of serious mental, physical, and developmental problems that may require costly and possibly lifelong medical care (Lucas et al. 1985; Wallis 1985).

As noted earlier, fewer adolescents are giving up their babies for adoption. The undesirable consequences of keeping these infants are striking. Some evidence indicates that the more time infants of adolescents spend with their mothers, the more handicaps the infants suffer and the poorer their cognitive development. They are less responsive to social stimulation, are less alert, and are less able to control motor behavior. Surprisingly, infants' physical irritability is more effective than their alertness in eliciting a positive response from their adolescent mothers. These young mothers will poke at their infants, perhaps to arouse irritability and create a mutual interaction. Children of adolescent mothers are more likely to be behaviorally, socially, intellectually, and perhaps even physically retarded in development compared with children born to older mothers (Roosa et al. 1982). Perhaps because adolescents, particularly the very young, are psychologically immature, they usually lack the cognitive maturity to consider the needs of others as more critical than their own. A secure sense of one's identity and the ability to place the needs of others first have been cited as central to adequate mothering (McAnarney et al. 1984).

It is not unusual for an adolescent to become pregnant again within two years after the first pregnancy. Gispert et al. (1984) found that adolescents who sought and received support from their parents during the first crisis were less likely to become pregnant again than were those who found little support at home.

When a teen pregnancy is brought to term, the extended family frequently assumes a paramount role in the child rearing, enabling many young mothers to cope successfully with the stresses of early parenthood. Ironically, this familial response may foreclose alternative sources of support, such as the father, who may be largely excluded from participating in the child rearing. It has been found that women who maintain strong ties with their parents are less likely to marry and are more likely to have insecure marriages. The existence of multiple family caretakers may be a boon at one stage of development and a liability at another (Furstenberg 1980).

The sexual activity of an adolescent male is often part of a larger pattern of rebellion, rejection of parental controls, aggressive acting out, alienation from school, and association with older peers who flaunt sexual experience as a badge of masculinity (Dreyer 1982). One study of sixteen unwed teen fathers found that almost one-third lacked basic anatomical knowledge and that three quarters did not know when ovulation occurs in the menstrual cycle. The researchers saw depression and an unmet need for counseling as significant problems for a number of these fathers (Hodgman 1983).

A study by the Bank Street College of Education funded by the Ford Foundation revealed that many young fathers were willing and eager to help their partner and offspring. At the end of a two-year program involving four hundred teen fathers in eight U.S. cities, 82 percent of the fathers reported having daily contact with their children; 74 percent said they contributed to their child's financial support; 90 percent maintained a relationship with the mother, who they had known for an average of two years. At the end of the program, 61 percent of the previously unemployed young men had found jobs, and 46 percent of the dropouts had resumed their education (Stengel 1985). Other studies have also found that when teen fathers are encouraged to remain involved with their children they were more likely to contribute to the support of

AN EXTRA SEVEN POUNDS COULD KEEP YOU OFF THE FOOTBALL TEAM.

Become a father before you're ready and you may always wonder what else you could have been.

THE CHILDREN'S DEFENSE FUND

their children and to get jobs and/or continue their education. (Robinson and Barret 1987; Marsiglio 1988; Barth et al. 1988).

Teen fathers usually have lower income, less education, and more children than do men who wait until at least age twenty to have children. One reason is that the teens who get a girlfriend pregnant often compound the first mistake with a second one: dropping out of school. Since their own father was likely a phantom parent, they do not have a good role model (Stengel 1985).

How well teen fathers manage the possibly simultaneous crises of pending parenthood and marriage may influence both their own and their partner's parental behavior. Lamb and Elster (1985) found that adolescent mothers and their partners interact with infants much as adult parents do. The teen parents also resemble adult counterparts in terms of parent-infant and parent-parent interactions. In particular, the quality of the father-infant interaction correlates significantly with almost all measures of the mother-father interaction.

Elster and Panzarine (1983) found that teenage prospective fathers who reported that they had expected a pregnancy to occur tended to have fewer concerns late in the pregnancy than did those who had not anticipated conception. Those young men who had dated their partner longer and were told of the pregnancy earlier had had a more stable relationship with their partner prior to conception. It also was found that unmarried fathers face similar stressors regardless of race or socioeconomic status; that the social situation surrounding adolescent pregnancy produces concerns common to all teen fathers; and that the younger the father at the time his first child is born, the less formal education he will complete (Elster and Panzarine 1983).

Runaways In the United States, 1.2 million teenagers leave home each year. Approximately 3,300 children a day run away from home (Children's Defense Fund 1990). Ten percent of all adolescent males and 8.7 percent of all adolescent females report running away from home at least once. Precipitating factors include delinquent behavior, drug usage, and sexual acting out. Some adolescents run away to escape restrictive parental control or difficulties in the school and community. Suicide attempts and psychotic breakdowns frequently are reported in families of runaways. These youths differ from others in terms of academic motivation and self-perception, and rejection seems to be the key ingredient. Time and again a runaway episode is precipitated by the underlying message from the parents (often nonverbal) that they have given up trying to set any limits and the child might just as well leave home (Ostensen 1981; Farber and Kinast 1984; Johnson and Carter 1980). School also serves as an arena for failure. "Rejects" at home become left out in school, where they are tracked into slow-learner classes, repeat grades, and are ostracized by teachers and peers. They respond with apathy, reduced ambition, and the expectation of defeat. Their chronic truancy from school is the functional equivalent of running away from home (Johnson and Carter 1980; Farber and Kinast 1984).

Runaways tend to leave impulsively, in a desperate flight from despair, self-abnegation, and loneliness. Approximately one-third of them do not return home, and those who attempt to survive on the streets face prostitution, drug abuse, AIDS, and criminal assault (Children's Defense Fund 1990).

Abused and neglected runaways have been told to leave home or have been abandoned. This group accounts for about 40 percent of runaways (Children's Defense Fund 1990). It is suspected that they have been severely and repeatedly abused. Of reported cases of child abuse, 30 percent involve adolescents. Twenty-four percent of all abuse-related fatalities and 41 percent of all serious abuse-related injuries occur to children between the ages of twelve and seventeen (Farber and Kinast 1984).

Sexual abuse, a prevalent form among abused adolescents, is so emotionally traumatic that it may be years before such incidents are revealed. One response is to run away, and another is for the molested to become the molester (Sugar 1983).

A surprising finding by Ostensen (1981) (which has not been supported by previously mentioned studies) is that the average runaway is a white female, age fifteen, who has attended school regularly and has had no previous involvement with police or probation. She leaves a home with one or both natural parents (half of Ostensen's subjects were from divorced families) and three siblings. Her mother is a homemaker, and her father is employed professionally. She has not run away before, is gone for only one night, and travels less than ten miles from home before being referred to the school counselor or juvenile justice personnel.

Mirkin et al. (1984) have identified three types of female runaways along a continuum of severity of family pathology: rootless, anxious, and terrified. The *rootless runaway* had extreme leniency as a young child and now seeks limitless pleasure and instant gratification in response to her parents' new attempts to set limits on her as an adolescent. The *anxious runaway* is leaving a more pathological family situation; she is put in the position of doing chores, rearing siblings, and worrying about finances as well as suffering abuse from an alcoholic father. The *terrified runaway* is traumatized by a sexually aggressive father or stepfather,

For an adolescent, age-mates from school or the neighborhood form the most significant peer group.

Cliques
A type of peer group that is small, with an average of six members.

Crowd
A type of peer group that is an association of two, three, or four cliques, with approximately fifteen to thirty members in all.

and her passive mother may be subtly encouraging the father's or stepfather's incestuous behavior.

Socialization

Influence of Peers

With friends, adolescents can test their developing identities, evolving independence, and attractiveness. They also have a good time with others who have similar interests. The concept of peer group refers specifically to a cluster of associates who know one another and who serve as a source of reference or comparison for one another. In adolescence, the significant peer group consists of age-mates in the neighborhood or school, that is, those who have a direct and dominant effect on the adolescent's daily life (Newman 1982).

For adolescents who have not formed their identity and self-concept, few situations are dreaded more than being rejected by peers or excluded from the group. The influence of peers becomes stronger as that of the family weakens. Adolescents with poor parental relationships will be more susceptible to peer group control.

Peer influences crest in the early junior high years, at about age twelve or thirteen (Curtis 1975). These young adolescents are likely to be self-conscious, have a shaky self-image and low self-esteem, and feel that others view them unfavorably. Environment may actually play a greater role than age in such concerns; that is, children of this age entering junior high appear more disturbed along these lines than do their age-peers still in elementary school (Simmons et al. 1973). In some school systems the sixth grade is the last year of elementary school, while in others it is the first year of junior high.

The peer group functions in several ways. It provides a supportive setting that permits the adolescent to establish increased autonomy from parents and older siblings. It offers an avenue for experimentation with cultural values and the opportunity to restate one's commitment or resistance to the family or cultural ways. Because peers are not family, adolescents can experience bondedness with or affection for a larger and more diverse segment of society than has been the case thus far. Peers also assist in directing the behavior of individuals, and the effect can be positive or negative. In some cases this control function moves toward deviance and impulsiveness. In other cases, peers encourage conformity within what is socially desirable and reduce egocentrism and tendencies to act in self-centered, antisocial ways (Newman 1982).

Although adolescents conform in general to the peer culture, they share values with their most immediate friends. Young adolescents usually hang out in **cliques** of up to half a dozen members of the same gender. **Crowds** have approximately fifteen to thirty members and are associations of two, three, or four cliques. Feelings of intimacy and closeness are major ingredients in a clique, while a crowd is created for larger social events, especially parties and dances. Clique membership is a prerequisite for crowd membership. The formation of these peer groups seems to develop along fairly well established lines. First, the same-gender clique is formed. Next, the girls' clique and the boys' clique interact in some group activity, such as a swimming party or volleyball game. Then, leaders of the two cliques meet individually, marking the beginning of dating. The cliques then become heterosexual and join with other cliques to form a heterosexual crowd. Most peer contacts, including friendships, dates, and larger group activities, are confined to other members of the crowd. Even-

The Transition to Junior High School

Moving from elementary school to junior high can be traumatic for many early adolescents. These youngsters begin having problems with subject matter, motivation, and self-esteem. In several studies, confidence in math ability and interest in mathematics dropped dramatically upon entering junior high school (Eccles and Midgley 1990; Harter 1981, 1982; Simmons and Blyth 1987). Harter (1981) reported a shift from a preference for challenges to a preference for easy work. Blyth et al. (1983) noted a decline in motivation. Simmons and Blyth (1987) found that girls but not boys experienced a significant decline in self-esteem.

Why would this transition create such a change in youngsters? Blyth et al. (1983) suggest that youngsters already are undergoing stress related to the onset of puberty. If the transition would occur a year or so later, perhaps it would be less traumatic. Studies testing this proposition have been inconclusive and inconsistent.

Thornberg and Jones (1982) compared students moving up a grade level within the same school structure with students moving up a grade level and into a new building. The new sixth graders who moved to the new building experienced feelings of lower self-esteem than did those who remained. No differences in self-esteem were found among the new seventh graders who moved to the new building or remained.

Nottelmann (1987) conducted a similar study of relocation effect on children moving between fifth and sixth grade and between sixth and seventh grade. She found self-esteem higher among the children in the relocation group than in the nonrelocation group. Even more surprising, Peterson, Ebata, and Graber (1987) found that children who made two consecutive location moves experienced greater long-term gains in self-esteem and self-image than did children who made a single location move from fifth to sixth grade or from sixth to seventh grade.

Why are these findings inconsistent? What variables could account for differences in self-esteem among early adolescents moving from elementary to junior high school? What role does the *nature* of the transition play? What roles does the *timing* play? What is the role played by environmental factors such as teachers, number of students per classroom, building design, and so forth?

---

tually the crowd disintegrates as couples begin to branch off (Csikszentmihali and Larson 1984; Dunphy 1963; Berndt 1982).

Cliques are often identified by the leader's name. Clique leaders are notable for participating in more advanced heterosexual activities, for being in touch with other cliques, and for serving as advisers or counselors in matters of dating and love. Clique leaders within a crowd form a special group that plans, executes, and promotes social activities. From this group a crowd or group leader emerges. The **sociocenter** is the crowd joker, who is usually popular and outgoing. The sociocenter's function is to maintain good feelings within the group and to provide a playful, congenial atmosphere. The more dominant and assertive the group leader is, the more clearly integrated is the role of the sociocenter (Dunphy 1963). Although the names and nature of cliques and crowds vary from school to school, examples are "dopers," "burnouts," "jocks," "brains," "head-bangers," "preps," "freaks," and "nerds."

Two influential sources pressure adolescents to identify with a peer group: parents and school adults. The latter encourage students to organize into peer groups, and they accept the students' groups as they exist, rarely attempting to bring members of different peer groups into a working relationship with one another. They acknowledge the students' right to establish boundaries, rivalries, and areas of cooperation in their relationships. School adults also reinforce some characteristics of the peer groups by selecting certain students for certain kinds

Sociocenter
The crowd joker, who is usually popular and outgoing and who maintains good feelings within the group and provides the group with a playful, congenial atmosphere.

of tasks. They often rely on leaders of various groups to convey and enforce school norms for acceptable behavior within their respective groups. Since the peer group structure provides an important means for maintaining order and predictability within the school, school adults usually make no effort to alter the structure, and if new groups begin to evolve, school adults may resist (Newman 1982).

Parental pressure to join or affiliate with a specific group of peers may be resisted or rejected by the adolescent. Many parents want their child to associate with the "right crowd," in hopes that the group will have a positive influence or to promote their child's "social prospects."

By far the greatest pressure to make some kind of peer group commitment comes from peers. The peer group structure is well established in most high schools, and members seek to persuade newcomers to affiliate with one group or another. Becoming a member of any group is considered more acceptable than remaining unaffiliated and aloof (Newman 1982). Adolescents tend to be mistrustful of those who do not wish to belong.

In offering membership to an individual, the peer group enhances the adolescent's feelings of self-worth and offers protection from loneliness. The adolescent can get support from these peers when conflicts develop within the family. In exchange, he or she must be willing to suppress some individuality and focus on attributes he or she shares with the peers. Although peer groups do not demand total conformity, they expect the unique characteristics of members to mesh with the group's self-image. Most adolescents find some security in demands to conform. A well-defined group identity lends stability and substance to an individual's self-concept. It allows the adolescent to feel that he or she is someone and that he or she belongs somewhere.

As important as peer groups are, it is not uncommon for adolescents to be preoccupied with their own feelings or thoughts. They may withdraw from social interaction and be unwilling to share areas of vulnerability and confusion that accompany physical, intellectual, and social growth. Most adolescents feel some loneliness and isolation. Even with peers there is a need to exercise caution in sharing personal concerns, for fear of rejection or ridicule. Maintaining one's "cool" and being perceived as "together," rather than appearing vulnerable, may hamper building a strong bond of commitment to a social groups (Newman 1982).

Some individuals do not exhibit a desire to belong to a group but instead are uneasy with peers. One reason may be that the parents are pressuring the adolescent to associate with a particular peer group, but that group does not accept the adolescent. Another reason may be that the individual does not view the existing groups as appropriate for his or her personal needs. Finally, if no group offers membership, the adolescent will gradually be shut out from the social environment (Newman 1982).

Influence of Family

Family communication patterns undergo change as adolescents grow older. According to Hunter (1985), adolescents' input into family decision making increases with age. Also, fathers maintain their authority while that of mothers declines.

The influence of parents and friends varies according to the type of activity or topic involved. For example, parental influence seems to prevail in future-oriented domains, such as finances, choice of schools, and career plans. Friends'

Life Skills

In order for youths to be prepared socially, physically, and emotionally to function in the adult world, the society needs to make a commitment to their education, health care, and occupational preparation. Youth also need a commitment from their society to help them develop life skills, which would involve bolstering their self-confidence, nonacademic skills, citizenship, and leadership. Some young people have this support and commitment from their families, but these youths still need help from outside sources that can provide positive interaction with adults and peers. Unfortunately, there are many youths who are from families that provide only the basics for survival. Minority and low-income adolescents in poor urban areas, rural youth, and youth under court supervision need services more than others, but they are the least likely to get them. These are the adolescents who are at risk.

The at-risk group of youngsters are more likely to have one parent at home. These parents often have little job flexibility, long work hours, and not much formal education. For example, four out of ten parents of Latino adolescents have less than nine years of formal education (Children's Defense Fund 1990). Family poverty and family structure—as well as neighborhood poverty, poor school quality, and inadequate and unaffordable facilities and programs—make these youths more at risk of not getting the support they need for personal and social development.

The Children's Defense Fund (1990) reports:

- In densely populated inner-city neighborhoods, violence and extremely high crime rates make safety an issue for children and adolescents. Recent news reports featured the sale of bullet-proof vests for children in such areas. Many of these youngsters are instructed to go straight home from school and lock the doors. They need programs in or near their housing complexes or schools and adults who are willing to supervise and take responsibility for them.
- Adolescents and youth, aged eighteen to twenty-one, who lack high school diplomas are twice as likely to be unemployed as those with diplomas. Almost four out of ten Latino adolescents do not have high school diplomas, compared with two out of ten white youngsters and three out of ten African-American youngsters.
- African-American males between fifteen and nineteen years of age are ten times more likely to be shot and five times more likely to be killed by other violent means than white males of the same age-group.
- Youths in the court system, such as in foster care, are disproportionately poor, minority, and behind in school or out of school. They often lack a consistent, caring adult in their lives.
- For rural adolescents, transportation is a problem. They have few opportunities to explore other communities or build relationships with peers and adults.

According to the Children's Defense Fund (1990) youths need the following:

- *Leisure-time activities*. These would include structured activities and supervised opportunities for interaction with peers and adults during the summer months, after school, and on weekends.
- *Nonacademic education*. Nonacademic pursuits could include physical education, recreation, exposure to the arts, development of social skills, and cultural education (developing an understanding of heritage and history, such as viewing the *Roots* series.)
- *Community involvement*. Youths need opportunities to have relationships and experiences that encourage a sense of community and link them with the adult world. They need to find ways to contribute to and participate in the world around them.
- *Opportunities to apply knowledge and develop leadership abilities*. This could be accomplished by getting involved in diverse projects and activities, which could provide opportunities to use their skills in ways that contribute to others.
- *Central places and central people*. Youths need places to go outside of the home where they can feel safe and be themselves. They also need relationships with key adults, not only within the family but also outside of the family. Key adults can assess the needs of the youths and link them with needed services, opportunities, and/or programs.

Female adolescents are more likely to accept the advice of parents regarding the future and the advice of peers concerning school-related issues.

influence centers around current events and such matters as dress, dating, drinking, social events, and joining clubs. Even the choice of reading material can be dictated by peer approval. Parents tend to explain their views more than they try to understand the adolescent's views in the academic-vocational, social-ethical, and family domains (Hunter 1985; Sebald 1986).

Which generational group is influential at any particular time depends on the issue the adolescent is confronting. When parents are seen as a better source, the adolescent is more parent oriented than peer oriented. Female adolescents are more likely to accept the advice of parents regarding the future and the advice of peers concerning school-related issues (Lerner and Shea 1982).

Adolescents want to talk about sex with their parents but believe they must be able to ask the right questions in approaching the subject. Consequently, friends and impersonal sources are the main "educators." Most adolescents assume that their parents prefer that they learn about sex from peers or other nonfamilial sources (Dickinson 1978; Sorenson 1973; Calderwood 1965).

Adolescents perceive their own attitudes as somewhere between those of their parents and their peers, between the "conservative" (where they put their parents) and the "liberal" (where they place their peers). Adolescents and their parents tend to agree on issues related to religion and marriage but not on those related to sex and drugs. Parents and adolescents also are similar on moral issues but not on matters such as style of dress, hair length, and hours of sleep. Although groups of adolescents as compared with groups of parents have somewhat different views about topics of contemporary social concern, most of these differences reflect contrasts in attitude intensity rather than attitude direction (Lerner and Shea 1982; Lerner and Weinstock 1972; Weinstock and Lerner 1972).

Adolescents report feeling more intimacy and openness of communication with, as well as seeking more advice and guidance from, mothers rather than

For a growing number of teenagers, the sentiment "I'm OK, who cares about you?" no longer prevails. Though there are no firm numbers on teen activism, many teachers and counselors predict a comeback. Granted, it's not yet a tidal wave of altruism. But in groups or on their own, teenagers are running recycling programs and peer hot lines, staffing soup kitchens and recording senior citizens' oral histories. Peter Scales, deputy director of the Center for Early Adolescence at the University of North Carolina, says, "The desire is there. We just have to tap into it."

The timing couldn't be better. As public funding falls short for everything from libraries to after-school programs, and as the traditional volunteer pool—i.e., housewives—shrinks, teenagers (as well as senior citizens) are the logical next wave of helpers. Many school systems now require community service, and teenage volunteerism may soon become part of the national agenda. The U.S. Senate has passed a youth-service bill that the House is now considering. Among its many components: funding for experimental Youth Corps programs in day-care centers and nursing homes. Even if the need for volunteers weren't so enormous, there would be good reasons for teens to pitch in. "It's a question of being part of a bigger cause," says Marc Miringoff, director of Fordham University's Center for Innovation in Social Policy in Tarrytown, N.Y. Or, as one Hudson, Ohio, teenager put it, "I used to say, 'Just let me lead my life.' But now I look around and see a world that needs me."

When the kids of Detroit's Westside Cultural and Athletic Center heard the first shots, they hit the dirt. There was no time to run for cover. In this patch of urban jungle, gun-play is commonplace, and war games look real. Soon, the WCAC kids were back

Human Development in the News: Kids with Causes

By KATRINE AMES

on their feet. "This time it was nothing," says George Smith, looking out over the weed-and-gravel field. "We just got up and played baseball."

It's experience, not nonchalance, that informs his speech. George, who began helping out four years ago, is the most dedicated volunteer at WCAC, a hardscrabble mecca for more than 400 children that runs on a tiny $16,000 budget. The 17-year-old high-school junior spends nearly every afternoon there tutoring and coaching sports. A "B" student who wants to study medicine, he brings his own books to the playground to show "that some kids actually do homework." George has become the best—and most accessible—role model many of these kids have. "It's in the simple things he does, like showing up on time or just listening to them," says WCAC director Erica Wright. Mario Henry, 10, says, "George is almost like a teacher but maybe a little better. He's easier to talk to." And Gabriel Knox, 14, calls him "calm and confident. He can get people to listen to him and motivate them real naturally."

George remembers kids from the first WCAC baseball team he played on, at 7. One boy is on drugs now; one is in prison; one is a crack dealer; one may be dead. Some would say George Smith—shy, lean, clean-cut—is lucky, but he has worked hard, too. And despite the praise he gets, he has no illusions about how much he can do for the WCAC kids. "I'm not a martyr," he says. "It can't be up to just me. A lot of people just don't seem to care." Yet George's realistic take on the future is suffused with dreams. "I

can see a lot of these kids ending up working at McDonald's. But then again, some are real smart, and maybe with the right push they'll do better. I guess that's why I'm out there, too. I can be part of that right push."

This fish story is true. Six years ago the fledgling ecology club at Casa Grande High School in Petaluma, Calif., a middle-class city 35 miles north of San Francisco, began to clean up Adobe Creek. The trout stream, once a healthy home for steelhead, was polluted and neglected. After reeling in 10 tons of junk—car parts, sofas, a washing machine—the students learned a painful lesson. "We cleared the garbage to create the proper environment for the fish to return," says vice president Brian Waits, 18. "What we didn't realize was that the community could put in litter as fast as we could clean it up."

With the help of teacher Tom Furrer, the students built a fish hatchery. Soon, they were fighting one another for the job of cleaning it out during their lunch hour; when the water got too hot, they raced to get ice. They released some 500 trout and catfish—fin-clipped so they could be recognized if they came back to spawn—into local waters. Then, officials ruled that the hatchery did not meet earthquake standards and had to close down. Initially devastated, club members soon resolved to build a better hatchery. It would release 20,000 steelhead and striped bass annually—and carried a $250,000 price tag. The students wrote a 186-page grant proposal and became articulate fund raisers. Donations flowed in (roughly $200,000 to date) and hatchery construction is now underway. "It will be our gift to the younger generation," says president Darcy Hamlow, 18. "Someday this stream will be full of life." This spring, a harbinger swam into view: a 29-inch steelhead, its clipped fins proof that it had been raised by the students.

Human Development in the News: Kids with Causes (continued)

If you're not involved, you'll never make a change," says Lizz Cohen, 17. "You can talk about it, but it's just talk." She's one of six girls from Saguaro High School in Scottsdale, Ariz., who are the impetus behind plans for a national freedom-of-speech museum in Washington. It began last year, after the sextet—Lizz, Ilene Mass, 16; Carol Mack, 18; Heidi Sherman, 16; Jaime Lewis, 17, and Carol Bien-Willner, 18—visited the Lincoln Memorial in Washington. They went to Capitol Hill and proposed installing a plaque to commemorate the spot where Martin Luther King Jr. delivered his "I Have a Dream" speech. They found out that an ordinance prohibits placing a memorial on a memorial, but were only momentarily deterred. When their history teacher, John Calvin, planted the idea for a First Amendment museum in a room to the left of the monument, they were off and running.

At the time Arizona was one of only three states that did not celebrate King's birthday—giving the girls further initiative. (This spring, the legislature voted to observe the holiday.) When they returned to Scottsdale, an affluent, almost exclusively white suburb of Phoenix, the students acted with the speed and single-mindedness of a commando unit. As Rep. Bruce Vento explains it: "Nobody told them they couldn't get things done." They sent out information packets and wrote letters outlining their proposal:

a museum with an exhibit depicting ways in which Lincoln inspired others—including King—to work for freedom and individual rights.

In March, armed with press clippings and letters of support from politicians and a variety of groups, the girls made a second assault on Washington. Pitching the Lincoln-King connection, they won over key government figures, including the regional head of the National Parks Service, Robert Stanton, and Vento, who chairs the subcommittee on National Parks and Public Lands. The museum should be ready in 1993. A structural assessment is being done, and the design team will hear the girls' ideas. Carol says, emphatically, "I don't think anything could stop us now."

Charity can also begin right across the border. From home base in Harlingen, Texas, Nora Morales, 17, and Mary Torres, 19, are running their own small-scale international relief effort. They have developed "adopt a school" programs that furnish Mexican pupils and teachers with critical supplies—and personal attention. The seeds were planted in 1987, when

Mary heard about a desperately needy school on the other side of the Rio Grande. As Mexican contacts led the girls to more schools, they solicited clothes, books and pencils in Harlingen. Community support has grown so strong that the girls now cross the border regularly with their bounty.

They raised money by selling flowers and balloons; they secured a loan to pay for a well at a school where water was dispensed from a can. Since help from Harlingen began arriving, says Jacinto Villega Garcia, headmaster of one school, teaching and learning have become easier. Many students who stayed away because they couldn't afford pencils and paper are back in class, where once bare walls are covered with maps. "Before we got them, we knew where we lived, but we didn't know where it was," says Jessica Loera, 13. The project has been especially rewarding for Mary, a native of Mexico who will become a U.S. citizen later this year. "We know we have a lot of privileges here," she says. Nora adds, "I have fun, and I'm not wasting my time." She has also paid a personal price—willingly. "I've lost some friendships. Friends say I don't have the time for them anymore, but I feel better knowing that I'm helping people."

fathers (Hunter 1985; Noller and Bagi 1985; Keith and Nelson 1991). Females respect the opinions of parents and friends more than do males. Girls also report more satisfactory relationships and seem to be attuned to their mothers' attitudes. Maladjusted girls often have mothers who are hostile and controlling, whereas popular and well-adjusted girls tend to have mothers who are social and outgoing and who grant their daughters autonomy. These mothers are also egalitarian and evaluate their daughters positively. In general, mothers are reported to be more nurturant, warm, and responsive, and they are cited as the preferred parent (Bayley and Schaefer 1963; Curtis 1975).

A family environment with open communication and authoritative parenting techniques seems to provide the context for successful resolution of role search. Adolescents with low self-esteem view communication with their parents as less facilitative than do adolescents with high self-esteem. Parents of low-self-esteem adolescents perceive their own communication with their spouse as less facilitative and rate their marriage as less satisfying than do parents of adolescents with high self-esteem (Lerner and Shea 1982).

There are empirical and theoretical reasons to explain the existence of a generation gap. Adolescents and parents may not perceive their relationship accurately; that is, adolescents may see their parents as less influential than they actually are, while parents may perceive themselves as more influential than is the case. On the one hand, adolescents overestimate the magnitude of differences between themselves and their parents, viewing parental attitudes as less congruent with their own than is actually the case. On the other hand, parents underestimate the extent of differences, perceiving their children's attitudes as very consistent with their own. Although only a small and selective generation gap exists in reality, parents underestimate this division, while adolescents overestimate it (Lerner and Shea 1982; Keith and Nelson 1991).

Families and Academic Success   Families can influence academic achievement and educational persistence. Zimiles and Lee (1991) found that adolescents from stepfamilies and single-parent families were three times more likely than adolescents from intact families to drop out of high school. They also found some complex interactive gender differences in conjunction with the nature of the family structure. Males were more likely to drop out of high school when living in either single-parent or intact families, whereas females were more likely to drop out if they are from stepfamilies. With a stepfather, females drop out of school more than males do; with a stepmother, males are more likely to leave school than females. To a lesser extent, dropout behavior among boys increases when their father remarries, while girls are less likely to drop out under this circumstance. In summary, the data indicate that the gender of the child or parent is not necessarily the important factor in dropping out. Rather, the gender match between the custodial parent and the child seems to be relevant, and the implications of that match differ according to whether a single-parent family or a stepfamily is involved.

SUMMARY

- Three major routes through the adolescent period have been identified: continuous growth (the majority of adolescents fall into this category), surgent growth, and tumultuous growth.
- Erikson's stage of psychosocial development is called identity versus role confusion. Identity involves a quest for personal discovery of "Who am I?" and it takes on the form of a social identity, sexual identity, and vocational or occupational identity. If the adolescent fails in his or her search for identity, then role confusion, identity diffusion, negative identity, or foreclosure may result. A moratorium gives the adolescent time to search for an identity.
- The social learning theory does not see the developing adolescent as any different than the developing younger child. The differences that do exist at the various age levels are the sociocultural expectations, with adolescents choosing different models than younger children.

Teen Employment

Should adolescents work during the school months? How many hours should they work each week? Is working harmful to them?

Since the early 1980s researchers and educators have questioned the advisability of the employment of adolescents during the school year (Greenberger and Steinberg 1981; Greenberger, Steinberg, and Vaux 1981; Steinberg, Greenberger, Garduque, Ruggiero, and Vaux 1982). In the United States, 43 percent of boys age sixteen or seventeen years and 37 percent of girls that age hold jobs (Greenberger and Steinberg 1986). In one study, one-sixth of fourteen- and fifteen-year-olds were working or looking for jobs (Nilsen 1984). Eighty percent of all high school students hold jobs at one time or another (Greenberger and Steinberg 1986).

In the past it was assumed that work for adolescents was beneficial and taught responsibility, punctuality, and dependability. It supposedly also taught them how to co-operate, interact socially, and be more tolerant of different age-groups and social classes. Greenberger and Steinberg (1986) did find that work taught adolescents to be responsible, on time, dependable, and self-reliant, but it did not increase cooperativeness, social interaction, or concern for others. They also found that the more hours worked in excess of fourteen hours a week, the more often the young people were absent from school, the less time they spent on homework and extracurricular activities, the lower their grades, and the less they enjoyed school. The more time they spent at their job, the less time they spent with their family and the less close they were to their friends. They had more negative attitudes toward work than those students who did not work. They were more tolerant of unethical work practices and were more prone to use drugs, alcohol, and cigarettes.

Steinberg and Dornbusch (1991) reported similar findings from their study of four thousand fifteen- to eighteen-year-olds. Long work hours during the school term were associated with lower investment and performance in school, greater psychological distress, drug and alcohol use, delinquency, and autonomy and independence from parents. Workers showed no marked difference from nonworkers in measures of self-reliance, work orientation, or self-esteem. In no areas was it found that extensive employment had positive effects.

Research findings differ as to the number of hours per week that may be worked without deleterious effects on school performance. Several studies place the break point at around twenty hours per week (Wirtz et al. 1987; Mortimer and Finch 1986; Bachman et al. 1986). Greenberger and Steinberg (1986) gave fourteen hours. Steinberg and Dornbush (1991) cited no specific number but did say that the more hours students work, the lower their grades. It seems safe to say that working more than fourteen to twenty hours a week could be harmful to an adolescent's school performance.

From your own observations, why do you think adolescents want to work? Why would working longer hours increase the likelihood of smoking and the use of drugs and alcohol? In what ways would working make an adolescent more independent from his or her parents?

Work teaches adolescents to be responsible, on time, dependable, and self-reliant, but it does not increase cooperativeness, social interaction, or concern for others.

- Self-esteem in adolescents is determined by the ideas and feelings they have about their own thoughts, body, appearance, personal characteristics; their view of others; and parental control.
- Various issues associated with adolescents are a result of poor self-esteem and the inability to form an identity. These issues include drug abuse, delinquency, suicide, sexual attitudes, pregnancy, and running away.
- Peers are a major factor in the socialization process of adolescents. Cliques and crowds are ways peers socialize, depending on their level of maturity. Peers have more influence on those adolescents who have poor relationships with their families. Peers are most influential regarding social events and activities.
- The family of an adolescent is another major factor in the socialization process of the adolescent. It is questionable if there truly is a generation gap. Families are influential regarding future-oriented subjects such as finances and college.

R E A D I N G S

Goldstein, A. P., Sprafkin, R. B., Gershaw, N. J., and Klein, P. (1981). *Skillstreaming the adolescent*. Champaign, IL: Research Press.
Set of exercises designed to improve social skills of adolescents.

Lightfoot, S. L. (1983). *The good high school*. New York: Basic Books.
A description of six high schools—two urban, two suburban, and two "elite." It stresses informal and formal education and the importance of administrative and faculty leadership necessary for success in high school.

Lipsitz, J. (1984). *Successful schools for young adolescents*. New Brunswick, NJ: Transaction Books.
Description of a sample of successful schools and the factors that contributed to their success.

Mead, M. (1971, originally published in 1928). *Coming of age in Somoa*. New York: Morrow.
A classic anthropological look at growing up in Samoa by Margaret Mead, the noted anthropologist. It changed the way Americans looked at adolescents.

Sizer, T. R. (1985). *Horace's compromise: The dilemma of the American high school*. Boston: Houghton Mifflin.
Discussion of how high schools transmit education and cultural and social values.

Steinberg, L. D. (1980). *Understanding families with young adolescents*. Carrboro, NC: Center for Early Adolescence.
Overview of simultaneous maturation of adolescents and their parents plus ideas for coping with an adolescent in the family.

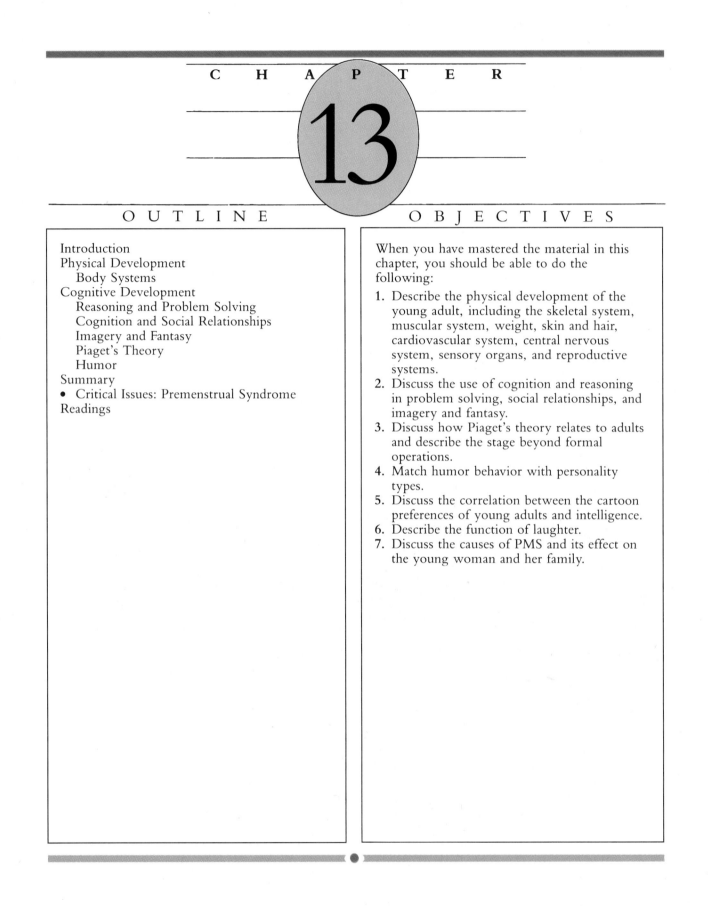

C H A P T E R

13

OUTLINE

OBJECTIVES

When you have mastered the material in this chapter, you should be able to do the following:

1. Describe the physical development of the young adult, including the skeletal system, muscular system, weight, skin and hair, cardiovascular system, central nervous system, sensory organs, and reproductive systems.
2. Discuss the use of cognition and reasoning in problem solving, social relationships, and imagery and fantasy.
3. Discuss how Piaget's theory relates to adults and describe the stage beyond formal operations.
4. Match humor behavior with personality types.
5. Discuss the correlation between the cartoon preferences of young adults and intelligence.
6. Describe the function of laughter.
7. Discuss the causes of PMS and its effect on the young woman and her family.

The Emerging Adult:
Early Adulthood—Physical and Cognitive Development

INTRODUCTION

Adulthood is characterized by both change and stability. Throughout adulthood changes occur in the individual's body, mental and cognitive capabilities, emotional and social ties, and feelings about self. Change can also be the result of a major disruption in everyday life, such as an accident or illness, or a "life event," such as a new job, marriage, the birth of a child, illness, divorce, grandparenthood, and widowhood. Other changes occur so gradually that they may not be obvious for some time. It is now recognized that adult life is neither fixed nor predictable. Major shifts in life-style are not uncommon. Divorce, a mid-life career change, remarriage, alternatives to traditional marriage, and redefinition of priorities and values are some of the more dramatic shifts (Whitbourne and Weinstock 1986).

Despite major changes during adulthood, there is a common thread that provides a sense of continuity and consistency. This common element is each person's identity, and it includes the collection of qualities uniquely his or her own, such as physical appearance, body system functions, age, gender, mental and cognitive abilities, values, goals, beliefs, and a set of roles within the family, at work, in the community, in the country, and in the world. The unique collection of these qualities that are attributes of the self differentiates an individual from others.

Recollections of earlier experiences are stored memories unique to each person. Future plans are related to what is *going* to happen to "me." Without continuity of identity, the individual would feel fragmented each time a new event occurred or when thinking about previous events. "Even when change is the predominant theme, there is stability provided by the recognition, through identity, that the change is 'mine' " (Whitbourne and Weinstock 1986).

When is an individual an adult? Who decides? Attempts have been made to identify the beginning of adulthood by legalistic means. The age at which legal adulthood is attained, or the age of majority, varies according to the type of behavior being regulated. For example, at one age a person is eligible to vote; at another, he or she may drink alcoholic beverages; and at another, he or she is free to marry without parental or guardian consent. There are also ages at which one legally can agree to engage in sexual relations (that age determines statutory rape), drive a car, open an independent banking account, or obtain medical treatment without parental or guardian consent.

If individuals are capable of passing these milestones, they supposedly are ready emotionally and mentally to take on the adult role. This assumption does not take into account the fact that young people may have no knowledge about what is considered appropriate behavior by the law. It also is assumed that there is no change in an individual's status for the next forty years or so after adulthood is legally achieved (Whitbourne and Weinstock 1986).

In later adulthood, an individual is once again limited by society's expectations and laws. There is an age at which he or she is eligible for retirement and receipt of Social Security and veteran's benefits, an age at which he or she qualifies for discounts on public transportation and at movie theaters, restaurants, hotels, and so forth. Behind these criteria exists the attitude that the older adult loses some competency with age and at the same time deserves special treatment and recognition for his or her contribution to society (Whitbourne and Weinstock 1986).

Adulthood is not a neat little package that is easy to describe. It encompasses both change and stability, and it can be inhibited by the age-related legalistic definitions that try to compartmentalize human development.

● PHYSICAL DEVELOPMENT

During the years of early adulthood (ages eighteen–forty), people reach their peak of physical well-being. (Bee, 1987) Good health and optimum strength are distinctive during this time, and few people notice signs of aging.

Body Systems

Skeletal System

By age eighteen all the skeleton is converted to bone. The smaller leg bones, sternum (or breastbone), pelvic bones, and vertebrae attain adult distribution of red marrow by twenty-five years of age (Lowrey 1978). (Red marrow produces blood cells and hemoglobin.) Although growth of the skeletal system is essentially completed around twenty-five years of age, the vertebral column continues to grow until age thirty, and three to five millimeters may be added to one's height (Tanner 1978). Although bones have achieved final growth, they retain the ability to form new bone at any time, an ability that is essential in healing fractures (Timiras 1972).

The mean height for men between eighteen and seventy-four years is 69 inches. Men can expect to lose less than one inch in a lifetime. Women between eighteen and seventy-four years have an average height of 63.6 inches. They can expect to lose about two inches during a lifetime (Abraham et al. 1979; Marshall 1973). The "settling" of the spinal column, which causes a decline in density of the long bones and vertebrae, may account for this decrease in height (Timiras 1972). Decreases in height start at about age fifty (Whitbourne and Weinstock 1986).

Muscular System

Efficiency in the muscular system reaches its peak between the ages of twenty and thirty. Muscular strength then declines, but the rate of decline is

Efficiency in the muscular system reaches its peak between the ages of twenty and thirty. Muscular strength then declines, but the rate of decline is dependent on the muscle group and the individual's activity level.

dependent on the muscle group and the individual's activity level (Whitbourne and Weinstock 1986).

The ability to incur *oxygen debt,* that is, to continue violent exercise without an adequate supply of oxygen, remains at its highest level. Lung efficiency in passing oxygen to the blood is beginning to decline, but strength and endurance are at their peak in the fourth decade. Some loss of speed and agility has taken place. In the Olympics, for example, athletes over age thirty are prominent in such events as long-distance running, fast walking, weight lifting, and wrestling; the more agile activities are the prerogative of younger athletes. Between thirty and forty-two years, joint cartilage begins to degenerate, eventually leading to arthritis (from which all elderly people suffer to some extent). Obesity accelerates the degeneration of joint cartilage (Marshall 1973; Newman 1982).

Weight

Several factors contribute to weight gain. The body increasingly stores excess fat under the skin as age increases. Decreased levels of physical activity mean that excess calories are not burned off but instead are stored as fat in the body (Whitbourne and Weinstock 1986; Timiras 1972). People not only become heavier as they age but also change shape. The waist and trunk thicken and the arms and legs become thinner. The bust and chest become smaller and the hips and abdomen become larger (Weg 1983).

Skin and Hair

The skin begins to lose moisture after adolescence, gradually becoming drier and more wrinkled with age. "Smile lines" and "crow's feet" usually appear during the early thirties and often are interpreted as one of the first signs of aging. Moisturizers are used to slow the process, and a well-balanced diet also helps (Whitbourne and Weinstock 1986).

Gray hair and baldness also may appear in young adulthood, and both seem to be influenced by heredity. Gray hair is simply hair without pigment (Ross-

People not only become heavier as they age, they also change shape. The waist and trunk thicken and the arms and legs become thinner. The bust and chest become smaller and the hips and abdomen become larger.

CHAPTER 13 *Early Adulthood—Physical and Cognitive Development*

TABLE 13.1 Desirable Weight Ranges (Men and Women Combined) at Various Ages

HEIGHT	AGES 20–29	AGES 30–39	AGES 40–49	AGES 50–59	AGES 60–69
4'10"	84–111	92–119	99–127	107–135	115–142
4'11"	87–115	95–123	103–131	111–139	119–147
5'0"	90–119	98–127	106–135	114–143	123–152
5'1"	93–123	101–131	110–140	118–148	127–157
5'2"	96–127	105–136	113–144	122–153	131–163
5'3"	99–131	108–140	117–149	126–158	135–168
5'4"	102–135	112–145	121–154	130–163	140–173
5'5"	106–140	115–149	125–159	134–168	144–179
5'6"	109–144	119–154	129–164	138–174	148–184
5'7"	112–148	122–159	133–169	143–179	153–190
5'8"	116–153	126–163	137–174	147–184	158–196
5'9"	119–157	130–168	141–179	151–190	162–201
5'10"	122–162	134–173	145–184	156–195	167–207
5'11"	126–167	137–178	149–190	160–201	172–213
6'0"	129–171	141–183	153–195	165–207	177–219
6'1"	133–176	145–188	157–200	169–213	182–225
6'2"	137–181	149–194	162–206	174–219	187–232
6'3"	141–186	153–199	166–212	179–225	192–238
6'4"	144–191	157–205	171–218	184–231	197–244

Source: Katchadourian, 1987.

man 1977). Baldness, which is thought to be caused by a gradual decrease in scalp circulation and adrenal secretion after the late twenties (Kimmel 1974), affects men more frequently than it does women.

Cardiovascular System

By age sixteen the cardiovascular system attains its adult size and rhythm. The total blood volume in a young adult is seventy to eighty milliliters per kilogram of body weight (Lowrey 1978). During childhood, blood pressure begins to rise. It sharply elevates in males during adolescence and again after age fifty. Females have a more gradual rise in blood pressure during childhood but have a higher level than males after age sixty. In normal, healthy men between thirty and forty years old, blood pressure rises slowly but steadily as a result of aging processes in the blood vessels.

The *aorta,* through which blood leaves the heart for distribution to the rest of the body, is a tube one inch in diameter with elastic walls that stretch with each beat of the heart. After the twenty-fifth year the elasticity of the aorta and

Fifty-eight percent of twenty-to-forty-four-year-olds participate in some form of sport.

its larger branches decreases steadily, even though the amount of blood pumped into them with each heartbeat remains the same. Blood pressure at the height of the heart's contraction *(systolic blood pressure)* therefore rises. Since smaller arteries in the limbs are narrowed by aging processes, resistance to the circulation of blood is increased, raising blood pressure further. Men and women in their thirties who are overweight are more likely than others to develop abnormally high blood pressure. This could lead to prolonged impairment of health and restriction of activity in later life (Marshall 1973; Newman 1982).

Choi (1978) found that younger persons exercise more regularly than do older persons—54 percent of twenty- to forty-four-year-olds compared with 42 percent of those sixty-five and older. Higher family income was correlated with exercise. Fifty-eight percent of twenty- to forty-four-year-olds participated in some form of sport, while only 10 percent of those sixty-five and older participated. Thirty-seven percent of women participated in one or more sport, while the figure for men was about 47 percent.

Cholesterol is both made by the body and consumed in foods of animal origin. Genetic differences affect how individuals produce and/or excrete cholesterol (Anderson and Van Nierop 1989). Cholesterol produced by the body increases from the age of twenty-one. This is of concern because high levels are correlated with fat deposits in blood vessels that lead to circulatory problems, especially in the heart muscle. Young adult men tend to have higher cholesterol levels than young adult women. Modifying the dietary intake of fats (including cholesterol) can reduce blood lipids (fats). Since cholesterol is a precursor of vitamin D and is closely related to some of the hormones, it should not be considered abnormal or eliminated entirely from the diet (Anderson and Van Nierop 1989; Anderson 1972). Many fast-food chains, in response to the increased concern for proper nutrition, now are advertising low-salt, low-fat, low-cholesterol products.

The heart rate is about 10 percent greater in women than in men (Marshall 1973). It is suspected that oral contraceptives increase the risk of cardiovascular disease, including high blood pressure, myocardial infarction (heart attack), and cerebrovascular diseases, which lead to stroke (Ashburn 1986).

Central Nervous System

The brain reaches physical maturity before age twenty (Lowrey 1978). Only slight changes can be detected in the brain and sensory organs during young adulthood. Final myelinization in the central nervous system occurs at about twenty-five years of age (Timiras 1972). The weight of the brain declines slowly at the rate of one gram a year from the twentieth year of life onward. There is an increase in moisture at the expense of solids in the cerebral cortex. It is uncertain whether this affects behavior. The average weight of a man's brain is slightly greater than that of a woman's. Size is no indicator of intelligence or wisdom; rather, it is the proportion of cerebral cortex to lower brain centers that seems to relate to the degree of intelligence of an organism.

The adult pattern of EEG activity appears to be established in the late teens and remains fairly constant until old age. There are, however, some changes in the alpha rhythms that are related to less attentiveness. *(Alpha rhythms* are the pattern of electrical activity of the brain of a normal, awake, but relaxed person.) These rhythms decrease with age, which may be related to disease rather than to aging. The chief behavioral effect of the changes in the nervous system during adulthood may be generalized as a gradual slowing of almost all functions and processes (Troll 1985; Marshall 1973).

Sensory Organs

Sensory organs show little change in young adulthood. A slight difference in hearing ability between the two sexes occurs: men are less able than women to detect high tones.

Because the lenses of the eye become less elastic, lessening the ability to focus, thirty-year-olds may find they cannot read small print as well as they could before. The eye lens begins to age during infancy, as it continues to grow without shedding older cells. It becomes thicker, less elastic, and more opaque with age. The changes may be so gradual that diminished visual acuity goes unnoticed.

Any slight loss of function in the senses is more than compensated for by training that makes fuller and more profitable use of the senses (Whitbourne 1985). For example, a manual laborer who is accustomed to carrying heavy tools and occasionally suffers a minor accident is less affected by pain than someone whose work is sedentary and who rarely experiences physical pain. A musician's keen sense of hearing can discriminate slight differences in sound and imperfections of pitch not noticeable to the untrained ear. Also, adults who suffer from a specific sensory deficit may compensate in relying more on another sensory organ.

Taste, touch, and smell remain intact during young adulthood. Deterioration in these three senses is not seen until after age forty (Hooyman and Kiyak 1988).

Reproductive Systems

Reproductive functioning begins in women at menarche, which occurs usually between ten and thirteen years of age. The reproductive organs are at peak function in women during their twenties. By age thirty, ovulation and menstruation may become less regular. The time between menstrual periods becomes shorter after about age thirty-five (Talbert 1977) and then lengthens

Human Development in the News: Why Isn't Our Birth Control Better?

PHILIP ELMER-DEWITT

A portrait in American fecundity: every day hundreds of young women, their bodies roundly pregnant, descend on the University of Southern California Women's Hospital. They overflow the available chairs and sprawl awkwardly on the floor. They come for prenatal checkups, gynecological care and, finally, to deliver their young. Last year more than 18,000 babies were born in this building, roughly 1 out of every 200 babies born in the U.S. "Sometimes they are lined up in the hallways and stacked up for C-sections like planes at LAX, six or seven deep," says obstetrician-gynecologist David Grimes.

But this busiest of U.S. obstetrics units also symbolizes an American failure: the extent to which the birth control revolution has not fulfilled its promise in the country where it began. Three decades after the Pill was introduced in the U.S., a shocking number of the 58 million American women of childbearing age still find it difficult to control their own reproduction, especially compared with women in other countries. Teenage pregnancy in the U.S. is more than double that of European countries, and the nation's abortion rate—1.6 million a year—is one of the highest in the developed world. All told, more than half of all American pregnancies—3.4 million out of 6 million each year—are accidents, the result of misusing contraceptives, using unreliable contraceptives or using no contraceptives at all.

The sorry state of birth control in America is underscored in a report prepared by the Population Crisis Committee, a nonprofit research group based in Washington. The committee found not only that Americans have fewer contraceptive options than their counterparts in most developed countries, but also that contraceptive devices are more expensive and more difficult to obtain in the U.S. than in some parts of the Third World.

While scientists around the globe are making rapid progress deciphering the dance of hormones that makes pregnancy possible—work that raises new strategies for blocking conception—the major American pharmaceutical companies have all but abandoned the field. Of the nine doing research in contraceptives 20 years ago, only one (Ortho Pharmaceutical) is still active. The others have been scared off by the fear of costly lawsuits like the one that drove the maker of the Dalkon Shield, an intrauterine device, into bankruptcy, and by public controversy such as that surrounding RU-486, the French "abortion pill."

Most of the world's governments encourage family planning and even subsidize the use of birth control devices. The U.S. stands out as the only major industrialized country that is moving in the opposite direction. Over the past decade, Washington has halted federal research on new reproductive technologies and declined to approve some of the most promising new methods of birth control.

There have been some improvements in U.S. contraceptive options, but they have been incremental rather than revolutionary. Manufacturers of the Pill have developed low-dose versions that avoid most of the side effects associated with earlier varieties. IUDs have improved greatly in the past decade and are now about as safe and effective as the Pill. And owing largely to the fear of AIDS, the condom, which dates back to the age of the Pharaohs, has come out from behind the pharmacists' counters and is now prominently displayed at stores across the U.S. in various colors, shapes and sizes.

Even the Food and Drug Administration-sanctioned Norplant—the long-lasting hormone implant hailed as the first new contraceptive device approved for use in the U.S. in three decades—is really a repackaging of the same chemical used in the Pill. Norplant is housed in matchstick-size tubes and inserted under the skin of a woman's arm. Its main advantage is that it does not depend on someone's remembering to take it every day. But it can cause irregular bleeding, and its cost (up to $1,000) puts it out of the price range of many who need it.

In Europe sexually active couples can choose from a wide selection of contraceptive approaches that includes more than two dozen different kinds of pills, monthly and bimonthly contraceptive injections, and an IUD that boosts its effectiveness with the slow release of hormones. The big news this summer is Britain's decision to become the second country—after France—to approve the sale of RU-486, the controversial postcoital contraceptive.

Carl Djerassi, the Stanford chemist who helped develop the original Pill in the early 1950s, calls RU-486 "the single most important new development in contraception of the past two decades." Reason: it gives women, for the first time, a relatively safe way to avoid pregnancy *after* they have had unprotected intercourse—thus fully removing the decision to exercise birth control from the decision to have sex. Basically, RU-486 is a menses inducer. Used in conjunction with a prostaglandin, it brings on a woman's period whether or not she is pregnant. Although there has been one death associated with its use (triggered by an allergic reaction to the prostaglandin), it is considered fairly safe. Several states, including conservative New Hampshire, are lining up to become test sites to speed its adoption in the U.S.

That is not likely to happen soon. Right-to-life groups have made opposition to the "French death pill" a rallying cry and have vowed to boycott not just it but all products made by any drug company that dares distribute it in the U.S. They argue that the notion of postcoital birth control is just abortion by another name; in addition, they are not enamored of the idea of separating sex from its consequences. "The problem is not that contraceptives are not available; the problem is that many people are not behaving responsibly," says Allan Carlson, president of the traditionalist Rockford Institute.

That attitude, which has come to dominate federal policy, indicates that the real dispute in America is not so much about abortion or contraception as it is about sex and values. American culture is a strange blend of prurience and prudery that tends to lead to the

worst of both worlds: movies and magazines that exploit sex and teach kids that it's glamorous and free of consequences, combined with a skittish denial of the facts of life that makes it hard to teach those kids how not to get pregnant.

"Many American women are grossly misinformed," says U.S.C.'s Grimes. For instance, 31% of American women in a 1985 Gallup poll indicated their belief that birth control pills cause cancer, when in fact the evidence shows that for nonsmokers the Pill actually reduces the risk of ovarian and endometrial cancer. Europeans are much better at putting sex—and birth control—in its place. Despite their Roman Catholic heritage, the French schools conscientiously provide sex education during which birth control and abortion are frankly discussed.

It would be a mistake, however, to blame the paucity of new contraceptive devices in the U.S. just on puritanical attitudes and conservatism.

One group that would have been expected to be contraception's natural constituency, feminists, has been more vocal in pointing out the dangers of various devices than in promoting their use. The positive result was the development of the new low-dose pills. The negative effect was that thousands of women abandoned the Pill altogether.

The National Academy of Sciences last year called for an infusion of federal dollars into contraceptive research, better sex-education programs and protection from liability suits for manufacturers who want to get back into the birth control business. But under the current Administration such actions are unlikely. Meanwhile, sexually active Americans are often left with an inadequate range of options: make the best of the contraceptives they have, choose to be sterilized, or turn to abortion when all else fails. With the last option under increasing legal challenge, the choices at the turn of the century are likely to be narrower than they are today.

Philip Elmer-Dewitt, "Why Isn't Our Birth Control Better?" *Time*, August 12, 1991.

during the forties, when some cycles are skipped altogether. The pituitary gland regulates the female sex hormones of estrogen and progesterone, which in turn control the menstrual cycle. The hormone levels in the blood vary at different stages of the menstrual cycle. At the midpoint of the cycle ovulation occurs, depending on the interaction of the pituitary gland, hypothalamus, and ovarian and uterine products. Estrogen reaches its peak shortly before ovulation, and progesterone peaks several days before menstruation, then declines rapidly.

Apparently, hormonal changes at different phases of the menstrual cycle cause changes in the direction of sexual impulse. Women have an active, extroverted sexual tendency in the first (estrogen-dominated) half of the cycle. They have higher self-esteem and lower anxiety and hostility. Shortly after ovulation a decrease is reported in "heterosexual tension," or in being "turned on" sexually. In the second (progesterone-dominated) half of the cycle, the mood shifts toward introversion, and dream material is often weighted with themes of pregnancy and mother-child relations. The incidence of coitus, as well as orgasm, is highest around midcycle, approximately the time when progesterone is at its highest. Ironically, significant increases in anxiety, depression, and hostility have also been noted during this time, which seems inconsistent with the increase in coitus and orgasm (Bermant and Davidson 1974).

Women in the age-group eighteen to thirty generally have lower food requirements than men. Women, however, need more iron in their diet to replace the loss due to menstruation. Mild anemia from iron deficiency is common. A pregnant woman's intake of calcium and iron should be higher than a man's. Women need energy foods and protein during lactation, when their calorie requirement is about three thousand, the same as that of a moderately active man. If a pregnant or lactating woman's diet is inadequate, her health will probably suffer before that of her baby (Story 1990). If her health is poor, her effectiveness as a mother could be so hampered that she could not properly care for her child.

After age thirty, the loss of elasticity in the pelvic tissues of women makes childbirth increasingly difficult. There is more resistance to the baby's head as it passes from the uterus to the outside world. A birth canal widened by previous births makes these aging effects less important. For some women over forty, the ovaries fail to ovulate and thus lead to the inability to become pregnant, but many women remain fertile until age fifty (Reeder and Martin 1987).

Reproductive functioning in men also begins at puberty. The Leydig cells apparently begin a slow decline in number around twenty-five years of age, accompanied by a gradual decline in androgen secretions. Because sperm can be produced throughout adulthood, the male's ability to father a child is not affected by these physiological changes (Schwartz et al. 1983; Swerdloff and Heber 1982). Even so, sperm produced later in life (beginning in the forties and fifties) are fewer, less viable (Swerdloff and Heber 1982), and less motile (Schwartz et al. 1983).

• COGNITIVE DEVELOPMENT

Cognitive theories have primarily addressed the intellectual development of children. Few have been concerned with mental growth and change after maturity. The development of adult intellectual ability has been approached primarily through empirical and descriptive strategies that focus on reasoning and problem solving, social relationships, imagery and fantasy, and, beyond Piaget's formal operational stage, problem finding and dialectical thinking.

Reasoning and Problem Solving

Although logical thinking is perfected in adolescence, it is not used much until adulthood. When individuals become committed and responsible, they apply their logical abilities to choosing the best course of action in problem solving. The problems faced in adulthood do not necessarily have a single correct solution. They tend to be more complex and long-term than the situations encountered during earlier stages. When individuals realize the complexity of various life challenges, they realize the necessity of a guiding philosophy or life plan that gives direction, emphasis, and style to the problem-solving task.

When a life problem is faced in an active, directed way, cognitive growth is stimulated. For example, when an individual recognizes that there is a discrepancy between what he or she wishes were true of reality and what he or she assesses to be true, the discrepancy encourages the person to move to a new level of arousal and attention (Schaie 1977–78; Schaie and Geiwitz 1982).

Searching for a solution can be stimulating. The search usually involves generating many solutions and then imagining the consequences of each one. Searching for solutions provides an opportunity to manipulate reality by modifying conditions to fit one's goals more satisfactorily (Newman 1982; Schaie 1977–78; Schaie and Geiwitz 1982).

Implementing a solution offers an opportunity for the individual to learn how closely his or her problem-solving skills predict reality. If the solution works, the individual feels a sense of success. If not, new opportunities are still opened up in the process. It is possible to become aware of new aspects of reality and to reevaluate personal resources used in problem solving (Newman 1982).

By young adulthood, cognition has reached the point at which abstractions, hypothesis testing, logic, and a capacity for the simultaneous manipulation of several variables emerge. Evidence exists, however, that the quality of reasoning and problem solving changes during adult life (Schaie and Geiwitz 1982; Newman 1982).

As Piaget's stage of formal operations asserts, adults direct their thinking not only toward finding solutions to problems but also toward thought itself. Monitoring one's thoughts, or metacognition, provides a means of detecting errors in logic or misunderstandings. Adults have the capability of imposing or removing constraints on their thoughts and thus solving the same problem under varied conditions. The mind operates at two levels simultaneously: one level generates ideas, and the other level keeps the usual constraints from interfering. In adult life, many levels of consciousness exist simultaneously. Each level offers a unique contribution to knowing.

Social Relationships

Adults often find themselves attempting to solve problems that center around interpersonal relationships. In fact, many of the same principles of thought that apply to solving mathematical or scientific problems also apply in these situations (Newman 1982).

Social relationships or face-to-face relations fit into one of six categories.

Single Encounters

People often become involved in first-impression relations, or "brief encounters" that may not go beyond a single interaction. These can be enriching and vitalizing, depending upon the situation and the attitude of the participants. The individuals involved often expose facets of themselves—such as beliefs, experiences, and feelings—that they ordinarily do not discuss with others. This type of interaction can occur with a seatmate on an airplane, with a salesperson, with another person in line at the grocery store, with a hotel clerk, and so forth (Newman 1982; Coleman and Edwards 1980).

Associational Relations

Group membership requires people to have repeated encounters with certain other people over time. There may be no great degree of intimacy, depend-

Work responsibilities require interaction with colleagues. The situational and job requirements affect the quality of interaction and define the degree of personal investment.

ing on the situation. It is these relations that help establish one's public image and reputation in a community.

Business or Collegial Relations

Work responsibilities require interaction with colleagues. Depending on the job requirements, people may work long hours with others, in close quarters; may experience a high degree of interdependence; and may have some emotional involvement. Relations with co-workers may be terminated because of transfer, dismissal, promotion, or job change. The situational requirements affect the quality of interaction and define the degree of personal investment. The uniqueness of business relations can simultaneously promote distancing and engagement (Newman 1982).

Friendship Relations

Adults have a small number of close relationships called friendships. Friends can be a source of support and warm emotional feelings. They can bolster our ego, self-acceptance, and self-definition (Tesch 1983). They provide intellectual stimulation, provide practical help, and can be just plain fun. Friends are usually of the same gender, and men's and women's friendships appear to be different. Female friendships are more personal, intimate, and emotional, while male friendships revolve around shared activities and are limited in self-disclosure (Wright 1982; Bell 1981). Unconventional adults—those who are more androgynous—may have close, personal, intimate friends of both genders (Bell 1981).

Family Relations

Families provide a whole network of relationships. On a day-to-day basis, they provide occasional interactions. Family members have a special feeling toward one another that is unique when compared with the feeling in other human relationships. The degree of interaction between family members de-

Families provide a whole network of relationships. The degree of interaction between family members depends on such factors as similarity of interests and values, physical attractiveness, and likeability.

pends on such factors as similarity of interests and values, physical attractiveness, and likability.

Intimate Relations

Intimacy usually occurs between husband and wife, parent and child, and lovers. Deep understanding and intense emotional commitment to the other, and to his or her development, characterize intimate relations (Newman 1982).

Most people cognitively focus on all these personal relationships every day. Considerable time may be devoted to thinking about these interpersonal systems, without the participant being aware of it. The thought processes involved in these relationships can be very stimulating. Each relationship is analyzed, evaluated, and monitored within its own context. Adults use intellectual activity to devise plans for social interaction that meet personal needs while conforming to "perceived societal norms for responsive and ethical relationships" (Newman 1982; Schaie and Geiwitz 1982).

Imagery and Fantasy

Mental images are central to the process of thinking. People often describe them as "pictures in the mind." They are most often associated with fantasy thought. Daydreaming usually involves sequences of images accompanied by feelings and sometimes by voices or other sensory experiences. In adulthood, mental images are used as a tool for problem solving, and they have qualities that make them valuable for this task. They permit the integration of several variables simultaneously. They also preserve three-dimensional space in a way that the written word or a drawing might not. Mental images permit the systematic modification of objects or relationships without feeling constraint. This quality is useful in finding solutions to problems involving social relationships (Newman 1982).

Mental images
Mental representations, or "pictures in the mind," associated with fantasy thought.

Intimacy occurs between husband and wife, parent and child, and lovers.

Images can aid an individual in planning and setting goals for the future. Levinson et al. (1978) note that to become a responsible adult, the individual needs to form a "dream," or ideal master plan for life, and give it a place of importance in his or her life structure.

Mental images can also help us cope with stress. They can enable us to retain a confident, calm emotional state even under the most tense conditions. Through a series of imaginary encounters, a person can learn to approach a feared event with more confidence.

The amount of mental imagery and fantasy thought varies from person to person (Newman 1982).

Piaget's Theory

Piaget's theory is based on the understanding that cognitive change is inevitable in neurologically intact children all over the world. The stages in a child's cognitive development emerge in a fixed order: sensorimotor functioning, preoperational functioning, concrete operations, and formal operations. (See earlier chapters.) Early formulations of Piaget's theory assumed that all individuals achieve mastery of concrete and formal operations at some point in young adulthood, usually in the late teens (Sinnott 1975, 1989). This assertion has been questioned extensively (Sinnott 1975, 1989; Flavell 1970; Riegel 1973; Youniss 1974; Piaget 1972). Large numbers of subjects studied in late adolescence, early adulthood, and middle age could not successfully complete formal operational tasks. In a study by Kuhn et al. (1977), only 30 percent of adults had achieved the transition to concrete operations. Most remained between concrete and formal operations, and about 15 percent showed no formal thought at all. It is not obvious that adults experience a biological process similar to that of children that correlates with changes in their stage of cognitive development.

According to Flavell (1970), the cognitive changes occurring in adulthood

CHAPTER 13   *Early Adulthood—Physical and Cognitive Development* appear to be more quantitative than qualitative and of lesser magnitude than the typical infant-to-adult changes. For example, young adults process information faster than children do (Hale 1990). These cognitive changes do not occur in all adults.

Cognitive challenges faced by adults tend to require judgment and relate to attitudes and beliefs rather than to skills. Learning does seem to be involved. Higher education and experienced-based changes in attitudes and beliefs are important variables in the cognitive level of adults (Blackburn 1984; Flavell 1970; Piaget 1972; Sinnott 1975).

Beyond Formal Operations

Neo-Piagetians have introduced the concept of a stage of cognitive development beyond formal operations, a fifth stage that is qualitatively higher. Arlin (1975, 1984) characterizes adult thought as *problem finding*. According to him, formal operational thinking functions as the tool for going one step further in identifying, or "finding," problems of the real world. Riegel (1973) and Basseches (1980, 1984, 1989) call this final stage *dialectical thinking*. They theorize that each new thought produces an awareness of opposing thoughts. That is, the pros and cons, advantages and disadvantages, and possibilities and problems are considered for each idea and course of action taken. Neo-Piagetians stress experience as an important factor in the ability to make these judgments. Adults use logical processes geared to the complexities and many issues they face that have no simple, clear-cut, logical solution. They see the evolution of the universe as a continuing, ongoing process, and they view the process of finding and creating order in the universe as basic to human life and understanding. While these dialectical reasoners recognize the relativity and transience of the world, they attempt to integrate and seek order in their understanding of life (Basseches 1984, 1989). Kramer (1983) questions whether this is truly a fifth stage and genuinely distinct from formal operational thinking. It is possible that formal operations and dialectical thinking are alternative modalities of adult thought and not separate stages (Whitbourne and Weinstock 1986).

Humor

We have noted the correlation between the stage of humor and the stage of cognitive development throughout the life span. There is a positive correlation between an individual's intelligence and his or her sense of humor. The more intelligent person is able to perceive a greater variety of humorous situations than is his or her intellectually less able peer. The degree of intelligence also influences the individual's preferences in forms and expressions of humor. Personality is another influencing factor. It helps account not only for variations in humorous expressive behavior but also for diverse tastes in humor. A composite of individual personality, gender, education, intelligence, emotional maturity, and experience determines humorous attitude and accounts for substantial differences in the appreciation of humor among people regardless of age (Kappas 1967). For example, McGhee, Bell, and Duffey (1986) found that young adult women, when compared with elderly women, reported significantly more clowning, joking, witty remarks, and strong laughter. The younger women also grew up in homes where different kinds of humor were modeled. They reported more joking, clowning, and playful teasing by their mothers and fathers during their childhood than the elderly women reported of their parents.

One dimension of personality that affects humor development is extroversion-introversion. Individual differences in this dimension appear early in childhood and remain highly stable throughout adulthood. Extroverts generally are social, lively, impulsive, emotionally expressive, and eager for novelty and change. Introverts are generally quiet, introspective, emotionally unexpressive, and orderly. They also prefer small groups of friends. Extroverts tend to prefer sexual and aggressive humor. Introverts tend to prefer nonsense or incongruity humor. In general, extroverts rate joking higher than do introverts. Extroverts tend to seek out and initiate all kinds of humor more often than do introverts. The greater emotional expressiveness of extroverts leads them to be generally more responsive to humor; for example, they laugh more. Introverts, who tend toward behavioral control and inhibition, are less responsive to humor and initiate it less frequently (McGhee 1986).

Another personality dimension related to a sense of humor is cognitive style, that is, the way an individual processes information. The degree of reflection-impulsivity, or conceptual tempo, is an aspect of cognitive style closely related to humor comprehension and appreciation. Reflection-impulsivity has been found to be stable over periods of several years. Impulsive individuals laugh more than reflectives do, even if they do not get the "point." Reflectives show better comprehension (McGhee 1986).

Parisi and Kayson (1988) assessed the preference of young adults for two different cartoons: Family Circus and the Far Side. The first has a family-oriented setting, with a mother, father, and children. It often focuses on the viewpoint of the children concerning some everyday event. The second involves animals, fantasy creatures, or people in very unusual situations. The Far Side was considered more humorous and likable by the more educated young adults surveyed, who appreciated its sardonic, satiric humor more than wholesome, simplistic humor of Family Circus.

Freud argued that part of the pleasure derived from humor merely results from exercising intellect in trying to understand a joke. Subsequent research has supported this view. Freud proposed that adults tire of functioning in the realm of logical and rational thinking, and they need periodic escape from such demands. They enjoy reverting back to the playful feelings, actions, and thoughts of childhood. Humor provides such an escape (McGhee 1979).

Freud, who distinguished between wit, humor, and the comic, also felt that in most cases, the main source of pleasure in humor stems from strong sexual and aggressive impulses or wishes at the unconscious level that are seeking expression. Humor provides an outlet for these impulses in a manner that is socially acceptable (McGhee 1979).

Laughter, one outcome of humor, performs important dynamic functions for people. It may release pent-up tension or energy, permit the expression of ideas or feelings that otherwise would be difficult to express, and facilitate coping with sources of conflict and distress (McGhee 1979). In describing the social significance of humor, Konrad Lorenz stated:

> Laughter (as the overt expression of humor) produces simultaneously a strong fellow feeling among participants and joint aggressiveness against outsiders. Heartily laughing together at the same thing forms an immediate bond, much as enthusiasm for the same ideal does. Finding the same thing funny is not only a prerequisite to a real friendship, but very often the first step to its formation. Laughter forms a bond and simultaneously draws a line. If you cannot laugh with the others, you feel as an outsider, even if the laughter is in no way directed against yourself or indeed against anything at all. (Lorenz 1963, 284)

Young adult women, when compared with elderly women, reported significantly more clowning, joking, witty remarks, and strong laughter.

S U M M A R Y

- During the young adult years, people reach their peak of physical well-being. During the thirties, some physical abilities slacken, but they are masked by greater experience. Only slight changes occur in the brain and sensory organs of the young adult.

- Women's reproductive organs peak during young adulthood. After the thirtieth year, childbirth becomes increasingly more difficult. Many women remain fertile until the early fifties. The menstrual cycle is correlated with various cycles of behavior.

- Reproductive functioning for men begins at puberty. The Leydig cells, a source of male hormones, apparently begin to decline slowly in number around twenty-five years of age, but this does not affect the ability to father children.

- When adults become committed and responsible, they use their logical abilities to choose the best course of action in problem solving. Problems are more complex and long-term than they were earlier in life, so there is more need for a guiding philosophy or life plan that gives direction, emphasis, and style to the problem-solving task. Adults can monitor their own thoughts, a process called metacognition.

- Adults attempt to solve problems that center around interpersonal relationships. Many of the same principles of thought that apply to solving mathematical or scientific problems also apply to understanding social relationships.

- Mental images are central to the process of thinking. They are "pictures in the mind." For adults, mental images are used as a tool in problem solving, making future plans, and coping with stress.

- Neo-Piagetians introduced the concept of a fifth stage of cognitive development that is qualitatively higher than formal operations. It has been characterized as problem finding or dialectical thinking.

- Humor and intelligence are related. The more intelligent person can perceive a greater variety of humorous situations. Personality also can influence a person's preferences with respect to forms and expressions of humor.

Premenstrual Syndrome

Premenstrual syndrome (PMS), or premenstrual tension, affects 85 percent of menstruating women, and 40 percent experience fairly regular symptoms. For the 5 to 10 percent of menstruating women who suffer from *severe* PMS, the days before menstruation are marked by physiological and psychological symptoms that disrupt their personal and professional lives (Norris and Sullivan 1983). According to the Banton Medical Dictionary, PMS is

> a condition of nervousness, irritability, emotional disturbance, headache, and/or depression affecting some women for up to about ten days before menstruation. The condition is associated with the accumulation of salt and water in the tissues. It usually disappears soon after menstruation begins. The hormone progesterone is believed to be a causative element, and a deficiency of essential fatty acids has also been observed.

Estrogen stimulates the uterine lining to form a bed of blood-filled tissue that will receive a fertilized ovum, while progesterone is necessary to help finish preparing the uterine lining in case of a pregnancy. Progesterone is also necessary if the fertilized ovum is implanted. If the ovum is not fertilized, both hormonal levels (estrogen and progesterone) drop, and a menstrual period occurs.

For a woman who does not have PMS, the estrogen and progesterone levels rise after ovulation and stay in correct balance during the *luteal phase* (which begins at ovulation and ends at menstruation). For a woman with PMS, the estrogen level rises, but the progesterone level does not achieve the high level it should (Bender 1989). PMS is not diagnosed by the symptoms themselves but by *when* they occur. (If the symptoms occur within ten days prior to menstruation, then it is believed PMS is responsible.)

There are approximately 150 symptoms of PMS. They are both physical and psychological.

Common *physical symptoms* are the following:

- bloating
- weight gain
- acne
- dizziness
- migraine headaches
- breast tenderness
- joint and muscle pain
- backaches

- changes in sex drive
- food cravings
- constipation
- diarrhea
- sweating
- shakiness
- seizures
- cold or flu symptoms

Common *psychological symptoms* include these:

- anger
- loss of control
- sudden mood swings
- emotional overresponsiveness
- unexplained crying
- irritability
- anxiety
- forgetfulness
- decreased concentration
- confusion
- withdrawal
- sensitivity to rejection
- depression
- nightmares
- suicidal thoughts

(Bender 1989)

Heilbrun and Frank (1989) found that women who experience high levels of premenstrual distress are more self-preoccupied and have a higher level of general stress than do other women.

Harrison et al. (1989) and Rosen, Moghadam, and Endicott (1990) compared PMS women who were psychologically healthy with PMS women who had mental disorders. Both groups had similar physiological symptoms except for breast pain, which was more severe among the healthy women. Those with mental disorders had higher scores on a number of psychological variables associated with depression, tension, and reduced performance, and the symptoms were exacerbated during the premenstrual period. For example, they reported more feelings of loneliness, stress, and pessimism, and they blamed others more. It also was found by Harrison et al. (1989) that both groups seeking treatment for premenstrual symptoms tended to have a lifetime history of depression, panic disorder, suicide attempts, and substance abuse. Among the

Premenstrual Syndrome (continued)

healthy women, 12 percent of those who experienced symptoms only during the premenstrual period had prior suicide attempts, compared with 32 percent of the psychiatrically ill. Both Harrison et al. (1989) and Paddison et al. (1990) suggest that women with persistent mental disorders find it more acceptable to attribute their symptoms to PMS and that many women with PMS are mistakenly diagnosed with mental disorders.

Harrison et al. (1989) found that their psychiatrically ill subjects experienced more severe premenstrual symptoms as they aged. In fact, none of the mentally ill women said their symptoms improved over time, while 10 percent of the healthy women reported improvement.

Sexually abused women are more likely to suffer from symptoms of PMS. Paddison et al. (1990) found that 40 percent of the PMS women in their study had been sexually abused. (The prevalence rate of sexual abuse in society is 18 percent.) Fifty-five percent of the sexually abused women had been abused as children and 45 percent as adults. Sexual abuse of females is more likely to occur among low-SES (low-socioeconomic-status) women than among high-SES women. Low-SES women were more likely to be abused by a relative, and high-SES women were more likely to be abused by a "friend." Both the low- and the high-SES abused women were similar regarding the severity of premenstrual symptoms. Although both groups showed elevated levels of anxiety and depression, the incidence of depression did not differ. However, depression was more severe for the low-SES group. The implications are that sexual abuse may sensitize women and predispose them to react to cyclic hormonal changes with premenstrual symptoms. It is also possible that sexual abuse sensitizes women to depression, and depression predisposes them to PMS (Paddison et al. 1990).

PMS has been implicated in a host of family-related problems, from general marital discord to separation, divorce, and child abuse. The woman, in turn, feels guilty and ashamed, which lowers self-esteem (Norris and Sullivan 1983). Because there are indications that the symptoms worsen over the years, women and their families may not even be aware of the pattern initially.

What can women do if they show the symptoms of PMS? What can spouses and other family members do to cope with the situation?

In France and England, PMS can be used as a defense if a woman commits a crime, especially a violent crime. Do you think American courts should take this into consideration when trying women for crimes?

• PMS affects 85 percent of menstruating women to some degree, while 5 to 10 percent of menstruating women suffer severely enough that it disrupts their personal and professional lives. There are 150 physical and psychological symptoms. Symptoms tend to increase as women age. Families are affected as well as the victims.

Gilligan, C. (1983). *In a different voice: Psychological theory and women's development.* Cambridge, MA: Harvard University Press.
    Author combines theories of moral development, research on moral development, and literary classics to demonstrate why women understand moral issues differently than men do.

Friedrich, J. C. (1987). *The pre-menstrual solution.* San Jose, CA: Arrow Press.
    Discussion of the problem of PMS and possible solutions to it.

Keen, S. (1983). *The passionate life: Stages of loving.* New York: Harper and Row.
    The author, influenced by Kohlberg, focused on the emotional/loving side of the adult developmental process.

Kegan, R. (1982). *The evolving self.* Cambridge, MA: Harvard University Press.
    Also influenced by Kohlberg, the author offers, in a clear and easy to read style, a view of the emerging adult.

READINGS

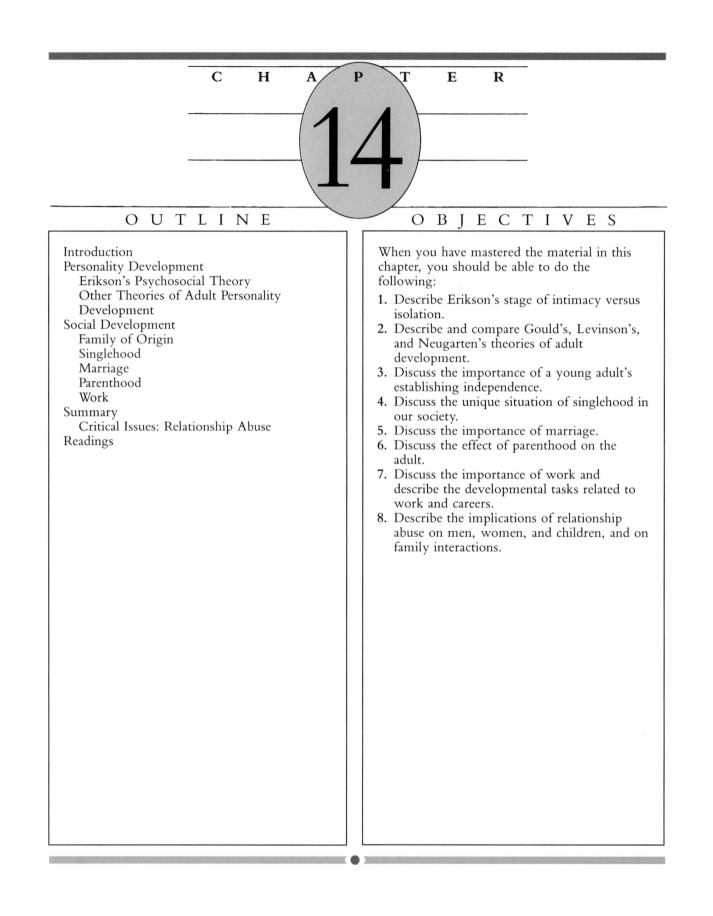

C H A P T E R

14

O U T L I N E

Introduction
Personality Development
    Erikson's Psychosocial Theory
    Other Theories of Adult Personality
    Development
Social Development
    Family of Origin
    Singlehood
    Marriage
    Parenthood
    Work
Summary
    Critical Issues: Relationship Abuse
Readings

O B J E C T I V E S

When you have mastered the material in this chapter, you should be able to do the following:

1. Describe Erikson's stage of intimacy versus isolation.
2. Describe and compare Gould's, Levinson's, and Neugarten's theories of adult development.
3. Discuss the importance of a young adult's establishing independence.
4. Discuss the unique situation of singlehood in our society.
5. Discuss the importance of marriage.
6. Discuss the effect of parenthood on the adult.
7. Discuss the importance of work and describe the developmental tasks related to work and careers.
8. Describe the implications of relationship abuse on men, women, and children, and on family interactions.

The Emerging Adult:
Early Adulthood—Psychosocial Development

INTRODUCTION

"**N**o single statement about any age is true of everybody. There is no monotonous sameness embracing all human beings" (Guntrip 1973, 69). For the adult, the individual personality is embedded in complex interpersonal networks and social systems, such as relationships between couples, within families, and in work environments.

PERSONALITY DEVELOPMENT

Erikson's Psychosocial Theory

Erikson was one of the first theorists to recognize that there is life after adolescence, and in doing so he identified three adult stages. He labeled the first adult stage "intimacy versus isolation." (The other two, generativity versus stagnation and ego-integrity versus despair, will be discussed later.) During intimacy versus isolation, either a young adult forms a commitment with another person so that a warm and meaningful relationship is established, or he or she has unsuccessful and superficial relationships with little or no intimacy, and a sense of ostracism or isolation occurs. Intimacy involves joining the separate identities of two individuals to form intense, durable, and close bonds (Whitbourne and Weinstock 1986). The young adult, after searching for and arriving at a personal identity, is now ready to fuse it with that of another. Each party to an intimate relationship influences the identity of the other. Most young adults attempt to accomplish intimacy through close friendships, sexual relationships, love relationships, and/or marriage. Erikson notes that the danger of this stage is that not only intimate but also competitive and combative relations can be experienced with the same person.

Erikson (1963) perceives intimacy as a combination of mutuality, sensitivity to a loved partner, physical closeness, willingness to share, and openness. In true mutual intimacy an adult retains his or her unique identity outside the fusion of the two identities but is still strongly committed to the relationship. It is only at this point that true *genitality* can fully develop. Much of sex before personal commitment is of the identity-seeking kind, whereas genitality is described by Erikson as a "permanent state of reciprocal sexual bliss." This utopia of genitality should include the following:

1. mutuality of orgasm
2. with a loved partner
3. of the other sex
4. with whom one is able and willing to share a mutual trust
5. and with whom one is able and willing to regulate the cycles of
   a. work
   b. procreation
   c. recreation
6. so as to secure to the offspring, too, all the stages of a satisfactory development
   (Erikson 1963, 266)

Although Erikson viewed intimacy in the context of a married heterosexual relationship, intimacy defined as mutuality can describe any relationship that involves emotional commitment between two adults. It can include close friendships between adults of the same or opposite gender, or homosexual and heterosexual adult relationships that have not been sanctioned by the legal system. The mutuality experienced in an intimate relationship incorporates deep and open communication and a strong commitment by both partners to one another and to the future of the relationship (Whitbourne and Weinstock 1986).

Carl Rogers (1972) stresses permanence of the intimate relationship and the enrichment that each partner contributes to it. Both partners need to work to ensure permanence and, in turn, provide a growth experience for the other. Enrichment of an intimate relationship is encouraged by communication, growth of each partner, and a lack of strict role expectations. Rogers believes that communication in true intimacy must allow each partner to reveal elements of self in an open and honest way and must contribute to an environment that encourages each partner to feel comfortable in being open. By eliminating strict role expectations, partners can accept, develop, and clarify roles as they relate to each other. This clarification enables each person to grow as an individual and become a fully functioning person while at the same time enhancing the growth of the other into a fully functioning person. These elements apply to any type of intimate adult relationship.

Isolation is the avoidance of contacts that commit to intimacy, and it leads to a deep self-absorption. Isolation can take the form of actually withdrawing from others within society and refusing to establish close friendships and relationships. In psychopathology, this disturbance can lead to severe "character problems." Partnerships can be formed between two isolated people, protecting both from the necessity to face the next critical development—that of generativity (Erikson 1963).

Erikson perceives intimacy as a combination of mutuality, sensitivity to a loved partner, physical closeness, willingness to share, and openness.

Other Theories of Adult Personality Development

Gould

Roger Gould's (1975, 1978) research supports a stage theory approach to adult development. While observing adults undergoing treatment in a psychiatric clinic, Gould concluded that the concerns prompting people to come to the clinic were related to age. He tested his ideas on a nonpsychiatric sample of more than five hundred men and women ranging in age from sixteen to fifty. According to Gould, over the years adults dismantle the protective devices they developed during childhood. These include a whole network of untested false assumptions that help protect the important illusion of absolute safety established during childhood. Gould (1978) theorizes that as young children, we maintained our belief in four major false assumptions:

1. I'll always live with my parents and be their child.
2. Doing it my parents' way, with willpower and perseverance, will bring results.
3. Life is simple and controllable. There are no significant coexisting contradictory forces within me.
4. There is no real death or evil in the world.

By the time of adulthood these assumptions are seen as factually incorrect, but they maintain a hidden control until significant events reveal them as emotional and intellectual fallacies. It is difficult to trust the new ability to think and judge as the only source of safety. Shedding these false assumptions marks the gradual shift from childhood consciousness into adult consciousness over the range of decades.

TABLE 14.1 Gould's Stages of Adult Personality Development

AGE	NAME OF STAGE	FALSE ASSUMPTION	CHARACTERISTICS
16–22	Leaving My Parents' World	I'll always live with my parents and be their child.	• Individual escapes from parental dominance. • Future is distant and unknown. • Substitute friends for family but still be a part of family.
22–28	I'm Nobody's Baby Now	Doing it my parents' way, with willpower and perseverance, will bring results.	• Individual becomes part of the "now" generation. • He or she develops more self-reliance and makes less use of friends.
28–34	Opening Up to What's Inside	Life is simple and controllable. There are no significant coexisting contradictory forces within me.	• Self-assurance waivers. • Individual is more self-reflective. • Marriage absorbs and reflects many stresses and strains. • Children become increasingly important. • Focus shifts from own parents to children.
34–45	Mid-life Decade	There is no real death or evil in the world.	• Friends and loved ones become increasingly important. • Time is visibly finite. • Personal comfort decreases. • Marital comfort is at a low level.
45 and beyond	Beyond Mid-life	No false assumptions.	• Feelings and relationships mellow. • Focus turns to what one has accomplished. • Individual is more interested in "everyday" experiences, no frills and glitter.

The first assumption, "I'll always live with my parents and be their child," is challenged in minor ways before the end of high school. From eighteen to twenty-two, however, it is challenged in more significant ways when events such as living away from home or joining a protest march bring the assumption into question. A great sense of liberation along with a potent new fear is the initial reaction when this tie to childhood is shed.

The second assumption, "Doing it my parents' way, with willpower and perseverance, will bring results," is challenged during the twenties. This period is marked by setting up an independent life and making major decisions that cannot be made by others, such as decisions about marriage, pregnancy, or a career. When this assumption is challenged, the young adult experiences a new sense of fundamental strength and independence. This new identity stimulates a feeling of competence.

The third assumption, "Life is simple and controllable. There are no significant coexisting contradictory forces within me," is challenged during the late twenties and early thirties. This is when most of the simple rules and "supposed-to-be's" about life prove ineffectual in the complicated real world. Once an individual becomes competent and independent in the external world, it is possible to get in touch with the "feared" inner world.

The fourth assumption, "There is no real death or evil in the world," is challenged during the early thirties and throughout the forties. This period is marked by mounting time pressures, others dying, parents becoming peripheral, and children preparing to leave home. The adult must get in touch with his or her own inner core without destroying other valuable parts of life.

Gould is quick to point out that the statements concerning each age-group are generalizations, but he believes the sequence is true for most people. The ages in which changes occur are a product of an individual's total personality, life-style, and subculture.

Levinson

Daniel Levinson and his colleagues (1978) conducted a longitudinal study of forty men, with the primary aim of identifying "a developmental perspective of adulthood in men." The common notion of adulthood as a fixed and unchanging state was rejected in favor of the concept of the life process as a sequence of seasons—periods or stages within the total life cycle. As a man progresses from one season to the next, he goes through alternating periods of stability and transition. Periods of stability involve building a structure around a series of choices, and these will determine the values and goals the man pursues during the ensuing six or seven years of stability. Then, internal factors interacting with external factors encourage the man to question and modify the existing life structure. During the transition period, which lasts about four or five years, new choices are explored that will form the basis for a new life structure. Inner conflict and a sense of crisis permeate the transition periods.

The first to occur is *early adult transition,* which links adolescence and early adulthood. It begins at age seventeen and ends at age twenty-two, give or take two years. Two tasks terminate pre-adulthood and begin early adulthood. The first is to move out of the pre-adult world, that is, "to question the nature of that world and one's place in it; to modify or terminate existing relationships with important persons, groups and institutions; to reappraise and modify the self that formed in it." The second task is to take a preliminary step into the adult world. This entails exploring "its possibilities, to imagine oneself as a participant in it, to consolidate an initial adult identity, to make and test some preliminary choices for adult living." The individual leaves the family during this time. The military or college may function as a transitional institution. An approximately equal balance exists between "being in" the family and "moving out." It is necessary to become less financially dependent, enter new roles and living arrangements, become more independent, and assume self-responsibility. This period lasts from three to five years.

The next period is the *first adult life structure—entering the adult world.* It extends from approximately twenty-two to twenty-eight years of age. A shift occurs in the center of gravity of a man's life, away from his family of origin. He must now become a "novice" adult with a home base of his own. Through peer friendships, love relationships, and occupational experiences, he arrives at an initial definition of himself as an adult. He needs to explore the possibilities for adult living, which means keeping his options open, avoiding strong commitments, and maximizing the alternatives. This is quite often reflected by a sense of adventure and wonderment. He also needs to create a "stable life structure" by committing himself to adult roles, responsibilities, and relationships that reflect his evolving set of priorities. It is not easy to find a balance between these tasks. Therefore, he may lay the groundwork for a career; or he may develop one career and then discard it; or he may drift aimlessly, creating a crisis at about age thirty, when strong pressures to achieve more order and stability occur.

The *age-thirty transition—changing the first life structure* extends roughly from age twenty-eight to thirty-three. This transition provides an opportunity to work on the limitations and flaws of the first adult life structure. Some men experience a smooth transition, without disruption or a sense of crisis. They modify their lives in certain respects but build on the past without making fundamental changes. For most men, however, Levinson found that this transition takes a more stressful form, that is, "the age-thirty crisis." A developmental crisis indicates great difficulty with the tasks required. A man feels that his life structure is intolerable but is unable to form a better one. A crucial step in adult male development is the shift from the age-thirty transition into the next period.

The second adult life structure—settling down usually begins in the early thirties and persists until about age forty. This is the culmination of early adulthood. The man invests himself in society and his future by building a nest and pursuing long-range plans and goals. His task during this time is to become a full-fledged adult within his own world. Advancement and a need for affirmation by others are central to this period. Advancement specifically refers to increases in social rank, income, power, fame, creativity, quality of family life, and social contribution. His sense of well-being depends on his own and others' evaluation of his progress toward these goals.

Toward the end of this period, approximately age thirty-six to age forty, there is a distinct phase called *becoming one's own man*. This represents the high point of early adulthood and the beginning of what lies beyond. A man frequently feels he is not independent no matter what he has accomplished so far. He believes that his superiors control too much and delegate too little. If a man has a mentor—a teacher, an experienced co-worker or boss—he is likely to give him up now.

The mid-life transition—moving from early to middle adulthood lasts roughly from age forty to forty-five. The disillusionment experienced during the mid-life transition involves the disappointment of not having one's "dream" or life goals come to fruition. The individual must come to terms with the reality of what he has achieved and revise his dream for the future in keeping with the true state of things. He questions his life structure again and asks: What have I done with my life? What do I really get from and give to my wife, children, friends, work, community—and self? What do I truly want for myself and others? He yearns to have his actual desires, values, talents, and aspirations expressed. Commonly he senses disparity between "what I've got now" and "what I really want," which leads to an interval of soul-searching. The majority of men experience a period of great struggle within the self and with the external world. The mid-life transition is a time of moderate or severe crisis. Every aspect of life is questioned, and the man feels he cannot go on as before. The end of the mid-life transition is marked by a series of changes rather than one dramatic event.

Entering middle adulthood—building a new life structure involves giving up the tasks of the mid-life transition. This occurs at about age forty-five. The life structure that emerges varies greatly in its suitability for the self and its workability in the world. Men who suffered irreparable defeats in childhood or early adulthood and had little time to work on their mid-life transition lack the inner and outer resources to build a new life structure. Others form a structure that is reasonably possible in the world but poorly connected to the self. That is, their life lacks inner excitement and meaning. Others find middle adulthood the fullest and most creative season. They are more deeply attached to others, while at the same time more separate and centered in the self.

Levinson and Gould had similar findings and perceive adulthood as a predictable series of stages. Levinson's small sample was not representative; half the subjects were extremely well educated and intellectually oriented, and another one quarter were top business executives. This extreme bias toward the upper end of the socioeconomic ladder jeopardizes the generality of the findings. Gould's sample consisted of both men and women, but its representativeness was not clarified, and there was no other descriptive information about the sample. Although flawed, these studies open up a number of issues about adult development and suggest that adulthood is not a time of boring stability or depressing decline.

Neugarten

Bernice L. Neugarten, a psychologist noted for her research on adult development, believes that a stage approach oversimplifies adult life, and she raises many important questions regarding the relevance of such an approach. People change as a result of accumulated experience. Due to complicated patterns of personal and social commitments, not only are adults more complex than children, but they also differ more from one another than do children. They become increasingly different as they move through life. The adult is also capable of manipulating the environment to reach his or her goals. The adult sense of time and timing is important to consider. By middle age, the highly refined powers

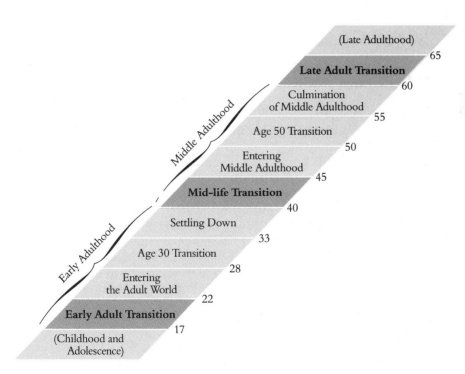

● **FIGURE 14.1**
Developmental Periods in Early and Middle Adulthood
As a man progresses from one season to the next, he goes through alternating periods of stability and transition.

Source: THE SEASON'S OF A MAN'S LIFE by Daniel J. Levinson. Copyright © 1978 by Daniel J. Levinson. Reprinted by permission of Alfred A. Knopf, Inc.

The timing of life events is becoming less regular in our society. It is no longer unusual to encounter the seventy-year-old student.

Age-grading
The traditional society's system of social expectations regarding age-appropriate behavior.

of introspection and reflection enable adults to reinterpret the past in order to establish coherence with the present. The ability to deal with both the past and the present simultaneously is a unique characteristic of the adult human personality. Middle-aged people use their memories in a different fashion than do the elderly. The former consciously draw from past experience in solving present problems, while the latter seem to put their store of memories in order so as to prepare for the end of their life story (Neugarten 1975).

Another issue in Neugarten's argument involves the ways in which individuals evaluate themselves in relation to socially defined time. In traditional societies **age-grading** provides a system of social expectations regarding age-appropriate behavior. Each individual follows a socially regulated schedule from birth to death. A socially prescribed timetable determines the order of major life events (marriage, birth of children, retirement). Age norms and age expectations function as a system of social controls. In modern society, men and women are aware of the social clocks that operate in various areas of their lives, know whether they are "early," "late," or "on time." This enables them to evaluate not only their family relations but also their occupational goals. They compare themselves with friends, classmates, and/or siblings to evaluate whether they have "made good." The timing of life events is becoming less regular in our society, however. Age is losing much of its customary meaning, and there is a trend toward a more fluid life cycle and an age-irrelevant society. It is no longer unusual to encounter the twenty-eight-year-old mayor, the thirty-year-old chief executive officer, the thirty-five-year-old grandmother, the fifty-year-old retiree, the sixty-five-year-old new father, and the seventy-year-old student (Neugarten 1975; Neugarten et al. 1968). Therefore, adulthood cannot be described as a series of discrete and neatly bounded stages. Many inner changes occur slowly across the life span and not in a stagelike fashion.

One study approached adult development from the perspective of roles and states of well-being rather than stages. Baruch, Barnett, and Rivers (1983) addressed the factors contributing to the well-being of adult women between ages thirty-five and fifty-five. A random sample survey of three hundred Caucasian

CHAPTER 14 *The Emerging Adult: Early Adulthood—Psychosocial Development* women was grouped into subsamples of "never married," "divorced with children," "married without children," and "married with children." All of the women in the first two groups and half of the women in the second two were employed outside the home. The women were asked about the rewards and pleasures in their lives. The analyses of the data revealed a two-dimensional picture of well-being. There was a strong statistical relationship among self-esteem, control over one's life, and levels of anxiety and depression. For example, women with high self-esteem and feelings of control typically scored low on the depression scale. This dimension of well-being, labeled "mastery," is related to the "doing" side of life, that is, the instrumental side. The second dimension, "pleasure," is related to the "feeling" side of life, that is, the quality of relationships with others. For example, a strong relationship was found among happiness, satisfaction, and optimism. This two-dimensional model provides a system for looking at how a whole range of issues affect women. It makes it easier to understand why a woman may feel good and/or distressed by certain circumstances. For example, why would a career woman who takes a year off to have a baby simultaneously feel intense joy and worthlessness? Perhaps she is nurturing the pleasure side of well-being while the mastery side is being neglected.

Women with the highest sense of well-being were those who took on several roles and had not confined themselves only to a career or only to home-making. Those women who were the most satisfied had taken on roles of marriage, motherhood, and employment outside the home, despite feelings of strain and stress. The rewards outweighed the stress for these women.

Stress was found to be greatest for women at home with children. They were more likely to feel role-strain by mid-life than were women employed outside the home. Homemaking is today's "high-risk job." Factors that left women in the role of homemaker were financial problems, the death of spouse, divorce, and changing personal and social needs. Women in low-status jobs also were more likely to feel stress than women in high-status jobs.

Satisfied married women felt that they had achieved economic security, intimacy, and sexual pleasure, and they experienced a sense of pleasure. Divorced and unmarried women employed outside the home reported strong feelings of mastery and had feelings of well-being comparable to the pleasure felt by satisfied married women.

The study found that no one "lifeprint" ensured all women a perpetual sense of well-being. American adult women are finding satisfying and fulfilling lives in a variety of role patterns. No one role pattern guarantees happiness or is problem-free. No single life pattern is hard or easy. Most role patterns involve trade-offs at different points in the life cycle.

"So for women, the 'age and stage' theories are not the answer to understanding the pattern of a life. Theories of women's lives that are now evolving take into account the fact that the times do change, and as environments change, people change with them" (Baruch et al. 1983, 242).

● SOCIAL DEVELOPMENT

Adulthood is a time of change and development. Involvement and interaction with others is as important for the young adult as it is for children and adolescents. Social development continues to be enhanced by family, friends, spouses, and fellow workers.

Family of Origin

Young adults must establish themselves as distinct from their family of origin. Some of the most difficult problems are forced on young adults by immature and anxious parents who think of them as "the children" and cling to the "right" to tell them what they ought to do. Emotional ties to parents persist long after economic and domestic independence is achieved. The unconscious persistence of parent-child relationships plays a large part in shaping all kinds of human relations at all ages, but this is most important during young adulthood.

As they move through their twenties, young adults become less dependent on, and have fewer contacts with, their parents. It is during this time that most of the momentous and significant relationships are entered into, such as marriage, parenthood, and professional and business commitments. In the process of committing to one or more of these areas, the young adult supresses some of the personality potentials with which he or she was born. Some individuals drift through the early twenties and delay making serious commitments until their thirties, or never do (Neugarten 1975; Rogers 1982; Donohugh 1981).

Autonomy does not necessarily follow when one leaves home and is free of excessive parental authority. A spouse, usually a wife, may transfer her dependency from her parents to her spouse, especially a domineering one (Rogers 1982).

Establishing economic and domestic autonomy is a major hurdle practically and emotionally. Most young adults leave home during their late teens or early twenties to establish their own home, but some remain with their parents while completing their education or working nearby. Some also return to live with their parents for various reasons, such as becoming unemployed, leaving a spouse, becoming an unmarried mother, or having to provide care or assistance to needy parents. More young adults today than a few years ago are residing with their parents: 37 percent of those eighteen to twenty-nine years of age in 1984, compared with 34 percent in 1970. Because women marry at an earlier average age than men do, fewer women than men were living with their parents in 1984 (Glick and Lin 1986).

The growth of the American economy has slowed since the early 1970s, and more young people are postponing marriage. The cost of housing has increased, the divorce rate has risen rapidly, and the proportion of babies born to unmarried women has reached a new high. In addition, the young adults born during the baby boom are faced with high unemployment rates, particularly in occupations usually filled by new entrants into the labor market. For these reasons, a rising proportion of young adults either still live with their parents or have moved back home (Glick and Lin 1986).

According to one study, of the young adults who are living with relatives, nearly half are married and living there with their spouses. Many of these "doubled couples" are near or below the poverty level, but some are living with well-to-do parents. The other half are either separated or divorced; very few are widowed. Young adults who remain in their parents' home risk creating stressful relations. Those returning after a period of absence also may find that personal relations in the family are not as cordial as they once were, especially if they have a spouse and/or children with them (Glick and Lin 1986). An older student, when discussing this topic in class, related, "I cried when he [her young-adult son] moved out, and I damn near cried when he moved back."

A significant task for young adults is to establish values that will be a basis for direction throughout life. Youthful ideals, expectations, and optimism about attaining goals change gradually to greater realism bordering on pessimism. As young adults become more conscious of their limitations, most of them accept their fate in life and do not seek dramatically different experiences. They have moderate goals centered around solid, satisfying jobs and a contented, loving family life (Rogers 1982).

Singlehood

Three or four out of every one hundred Americans never marry. Remaining single has become a trend, and in 1982 there were 19.4 million single adults. Never-married men and women had been viewed negatively by our society, men less so than women. Single women were seen as less feminine, less loving and nurturing, less sexually attractive, and more selfish. During the past twenty years, however, singlehood has become more socially acceptable and is perceived increasingly as a deliberate choice by the individual (Cockrum and White 1985).

The median age for first marriages in the United States is 23.3 years for females and 25.5 years for males. The median age has risen since 1978 from 21.8 years for females and 24.2 years for males. The largest increase in singlehood has been among men and women between ages twenty and twenty-nine, an age-group representing almost 25 percent of young adults. The longer marriage is postponed, the more the likelihood of lifelong singleness increases (Doherty and Jacobson 1982; U.S. Bureau of the Census 1985). It is not yet clear whether the trend is toward postponed marriage or more lifelong singleness. Traditionally, most people who married did so by age forty. Unwed men were usually less educated, held lower occupations, and had lower incomes than those who married. Women who did not marry tended to have above-average educational levels and higher incomes (Kennedy 1978).

Individuals remain single for many reasons: Many prefer this life-style. Others lack the opportunity to marry. Some choose life commitments such as religious orders that require celibacy. A few are physically or emotionally ill and live in institutions. Many have financial needs or professions that preclude marriage. The statistics usually include homosexuals who may be unmarried but do not live as singles (Kennedy 1978).

Singlehood is becoming a subculture identified as a market area by housing and various other merchandising groups. Recreational, educational, and other kinds of programs have been tailored for singles. Within this broad category are several subgroups that have little interaction with one another. These include young nonmarrieds who may eventually marry, older nonmarrieds who may choose to remain so, and divorced or widowed people who may remarry. Each group has special interests and needs, as well as the distinction of not having a clearly defined social pattern in our society.

Social support serves a vital function for singles by validating singlehood as an acceptable adult status. Friendships are an important source of self-worth, comfort, and connection with the world. Similar values shared with friends reinforce the single adult as he or she functions in a marriage-based society. Friends of both genders are important to the happiness and life satisfaction of single adults. Visiting friends is one major way single adults reduce loneliness and unhappiness. Social support has been found to be a better predictor of life satisfaction than is marital status (Cockrum and White 1985; Block 1980).

Loneliness has been identified as a major problem for singles, especially

Three or four out of every one hundred Americans never marry. Remaining single has become a trend, and in 1982 there were 19.4 million single adults.

those who do not wish to be single. Men experience loneliness more often than women do. Many men do not develop the skills needed to build social and emotional support systems that can be used to reduce loneliness, and men are not socialized to be expressive and sharing. In contrast, women are encouraged to express themselves and be open about their feelings, so they are more likely to have support systems and to utilize their family network. Male life satisfaction is related to the availability of social relationships or the presence of a network of individuals who share interests and values. Female life satisfaction is related to affectional, close relationships that provide a sense of security and peace (Cockrum and White 1985).

Marriage

Along with birth and death, marriage is considered by many as one of the three great events in life. Unlike birth and death, marriage is largely within our control; we may choose when and who to marry. The adjustment to marriage requires significant changes in adulthood. It is probably the most influential relationship of adult life and the major source of demands for socialization upon the young adult. During the past fifty years, personal fulfillment both inside and outside marriage has been perceived as important as marital stability. The emerging norm of male-female equality in marriage has emphasized the importance of personal growth. The result is that contemporary marriage is more intense as well as more fragile than traditional marriage (Doherty and Jacobson 1982).

Evidence indicates elements of both stability and drastic change in the institution of marriage. Stability is indicated by the fact that Americans continue to marry and have children. More than 90 percent of American adults marry at some point in their life. Although most young adults marry, many are breaking tradition by living with someone of the opposite sex outside of marriage. In 1985 approximately two million households were unmarried couples (U.S. Bureau of Census 1985).

During early adulthood, the marriage choice is based on a realistic, objective attraction to someone who is physically, temperamentally, intellectually, and socially a genuine partner; the choice may also be based on an unconscious emotional attraction or repulsion due to childhood relationships. For example, the marriage choice may be influenced by the search for something in a personal relationship that a parent was unable to give. It may also be influenced by the need to continue a struggle with a parent through a substitute person, (resulting in a bad marriage that may prove impossible to break or to mend) (Guntrip 1973). The timing of marriage and parenthood may have as much consequence on the social development of the adult as the events themselves. Those who marry early have more children, usually more closely spaced, as well as lower educational achievement, lower occupational attainment, lower income, and higher marital instability. Delayed marriage for women until their late twenties has been found to enhance social-class status. Other variables affecting the social development of the adult include societal norms for marital- and family-role behavior and historical events impinging on the family. An additional factor is that adults are engaged in multiple-role careers (such as education, work, community involvement, as well as family), each role having its own socialization requirements and timetable (Doherty and Jacobson 1982).

Married people report the highest levels of happiness. Among the never

The adjustment to marriage requires significant changes in adulthood. It is probably the most influential relationship of adult life and the major source of demands for socialization upon the young adult.

married, men have less life satisfaction than women do. Married people have the lowest rates of mortality, physical and mental illness, and institutionalization. Widowed people have the second lowest rates of physical and mental illness, followed by single people. Separated and divorced people have the poorest health and the highest mortality (including rates of suicide, homicide, and accidental death). They have the highest rates of acute conditions, chronic conditions that limit social activity, health-related disability, and admission to both outpatient and inpatient psychiatric facilities. Being married may offer social support that decreases a person's vulnerability to physical and mental disorders. Separation, divorce, and death mean the loss of this support and require difficult adjustments that make a person more vulnerable to physical and mental disabilities (Doherty and Jacobson 1982).

Parenthood

Increasingly, parenthood has come to be viewed as an important social transition that produces various stresses, strains, rewards, and gratifications. Contemporary parenthood has elements of both continuity and change. Two demographic trends have been noted in the twentieth century: the increased proportion of couples who have children and the decreased number of children they have. Among married American women between the ages of fifteen and forty-four, 2 percent are voluntarily childless, 2 percent are involuntarily childless, and 15 percent are temporarily so, that is, they plan to have children in the future (Bachrach and Mosher 1982). There is some indication that the proportion of couples who want child-free life-styles is increasing, but the most impressive change in parenthood is the trend toward fewer children rather than no children. Three to four children per family was the average from the early twentieth century through the 1950s, but couples who married in the late 1970s reported that they expected to have only two children. There also is a longer wait before the first child. This lower fertility rate along with a higher life expectancy has created a major change in the family life cycle. Married couples now have a longer period together without children at home. Since the early 1900s, fourteen years of child-free living have been added to the family cycle. The amount of childless time may have implications for the couple's marriage and life course (Doherty and Jacobson 1982; LaRossa and LaRossa 1981).

Teachman and Polonko (1985) noted in their review of the literature that the timing of the first birth affects a woman's career, the material assets of the household, the risk of marital dissolution, and the number and timing of additional children. The first birth may influence the physical and emotional well-being of the child and the mother's sense of self-worth. There are also implications for the household division of labor and patterns of leisure and companionship.

Women who delay their parenting role have a higher education level (education affects birth timing by influencing when marriage occurs), are older at marriage, are less involved in religion, are non-Catholic, have labor-market experience, come from a nonfarm background and a stable parental home, have fewer siblings, and come from a region other than the South. In addition, Spanier and Roos (1985) found that education is associated with the timing and occurrence of most life-course events. There is also an association between smaller families and higher education. The childbearing period is shorter for women with higher levels of education.

The arrival of a child into the two-person marriage changes and redefines the family system. As the child develops, the family will continue to change and its relationships will continue to alter. A major function of the family is to rear children, which in our society involves helping them grow, develop, and socialize. We now use the word *rear,* but prior to the Reformation the word used was *raise,* which meant literally to lift the newborn into the air as a public act of declaring paternity and accepting the infant into the social group. Not to "raise" a child meant literally to leave it on the ground to die (Zeits and Prince 1982).

Pregnancy may trigger dramatic changes in the roles of family members, particularly the husband and wife. The coming of the first child has been found to reduce the level of marital satisfaction for many couples (Belsky et al. 1985). Yet Harriman (1986) found that the birth of a child apparently precipitates a higher degree of positive change among husbands and wives who score high on marital adjustment compared with those who score low. Happiness in one's marriage seems to accentuate any positive changes and minimize any negative ones occurring with the parenting experience.

Specific complaints center around issues of restricted freedom and the wife's overinvolvement with mothering and reduced involvement with her husband. Subsequent pregnancies also lead to changes for older children in terms of decreasing maternal warmth, intensity, and duration of contact. Individuals with children, especially mothers, are susceptible to mental health problems and psychological stress. For example, those with a child under five have the highest average psychiatric-symptoms scores, with housewives scoring slightly higher than women working outside the home. These housewives also score highest on the experience of excessive demands, the desire to be alone, and the degree of loneliness. Two factors that can offset the stressors of motherhood are employment outside the home and having a husband or male friend who is considered a confidant (Doherty and Jacobson 1982; Zeits and Prince 1982).

When both parents are involved with childrearing, both feel more positive toward parenthood. When parents talk about the infant frequently, fathers are

Two factors that can offset the stressors of motherhood are employment outside the home and having a husband or male friend who is considered a confidant.

much more involved with their infant. It appears, then, that mothers can exert an indirect influence on father-infant interactions by helping the father understand the normal developmental processes of the infant. Happily married couples function as sources of mutual support and encouragement. This makes childrearing easier and problems less difficult. Some men report that becoming a father gave them the incentive to "make it" in their job and intensified their sense of financial responsibility (Belsky 1979; Crnic et al. 1983). Also, fathers often see their children as a source of refuge from the outer world, but they feel the worth of the parents is reflected by the child's public behavior. Because the father represents the nonfamily world, he may be more embarrassed than the mother when the child misbehaves in public. Fathers from middle-class families are less likely to be annoyed by a child's behavior than are lower- and upper-class fathers (Zeits and Prince 1982).

The social class of the parents influences the techniques used in childrearing. Working-class parents punish for the consequences of the child's act, while middle-class parents tend to punish on the basis of the child's intent (Zeits and Prince 1982).

Pratt (1976) identified several characteristics of a healthy, or "energized," family. These included the active engagement of all members in varied and regular interaction with one another; family ties to the broader community through the active participation of family members; a high degree of family autonomy and a tendency to encourage individuality; and engagement in creative problem solving and active coping.

Work

"It is work which occupies most of the energies of the human race. . . A person's work is undoubtedly one of the most decisive formative influences of his character and personality" (Schumacher 1979, 2–3).

Work is intertwined in the definition of adulthood. It begins with the entry into the first job and ends with retirement. When Freud was asked what he thought a normal person should be able to do well, he answered "to love and to work" (Erikson 1963). As children we talk about the job we will have "when we grow up." A job usually takes the person outside the home, involves specific activities, is on a time schedule, and provides income. It is considered part of a career if it is related to a person's training, to previous jobs, and to anticipated jobs (Troll 1985).

Work involves a continuing connection to the human community, with its changing patterns of options and contingencies. Social and economic conditions determine the realities of the work situation. Work, a major socializing force, is a complex social role, with a set of expected behaviors, skills, and attitudes. Work provides individuals with an identity, a self-concept, and a forum for social and personal interactions. It trains the adult in the values and mores of our society, which in turn adds to his or her competencies (Henry 1975; Havighurst 1982).

Work has different meanings for different people. For some it is a source of prestige and social recognition and a basis for self-respect and a sense of worth. For others it is an opportunity for social participation or a way to be of service. For many it is enjoyment of the activity itself or a means of creative self-expression. It may also be just a way to earn a living (Troll 1985).

The average American's work life is about fifty years, that is, from eighteen to sixty-eight years of age. Because this period is so long and complex, Havinghurst (1982) found it necessary to view it in developmental phases or stages that present different challenges and opportunities. Each stage or phase has its own developmental task. "A developmental task arises at or about a certain period in the life of the individual, successful achievement of which leads to his/her happiness and to success with later tasks, while failure leads to unhappiness in the individual, disapproval by the society, and difficulty with later tasks" (Havighurst 1982, 775).

The developmental tasks related to work and careers begin during adolescence. The first is *preparing for an economic career.* The great majority of boys and girls ages fifteen to twenty have occupational learning and preparation as a principal interest, and this focus may remain significant for up to sixteen years. The career is often the organizing center for young men and women. "A career in which a person can grow in responsibility and competence as well as income, can plan for the future and can invest his/her time and energy with the certainty of future gain has been called . . . an 'orderly career' " (Havighurst 1982, 775). Adolescents find that getting started on an "orderly career" is a decisive task for them. There is a great deal of fumbling about, with little or no guidance, resulting in a number of vocational misfits. College students are advised not to make a vocational choice until they have completed two years of general education. The two most common choices are business and teaching. Those young people who choose teaching prepare explicitly for that occupation in college. Those who are going into business major in economics or business administration in college. The long period of preparation required for many middle-class occupations is the top priority among most young men and women in their twenties. This task may interfere with other developmental tasks, such as becoming a responsible citizen and starting a family.

The second major task related to careers is *getting started in an occupation.* This consumes so much of the energy and time of young people that they may become engrossed in it, ignoring or neglecting other tasks. The process is more difficult for middle-class young men than it is for upper- and lower-class young men. Success in an occupation is imperative in order for a middle-class man to maintain his social position. For some women this task may interfere or conflict with the tasks of finding a mate and starting a family. This can be a major problem of early adulthood for some middle-class women.

The third major development task related to work is *reaching and maintaining satisfactory performance in one's occupational career.* During their middle-adult years, men achieve the highest status and income of their career. If women have been employed all of their adult life, this is true for them as well. Some people in middle adulthood start over in new careers, deliberately changing from routine jobs to work that is more interesting and/or rewarding to them in other ways. Approximately 53 percent of women, ages forty to fifty-nine are in the U.S. labor force, which many seek to enter after rearing their children. Approximately 10 percent of men change the nature of their work between the ages of forty and sixty, either due to their own initiative or for reasons beyond their control. Some men (professional athletes, policemen, firemen, army officers, and so forth) change jobs because they are no longer physically fit for their work after a certain age. Many of these people move into supervisory roles, while others change careers entirely. For many individuals the career task becomes not reaching and maintaining their peak of prestige and income but achieving a work role that is flexible, interesting, productive, and/or financially more satisfactory. Retraining may be required in changing careers.

The final developmental task is *adjusting to retirement and reduced income,* which occurs for most people between the ages of sixty and seventy. For those people whose job was the "axis of life," this is a difficult and unwelcome period. Others may savor the freedom and seek out interesting leisure, social, and/or civic activities. Society's goal should be to make this task flexible so that the needs of people with a variety of attitudes are addressed. A problem facing

Work provides individuals with an identity, a self-concept, and a forum for social and personal interactions. It trains the adult in the values and mores of our society, which in turn adds to his or her competencies.

Approximately 53 percent of women ages forty to fifty-nine are in the U.S. labor force.

many who retire is reduced income and less purchasing power due to inflation's effect on a fixed income.

In conclusion, work has different meanings for different people. Work can be intrinsically or extrinsically motivating. Some intrinsic factors contributing to work satisfaction are the degree of interest and variety, the opportunity for self-direction and autonomy, the amount of challenge and stimulation of personal growth, the ability to see the results of work efforts, and recognition of these efforts by others. Extrinsic factors include salary and status, the comfort and convenience of the work environment and hours, the friendliness and attitudes of co-workers, employment policies and supervision, and opportunities for advancement (Whitbourne and Weinstock 1986).

SUMMARY

- Erikson's stage of intimacy versus isolation involves fusing one's identity with that of another. The avoidance of intimacy leads to a deep sense of isolation and self-absorption.
- Gould's research supports a stage theory approach that recognizes a developmental sequence in the early- and middle-adult years.
- Levinson and colleagues, based on a study of male subjects, perceive adulthood in developmentally fixed stages. They see a pattern of transitions that produce predictable crises and behavior. They view the overriding task of adulthood to be that of creating a structure of life.
- Neugarten believes that a stage theory approach oversimplifies adult life. Adults judge and evaluate themselves and others in relation to socially defined time. In traditional society, a prescribed timetable determines the order of major life events.
- Baruch, Barnett, and Rivers' (1983) study of adult women indicates that age and stages are not relevant to women's roles and state of well-being.

Relationship Abuse

Most studies on relationship abuse focus on the violent male in a marital relationship, but studies have revealed that courtship violence usually precedes marital violence and that females also initiate violent encounters (Flynn 1990, 1987; Edleson and Brygger 1986; Makepeace 1986; Straus and Gelles 1986).

In terms of courtship violence, males and females have similar rates (Makepeace 1986; Straus et al. 1980). Henton et al. (1983) found that 78 out of 644 high school students had experienced courtship violence. Fifty of the 78 students, or 71.4 percent, reported that at some point each partner had been either a victim or an aggressor. Of the remaining 28.6 percent, 1.4 percent were male abusers only, 5.7 percent were female abusers only, 8.6 percent were abused males only, and 12.9 percent were abused females only. In a college sample, Cate et al. (1982) found that abuse was mutual in nearly 70 percent of abusive relationships. These studies indicate that females are just as likely as males to be the sole abuser in courtship violence.

Courtship violence is about as common as spousal violence (Cate et al. 1982; Lane and Gwartney-Gibbs 1985). Straus and Gelles (1986) found that the rate of overall abuse by husbands dropped from 12.1 percent in 1975 to 11.3 percent in 1985. The rate of overall abuse by wives increased from 11.6 percent in 1975 to 12.1 percent in 1985. (Note: Overall abuse is not as violent as severe abuse, which has a high probability of causing an injury.)

Although the rates of violence by men and women are about equal, the motives and effects are not. Women are more likely to use violence to pull away from their husband's grasp or in reaction to his violence (Walker 1984). Most violence committed by women is in self-defense or in retaliation against their husband (Strauss 1980; Makepeace 1986).

Men inflict more severe damage on their lovers or wives than do women (Flynn 1990), probably because of their superior size and strength. Approximately 7.0 percent of wives and 0.6 percent of husbands are *severely* abused by their spouse. Because the abuse perpetrated on women is more severe, their victimization is more visible.

What about the men who are abused? They are reluctant to acknowledge that they have been beaten by their wife. Embarrassment and humiliation are felt by victims of both genders, but a husband usually feels these more keenly because of society's view of the traditional male role.

Men and women often remain in abusive relationships for the same reasons. As long as the abuse and violence are not severe and are relatively infrequent, the victims tend to stay. They are more likely to do so if they were abused as children (Gelles 1976). Also, abused men and women may stay because they love their spouse; the spouse is genuinely apologetic; the disclosure would cause embarrassment; or they make excuses for the perpetrator, such as stress or substance abuse. Even after repeated attacks, men and women may remain because of economic and material concerns, for the safety of their children, or because of psychological dependency (Pagelow 1984). Children's safety is a major concern of abused husbands, and they may stay in order to protect them. The welfare of the children is more important than the men's own safety, and often the men are abused when trying to protect the children from the abusive mother (Steinmetz 1977–78).

Those who abuse or batter their spouse and those who are victims often come from abusive households. In her study of four hundred battered wives, Walker (1984) found that 29 percent of the wives and 35 percent of the battering husbands were from homes in which they had viewed their mother inflicting violence on their father. It is, therefore, necessary to help children and adolescents learn effective techniques for resolving conflicts in relationships so that intergenerational patterns are broken and violence does not remain an acceptable model. Also, relationship violence is interactive; that is, certain characteristics of the family system and certain interactional sequences generate violence. Each person in the relationship must "view relationship violence as a mutual problem and accept responsibility for his/her actions" (Flynn 1990, 197). The majority of cases involve mild to moderate violence. Situations of severe and life-threatening abuse would not benefit from a prevention or intervention approach (Flynn 1990).

What are some of the long-term effects on children who witness abuse between their parents? What are some consequences of relationship abuse for our society? Recently in some states, women who had been convicted of murdering their partners were released from prison on the ground that they were suffering from "battered wife syndrome." Do you think this is an appropriate defense? Why or why not?

- Establishing independence is one of the most important tasks of the young adult. The primary agents of adult socialization are spouse, employer, and children. Marriage and parenthood provide the primary social roles for most people in most societies.
- Remaining single has become a national trend. It is not clear whether this indicates that marriage is being postponed or that an increasing number of individuals will remain single throughout life. Various subgroups exist in the singlehood category.
- Marriage is probably the most influential relationship of adult life and the major source of demands for socialization upon the young adult. Contemporary marriage is more intense as well as more fragile than traditional marriage.
- Parenthood is an important social transition. Contemporary parenthood demonstrates both continuity and change. In this century the proportion of people who have children has increased, and number of children they have has decreased. Having children can be stressful, especially for the mother. The involvement of both parents and maternal employment can alleviate the stressors.
- Work is intertwined with the definition of adulthood. It is a main socializing agent as well as a major source of an adult's self-concept.
- Courtship violence usually precedes spousal violence. Both men and women are abusers as well as victims in relationship abuse. Men and women stay in violent relationships for similar reasons. Prevention and intervention programs are beneficial in overall abuse but not in severe abuse situations.

R E A D I N G S

Anderson-Khleif, S. (1982). *Divorced but not disastrous.* Englewood Cliffs, NJ: Prentice-Hall.
  A review of the literature on divorce and along with the results of the author's own study. Offers divorced parents some possible solutions to their unique problems.
Appleton, W.S. (1981). *Fathers and daughters.* New York: Doubleday.
  Discussion of early father/daughter attachment and how the relationship affects women's choices of spouses and careers.
Burgwyn, D. (1981). *Marriages without children.* New York: Harper and Row.
  Discussion by individuals who choose not to have children.
O'Kane, M.L. (1981). *Living with adult children.* St. Paul, MN: Diction Books.
  A guide for parents who have adult children who live in their home.
Sheehy, G. (1976). *Passages.* New York: Dutton.
  A lay person's account of the stages of adult development drawn from several research studies, including Gould and Levinson.
Sheehy, G. (1981). *Pathfinders.* New York: Morrow.
  This book suggests ways adults can overcome crises and find their "path" to well-being. A sequel to *Passages.*

C H A P T E R

15

O U T L I N E

Physical Development
    Body Systems
    Behavior Patterns and Health
Cognitive Development
    Cognitive Functioning
    Intelligence
    Moral Judgment and Personal Philosophy
    Humor
Summary
• Critical Issues: Stress
Readings

O B J E C T I V E S

When you have mastered the material in this chapter, you should be able to do the following:

1. Describe the physical development of the middle adult, including the skeletal system, muscular system, skin and hair, cardiovascular system, central nervous system, sensory organs, and reproductive systems.
2. Discuss how the behavior patterns of adults, including Type A and Type B behavior, affect health.
3. Discuss conditions that are related to overall cognitive functioning.
4. Discuss how intelligence changes throughout the adult years and how it differs between men and women.
5. Describe judgment development during adulthood as it relates to morality, Fowler's theory of faith, political thought, and personal philosophy.
6. Identify the mental and physiological benefits of humor.
7. Describe how cartoons or comic strips offer a reflection of long-term male-female relationships and discuss the four interrelated themes.
8. Describe how humor is a tool of social status.
9. Discuss how stress has major internal and external influences on health.

Mid-life: Middle Adulthood— Physical and Cognitive Development

PHYSICAL DEVELOPMENT

Physical development in the middle-adult years (40–65 years) differs more between individuals than between age-groups. Individuals throughout life vary widely in their energy level, capacity for work, and general health. These individual differences increase as people age (Weg 1983). Also, aging does not occur uniformly in one individual; one physical system may deteriorate while others function well. For example, a forty-seven-year-old woman may have degenerative arthritis but a sturdy heart. Another woman of the same age may have strong bones and muscles but a weak heart. Some people appear and act old at forty-five, while others are active, outgoing, and youthful at seventy.

The frequency of illness and disability increases with age, but the frequency of accidents decreases. As people grow older they are less susceptible to colds and allergies, but they tend to tire faster, have more dental problems, have higher blood pressure, and need more time to recuperate from fatigue or illness. This does not mean middle-aged people are in poor health. Many individuals live all of their adult years without being sick or incapacitated in any way (Troll 1985).

Two types of aging have been identified. *Primary aging* is normal, unavoidable, and universal. *Secondary aging* is the product of physical disease, abuse, and disuse (Busse and Maddox 1985). It is not universal or unavoidable. Changing the environment or personal practices, such as discontinuing tanning or smoking, can avoid secondary aging.

Body Systems

Skeletal System

After the fortieth year, the balance between physical growth and degeneration shifts more to the side of degeneration. The average man still has about thirty more years to live, and the average woman, about thirty-five more years. After age forty-five or fifty, stature begins to decline. The only part of the skeleton in which positive growth continues is the head and face, which increases in measurement at least up to age sixty. The increase between the ages of twenty and sixty is only 2 to 4 percent.

From the fortieth year, bone mass begins to decrease (Horsman and Cury 1983). Calcium loss from bone tissues is more apparent in women during and following menopausal changes, with *osteoporosis* (calcium loss leading to decreasing bone density and mass) representing a truly age-related and age-determined process (Riggs et al. 1981). Data indicate that 35 to 40 percent of all females will develop osteoporosis, which increases the possibility of fracture from minor incidents (Bart 1971; Riggs et al. 1981).

Loss of calcium in males may not start until age fifty-five or sixty, and it occurs at a slower rate than for females. The male skeleton contains more calcium and is heavier than that of a female of the same size. Thus, males in this age-group have more bone strength than females (Mazess 1982).

Muscular System

Muscular strength and the ability to maintain maximum muscular effort decline steadily. Loss of strength is not due to weakening of the muscle fibers themselves but to their reduction in quantity and to changes in the elasticity of the fibrous tissue within which muscle fibers are embedded. Muscle strength and mass also are related to activity; when muscles are not used, they weaken.

A sedentary individual can show a gain in strength by participating in a short-term exercise program (Aniansson and Gustafsson 1981; Sidney 1981; Grimby and Saltin 1983). A study of sixty-two-year-old male machinists who had to exert themselves strenuously found they had the endurance and muscle strength of twenty-two-year-olds (deVries 1983).

By age forty-five, the strength of the back muscles in men declines on the average to 96 percent of its maximum value. By age fifty it declines to 92 percent. Lower back pain at this stage may be related to impaired flexibility of the hip and back and reduced elasticity of the hamstring muscles. This rapid decline continues (Marshall 1973). As the muscle cells atrophy and die, fat cells increase, resulting in a body with less muscle and more fat (Borkan et al. 1983).

The time required to carry out movements increases at a steady rate in the forties and fifties. The slowdown is not due to the inability of muscles and joints to move quickly but to a message delay in the brain and spinal cord, where a longer period is needed to initiate and guide muscular activity (Whitbourne and Weinstock, 1986).

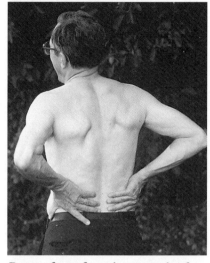

By age forty-five, the strength of the back muscles in men declines on the average to 96 percent of its maximum value. By age fifty it declines to 92 percent. Lower back pain at this stage may be related to impaired flexibility of the hip and back and reduced elasticity of the hamstring muscles.

Skin and Hair

The tissues of the skin remain healthy and intact with a glowing appearance until approximately age fifty to fifty-five. This is especially true of nonsmoking individuals who receive adequate vitamins, minerals, nutrients, and fluids. Wrinkles gradually appear. During the period from age twenty-five to seventy, the thinning of fat and muscle under the skin and diminished activity of the sweat glands and sebaceous glands that lubricate the skin surface contribute to wrinkling and sagging (Whitbourne and Weinstock 1986). Water loss in the skin causes dryness in middle adults and in the elderly. Increased exposure to the sun over a long period accelerates the drying and wrinkling. It takes longer for skin wounds to heal, possibly because of the decreased rates of resynthesis of cells needed for healing and collagen formation. (Collagen fibers and elastin fibers make up the greatest percentage of connective tissues.) After forty-five years of age, women have less skin thickness and less total skin collagen than men (Hooyman and Kiyak 1988). Men and women lose some subcutaneous fat during this stage. Women have increased fat deposits under the arms, in the breasts, and in the groin area after menopause (Budoff 1983).

The hair changes noticeably during middle age. The hairline recedes and thins out during the forties. Baldness and graying increase. By the time most men and women are in their fifties they are gray-haired (Whitbourne and Weinstock 1986; Rossman 1977). Less noticeable changes include stiff hairs appearing in the nose, ears, and eyelashes of men. Hair on the upper lip and chin, neck, arms, and hands becomes coarser in both men and women. Both lose some hair from their scalp as they age. For example, the scalp hair of a fifty-year-old man or a woman thins from 615 follicles per square centimeter to only 485 (Rockstein and Sussman 1979).

"Bags" under the eyes, which are so common during the middle-adult years, are caused by weakening of the underlying muscle and fibrous tissue. The lower eyelid drops in folds, and the subcutaneous fat herniating the weakened muscles makes the skin balloon (Schuster and Ashburn 1986).

Cardiovascular System

During the middle-adult years the functions, rate, and rhythm of the heart are maintained through a system of activity and quality exercise, such as aerobics. After age forty-five, if work and leisure activities become more sedentary,

Women under age fifty who smoke heavily may be more likely to have heart attacks than nonsmoking women.

the heart begins to lose its tone and rate, and rhythm changes emerge. Blood pressure should be under 150/90 (Brunner and Suddarth 1984).

The cardiovascular system is composed of cells that do not renew themselves. As they age, they lose elasticity and undergo other degenerative changes (Whitbourne and Weinstock 1986). The majority of deaths after age fifty are due to cardiovascular failures. Since environmental conditions strongly influence hypertension, or elevated blood pressure, it is possible to prevent or delay cardiovascular disease through behavior modification. Less-advantaged or poorer people have significantly higher blood pressure than those better off. According to one study, race, gender, and weight influence blood pressure even in young adults (Johnson et al. 1975). African-American females have the highest incidence of high blood pressure, followed by African-American males, white males, and white females. The greatest influence on blood pressure for African-American and white females and white males is obesity. Stress, smoking, and diet affect blood pressure. Exercise, stress reduction, smoking cessation, and a low-fat, low-salt diet will reduce it (Kohn 1977).

Although deaths from cardiovascular disease have decreased substantially over the last two decades, diseased coronary arteries continue to kill more than 500,000 Americans each year. More than six million persons have symptoms of coronary artery disease, to which genetics and life-style place the individual at risk. Men are at greater risk than women. Risk factors include a family history of premature heart attack, increasing age, cigarette smoking, high blood pressure, obesity, abnormal levels of cholesterol, and a sedentary life-style (Dacy 1988).

Coronary heart disease (CHD) is the major cause of death among postmenopausal women and is related to behavioral risk factors. Major among these are diet, cigarette smoking, and blood pressure. The role of psychological symptoms and behavior in the onset of CHD in postmenopausal women is unclear. If hormonal and behavioral changes during menopause could be related to such variables as obesity, diet, exercise, smoking, and alcohol, then a more scientifically based prevention program could be developed (Kuller et al. 1984). Women under age fifty who smoke heavily may be more likely to have a heart attack than nonsmoking women, and the risk is even higher if they take birth control pills. Compared with nonsmoking women using oral contraceptives, women who smoke twenty-five or more cigarettes daily and take the pill have twenty-three times the risk of heart attack. Women smoking fewer than fifteen cigarettes a day are almost one and a half times more likely to have a heart attack as compared with nonsmoking women. Compared with men, postmenopausal women have a higher risk of heart attack because of factors such as high blood pressure or elevated cholesterol, and their chances increase even more if they smoke. The blood flow to the brain greatly improves by quitting smoking. It also has been found that the fertility of female smokers is estimated to be about 72 percent of that of nonsmokers. The smokers are nearly 3.5 times more likely to have taken more than a year to conceive (Siegler and Costa 1985; Schaie and Geiwitz 1982; Whitbourne and Weinstock 1986).

The coronary arteries, which supply blood to the heart muscle itself, become narrowed in apparently healthy forty- and fifty-year-old men. The efficiency of the heart during exercise is impaired by the lack of blood for its own use. For many men this causes pain during exercise, known as *angina of effort* or *angina pectoris*. The latter term refers to the fact that the pain is felt in the shoulder, even though it originates in the heart muscle. Narrowing of the arteries that supply blood to the leg muscles may cause similar pain there. These pains have protective value in that when sufficiently severe, they restrict the activity of the individual. It is not uncommon during the fiftieth year for a complete blockage of a coronary artery (also known as *acute coronary occlusion* or *sudden heart attack*) to occur. This blockage will cause destruction of part of the heart muscle and may be extensive enough to prevent heart function and cause death. Usually, however, the patient recovers (Whitbourne and Weinstock 1986).

Central Nervous System

The central nervous system in the middle adult is similar to that of the young adult. Physiologically the middle adult functions at a highly complex cognitive level. Maturity and experience are advantageous when critical decisions or organizational skills are needed. Individuals may experience a slight delay in reflexes and a slower response to sudden changes. Although brain cell loss increases, there are still plenty of functioning cells in the human brain (Burnside 1981).

Sensory Organs

Hearing, smell, taste, and touch are generally maintained during the middle-adult years. Around fifty years of age, however, there may be obvious losses in hearing and the sense of smell (Whitbourne and Weinstock 1986).

Changes in vision may become apparent during early middle adulthood. The most common one is impaired sight due to the loss of elasticity in the crystalline lens of the eye. It usually begins around age forty and in most cases can be corrected with glasses or contact lenses. After age forty-five the eye lens may gradually become more opaque (Schuster and Ashburn 1986). After age forty, *glaucoma,* a disease in which fluid within the eyeball increases, becomes more common. It is the leading cause of blindness during the middle-adult years (Johnson and Goldfinger 1981). After age fifty other vision changes include decreasing depth perception, muscle weakness that makes it difficult to focus on small print for several hours, and slower adaptation to darkness (Whitbourne 1985).

Reproductive Systems

Throughout the forties women begin losing their capacity to have children, and by the mid-fifties the capacity ceases completely for most women. The **climacteric** encompasses the entire transition: from the time reproductive ability begins slowly to diminish, through the degeneration or involution of the ovaries and their various processes, to the final cessation of reproductive ability (Whitbourne and Weinstock 1986). **Menopause,** the time during which menstruation ceases completely, marks the end of the climacteric.

Most women experience menopause at around fifty years. Blood pressure rises abruptly and remains a little above the male value from then on. This is only part of the physiological change. The end of the menstrual flow is usually the final event in a series that began five or more years earlier with aging changes and the loss of the function of the ovaries. As long as two years before menstruation stops, the failure of ovulation and loss of capacity to have children may occur. The symptoms widely associated with menopause include hot flashes or flushes; sweating; chills; cold, moist, and numb extremities; palpitations; vertigo; headaches; fatigue; nervousness; insomnia; osteoporosis; and depression. But there is little empirical evidence that these symptoms are experienced by substantially larger numbers of women during menopause than during other

Climacteric
In women, the transition from the time reproductive ability begins to diminish, through the degeneration or involution of the ovaries and their various processes, to the final cessation of reproductive ability.

Menopause
The time in a woman's life during which menstruation ceases completely.

times in life. Therefore, these symptoms may be hormonal or psychosocial in origin. Depression, for example, is more likely to be associated with such psychosocial factors as family relations and socioeconomic experiences in mid-life than with endocrine changes. The one symptom most clearly associated with menopause is hot flashes, which affect 68 percent of menopausal women. No other specific symptom significantly differentiates menopausal women from all other age-groups. Considerable variation exists in the subjective reports of symptoms, with 10 percent of women claiming incapacitation by menopausal symptoms and 16 percent claiming to be completely symptom-free. Women who report a high number of symptoms tend to be less educated, are less likely to be working, and view themselves as in poorer health than subjects with fewer or no symptoms. The so-called menopausal syndrome may be more strongly related to a woman's personality than to menopause itself. The view that women see menopause as a loss of femininity is not supported by data (Whitbourne and Weinstock 1986; Marshall 1973; Polit and LaRocco 1980; Notman 1984).

Younger woman (twenty-one to forty-four years) hold more negative views of menopause than do older women (forty-five to sixty-five years). The middle-aged woman sees the postmenopausal period as a time when she will be happier and healthier, which emphasizes the belief that the unpleasantness will be temporary. This attitude has been substantiated by interviews with postmenopausal women:

"My experience has been that I've been healthier and in much better spirits since the change of life. I've been relieved of a lot of aches and pains."

"Since I have had my menopause, I have felt like a teenager again. I can remember my mother saying that after her menopause she really got her vigor, and I can say the same thing about myself. I'm just never tired now." (Neugarten et al. 1975).

When menopause occurs on time, that is, during mid-life, it is not associated with psychological distress. This is not true when menopause occurs at earlier or later stages of the life course (Lennon 1982). Several studies demonstrate that the timing of life events is an important element in psychological effect.

Stress at this time in a woman's life has been shown to have a significant influence on menopausal symptoms. The symptoms almost invariably increase for women who experience a divorce or the death of a loved one during this period. In other words, life stress, particularly a personal loss, plays a more powerful role in intensifying symptoms than does the menopause itself (Greene and Cooke 1980; Cooke and Greene 1981; Cooke 1981). The advent of menopause brings with it freedom from the fear of pregnancy, and loving intimacy can be enjoyed in a secure way.

Clinical symptoms associated with menopause include vasomotor symptoms (heart rate and blood pressure) changes in skin and bone metabolism, and heightened risk for coronary heart disease and endometrial cancer (Soules and Bremner 1982).

The term **male climacteric** is quite often used with regard to middle-aged men. It is somewhat a misnomer since there is no male equivalent to female menopause. Whereas women's ovaries do not function after a definite time in mid-life, men's potency gradually diminishes. The male climacteric commences

Male climacteric
A slow decline in the sexual potency of men during the sixties and seventies. Most men do not lose their ability to father children.

in the sixties or seventies, and it advances at a much slower rate than the female climacteric. Most men do not lose their ability to father children. They experience less extensive hormonal changes than women do (Swerdloff and Heber 1982).

Testosterone production begins to decline about 1 percent a year during middle adulthood and contributes to a decline in physical energy. Sexual functioning also changes; a man may take longer to attain erection, but he can maintain it longer. Some secondary sex characteristics change: the voice may become higher pitched, facial hair may grow more slowly, and flabbiness may replace muscle (Lewis 1978; Bermant and Davidson 1974; Soules and Bremner 1982).

The male climacteric is also related to irritability, depression, and certain syndromes thought to result from decreased hormonal levels. Some men experience such testicular hormone loss that their condition is similar to female menopausal symptoms, complete with hot flashes, nervousness, fatigue, psychological depression, and loss of energy. They may even become impotent, although impotence at this age often is due to male expectations and psychological factors rather than physiological alterations. Nevertheless, the effect can be a decline in sexual activity, if not in reproductive powers, and a diminished sense of sexual well-being. Our society contributes to this attitude by regarding aging persons as nonsexual or asexual (Lewis et al. 1978; Bermant and Davidson 1974; Soules and Bremner 1982; Weg 1983; Whitbourne and Weinstock 1986).

Until puberty, the prostate gland shows little activity, but from then until the fifth decade its well-developed tubulo-alveolar glands make an important contribution to ejaculation. Changes in the male reproductive function during middle adulthood are generally gradual, often related to the overall fitness of the individual, and degenerative. The prostate gland becomes enlarged and increasingly coarse. Since the function of the prostate is to force semen from the penis at ejaculation, the strength of the response declines as a man gets older. The risk of cancer of the prostrate reaches its highest level during middle age (Koch 1980).

Despite decline, all parts of the system retain sufficient capability to make reproduction possible, in many cases, into extreme old age. The oldest new father on record was ninety-four years old. The rate of and age at decline in the function of the testes are quite variable (Weg 1983).

The crises to which climacteric men are susceptible include frustration in career pursuits, separation from a late-adolescent child, awareness of some decline in sexual potency, and symptoms of ill health associated with aging. Interviews with middle-aged men reveal an underlying theme of the desire to be an adolescent again in order to start life anew. The central tasks of a climacteric man are to accept the reality that he is middle-aged, to appreciate the good things in his life as well as his past accomplishments, to give up some of his unrealistic goals, and to recognize that he has unrealized potential that he can seek to develop for the rest of his life (Schaie and Geiwitz 1982).

Behavior Patterns and Health

Patterns of behavior affect the health of the adult. An important study (Friedman and Rosenman 1974) has identified two types of behavior, *Type A* and *Type B,* with accompanying health characteristics. The **Type A** pattern of personality traits includes excessive competitive drive, aggressiveness, impatience, and a harrying sense of time urgency. Type A individuals "seem to be engaged in a chronic, ceaseless, and often fruitless struggle—with themselves,

Type A behavior
A pattern of personality traits including excessive competitive drive, aggressiveness, impatience, and a harrying sense of time urgency.

with others, with circumstances, with time, sometimes with life itself." They exhibit a well-rationalized form of hostility (Williams and Barefoot 1988) and almost always deep-seated insecurity. They are more motivated to win in conflict situations than are Type B people (Smith and Brehm 1981). They are involved in an incessant effort to achieve more and more in less and less time (Strube et al. 1984). At some point in life they measure the value of their total personality or character by the number of their achievements. Their innermost security has been staked on the pace of their status enhancement, that is, on a maximum number of achievements accomplished in a minimum amount of time. Because Type A people try to accomplish so much so quickly, their creative powers as well as the acuity of their judgment are impaired. Rhodewalt et al. (1984) found that Type A administrators under high stress report more psychological impairment and cardiovascular-related health problems than do high-stress Type B's or low stress A's or B's. This reinforces the importance of situational factors when studying Type A subjects.

Physiologically, the serum cholesterol level is much higher in Type A people (Friedman and Rosenman 1974), and they show higher blood pressure when performing a competitive task or when challenged (Goldband 1980). The brain and its functions can alter the blood or serum cholesterol level and make them more coronary prone. Friedman and Rosenman (1974) monitored the serum cholesterol level of a group of accountants from January to June.

When the April 15 tax deadline approached, and the sense of time urgency of these accountants rose sharply, so did the level of their serum cholesterol. Conversely, in May and early June, when their sense of time urgency almost disappeared, their serum cholesterol fell. This change in serum cholesterol, then, could only have been due to their emotional stress—because neither their food, smoking, or exercise habits had changed during the period of our surveillance.

The Type A person appears to be trying to get control of every situation. This may be necessary in some cases, but it is not possible in all cases. Such an intense desire for control causes Type A people to blame themselves for failure more often than Type B people do (Musante et al. 1983).

Type B people do not push themselves to obtain material things or squeeze an endless series of events into an ever-decreasing amount of time. Their intelligence is as high or higher than that of Type A's, and they may be just as ambitious or more so. They may also have a considerable amount of drive, but it is more steady and provides more confidence and security. Intelligent Type B's are capable of assuming a nonstereotypical role and find time to ponder leisurely, weigh alternatives, and experiment. They also find time "to indulge in dialectical reverie from which two, three, or even four seemingly totally disparate events, facts, or processes can be joined to produce strikingly new and brilliant offshoots."

Most urban Americans fall into one of these two groups. Among samples tested, Type A accounts for 50 percent; Type B, 40 percent, and mixed characteristics, 10 percent. No clear correlation has been found with socioeconomic status or occupational position. Several reasons may explain the lack of correlation between Type A subjects and their occupation. First, their sense of urgency is not synonymous with a sense of job or position responsibility. Second, excessive drive and competition may be wasted on economic trivia rather than more important affairs. Finally, most promotions, especially in corporate and

Type B behavior
A pattern of personality traits opposite of Type A behavior. Type B personalities take time to ponder leisurely, weigh alternatives, and experiment.

professional organizations, go to the wise rather than the hasty, to the tactful rather than the hostile, and to the creative rather than the competitive.

Hart (1983) found that Type A's reported relatively fewer physical symptoms and perceived themselves as being more healthy than did Type B subjects. Unlike B's, Type A's rated themselves as healthier than their peers, and they reported higher self-esteem and greater life satisfaction. They also feel more involved in their work than do Type B people (Matthews 1982).

Type A American women have a much higher serum cholesterol level than Type B women and, on average, a higher level than Type A men. Coronary heart disease is more frequent in Type A women than in Type B women, and it is as prevalent in Type A females as in their male counterparts. Although American white women have less coronary heart disease than American males, they still exceed males from many non-Western countries (Hart 1983).

In a fourteen-year study, it was found that Type A women, as compared with Type B women, are significantly heavier and are more likely to be employed outside the home most of their adult years. This research, like Hart's study (1983), found that Type A women are more likely to develop coronary heart disease than are Type B women (Eaker and Castelli 1988).

Gilbert (1983) found that the most significant instruction for the individual who seeks a stress-minimizing lifestyle is to avoid "motivational overdetermination," that is, do not strive for several goals concurrently. Many clinics now treat Type A cardiac patients by educating them in Type B behavior.

In a more recent study, Ragland and Brand (1988) disputed some of the earlier findings concerning the Type A personality. They found that Type A's who suffer a heart attack should resume their "hard-driving" styles because it may actually help them live longer. These patients survived at twice the rate of recuperating Type B's. The clinical implication is that an intervention to change Type A behavior after a coronary event will not increase the individual's chances of survival.

The way people respond to life circumstances can affect their health and mortality. Death rates for men under seventy-five who lose a spouse are significantly higher than normal. Women who are widowed are also at risk of death from various diseases. The way a woman responds emotionally to breast cancer may predict the outcome. Those who are more depressed have higher rates of cancer recurrence and lower levels of white blood cells, which fight cancer cells. During times of emotional stress, a person's platelets secrete more of two proteins linked with clotting and heart disease (Orioli 1985).

Research has found that women who were separated or divorced for a year or less had "significantly poorer immune function" than the married women studied. Among the divorced and separated women, those who harbored feelings of anger, resentment, or love for their former or estranged husbands had poorer immune function than did those who were less attached. Among the married women, those who rated their marriage as poor had weaker immune systems than those who said they were happily married (Kiecold-Glaser et al. 1987; Kennedy et al. 1988).

COGNITIVE DEVELOPMENT

Changes in cognitive functioning are slow but incremental between the twenties and sixties. Still, adults are capable of "getting smarter" as they get older. Middle-aged adults, for example, make better use of education and handle problems better than do twenty-year-olds. The total person should be considered within the environmental situation. If an individual is in an environment that requires only a low level of cognition, then he or she will adapt and function at that level. Therefore, ability or competence does not necessarily predict performance. The functioning of the sensory organs and the general state of the body also can affect the efficiency of learning and memory. Reduced functioning in vision, hearing, or touch not only can hamper the learning of new information but also will contribute to a decline in interest in the environment.

Cognitive Functioning

Speed, arousal, attention, and caution are conditions related to overall functioning. **Speed** refers to the rate of cognition. Complex cognitive functioning slows at an earlier age than simpler functioning. Also, slowing occurs later in healthier people. Generally, during most of the adult years, there is little change in the speed of functioning, which decreases about four milliseconds per decade between ages twenty-eight and ninety-nine. The only function that decreases noticeably is psychomotor ability. The main problem older adults have with intelligence tests are time limits. Other factors that can affect speed include unfamiliarity with the kinds of tasks assigned, meaninglessness within the person's own microsystem, and the tendency to be more cautious. Middle-aged

Speed
The rate of cognition.

adults with equivalent alpha patterns act as quickly as younger adults. Therefore, general slowing could be attributed to central nervous system deterioration caused by a disease rather than aging. Adults who are regularly involved in vigorous physical activity, whether they are young or old, have faster reaction times than those who are not. For example, older athletes are faster than younger nonathletes.

Arousal, or alertness, can also affect intellectual functioning. Some individuals are "morning" people, others are "night" people. Different people work best at different times because they are aroused at different times. Younger adults can reach a high state of arousal, perform their task, and then quickly return to their base level. Middle-aged adults take longer to reach an adequately high arousal level, and after they finish their task, they take longer to return to base level. An optimal level of arousal is apparently necessary for efficient performance; too little or too much arousal in a particular situation does not help people function efficiently. Middle-aged people keep moving to higher and higher arousal levels (overarousal) before they drop back again, and practice improves their performance because it decreases this tendency. As they get used to a situation, they are less anxious and less tense. The process of becoming aroused is accompanied by slower heartbeats and by changes in blood pressure, especially the diastolic pressure (Troll 1985).

Arousal
Alertness.

Attention refers to the manner in which we focus on what we are doing, how "tuned in" we are to what is going on around us. People vary in the degree to which they focus their attention and in how wide their focus is. Some people can take in only a small amount of information at a time, while others can absorb a larger amount of information in a short period. If the focus is too narrow, then much information is lost; if it is too wide, then it is harder to distinguish what is relevant. Attention is focused by selecting out those stimuli that are relevant to the current interests of the individual (Troll 1985).

Attention
The manner in which we focus on what we are doing.

Caution, or rigidity, is occasionally perceived as a style or personality variable and sometimes as an organic variable associated with getting older. As individuals age they *prefer* more time for problem solving but do not *need* more time. Young and middle-aged adults do not differ in response when risk taking is necessary. Age-associated value systems, rather than fundamental personality or organic characteristics, explain any difference. For example, what is considered versatile and flexible by a young adult may be considered rash by an older person, and what a middle-aged adult considers a well-thought-out approach might be considered slow and indecisive by a younger person (Troll 1985).

Caution
Rigidity.

Intelligence

The number of years of school is related to the level of measured general intelligence. The more education people attain, the higher their initial scores and the higher these remain throughout life, compared with the scores of their peers. Most younger people over the last few decades have more education and higher IQ scores than their parents and grandparents do. When the young people reach their parents and grandparents' ages, their respective IQ scores will still be higher (Schaie 1983).

Longitudinal studies of intelligence tests indicate some increase in IQ scores at least through the twenties and no general decline until about age sixty. Scores tend to increase more among the better-educated people (Bray and Howard 1983; Cunningham and Owens 1983; Schaie 1983).

Longitudinal studies of intelligence tests indicate some increase in IQ scores at least through the twenties and no general decline until about age sixty. Scores tend to increase more among better-educated people.

There is an increase in general IQ for men between ages sixteen and thirty-six and a slight decline for women from age twenty-six to thirty-six. Dependent women are more likely to have declining IQs than are those less characteristically sex-typed. Women are superior in verbal meaning, reasoning, and word fluency. Men are superior in space, number, and general intellectual ability (overall score) (Troll 1985).

Schaie's (1983) longitudinal study found that the pattern of intellectual change in adulthood is not fixed. It differs from person to person, is multidirectional, varies according to the type of ability tested, is affected by the environment as well as aging, and, in cases of decline, is not irreversible. Schaie points out, however, that although individuals of the same age vary widely and there is no pattern of change across abilities among adults, there is some decline by age sixty and even more by age seventy-four; by age eighty-one the average adult scores below the middle range of adults in their twenties.

Schaie (1983) noted that health and environmental stimulation influence intelligence test scores. Cardiovascular disease appears to have indirect effects because of its effects on central and autonomic nervous system functioning. Arthritis also correlates with lower scores. Environmental stimulation is related to life complexities, including satisfaction with life status and social status, amount of surrounding noise, exposure to cultural influences, employment status (for female subjects), and whether or not the family is intact. Subjects who score high on life complexity either maintain or increase their intelligence test scores. Those whose lives are the least complex score lower on intelligence tests.

Moral Judgment and Personal Philosophy

Moral judgment and personal philosophy govern social behavior, political thought, and social responsibility for the adult.

Piaget and Kohlberg saw changing cognitive capacities as being related to changes in moral thought. As stated earlier, the emergence of formal operations is a prerequisite to the emergence of principled moral judgment. Kuhn et al. (1977) found that among subjects who had attained some level of formal operational thought, less than one quarter showed any emergence of principled moral reasoning. Most adults continue to function at an intermediate level of Kohlberg's stages of moral development (stages 3, 4, and/or 5) (See Chap. 10). Walker (1984) found that moral reasoning among men and women is remarkably similar. Gilligan (1982) argues, however, that males and females differ significantly, noting that they are socialized to approach moral questions in different ways. Females give greater consideration to human relationships, and they are reluctant to judge right and wrong in absolute terms because they are socialized to be caring, nurturing, and nonjudgmental.

Rest and Thoma (1985) found that education correlates with moral development. Their high-education group showed increasing gains, while the low-education group leveled off. The number of years in college added significantly to the predictability of moral judgment in young adulthood, above and beyond that accounted for by initial high school scores.

Kohlberg (1981) suggests a stage-seven response to ethical and religious problems, based on "constructing a sense of identity or unity with being, with life, and with God." Stage-seven thinking goes beyond postconventional justice reasoning (stage six) (Kohlberg, Levine, and Hewer 1983). It involves a cosmic orientation that includes an awareness of the "reason for existence" for the individual. Internalized principles go beyond the teachings of an organized religion to a consideration of the self as a part of the cosmic order. Persons in stage six may be willing to *die* for their principles, but persons in stage seven are willing to *live* for their beliefs—a much more difficult task. Kohlberg points out that few individuals achieve this level. Examples are Socrates, Joan of Arc, Martin Luther King, Jr., and Mother Teresa (Kohlberg 1981).

Fowler (1981, 1983) goes beyond questions and stages of moral reasoning as stated by Kohlberg and Piaget. He is concerned about each individual's "world view" or "model" of his or her relationship to others and to the universe. *Faith* is used to describe such a personal model, not to be confused with a set of specific religious beliefs. Each of us has a faith, according to Fowler, whether or not we belong to any particular church or organization. Moral reasoning is only a small part of faith. Faith is both social and relational; that is, it deals with our understanding of our connections with others and with finding meaning in those relations. Fowler proposed a stage theory of faith, with each succeeding stage representing a higher level or depth of "selfhood" and an increased capacity for intimacy with others in our world (Fowler 1981).

Primal Faith (Infancy) A prelanguage sense of trust forms, similar to the trust in Erikson's first stage (trust versus mistrust). A mutuality forms between parent and child to offset the anxiety caused by separations during infancy.

Intuitive-projective Faith (Early Childhood) The child's imagination (stimulated by stories, gestures, and symbols), combined with thinking that is not yet logical, provides long-lasting information about protective or threatening powers surrounding him or her.

Mythic-literal Faith (Childhood and Beyond) The developing ability to think logically allows children and adolescents to search for rules and systems. They are able to capture the meanings of life in stories about death, life, God, and why people are in the world, but they take the stories quite literally. They then,

Primal faith
In Fowler's theory, the first stage of moral development, in which a prelanguage sense of trust forms. A mutuality develops between parent and child to offset the anxiety that occurs from separations during infancy.

Intuitive-projective faith
In Fowler's theory, the second stage of moral development, in which a child's imagination provides long-lasting information about protective or threatening powers surrounding him or her.

Mythic-literal faith
In Fowler's theory, the third stage of moral development, in which children, adolescents, and some adults adopt specific beliefs and observances as part of their "faith community," literally without reflection.

Synthetic-conventional faith
In Fowler's theory, the fourth stage of moral development, in which new cognitive abilities allow the adolescent to create a personal ideology of beliefs and values. The individual at this stage chooses a set of beliefs from those available.

Individuative-reflective faith
In Fowler's theory, the fifth stage of moral development, in which the young adult is in a transition to finding a genuinely individual set of principles or beliefs.

Conjunctive faith
In Fowler's theory, the sixth stage of moral development, in which the middle adult is ready to hear about beliefs other than his or her own. This stage tries to unify opposites in mind and experience.

Universalizing faith
In Fowler's theory, the seventh stage of moral development, in which the person steps beyond individuality to a feeling of oneness with the power of being.

literally without reflection, adopt specific beliefs and observances as part of their "faith community." Some adults show faith of this kind.

Synthetic-conventional Faith (Adolescence and Beyond) The new cognitive abilities that involve reexamination of beliefs and a search for identity allow the adolescent to create a personal ideology of beliefs and values. The individual at this stage chooses a set of beliefs from those available. Authority is perceived as being outside the individual and truth as coming from external sources. The beliefs and values chosen at this stage are designed to unite one in emotional solidarity with others.

Individuative-reflective Faith (Young Adulthood and Beyond) In young adulthood there is a further transition to finding a genuinely individual set of principles or beliefs. This transition involves a critical reflection upon one's beliefs and values. There is a more attuned understanding of self and others as part of the social system. Responsibility is assumed for making choices involving ideology and life-style that in turn open the way for commitments in relationships and vocation.

Conjunctive Faith (Mid-life and Beyond) Conjunctive faith is not typically found before mid-life. It is marked by the "embrace of polarities in one's life, an alertness to paradox, and the need for multiple interpretations" (Fowler 1983, 58). There is also a realization that many different systems of belief can all be partially true. There is a readiness to hear about beliefs other than one's own. This stage tries to unify opposites in mind and experience.

Universalizing Faith (Mid-life or Beyond) The transition to universalizing faith, which is relatively rare even in late adulthood, involves a step beyond individuality to a feeling of oneness with the power of being. People in this stage are heedless of self-preservation and may even be seen as subversive to traditional organized religion. "Their visions and commitments free them for a passionate yet detached spending of the self in love, devoted to overcoming division, oppression, and brutality" (Fowler 1983, 58). Gandhi's mature life exemplifies this oneness. He formed a vision of unified being that went beyond the barriers of caste, religion, race, and nationality. Gandhi believed that to love life in all its fullness, and to be faithful to the vision of oneness, a person must be ready to lay down his or her life in order to overcome injustice.

Although these stages of faith resemble the formal structure-developmental modes proposed by Piaget and Kohlberg, Fowler emphasizes emotions and feelings. More than Piaget and Kohlberg, Fowler has tried to avoid the separation of cognition and emotions. He has systematically given attention to the role of imagination in the knowing and committing that is faith. Data collected by Fowler, Piaget, and Kohlberg suggest that there is some basic stable meaning to life that we adhere to throughout life.

Adopting a personal philosophy is an indicator of a mature mind. That philosophy is a guide to the meaning and purpose in experience and determines the quality of relations between individuals. It is formed from analyzing past experiences and anticipating future possibilities. It is based on interactions from almost every dimension of social relationships. Factors that are important in the maturation of a personal philosophy include work, a relationship with a loving companion, parenting, and encounters with political and/or historical events. "A personal philosophy is a creative reduction of enormous amounts of data into a few convincing principles." Once established, it is more likely to be a "lens through which events are interpreted than to be the object of interpretation itself" (Newman 1982, 632).

Adopting a political ideology is one factor that contributes to a mature personal philosophy.

Political thought is a "system that governs a person's relationship with community, county, state, or federal levels of organization" (Newman 1982, 631). Political thought is not highly developed for many adults. The low percentage of voters in state and local elections indicates that the majority of adults do not exercise their political conceptualizations by trying to change the direction of government. Apparently, politically inactive adults are aware of the nature and organization of the political system that operates in this country. One view is that successful political socialization has created a pool of individuals who identify strongly with the United States, support its government, and do not feel the need to actively influence the political system.

The widespread influence of television has challenged today's adults to adapt their political ideology to the reality of political life. Adults feel uneasy about the gap between the enormity of the political and governmental systems and their own capacity to understand, predict, or influence the pattern of events.

Individuals do not acquire a political ideology haphazardly, nor are they inconsistent. Personality traits that correlate with a particular ideology are stable over time. For example, adolescents who are anti-authoritarian, and non-ethnocentric tend to develop into politically liberal adults. Mussen and Haan (1981) found that those who adopt a liberal political ideology tend to be independent, rebellious, unconventional thinkers, concerned with philosophical and intellectual matters, proud of their objectivity, and more accepting of their own and others' feelings, motivations, and emotions. Those who adopt a conservative political ideology tend to be submissive, dependent on others, in strong need of reassurance, moralistic, little inclined toward introspection, and uncomfortable with uncertainty and ambiguity. It is not fully understood why an individual will be a liberal or a conservative, but the implications drawn by Mussen and Haan (1981) point to early socialization and parents' child-rearing techniques. Other factors may relate to the individual's social and economic fortunes or to social, historical, and/or economic events. Moral judgment and personal philosophy are also elements that interact to help form an individual's political ideology.

Humor

Individuals involved in comedy have been studied to identify any personality characteristics that set them apart from the general population. Fisher and Fisher (1981, 1983) found that clowns, comics, and comedy writers had at least one parent or another close relative who did a lot of joking and clowning during their childhood. Amateur comics have the following attributes: aggressiveness, spontaneity, unconventionality, leadership, social ambition, impulsivity, self-confidence, outspokenness, self-centeredness, and verbal fluency. (Fisher and Fisher 1981; Salameh 1980). Professional comics show high concern about issues of good and evil; a preoccupation with size, particularly smallness; a concern with things not always being what they seem; and a conviction that life is full of contradictions (Fisher and Fisher 1981, 1983).

Humor can contribute to an individual's mental well-being. One of its functions and properties is to release tension. Wolfenstein (1954) points out that in joking we downplay disappointment and transform painful feelings. Humor is one of the most complex products of the human mind and is a distinctly human achievement. The ability to joke is an important emotional resource, and the psychological process involved is exceedingly complicated. We have mixed feelings about joking. We tend to value the capacity for joking and to discredit the individual who has no sense of humor. We generally correlate a good sense of humor with good mental health. We regard people who rarely laugh or who have little sense of humor as being poorly adjusted. Yet we also question the adjustment of those who laugh indiscriminately or in inappropriate situations (McGhee 1979). Joking is an attempt to overlook or forget life's problems. Adults need a temporary escape from the burdens of reality, and humor is an easy and socially acceptable way to accomplish this. The primary concern is the fear of appearing immature (Wolfenstein 1954; McGhee 1972). The degree of humor appreciation among adults is positively correlated with other psychological measures of maturity and seems to be a fairly stable personality characteristic (McGhee 1979).

Cartoons or comic strips offer a mirror that can reflect marital and social realities. Long-term male-female relationships in mid and late life appear to offer a wide range of opportunities for cartoon humor. Ansello (1986) did a content analysis of ninety cartoons and comic strips, published between 1979 and 1984, that featured at least four interrelated themes within long-term male-female relationships: (1) traditional antagonism between the sexes, (2) tension release, or catharsis, (3) shared intimacy, and (4) accommodation to gender-role changes.

Antagonism between genders is readily recognizable and stereotypic. For example, themes include male superiority, female troublesomeness, the nagging wife, and the struggle for the upper hand. Control is the major source of antagonism.

Catharsis, or tension release, is one of the healthiest consequences of long-term relations. While one partner may be the cause of the stress, the continued relationship allows enough security to purge emotions and ease frictions between the couple. Proximity or physical closeness may be the underlying dynamic for this tension release.

Example of Shared Intimacy

Example of Antagonism

Reprinted with special permission of King Features Syndicate, Inc.

Example of Accommodation

"NOW I REMEMBER WHAT I WAS DRINKING TO FORGET."

Reprinted with special permission of King Features Syndicate, Inc.

"You must be getting tired, dear . . . Do you want me to drive on my own for a while?"

Reprinted with special permission of North America Syndicate, Inc.

Example of Catharsis

Reprinted with special permission of North America Syndicate, Inc.

Shared intimacy is necessary for life satisfaction. The key is the opportunity to share personal beliefs, confide in one another, and know one another. People in long-term relationships develop a special awareness of and appreciation for their partner's idiosyncrasies. Familiarity is the underlying dynamic here; that is, "familiarity breeds humor."

In a similar vein, Warner (1984) discusses humor as a subset of self-disclosure in that the practice of sharing a joke, laughter, wit, or humor discloses specific knowledge, and the person is motivated to share that content with a specific, significant person in a given situation. The context of Warner's study was the relationship between a withdrawn patient/client and a therapist. Humor tends to pull withdrawn patients out.

Accommodation is a "return of the repressed" in both genders. Men relinquish their competitive and production orientation to the more social and nurturant aspects of their personality. Women abandon their social and nurturant characteristics for the more managerial and assertive aspects of their personality (Gutmann et al. 1980). Adjustment to new roles is the underlying dynamic. The object of some of the humor may be the dominant or powerful older woman or the man who whines or commiserates. The older man may try to deny through alcohol, and the barroom is the common setting in this theme. Thus, humor plays a role in illustrating late-life transitions.

Laughter and humor have been identified as "good for the body." They restore homeostasis (the physical process by which internal systems of the body such as blood pressure and body temperature are maintained at equilibrium), stabilize blood pressure, oxygenate the blood, stimulate circulation, ease digestion, and generally produce a feeling of well-being (Keith-Spiegel 1972). Norman Cousins (1979), in *Anatomy of an Illness as Perceived by the Patient,* supports this assertion and relates how he recovered from a life-threatening illness with the aid of humor.

> It worked. I made the joyous discovery that ten minutes of genuine belly laughter had an anesthetic effect and would give me at least two hours of pain-free sleep. When the pain-killing effect of the laughter wore off, we would switch on the motion-picture projector again [he had several comedy movies], and, not infrequently, it would lead to another pain-free sleep interval. Sometimes, the nurse read to me out of a trove of humor books. Especially useful were E. B. and Katherine White's *Subtreasury of American Humor* and Max Eastman's *The Enjoyment of Laughter.* How scientific was it to believe that laughter—as well as positive emotions in general—was affecting my body chemistry for the better? If laughter did in fact have a salutary effect on the body's chemistry, it seemed at least theoretically likely that it would enhance the system's ability to fight the inflammation. So we took sedimentation rate readings just before as well as several hours after the laughter episodes. Each time, there was a drop of at least five points. The drop by itself was not substantial, but it held and was cumulative. I was greatly elated by the discovery that there is a physiologic basis for the ancient theory that laughter is good medicine.

By the end of one week Cousins was completely off drugs and sleeping pills. "Sleep—blessed, natural sleep without pain—was becoming increasingly prolonged" (Cousins 1979).

Humor can be a tool of social status. Status differences between employees in occupational settings are reflected in individuals of higher status or rank initiating more jokes and other witty remarks than low-status people. This supports the view that humorists have more social power than others. Lower-status employees feel they are stepping beyond the bounds of their position by taking the assertive role of jokester (Smeltzer and Leap 1988). Not only do authoritative individuals initiate more jokes, but their humor quite often is at the expense of others. Thus high-status employees are free to put down lower-status employees, but the latter do not enjoy the same privilege and are more likely to tell self-deprecating jokes (Duncan 1985).

Vinton (1983) noted three types of joking behavior in work settings. The first was *bantering*. Employees used this type of joking behavior to communicate a desire to work on an equal basis with others. *Teasing* was the second type, and it was used to send a serious message in a nonthreatening manner. Third, *self-ridiculing jokes* communicated an intention to engage in joking behavior and lessen established status boundaries.

Humor about sex roles often is based on the perspective that women have a lower status than men. McGhee and Duffey (1983) found that not only do women see great humor in women being victimized in jokes, but they also rate such jokes as even funnier than males do. That is, men prefer jokes in which women are put down, but women seem to enjoy them even more. This strengthens the view that self-disparagement may play a unique role in establishing a female sense of humor. A female-disparaging joke will be funnier to women when told by another woman rather than a man, however. And if told by a man or woman who supports the feminist movement, such a joke is funnier than if told by a woman known to be against the movement. Women who identify strongly with the feminist movement show the male pattern of preferring jokes in which the opposite sex is disparaged. Females give a higher funniness rating than males to self-disparaging jokes, regardless of the sex being disparaged. This may reflect the fact that females typically are less concerned than males with the issue of dominance and infallibility. Even though they are humorous in context, self-disparaging acts may be threatening to men. If so, it is not surprising that men do not find humor in the putting down of other men, especially by a woman (McGhee 1979). In another study, Smeltzer and Leap (1988) found that women regarded sexist jokes as less appropriate than men did. Men considered sexist jokes as more appropriate than females did in a mixed group. They also found that African-Americans were less offended by racist jokes than whites were. Females rated racist jokes as more offensive than sexist jokes.

Women seem to be generally more sensitive to the reactions of others than are men. Laughing at someone else's jokes, whether funny or not, assures continued liking and acceptance by others, which suggests why women are likely to do it. They laugh at jokes or events they do not find funny in order to present a "charming" personality in public (McGhee 1979). To maintain this frame of mind, however, a woman must be confident that a joke, even against her own sex, is meant only in a playful sense.

An individual with a good sense of humor does not let the desperateness of his or her situation interfere with the enjoyment of potentially comical events when they occur.

SUMMARY

- Middle-aged adults are less susceptible to colds and allergies, but they tend to tire faster, have more dental problems, have higher blood pressure, and need more time to recuperate from fatigue or illness.
- Appearance changes a great deal during middle age. These changes involve skin, hair, muscles, and height.
- Menopause represents the major physical change in middle-aged women. Hot flashes are the most common symptom of menopause. Younger women have more negative attitudes concerning menopause than do older women.
- The male climacteric involves very slow hormonal changes. Sexual functioning alters slightly, and there is a decline in physical energy. These changes are psychological as well as biological.
- Behavioral patterns have a strong influence on the health of adults. Two major patterns are Type A and Type B behavior. The Type A person has an excessive competitive drive, is aggressive and impatient, and has a harrying sense of time urgency. The Type B person is just the opposite. He or she finds time to ponder leisurely, weigh alternatives, and experiment. Life circumstances can also affect the health of the adult.
- Cognitive functioning is dependent on speed, arousal, attention, and caution. When adults become committed and responsible, they use their logical abilities to choose the best course of action in problem solving. Problems are more

Stress

Stress is an inevitable part of life and offers challenges to learn and master new skills and behavior patterns. Excessive stress, however, can disrupt emotional, cognitive, and physiological functioning. Chronic stress is related to the incidence of life-threatening physical conditions such as high blood pressure and heart disease. Managing stress has become a priority for physicians and the general public.

What stressors affect individuals during their adult years? According to Hurrelmann (1989), the most prominent areas from which stressors emerge are professional life, family life, and leisure time. Through professional life the individual is integrated into the production and service domain of society. Family life and leisure time encompass nonprofessional forms of living and working, that is, the reproductive domain of society. The professional and personal domains mutually influence each other.

Work in the professional domain often determines social acceptance, social prestige, and financial status. Unemployment is highly stressful for a number of reasons:

1. loss of the structure provided by the workday
2. loss of financial security and the ability to satisfy material needs
3. loss of new vistas related to work (individually in the form of a career, socially in the form of acknowledgement)
4. loss of social contacts with colleagues
5. loss of the ability to express oneself through work
6. loss of the possibility for satisfying one's need to be productive
7. loss of one's sense of importance in society
8. loss of stimulation through the social environment
9. loss of the role as wage earner and provider for the family (Hurrelmann 1989, 52)

Even the threat of unemployment leads to an increase in health problems and psychosomatic symptoms, such as heart disease, high blood pressure, and digestive disorders (Hurrelmann 1989).

Work overload, another stressor, takes two forms. One occurs when time runs out to complete a specific project. The other occurs when performance standards are set so high that they cannot be met regardless of the time allowed (Ivancevich and Matteson 1980).

Relocation due to promotions and job changes has increased noticeably in the past twenty years. In any year, about one-fifth of the population moves. The situation is

Relocation is stressful to the family. Spouses of transferred executives react with depression, and adolescent children experience a lengthy period of poor peer relationships.

The death of a loved one is one of the three most stressful events in an individual's life. The stress syndrome of grief includes physiological distress, such as shortness of breath, tightness in the throat, fatigue, and loss of muscular strength.

Stress (continued)

especially stressful to the spouse and children. Spouses of transferred executives react with depression, and adolescent children experience a lengthy period of poor peer relationships (Brett 1980).

Role conflict is another stressor in the workplace. It occurs when the performance of one job-related task competes with the performance of an equally important task. For example, if one superior gives instructions that conflict with those of another superior, an employee will experience role conflict. How would you handle such a situation? Role conflict also occurs when an employee is asked to do a task that violates his or her values or beliefs, such as selling a product that he or she knows will not meet the needs of a customer. Role conflict produces tension and anxiety, reduces the quality of performance, and often results in antagonism toward fellow employees.

Separation and loss are the most serious stressors in family life. The death of a spouse, divorce, and marital separation are the three most stressful events for most people. They mean the end of a valued relationship and force a person to make major readjustments in life-style. Divorced and separated people are more anxious, feel more helpless, and have lower self-esteem than married people. They are also more frequently admitted to mental hospitals, are physically ill more often, and are more likely to commit suicide than married people (Doherty and Jacobson 1982).

The death of a loved one may be even more devastating. The stress syndrome of grief includes physiological distress, such as shortness of breath, tightness in the throat, fatigue, and loss of muscular strength. The griever often feels guilty about real or imagined slights to the deceased (Kalish, 1985).

How do people cope with these stressors? One way to cope is to use defense mechanisms, such as denial and intellectualization. Defense mechanisms are usually unconscious and automatic methods of reducing stress when the situation makes it difficult to use more direct coping methods. *Denial* blocks the ability to perceive reality and thus the ability to act on external threats. For example, the terminally ill cancer patient who plans for retirement is using denial. *Intellectualization* does not distort perception but blocks from conscious awareness the emotional arousal that accompanies stress. The individual appears to remain calm and detached in a stressful situation.

Reappraising the situation, another way to cope, reexamines the initial perceptions of a stressful situation. This method relies on the ability to weigh evidence and convert a negative appraisal into a positive one. This method fits the old saying "look on the bright side."

Many people use tension-reduction techniques, such as sedative drugs, physical exercise, and training in the relaxation response. *Sedative drugs* include ethyl alcohol, the barbiturates, and the benzodiazepines. These sedative drugs reduce stress-related physiological arousal and induce sleep immediately. Sedatives help in the short run, but long-term use can lead to substance abuse.

Physical exercise is an active approach to dealing with physiological reactions to stress. How can exercise reduce stress when it creates almost the exact same physiological reactions that stress does? One theory is that exercise is voluntary and enables the individual to stay in control of his or her physiological arousal. At the same time it promotes a sense of mastery over stress reactions and produces a postexercise state of relaxation.

The *relaxation response,* or deep relaxation, is at one end of the continuum of physical arousal; a highly aroused state of stress reaction is at the other end. Three techniques for learning the relaxation response are hypnosis, meditation, and progressive relaxation. Hypnosis uses direct suggestion and relaxing mental images, such as imagining lying on a deserted beach. Meditation focuses attention on a mental image for several minutes. The continued practice of hypnosis or meditation produces an altered state of consciousness that leads to a person's feeling temporarily disengaged from his or her immediate surroundings. Progressive relaxation consists of alternately tensing and relaxing the individual major muscles of the body. This method teaches how to recognize the difference between tension and relaxation and then voluntarily progress to a state of deep relaxation.

Why are some situations more stressful to one individual than to another? What coping methods do you use when you are in a stressful situation? Some school systems have adopted life-skill programs that include teaching stress-reduction techniques to children. Many parents are opposed to such programs. What do you think?

complex and long-term than earlier in life, so there is more need for a guiding philosophy or life plan that gives direction, emphasis, and style to the problem-solving task.

- The number of years of school correlates with the level of general intelligence. The more education people attain, the higher their initial intelligence scores and the higher those scores remain throughout life.

- Moral judgment and personal philosophy are related to cognitively evaluating one's place in the world, assessing one's relationships with others, and determining one's selfhood. They also are related to an individual's political ideology. The stage theories of Piaget, Kohlberg, and Fowler address the development of morality and personal philosophy from different perspectives.

- Humor is an indicator of mental well-being and has been correlated with physical healing.

- Cartoons and comic strips offer a reflection of long-term male-female relationships with four interrelated themes. Humor can be a tool reflecting higher or lower social status, occupational status, and the sex-role dilemma.

- Adaptation to stress has major internal and external influences on health. Stressors emerge mainly from professional life and from family life and leisure time. Adults use several ways to cope with stress, including defense mechanisms (denial and intellectualism) and tension-reduction techniques (sedative drugs, physical exercise, and training in the relaxation response).

READINGS

Charness, N. (1985). *Aging and human performance.* New York: Wiley.
Reviews of research concerning age-related differences in a variety of cognitive performances.

Fince, C. E. and Schneider, E. L. (1985). *Handbook of the biology of aging.* New York: Van Nostrand.
Reviews of recent work on the biology of aging.

Fries, J. F. and Crapo, L. M. (1981). *Vitality and aging.* San Francisco: Freeman.
Authors explain how death and disease can be postponed and how everyone can be able to live a vital life right up to when they die.

Ghandi, M. K. (1983). *Autobiography: The story of my experiments with truth.* Boston: Beacon Press.
A perspective of how Ghandi reached his moral and political philosophy.

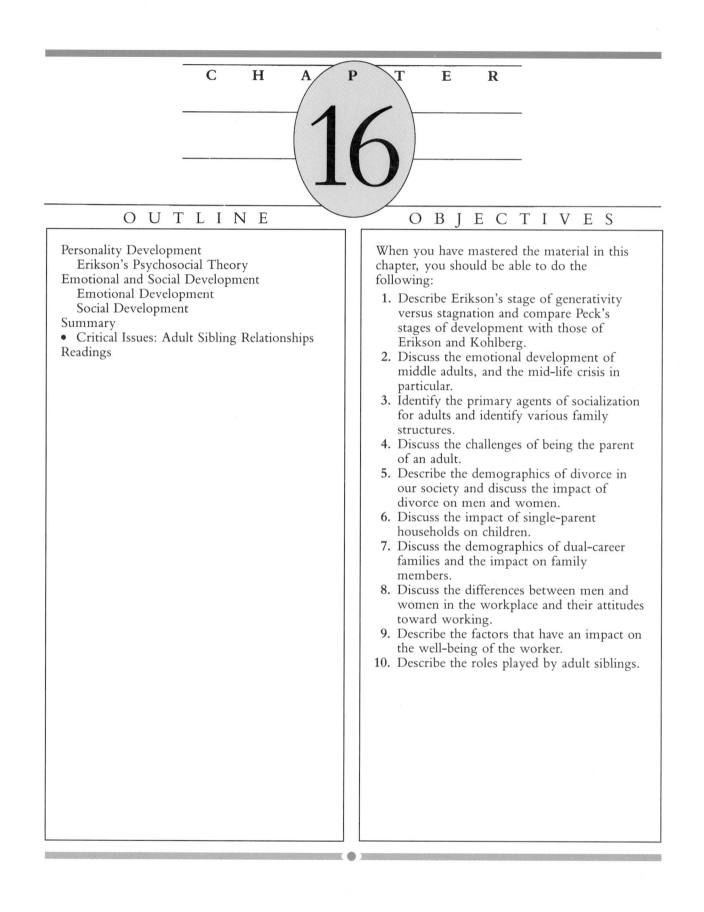

CHAPTER 16

OUTLINE

Personality Development
    Erikson's Psychosocial Theory
Emotional and Social Development
    Emotional Development
    Social Development
Summary
• Critical Issues: Adult Sibling Relationships
Readings

OBJECTIVES

When you have mastered the material in this chapter, you should be able to do the following:

1. Describe Erikson's stage of generativity versus stagnation and compare Peck's stages of development with those of Erikson and Kohlberg.
2. Discuss the emotional development of middle adults, and the mid-life crisis in particular.
3. Identify the primary agents of socialization for adults and identify various family structures.
4. Discuss the challenges of being the parent of an adult.
5. Describe the demographics of divorce in our society and discuss the impact of divorce on men and women.
6. Discuss the impact of single-parent households on children.
7. Discuss the demographics of dual-career families and the impact on family members.
8. Discuss the differences between men and women in the workplace and their attitudes toward working.
9. Describe the factors that have an impact on the well-being of the worker.
10. Describe the roles played by adult siblings.

Midlife: The Middle Adult—Psychosocial Development

PERSONALITY DEVELOPMENT
Erikson's Psychosocial Theory

Erikson labeled the second adult stage "generativity versus stagnation," and it corresponds to middle adulthood. Generativity emphasizes continuity with the preceding stages, but it is primarily concerned with supporting and encouraging the development of future generations. This involves establishing and guiding the next generation. Having or even wanting children, however, does not "achieve" generativity. There are individuals who, for various reasons, do not apply this drive to their own offspring. Some parents have difficulty developing this stage. They are self-centered and lack the capacity to see that children are a necessity to continue the species and are a welcome trust to the community.

Generativity should be regarded in relation to an individual's production as well as his or her progeny. Mature adults need to be needed. The concept of generativity encompasses productivity and creativity. This may involve leaving something of one's self, such as art or literary works, to future generations (Erikson 1963).

If such enrichment does not occur, then a pervading sense of stagnation and personal impoverishment occurs. When middle adults do not establish continuity with the next generation, they may become overly absorbed in self and ignore the needs of others. Individuals often begin to indulge themselves as if they were their own or another's only child. Early invalidism, physical or psychological, may result.

Robert Peck (1960) has proposed a theory parallel to Erikson's stages of psychosocial development and Kohlberg's stages of moral development. His theory may be viewed in chronological stages that parallel the specific developmental stages (see page 430).

According to Erikson, generativity emphasizes continuity with the preceding stages, but it is primarily concerned with supporting and encouraging the development of future generations. This involves establishing and guiding the next generation.

Generativity should be regarded in relation to an individual's production as well as his or her progeny. This may involve leaving something of one's self, such as art or literary works, to future generations.

EMOTIONAL AND SOCIAL DEVELOPMENT

Emotional Development

Neugarten (1968), in her classic studies of adulthood, noted that middle-aged men and women constitute a powerful age-group. They are the "norm bearers" and "decision makers" although they live in a youth-oriented society. Middle-aged individuals experience a heightened sensitivity to their position within a complex social environment. They are highly introspective and verbal, with considerable insight into changes that take place in their careers, families, status, and the way they deal with both their inner and outer worlds. The higher an individual's career position, the more likely he or she is willing to explore the various issues and themes of middle age.

Some of the issues of middle age are related to new family roles. These roles include the reversal of authority when the middle-aged child becomes the decision maker for the aging parent. Becoming a father- or mother-in-law and attempting to establish an intimate relationship with a child's spouse under short notice is another role. Grandparenthood is also a new and challenging role. The middle-aged individual is aware of becoming a bridge between the generations. He or she faces increased stock-taking and heightened introspection and reflection. Also, time is restructured in terms of "time left to live" rather than "time since birth." Death becomes personalized in the sense that middle adults realize "I am going to die." For women this involves preparation, or rehearsal for widowhood; for men, the preparation, or rehearsal, for illness; and for both, a new attention to body-monitoring (Neugarten 1975).

Middle-aged individuals are past the period of idealism that is characteristic of young adulthood. Middle-aged adults recognize that although early commitments often remain unchanged, the basis or foundation underlying these ideals was excessively high and/or inappropriate. The theme of this stage should be

Peck's Theory

The *amoral* individual has "infantlike" inaccurate perceptions, emotional immaturity, and the inability to control himself or herself in adequately meeting the demands of social living. Behavior is impulsive, insensitive, and done without regard to its effects on others. Those who remain at the amoral stage are called "sociopathic." They have no internalized moral principles. Their interpersonal relationships are egocentric, and they feel no remorse or guilt when they violate societal expectations. They are blind to the moral implications of their behavior and its impact on others.

The *expedient* individual comes to terms with society in his or her own way. However, his or her way is that of a young child who conforms in order to avoid adult punishment or disapproval. This individual is no different than the amoral individual in the lack of concern about others. Others are seen as a means to satisfy present, pressing wants and needs. Expedient individuals behave subtly in order to manipulate others for their own selfish ends. When external authority is not present, they do what they want to do. They have no internalized set of moral behavior codes. They give little of themselves to others and tend to manipulate their interpersonal relationships.

The *conforming* individual is similar to a child who accepts the dictates of his or her family and society in a placid and uncritical way. He or she conforms to the group's demands. If the peer group expects specific social or religious behaviors, the individual behaves according to these expectations. If immoral or socially nonconforming behavior is rewarded, the individual does what the crowd expects, even if it violates earlier training. The situation, rather than a core set of principles, determines the ethics. Conforming individuals may be faithful to their marriage commitments and church vows at home. However, when they are away from home, such as at a conference, they may "forget" their marital commitments. Some will feel shame if they are concerned about what others think of them, but they will not feel guilt for violating principles of honesty, loyalty, and truthfulness. They feel little guilt if they break a rule. They have not internalized many principles of moral responsibility. These individuals, like older children, know how to live at peace in their familiar world. However, they do not ask questions about its fundamental traditions and take these for granted as absolutes.

The *irrational-conscientious* individual is much like a child or early adolescent who lives by absolute rules. This individual has an internalized code of moral behavior that he or she rigidly follows and applies to others as well. The rules must be followed and enforced, with a penalty applied without mercy. Extenuating circumstances or motives are not taken into consideration. These high personal expectations and an intolerance of personal failure leave irrational-conscientious individuals with deep feelings of guilt and shame if they fail to act in a morally acceptable manner. Psychotherapy might be necessary in some cases to help free them from irrational guilt. The positive side of this stage is that these people try hard to behave morally and uphold the moral expectations of their society and religious faith. They are prone to become involved in social issues, and because of them, the quality of life in their communities is significantly better.

The *rational-altruistic* individual goes beyond fulfilling legal rules to implementing internalized principles. He or she is a continuously maturing person. Articulated rules are not abandoned but instead are used as guides for moral behavior. The "good of others" principle is the value system under which rational-altruistic people operate. Their courses of action are based on reason rather than impulse. The welfare of others is as important as their own. Individuals at this level work with others in constructive ways. They enjoy life, and they are not afraid to appropriately express their emotional reactions. These individuals are authentic. They are well-adjusted and quite undefensive about their actions. They feel guilt and shame at times, and admit their errors. They make a sincere effort to rectify their mistakes, make amends, and restore the damaged egos of others. Thus, they are fully developed moral persons, who try to behave conscientiously and morally because it is the right thing to do. Their motive is not to escape a guilty conscience or censure by society.

"attainment of our potentials" (Donohugh 1981, 209). During this period the individual is beginning to discover himself or herself and question earlier values and where they have brought him or her.

Women tend to define their status in relation to events within the family cycle. Married middle-aged women are closely tied in launching their children into the adult world. Unmarried middle-aged career women often discuss middle age in terms of the family they might have had. Often men perceive the onset of middle age by cues presented outside of the family, usually in the workplace. Men are more likely to see a close relationship between one's "life line", that is, the amount of time one has to live, and one's "career line." They take stock and note any disparity between career expectations and career achievements. However, the most dramatic cues for men are often biological. An increased interest in health, a decrease in the efficiency of the body, and the death of friends of the same age are signs that prompt many men to describe bodily changes as the "most salient characteristic of middle age" (Neugarten 1968).

The *mid-life crisis* has received considerable publicity. Several studies indicate that many men and women experience a stressful period in mid-life (Livson 1981; Gould 1978; Levinson et al. 1978), but it is not necessarily a crisis. Some people go through a transition, while others experience no overwhelming feelings of change. A life-threatening illness can contribute to the onset of the mid-life transition as well as to the intensification of the experience.

Men experience this time period differently than women do. For men, the concern at mid-life is with mortality and time running out. This concern is probably based on the physical realities of being male. Men are more prone to life-threatening diseases, such as heart disease, that strike at mid-life. How they tackle the reality of eventual death—whether they face this reality or deny it—will depend on how they worked through earlier crises. Some behaviors that emerge during this time include hypochondriacal concern with health and appearance, emergence of sexual promiscuity, and increased religious concern (Cytrynbaum et al. 1980). Baruch, Barnet, and Rivers (1983) found no evidence that anxiety and depression associated with a mid-life crisis appear in women around age forty or fifty. Their sample of women rarely spoke of time running out. The concerns women expressed about aging centered not on having too little time left, but on having too much. Middle-aged women know they are likely to live past seventy and fear they will lose their independence and will not function as active adults.

For women, the experience of "empty-nesting" ranges from distress to relief and varies in meaning and timing. The degree of investment in parenthood, individual differences in personality, simultaneous changes in the couple's relationship, and the woman's sense of security in what lies ahead all shape the experience. Menopause has also been seen as a major biological determining event of mid-life (Neugarten 1968; Cytrynbaum et al. 1980).

The mid-life transition can be conceptualized through a series of interrelated tasks to be mastered. These tasks include acceptance of death and mortality; recognition of biological limitations and health risks; restructuring of sexual identity and self-concept; reorientation to work, career, creativity, and achievement; and reassessment of primary relationships. Commitment to these tasks signals one's entry into and participation in mid-life. The work of mid-life involves continual and deep examination of inner experiences, feelings, fantasies, conflicts, values, and attitudes. The quality of work carried on during mid-life in mastering these developmental tasks can set the stage for considerable growth and adaptation. Failure to do so may predispose post-mid-life people to distress (Cytrynbaum et al. 1980).

Gutmann and his colleagues' cross-cultural studies (1975, 1980) indicate that a massive turnover of sex roles takes place in middle life. Men can adopt out-

Berry's World

© 1986 by N.E.A. Inc 7-E

"I've forgotten! Is it married women who want romance and married men who want a nest, or the other way around?"

ward passivity, sensuality, and tenderness—attributes that were previously repressed. Women are free to become domineering, independent, and unsentimental. Without the responsibility of growing children, wives and mothers no longer need to admire male assertion and are now free to recognize and enjoy such energies in themselves. In other words, the sharp distinctions of earlier adulthood break down and each sex becomes, to some degree, what the other used to be. The resulting sexual bimodality and refocusing of energy occurs as the sense of parental imperative lessens. (*Parental imperative* means the culturally imposed requirement that certain potentialities be blunted in the service of procreation and parenting tasks.) According to Gutmann et al., it is the requirements of parenthood that establish traditional sex-role distinctions in early adulthood. Masculine and feminine qualities are distributed not only by sex but by life period and requirements of parenthood. Middle and later life are periods during which men and women move toward "normal unisex of later life." Such developments can be stressful, especially for couples and families.

Emerging opposite-gender components can precipitate pathological symptoms for men and women. The emerging passive-dependent needs of men may not be gratified by their new, more autonomous, independent, and assertive wives or other female partners. Men may then develop alcoholic or psychosomatic symptoms. The mid-life husband who leaves his wife for a younger, more dependent woman may do it not to prove sexual potency, but to help him deny his emerging passivity. Thus, those who fail to resolve, or who deny, these conflicts may suffer from distress and despair or are more predisposed to these symptoms in later years.

Dual-career families may experience problems with the emerging opposite-sex components. Emerging passive-dependent needs in the husband can lead him to have powerful wishes to be cared for, to be loved, and to love. The need for a more intimate, caring relationship may come at a time when his wife is moving toward autonomy, independence, and assertiveness that are necessary in continuing a career. (Cytrynbaum et al. 1980).

Social Development

Adult personality changes often occur as a consequence of changes in the adult's social roles. After childhood, socialization consists of learning the skills, attitudes, and knowledge necessary to successfully perform the major roles of adult life, including spousal and parental roles. The primary agents of adult socialization are the various role partners one encounters, such as spouse, employer, child, friends, and so on. Each of these partners influences the adult's personality and behavior. The socialization agents who have the strongest influence are those who have the highest frequency of controlling behavior, those who are most important to the adult, and those who have the most control over rewards and punishments. Marriage, parenthood, and work provide the primary social roles for most people in most societies. These are paramount in influencing adult development and mental health (Doherty and Jacobson 1982).

Family

Every society has its own rules and regulations that emphasize its expectations of its citizens. The family within a society reflects the expectations of that society. Each individual, therefore, is socialized through the family unit or structure. Family structures are different in various societies. However, no matter what the structure, it seems natural and correct for most of the individuals living in it. A family system has been defined as being "composed of intimately interrelated individuals who have close emotional and behavioral ties to each other. The tasks of such systems change over the course of the life cycle of the family" (Cytrynbaum et al. 1980).

The **nuclear family** is found in most societies. This unit consists primarily of father, mother, and child(ren). **Conjugal family** is another name often applied to nuclear family and is based on the marriage relationship of the husband and wife. Marriage establishes and regulates the nuclear family. In Western society the nuclear unit of a married couple and their children is viewed as the most important and usual family form. A nuclear family functions only as long as its two focal members, that is, the husband and the wife, are together, since the conjugal relationship is what holds the unit together. Even in areas where the nuclear unit is the norm, other structures of families exist.

A nuclear family is connected with individuals and other family units called **kin.** Kin include grandparents, aunts, uncles, cousins, nieces, nephews, brothers, sisters, brothers- and sisters-in-law. Our society does not have a definite policy on how we treat and how much attention we pay to these kin. Each family is different in this regard.

The **extended family** is an integration of a more complicated family structure resulting in families that may last for several generations. An extended family includes two or more nuclear units operating as a recognized social unit. The emphasis is on parent-child bonds and relationships between siblings. These families can perform more functions than a nuclear family. The extended family is often organized around a business or occupation that provides work and income for everyone. The conjugal relationship is weakened in intensity and concentration compared with the husband-wife relationship in the nuclear family, where much of daily life is shared only by the pair. Child rearing is also different in aims and methods.

Some extended families exist among lower-class ethnic groups in North America. Several generations may live in one house. Upper-class extended

Nuclear family
A family unit that consists of mother, father, and child(ren).

Conjugal family
A nuclear family unit in which the husband-wife relationship is of primary importance.

Kin
Family members including grandparents, aunts, uncles, cousins, nieces, nephews, brothers, sisters, brothers- and sisters-in-law.

Extended family
An integration of a complicated family structure resulting in families that may last for several generations.

families, although they do not live in the same house, may own joint property. They may build their homes, especially their summer homes, in clusters. For example, the Kennedy family has its cluster of family homes in Hyannis Port, Massachusetts. Upper-class North American extended families are similar to Asian extended families. The conjugal pair is less central than in the middle-class nuclear family, while blood relations are very important. Older members have power and status. Because women usually outlive men, the leader or high-status member of an upper-class extended family is likely to be a woman. She usually has a great deal of financial power. The upper-class family may control the choice of marriage partners, more than middle-class nuclear families do and less than Asian extended families do.

Parenthood

Parenting of adults adds another dimension to the parenting role. Eighty percent of the present-day middle-aged and older people who have ever married have living children. Ten percent of those over age sixty-five have children who are over sixty-five (Troll 1985).

When children leave home as young adults, their parents feel both loss and gain. The gains include an increased sense of personal freedom and relief from parental responsibilities. The parents also gain a new set of resource people: their children. Fathers gain less conflict, but also less pleasure. The loss felt by the parents is compounded by the concurrent biological changes and career changes. Women anticipate this event more than the men do and are better prepared. The independence of the children comes at a time when most men are getting ready to get close to them. The interaction between parents and their adult children appears to be carried on more through the mother's linkage than through the father's. Due to this situation, the father of adult children may assume an even more peripheral role than he had when the children were small (Troll 1985).

Developmental changes and transformations occur in fathers when their children become adults. The number of functions the fathers perform drops from eight or nine when their children are preadolescents to one or two when they become adults. Usually the first function to drop is authority, followed by protecting, teaching, providing, and counseling (if this was ever done at all). The only function to remain and develop is friendship. Middle-aged women report that their daughters become their friends (Troll 1985).

Parents of adult children are not always "in tune" with their children. They quite often assume that their children adopted their opinions and values. However, a study by Thompson et al. (1985) found that mothers and fathers were equally inaccurate in perceiving the opinions of their young-adult sons. Mothers were slightly above fathers in perceiving the opinions of their young-adult daughters, especially in areas concerning women's rights. Specifically, parents have limited ability to gauge what their children believe on several issues they face as they enter adult status. Parents also show little agreement among themselves about what their children think. The only areas in which parents accurately predict and share the viewpoints of their children are fundamental religiosity and sexual permissiveness.

Parents report that their adult children try to change them. The children are partially successful. Mothers are influenced in activities outside the home, in areas such as work, leisure, or education, with many returning to school or work. Fathers are more influenced concerning their physical appearance and

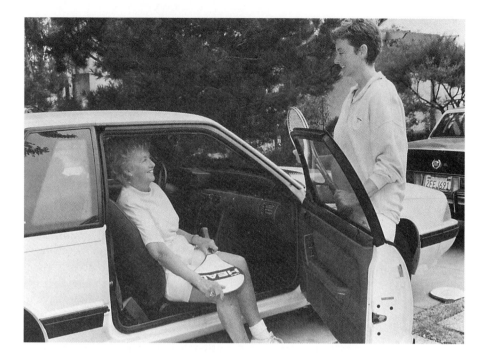

The mother-daughter dyad is perceived as the most balanced or reciprocal. Mothers are about three times more likely than fathers to discuss personal problems with their adult children.

views on current issues. Generally mothers are more accepting in being influenced than are fathers (Troll 1985).

The mother-daughter dyad is perceived as the most balanced or reciprocal, and the father-daughter dyad the most imbalanced, with the daughter giving much more than she receives. Most mothers and fathers perceive their adult children as sensitive to their feelings and moods. Mothers are about three times more likely than fathers to discuss personal problems with their children. Most middle-aged and older parents prefer "intimacy at a distance." Feelings of closeness accompany a need for some separateness (Troll and Bengston 1982).

Adult children who have to place their elderly parents in a nursing home feel guilty, strained, and bereaved. Such a situation represents a family crisis and opens up old wounds. Quite often a least-loved child may emerge as the caretaker because of the wish to try for that love one more time, even at the cost of more sacrifice (Hooyman and Kiyak 1988).

Daughters are more likely than sons to live close to their mothers, to visit them frequently, and to help them. Daughters are more attached to their mothers than to their fathers, and they are more attached to their mothers than sons are. Middle-aged mothers expect a lot from their young-adult daughters, but rarely give the daughters credit when they fulfill these expectations. Middle-aged mothers expect little from their sons and then lavish praise when the sons do something for them. Daughters are more bothered and upset by their parents, are more resentful, and are less satisfied with the relationship (Troll and Bengston 1982).

Daughters become closer to their mothers after they marry and become mothers. When young adult daughters get more help from their mothers than they give, the relationship is less intimate than when aid is balanced. But the reverse is not true. When middle-aged daughters give lots of help to their sick mothers, neither they nor their mothers report less attachment (Troll 1985).

Divorce

In 1989, the divorce rate was 4.7 per 1,000 population, down from a high of 5.3 per 1,000 population in 1979 and 1981 (Kitson and Morgan 1990). The most prevalent period in which divorces occur was in the age-group of twenty-five to thirty-nine years. If history is an indicator, they will spend an average of three years in the divorced role before they remarry (Doherty and Jacobson 1982; Glick 1989, 1990; Spanier 1990).

A mutually shared decision to separate or divorce is uncommon. Usually one partner wants to terminate a marriage more than the other does, creating a psychological imbalance in which one spouse is actively shutting the door on the marriage while the other continues to be attached to, or dependent upon, the marriage. Only one couple in sixty have made a truly mutual decision to divorce. It appears that women take the initiative more often than men do in seeking a divorce. Men are significantly more opposed to the separation than women are (Kelly 1982).

Men who marry before the age of twenty are twice as likely to divorce than those who marry after twenty. The same is true for women who marry before they are eighteen. Men and women who fail to complete high school have a higher divorce rate, as do men on the lower income scale. The relatively disadvantaged have disproportionately more divorces, but the socioeconomic gap is closing. African-Americans divorce more often than whites. The instability of the husband's employment and income in any given year increases the probability of divorce, independent of income level. There is also a higher likelihood of divorce when the husband's income decreases extensively from the previous year. Wives with higher wages are more likely to divorce than women who have lower wages (Kelly 1982). Remarried mothers entered into their first marriages at younger ages. This supports the common contention that young marriages are less stable (Spanier and Roos 1985).

Premarital pregnancies increase the probability of eventual divorce. It is estimated that one woman in four is pregnant at the time of her marriage. Premarital pregnancies occur across all socioeconomic, racial, and religious groups (Kelly, 1982).

Impulsive decisions to divorce do occur; however, it is more common for the adult to contemplate the possibility for months or years before making a firm decision. In some cases a "last straw" phenomenon occurs, when some specific event triggers the decision to separate. The three most common experiences that trigger the decision include infidelity; outside events (such as moving, graduating, and/or a new job) intruding on the relationship; and some situation that becomes intolerable, such as a second suicide attempt or alcoholism. In other cases, a "buildup," or combination of things, precipitates the divorce or separation. The adults facing this situation, most often women, indicate a growing sense of dissatisfaction and emptiness, which causes a slow, stubborn move toward the end of the relationship. After the realization that divorce is an option, the complex process leading to separation is set in motion, involving turmoil, indecision, and apprehension about the future. Counseling experiences, even when short-term, are useful in helping to clarify thoughts and feelings about the relationship (Kelly 1982).

The spouse who does not initiate the separation or divorce undergoes an extraordinarily stressful experience when told he or she is no longer loved or wanted. The stress of divorce is second only to the death of a spouse in terms of the demands made to reorganize one's life in a major way. Feelings of humiliation and powerlessness overwhelm the rejected spouse as he or she acknowledges the inability to make the departing spouse stay married. A common response to this shattered self-esteem is usually immense anger, depression, and a surprising degree of regressive behavior. Many are completely unprepared for their spouse's decision to divorce. Many had felt ungratified in their marriage but were not actively contemplating divorce and were shocked and upset by their spouse's decision. Spouses who initiate divorce often do so with sadness, guilt, apprehension, relief, and occasionally anger. However, they are definitely different from the rejected spouse in their sense of control and the absence of profound feelings of humiliation. For spouses who initiate divorce, the period of greatest stress may be prior to the separation. Symptoms they experience during this time include weight change, upset stomach, headaches, nervousness, dizziness, and general weakness (Kelly 1982).

Being divorced is a stressful situation for most people. Weingarten (1985) found that those who are currently divorced are considerably less exuberant about life than their first-married and remarried counterparts. This does not mean that being married reduces vulnerability to stress; rather, being divorced increases stress relative to being in an intact first marriage. For a minority of men and women who are overwhelmed and disorganized beyond their ability to recuperate, divorce caused symptoms of mild to extreme psychopathy. For example, some experience depression or symptoms such as sleeplessness, decreased self-esteem, lack of energy, and weight changes clinically associated with depression; others become suicidal (Kelly 1982). Menaghan (1985) found that individuals, four years after their divorce, had higher distress levels than the married, with economic problems, unavailability of confidants, and a deteriorating standard of living contributing to the distress.

Despite the critical amount of stress during the separation period, the sudden and painful economic and social changes, and the continued loneliness experienced by many divorced men and women, divorce potentially frees men and women from destructive and unsatisfactory relationships. Divorce represents the death of a relationship, but it can also be the rebirth of an individual. It can allow him or her to develop and change in fulfilling ways.

Single-parent Families

The single-parent family is the fastest-growing family form in the United States. Some of the many reasons a person may become a single parent include separation, divorce, widowhood, adoption, and premarital birth (Current Population Reports 1984; Hanson and Sporakowski 1986; Greif 1986; Hanson 1986). By 1984, 25.7 percent of all family groups were headed by one parent. About 89 percent of one-parent families who had children under eighteen years of age were headed by women. A majority (69 percent) of these women had never been married or were divorced. In 1984, over one-half of all African-American children lived with one parent, while one-sixth of all white children and one-fourth of all children of Spanish origin did (Norton and Glick 1986). More than one-half of all children born in 1990 will spend part of their childhood in a single-parent home (Children's Defense Fund 1990).

Approximately 800,000 fathers in the United States are rearing minor children without a mother in the home. Generally, they are financially better off than single-parent mothers. They rarely solicit help from relatives and rarely pay someone to do household tasks. Homemaking does not appear to be a problem for single fathers. Although these fathers do report some problems, such as worrying about their daughters' lack of a female role model, most feel satisfied and competent as a single parent (Risman 1986; Hanson and Sporakowski 1986). Greif (1985) found that as the children get older, they participate more in housework. Single-parent fathers receive more help from teenage daughters than from teenage sons. These fathers also expect less from their children in the way of housework than would be expected in a two-parent family.

Less than half of the women who are supposed to receive child support from the father receive the full amount. Approximately 14 percent of noncustodial mothers pay child support. Noncustodial mothers who pay child support earn a higher income than those who do not. Also, noncustodial mothers who pay feel more involved and are consulted more. This is often an indicator of a good relationship between all the family members (Greif 1986).

Both male and female single-parent households can provide healthy environments in which to grow and live. Parents need to know that their own health status can make an impact on the health status of their children. Good health in parents is associated with good health in children. Hanson (1986) found that children living with mothers reported higher overall physical and mental health than children living with fathers. Boys display higher levels of health, especially mental health, as compared with girls. Boys living with their mothers have the best overall health, whereas girls living with their fathers have the worst. Single mothers have poorer overall health than single fathers. Fathers with sole custody of boys report the highest level of mental health, and mothers with sole custody of boys report the lowest mental health. Joint-custody parents are equal. Sole-custody fathers are significantly higher than sole-custody mothers in terms of education, occupation, and income. Joint-custody male and female parents are about equal in these terms. In sum, although single-parent families may experience many problems, they are not necessarily less able to manage them than other types of families.

Young adults reared in single-parent families differ from those reared in traditional two-parent families (Mueller and Cooper 1986). Those reared in single-parent families tend to have lower educational, occupational, and economic attainment than their counterparts. They are also more likely to have their first child at a younger age and to become separated or divorced rather than stay married.

Dual-career Families

Dual-career families
An intact family unit in which both parents work outside the home.

Dual-career families are those in which the family is intact and both the father and the mother are employed. Working mothers report they are more satisfied with their lives than nonworking mothers (Ferree 1976; Burke and Weir 1976). They view work as a right rather than an option. They now bargain for and receive assistance with housework and child care from their husbands when they go to work (Scanzoni and Fox 1980). Women accommodate their careers to meet the needs of their families. Some follow a sequential pattern, either having children early and starting a career later, or first pursuing a career and then having children. Others follow a simultaneous pattern. Working wives contribute substantially to the economic support of their families. Wives who work full-time contribute 40 percent to the family income (U.S. Department of Labor 1985).

The majority of all families have spouses who are working or looking for work. By 1995, two out of three preschool children and four out of five school-

age children will have mothers in the work force (Children's Defense Fund 1990).

Dual careers can contribute to marital happiness when both spouses are satisfied with their occupations. For working wives as well as their husbands, the effects of job satisfaction interact with the effects of marital happiness in producing overall happiness, indicating a spillover effect; that is, satisfaction in one domain of life overflows into other areas of life. Benin and Nienstedt (1985) found that the happily married housewife who prefers to work but does not because of her husband's preference is more likely to be unhappy than a happily married working wife who would prefer not to work. Similar results were found by Ross et al. (1983) and Mirowsky and Ross (1986). Wetherington and Kessler (1989) found that when wives move from homemaking to full-time or close to full-time employment, there are positive effects; the reverse, that is, moving from full-time work to homemaking, has negative effects. Coleman and Antonucci (1983) found that middle-aged working women have higher self-esteem and less psychological anxiety than homemakers. These working women also report better physical health than homemakers do. Therefore, work may function as a stabilizing force for women during critical periods throughout the life cycle.

The extent of the husband's participation in family tasks also affects the wife's feeling of well-being. Ross and Mirowsky (1988) and Ross et al. (1983) found that both employed and unemployed wives were not as stressed when their husbands participated equally in household tasks. *But,* sharing was rare. Only 20 percent of dual earner couples shared household work, and only 7 percent of the couples with a female homemaker shared these duties. However, Thornton's (1989) analysis of survey data shows a strong and continuing trend toward greater support of women's outside employment and men's household participation.

Fathers in dual-earner families are more involved in child rearing than fathers in single-earner families. Also, parents in dual-earner families do not emphasize traditional sex-role training as do parents in single-earner families (Scanzoni 1978; Rapoport and Rapoport 1971).

Working mothers serve as more appropriate role models for their children. Children from dual-earner families are more responsible, become more independent, and develop higher self-esteem. They are highly supportive of their families' dual-career life-style and perceive their families as high in family strengths, especially concern, respect, and support. The children point out that time constraints are a primary problem associated with dual-career living. The families attempt to cope with this problem by purposefully planning family activities (such as weekend trips, vacations, and holidays) to develop closeness, and they set aside time for routine communication on a regular basis (Knaub 1986).

Sons from dual-career families are more likely than sons from traditional families to support the idea of dual-career families for themselves and their future spouses (Stephan and Corder 1985; Knaub 1986). Sons of working mothers are above average in social and personality adjustment (Gold and Andres 1978a, 1978b). They also see men as warmer and more expressive (Hoffman and Nye 1974).

Adolescents of both sexes from dual-career families hold more egalitarian sex-role attitudes than do adolescents from traditional families. Also, adolescents from dual-career families perceive that a wife who is employed outside of the home has higher prestige than a wife who does not work outside of the home (Stephan and Corder 1985).

Work

Men and women experience an increasing disparity as they progress along their career paths. Even in situations where they have been pursuing career paths to the same extent, men earn higher salaries, reach higher positions, and reach those positions more easily (Havighurst 1982). Women's jobs are more likely to involve the combination of high job demands and low decision latitude. Such job characteristics are associated with greater mental and physical distress on the part of the worker (Karasek et al. 1981; House et al. 1986). Other occupational conditions that are linked to stress, especially for women, include depersonalization, noxious job conditions, poor earnings, few opportunities for advancement, time pressures, and long work hours (Menaghan and Merves 1984; Voydanoff and Donnelly 1989).

The quality of interpersonal relations with job supervisors and co-workers in the workplace can also make an impact on the well-being of the individual worker. One study found that feeling socially supported at work is associated with better physical and mental health for men and women. For nonmarried mothers, low support at work has particularly negative effects (Hibbard and Pope 1987). Married women's job satisfaction suffers when the negative effects of a poor social climate on the job, low supervisor support, and low job satisfaction are combined with the inequality of their husbands' time spent on household work and child care (Repetti 1988).

For men and women, economic pressures affect parental feelings of mastery, efficacy, and distress (Downey and Moen 1987; Duncan and Liker 1983; Duncan and Morgan 1981), and an increase in parental distress affects parent-child interaction (Conger et al. 1984; Piotrokowski et al. 1987; Voydanoff 1987). Economic deprivation, to some extent, affects the child's perception of his or her parents, which in turn impacts on the child's behavior towards adults. In particular, the father-son relationship is more likely to be hurt by economic deprivation than any other parent-child dyads (Siegal 1985). Thus, both unstable employment and low-wage employment are associated with less optimal home environments (Voydanoff 1990; Ellwood 1988).

Daughters of working women are more likely to work and combine work

Although most women do paid work and contribute 40 percent to the family income, men still receive recognition and responsibility for providing for the family. Both men and women feel an "enhanced well-being" when they have satisfying, well-paid jobs and/or professions.

and family when they grow up. Women with a higher education are more likely to be employed before the birth of their first child and more likely to return to work during the baby's first year. Women who have been raised to expect more than becoming a wife and mother cope better with conflicts between their family and work roles and tend to be more satisfied with their lives. High-status fathers tend to encourage achievement in their daughters, particularly in their oldest daughters and when there are no sons. Middle-aged executive women are usually first-born children of successful fathers and nonworking mothers. They perceived their fathers as being supportive and encouraging them to achieve while they grew up (Troll 1985).

Paid and unpaid work is central to family life. Berk (1985) and Pleck (1985) found that men and women spend about the same total hours working, including both paid and family work. Women, however, are more likely than men to shift their time back and forth between paid and family work in order to sustain family life. Women are much more visible in the labor force than they once were. However, unpaid family work remains "invisible," even to the women who do it (DeVault 1987). It is unacknowledged and invisible because it is private, commonplace, unpaid, done by women, and combined with leisure and love (Daniels 1987).

Although most women do paid work and contribute 40 percent to the family income, men still receive recognition and responsibility for providing for the family (Szinovacz 1984). Both men and women feel an "enhanced well-being" when they have satisfying, well-paid jobs and/or professions (Baruch and Barnett 1986; Coleman et al. 1987; Staines and Libby 1986). The meaning of paid work, however, is different for men than it is for women. A woman's feelings are "Work is what I do, not what I am," but a man is likely to give his occupation when asked "Who are you?" Men and women have different atti-

Human Development in the News: Shape Up—Or Else!

ANNETTA MILLER and ELIZABETH BRADBURN

Employees at Hershey Foods Corp. may want to lay off the chocolate Kisses for a while. Later this summer some 650 nonunion workers at the candy conglomerate will be asked to report to a company health-screening site where they will be weighed, measured, pricked and prodded for details about their smoking and exercise habits. It's not a tryout for the company Olympics. It's part of an experimental program designed to cut health-care costs by penalizing the flabby and rewarding the fit. Under the plan, employees who fall short in five risk categories—and fail to mend their ways—could lose as much as $1,404 a year worth of health-care benefits (chart). While Hershey officials see the plan as a way to stop subsidizing unhealthy behavior, union leaders view it with suspicion. "This will cause an outcry," says Earl Light of Chocolate Workers' Local 464. "It's like [the company's] saying, 'Think the way I think, or you won't get as many benefits.' We see that as potentially dangerous."

Get out your jogging shoes. The health police are after you. Group insurance used to charge every employee the same amount. But with corporate America in the throes of double-digit health-care inflation, a small but growing number of companies is sending employees a message: shape up or else. U-Haul in Phoenix, Ariz., makes smokers and the seriously overweight pay a $120-a-year insurance premium; fitter employees get their premiums waived. Adolph Coors Co. in Golden Colo., will foot 90 percent of employees' medical bills (instead of 85 percent) only if they're fit or swear to follow a health program. And Foldcraft in Kenyon, Minn., requires workers to pay at least a $900 deductible unless they score well on a variety of tests, includ-ing blood-pressure readings and body-fat analyses. Says Michael Carter, of the benefits-consulting firm Hay/Huggins: "Management is saying, 'No more Mr. Nice Guy. When it comes to spending our money, you're going to play by our rules'."

Why are companies tightening their grip? Nothing else has successfully controlled health-care costs. Despite the advent of "wellness" programs and attempts to rein in doctors and hospitals, the cost of corporate medical plans grew 22.6 percent in 1990, according to the benefits-consulting firm A. Foster Higgins. So far most cost-cutting efforts have been directed toward treating illnesses rather than preventing them. But according to a study by Johnson & Johnson, 15 to 25 percent of the health-care costs incurred by employees are due to preventable illnesses. Moreover, officials at Southern California Edison Co. have found that individuals with three or more coronary-risk factors had health-care claims twice as high as those with no risks. With employers demanding more preventive care, Blue Cross and Blue Shield announced last week it will offer coverage for periodic screenings.

Conventional wisdom holds that all this prevention will lead to healthier workers and, therefore, a healthier bottom line. It may not be that simple. Some research actually supports the argument that prevention does *not* pay. Louise Russell, professor at Rutgers University's Institute for Health-care Policy, says preventive screenings may make people live longer and have fewer illnesses but won't necessarily lower health-care costs. Take high-blood-pressure testing. While most Americans get their blood pressures measured regularly, only about 10 percent will ultimately succumb to hypertension. Says Russell: "It costs more to screen and treat high blood pressure than it does to leave it alone and pay for the consequences."

Such arguments don't faze employers who have called out the lifestyle inspectors. A recent Harris poll for Metropolitan Life showed that 86 percent of corporate executives believe in increased premiums for people with unhealthy habits. To that end, firms are resorting to everything from pampering to pointed nudges to make workers toe the line. To avoid a sledgehammer approach, most portray their incentive programs as rewards for good health habits rather than as penalties for bad ones—and insist participation is voluntary. A few take an openly tougher stand. Baker-Hughes in Houston collects $10 a month from workers who use tobacco. The company also requires employees to score in an acceptable range on three out of four health tests (cholesterol and triglyceride levels, height-weight ratio and blood pressure) in order to collect a $100 annual reward. No one gets a break. In April, Joe Vinson, Baker-Hughes's compensation-and-benefits director, flunked the tests for cholesterol and triglycerides. "The majority of my department took it and passed," he admits. "Looks like I need to cut back on the Mexican food."

Executives at Mesa petroleum don't just get ribbing from their underlings. The pressure to measure up comes di-

tudes in their perception of paid work because of the connection between paid work and family. Men can keep paid work and family as separate spheres of life better than women can. Women tend to shape their paid work responsibilities to the needs of their families (Gerson 1985; Zussman 1987).

SUMMARY

- Erikson's stage of generativity versus stagnation, the middle-adult years, involves establishing and guiding the next generation. The concept of generativity encompasses productivity and creativity. If such enrichment does not occur, then a pervading sense of stagnation and personal impoverishment occurs.
- Middle-aged men and women constitute a powerful age-group. They are the norm bearers and decision makers. Introspection and reflection increase during middle adulthood. A mid-life crisis may occur during this period. Men and women begin to exchange roles as they get older.
- The primary agents of adult socialization are spouse, employer, and children. The nuclear family is the most common family form.
- Parents of adult children take on new roles. They feel both gains and losses.
- The divorce rate is about 50 percent but recent data indicate that it is leveling off. People divorce for many different reasons. Divorce can be devastating to some people, and it can offer a new beginning to others.
- Single-parent families are primarily headed by women (89 percent). Single-parent fathers are definitely in the minority, but they are financially better off than single-parent mothers.

Adult Sibling Relationships

The relationships between brothers and sisters generally last longer than the relationships between parents and children. The sibling relationship is an unearned relationship in which there is relatively equal power and freedom (Cicirelli 1982). During middle adulthood, sibling ties become loosened and diffused, and contact becomes voluntary. Factors such as emotional closeness, sibling responsibility expectations, income level, the nature of competing activities and responsibilities, and geographical proximity determine how often adult siblings interact (Goetting 1986). Cultural expectations indicate that a sibling relationship should be more emotionally close, meaningful, and enduring than most other interpersonal relationships (excluding husband-wife relationships). (Lee, Mancini, and Maxwell 1990).

Emotional closeness between siblings involves trust, enjoyment of the relationship, concern, and shared experience. Common interests and admired personality characteristics add to the emotional closeness and are among the reasons siblings stay in touch and in some cases choose to live together in their later years (Borland et al. 1981).

In a study involving middle-aged adults, Circirelli (1982) found that 19 percent saw their siblings on a weekly basis; 41 percent, at least monthly; 36 percent, several times a year but less often than once a month. Three percent had not seen their siblings in over two years (their siblings lived outside of this country). Lee et al. (1990) found that sister-sister pairs had the most contact, and females were more likely than males to make contacts. Feelings of responsibility and emotional closeness are motivations for contact with siblings. Siblings from large families are less likely to maintain contact than siblings from small families. (Lee et al. 1990). This finding contradicts Schvaneveldt and Ihinger's (1979) finding that greater family size is related to greater sibling solidarity.

Having children and whether or not they are at home can determine the amount of sibling contact during the adult years. Lee et al. (1990) found that those without children felt obligated to maintain contacts with siblings. Those who had children at home felt that attention to their children was higher in priority and, therefore, that they had freedom from obligation to their siblings. Having children did not affect the *desire* to contact siblings, but only acted as a rationale for relieving the obligation to do so.

Except for companionship and socio-emotional support, the common tasks of "siblingship" during early and middle adulthood are related to the care of elderly parents and later to the dismantling of the parental home (Bank and Kahn 1982; Cicirelli 1982; Matthews and Rosner 1985). Parents' failing health and loss of independence reactivates sibling interaction during the middle-adult years. Initially the sibling bond may be reactivated to address a particular crisis, but then it may continue to serve as a base during the period of parental decline and death (Goetting 1986).

Other circumstances may affect sibling relationships and task performance during adulthood. For example, family structure and cultural expectations may be factors. Johnson's (1982) study with Italian-American families found that due to frequent contact with the family after marriage, an Italian-American individual is as likely to go to a sibling as to a spouse when problems arise.

Marital disruption will also cause more interaction with siblings. Cicirelli (1984) found that maritally disrupted individuals were more likely than their maritally intact counterparts to believe that the burden of helping elderly parents should be shared with all the siblings and they depended more on siblings to provide aid to elderly parents. Brothers of maritally disrupted sisters were more likely to act as a male role model for their nieces and nephews when there was no husband present.

Apparently siblings maintain a wide variation of interaction and commitment to each other during their adult years. They continue to care about and for one another and remain on call as a source of aid and/or a support system. Their common heritage binds them together in a unique way.

What factors contribute to the interaction of adult siblings? How can dismantling the parental home draw adult siblings together? How can it create dissension?

- The happily married housewife who prefers to work but does not because of her husband's preference is more likely to be unhappy than a happily married working wife who would prefer not to work. Working mothers serve as more appropriate role models for their children. Adolescents from dual-career families hold more egalitarian sex-role attitudes than do adolescents from traditional families.

- Men and women experience an increasing disparity as they progress in their career paths. Occupational conditions are related to feelings of success or feelings of stress.

- Sibling relationships last longer than relationships between parents and children. During middle adulthood, sibling ties become loosened and diffused, and contact becomes voluntary. Responsibilities for elderly parents create a unity bond between adult siblings.

READINGS

Filene, P. (1981). *Men in the middle.* Englewood Cliffs, NJ: Prentice-Hall.
Discussion of how middle-age men cope with the problems of work and family.
Kessler-Harris, A. (1982). *Out of work.* New York: Oxford University Press.
A history of women who have earned wages and worked outside of the home in America.
McGill, M. E. (1980). *The 40 to 50 year old male.* New York: Simon and Schuster.
Acknowledges that most men do not have midlife crises and offers advice for those who do.
Shahan, L. (1981) *Living alone and liking it.* New York: Harper and Row.
Discusses issues, problems, and benefits of living alone.

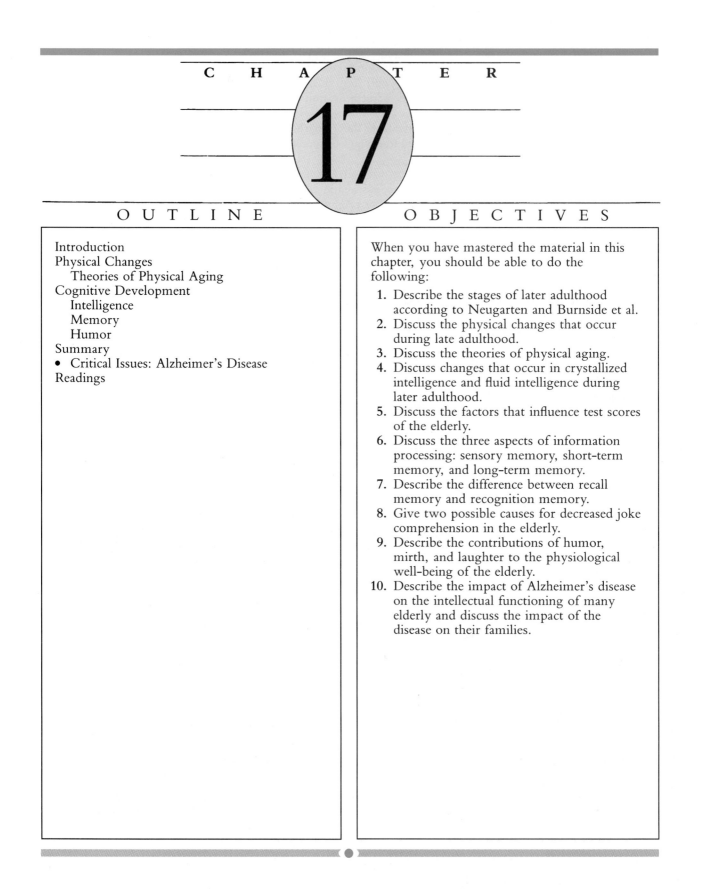

C H A P T E R

17

O U T L I N E

Introduction
Physical Changes
    Theories of Physical Aging
Cognitive Development
    Intelligence
    Memory
    Humor
Summary
● Critical Issues: Alzheimer's Disease
Readings

O B J E C T I V E S

When you have mastered the material in this chapter, you should be able to do the following:

1. Describe the stages of later adulthood according to Neugarten and Burnside et al.
2. Discuss the physical changes that occur during late adulthood.
3. Discuss the theories of physical aging.
4. Discuss changes that occur in crystallized intelligence and fluid intelligence during later adulthood.
5. Discuss the factors that influence test scores of the elderly.
6. Discuss the three aspects of information processing: sensory memory, short-term memory, and long-term memory.
7. Describe the difference between recall memory and recognition memory.
8. Give two possible causes for decreased joke comprehension in the elderly.
9. Describe the contributions of humor, mirth, and laughter to the physiological well-being of the elderly.
10. Describe the impact of Alzheimer's disease on the intellectual functioning of many elderly and discuss the impact of the disease on their families.

Mature Adults:
The Elderly — Physical and Cognitive Development

INTRODUCTION

Aging is a natural and normal phenomenon for all living things. It begins at fertilization and continues throughout the life cycle. A disproportionate amount of attention has been focused on the first half of life, and only recently has theory and research been directed to the older adult. The sixties mark the passage from middle to old age, bringing a range of demands and challenges that the individual has never experienced before.

By the end of this century, the number of people under sixty-five will increase by 17 percent, while those sixty-five to seventy-five will increase by 14 percent. The greatest increase, 53 percent, will occur among those seventy-five and older (Steinmetz and Amsden 1983). With the larger population of elderly, we are witnessing the emergence of an unprecedented group of healthy, educated, retired workers. Such a phenomenon will make us revise our stereotypes of late adulthood as being inactive, decrepit, and frail (Neugarten 1978).

Later adulthood is a long, significant part of life. It is not a stage in which everyone should be "lumped" into one group. People are perhaps more heterogenous at this stage than they were at earlier stages in the life cycle, but they vary in physical health and aging factors. For example, a newly retired sixty-five-year-old may be caring for an eighty-five-year-old parent. These two individuals represent two separate generations. They have experienced two separate historical eras.

Late adulthood can be broken down into various stages. Neugarten (1982) separates this stage into the young-old and the old-old, the competent and the frail. These distinctions are based on social and health characteristics, not on age. The young-old are the majority of persons over sixty-five. These men and women are healthy and active, well integrated into their families and their communities, relatively well educated, and involved politically. They use their time in a meaningful way. Some want to continue to work; some pursue fulfillment through education or various types of leisure activities; some do volunteer work. These people are an underutilized resource in our communities. The old-old or frail are the minority of older persons. They have suffered major physical or mental deterioration or losses in their support systems, and they require a range of special supportive and restorative health and social services.

Burnside et al. (1979) divide the stage of later adulthood according to decades. The sixty- to sixty-nine-old-year olds are the young-old. This is a major transitional period in which the individual must adapt to new roles and new means of coping with losses and gains. Friends and colleagues start to disappear. Income is reduced. Societal expectations change by demanding less energy, less independence, and less creativity. This can be demoralizing and may lead to the individual's slowing down his or her pace in a self-fulfilling prophecy. Many people in their sixties look for new and different activities if they have retired. Some retirees remain givers, producers, and mentors. They may become volunteer executives in small businesses, visitors to hospitals, or foster grandparents.

The seventy- to seventy-nine-year-olds are the middle-age old. This decade is marked by loss and illness. Family and friends may begin dying at an increased rate. The individual's social world becomes smaller, and he or she must cope with reduced participation in formal organizations. Health problems become more severe, and the individual is more restless and irritable.

The eighty- to eighty-nine-year-olds are the old-old. These individuals find it more difficult to adapt to and interact with their surroundings. They need an

Later adulthood is not a stage in which everyone should be "lumped" into one group. A sixty-five-year-old retiree may be caring for an eighty-five-year-old parent. These two individuals represent two separate generations. They have experienced two separate historical eras.

environment that is streamlined and barrier free, that offers both privacy and stimulation. They need help to maintain social and cultural contacts.

The ninety- to ninety-nine-year-olds are the very old-old. Little is known about this age-group. Although their health problems may be more severe, they can alter their activities to make the most of their present situations. If previous crises were resolved in a satisfactory way, then the nineties may be joyful, serene, and fulfilling. Burnside et al. (1979) did not identify stages beyond one hundred years of age.

● PHYSICAL CHANGES

Studies of people who age successfully indicate that they maintain regular and vigorous physical activities, have extensive social contacts, and pursue intellectually and emotionally stimulating activities. The decrease or disuse of functions can lead to unnecessary physical limitations, social isolation, disorientation, and apathy (Pfeiffer 1974, 1975, 1977). By age sixty, many people eagerly look forward to retirement, while others are highly active, both physically and mentally, and they dread the inactivity that retirement might bring.

Men who reach their sixty-fifth birthday can expect to live another 14.1 years, while sixty-five-year-old women can expect to live another 18.3 years (Verbrugge 1984). In determining the extent of an individual's life span, the age at which his or her mother died appears to have a greater influence than the age at which his or her father died (Rockstein 1977).

Tissues

Physiologically, the tissues of old people are less capable of carrying out their functions. The loss of function is due partly to degenerative changes in the

According to Neugarten, the young-old are the majority of persons over sixty-five. Regardless of their age these men and women are healthy and active.

Studies of people who age successfully indicate that they maintain regular and vigorous physical activities, have extensive social contacts, and pursue intellectually and emotionally stimulating activities.

It is now known that many individuals can forestall or blunt the process of physical aging through regular exercise.

Osteoporosis
A physical condition in which bone marrow gradually disappears in the arms and legs and becomes concentrated in the bones of the trunk. A loss of calcium makes the bones more brittle, hollow, weak, and porous.

active cells themselves and partly to the increase in the amount of inactive fibrous tissue by which the active cells are surrounded. Cells that do not divide during life (such as those found in the brain) may gradually deteriorate and become less fit for their job. Where cells divide, there may be changes that cause daughter cells to be less well adapted to their tasks than the parent cells from which they were derived. Obvious manifestations of aging include wrinkling of the skin, slowness of movement, and the inability of the eye to see close-by objects. Wrinkles in old age are caused by the loss of fat tissue under the skin. The skin has the crisscrossed look of soft, crumpled paper or fine parchment (Hooyman and Kiyak 1988).

Muscular System

A pronounced stoop or slump in posture is common among old people. The head is positioned slightly forward from the rest of the body. Shrinking muscles, a decrease in muscular elasticity, calcification of ligaments, shrinking and hardening of tendons, and some loss of space between the vertebral disks are accentuated by years of poor posture. Shoulder width decreases, but chest and pelvis width increases. An old person shrinks and appears to be a disproportionate individual who needs to be stretched out. This is due to multiple developmental factors, including skeletal, muscular, subcutaneous tissue, fat, and dermal structural changes (Ebersole and Hess 1985).

A rapid decline of muscle tissue occurs after age fifty (Rossman 1980). The greatest loss appears to be in the "fast twitch" muscle fibers, which are primarily involved in rapid bursts of strength such as sprinting. There is a slower loss in "slow twitch" fibers, which are involved in prolonged activity such as jogging (Ostrow 1984).

It is now known that many individuals can forestall or blunt the process of physical aging through regular exercise. A portion of the body-system changes that are commonly attributed to aging are really due to disuse and lack of exercise. In other words, a physically active life may allow an individual to approach his or her true biogenetic potential for longevity (Bortz 1982). Spirduso (1975) found that a highly active sports life appears to contribute substantially to faster central nervous system processing and faster muscular movement in older men. There is a possibility that the older men in this study may have had inherently faster reaction times and movement times and thus selected a more active life-style, but daily vigorous exercise may be a substantial reason why they performed almost as well as young college men. These results support vigorous sports participation as a significant factor in retarding the onset of aging.

Muscle weight decreases with age. As muscle cells accumulate more fat, their structure and composition are altered. Muscle function slows down, which in turn causes the muscle to take longer to achieve a state of relaxation after exertion (Guttmann 1977). Muscle function is affected by the changing structure and composition of the skeleton.

Bones

Several significant changes associated with age occur in bones. Bone marrow gradually disappears in the arms and legs and becomes concentrated in the bones of the trunk. A loss of calcium makes the bones more brittle, hollow, weak, and porous. This process is called **osteoporosis.** This condition can be greatly minimized through proper diet, exercise throughout one's life (bones must be stressed to some degree to maintain minerals), and sufficient amounts of estrogen. Bedridden patients lose not only muscle tissue but also bone. In women who are postmenopausal, hormone replacement therapy is of great value. Osteoporosis is four times more prevalent in women than in men. As implied above, it becomes more apparent with the decline of estrogen. Since the bones are more porous, they are more likely to fracture and are slower to mend. As a result, bone fractures occur more often after age forty-five for women and after age seventy-five for men (Ebersole and Hess 1985). Changes in the bones of the joints, called **osteoarthritis,** are due to the wear and tear of years of body movements. This appears to occur with equal frequency in later adult men and women (Rossman 1980).

Osteoarthritis
Changes in the bones of the joints.

Skin and Hair

In later adulthood, pigment spots enlarge and multiply with exposure to natural and artificial light. Hair distribution becomes more sparse in both sexes. Hair on the head thins, and leg hair quite often disappears. Asians and African-Americans have less hair than whites, while Native Americans have little or no hair on their bodies. Hair that was once dark, thick, and abundant becomes thinner, lighter, gray, and less full. Hair becomes gray because the production of melanin in the hair follicles decreases. About 50 percent of the population (male and female) over fifty has gray or graying hair. Women have some hair loss but not as much as men (Hooyman and Kiyak 1988).

The aged skin loses resilience and moisture, and appears dry. Face and neck wrinkles, because of lessened elasticity in the muscles, mirror facial expressions acquired over a lifetime. Exposure to the sun increases changes in the skin tissue by altering collagen formation which in turn, leads to loss of elasticity (Hooyman and Kiyak 1988).

The Heart and Cardiovascular System

The established and significant changes that occur in the heart of an elderly person include decreased cardiac output, a heart rate that remains unchanged or only slightly slows when the person is at rest, and an increase in the time required for the heart rate to return to normal once it is elevated (Ebersole and Hess 1985). Between the ages of twenty and ninety, the amount of blood pumped by the heart decreases by 50 percent. Vascular changes that affect blood flow to body organs, including the heart, liver, kidneys, and pituitary gland, are caused by the decreased elasticity of arteries and arterioles. The aorta enlarges, and circulation in the coronary arteries decreases by approximately 35 percent after sixty years of age (Ebersole and Hess 1985).

Pulmonary System

While an elderly individual is resting, it is not obvious that there are changes in lung performance. A little exertion or stress during awake hours will bring on *dyspnea* (difficulty in breathing) and other symptoms. The lungs have difficulty expanding due to alterations in the thorax or diaphragm areas. Also, the ribs restrict the function of the lungs because they do not move as freely when the individual inhales. Although the lungs do not shrink in size, they do become more rigid. The rigid lung tissue in the elderly individual may explain why his or her lungs are less likely to collapse if the chest is opened or pneumonia develops. Total lung capacity is not altered but is instead redistributed. Incomplete lung expansion leads to the collapse of the base of the lung. Exercise will help maintain the flexibility of lung tissue and facilitate lung expansion (Ebersole and Hess 1985).

The anatomical changes that occur in the structure of the chest along with altered muscle strength make it difficult to cough up any material that accumulates or causes an obstruction in the lungs. The elderly, therefore, have a less effective cough response, which can potentially cause more problems for those who are sedentary, bedridden, or limited in activity (Hooyman and Kiyak 1988).

Gastrointestinal System

The gastrointestinal system handles age change better than other body systems do. Teeth are an important aspect of digestion and the gastrointestinal system because chewing food prepares it for digestion. Today's elderly are primarily dependent on dentures. Many of the elderly who have dentures choose not to use them, while others cannot afford them. Because of this, many elderly are placed on pureed diets. Such diets are unappealing and tasteless, and they lack the texture needed to stimulate appetite, gastrointestinal motility, enjoyment of eating, as well as the maintenance of a nutritional diet. In elderly people, the secretions produced by the intestinal tract are less than in younger people. The secretion of saliva, *ptyalin* (which is responsible for starch breakdown), as well as the amount of free and total gastric acids, decreases. Hydrochloric acid reduces in the stomach at about age sixty. The pepsin (an enzyme in the stomach that begins the digestion of proteins) level begins to fall during the forties decade and declines sharply to about age sixty, then evens out and remains a constant low. The elderly become unable to tolerate the ingestion of large amounts of fat-containing food. The body's use of calcium is affected by the lack of adequate gastric acid and slower active transport in the body.

The large intestine's internal sphincter loses its muscle tone and can, in turn, create problems in bowel evacuation. The external sphincter, which does not lose its muscle tone, cannot control the bowels by itself. Neural impulses are transmitted slower, lessening the awareness of sensations of an impending bowel evacuation (Hooyman and Kiyak 1988).

Bowel and bladder problems can interfere with independent living, as well as threaten the body's capacity to function and survive. Elimination is a private matter. Society has emphasized appropriate procedures for eliminating and disposing of body waste, and when deviations occur, the elderly suffer chastisement, ostracism, and the desire for social withdrawal. Attention to the bowel function occurs when elimination is perceived as abnormal. The elderly are known for their overriding concern with their bowel function, and frequently they complain about problems, especially constipation (Ebersole and Hess 1985).

Nutritional Requirements

Lifelong eating habits influence the nutritional state of an individual. These habits are established out of tradition, ethnicity, religion, and culture. Eating habits do not necessarily correspond with nutritional needs. Poor health among the elderly may be due to poor diet or improper nutrition.

The elderly do not require as much food as younger adults. This is due to lessened physical activity and slowdowns in body metabolism. General metabolism decreases, and the total requirement for food becomes less. However, many elderly are overweight because it is difficult to change the eating habits of

Men living with a spouse have better dietary patterns than either men living alone or men living with someone other than a spouse.

a lifetime. On the other hand, many are anemic and malnourished because they are financially poor or have no knowledge about nutritious food. Lessened adaptability to various nutrients leads to undereating, overeating, dehydration, or too-rapid fluid intake. These situations lead to more serious consequences during old age than they would have during youth (Ebersole and Hess 1985). By age sixty-five, individuals require at least 20 percent fewer calories than younger adults. It is not unusual for older Americans to be both overweight and undernourished (Anderson and Van Nierop 1989).

A diet high in quality, rich in proteins, minerals, and vitamins, is just as necessary in old age as it is in childhood. However, there is a tendency toward vitamin and mineral deficiencies. This can be due to the faulty absorption of vitamin B_1 and B_2, calcium, and iron, as well as to inadequate diet. Minerals such as iron and calcium and vitamins K, B_1, and B_{12} are the most frequently deficient. Because of the cost of, and the difficulty in chewing and digesting, meat, the consumption of protein is less than earlier in life (Ebersole and Hess 1985). Changes in bones and muscles require changes in diet. Over the years, bones lose more calcium than they absorb from food. As the muscle tone in the intestines decreases and constipation occurs, the elderly need more high-fiber foods such as bran. Fiber is an important dietary supplement. (*Fiber* is the undigestible material that is abundant in raw fruits, raw vegetables, and unrefined grains and cereals. It encourages the absorption of water, increases bulk, and improves intestinal movement. It prevents constipation, hemorrhoids, and diverticulosis. It also helps reduce caloric intake, helps control obesity, and is thought to aid in preventing heart disease and colon cancer [Ebersole and Hess 1985].)

Davis et al. (1985) found that men living with a spouse have better dietary patterns than either those living alone or those living with someone other than a spouse. Low-income men who are not living with a spouse are at the highest risk of poor dietary intake. Older men who live alone have less adequate diets than older women who live alone, less dietary variety and intake of fruits and vegetables, and lower serum nutrient levels. The dietary patterns among older women seem to vary less in relation to living arrangements than they do among older men (Brockington and Lempert 1966; Monagle 1967; Krondl et al. 1982; Burr et al. 1982).

Senses

Everyone will eventually experience a decline in visual acuity. The decreased ability of the eyes to adjust for close and detailed work begins at about forty years of age. The rate of blindness and loss of visual acuity increases sharply after the age of sixty. Less than 30 percent of seventy-year-olds have 20/20 vision. The hardening of the lens causes difficulty in focusing, and this hardening is often accompanied by brownish discoloration, which causes further impairment (Schaie and Geiwitz 1982). The lens sometimes becomes increasingly opaque, and a complete loss of vision ultimately results. This is called **cataract.** Cataracts are found in 20 to 25 percent of seventy-year-olds. The most common form of cataract is apparently not the result of any ocular disease and must be regarded as a continuation of the normal processes of degeneration associated with old age (Botwinick 1984).

Most older adults need more illumination to see well, and they see less well in the dark. They need about twice as much light to see things as they did when they were twenty years old. More light is needed for all visual perception. This change involves the basic receptor cells for light in the retina. The retinal cells are destroyed or malfunction due to decreased blood circulation and their resulting starvation. Retinal cell damage has been detected in most people by the age of fifty-five to sixty-five. As mentioned above, the loss directly affects sensitivity to low levels of illumination. This makes night driving hazardous. Color vision is also affected, making it difficult to identify the color of objects (Schaie and Geiwitz 1982).

Adults over sixty find it takes longer for their eyes to adjust to abrupt changes in light or darkness. The reflexive adjustments of the eye lens to light or darkness are slowed because of the general loss of tissue elasticity that accompanies aging (Bee 1987; Ebersole and Hess 1985).

Vision impairment is often the most important factor that limits the activity of otherwise healthy elderly people. The main cause of the elderly's proneness to accidents on the road and in the home is the combination of vision deterioration and the decreasing ability to react quickly in emergencies.

Auditory changes are subtle. The greatest loss takes place in the ability to hear higher frequency tones that occur in speech sounds, such as "s," "sh," "ch," and "f." Vowels, which have a low pitch, can be heard more easily. High-frequency-pitched language becomes disjointed and misunderstood without vowels. *Noise masking* occurs, which means background noise interferes with conversation so it is difficult to understand what is being said. Rapid speech, when conversing with an elderly individual, will make words garbled and unintelligible (Thomas et al. 1983). All adults lose some auditory acuity from about age fifty onward. Approximately 15 percent of adults over seventy-five can be classified as deaf (Corso 1977). Another 15 to 20 percent have serious difficulty with hearing (Darbyshire 1984; Verbrugge 1984). Adults with major hearing losses experience great difficulty in social situations. This is especially true in situations where several conversations are going on at once.

For the elderly, taste-detection decreases are minimal in tasting salty and

Cataract
A condition of the eye in which the lens becomes increasingly opaque and a complete loss of vision ultimately results.

sweet flavors. Moore et al. (1982) found a small gradual loss in sweet sensitivity among the elderly. They also found large individual differences among the older people in their study. Grzegorczyk et al. (1979) found, among their sample of twenty-three- to ninety-two-year-olds, a continuous but small loss in salt sensitivity. The elderly who are institutionalized have a higher ability to detect sour substances, which may be due to medication (Weiffenbach et al. 1982).

The sense of smell is one of the first senses to develop during the fetal period and is the last of the senses to decline among the elderly (Rovee et al. 1975). The sense of smell declines slowly until about age seventy, and then it declines rapidly. Sixty percent of adults between sixty-five and eighty have severe loss in the sense of smell, with one quarter of the 60 percent losing all sense of smell (Doty, Shaman, and Dann 1984). This loss may be partly responsible for the poor nutrition and lack of interest in food found among many elderly people.

Brain and Nervous System

The central nervous system shows a decline in cell number with advancing age. Unlike neurons (nerve cells specialized to transmit information from one part of the body to another) outside of the central nervous system, central nervous cells do not regenerate when they are injured or destroyed. The brain loses cells and loses weight as an individual ages. This is one possible explanation for the forgetfulness and the more circumscribed outlook that the aged develop over time (Ebersole and Hess 1985; Rockstein et al. 1977). Connections between nerve cells become less numerous from disuse (Birren, Woods, and William 1980). Rat studies found that continued exercise and stimulation of the brain results in new brain cell connections and a heavier brain in old rats (Conner, Diamond, and Johnson 1980). With humans, the nerves "fire" somewhat more slowly in older adults than in younger adults (Smith, Thompson, and Michaelewski 1980). In general, however, the cerebral function does not deteriorate as rapidly as many people imagine, unless degenerative processes in the cerebral arteries are unusually advanced.

The brain influences the sleep-wake cycle. The elderly experience variations in sleep pattern, quality, and requirements. It is unusual for elderly individuals to sleep all through the night. They comment about how poorly they slept. It is not unusual for an elderly person to awaken for periodic trips to the toilet to empty his or her bladder; this is especially true of men over the age of sixty-five. Insomnia should be viewed as a response to various discomforts or psychological upsets. Poor sleep may be related to emotional causes such as depression (Drachman 1980). The elderly experience less rapid eye movement (REM) and deep sleep than when they were younger. They spend most of their sleep time alternating between REM and light sleep levels. Drugs used to aid sleep may be more harmful than helpful, since they interfere by depressing REM sleep, which is necessary for relieving tension and anxiety. A drug-induced sleep causes the elderly individual to feel tired and unrested when he or she wakes up (Ebersole and Hess 1985). People who are sixty and older consume 40 percent of the sleep medications sold (Schaie and Geiwitz 1982).

Age changes in the brain can be detected by monitoring brain waves with electroencephalograms (EEGs). Age differences are not usually detectable until the late fifties or early sixties. The alpha waves appear to slow down. Young adults usually average ten or eleven cycles per second; sixty-year-olds average nine cycles per second; eighty-year-olds average eight cycles per second. Thus EEG results suggest an increasing sluggishness of the brain and central nervous system in old age. It is not clear how this correlates with intellectual performance (Schaie and Geiwitz 1982).

Health

Arteriosclerosis, hypertension, arthritis, and various cancers are pathologies associated with aging. They have some important characteristics in common. They begin insidiously and may progress without symptoms for several years before subjective physical stress or observations by medical advisers reveal something is wrong. Most cancers are amenable to treatment if recognized early, but many elderly do not seek medical treatment. This is another obstacle to effective prevention.

The presence of these common diseases tends to increase vulnerability to other illnesses, particularly infections such as pneumonia. Finally, the course of all these diseases leads to a prolonged period of disability before death results, either from the diseases or from another cause such as an acute infection (Schaie and Geiwitz 1982).

Sexual Functioning

Physical infirmities that reduce or eliminate sexual capacity and functioning can develop at any age. However, male and female sexual functioning undergoes a steady decline at around age fifty. However, this decline appears to cease after age sixty. Changes are variable in different individuals. Sexually active and unanxious men who are accustomed to prolonged sexual play in intercourse are not negatively affected by these changes. However, men whose stereotype of virility is hurried sexual play and intercourse might interpret these changes

Arteriosclerosis, hypertension, arthritis, and various cancers are pathologies associated with aging. The course of these diseases leads to a prolonged period of disability before death results.

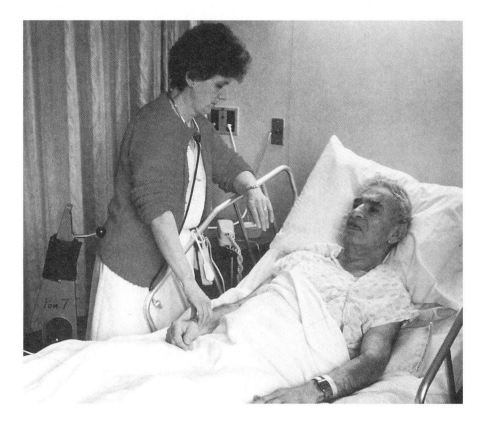

negatively and as loss of function. The resulting anxiety may lead to impotency. *Impotence* means that they fail to induce or sustain penile erection in at least 25 percent of their coital attempts (Comfort 1980). Impotency is never a consequence of chronological age alone. Its frequency with age is due to a variety of reasons. Some of the causes of impotence in the older male are the increasing prevalence of diabetes; hypertension; prostatic enlargement (ninety percent of men over eighty years of age experience enlargement of the prostate gland), which may lead to medications that cause impotency; needless radical or negligent surgery; and, above all, the social expectation of impotence with age (Botwinick 1984), reinforced by obesity, sensitivity to alcohol, and depression (Comfort 1980).

Beyond sixty years, the physical infirmity of the female partner is also an important factor. If the wife is physically infirm, the elderly male is restricted in sexual opportunity. Regularity of sexual expression is the key to sexual responsiveness for the elderly male. With the loss of their wives as a sexual outlet, many elderly males report a rapid loss of sexual tension and an increase in impotency (Silber 1981).

The sexuality of elderly females is more complex than that of elderly males because much of the sexual activity of women does not involve coitus and does not result in orgasm. However, Starr and Weiner (1981) found that when the sexual activity was coitus, 98.5 percent of the older women in their study experienced orgasm. Eighty-six percent of the women in the survey said they achieved orgasm at a rate equal to or greater than when they were younger. When sexual waning does begin among women, it is of a lesser extent than that among men. The sexual frequencies reported by women are profoundly influenced by the age, health, and level of sexual functioning of their husband or partner (Brecher 1984).

Sexual relations among the elderly are not unusual and should not be thought of as immoral. It is grossly unfair to place restraints on the elderly because of false beliefs that old people are sexless people (Botwinick 1984). Traditionally, appropriate behavior for young adults was seen as inappropriate for older adults. An older man was viewed as a "dirty old man" if he was interested in sex. His age was what made him "dirty." The older woman who was interested in sex was viewed in the same negative way. The elderly often accepted the myth that old people should not be interested in sex. They, then, denied themselves pleasurable release from sexual tensions, as well as the tender feelings of loving and being loved, being needed, and being intimate (Schaie and Geiwitz 1982). However, attitudes of elderly men and women toward sex have

TABLE 17.1 Sexual Activity of the Elderly

	50 DECADE	60 DECADE	70 AND OVER
ALL WOMEN	(N = 801)	(N = 719)	(N = 324)
Sexually Active	93%	81%	65%
ALL MEN	(N = 823)	(N = 981)	(N = 598)
Sexually Active	98%	91%	79%

Source: Brecher 1984.

Sexual relations among the elderly are not unusual and should not be thought of as immoral. It is grossly unfair to place restraints on the elderly because of false beliefs that old people are sexless people.

changed in the past few years. Starr and Weiner (1981) conducted a study with men and women aged sixty to ninety-one, regarding sexual experience. One question Starr and Weiner asked their respondents was, "How do you feel about older people who are not married having sexual relations and living together?" Ninety-one percent approved! Ninety-five percent of the men and 89 percent of the women gave similar responses. Therefore, it may be assumed that the elderly are participating in their own sexual revolution.

Theories of Physical Aging

"Aging" intrinsically means a definite time course and direction for individual changes in the various parts of an organism, the sum total of which results in the failure of the organism to withstand the stress of the environment, ultimately leading to death. Therefore, the life span is really a reflection of the sum total of deleterious changes accumulated during a lifetime (Rockstein et al. 1977).

The cumulative biological changes that occur in all species ultimately result in the individual's decreased ability to function in his or her environment. Although maximum longevity appears to be universally genetically determined, the individual's potential life span depends upon the physical and biological factors in his or her environment (Rockstein et al. 1977).

The numerous changes that take place in an aging organism are sometimes deleterious, sometimes neutral, and sometimes helpful. Changes that do impair the function in one or another particular area may have a negligible effect on the aging of the organism as a whole (Spiegel 1972). Many theories have been proposed concerning the process of biological aging. Many have merit, but none are conclusive. Some are too complex to discuss here, but the central issues are worth consideration.

Some theories of aging identify environmental factors as the primary cause of aging. Those factors that affect our health and life expectancy include air pollution, nutritional deficiencies, obesity, smoking, driving habits, and emotional pressures. Some of these factors can be controlled by individuals. Other factors can be controlled if effective political and legal steps are taken.

The **wear and tear theory** states that simple mechanical wear and tear occurs with age. Every machine and organism has a preprogrammed obsolescence and each species has a biological clock that determines the maximum life span and the rate that each organ system will deteriorate. Cells continually wear out and surviving cells cannot repair their own damaged parts.

The **cytologic theory** of aging sees the body as being victimized by additive effects of insults and injuries to individual cells. The "insults" are ionizing radiation; chemical, mechanical, and thermal alterations; stress; rebounding imbalances in which a domino effect takes place from a single physiological malfunction; and a progressive "glut of insoluble elements" within specific cells (Timiras 1972).

"The machine breaks down" is another theory of aging. There are no specific aging genes, but as time goes on, the body cells, in the course of living, dividing, and growing, are subject to environmental influences as well as biochemical changes. Molecules within the cells become damaged in some way, causing breakdowns in cell machinery and subsequent errors in function. The precise nature of this sort of damage really is not understood, but it is known that such errors or changes, which may be mutations, do occur. Possibly the known repair systems that the body cells contain become inefficient or defective. Accumulated errors and changes could cause sufficiently dangerous malfunctions that lead to cell and then body death. The external environment cannot be overestimated.

With the **deterioration of the immune system,** viruses may persist in tissues throughout one's life, in spite of a continuous effort by the body to fight them with antibodies. The battle between antibodies and invading viruses may injure cells and bring on degenerative diseases, such as presenile dementia, in adulthood (Milunsky 1977).

Most of the current research sees aging as emanating from the organism itself, rather than from the external environment. **Genetic preprogramming** suggests that there is a blueprint for the total life span "written in your genes." A tiny pinch of skin grown in a tissue culture in the laboratory has cells with a fairly fixed life span. These cells, or *fibroblasts,* have been grown from the skin of many persons. Each cell is able to grow and double itself about forty to sixty times over. After that it dies. Similar studies with different animal species have also demonstrated a limited life span of cells. It appears that the lifetime of each cell is directly proportional to the average life span of the species involved. Therefore, for men and women, fibroblast cells double, on the average, about fifty times before dying and relate to the usual human life span of about seventy years. Evidence indicates that the number of times a cell can divide is fixed in the inborn genetic messages. Cells grown from the skin of an old person were found to have curtailed life spans when compared with cells grown from the skin of an infant. The implication of this information is that aging is basically fixed from the start by "aging genes" that program our cells for a certain span, at the end of which the cells cease to function normally. This theory is supported by the occurrence of predictable specific changes in the human body, such as puberty and menopause. The exact timing of the changes is probably influenced or controlled by heredity (Milunsky 1977; Hayflick 1980).

Wear and tear theory
A theory of aging that views aging as a product of gradual deterioration, particularly in relation to bone or parts of the circulatory system.

Cytologic theory
A theory of aging that sees the body as being victimized by additive effects of insults and injuries to individual cells.

"The machine breaks down"
A theory of aging in which the body cells, in the course of living, dividing, and growing, are subject to environmental influences as well as biochemical changes.

"Deterioration of the immune system" theory
A theory of aging in which viruses are seen as culprits that the body fights continuously with antibodies. The battle between antibodies and the invading viruses may injure cells and bring on degenerative diseases.

Genetic preprogramming
A theory of aging that suggests there is a blueprint for the total life span "written in your genes."

"Mean time to failure" theory
A theory of aging that suggests aging is a product of gradual deterioration of various organs. That is, organs deteriorate gradually and separately.

Planned mutations
A theory of aging in which some genes have the specific function of causing mutations in other genes, which may have deleterious effects on the individual organism during its life span, thus accelerating the aging process.

Accumulation error theory
A theory of aging involving the possibility that in the course of protein production, one or more of the components of the process will not function properly and will make a mistake resulting in an incorrect amino acid being inserted into a protein. Over the years these mistakes will accumulate and reduce the efficiency of the body or keep it from working altogether.

Collagen theory
See Cross-link theory.

Cross-link theory
A theory of aging that suggests living cells age when connective tissue binds together, becomes rigid, and loses its function.

Autoimmune theory
A theory of aging that attributes aging to the development of antibodies that destroy normal cells. That is, human beings, as they age, show an increasing tendency to reject their own tissues.

The **"mean time to failure" theory** suggests that aging is a product of gradual deterioration of various organs. The process of aging is compared to what happens to automobiles or washing machines. Without repairs they might function well for a few years, and with perfect repairs they might last indefinitely, as long as spare parts are available. However, the lack of perfect repairs or spare parts means that the machines will ultimately end up in a scrap heap. For human beings, "spare part" surgery is limited to a few organs. Also, the "spare parts" are not perfect (Hayflick 1980).

Planned mutations is another theory. Genes with the specific function of causing mutations in other genes have been identified in a number of organisms. These mutations may have deleterious effects on the individual organism during its life span, thus accelerating the aging process. Generally, however, mutations in themselves do not play a major direct role in aging, but may interrelate with other factors to affect the aging process (Spiegel 1972).

The **accumulation error theory** involves the possibility that in the course of protein production, one or more of the components of the process will not function properly and will make a mistake by incorrectly reading the language of the genetic code, resulting in an incorrect amino acid being inserted into a protein. Sometimes the functioning of a protein, itself a part of the apparatus for making proteins, may be affected. If an error is made and inserted into a protein, it will in turn cause other errors. This situation is parallel to an error in the instructions to an automatic machine tool. The tool would create faulty parts that, when they were assembled in the final product, would reduce the product's efficiency or keep it from working altogether (Timiras 1978; Hayflick 1980).

The **cross-link theory,** or **collagen theory,** suggests that living cells age when connective tissue binds together, becomes rigid, and loses its function. The concept of cross-linkage can be described in terms of the behavior and characteristics of collagen and elastin, which are the components of connective tissue. Changes in connective tissue indicate that cross-linkage has occurred. These changes lead to a loss of elasticity in blood vessels, muscle tissue, skin, the lens of the eye, and other organs, and to slower healing of wounds. Also as a result of cross-linkage, tendons become dry and fibrous and may loosen; arterial walls lose the smooth muscle fibers; and the linings of the lungs and gastrointestinal tract decrease in efficiency. Another visible effect is that the nose and ears increase in size.

The **autoimmune theory** attributes aging to the development of antibodies that destroy normal cells. That is, human beings, as they age, show an increasing tendency to reject their own tissues. Autoimmune diseases increase with age, with age-related increases in autoimmune serum antibodies. These diseases include rheumatoid arthritis, cancer, diabetes, vascular diseases, and hypertension. There is also evidence that autoimmune reactions may play a role in neuronal degeneration. Preliminary human data show an increase in brain-reactive antibodies with age (LaRue and Jarvik 1982).

● **COGNITIVE DEVELOPMENT**

In the United States there is a common attitude that older means "dumber" and that somehow the peak years for learning are over by twenty or thirty. Yet in many cultures, only the old are regarded as wise.

One of the most studied aspects of aging is cognitive functioning. Older individuals who have trouble with cognitive functioning will eventually experience stress in work, leisure activities, relationships with family and friends, and roles in the community.

Longitudinal studies suggest that intelligence during maturity and old age does not decline as soon as people originally assumed. If illness does not intervene, cognitive stability is the rule and can be maintained into the ninth decade (Jarvik 1973). Different intellectual measures show different rates of decline. On measures of vocabulary and other skills reflecting educational experience, most individuals seem to maintain their adult level of functioning into the sixth and seventh decade (Baltes and Schaie 1975).

Some mental activity may be noticeably impaired in some people by the end of their sixties. Memory, especially for names, may be impaired. Such changes are partly caused by degenerative processes that affect the blood vessels of the whole body and, as a result, reduce the supply of oxygen to the brain. This may lead to damage of the brain cells themselves. Changes in motor, cognitive, and brain electrical behavior are correlated with changes in heart rate and blood pressure in the aging individual (Botwinick 1984).

Cardiovascular disease is widely suspected of being one type of pathology that can result in decrement in cognitive functioning. In general, individuals with cardiovascular disease appear to be most impaired in the speed of psychomotor performance and on highly speeded tests of cognitive ability (Hertzog, Schaie, and Gribbin 1978; Whitbourne and Weinstock 1986).

The elderly perform a variety of cognitive tasks at a less complex level than do middle-aged subjects. An example is the game of "Twenty Questions." Adolescents and middle adults generally approach this game by asking questions that eliminate large groups of possibilities, such as, "Is it alive?" The elderly, like young children, ask specific questions to test specific hypotheses, such as, "Is it my shoe?" The supposition is that the elderly are still capable of using abstract problem-solving strategies but are not inclined to approach tasks from that orientation. It could be hypothesized that as adults narrow the focus of their attention more and more to immediate needs and immediate obstacles to the gratification of needs, they stop using multifaceted, flexible problem-solving strategies that were used during the earlier adult years (Newman 1982).

The elderly appear to be accident prone. However, evidence suggests that it is not necessarily a decline in motor response or muscular strength that leads to accident-prone behavior, but rather slowness of decision time and the inability of the older person to rapidly discriminate relevant information from irrelevant information. Automobile accidents and pedestrian accidents often indicate failure of judgment. Scanning traffic flow, traffic lights, and other information and arriving at a relevant decision at an appropriate time is often not possible due to the timing characteristics of the older nervous system (Sterns, Barrett, and Alexander 1985).

Intelligence

Cattel (1963) and Horn (Horn and Cattel 1966; Horn 1982) propose that primary mental abilities fall into two principal dimensions: *crystallized* and *fluid* intelligence. **Crystallized intelligence** encompasses the sorts of skills one acquires through education and acculturation, such as verbal comprehension, numerical skills, and inductive reasoning (Horn 1982). To a large degree it reflects the extent to which one has accumulated the collective intelligence of one's own

Crystallized intelligence
The sorts of skills one acquires through education and acculturation, such as verbal comprehension, numerical skills, and inductive reasoning.

culture. It is the dimension tapped by most traditional IQ tests (Baltes and Schaie 1975). Crystallized intelligence increases over the life span (Neugarten 1976).

Fluid intelligence
Intelligence based mainly on the speed and effectiveness of neurological and physiological factors.

Fluid intelligence is based mainly on the speed and effectiveness of neurological and physiological factors (Horn 1982). Abilities within this area include motor speed, memory, and figural relations (for example, embedded figures). This type of intelligence can "flow into" various activities, such as perceiving, recognizing, and cognitively dealing with new information. Fluid intelligence seems to increase until late adolescence and gradually decline throughout adulthood (Neugarten 1976; Hooper, Fitzgerald, and Papalia 1971). The neural structures that are thought to be affected by aging are responsible for fluid intelligence (Whitbourne and Weinstock 1986).

Although there are differences between fluid and crystallized intelligence, the two are actually somewhat interdependent. A person must possess the fluid ability to learn new information in order to acquire the skills and knowledge that are specific to his or her culture and educational system. If an individual has the ability to follow the logic of a mathematical equation, it is much easier for him or her to acquire knowledge of advanced physics. On the other hand, training and experience in mathematics gives the individual the crystallized ability that makes it easier to learn new formulas (Whitbourne and Weinstock 1986).

As an individual ages, crystallized intelligence compensates in some ways for losses in fluid intelligence. Losses in speed and memory, which begin in late middle age, are often offset by gains in reasoning and understanding. In fact, crystallized intelligence increases as long as a person is alert and capable of taking in new information. In longitudinal studies that rated subjects on their performance of skills that use crystallized intelligence, individuals often scored higher in their fifties than they did in their twenties (Cunningham and Owens 1983). Perhaps this explains why scholars and scientists, whose work is based on accumulated knowledge and experience, are more productive in their forties, fifties, sixties, and into their seventies than they were in their twenties.

Older adults, those in their seventies and eighties, can perform quite effectively on tests of intellectual functioning. Physical health and morale are found to be important in enabling the subjects to demonstrate and use their abilities. Those who are free of disease, especially of the cardiovascular type, and who are adequately stimulated socially and emotionally, perform as well as younger adults, particularly on verbal materials and also where speed of response and motor coordination are not involved (Whitbourne and Weinstock 1986). One area of elderly cognition that is well documented is the decline in speed, or "slowing down," in both mental and physical performance. On speed-related tests, older subjects consistently score lower than younger ones (Monge 1975; Cerella 1985). Elderly subjects can learn as well as younger ones when the factor of speed is eliminated with respect to stimulus presentation and response requirements. The quality of learning of the elderly compares favorably with that of young adults (Granick and Friedman 1973).

Age, in general, is not a reliable index of cognitive performance. Tests used to assess intelligence may contribute to the apparent decline that is sometimes observed in elderly subjects. The concept of intelligence and the instruments to measure intelligence are based on the abilities that are most important during youth and young adulthood. Older people tend to do relatively poorly on tests employing technical language, such as the terminology of physics or computer programming, because they did not experience it in their education. Their

Scholars and scientists, whose work is based on accumulated knowledge and experience, are often more productive in their forties, fifties, sixties, and into their seventies than they were in their twenties.

performance is better if items are worded in terms of everyday experiences. An additional problem is the distinction between a person's competence and his or her actual performance. Handicaps that have nothing to do with intrinsic ability may affect the way a person performs on a test. For example, the aged are especially susceptible to the effects of fatigue. Pretest fatigue can considerably lower the scores of older subjects, but does not affect the performance of younger ones (Baltes and Schaie 1975; Baltes et al. 1984).

Research on age stereotypes indicates that some young people hold a negative view of old age. This view may influence young people to withdraw reinforcements for competence in the elderly, or even to punish such competence. The aged then may eventually accept the stereotypes and view themselves as deficient, putting aside intellectual performance as a personal goal. The intellectual deficit becomes a self-fulfilling prophecy (Lachman and Jelalian 1984).

Baltes and Schaie (1975), in their longitudinal study, found, among the elderly, a decline only in one measure of cognitive functioning out of four. The decline was in *visuomotor flexibility,* which involves the skill in shifting from familiar to unfamiliar patterns in tasks requiring coordination between visual and motor abilities (for example, when one must copy words but interchange capital letters with lowercase letters). There was no age-related change in *cognitive flexibility,* which involves the ability to shift from one way of thinking to another. (For example, the individual must provide either an antonym or a synonym to a word, depending on whether the word appears in capital or lowercase letters.) The measures of crystallized intelligence and visualization showed an increase in scores for the various age-groups, right into old age. Even people over seventy improved from the first testing to the second, after seven years. *Visualization* is the ability to organize and process visual materials, and involves tasks such as finding a simple figure contained in a complex one or identifying a picture that is incomplete. As stated earlier, crystallized intelligence encompasses the sorts of skills one acquires through education and acculturation and reflects the extent to which one has accumulated the collective intelligence of one's own culture.

One can only speculate about the reasons for generational differences in intelligence. Perhaps the answer lies in the substance, method, and length of education received by different generations. When the history of our educational institutions is considered and census data are gathered on the educational levels attained by members of specific generations, it seems fair to assume that the older people were exposed to shorter periods of formal education. Also, their education probably relied more heavily on the principle of memorization and less heavily on that of problem solving (Baltes et al. 1984).

An analysis of a longitudinal study involving those in the sixty to seventy-nine age-group demonstrated that persons with initially higher IQ scores (as measured by the Wechsler Adult Intelligence Scale [WAIS]), show a better prospect for longer life and have more stable ability levels (Eisdorfer and Wilkie 1973). Hall and her colleagues (1972) also found, in their longitudinal study, that a deficit in WAIS performance is significantly related to death in the elderly. When intellectual decline does occur, it comes shortly before death. A sudden deterioration during a year or so immediately prior to a natural death is called a **terminal drop** (Baltes and Schaie 1975; Baltes et al. 1984; Schaie and Geiwitz 1982).

Levinson and Reese (1967) compared the performance of children, college students, institutionalized and community-dwelling aged, and retired college faculty on a classic object-quality discrimination learning set series. Performance increased with age in the early years, reaching a peak in the college-age group, and decreased with age thereafter. Of particular interest was the finding that the retired college faculty were markedly superior to the other aged subjects. The longer a person is in the academic environment, the better the test score. Since the professor continues to accumulate crystallized intelligence and is exercising fluid skills, he or she should be increasing his or her raw scores on the standardized tests. Apparently an initially high IQ and/or considerable educational achievement may be significant variables in retaining intelligence.

The aged have the intellectual potential and ability to learn and benefit from education. The well-known productivity, high-level mental functioning, and creative output of many elderly individuals who remain active and involved in new learning experiences suggest that educational stimulation may accomplish this for many others. Education can play a significant role in enabling the aged to maintain their intellectual effectiveness. It appears that those who already have a good deal of education and exposure to learning are the most likely to continue adding to their knowledge and to maintain their intellectual effectiveness. Throughout the adult years, life goals change from success in traditionally defined intellectual tasks to success in more practical situations involving decision-making ability, life adaptation, judgment, or "wisdom." If intelligence tests took these abilities into account, it would be easier to estimate the elderly individual's true cognitive ability.

Memory

Memory is sometimes impaired during late adulthood. Memory is seen as a flow of information through the human thinking system. Memory has three storage systems in which information is stored for later use. The three storage systems are sensory memory, short-term memory, and long-term memory.

Terminal drop
Sudden intellectual deterioration during a year or so immediately prior to a natural death.

Sensory memory involves a brief sensory impression; that is, it is a memory system of extremely short duration. Immediately after the removal of a stimulus, a sensory representation of the stimulus is suspended in the mind for a brief time. Because many older adults have poor vision and poor hearing, there are some things they do not perceive well. But when they do perceive something, they have a sensory memory as good as that of younger adults (Craik 1977; Labouvie-Vief and Schell 1982).

Short-term memory is memory for information that has received minimal processing or interpretation. Short-term memory has a capacity limited to seven or so items. Material in short-term memory is thought to be held by the operation of rehearsal (a repetitive review of the material to be remembered) and if rehearsal is interrupted, the material has a half-life of no more than ten or fifteen seconds. There appears to be a slight decline in short-term memory with age. The effect of age on short-term memory is much larger if the person is asked to change the given information, for instance, rearrange it, or recall it in some order other than the one in which it was given. Thus, on simple short-term memory tasks, there is a slight age difference; however, when the task is made more complex, older subjects are more disadvantaged (Botwinick and Storandt 1974).

Long-term memory is memory for information that has been processed or stored in a reasonably deep fashion. It is presumed that long-term memory is not limited in either the capacity to store information or the duration for which it is stored. The largest age differences are found in long-term memory. Retrieval becomes slower with age (Cerella 1985; Madden 1985).

Recall memory is the ability to retrieve information about objects or events that are not present or currently happening. Recall requires the generation of information from the short- or long-term memory without a related object being present. **Recognition memory** is a retrieval system in which information is matched with stimulation information in the environment. It is easier than recall.

Macht and Buschke (1984) investigated age differences in the speed of verbal recall under controlled conditions that induced both aged and young adults to carry out the same kinds of processes during learning and recall. Memory for the target items was tested by free recall and cued recall in which each item was cued by its category label. There were no age differences in either the rate of free recall or the speed of cued recall under these conditions. Older adults are a bit slower in bringing things to memory. Their greatest difficulties are not with short-term recall but with longer-term recall.

Adults over fifty-five years of age do not show much forgetting in recognition tests but do in recall tests. Recall scores are lower than recognition scores at all ages (Walsh 1983). When comparing young adults (eighteen to twenty-four years) with older adults (sixty to seventy-four years), Madden (1985) found that age differences in memory performance were determined by quantitative changes in the speed of information processing rather than by qualitative changes in attention. The older adults had more difficulty in assimilating incoming information that was complex and unfamiliar and had to be handled with speed.

Humor

Getting the joke is an intellectual process, while enjoying it is an affective, or emotional, experience. Much of the scientific study of humor development

Sensory memory
A memory system of extremely short duration.

Short-term memory
Memory for information that has received minimal processing or interpretation.

Long-term memory
Memory for information that has been processed or stored in a reasonably deep fashion.

Recall memory
The ability to retrieve information about objects or events that are not present or currently happening.

Recognition memory
A retrieval system in which information is matched with stimulation information in the environment.

follows a cognitive model (Nahemow 1986). Although a maturational framework outlines various developmental levels in the kind of humor children understand and appreciate, it is unlikely that adults would fit into such a framework. Their appreciation and understanding of humor is more related to cognitive ability, cognitive style or strategy, and temperament or personality combined with experience. As the cognitive ability of children develops and matures, they are increasingly able to comprehend and appreciate humor. Also, as their cognitive ability increases and a joke becomes too easy, they appreciate it less.

There is some evidence that logical thinking may regress somewhat and become more disorganized during old age. Schaier and Cicirelli (1976) tested three groups of older adults (aged fifty to fifty-nine, sixty to sixty-nine, and seventy to seventy-nine) on their appreciation and comprehension of twelve conservation and twelve nonconservation jokes. (As you may recall, elementary-age children begin to comprehend the concept of conservation as their cognitive abilities mature.) The conservation jokes included conservation of mass, weight, and volume. Cognitive ability on these three conservation tasks were also tested. Schaier and Cicirelli found that in the elderly, appreciation of these jokes increased with age, but comprehension decreased with age. (The older subjects tended to understand the jokes less well, but thought they were funnier.) Schaier and Cicirelli also found that as age increased, more individuals no longer had the ability to conserve volume on the Piagetian task.

Examples of some of the jokes used in the study:

Conservation of mass. "Mr. Jones went in to a pizza parlor and ordered a whole pizza for his dinner. When the waiter asked if he wanted it cut into six or eight pieces, Mr. Jones said, 'Oh, you had better make it six! I could never eat eight pieces.'"

Conservation of weight. "George and Bob had a raft made out of old logs. One day they took the raft out into the middle of the lake for a picnic lunch. As soon as they finished their lunch, the raft began to sink. George said, 'Oh no! We've eaten too much.'"

Conservation of volume. "Shawn wanted to clean his toy truck, so he put it into a pail of water, but the water overflowed. His little brother said, 'Take the truck apart and then you'll have room.'"

Sometimes older individuals do not understand a joke because it is related to a contemporary topic to which they do not have access. Older adults come from a different time. They are often left out of the common culture, making it difficult for them to get a joke. On the other hand, a younger individual might not get a joke because it relates to an earlier time period and he or she does not have the background to appreciate it. For example, "Did you know that the natives like potatoes even more than missionaries? Yes, but the missionaries are more nutritious." This joke may not make sense to a young person who knows about Third World people but not about "natives" (Nahemow 1986).

"Aging is unbearable without humor" (Datan 1986, 161). Humor by and about old people deflects the painful truths of biological decline and inevitable death, thus converting the unbearable into the humorous. For example, Reggie the Retiree (1982) wrote a book, *Laughs and Limericks on Aging in Large Print,* addressing the elderly's fears of physical loss.

My bifocals are the best you can find
My teeth fit and don't bind
My ear plug's o.k.

and so's my toupee
but I sure do miss my mind.

(P. 16)

Humor also serves as a self-defense, that is, "the humor of the resilient underdog." The "resilient underdog" laughs at himself or herself, not others. An example would be the elderly man who can laugh at sex, sensuality, and fear of biological decline.

Humor, mirth, and laughter contribute to the physiological well-being of the elderly (Fry 1986). Physical deterioration lessens, and the elderly can take greater control of their life experiences. For example, it has been found that humor positively affects the autonomic nervous system (Schacter and Wheeler 1962; Levi 1965; Langevin and Day 1972). Levi (1965) found that after humor exposure, subjects' urine samples demonstrated adrenaline and noradrenaline excretion. He concluded that "emotional responses rated by the subjects as pleasant may be accompanied by increased sympatheticoadrenomedullary activity" (p. 85). Langevin and Day (1972), in assessing the autonomic function, found that increases in galvanic skin response and heart rates were positively correlated with humor ratings. Humor also affects the circulatory system (Averill 1969; Fry and Rader 1969; Jones and Harris 1971; Langevin and Day 1972; Sroufe and Waters 1976; Godkewitsch 1976; Fry and Savin 1982). For example, there is a correlation between the degree of laughter elicited by humor and the activity of the pulmonary-cardiac reflex, as well as increases of both the systolic and the diastolic blood pressure levels. After laughter ceases, there is a short period when blood pressure levels go below those of the prelaughter period, revealing a stimulation-relaxation pattern (Fry and Savin 1982). Other systems affected positively by humor include the respiratory system (Fry and Rader 1977; Svebak 1977; Fry and Stoft 1971; Young 1982), the skeletal muscular system (Schwartz 1974; Svebak 1975; Chapman 1976), and the central nervous system (Svebak 1982). Therefore, the quality of life for the elderly and their relationships with others can significantly improve through involvement in humor and encouraging involvement in humor, mirth, and laughter (Stevens 1986). Humor is advantageous emotionally, psychologically, physiologically, as well as cognitively. Perhaps that is why people who live longer tend to have a good sense of humor (Fry 1986).

SUMMARY

- Later adulthood includes various stages. Neugarten separates this time period between young-old and old-old. Burnside and colleagues divide the time period according to decades: young-old (sixty to sixty-nine years), middle-age old (seventy to seventy-nine years), old-old (eighty to eight-nine years), and very old-old (ninety to ninety-nine years).
- People who age successfully maintain regular and vigorous physical activities, have extensive social contacts, and pursue intellectually and emotionally stimulating activities. Disuse of functions can lead to unnecessary physical limitations, social isolation, disorientation, and apathy.
- Men who reach their sixty-fifth birthday can expect to live another 14.1 years, while sixty-five-year-old women can expect to live another 18.3 years.
- The elderly undergo many physical changes, including changes in tissue, musculature, bones, the circulatory system, nutritional requirements, the senses, the nervous system, health, and sexual functioning.

Alzheimer's Disease

Alzheimer's disease (AD) is one of the most threatening and disabling disorders found among the elderly. It involves deterioration in intellectual performance, characterized by memory loss, and interferes with work and/or social activities (Davies 1988). It is the fourth leading cause of death among older adults (Blieszner and Shifflett 1990). Although fewer than 1 percent of all people are affected at age sixty-five, the figure rises steeply to 20 percent at age eighty and older (Davies 1988).

The onset of AD is usually subtle, with lessened initiative and some forgetfulness. Other symptoms include a decline in judgment, progressive difficulty with word finding, and loss of recent memory in particular. Personal hygiene habits, interest in the environment, and insight diminish. In later stages, the individual suffers increased mental deterioration, lethargy, and total helplessness. The individual requires total nursing care and ultimately dies (Crystal 1988; Blieszner and Shifflett 1990). Death is usually caused by a bacterial or viral infection. However, rates for accidents, vascular disease, and neoplasia (any benign or malignant tumor) are also elevated in AD patients (Terry and Davies 1980).

It has been suggested that there is an autosomal dominant gene for AD that may or may not express itself when the individual gets older, with a 50 percent chance of it appearing by age ninety. Many families have been found to be carriers of the dominant gene. There appears to be an increased risk of the disease among first-order relatives of patients with the disease if the disease has been found in three or more successive generations. About half of the first order relatives will eventually develop AD. Rates are high among both monozygotic and dizygotic twins. Approximately equal numbers of males and females are affected (Breitner 1988).

AD has a tremendous impact on the family and friends of the patient. It is especially difficult for spouses and adult children who function as caregivers. George (1984) found that spouse caregivers had poorer health, were more likely to use psychotropic (mood altering) drugs, had more financial problems, and had less leisure time than adult-child caregivers. Adult-child caregivers, on the other hand, reported more stress and unhappiness than spouse caregivers. Both the spouses and the adult children had lower well-being than more distantly related caregivers, such as nieces, siblings, and daughters-in-law.

Spouses who were caregivers noted changes in their marital relationship during the early stages of AD. Primarily they were aware of changes in marital role patterns, especially the loss of egalitarian division of labor. Also, sharing sexual expression with and communicating love to each other declined during the early stages. During the later stages of AD, the spouses experienced guilt feelings about the conflict between their marital commitment and their interest in developing new relationships and interests (Kvale and Bohlen 1985).

The breakdown of the marital relationship with an AD patient is unique, with implications for the spouse's future life-style and life satisfaction. When a marital relationship ends in divorce or the death of one's partner, a new close relationship can replace it. However, the spouses of AD patients are unable to complete the grieving process that normally follows divorce or a death. Neither can they focus on other primary relationships to replace the lost one, because the relationship continues, even though it is in a drastically altered form (Blieszner and Shifflett 1990).

What can be done to help the individuals and families who are, in a sense, trapped? What about foster care for AD patients? What other intervention programs could be designed for AD patients and their families? Should the government consider paying for nursing care of *all* AD patients, despite the family's ability to pay? Would you place your parents in a nursing home? Why or why not?

- Many theories have been proposed concerning the process of biological aging. Many have merit, but none are conclusive. Some theories identify environmental factors as the primary cause of aging, and other theories see aging as emanating from the organism itself, rather than from the external environment.
- Most people do not suffer substantial losses of overall cognitive power in old age. Crystallized intelligence increases as long as a person is alert and capable of taking in new information. Fluid intelligence, which includes motor speed, memory, and figural relations, seems to increase until late adolescence and gradually decline throughout adulthood.

- There is a general age-related slowing in the speed of information processing, sensory memory, short-term memory, and long-term memory. During later adulthood, recall memory suffers a consistent drop, while recognition memory shows no deterioration.
- As individuals get older, they tend to understand jokes less well, but think they are funnier. Humor, mirth, and laughter contribute to the physiological well-being of the elderly.
- Alzheimer's disease is one of the most threatening and disabling disorders found among the elderly. It makes a tremendous impact on the family and friends of the patient. It is especially difficult for spouses and adult children who function as caregivers.

READINGS

Aronson, M. K. (1988). *Understanding Alzheimer's disease*. New York: Charles Scribner's Sons.
Provides a comprehensive guide to Alzheimer's disease.
Brecher, E. M. (1984). *Love, sex, and aging*. Boston,: Little, Brown.
Reports survey of sexual behavior of over 6000 individuals over the age of fifty.
Ostrow, A. C. (1984). *Physical activity and the older adult*. Princeton, NJ: Princeton Book Company.
Discussion of exercise as it relates to the physical changes in the older adult.
Simonton, D. K. (1984). *Genius, creativity, and leadership*. Cambridge, MA: Harvard University Press.
Examination of historical data that indicates the relationship of age to creativity, genius, and leadership.
Wantz, M. S. and Gay, J. E. (1981). *The aging process: A health perspective*. Winthrop.
Discussion of psychological and physical aging, as well as disease and health enhancement.

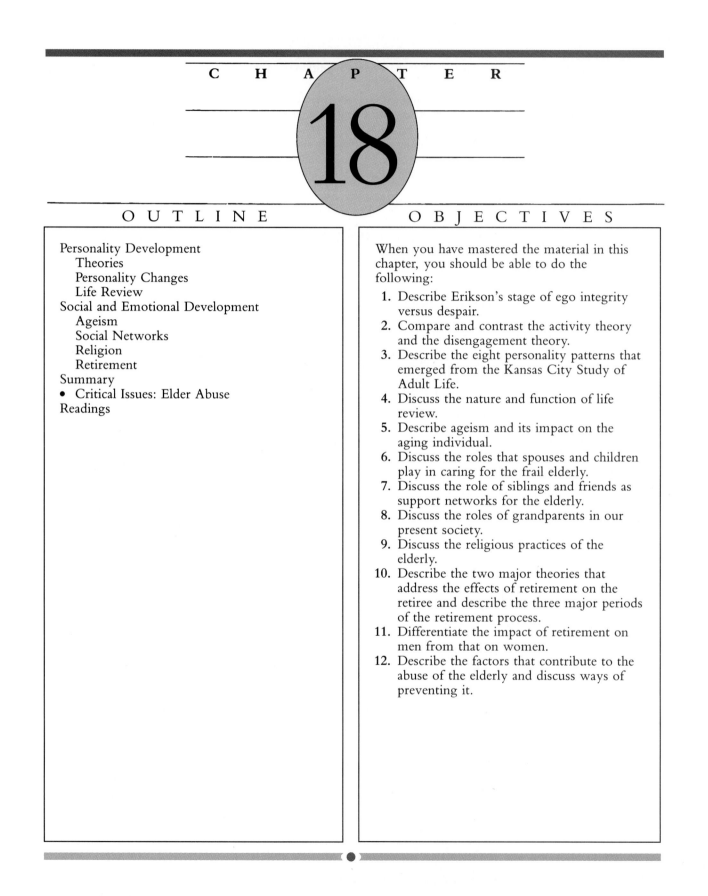

C H A P T E R

18

O B J E C T I V E S

When you have mastered the material in this chapter, you should be able to do the following:

1. Describe Erikson's stage of ego integrity versus despair.
2. Compare and contrast the activity theory and the disengagement theory.
3. Describe the eight personality patterns that emerged from the Kansas City Study of Adult Life.
4. Discuss the nature and function of life review.
5. Describe ageism and its impact on the aging individual.
6. Discuss the roles that spouses and children play in caring for the frail elderly.
7. Discuss the role of siblings and friends as support networks for the elderly.
8. Discuss the roles of grandparents in our present society.
9. Discuss the religious practices of the elderly.
10. Describe the two major theories that address the effects of retirement on the retiree and describe the three major periods of the retirement process.
11. Differentiate the impact of retirement on men from that on women.
12. Describe the factors that contribute to the abuse of the elderly and discuss ways of preventing it.

Mature Adults:
The Elderly—Psychosocial
Development

PERSONALITY DEVELOPMENT

Theories

Erikson's Psychosocial Theory

Erikson calls the final crisis of adult development "ego integrity versus despair." Those individuals who can look back on their lives and feel satisfied have a sense of integrity. They have accepted the fact that one's life is one's own responsibility. They feel that their lives have been meaningful and whole. These individuals accept the inevitability of mortality. People who successfully resolve the conflict of ego integrity versus despair emerge with a sense of wisdom, one of the true strengths of old age. The individual who possesses integrity is ready to defend the dignity of his or her own life-style against all physical and economic threats. "For he knows that an individual life is the accidental coincidence of but one life cycle with but one segment of history, and that for him all human integrity stands and falls with the one style of integrity of which he partakes" (Erikson 1968b, 139).

The absence of this ego integration is signified by disgust and despair. The individuals who look back on their lives and see nothing but a succession of missed opportunities and wrong decisions feel despair. They feel that time is short, too short for the attempt to start another life and try out alternate roads to integrity. Their despair is often disguised behind a show of disgust, misanthropy, or chronic contemptuous displeasure with particular institutions and particular people. This disgust and displeasure only signifies the individual's contempt for himself or herself (Erikson 1968a, 1968b). Without ego integrity, the individual may fear death.

Social Theories of Aging

There are two general points of view regarding optimum patterns of aging. Both are based on the observations that as people grow older their behavior

According to the activity theory, the optimal way to age is to stay active and to resist the shrinkage of the social world. The activities of middle age should be maintained as long as possible.

changes, the activities that characterized them in middle age become curtailed, and the extent of their social interaction decreases. The two theories then diverge. The first theory is called the **activity theory.** This theory implies that except for the inevitable changes in biology and in health, older people are the same as middle-aged people, with the same psychological and social needs. The decreased social interaction that characterizes old age results from society's withdrawal from the aging person. This decrease in interaction proceeds against the desires of most aging men and women. The optimal way to age, then, is to stay active and to resist the shrinkage of the social world. The activities of middle age should be maintained as long as possible. Then the individual should find substitutes for activities that have to be relinquished, substitutes for work after retirement, and substitutes for friends and loved ones after their deaths (Havighurst, Neugarten, and Tobin 1968).

The second theory is called the **disengagement theory.** This theory argues that both society and the aging person mutually withdraw, with the aging individual accepting and perhaps desiring decreased interaction. This theory suggests that the individual's withdrawal has intrinsic, or developmental, qualities as well as responsive ones. Social withdrawal by the aging person is seen as corresponding with increased preoccupation with the self and decreased emotional investment in persons and objects in the environment. Disengagement is, therefore, a natural rather than an imposed process. From this viewpoint, the older person with psychological well-being reaches a new equilibrium. This equilibrium is characterized by a greater psychological distance from others, altered types of relationships, and decreased social interaction (Havighurst, Neugarten, and Tobin 1968).

Activity theory
A social theory of aging that implies that except for the inevitable changes in biology and in health, older people are the same as middle-aged people, with the same psychological and social needs.

Disengagement theory
A social theory of aging that argues that both society and the aging person mutually withdraw, with the aging individual accepting and perhaps desiring decreased interaction.

According to the disengagement theory, both society and the aging person mutually withdraw, with the individual accepting and perhaps desiring decreased interaction.

Personality Changes

There is a relatively high degree of consistency in personality traits among the elderly. However, these traits are subject to variability with extreme changes in circumstances, such as major changes in health or environment. This position was supported in the classic Kansas City Study of Adult Life. Neugarten, Havighurst, and Tobin (1968) found that neither the activity nor the disengagement theory seemed adequate. They found that certain individuals, as they aged, disengaged with relative comfort and remained highly contented with life. Others disengaged with great discomfort and showed a drop in life satisfaction. Others had long shown low levels of activity accompanied by high satisfaction. These people showed relatively little change as they aged. Personality type was the important variable. Neugarten, Havighurst, and Tobin identified four major personality patterns in the individuals in their study: *integrated, defended, passive-dependent,* and *disintegrated.* These four patterns were further divided according to role activity and life satisfaction, yielding eight patterns.

The **integrated** personalities were well-functioning persons who had a complex inner life and, at the same time, intact cognitive abilities and a competent ego. These individuals maintained a comfortable degree of control over their lives. They were flexible, open to new stimuli, mellow, and mature. All of the people in this group were high in life satisfaction, but they were divided regarding their amount of role activity. Three patterns reflecting role activity emerged from this group: the reorganizers, focused, and the disengaged. The *reorganizers* engaged in a wide variety of activities. They could be described as the optimum American agers; that is, they placed a high value on "staying young, staying active, and refusing to grow old." They substituted new activities for lost ones, and when they retired from work, they gave time to community affairs, church, or other organizations. They reorganized their patterns of activity.

The *focused* showed medium levels of activity with high life satisfaction. They became selective in their activities and devoted energy to, and gained their major satisfaction from, one or two role areas.

The *disengaged* showed low activity with high life satisfaction. They voluntarily moved away from role commitments, not in response to external losses or physical deficits, but because of preference. They were self-directed persons with an interest in the world, but that interest that was not imbedded in a network of social interactions. They experienced high feelings of self-regard and chose what might be called a "rocking chair" approach to old age, that is, a calm, withdrawn, but contented pattern.

The **defended** personalities were described as the striving, ambitious, achievement-oriented personalities, with high defenses against anxiety and the need to maintain tight controls over impulse life. This personality type provided two patterns of aging: holding on and the constricted. The *holding-on* group saw aging as a threat and, therefore, responded by holding on as long as possible to the patterns of their middle age. They were successful in their attempts, thus maintaining high life satisfaction with medium or high activity levels. These persons would say, "I'll work until I drop," or "As long as you keep busy, you will get along all right." The *constricted* persons busily defended themselves against aging. They were preoccupied with losses and deficits and dealt with these threats by constricting their social interactions and their energies and by closing themselves off from experience. They seemed to structure their worlds to avoid what they regarded as imminent collapse. And while this constriction

Integrated
The personality pattern of well-functioning elderly persons who have a complex inner life and, at the same time, intact cognitive abilities and a competent ego.

Defended
The personality type of elderly persons who are striving, ambitious, and achievement oriented, with high defenses against anxiety and the need to maintain tight controls over impulse life.

resulted in low role activity, it worked fairly well, given their personality pattern, and kept them high or medium in life satisfaction.

The third group of personalities were **passive-dependent,** which included two patterns of aging: succorance-seeking and the apathetic. The *succorance-seeking* were those individuals who had strong dependency needs and sought responsiveness from others. These persons maintained medium levels of activity and medium levels of life satisfaction, and seemed to maintain themselves fairly well as long as they had at least one or two other persons whom they could lean on and who met their emotional needs. The *apathetic* pattern represented those persons in whom passivity was a striking feature and who had low role activity and medium or low life satisfaction. They were also "rocking chair" people, but with a different personality structure than the disengaged had. The apathetic pattern seemed to occur in persons in whom aging reinforced long-standing patterns of passivity and apathy.

Finally, there was a group of **disintegrated** personalities who showed a *disorganized* pattern of aging. They had gross defects in psychological functions, loss of control over emotions, and deterioration in thought processes. They maintained themselves in the community, but they were low both in role activity and in life satisfaction.

Neugarten, Havighurst, and Tobin (1968) concluded that people, as they age, seem to be neither at the mercy of the social environment nor at the mercy of some set of intrinsic processes. In fact, the individual seems to continue to make his or her own "impress" upon the wide range of social and biological changes. Each person exercises choice and selects from the environment according to long-established needs. Individuals, therefore, age according to a pattern that has a long history and that maintains itself, with adaptation, to the end of life. In normal men and women there is no sharp discontinuity of personality

Passive-dependent
The personality type that includes the succorance-seeking elderly (those who have strong dependency needs) and the apathetic elderly (those who are passive and have low role activity and medium or low life satisfaction).

Disintegrated
A personality type with gross defects in psychological functions, loss of control over emotions and deterioration in thought processes.

Disintegrated personalities show a disorganized pattern of aging. They have gross defects in psychological functions, loss of control over emotions, and deterioration in thought processes.

with age, but instead an increasing consistency. Characteristics that have been central to the personality seem to become even more clearly delineated. Those values that have been cherished become even more salient. Patterns of overt behavior are likely to remain compatible with the individual's underlying personality needs and desires as long as the environment permits.

Gutmann (1968, 1977), in his comparative studies, has documented a difference in the way aging affects men compared to the way it affects women. Men tend to move from an active to a passive style, while women tend to move from a passive to an active style. Men appear to feel that after a lifetime of responsibility, breadwinning, and decision making, they can now express the complexity of their personalities, including traits that are considered feminine. Women, on the other hand, seem to become more aggressive, instrumental, and domineering. Gutmann's hypothesis is that both sexes are responding to liberation from the "parental imperative," that is, the social pressure for women to conform to the nurturing role necessary in parenting and for men to be financially responsible for the family and suppress any conflicting traits.

Changes within an elderly individual's daily life and immediate environment can alter his or her perception of life to some degree and affect his or her physical and mental health. The elderly, who are more susceptible to illness, are also subject to a variety of significant life changes, including the loss of the work role, declining income, changes in physical functioning, the death of friends, and the illness or death of spouse. A correlation has been noted between such life changes and a variety of psychological and psychosomatic complaints, including depression. Change alone, however, does not influence emotional well-being, even when the change is brought about voluntarily, except when it leads to hardships in key conditions of living (Pearlin 1980).

Older persons are also susceptible to chronic daily stresses, called "daily hassles," which are repetitive and stable (Lazarus 1981; Lazarus and Cohen 1977). They are irritating, frustrating, and distressing daily occurrences, including practical problems, environmental irritants, and concerns related to family, health, and finances. These chronic daily hassles eventually bring about the same psychological symptoms that are related to major life events and changes.

The majority of elderly persons have sound mental health. The percentage of the elderly who have mental problems is similar to that of the general population. Positive features of mental health include such characteristics as a positive self-attitude, growth and self-actualization, integration of the personality, autonomy, and being in touch with reality (Birren and Renner 1980). Four in five older people look back on their lives with satisfaction, and three in four feel their lives are as interesting as ever. Psychological functioning in the elderly is complex, involving an interaction between factors in the social environment and a sense of self and personal competencies (Simon 1980; Harris et al. 1975). Holahan et al. (1984) found that in the elderly, perceptions of self-efficacy in dealing with daily hassles and negative life events were related to successful adjustment. Higher levels of self-efficacy were associated with lower levels of depression for both sexes, with lower levels of other psychological distress for women, and with fewer psychosomatic complaints for men. Overall, the results of this study imply that both the perception of self-efficacy in dealing with hassles and the frequency of hassles are important predictors of psychological distress and psychosomatic complaints in elderly persons. Therefore, when hardships arise from conditions of living, even if based on voluntary decisions, emotional well-being may be altered.

Life Review

Many of the elderly engage in an evaluative backward glance at their life and weigh their accomplishments and failures, their satisfactions and disappointments. They initiate a new process of self-reflection that results in a new perception of and relationship with their own mortality. This process is called **life review.** Some elderly are essentially seeking to delineate a final identity as they approach death (Pfeiffer 1977). However, the individual's self-reflection may not be related to chronological age or distance from death but instead to his or her perceived control over the environment, or how much independence he or she can maintain in his or her life circumstances. Some people indulge in life review during early adulthood, while others, who are less self-reflective, approach old age with a "one day at a time" attitude. Some clues that an individual has involved himself or herself in life review would be a newly established will, a revised will to keep up with changed circumstances, or changes in exercise, diet, and drinking habits out of concern for longevity. Does he or she quit smoking because of, or continue smoking despite, warning symptoms? Does he or she visit or avoid seriously ill friends and relatives? Does he or she skip over the obituary section of the newspaper or immediately turn to it? The answers to these questions would provide insight into *how* the individual involved himself or herself in life review (Kastenbaum 1985).

Life review
A process of self-reflection that results in a new perception of and relationship with one's own mortality.

The personal sense and meaning of the life cycle are more clearly unfolded by those who have nearly completed it. The older person provides an inkling of the nature of the forces shaping life and the effects of life events. Life review should be recognized as a vital process, which may help others to listen, to tolerate and understand the aged, and not to treat reminiscence as insignificant.

It is important for the elderly person to integrate his or her past life experiences as they have been lived, not as they might have been lived. Probably at no other time in life is there as powerful a force toward self-awareness as in old age. The task that needs to be accomplished is to find an identity that integrates the diverse elements of an individual's life and that allows him or her to come to a reasonably positive view of his or her life's worth (Pfeiffer 1977).

● SOCIAL AND EMOTIONAL DEVELOPMENT

Ageism

Age stereotyping, or *ageism,* is a form of discrimination against older adults. It can make a negative impact on the emotional well-being and social interaction of the elderly individual. Ageism insinuates that an older person is less competent, less intelligent, more infantile, less attractive, and has lost his or her memory. Studies have found that these discriminatory accusations are unfounded, although many people believe them (Green 1981; Levin and Levin 1980; Puckett et al. 1983; Schonfield 1982; Levin 1988).

Social Networks

An individual's social networks includes those people who provide social support. Social competence is distinctly related to the use and misuse of social support. The person who is socially competent is more likely to acquire support-network members and be able to activate their aid in problem solving.

Thus, such a person will experience a better quality of life and fewer negative outcomes than less socially competent individuals (Antonucci 1985).

Most old people are surrounded by a support network of family and friends. The isolated elderly may be continuing a lifelong pattern of isolation, as indicated by studies of people living in single-room-occupancy hotels. There is relatively little change in the number of people from whom an individual receives support. Women have significantly larger and more multifaceted social networks than men do. Wives provide more support than husbands do, but husbands say they provide more support to their wives than wives report they provide to their husbands. Women are significantly more satisfied with their friends, but there are no differences in satisfaction with family. Men report higher levels of marital satisfaction than women do; however, both men and women generally report higher levels of marital satisfaction with age. The social ties of women are different than those of men. Men turn to their wives for support, while women turn not only to their husbands but also to children, other family members, and friends. Women have better interpersonal skills than men do, and these skills become important and highly functional in old age. Women report providing and receiving more support from their children than do men (Hooyman and Kiyak 1988).

Marital status definitely affects social-network status. Married people have larger networks than people who are separated, divorced, or widowed, or those who have never married. Married women have the largest support networks, and unmarried males have the smallest. Unmarried women have better support networks than unmarried men. Widows are generally involved in extensive support networks, and the role of children, especially daughters, is crucial. It has been noted that, in general, men are absent from the support networks of widowed women (Hooyman and Kiyak 1988).

People who have lower socioeconomic status, lower income, and less education tend to have smaller networks that consist mainly of family members. People who have higher socioeconomic status, higher income, and more education generally report larger networks with diverse membership consisting of both family and friends. Older people with less education and less income are more likely to report feelings of loneliness, compared with those with more education and more income (Antonucci 1985).

Rural farm and nonfarm couples have a great deal of continuity in the frequency of social interactions with family and friends from the pre- to post-retirement period. Urban residents, compared with rural residents, have fewer relatives among their network members. They tend to have networks that are less dense, that is, fewer members of their support networks are relatives. Urbanites are likely to have uniplex relationships with their network members, that is, different members occupying different support roles rather than the same members occupying multiple support roles (Antonucci 1985).

Family

For physical health, mental health, and economic reasons, old people should live independent lives in their own homes as long as they can maintain a satisfactory standard of living (McAuley and Blieszner 1985). The elderly adult's preferred living arrangement is with a spouse, with a second choice of living alone, and finally, living with an adult child. Older men, people who are divorced, and those with higher incomes are least likely to live with other family members. For the elderly in the community, health, finance, and informal supports play important roles in determining how long they will be able to maintain their preferred living arrangements (Antonucci 1985).

The Elderly and Their Adult Children   Family bonds override distance and separation regardless of age or generation placement. Most adult children and their elderly parents maintain a relationship based on the affectional bond between them. While the relationship is not one of day-to-day contact or close personal intimacy, neither is it one of mere obligation, pseudo-intimacy, or estrangement. The relationship is characterized by a closeness of feeling between parent and child, an easy compatibility between them, a low degree of conflict, and a good deal of satisfaction. The amount of interaction between parent and child depends on the closeness of the affectional bond, although other factors (duty, parent dependency, other responsibilities) may also have an effect (Cicirelli 1983).

Brody et al. (1984) interviewed three generations of women regarding their opinions about what adult children should do for their elderly parents. The large majority of each generation indicated that adult children, regardless of gender, marital status, or work status, should adjust their family schedules and help meet the expenses of professional care for the impaired elderly parent when needed. However, they did not believe it was appropriate to adjust work schedules or share households. The elderly women in the sample preferred adult children as providers of emotional support and financial management but not income. The middle generation of women were least in favor of parents' receiving financial help or instrumental help from their children, preferring formal services to provide this assistance.

When the elderly live in the homes of other family members, usually their children, day care is a viable option to relieve the family from the stress of constant daily care or concern about the older adult's safety while family members are at work. This option is especially helpful if the elder is somewhat able-bodied, independent, and not bedridden. Day-care centers are often supported by community agencies or churches. They provide recreational opportunities, socializing activities, lunch, and companionship. Centers usually stay open during the workday hours. Adult day care offers the elder a chance to be cared for and independent from the family (Eagen 1986).

Frail Elderly   The needs of the frail elderly pose a special demand on the support network. The frail elderly typically are cared for by spouse, children, and other family and friends. The support provided determines whether the older person is able to maintain independent living quarters and avoid institutionalization (Blieszner and Alley 1990). Elderly parents who have lost their adult children are particularly at risk, since they may not have developed a means of coping that makes use of other available sources of support.

The frail elderly prefer to obtain support from informal sources such as friends, spouse, and family. The most typical situation is the frail older man cared for by an only-slightly-less-frail older woman, usually his wife (Blieszner and Alley 1990). It is when the older woman herself becomes too frail to care for her spouse or is unable to care for herself that the extended family becomes involved. In the context of caring for the elderly, the word *family* most often means the women in the family. The people, other than spouses, that most elderly people turn to for help in a health crisis are women in middle-age, usually daughters and in some cases daughters-in-law (Cantor 1983; Stone et al. 1987).

The daughter is often called the "sandwich generation" because she is centered between concern for her young-adult children, who are just making a place for themselves in the adult world, and responsibility and concern for her elderly parent(s). The amount of help the middle-aged daughter is able to provide is related to whether she is married and whether she is employed. Older middle-generation women are more likely than younger middle-generation women to have an elderly mother in the household (34 percent of those fifty or older compared with 9 percent of those in their forties). The childless elderly woman is at a much greater disadvantage than the spouseless elderly woman (Lang and Brody 1983).

Family and work obligations often conflict with caregiving responsibilities. Employed adult children provide about the same number of caregiving hours as unemployed adult children, although they are less likely than the unemployed children to perform personal care tasks and cooking. They usually give up hobbies and social activities rather than time in the workplace (Brody and Schoonover 1986; Cantor 1983; Soldo and Myullyluoma 1983).

According to Cicirelli (1983) there are two areas in which adult children need support in relationships with elderly parents. First, they need to develop better communication with their elderly parents in order to reach an understanding of what the parents' most important needs are and how they, the adult children, can best make a contribution. Second, adult children need help in coping with the stresses that seem to be an inevitable side effect of helping elderly parents. Supplementary or backup services, such as part-time day care or respite care, need to be provided. This can do much to prevent an excessive buildup of strains that could result in a family breakdown or lead to parent abuse. Self-help groups help adult children share strains and feelings, as well as gain emotional support. Counseling activities can also help adult children develop skills for dealing with elderly parents and coping with the stresses of helping. Such supportive services are especially important in situations where an adult child is bearing an unusually heavy burden, such as an intergenerational household or limited financial resources.

Sibling Relationships   Little is known concerning sibling relationships in the family support network of older adults. A sibling relationship can have the longest duration of any kin relationship and may be more egalitarian than any relationship in the family. Siblings usually share a common past and are relatively close in age, making the sibling tie a unique family relationship, one that may contribute to the ability of siblings to provide a unique kind of kin support for each other in later life. Although the number of living siblings declines with age, most older adults have at least one living sibling. Among adults age sixty-five or older, 75 to 93 percent report at least one living brother or sister. A lack of proximity to siblings limits the degree and type of support that siblings can offer. Widowed, single, and childless older adults have greater contact and express greater closeness with siblings than do married older adults and those with children. Siblings provide an important source of social and psychological support in later life, with older adults reporting greater closeness with siblings than younger adults do. Closeness between siblings develops in childhood and is relatively stable and consistent over the life course (Scott 1983).

Factors important in older siblings' relationships include physical, emotional, psychological, and financial support. Communication and memory-sharing among older siblings validates perceptions of self and maintains closeness. Sibling relationships are influenced to a great extent by the existing family structure. Sisters appear to provide more emotional support to their siblings than do brothers. The sex composition of the sibling dyad appears to have an influence on the degree of attachment in later life, the sister-sister dyad being especially strong. Same-sex siblings who were nearest in birth order tend to form stronger relationships than other sibling combinations. Older siblings, whether male or female, are influenced to a greater extent by sisters than by brothers. Rivalries subside in later life (Scott 1983).

The help most frequently exchanged between older siblings includes assistance during illness, help in making important decisions, and transportation. Older siblings appear to keep in touch via writing, telephoning, getting together for special occasions, brief visits, and home and commercial recreation. These activities are the major channels for sibling interaction in later life (Scott 1983).

Institutional Care

Stress on caregivers may make them look for relief through institutional care. Such a decision is multifaceted. Usually institutionalization is the last resort after all of the family's resources have been depleted. Such a move often results in feelings of grief, guilt, shame, anxiety, fear, and also may renew old family conflicts.

Most families continue to visit their older family members. Some experience an improvement in their relationship with the institutionalized family member. Institutional residents who receive frequent visitors become less impaired than those who do not. Institutionalized elderly who report greater support ties with the staff and greater ties outside the institution to family and friends make better adjustments (Hatch and Franken 1984). The relationship between social support and residential environment is both important and complicated. The better the social interaction and support the resident perceives, the better the adjustment and morale of the individual. For example, age-segregated community dwellings and retirement communities are more conducive to the exchange of informal supports than age-heterogeneous settings (Antonucci 1985).

Institutional care has received much adverse publicity during the past fifteen years. Only 5 percent of those people over sixty-five are institutionalized. Many nursing homes have been reported to be boring, meaningless, nonstimulating places where people have little to do but wait to die. The general public's attitude toward such institutions is negative. However, not all institutional care is bad. Those facilities that give their residents responsibility and encourage independence have residents who are motivated and who live longer.

The majority of nursing home residents are functionally impaired and cannot live independently in a community setting. However, for every impaired older person in a nursing home facility, there are at least two and maybe even five equally impaired individuals living in the community (Duke Center for the Study of Aging and Human Development 1978). Therefore, poor physical health and medical need alone does not explain institutionalization. In fact, the variable that appears to distinguish nursing home residents from community-based impaired individuals is the absence of a caregiver or support network for those who are institutionalized (Noelker and Bass 1989).

Geriatric foster-care homes offer a viable alternative to nursing home care. *Geriatric foster care* is a program in which trained and supervised families "adopt" and care for one or more (depending on state laws) unrelated older individuals who would otherwise enter a nursing home. The rationale for this type of care is that a family setting is the best environment for promoting quality of life and

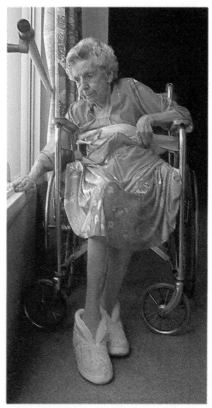

Only 5 percent of those people over sixty-five are institutionalized. Many nursing homes have been reported to be boring, meaningless, nonstimulating places where people have little to do but wait to die. However, those facilities that give their residents responsibility and encourage independence have residents who are motivated and as healthy as possible.

maintaining the feeling of humanness. The foster family becomes a surrogate for the elderly individual's family. Several studies have found that foster-care programs have higher patient satisfaction—including more patient improvement, patient satisfaction with activities, patient friendships, and privacy—than nursing homes do (Dale 1980; Oktay and Volland 1981; Talmadge and Murphy 1983; Braun and Rose 1987).

Grandparenting

The chances of a young person having a living grandparent are higher than at any other time in history. There are approximately forty-eight grandparents per one hundred parents, as compared to fourteen grandparents per one hundred parents at the turn of the century (Serow 1981).

Rev. John Robinson, pastor to the Pilgrims in Holland before their departure to Plymouth in 1620, commented:

> Grandfathers are more affectionate towards their children's children, than to their immediates. . . . And hence it is, that children brought up with their grandfathers and grandmothers, seldom do well, but are usually corrupted by their too great indulgence. (Greven 1977, 27)

John Wesley, a century and a half later, warned mothers:

> Your mother, or your husband's mother, may live with you; and you will do well to shew her all possible respect. But let her on no account have the least share in the management of your children. She would undo all that you have done; she would give them their own will in all things. She would humour them to the destruction of their souls, if not their bodies, too.

He added:

> In four-score years, I have not met with one woman that knew how to manage grand-children. My own mother who governed her children so well, could never govern one grand-child. In every other point obey your mother. Give up your will to her's. But with regard to the management of your children, steadily keep the reins in your own hands. (Greven 1977, 27).

References to grandparents in two *Good Housekeeping* volumes from the 1880s and two from the 1970s, were compared. In both centuries, items typically pertained to grandmothers. In the 1880s it was taken for granted that grandmothers were old. No specific age was mentioned in the majority of items, but physical descriptions provided indications that grandma had lived a long and hard life: "Silvered head, eyes grown dim with the mist of age." The grandmother of the late nineteenth century had toiled for decades and now had her "hands stilled from loving service" as a reward. She was frequently described as sitting in a chair by a fire or lamp. When grandchildren were mentioned, they tended to be very young. Seldom was the 1880s grandmother described as dealing with the nitty-gritty aspects of everyday family life. The frail figure by the fire was not *withdrawn* from everyday living, but was *above* it. She had a place on a pedestal, and she had earned it.

The 1970s grandmother presented different images. It was difficult to find any themes in these descriptions. There was no ready replacement for the weary, quiet figure by the 1880s fire. No uniform, consistent picture of grandma emerged. It appeared that there were as many styles of grandmothers as there were grandchildren. Grandmothers' ages ranged from the fifties to past one hundred. Grandchildren ranged from toddlers to adults. Also, there appeared to be a new uncertainty about what it meant to be a grandmother. Members of several generations puzzled over what grandmothers were supposed to do. The magazine items from the 1880s and the 1970s are probably good mirrors of grandparenthood over the last century. Grandma is definitely not what she used to be, and simple categories and expectations cannot capture the current spectrum of grandparenting styles and grandparenting experiences (Hagestad 1985).

Grandparenting is not parenting at an older age. Whereas parenting tends to shape and alter all other parts of life, grandparenting tends to be shaped by other events going on in life. People usually make a decision to become parents and then keep making decisions about how to be parents. But no matter how much people want to be grandparents, someone else must make the decision. Many grandparents interpret grandparenting as a reflection upon the quality of their parenting.

> If their children make them grandparents too early, they must have done something wrong. If their children never make them grandparents, they must have done something wrong. If their children do not raise their grandchildren as they—the grandparents—would have wished, they—the grandparents—must have done something wrong. (Troll 1985, 135)

Few grandparents wish to return to parenting with their grandchildren, but they do remain alert to what goes on. If all is well, they prefer to remain formal and distant or indulgent grandparents, visiting their children and grandchildren as one part of their regular life activities but otherwise enjoying their own life. It is more interesting to be with peers, who are likely to share more recreational interests, than to help out with needy children who remind them of their lack of success in parenting. If there is trouble, however, they may have to give up much of their personal, nonfamily life to meet the needs of their family (Troll 1983).

Grandparents could best be viewed as the "family watchdogs." Grandparenting is generally a secondary activity in most grandparents' lives unless they have reason to believe that their values are not being handed down, or unless trouble in the lives of their children leads them to pitch in and help. Thus, those older people who are the most involved with their families have the lowest morale; finding your children and grandchildren in trouble does not make for happiness. It is much more fun to do your own, new thing and be with your own friends than to repeat earlier behaviors, no matter how enjoyable they were the first time around (Troll 1985).

Grandparenting is a process shaped by the synchrony of its timing with previous expectations and other ongoing life processes. Physical, psychological, and social development determine its meaning and behaviors. Marital, filial, and parental status and events may shape grandparenting, as may employment or social involvement. Healthy, vigorous, and intelligent grandparents probably interact with their grandchildren quite differently from physically weak or mentally confused grandparents. Married or employed grandparents may be different from those who are widowed or retired (Troll 1985). Older grandparents tend to be more formal; younger grandparents represent more the "fun seeker" enactment of the role. Older grandparents more than younger grandparents, minimize the differences between themselves and their children or grandchildren. "On-time" grandmothers (the mothers are over twenty-one) tend to welcome the birth of grandchildren and greatly facilitate the mothers' transition.

Grandparents are seen as a moderating force whose presence softens the intensity of modern family life.

On the other hand, "off-time" grandmothers (the mothers are eleven to eighteen years of age) are reluctant to accept their role and deny it in some cases (Bengston 1985).

Thomas' (1986) study considered age and sex differences in grandparenting satisfaction and in perceived grandparenting responsibilities. Her sample consisted of three age-groups: forty-five to sixty, sixty-one to sixty-nine, and seventy to ninety. She found that younger grandparents expressed greater responsibility for disciplining, caretaking, and offering child-rearing advice, regardless of the grandchildren's ages. Grandfathers in all three groups, compared to grandmothers, expressed greater responsibility for disciplining, caretaking, and offering child-rearing advice, but less satisfaction with grandparenting, regardless of the number of grandchildren or the grandchildren's ages. Grandmothers of all ages expressed high levels of satisfaction—again, regardless of the grandchildren's ages.

Current grandparents are demographic pioneers. In our society, grandparents range in age from thirty to one hundred ten, and grandchildren range from newborns to retirees. It should not be surprising to find a wide variety of grandparenting styles (Hagestad 1985).

Grandparents today are seen as a moderating force whose presence softens the intensity of modern family life. Because of reduced family size, altered expectations of goals, and a weakening of community ties, nuclear families have become increasingly intense socioemotional environments. Grandparents can deflate some of the intensity by giving the other two generations "a place to go." They may also serve as "interpreters" or mediators between the two generations. Grandparents can help make parents more understandable to their children or become arbitrators in conflicts between parents and children. Grandmothers of adolescent girls frequently serve as confidants when the girls have trouble with their parents (Hagestad 1985).

As of 1980 an estimated three quarters of Americans over the age of sixty-five were grandparents. Two key demographic changes have altered the nature of grandparenthood in our society: increased life expectancy and new rhythms in the family cycle. First, more people become grandparents than ever before. Entry into grandparent status typically occurs at mid-life, and many people spend four or more decades as grandparents. Nearly half of all grandparents will become great-grandparents. Some will also become great-great-grandparents. A growing number of women will spend a few years when they are both grandmothers and granddaughters. Second, parenthood and grandparenthood have become more distinct, both as individual life experiences and as two kinds of family status (Hagestad 1985).

For most people there are two opportunities within their own life cycle to interact with their actual grandparents: as children and as adolescents. Children tend to interpret the grandparent as a strong, foundational element in the family experience. The relationship between grandparents and grandchildren represents a link that bonds the family longitudinally. Continuity and a sense of belonging are symbolized by the grandparent-grandchild relationship. It may not be as important for grandparents and grandchildren to actually be in communication with each other as to have been in communication with each other at one time, so that symbolically memories and experiences can be recalled, relived, and reused throughout the life cycle (McCready 1985).

Grandmothers and grandfathers assume different roles. Grandfathers emphasize task-oriented involvements in spheres outside the family. Grandmothers

Nearly half of all grandparents will become great-grandparents and some will become great-great-grandparents. A growing number of women will spend a few years when they are both grandmothers and granddaughters.

emphasize interpersonal dynamics and quality of ties in the family. Grandfathers are seen as "ambassadors" or "foreign ministers," while grandmothers are seen as "ministers of the interior." Contact and exchanges between generations to a large extent are facilitated and carried out by women, that is, the **kin-keepers.** Women bring families together. They organize get-togethers, remember birthdays, write Christmas cards. Women are also "family monitors" and, more than men, observe the course of relationships and register changes in them. The closest grandparent-grandchild relationship is between maternal grandmothers and granddaughters. Young adults are closer to maternal than to paternal grandparents. Warm and emotionally complex relationships are more common among maternal grandparents and grandchildren than among paternal grandparents and grandchildren. This strongly suggests that the quality of bonds between grandparents and grandchildren reflects the work of a kin-keeper in the middle generation—a mother. Women in different generations, as compared with the men, can more easily see the core of continuity in key life roles. Even though more and more women are active in nonfamily spheres, they are not relinquishing their position as minister of the interior, focusing strongly on the inner familial world and its workings. Overall, grandmothers cover a wider spectrum of influence than grandfathers in their conversations with grandchildren. Like the grandfathers, they talk with grandchildren about practical issues of adult life in society, but they add concerns about friendships and family relations. Grandmothers also distinguish less between grandsons and grand-

Kin-keepers
Women who maintain contact and exchanges between generations.

Closer links have been observed with grandparents' same-sexed grandchildren. For grandfathers, the widest spectrum of influence is reported in families where the grandchild is the son of a son. Among grandmothers, the most involvement appears to be with daughters of daughters.

daughters than do grandfathers. Grandmothers have assimilated more of the cultural changes in the roles of men and women than have grandfathers. Grandfathers see it as appropriate to influence their grandchildren regarding instrumental matters: getting an education, finding a job, dealing with money, managing life's responsibilities and challenges. They consider interpersonal issues to be outside of their domain. They have clear notions of what constitutes "man talk," and they concentrate most of their influence on grandsons. Closer links to their same-sex children and grandchildren have been observed. For example, for grandfathers, the widest spectrum of influence is reported in families where the grandchild is the son of a son. Among grandmothers, the most involvement appears to be with daughters of daughters (Hagestad 1985).

Contrasts are noted between grandmothers and grandfathers when they are asked about strain and conflict across generational lines. They tended to avoid open conflict, both saying, "We never have arguments." Younger generations are more ready to report family strain and conflict than are older generations. Race relations, social policy, and sex roles are identified as "touchy subjects" around grandpa. Trouble spots for grandma are interpersonal issues, particularly in the family realm (Hagestad 1985).

Kahana and Kahana (1975) found that children's views of and relationships with their grandparents change as they grow older. Younger children, four to five years old, value grandparents for their indulgent qualities. Eight- to nine-year-olds prefer fun-sharing, active grandparents. Eleven- to twelve-year-olds reflect distance from their grandparents.

Cherlin and Furstenberg (1985) identified three styles of grandparenting. **Detached grandparents** seem remote from all of their grandchildren. They are truly distant figures for whom intergenerational ties, by choice or by circumstance, play a small role in life. Older, with less familistic values, perhaps removed geographically or emotionally from their children, these people are grandparents only in a symbolic sense. They are recognized by kin and friends as grandparents, but they only fill slots in a genealogy. Other grandparents, however, may be detached from some but not all of their grandchildren. They

Detached grandparents
Grandparents for whom intergenerational ties, by choice or by circumstance, play a small role in life.

have adopted a strategy called "selective investment." They focus their efforts and emotions on one or more of their grandchildren who live nearby or are especially personable or in need of help. They are able to act as grandparents and to compensate for weak ties to other kin.

Passive grandparents differ from detached grandparents by regular contact. They stand ready to offer assistance when needed but otherwise are loath to interfere in rearing grandchildren. Most passive grandparents derive substantial satisfaction from relationships with their grandchildren. They best fit the popular image of the American grandparent—that is, the loving older person who sees the grandchildren fairly often, is ready to provide help in a crisis, but under normal circumstances leaves parenting strictly to the parents.

Influential grandparents are younger and more energetic. They see their grandchildren more often, are major figures in their grandchildren's lives, and tend to have a familistic value orientation. They have frequent, almost daily contact with their grandchildren, committing time, energy, and sometimes money.

Bengston (1985) identified four symbolic functions of grandparents. The first function is *"being there."* This function involves helping their families in times of trouble more by affirming their availability than by any specific act of intervention. "Being there" provides a potential deterrent to familial disruption. "Being there" maintains the identity of the family and provides a buffer against its mortality. The simple presence of the older generation during divorce or the transition to parenthood exudes a calming influence.

A second symbolic function is the *"Family National Guard."* Grandparents are often called upon to go beyond the passive or ready-reserve situation into the active frontline management of supporting children and forming active intergenerational relationships.

Another symbolic function is that of *arbitration.* Grandparents negotiate carefully between parents and children concerning values and behaviors that may be central, in the long run, to family continuity and individual enhancement.

The final function involves the *social construction of biography.* Grandparents play an enormous role in building reasonable connections between our past, present, and future. The oldest generation has the greatest stake in the grandchild's continuity with the past.

Grandparenting is a tenuous role, a social status without clear normative expectations attached to it. Our society is not clear as to what the rights and obligations of grandparents are. Because of congressional hearings and a push for legislation, legal protection of grandparents' rights has received a great deal of publicity. During divorce, custody still goes to the mother, rather than the father, in nine cases out of ten, which means that paternal grandparents are more likely to have problems gaining access to their grandchildren (Matthews and Sprey 1984). Patterns of remarriage and family reconstitution add more challenges. The majority of divorced people remarry within three years. Many remarriages result in some form of "blended family." A growing number of children spend part of their childhood living with a stepparent and stepsiblings or half siblings. This could perhaps provide the children with opportunities for enriched intergenerational ties with multiple sets of grandparents (Hagestad 1985). For grandparents, there are ambiguities in relating to grandchildren with whom they have no blood ties.

Among children whose divorced mothers remarried in the 1970s, close to 50 percent will experience the mothers' second divorce. There will be no legal

Passive grandparents
Grandparents who have regular contact with their grandchildren and are ready to offer assistance when needed but refuse to interfere in rearing them.

Influential grandparents
Grandparents who see their grandchildren often, are major figures in their grandchildren's lives, and tend to have a familistic value orientation.

protection for the stepparents and stepgrandparents. These individuals will have had the experience of spending a great deal of effort on making step-relationships work, only to find them dissolved (Hagestad 1985).

Because of factors such as women's role as kin-keepers, trends in custody arrangements, and sex differences in remarriage patterns, one could make two predictions about grandparent-grandchild relations in the future: First, the most vulnerable bond will be between the paternal grandfather and the grandson. Second, our society will become increasingly matrilineal in its patterns of intergenerational continuity (Hagestad 1985).

Friendship

Friendships are important to the psychological as well as the social well-being of the elderly. Through friendships, they find the companionship, acceptance, and support that is necessary for a healthy self-concept. In many ways the patterns of friendship in the elderly are similar to patterns observed in mid-life adults. Evidence indicates that contacts with friends are more frequent among seniors of high socioeconomic status. Older people from the working class are more dependent on the neighborhood as a source of friends than are those from the middle class (Dickens and Perlman 1981). The middle class is more likely than the lower, or working, class to draw friendships from a wider circle. Their friends also may be considerably younger than they are (Reisman 1981).

Friendships contribute more to morale than do relations with kin. Blau (1981) suggested that friendships help individuals sustain a sense of usefulness and self-esteem more effectively than relationships with their children, because friendships are based on mutual needs and involve a voluntary exchange of sociability between equals. At the end of the life cycle, contact with children may be a consequence of poor health and other needs (Dickens and Perlman 1981).

There are several problems faced by the elderly in forming or maintaining friendships. One problem is retirement from paid work. Working with others at a similar level was a useful source of friendships (Chown 1981). Illness is a problem that hampers maintaining friendships. Chronic conditions associated with old age, such as rheumatism, bronchitis, and arthritis, result in lessened physical mobility. Lowered ability to use public transport and the decreased likelihood of driving a private car also result in lessened mobility. Less-specific ill health depletes general energy, so just the chores of living take a greater proportion of time and leave a person unwilling or too tired to face "social" relaxation. When hearing losses occur, it makes social interaction difficult and reduces the pleasure of social occasions. As physical capabilities decrease, the elderly individual is likely to change living quarters, which in turn may increase the physical distance from existing friends without providing opportunities to meet new people. Even if the elderly individual stays in the same home, his or her friends may move (Chown 1981).

One important function of friendship is assistance. Friends often call upon one another for instrumental as well as emotional support. However, friends may find that the "costs" of helping elderly friends are so great that they withdraw from the friendships. Or an elderly person may feel so "in debt" to someone for help received that ending the friendship may be preferable to the discomfort of the debt (Chown 1981). Roberto and Scott (1986) found that older individuals with equitable friendships reported less distress with their relationships than those who perceived their friendships as inequitable. They also found that overbenefited individuals felt angrier than underbenefited individuals and those in an equitable relationship. The inability to reciprocate can undermine an individual's sense of independence and self-worth. The realization that one is less capable of doing for oneself than in previous years can be stressful to an elderly adult.

Friendships and social interaction go with high morale and satisfaction with life. When people become socially isolated, they become depressed. Having a confidant is of central importance in old age. It allows people to withstand much better the crises they have to face. A confidant is usually a sister, a daughter, or a friend of the same age and sex as the older person (Chown 1981). The more older people's social life is exclusively with their children, the lower their morale. Socializing with friends is much better for them (Troll 1983).

Religion

In the past, research on the religion and religious behavior of the elderly concluded that there was a decline in the religiousness of older people (Orbach 1961; Wingrove and Alston 1974). These conclusions were based on a too-narrow conceptualization of religion in terms of participation in an organized religion. Mindel and Vaughan (1978) argued that by focusing attention on the nonorganizational aspects of elderly people's religious participation (such as prayer, Bible reading, private devotion, and listening to religious radio programs), it becomes readily apparent that "religion is still a salient factor in their lives as they understand it, despite the lack of participation in its formally organized forms" (p. 108). Ainlay and Smith (1984) also found that private, nonorganizational participation is important for the religious lives of the aged. For the elderly, the form or level of participation in an organized religion may change while leaving a strong psychological relationship within the life of the individual.

Hunsberger (1985) found a tendency toward increased religiosity in older people. However, he also found that while highly religious persons reported an increase in religiousness during old age, those who had always been low in religiosity reported a decrease. The mothers of the elderly were reported to have had the strongest proreligious influence, although both parents were generally perceived to be important influences in religious development. Hunsberger found a positive relationship between religiosity and life satisfaction.

In summary, the religious activities of individuals do not cease with advancing age. Religious practices apparently become more determinate with age. As people proceed through late life, their age becomes increasingly influential on their nonorganizational and organizational activities in the church, as well as their attitudes toward participation. Limitation in physical mobility makes an impact on religious behavior.

Retirement

Retirement is one of the most important events for older workers. Clearly, it affects the way the elderly spend their time, the amount of their income, and who they interact with. It has also been assumed that it affects their physical and mental health, self-esteem, happiness, and life satisfaction. People who continue to work well into their old age nearly always score high on inventories inquiring into morale, happiness, and adjustment (Chown 1977). In 1981, the median age of retirement for males was 64.3 years, and for females, 62.9 years (Harris et al. 1981).

Two major theories address the effects of retirement on the retiree: the *crisis theory* and the *continuity theory*. The **crisis theory** assumes that retirement has negative and degrading effects because occupational identity is the basic legitimizing role for people in our society. Loss of this role through retirement implies inability to perform, which reduces self-respect and status, which leads to further withdrawal from social participation, which leads to isolation, illness, and decline in happiness and life satisfaction. The **continuity theory** assumes that occupational identity is not the central role for many workers. Retirement is seen as a legitimate and desirable role with opportunities for the continuation of other roles and the development of new leisure roles, providing a continuation of self-esteem and status. This theory sees no long-term negative effects of retirement (Palmore et al. 1984).

Both of these theories are seen as being too general and too sweeping. The crisis theory mistakenly assumes that occupational identity is necessarily the central and legitimizing role in our society. Many workers see their job as primarily a means of earning a living so they can carry out the roles more important to them. Retirement does not necessarily mean the inability to perform; in fact, many people retire voluntarily to take advantage of leisure opportunities. Our society now sees retirement as a respectable and desirable position. The continuity theory, on the other hand, does not recognize that retirement may have significant negative effects for some workers in some situations. Almost all retirees experience a reduction in income. Many are forced to retire early or before they wish because of disability or mandatory retirement. These retirees may experience severe negative effects (Palmore et al. 1984).

The Harris poll (1981) found that adults nationwide (90 percent) agree that "nobody should be forced to retire because of age, if he wants to continue working and is still able to do a good job." At the same time, however, nearly eight in ten believe that "most employers discriminate against older people and make it difficult for them to find work." Most working Americans in all age-groups do not look forward to retirement, and nearly half of the retired Americans (46 percent) say they did not look forward to their retirement. Most retired Americans (62 percent) say they retired by choice. However, nearly four in ten (37 percent) say they were forced to retire because of poor health or disability. Over 90 percent of retired adults who looked forward to retiring feel they retired at the right time. When the time comes to retire, most of the people who are presently working would like to be given the option of working part-time instead of retiring completely. This appeals to a large extent to all age-groups. Among those who want to continue working part-time, the age-group of fifty-five and older would prefer to stay with the same kind of job they are presently in. Younger adults would be more interested in a part-time job that is different from their present job.

The retirement process involves three major periods: *preretirement, retirement transition,* and *postretirement.* **Preretirement** involves looking ahead to retirement, to what life in retirement will be like. Decisions about whether one will retire—and if so, when—are made during this time. **Retirement transition** involves leaving the job and taking on the role of a retired person. **Postretirement** is life without a job, plus factors such as health, activity level, and perhaps having to live alone (Atchley 1982). Emotional support and acceptance of retirement by an elderly individual's family are important elements in his or her adjusting to retirement. Through the family, the retired individual can obtain status, high morale, and feelings of usefulness (Chown 1977).

All in all, both men and women typically adjust well to the retirement transition. Some retirees are active and organized, substituting nonwork activities for work activities, while others choose to become "rocking chair" types. For the most part, people maintain their previous levels of social activity (Hooyman and Kiyak 1988). The best predictors of positive adjustment to retirement are good health and adequate income, while the recent death of a spouse is the most significant negative predictor.

Older women are a heterogeneous subgroup in the labor market. Women enter the labor market at various stages of the life cycle. This heterogeneous subgroup includes the woman who has devoted most of her life to a paid work career, the woman who has left the workplace at different times and later returned, and the "displaced homemaker" who is seeking work for the first time in her later years (Paul 1984). Older women are now active in various roles. Two-fifths, or 44.1 percent, of women fifty-five to sixty-four years are in the labor force. Some have children still at home or elderly parents needing assistance (Aldous 1985).

There are different factors that contribute to the variation in ages at which mature workers retire. These factors differ for older males and older females. Older men who prefer to continue to work have an expectation of adequate retirement income, high employment wages, good health, and high occupational status. Essentially, high preretirement income, adequate retirement income, and good health are most often correlated with the high occupational status of men who prefer to delay retirement. Higher occupational status and better wages correspond with reluctance to retire. Between the ages of sixty and sixty-five, men are more likely to leave the work force if their health declines and retirement income becomes available. That is, males of this age who are in poor health and who believe that they can afford to retire are more likely to leave the work force than any other group of older workers.

Factors that encourage continued work among older women are not the same as those that encourage continued work among older men. The decision to continue employment is more complex for older women, since many have entered and exited the work force several times during their life course. Generally, the availability of Social Security income and employer pension eligibility do not decrease their participation in the labor force, as is the case with older men. However, women, like men, are more likely to stay in the work force when they receive higher wages. Dependent parents in the home lower the likelihood of their staying in the labor force. Recently, it has been noted that the decision to postpone retirement and continue working is made jointly among dual-career couples. Therefore, one spouse in the work force increases the probability of participation of the other spouse, especially in the case of the male. Essentially, the variables affecting the decision to extend the work life in two-earner households appear to differ from those operating in the traditional one-earner family. As the number of dual-career families increases, it is possible that the labor force participation of older males and females will not decline as rapidly with age as is presently the case (Paul 1984).

Atchley (1982) compared women to men concerning the process of retirement. He found that women were more likely than men to say they did not plan to retire. Men and women were quite similar in terms of their attitudes toward work and retirement and the average age at which they planned to retire. But the

Elder Abuse

Elder abuse and neglect has been identified as a major social and individual problem. *Elder abuse* has been defined as "those actions that have negative or harmful consequences on the psychological, physical, or financial conditions of the elderly"; and *elder neglect* has been defined as "the failure to meet important physical, social, and emotional needs of older people" (O'Malley et al. 1983, 998).

Abuse of the elderly is one of the most tragic outcomes of caring for the elderly. Seventy-five percent of the elderly who are abused live with the abuser, and in over 80 percent of the reports the abuser is a relative (Steinmetz and Amsden 1983; Pillemer 1986; Pillemer and Finkelhor 1988; Paveza 1987). Early evidence (Steinmetz and Amsden 1983; Stever and Austin 1980) indicated that the overwhelming majority of the caregivers (90 percent) and the vulnerable elderly (over 82 percent) were women and that frail, dependent elderly women were the most likely to be abused by adult children. However, more recent evidence (Pillemer 1986; Pillemer and Finkelhor 1988; Paveza 1987) indicates that abuse of males occurs more frequently than abuse of females. It also shows that spouses are more likely to abuse spouses than adult children are to abuse parents.

Although violence on elders has been sensationalized in the media, violence by elders on their adult children or caregivers has remained hidden. This type of violence is more likely to occur when the elderly individual is demented and lacks impulse control (Steinmetz and Amsden 1983; Pillemer and Finkelhor 1988).

The tasks required in caring for an elder, the stress resulting from the dependence of the elder, and an overall sense of burden interact to increase the likelihood of abusive and disruptive family interaction. Other factors that can increase stress are physical health problems of the elder, unresolved conflicts that began between parents and children during the adolescent years, elder-caregiver conflicts over power, and as mentioned earlier, shared family residence (Gold and Gwyther 1989). Depletion of family resources, especially in cases of shared family residence, with added financial and emotional burdens can ignite violent behavior (Kosberg and Cairl 1986; Brody 1981).

The lack of hands-on experience for dealing with an elder who may need to be fed, restrained, or medicated against his or her will may also result in abuse. Families need to understand the developmental characteristics of aging and accurately assess the limits of their ability to

TABLE 18.1 Perpetrator-Victim Relationship (Including Proxy respondents, unweighted data)

	ALL TYPES★	PHYSICAL VIOLENCE	CHRONIC VERBAL AGGRESSION	NEGLECT
HUSBAND TO WIFE	14 (22%)	7 (17%)	7 (27%)	2 (29%)
WIFE TO HUSBAND	23 (36%)	17 (43%)	7 (27%)	—
SON TO MOTHER	5 (8%)	4 (10%)	2 (8%)	—
SON TO FATHER	5 (8%)	3 (7%)	3 (11%)	—
DAUGHTER TO MOTHER	4 (6%)	1 (3%)	2 (8%)	2 (29%)
DAUGHTER TO FATHER	1 (2%)	1 (3%)	—	—
OTHER	11 (18%)	7 (17%)	5 (19%)	3 (42%)
TOTAL	63	40	26	7

★The total number of cases in specific categories exceeds the All Types category, because more than one type of abuse was sometimes present.

Source: K. Pillemar and D. Finkelhor, The Prevalence of Elder Abuse: A Random Sample Survey, *The Gerontologist*, vol. 28, No. 1, February 1988, 51–57.

Elder Abuse (Continued)

provide care. Other abuse-prevention approaches include teaching older individuals and their family members how to cope with common sources of stress and conflict, how to effectively communicate with each other, and how to use family and community resources (Gold and Gwyther 1989).

There is a point when even the most loving child has difficulty dealing with the personal grooming, physical, social-emotional, and mental health needs of an elderly parent. Support services are needed to relieve these pressures. Such services may include visiting nurses, geriatric

aides, friendly visitor and respite programs. Support services can relieve the family of daily tasks, or relieve the frustration and stress caregivers feel from performing these tasks, and thus enhance the caregiver-elder interaction. They also provide positive role models for future generations (Steinmetz and Amsden 1983).

Why do you think elderly victims of abuse refuse to acknowledge they are being abused? What are some ways of preventing elder abuse? What options are available to the elderly if they are abused?

TABLE 18.2 Rates (Per Thousand) of Elder Abuse by Characteristics of Victim

	ALL TYPES	PHYSICAL VIOLENCE	VERBAL AGGRESSION	NEGLECT
MALE	51★	37★	21	1
FEMALE	23★	13★	9	5
MARRIED	49★	32	19	4
WIDOWED	22★	16	9	3
DIVORCED	28★	25	18	9
NEVER MARRIED	7★	25	—	—
LIVE ALONE	15★★	7★	6	5
SPOUSE ONLY	41★★	33★	19	2
CHILD ONLY	44★★	25★	18	4
SPOUSE AND CHILD	67★★	42★	23	11
OTHER	16★★	16★	—	—
HEALTH				
EXCELLENT	17★	12	5	—
GOOD	31★	24	13	—
FAIR	36★	18	12	8★★★
POOR	77★	47	30	22★★★
NO HELPER	35	—	9	26★★
HELPER	33	23	14	2★★

★ = .01   ★★ = .001   ★★★ = .0001

Source: K. Pillemer and D. Finkelhor, The Prevalence of Elder Abuse: A Random Sample Survey, *The Gerontologist,* vol. 28, No. 1, February 1988, 51–57.

dynamics of planned retirement were different for women. Among the women who planned to retire early were upper-status married women in good health who looked forward to retirement. Those who planned to retire late had lower status, tended to be unmarried, and had a less positive view of retirement. Negative economic factors seemed to play a strong part in a woman's decision to retire later. Among men, retirement was more likely to occur at or near the traditional age of sixty-five rather than earlier or later. Those who planned to retire later (only about 6 percent) were motivated more by positive attitudes toward retirement than by negative economic factors.

In retirement, women were significantly more positive toward retirement than men were, although both sexes were quite positive. Both sexes were quite active in retirement. Health was a major determinant of activity level. Life satisfaction was high and showed no gender difference. Life satisfaction was influenced by activity level for both sexes. Women's high life satisfaction was related to good health and older age, while men's depended on income adequacy and having many goals. Retirement was very positive for the vast majority of people in this study.

In a similar study of 179 retired professional women, Block (1982) also found that resources such as health and income were prerequisites for successful adaptation to retirement. For professional women, retirement planning played an important role in subsequent adjustment to retirement transition.

Keith (1985) conducted a longitudinal study that investigated factors associated with evaluations of work, retirement, and well-being by 1,398 never-married, widowed, and divorced/separated men and women. Formerly married women identified work as less important than men did, while never-married women were as committed to work as their male counterparts. Those who assigned great importance to work were not less happy. Divorced/separated men and women were the most economically disadvantaged, so employment may have been a financial necessity for them. Although health was important to all of the groups, it was particularly salient to the never-married. Health may be especially important to maintain independent living by the never-married because they have fewer family ties than the formerly married. Widowed and divorced/separated women seemed especially vulnerable compared to never-married women. Formerly married women were somewhat less happy with their lives and also held more negative attitudes toward retirement than never-married women. Never-married women enjoyed retirement and indicated greater happiness with retirement than formerly married women. Never-married women had more sustained work histories than formerly married women, and their career fatigue paralleled that of men, thus contributing to their approval of retirement. Never-married women had better economic circumstances at retirement than did widowed and divorced/separated women. The never-married status was less consequential for the retirement attitudes and well-being of men than of women. Generally, attitudes associated with work, retirement, and happiness were fairly similar across the three marital statuses. Attitudes toward work and retirement were independent of socioeconomic circumstances, which contradicted other studies (Foner and Schwab 1981) that found that higher income was positively correlated with adjustment to retirement.

As mentioned earlier, most retirees are satisfied with their lives and adjust well to this important transition. In sum, those with good health, higher-status jobs, adequate incomes, social networks, and leisure interests are more likely to be satisfied.

A major new study of older workers concludes that they not only earn their keep, but they also do a better job than their younger counterparts.

The study, commissioned by the Commonwealth Fund, a non-profit philanthropic organization, found that older workers are flexible in accepting work assignments, that they master new technologies as quickly as younger people and that they often are better sales people. In addition, they score higher than their juniors in two important categories that directly affect business costs:

- Older workers have lower turnover and absenteeism rates—they don't switch jobs as frequently.
- They're more likely to show up when scheduled to work.

In releasing the study, Thomas W. Moloney, senior vice president of the Commonwealth Fund, noted, "This study for the first time provides numerical results from real companies that have hired older workers. The bottom line speaks for itself. The case studies prove that hiring older people makes good business sense."

But even this proof may not be enough, say experts.

"Managerial stereotypes still exist as well as employer concerns with the cost of employing older workers," says Robert C. Levin, director of the Institute on Aging, Work and Health, a Washington, D.C., research group.

AARP labor economist Judy Hushbeck agrees, "Sure, there's real world evidence that elders make good workers," she says. "There also are laws against discriminating against them. But attitudes are hard to change."

The Commonwealth Fund commissioned ICF Inc., a Washington consulting firm that specializes in labor studies, to compare older and younger workers at Days Inns of America, Inc.; The Travelers Corp.; and B & Q, the largest do-it-yourself home-improvement firm in Great Britain.

Days Inns records show that it takes younger and older workers the same amount of time—two weeks—to be trained on the sophisticated computer equipment, but that older workers stay with Days Inns longer, thereby cutting overall training and recruiting costs.

Further, according to the study, while older workers in Days Inns' two reservations centers take longer to handle each telephone call, they also book more reservations than younger employees. And, company records also show they're flexible in accepting work assignments.

Similar success stories were found at Travelers, an insurance firm that established a job bank for its retirees 10 years ago.

At the British retail chain, B & Q, management staffed an entire store with workers 50 and older in 1988 to test the seniors' potential. The store was 18 percent more profitable than average when compared to five other B & Q stores, employee turnover was six times lower, there was less absenteeism and the store's inventory suffered less "leakage," i.e., damage and theft.

"In no instance were these companies motivated by compassion or social justice," said Maloney. "They were motivated by profitability and the availability of skilled workers."

Source: *AARP Bulletin,* July–August 1991, Vol. XXXII, No. 7.

- Erikson's final stage of development is ego integrity versus despair. Those who look back on their lives and feel satisfied have a sense of integrity, while those who look back and see nothing but a succession of missed opportunities and wrong decisions feel despair.
- There are two general points of view regarding optimum patterns of aging. The activity theory implies that except for the inevitable changes in biology and in health, older people are the same as middle-aged people, with the same psychological and social needs. The disengagement theory argues that both society and the aging person mutually withdraw, with the aging individual accepting and perhaps desiring decreased interaction. Neither theory seems adequate.
- Four major personality patterns have been identified among the elderly: integrated, defended, passive-dependent, and disintegrated. These four patterns are

SUMMARY

further divided according to role activity and life satisfaction, yielding eight patterns altogether.

- Men and women appear to differ in the way aging affects them. Men move from an active to a passive style, while women move from a passive to an active style.
- Aging is a highly individualized process. Some old people manage poorly, some manage well. The major factor in this variation is the extent of the actual deterioration of the elderly individual's life circumstances.
- Many of the elderly engage in an evaluative backward glance at their life and weigh their accomplishments and failures, their satisfactions and disappointments. This process is called life review.
- Ageism is a form of discrimination against the elderly. It can make a negative impact on their emotional well-being and social interaction.
- An individual's social network includes those people who provide social support. Networks vary according to socioeconomic status, level of education, whether a person lives in an urban or a rural setting, marital status, and so on. Social networks include children, spouses, siblings, grandchildren, and friends.
- The frail elderly present a special burden to the family. The family can care for a frail elderly individual in a home setting, or use an institutional setting such as a nursing home or a geriatric foster-care facility. There are positive and negative factors in either option.
- Grandparenthood is a social status without clear normative expectations attached to it. Grandmothers and grandfathers assume different roles. Three styles of grandparenting have been identified: detached, passive, and influential.
- Friendship patterns among the elderly are similar to friendship patterns observed among mid-life adults. However, many environmental factors hamper the maintenance of friendships in later adulthood.
- For the elderly, the form or level of participation in an organized religion may change, while leaving a strong psychological relationship within the life of the individual.
- Retirement is one of the most important events for older workers. It affects the way they spend their time, the amount of their income, and with who they interact. Two major theories address the effects of retirement on the retiree: the crisis and continuity theories. The best predictors of positive adjustment to retirement are good health and adequate income.
- Elder abuse and neglect has been identified as a major social and individual problem. Most of the elderly who are abused live with the abuser. Recent data indicate that abuse of males is more frequent than abuse of females. Also, spouses are more likely to abuse spouses than adult children are to abuse parents.

R E A D I N G S

Binstock, R.H. and Shanas, E. (1985). *Handbook of aging and the social sciences.* New York: Van Nostrand.
Review of social science research concerning social aspects of aging, social systems, social interventions, and social structures.

Brubaker, T.H. (1985). *Later life families.* Beverly Hills, CA: Sage.
Complete and detailed description of families from middle age and beyond.

Michaels, J. (1983). *Prime of your life: A practical guide to your mature years.* Boston: Little, Brown.
Practical information concerning finances, health, and leisure time for the elderly.

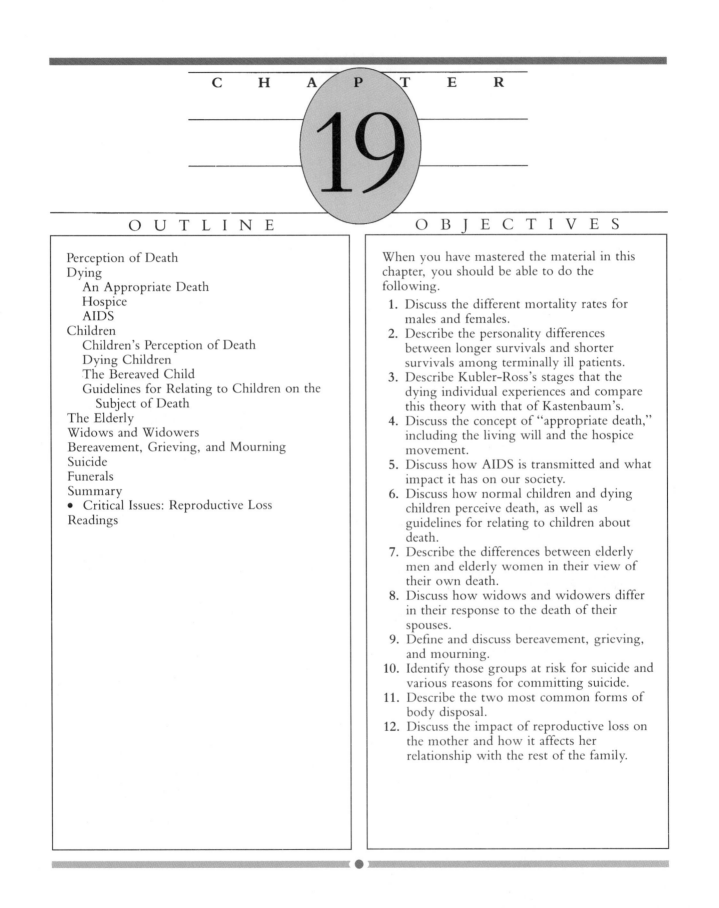

C H A P T E R

19

O U T L I N E

Perception of Death
Dying
   An Appropriate Death
   Hospice
   AIDS
Children
   Children's Perception of Death
   Dying Children
   The Bereaved Child
   Guidelines for Relating to Children on the
     Subject of Death
The Elderly
Widows and Widowers
Bereavement, Grieving, and Mourning
Suicide
Funerals
Summary
• Critical Issues: Reproductive Loss
Readings

O B J E C T I V E S

When you have mastered the material in this chapter, you should be able to do the following.

1. Discuss the different mortality rates for males and females.
2. Describe the personality differences between longer survivals and shorter survivals among terminally ill patients.
3. Describe Kubler-Ross's stages that the dying individual experiences and compare this theory with that of Kastenbaum's.
4. Discuss the concept of "appropriate death," including the living will and the hospice movement.
5. Discuss how AIDS is transmitted and what impact it has on our society.
6. Discuss how normal children and dying children perceive death, as well as guidelines for relating to children about death.
7. Describe the differences between elderly men and elderly women in their view of their own death.
8. Discuss how widows and widowers differ in their response to the death of their spouses.
9. Define and discuss bereavement, grieving, and mourning.
10. Identify those groups at risk for suicide and various reasons for committing suicide.
11. Describe the two most common forms of body disposal.
12. Discuss the impact of reproductive loss on the mother and how it affects her relationship with the rest of the family.

Dying and Death: The Final Stage of Life

PERCEPTION OF DEATH

Human beings are the only living creatures that can contemplate and thus plan for their own deaths. Death awareness comes from directly or indirectly experiencing others' deaths. Becoming an adult does not guarantee an appreciation of one's own mortality. Evading the topic is common. It is easier to believe and accept the general proposition that humans are mortal without seeing the personal implications. Not only do we as individuals differentiate ourselves from those who are dying, but we tend to control our own anxieties through personal denial and expect unrealistic responses from the terminally ill. There is also a tendency to deny a death threat to one's own body even when the symptoms are unmistakable (Kastenbaum 1986).

Males and females have different mortality rates and life expectancies. In fact, the differences are systematic throughout the life span. Males at every age level have greater odds against continued survival. Only one female in two thousand will die between the fifteenth and sixteenth birthdays, as compared with one male in one thousand. Also, a female at this age has an average life expectation of at least sixty-one more years, as compared with fifty-four more years for the male. Females maintain about a seven-year advantage in average life expectation (Kastenbaum 1986).

DYING

A **mutual pretense,** in which both the dying person and those relating to the dying person pretend they do not know the prognosis, serves to isolate the parties from each other, since neither can then discuss what is uppermost in their mind (Kubler-Ross 1969).

The terminally ill people who function most successfully are those who previously showed high coping skills, high life satisfaction, and good marital relationships (Kalish 1985). Weisman and Worden (1975), in a study involving terminally ill cancer patients, found that interpersonal relationships affected the patients' length of survival. They found that patients who maintained active and mutually responsive relationships survived longer than those who brought poor social relationships with them into the terminal stage of life. Weisman and Worden developed a composite profile of longer survivals and shorter survivals. The longer survivals had good relationships with others and managed to preserve a reasonable degree of intimacy with family and friends until the end. They asked for and received much medical and emotional support. As a rule, they accepted the reality of serious illness but did not believe death was inevitable. At times they denied the gravity of the illness or seemed to repudiate the fact that they were becoming more feeble. They were seldom deeply depressed, but they did voice resentment about various aspects of their treatment and illness. When anger was displayed, it did not alienate others but commanded their attention. The longer survivals were afraid of dying alone or untended, so they refused to let others pull away without taking care of their needs.

The shorter survivals reported poor social relationships, starting with separation from their family of origin early in life. Some of them had psychiatric disorders including depression. They also talked about repeated mutually destructive relationships with people over the years. When treatment failed, their depression deepened, and they became highly pessimistic about their progress.

Mutual pretense
A context in which both the dying person and those relating to the dying person pretend they do not know the prognosis.

They had considered suicide at times. They wanted to die, which reflected more conflict with reality than acceptance of it.

Those who say they want a sudden and/or unexpected death probably wish to avoid physical pain and suffering, as well as emotional stresses for themselves and their survivors. However, an unexpected death can be very difficult for survivors. They did not get the opportunity to prepare, and the deceased person did not get his or her affairs in order, or try to finish important projects, or participate in the grieving process with loved ones. A sudden and unexpected death has less impact on the survivors of an elderly person, in which case rehearsal for death has probably been in process for some time and preparations for death are probably already made (Sanders 1982–83).

Kubler-Ross (1969, 1975), a well-known authority on death and dying, established a model in which the dying person experiences five stages, which begin when the individual is aware of the poor prognosis. These stages should be perceived more as normal emotional responses to the prospect of death and the miseries associated with dying. They are experienced differently by each individual depending on his or her particular illness, age, sex, personality, religious orientation, and situation. Not all of them will necessarily appear, nor will they occur in a particular order. The stages are denial, anger, bargaining, depression, and acceptance.

Denial is a temporary defense. "No, not me! It cannot be true!" is the typical response. *Anger* boils up after the initial shock, when the denial response has passed. "Why me?" There is a feeling that someone must be blamed for this overwhelming disaster. It is common for the patient to become difficult to deal with during this time. In *bargaining* the individual tries to make some kind of deal with fate. The bargaining process may be between the patient and his or her family, caregivers, and friends, or it may be between the patient and God. *Depression* begins to occur as the individual begins to weaken, feel some discomfort, and experience physical deterioration. As the symptoms become too obvious to ignore, strain and stress take their toll. Feelings of guilt and unworthiness, the explicit fear of dying, and a loosening of relationships occur during this stage. The thoughts and feelings of the dying individual are dominated by a great sense of loss. The final stage, *acceptance,* allows the patient to let go. The depression lifts during this period. This does not mean that acceptance is a happy or blissful stage; it is more of a state of detachment from people and things formerly valued. It is a quiet expectation of the next step to come. Many people do not experience acceptance but may stop at any one stage on the way. Each individual may have a different tempo or rate of movement through the stages. Kubler-Ross notes that the stages will not necessarily appear in the order listed.

Kastenbaum (1986) questions Kubler-Ross's stage theory approach, although he acknowledges that it is valuable not only for specific observations and insights made along the way, but also because it proposes that there might be some basic, universal modes of adaptation to terminal illness. He notes that other variables should be taken into consideration when discussing dying in terms of stages. For example, he believes that the specific disease and treatment must be taken into account. When ignoring the symptoms and *trajectory* (that is, the physical, social and emotional progression) of a particular life-threatening illness, it is easy to develop an unrealistic view of the dying process. Differences and similarities in the dying experience are related to age and personality, as well as to the types of pain, discomfort, or disfiguration associated with a particular illness and its treatment. Also, even if an individual experiences some feelings in common with another dying person, he or she does so within a unique pattern of life and environment that no other person has experienced.

An Appropriate Death

In recent years, there has been a movement in our society that supports letting each person die an **appropriate death,** which means permitting each individual the opportunity to die as he or she wishes to die, at least to the extent that this is possible. According to Kalish (1985), three factors are necessary in allowing people to die an appropriate death, assuming their health and cognitive condition permit:

1. a warm and intimate personal relationship, preferably with a family member or friend, but if necessary, with a caregiver
2. an open-awareness context, in which the dying person and people within the social environment are aware of the prognosis and can relate to each other in terms of the terminal condition
3. a belief system that provides for meaning

The three circumstances can be integrated with one another to provide a sense of transcendence that permits the dying person to retain self-esteem and believe that his or her future and life in general have significant meaning.

An appropriate death involves the right of the individual to determine the time and conditions of his or her own deaths. Technology has increased the length of existence, but not always the quality of that existence. **Euthanasia** has become an alternative for many who are facing a prolonged painful period of dying. *Euthanasia* means "easy death" (from the Green *eu* meaning "good" or "well" and *thanatos* meaning "death"). It is the act of painlessly putting to death someone who is terminally ill. There are three types of euthanasia: *passive, active,* and *voluntary.* **Passive euthanasia** allows a person to die by withholding treatment and heroic measures. For example, a comatose patient would not be attached to a support system. **Active euthanasia** is another name for mercy killing. Another person, such as a physician, friend, or family member, actually helps the terminally ill patient die, in order to prevent long-term suffering. For example, an elderly Florida man shot and killed his wife, who was suffering from Alzheimer's disease and osteoporosis. He was convicted of murder. **Voluntary euthanasia** is the act of killing oneself or letting oneself die when there is no hope of recovering from a terminal illness. An individual may refuse food, medication, treatment, and/or the use of heroic measures such as life support systems, like a respirator. Morgan (1988), a death educator, declares that the right to refuse treatment is a constitutional right of self-determination and privacy. If there is a possibility that the individual can lead a fairly comfortable, meaningful life, then the act of refusing treatment is considered suicide. Individuals who are incapacitated physically through a stroke or advanced cancer, or are incapacitated psychologically through cognitive losses, lack the potential to perform voluntary euthanasia.

A **living will** is a document to formalize and declare an individual's wishes in specifying treatment limitations in the event of an irreversible, serious, and long-term illness. Recently the living will has become either a legally enforceable or an advisory document. The living will states conditions under which an individual, in good health and cognitively alert at the time of the signature,

Appropriate death
Permitting each individual the opportunity to die as he or she wishes to die, at least to the extent that this is possible.

Euthanasia
The act of painlessly putting to death someone who is terminally ill.

Passive euthanasia
To allow a person to die by withholding treatment and heroic measures.

Active euthanasia
Mercy killing; to actively aid in the death of a terminally ill person.

Voluntary euthanasia
The act of killing oneself or letting oneself die when there is no hope of recovering from a terminal illness.

Living will
A document to formalize and declare an individual's wishes in specifying treatment limitations in the event of an irreversible, serious, and long-term illness.

502

To my family, my physician, my lawyer and all others whom it may concern: Death is as much a reality as birth, growth and aging—it is the one certainty of life. In anticipation of decisions that may have to be made about my own dying and as an expression of my right to refuse treatment, I, _____, being of sound mind, make this statement of my wishes and instructions concerning my treatment.

Claire Angel, a Manhattan pianist, is active and healthy. Yet recently she had her lawyer draw up a living will, a signed, dated and witnessed document that allows people to state in advance their wishes regarding the use of life-sustaining procedures. Why such concern? "My life experience has prepared me to consider my own mortality," says Angel, 58, whose husband and mother are in nursing homes. "I would like to protect my children from having to make a difficult decision on my behalf."

More and more Americans are taking similar legal precautions in the hope of dying with dignity. "If you're incompetent or unconscious at the end of your life, someone will make the choice," says Fenella Rouse, executive director of the Society for the Right to Die. "If you don't want to make that decision, fine. But this is one of the ways of retaining control." Two groups, the Society for the Right to Die and Concern for Dying, both located in New York City, have distributed millions of living-will forms

over the past 20 years. Other organizations, including the National Academy of Elder Law Attorneys in Tucson, provide information on how to locate lawyers who specialize in drawing up such legal tools. In addition, many right-to-die advocates recommend the use of health-care proxies, documents authorizing another person to make medical decisions on one's behalf in the event of an incapacitating accident or illness.

Living wills usually serve two purposes: they describe what sort of physical condition is intended to trigger the document's provisions and list the types of treatment the person wishes to avoid. Experts recommend making the language as specific as possible, although there are no absolute guarantees. "You never know what a local prosecutor or doctor may do," says Giles Scofield, legal-services director of Concern for Dying. "There's no language that will always be perfect."

The main shortcoming of the living will is that it does not take effect unless a patient is terminally ill. State definitions of terminal illness vary, ranging from "imminent" death to

death within a number of months. Thus people with debilitating strokes or Alzheimer's disease or those in permanent comas are unlikely to be protected by most living-will statutes. "Many people think they will be aided in these situations, but they may not be," says Leslie Pickering Francis, a law professor at the University of Utah. "For example, Nancy Cruzan's case does not fit most states' definitions of terminal illness."

Still, living wills and health-care proxies are the best means available to enforce one's wishes. For those who choose this route, experts make the following suggestions:

- Obtain the proper forms or the help of an attorney.
- Discuss your living will and proxy with your doctor. Make sure that copies are included in your medical records.
- Be certain your living will reflects your precise wishes. Be aware of the limitations your state imposes.
- Inform your family and friends that you have signed these documents. Give copies to those most likely to be contacted in case of an emergency.
- Update the documents once a year.

requests that no medically heroic methods be used to sustain his or her existence; the request can be extended to the elimination of life-sustaining equipment and medications.

Hospice

An ongoing effort to provide care for the terminally ill patient and his or her family is the **hospice** movement. It is, in fact, a system of care for the terminally ill. The hospice movement has its base in two historical sources:

Hospice
An institution and/or organization devoted to making the lives of dying people as **dignified** and **comfortable** as possible.

1. In Europe, during the Middle Ages, tired and hungry pilgrims could rest at "hospitable places," which were like refuges or inns. The term *hospice* continued to be used in France, where it evolved to mean a shelter for people in need, including the elderly, foundlings, and incurables. During the nineteenth century, the Irish Sisters of Charity established hospices specifically for the chronically and terminally ill.
2. During the Middle Ages, the impoverished and seriously ill "were literally dying in the streets through cold and malnutrition." Sympathetic people took these unfortunate people to a place of shelter and care. This eventually led to establishing *hospitals,* with the gradual professionalization of care (Kastenbaum 1986).

Hospice was given new meaning in 1967 when Saint Christopher's Hospice was formed in London by Cicely Saunders. It was designed as a place where the dying could live out their lives as fully and comfortably as possible with loved ones around them. The goal was for the patients to be free of pain and to have a place to die with dignity (Morgan 1988).

Hospice programs have many models available today. Some are housed on wards of existing hospitals, while others are freestanding; some link into other community health services, while others have created their own autonomous care system; some have elaborate facilities, while others restrict themselves to outpatient programs and services and follow-ups on patients in whatever hospitals or other institutions they go to. Most hospices in the United States only help care for individuals in their own homes. There are approximately 1,600 organizations. Hospices are viewed more as a philosophy of health care for the terminally ill than as a specific building or facility (Morgan 1988).

In order for a patient to be eligible for care by most hospices, his or her death must be anticipated within a limited time, which is usually six to twelve months. Cancer patients make up about 80 percent of hospice patients, while individuals with AIDS, Alzheimer's, and other conditions are also served (Morgan 1988). The emphasis is placed on the total well-being of the terminally ill patient and the family. The social and physical environments of the hospice are designed for *life*. An important feature of the physical environment is flexibility and freedom, so the terminally ill patient can have the important people in his or her life nearby every step of the way. The hospice stresses comfort and hope rather than prolonging life through extraordinary means. Its environment and interpersonal system are designed to support the continuation of the individual's life-style until the very end of life (Kastenbaum 1986).

Hospice care contributes to the quality of life for terminally ill patients. A group of New Haven, Connecticut, hospice patients who were cared for at home were compared with a control group that received no hospice support. The hospice home-care patients were significantly better off in terms of anxiety, depression, and hostility, and their family members also appeared more satisfied. (Lack and Buckingham 1978). In a similar study in England, hospice patients were less anxious and less depressed than comparable hospital patients. Hospice patients approved warmly of the opportunity for open communication concerning their terminal status, and they rated the staff and treatment program higher in general than did persons dying in hospitals (Hinton 1979).

For the most part, hospices underserve the elderly in comparison to other age-groups. This is because programs usually are geared for people who are cognitively intact, who are living with someone who could provide at-home

AIDS... don't use needles

Harold Washington, Mayor, City of Chicago
Lonnie C. Edwards, MD, Commissioner of Health

Even if people infected with the AIDS virus have no symptoms, they may spread the virus to others through the sharing of IV needles. The virus can also be spread through unprotected sexual contact and transmission during pregnancy or childbirth.

care with help, and whose dying trajectory will not be long or drawn out (Kalish 1985).

AIDS

Acquired immune deficiency syndrome (AIDS), which one could say is fast becoming a modern-day "plague," was first reported in the United States in mid-1981. The Center for Disease Control (CDC 1990) estimates that 1.0 to 1.5 million people are infected by the human immunodeficiency virus (HIV). There is no cure, and it is expected to claim an increasing number of lives. At least one-third of those infected with HIV may develop AIDS within a six-year period. It is projected that by 1992, 270,000 persons will have developed AIDS, and 180,000 will have died. In 1991 alone, 54,000 persons are predicted to die with AIDS. The three major cities for AIDS cases in the United States are New York (287.7 cases per million population, or 28 percent of cases nationwide, San Francisco (254.1 per million, or 10 percent), and Los Angeles (97.6 per million, or 8 percent) (The Facts about AIDS 1987).

The AIDS virus, like other sexually transmitted diseases, is transmitted by certain behaviors. The virus, present in semen and vaginal fluid, can be passed to others by intimate sexual contact. It can also be passed to others by sharing intravenous (IV) needles contaminated with blood, and it can be transmitted from a mother to a fetus during pregnancy. All present evidence indicates that the AIDS virus is not transmitted by any form of casual, nonsexual contact (Macklin and Needle 1987).

The majority of AIDS patients die within two years of being diagnosed. AIDS is characterized by a defect in an individual's natural immunity against disease. The AIDS virus, HIV, attacks the white blood cells which help protect the body from infections. AIDS victims are vulnerable to serious illnesses that are not life-threatening to those with normally functioning immune systems. Common illnesses that are life-threatening to AIDS-infected persons are infections caused by certain bacteria, fungi, viruses, protozoa, and cancers. These illnesses are called "opportunistic." This means they take the "opportunity" to attack when natural immunity is weakened. It was the unexpected presence of such illnesses in groups of young men in 1981 that first led to the identification of AIDS.

AIDS-related complex (ARC)
Chronic symptoms, such as fever, weight loss, diarrhea, and swollen lymph nodes, found in patients infected with AIDS.

Even if people infected with the AIDS virus have no symptoms, they may spread the virus to others through unprotected sexual contact, the sharing of IV needles, and transmission during pregnancy or childbirth. Some infected persons may have chronic symptoms such as fever, weight loss, diarrhea, or swollen lymph nodes. Such symptoms are sometimes called the **AIDS-related complex (ARC).** From 200,000 to 300,000 persons exhibit ARC. In one study of persons infected with the AIDS virus, over a period of six years 30 percent developed AIDS, 22 percent developed swollen lymph nodes, 27 percent developed other chronic symptoms, and 21 percent remained free of symptoms (Macklin and Needle 1987).

When moderate damage to the immune system is caused by the AIDS virus, symptoms of chronic infection may occur and may include tiredness, fever, loss of appetite and weight, diarrhea, night sweats, skin rashes, yeast infections of the mouth, and swollen glands in the neck, armpits, or groin. Most of these symptoms are not unusual in people without the AIDS virus, and they do not usually indicate immune deficiency. However, if they persist for more than two weeks, a person should see a doctor so that the cause can be identified with certainty.

The serious opportunistic infections of AIDS are likely to occur if the damage to the immune system is substantial. Most adult victims with AIDS have had one or both of two rare diseases: a parasitic infection of the lungs known as *Pneumocystis carinii pneumonia* (PCP) or a type of cancer known as *Kaposi's sarcoma* (KS). The symptoms of PCP are similar to those of other forms of severe pneumonia, such as persistent cough, fever, and difficulty in breathing or shortness of breath. Kaposi's sarcoma is a malignant tumor arising from blood vessels in the skin or mouth or inside the body. The tumors may appear as purple, blue-violet, or brownish spots or bumps. Other opportunistic infections seen in AIDS patients include unusually severe infections with yeast (candida), cytomegalovirus, herpes virus, and various parasites. When the AIDS virus attacks the brain and nervous system, symptoms may include memory loss, indifference, loss of coordination, partial paralysis, or mental disorders. These symptoms may develop slowly over a long period of time (CDC 1990).

Children who are AIDS victims tend to have different opportunistic infections than adults. Children with AIDS experience poor growth, enlargement of the liver and spleen, and a form of pneumonia in which white blood cells (lymphocytes) are found in large numbers in the lungs. Among children, PCP is less common and KS is very rare (Macklin and Needle 1987).

Homosexual men presently make up 65 percent of all persons with AIDS. An additional 8 percent of cases occur in men who both have sex with men and use IV drugs. It is believed that the practice of anal intercourse is more likely than other forms of intercourse to transmit the AIDS virus because of the vulnerability of the rectal lining. Heterosexual couples who engage in anal intercourse are also at higher risk for AIDS than those who do not. Other sexually transmitted diseases that cause inflammation may also increase the risk of infection with the AIDS virus.

As noted earlier, the sharing of needles by IV drug users increases the risk of infection with the AIDS virus. Up to 17 percent of persons with AIDS are IV drug users. A higher proportion of these cases occur in African-Americans and Hispanics. It is more common for African-Americans and Hispanics to share needles than it is for whites (CDC 1990).

The women who transmit AIDS to their children during pregnancy either use IV drugs or have sexual contact with IV users or with men who have sex with someone who is infected. Currently there are more than five hundred documented cases of AIDS in children under age thirteen. It is estimated that three thousand more children have other serious illnesses resulting from the AIDS virus. And it is estimated that three thousand additional infected children are born each year. Eighty percent of all children with AIDS were infected during pregnancy or at the time of delivery. Another 12 percent received transfusions of infected blood before the blood supply was protected. Five percent of the children with AIDS are hemophiliacs (Macklin and Needle, 1987).

Four percent of all persons with AIDS are heterosexuals. About half of these cases involve persons from other countries (mainly Africa). In these other countries, the equal incidence of AIDS among men and women suggests heterosexual transmission. The other half of heterosexual AIDS victims consist almost exclusively of individuals who have been the sexual partners of bisexual men or IV drug users. Heterosexuals who have sexual contact with people in risk groups can set in motion a cycle of heterosexual transmission. This makes it possible for the virus to spread through all parts of society, like other sexually transmitted diseases. Recommended ways to prevent this from happening are through abstinence, monogamy, and the use of condoms (The Facts about AIDS 1987).

Individuals who abstain from sexual relations, as well as couples who are not infected with the AIDS virus and have monogamous sex, are not at risk through sexual transmission. Just as with virtually all sexually transmitted diseases, the more sex partners a person has, the greater the risk of being infected with AIDS. But for homosexuals and for those who have sex with persons who share needles, unless protection is used, even one new sex partner greatly increases the probability of infection. It has been found that the regular use of latex condoms can help prevent sexual transmission of the AIDS virus, because the virus is less likely to pass through them. The effectiveness of condoms is increased if they are used together with nonoxynol-9, a spermicide that has been shown to kill the AIDS virus. In order to provide protection, condoms must be used from start to finish of the sexual encounter and must be used during every encounter (The Facts about AIDS 1987).

The AIDS virus, unlike many other viruses, is weak, fragile, and easily destroyed outside of the body. This is why it can be transmitted only by sexual contact, introduction into the bloodstream, or pregnancy. *AIDS is not transmitted by casual contact of any kind.* Casual contact includes the following

- shaking hands
- hugging
- social kissing
- crying
- coughing
- sneezing
- swimming in pools
- massaging
- preparing food or beverages
- sharing bed linens, towels, cups, dishes, straws, or other eating utensils
- sharing toilets, telephones, office equipment, or furniture

Although the virus has been detected in small amounts in tears and saliva, there are no documented cases of transmission from these fluids. Also, there is no evidence that the virus is transmitted by mosquito or other insect bites. The AIDS virus does not infect the mosquitoes' salivary glands, unlike diseases that are transmitted by mosquitoes, such as malaria and yellow fever (The Facts about AIDS 1987).

The best weapon against the spread of AIDS has and will be our understanding of the disease and how it is transmitted. For example, an understanding of AIDS has generated a behavioral change such that there has been a virtual elimination of the AIDS virus from the nation's blood supply. Individuals at risk have responded to requests that they not donate blood, thereby contributing to a safe supply of blood. The testing of donated blood supports this fact. There has been a decline in the rate that AIDS is spreading in certain cities. Education has also contributed to a sharp decline in other sexually transmitted diseases among homosexual men in certain cities, as well as a decrease in their sexual practices that increase the risk of AIDS. Intravenous drug users are more difficult to reach and to influence (Macklin and Needle 1987; The Facts about AIDS 1987).

AIDS victims suffer from discrimination and ostracism. Children with AIDS are humiliated in school and in the community by children and adults. Some communities have barred them from the schools (although the courts have ruled in favor of the AIDS children in each case). Infants with AIDS have been abandoned in hospitals where many health-care people have refused to care for them. Adult male and female victims are scorned and avoided, whether they are homosexual or heterosexual. The disease has created a lower class of people who do not have the means—socially, emotionally, physically, or financially—to defend themselves or fight back. Education has helped alleviate some of the discrimination, but the problem is far from being resolved.

● CHILDREN

Children's Perception of Death

Death themes are common in the world of childhood. Television is one of the current sources of influence in a child's discovery and understanding of death. It explicitly displays death encounters all of the time. The effects of television may vary from child to child, depending on the socioeconomic level. Lower-class urban children are more aware of the concept of death because they are exposed to more real violence. It appears that many children have a practical, matter-of-fact approach to the interpretation of death. Children are acquainted with death, but we as adults are not fully aware of their actual thoughts and experiences (Kastenbaum 1977).

The child's game ring-around-the-rosy was popular during the peak years of the plague in medieval Europe. "Ashes, ashes, all fall down" illustrated that the children were acutely aware that people all around them were dying. In the game, security was gained by joining hands. The ritual impersonated and, in its way, mastered death. Also, the variety of tag games include some that make the death theme quite explicit. *Peek-a-boo,* an old English phrase meaning "Alive or dead?" represents an attempt at active mastery of the gap between being and nonbeing. Thus the concern with death has been a common theme in children's play throughout the centuries (Kastenbaum 1986). Today these games do not hold the same significance that they once did.

Healthy children view death according to their stage of cognitive development. Maria Nagy (1948) conducted a study in Budapest, Hungary, with 378 children ages three to ten years. The children were asked to express their death-related thoughts and feelings. Older boys and girls drew pictures and also were asked to "write down everything that comes to your mind about death." The results indicated a clear developmental progression. Three age-related stages of death interpretation were identified. Stage 1 included the youngest children, three to five years. Death was seen as a continuation of life but on a reduced level. The dead are, in effect, less alive. They cannot see and hear very well. They are not as hungry as the living. They do not do much. Being dead and being asleep are similar conditions; that is, life is diminished, not finished. Death is temporary. The dead might return, just as the sleeping might awake. The preschoolers were also very curious. They asked questions about the details of the funeral, the coffin, the cemetery, and so on. This fascination with the practical or concrete aspects of death is often overlooked. Even though these children did not understand death by adult standards, they did have negative feelings about it. Death did not appear to be much fun. The dead might be sleeping, which was acceptable but boring, or they might be scared and lonely away from all their friends.

Stage 2 included five- or six-year-olds to nine-year-olds. A major advance in the understanding of death was noted in these children. They recognized that death was final. The older the child in this age range, the more firm the conclusion. Many of the children represented death as a person. (Personification is one of humankind's most ancient modes of expressing the relationship with death.) Personification of death as a skeleton was fairly common. Death personifications were often fearful, representing enormous, often mysterious power. Some children added threats or lethal wishes against their personifications, such as "Kill the death-man so we will not die." The realization of death's finality was accompanied by the belief that this fate might still be eluded. The clever or fortunate person might not be caught by the "death-man." The children did not recognize mortality as universal or personal. Stage 2, then, combined finality with an escape hatch.

Stage 3 began around nine or ten years and was assumed to continue thereafter. The child at this age understood death to be personal, universal, inevitable, as well as final. Discussions of death showed adult reasoning capabilities. All that lives must die, including oneself. This new awareness was compatible with belief in some form of afterlife.

Safier (1964), in a study involving thirty boys ages four to ten years, also found a three-stage developmental progression. The youngest children seemed to interpret both life and death in terms of a *constant flux*. There was an absence of the idea of absolutes. Death, as well as life, comes and goes.

In the intermediate stage, the dominant idea was the *outside agent*. The boys saw both life and death as things that are given and taken away. They saw the imploring presence of an external force. They also showed an interest in scientific explanation and expressed more curiosity about life and death.

At the highest level, the *internal agent* was dominant. "Something goes by itself, something stops by itself." These children, at about ten years, were developmentally advanced enough to manipulate ideas with some skill. They were beginning to establish a mental framework in which a variety of thoughts and impressions could be integrated, including thoughts of life and death. Safier's findings support those of Nagy. They also follow the developmental principles of Piaget.

Koocher (1973) also found that children's thoughts were closely related to their developmental levels. Children at the higher developmental levels were more realistic and objective in their answers to death-related questions. Their understanding of death was fairly consistent with their overall way of understanding the world. This study did not support Nagy's findings of a personification-type response when children were asked what would happen at the time of death.

In a review of literature concerning children and death, Speece and Brent (1984) found that the majority of healthy children between the ages of five and seven years in modern urban-industrial societies achieve an understanding of three components of the concept of death: *irreversibility, nonfunctionality,* and *universality.* Since this is also the age at which children make the transition from preoperational to concrete-operational thinking, some relationship between concrete-operational thinking and the understanding of death seems likely. (Speece and Brent's findings do not support those of earlier studies regarding the age at which a child comprehends the universality of death. Earlier studies [Nagy 1948; Safier 1964] indicated that children were much older [ten years or older] before they understood death to be universal.)

Irreversibility refers to the understanding that once a living thing dies, its physical body cannot be made alive again. Phrases such as "Death is final," "Death as irrevocable," and "Death is permanent," have been used to describe this concept. The question of whether the physical body itself can come back to life after death is separate from the belief in a spiritual afterlife.

Nonfunctionality refers to the understanding that all life-defining functions cease at death. Alternate terms are *dysfunctionality* and *cessation.*

Universality refers to the understanding that all living things die. Other phrases for this general notion include "Death as an immediate possibility," "Death as a personal event," and "Inevitability."

Before children understand irreversibility, they often view death as temporary and reversible. As these children see it, dead things can become alive again spontaneously as a result of medical intervention, magic, eating, drinking water, or the wishful thinking and prayer of others. These young children tend to see death as sleep (from which you can wake up) or like a trip (from which you return). Also, the fact that a large number of children mention medical intervention (e.g., going to a hospital, getting a shot) as a method for reversing death suggests that some children see death as similar to being sick.

Before understanding universality, children often believe that there are certain actions that can be taken to avoid death, or that certain "special" classes of people do not die. For example, young children think death can be avoided by being clever or lucky. People thought to be excluded from dying include teachers, members of the child's immediate family, children in general, and the individual child himself or herself. Before they understand that they themselves will die, children understand that others will die. However, very few children exclude only themselves from dying. Many children who apparently do understand the inevitability of their own death have a tendency to say that their death will occur only in the remote future, when they get old. They seem unable to grasp the possibility that their own death can occur at any time.

Before understanding nonfunctionality, children view death as somewhat different from life in that either dead things do not possess all of the functional capabilities of alive things, or dead things have diminished capabilities for specific functions. For example, dead things cannot hear as well as alive things.

Irreversibility
The fact that once a living thing dies, its physical body cannot be made alive again.

Nonfunctionality
The fact that all life-defining functions cease at death.

Universality
The fact that all living things die.

Children realize that certain functions cease at death before they realize that other functions cease. They first understand the cessation of the most visible aspects of functioning, such as eating and speaking, and only later recognize that more subtle, cognitive aspects, such as dreaming and knowing, also end with death. These children already understand the states of alive and dead as mutually exclusive. Therefore, their principal difficulty in understanding nonfunctionality is their uncertainty about which functions cease at death (Speece and Brent 1984).

Most of the studies concerning children's understanding of death indicate that realistic or adult-level death concepts are grasped by children who are at a relatively advanced level of thought. According to Piaget, the flexible and integrative qualities found in adult thought are not established until early adolescence. Therefore, the ten-year-old may know some of death's most distinctive characteristics but is limited in relating this knowledge to his or her total understanding of the world. Once the child reaches formal-operational thinking, he or she is capable of thinking about death and anything else in an abstract and systematic matter.

Dying Children

Children who are dying tend to view dying differently than other children do. Myra Bluebond-Langner (1975, 1977) worked with terminally ill children ages three to nine years. She spent many hours with them at the hospital, listening to them and observing their interactions with parents and staff. The children went through various stages of acquiring of information, which appeared to be related to their treatment experiences and the treatment of the other ill children with whom they came in contact. The stages were as follows:

1. I have a serious illness.
2. I know what drugs I am receiving and what they are supposed to do.
3. I know the relationship between my symptoms and the kind of treatment I am getting.
4. I realize now that I am going through a cycle of feeling worse, getting better, then getting worse again. The medicines do not work all the time.
5. I know that this will not go on forever. There's an end to the remissions and the relapses and to the kind of medicine they have for me. When the drugs stop working, I will die pretty soon. (Bluebond-Langner 1977)

Bluebond-Langner's study illustrates how seriously ill children work hard at trying to understand what is happening to them. They become aware of the possibility of death, note the specific changes that occur in their bodies, the kind of treatment they are receiving, and the responses from family and friends. Even the terminally ill children who are considered too young to understand do grasp the finality and inevitability of death.

Natterson and Knudson (1960) also found that dying children view death differently than well children do. They studied children ranging in age from less than one year to almost thirteen years. All of the children were suffering from cancer-related conditions with poor prognoses. The youngest children were most alarmed about separation from their parents. These were preschool boys and girls who would have been at home with their mothers if they had not had a severe illness. Five- to ten-year-olds appeared to be most upset by the nature of the diagnostic and treatment procedures. Their fear and distress had "strong

When there is a death in the family, it can draw attention and energy away from the needs of the children. It is difficult to care for the emotional or even physical needs of the children when one spouse dies.

roots in reality." Procedures such as bone marrow aspiration and venipuncture were seen as physical invasions of the integrity of the body. Pain and mutilation (even as medical treatment) were threatening. Anxiety about dying and death was found mostly among the oldest children. Like healthy children their age, the eleven- and twelve-year-olds grasped the finality and universality of death.

The Bereaved Child

When there is a death in the family, it can draw attention and energy away from the needs of the children. It is difficult to care for the emotional or even physical needs of the children when one spouse dies. Those parents who do try to meet the needs of their children, and try to make their relationships with the children a core around which their lives can be steadied and reorganized, may have difficulty managing both their own sorrow and the needs of the children. When a child is dying, the parents become so involved that their other children may be neglected. Parents and professional caregivers in our society are so traumatized by the death of a child that it may be difficult to have the perspective and emotional energy to recognize the impact of this loss on the child's brothers and sisters, as well as the other children in the neighborhood or school.

Thus, the bereaved child will probably face two sources of stress. First, he or she may be deprived of some of the normal support usually provided by the parents, because of their own involvement in the bereavement. The child may not eat as well or be properly clothed, be protected from accidents and mishaps, and/or have the availability of the normally loving and receptive parent. Second, the child has to suffer through his or her own bereavement response. It is easy for the child to become isolated. This is especially true if the adults in the child's life fail to appreciate his or her level of understanding or to accurately read his or her bereavement response. The child's developmental level and the role that the deceased person played in his or her life should be taken into account. The bereaved child may express his or her distress in ways that seem unrelated to the loss. For example, serious problems in school may appear for the first time, and he or she may suddenly turn on playmates in anger. Fear of the dark or of being alone may reappear.

In the case of the death of a parent, the child can show the effects of bereavement without showing sorrow. When a surviving parent does not show his or her own tears and tells the child to be brave, it is difficult then for the child to show his or her own feelings openly. The child's memory is likely to be focused around a relatively few strong images of the deceased, while the bereaved spouse has many recollections stretching over the years. The child, therefore, carries memories of the lost parent in the form of highly emotionally invested scenes and activities and may have overwhelming recollections of them years later (Berlinsky and Biller 1982).

Bereaved children are capable of experiencing emotional suffering for a long time. The mental image of the lost parent remains with them. Adults delude themselves by assuming that the child forgets easily. The child may contribute to this assumption because he or she does not grieve or mourn as an adult does. Quite often the child will express anger toward the deceased. This may horrify the surviving parent, but it may be a necessary exercise in order for the child to accept the loss. This does not mean that the child does not love and miss the lost parent. The adult may also be experiencing some similar mixed feelings toward the deceased (Kubler-Ross 1983).

Childhood bereavement has long-term effects on subsequent development. Five or ten years after a parent dies, bereaved children tend to be more submissive and introverted than other children (Berlinsky and Biller 1982). Adults who were bereaved as children suffer more from physical and mental illness than the norm. Evidence indicates that the child who suffers loss by the death of one or both parents is likely to be more vulnerable to emotional and physical problems as an adult than the child who does not (Kastenbaum 1977).

Guidelines for Relating to Children on the Subject of Death

Kastenbaum (1986) offers some guidelines for relating to children on the subject of death.

1. *Be a good observer.* See how the child is behaving and listen to what he or she is really saying. Unless there is an overriding necessity to do so, do not rush in with explanations, reassurances, or actions. Be relaxed, patient, and attentive enough to develop a better idea of what questions or needs the child actually is expressing.
2. *Do not wait or plan for "one big tell-all."* A continuing dialogue should be maintained. Opportunities for discussion include the deaths of pet animals, deaths reported in newspapers, and deaths portrayed in the movies or on television. Death should be one of many topics that adults and children can discuss together. It is more natural and effective this way.
3. When the situation centers around an actual death, *do not expect all the child's responses to be obvious and immediate.* Be patient and available. The total realization and response takes time to unfold. Then it will express itself in many ways, including changes in sleeping habits, mood, relationships with other children, demands on adults, and so on.

4. Children are truly a part of the family. *Let them remain with the family and household after a death.* Do not send them to a neighbor or relative. Examine such impulses before acting on them. Keep in mind what the child might learn from the opportunity to participate in the family's response. Also, lingering questions and misinterpretations might remain with the child if he or she is excluded.

5. *Simple and direct language is best.* Fanciful, sentimental, and symbolic meanderings quite often turn into a mini-sermon, peppered with words and concepts that have little meaning for the child. Provide accurate information that he or she can repeat in his or her own words. This will also make it possible to determine if the child understands what has been said.

6. *The child's sense of comfort will be strengthened by the very fact that an adult is available to talk about death with him or her.* Your natural feelings expressed in the situation are not likely to harm the child but instead may provide him or her with a basis for expressing and sorting out his or her own feelings.

● THE ELDERLY

We as a society have difficulty believing that young people can die and view such death as untimely. This implies that death is not untimely for the elderly. Aging and death are perceived as a cloudy, dimly perceived existence in the far future. Older people have had many more death-related experiences than younger people have had. They have experienced the deaths of both parents; they have experienced the deaths of more family members and friends; they have attended more funerals and visited more people who were dying; and they are more likely to have had one or more personal encounters with their own possible death and are more likely to be suffering from life-threatening health conditions (Kalish 1985).

Five aspects of death awareness emerge as age increases. *The anticipated life span is foreshortened,* and the future seems finite rather than virtually infinite. Such awareness requires ongoing restructuring in allocation of time, effort, and other resources. That is, "the closer we get to death, the more we shift our priorities and reallocate our energies." *Society realizes that the elderly do not have a future,* so they do not receive a major investment of resources from others (i.e., the state, the family, the community, and the work organization). *Desirable roles are closed to the elderly,* although other desirable roles may emerge. *The elderly are likely to see the future as requiring increasing effort* in order to maintain the status quo or a minimal decline. When people face their imminent death at a later age than they anticipated, they feel they have received their entitlement; when faced with their own foreseeable death in advance of that time, they may feel deprived. As more and more of their same-aged peers die, the surviving elderly cannot help but be affected. They experience a combination of loneliness, sadness, fear, and anxiety, as well as pleasure and guilt that "it wasn't me." *Changing health status can make an impact.* Death is usually due to a chronic condition (Kalish 1985).

Over 20 percent of the death certificates for persons sixty-five years of age or older stipulate that a long-term-care facility was the residence at the time of death; however, only 5 percent of the elderly are in a long-term-care facility at a given time. When asked where they want to die, most people of all ages would prefer to die at home. Dying at home is most appropriate when the individual

Death appears less frightening for those who are older. Women find the prospect of their own death to be more fear-arousing than men do, but women simultaneously have greater acceptance of their own death.

is reasonably alert and capable of interaction with others; when his or her health condition is beyond effective treatment, or effective treatment is possible at home; when being home will provide something important, such as frequent or meaningful personal relationships, familiarity, or privacy; and when death is imminent and final weeks, days, or hours are most fruitfully spent in familiar surroundings with loving people (Kalish 1985).

Death appears less frightening for those who are older. Women find the prospect of their own death to be more fear-arousing than men do, but women simultaneously have greater acceptance of their own death. The greater the extent of religious feeling, the less the fear of death. The fear of death is least among both the deeply religious and the deeply irreligious, while people who are uncertain or uncommitted exhibit the greatest anxiety (Kalish 1985).

● WIDOWS AND WIDOWERS

In the United States, over 50 percent of all women over sixty-five are widows, and the proportion goes up to 70 percent among women over seventy-five. Widows outnumber widowers six to one among those sixty-five to seventy-five. The ratio is nearly five to one for those over seventy-five (Kalish 1985).

When the death of a spouse is sudden and there is no opportunity for emotional preparation, the survivor may experience extensive haunting experiences. For most widows it is comforting to feel that the husband is still there somehow. Even on the occasions that the sense of his presence has hallucinatory

TABLE 19.1 Death Rates for Ten Leading Causes of Death among Older People, by Age: 1984 (rates per 100,000 population in age-group)

CAUSE OF DEATH	65+	65–74	75–84	85+
ALL CAUSES	5,102	2,848	6,399	15,224
DISEASES OF THE HEART	2,186	1,103	2,749	7,251
MALIGNANT NEOPLASMS	1,042	835	1,272	1,604
CEREBROVASCULAR DISEASES	476	177	626	1,884
CHRONIC OBSTRUCTIVE PULMONARY DISEASES	199	141	270	331
PNEUMONIA AND INFLUENZA	182	54	216	883
DIABETES	95	59	126	217
ACCIDENTS	87	50	107	257
ATHEROSCLEROSIS	83	17	88	488
NEPHRITIS, NEPHROTIC SYNDROME, NEPHROSIS	58	27	76	201
SEPTICEMIA	41	20	52	142
ALL OTHER CAUSES	654	365	816	1,965

SOURCE: National Center for Health Statistics. "Advanced Report of Final Mortality Statistics, 1984." *Monthly Vital Statistics Report* Vol. 35, No. 6, Supplement (2) (September 1986).

Widows outnumber widowers six to one among those sixty-five to seventy-five; the ratio is nearly five to one for those over seventy-five.

Obsessional review
To relive the events surrounding the death of a loved one.

vividness, the widow can usually differentiate between the reality of his death and the impression that he is still with her. It is considered neither unusual nor crazy for a widow to have this sense of presence (Kastenbaum 1986).

A dying elderly man has his wife to take care of him, but when his widow becomes terminally ill, she has greater difficulty in finding a caregiver. On the other hand, if the husband survives his wife, there are many widows who might be available for companionship, sexual intimacy, and living together or marriage. For the older widow, the pool of available men is quite small. Because of this imbalance, widows are more likely than widowers to live alone (Kalish 1985).

Widows and widowers differ in their response to the death of their spouses. In general, the men seem to accept the reality of the death more rapidly and completely. Although the newly bereaved man is likely to feel the presence of his wife soon after the bereavement, such a feeling is much less common as time goes on than it is for a widow. The man is likely to engage in **obsessional review,** reliving over and over again the events surrounding his wife's death, but he usually cuts it off after a few weeks. A widow engages in obsessional review and does so for a longer period of time. The widower is more likely to push himself back to the immediate realities of his situation and is less likely to speak openly about his feelings. He has a greater concern about the practical problems of running the household. Also, the people who rally around him tend to concentrate on helping him manage the house and the children. Widowers may make a more rapid social recovery than widows do, but they are slower in making an emotional recovery. A widower usually starts dating sooner, and gets remarried sooner, than a widow does (Kalish 1985; Kastenbaum 1986; Stroebe and Stroebe 1983).

Another way widows cope with their loss, other than through obsessional review, is through "sanctifying" their deceased husbands, idealizing both the person and the past relationship. This appears to give meaning to the previous life of the widow while simultaneously justifying any tendency she might have to avoid the risk of new relationships (Kalish 1985; Kastenbaum 1986).

The major problem facing widows is loneliness. Widows are also more likely to mention problems with finances, making decisions alone, and doing things by themselves (Smith and Zick 1986).

● BEREAVEMENT, GRIEVING, AND MOURNING

Bereavement is "a status of being deprived by loss" (Kalish 1985). It is an objective fact. People are bereaved when a person close to them dies. Bereavement is, therefore, a recognized social fact as well as an objective fact. The bereavement status suggests what the survivor might be experiencing or how he or she has adapted to the loss. It is a clue to possible psychological distress (Parkes and Weiss 1983).

Survivors have several behavioral responses to loss. First, *anger* is often accompanied by expressions of blame directed against others who might or might not have had any objective role in the death (for example, physicians and other caregivers, God, another member of the family). *Guilt* is based on real or fantasized responsibility for the death or on real or fantasized inadequacies in the course of the relationship, increased by the realization that it is too late to make amends. *Depression* is episodic and acute rather than chronic and prolonged. *Anxiety and restlessness* occur, with the inability to sit still. All actions, however, are accomplished without zest. *Images of the deceased* are often vivid, real, and immediate. Those suffering recent losses frequently feel they have encountered the dead person in reality, while simultaneously knowing it is impossible (Kalish 1985). These stages are similar to those experienced by the dying.

In the case of marital bereavement, the absence of an opportunity to prepare oneself emotionally has a major impact on the intensity and duration of the trauma. Glick et al. (1974) noted that slightly more than a year after the death of a spouse, subjects who had experienced sudden, unexpected bereavement were more socially withdrawn than those who had had advanced knowledge. They were more preoccupied with details of the death, had more difficulty accepting the reality of the loss, and in general were experiencing more disorganization throughout their lives. They were more likely to be anxious and to have a pessimistic outlook on the future.

Osterweis et al. (1984), Stroebe and Stroebe (1987), Raphael (1983), and Shuchter (1986) noted a decline in health and great distress in the surviving spouse. Bowling and Cartwright (1982) found that breathlessness, indigestion, depression, backaches, rheumatism, trouble with teeth and gums, sleeplessness, and loss of appetite were reported more frequently among surviving spouses than among comparable persons. Perkins and Harris (1990) found that the death of a spouse, a sibling, or sibling-in-law contributed to the adverse health of middle-aged adults.

Grief encompasses feelings engendered by the loss of a loved one and a process of adapting to the loss. It is the way the survivor feels. It is a state of shock, sorrow, and anxiety, including physical and emotional distress. When a person is said to be "grief-stricken," it indicates that the individual's total way of being has been affected by the loss. In the case of the death of a spouse, the course of the grieving process can be predicted to some extent by the quality of the marital relationship. The grief is more disturbing when the partners had mixed feelings toward each other. The adjustment is more difficult if the relationship was based on dependency (Parkes and Weiss 1983).

Bereavement
A status of being deprived by loss.

Grief
Feelings engendered by the loss of a loved one and a process of adapting to the loss.

Anticipatory grief
The initiating of grief and mourning in anticipation of someone's death.

Grief work
The process in which the bereaved person must slowly detach his or her intense feelings from everything that linked him or her with the deceased.

Mourning
Grief and bereavement that is, in varying degrees, determined by custom and expressed through ritual.

Cultures reflect specific and different signs of mourning, such as wearing black. It is almost universal that the bereaved engage in some type of public behavior that acknowledges the death.

Anticipatory grief is the initiating of grief and mourning in anticipation of someone's death (Horowitz et al. 1980).

Grief work is the process in which the bereaved person must slowly detach his or her intense feelings from everything that linked him or her with the deceased. This process takes time and effort.

The manifestations of grief are necessary to help the bereaved individual return to a normal life. The first stage involves shock, numbness, and disbelief. The second stage involves painful longing, yearning, and a preoccupation with memories and mental images. Depression follows, with people feeling lethargic, passive, and defeated. Panicky feelings emerge. Although grief attacks become less frequent, survivors experience an overwhelming desire to run away. Widows are more susceptible to these feelings than widowers are (Parkes and Weiss 1983).

Mourning is grief and bereavement that is, in varying degrees, determined by custom and expressed through ritual. Cultures reflect specific and different signs of mourning. However, it is almost universal that the bereaved engage in some type of public behavior that acknowledges the death. Mourning behavior can change within the same culture over a period of time. The practice of wearing black for a year after a spouse's death, which was common at the turn of the century, is no longer practiced today (Kalish 1985; Kastenbaum 1986).

A death affects the family structure in many ways. First, it removes the person from the family system. Some of that person's roles may require replacement. The existential reality of the dead person often continues meaningfully in the lives of the survivors, that is, sometimes the deceased is seen, heard, felt, or otherwise sensed by survivors. Second, death sets into motion series of events that affect the family and the general community. One series involves the funeral arrangements, including the wake and the funeral-burial ceremony. An-

other series involves the transfer of property. Another concerns the possibility of autopsy, issuance of a death certificate, and recording the death. Other series involve contacting family members around the country, informing employers or other relevant persons, and deciding about changes in living arrangement for surviving household members. Third, the economic effects of the death may influence the wealth and income of the survivors. This effect is not spread evenly over all the survivors, nor is it spread evenly over time. The surviving spouse may immediately accumulate more money through insurance and other benefits, but his or her long-term income may diminish. Adult children may not receive what each considers a fair allocation of a deceased parent's wealth, which may lead to tension among them. Finally, the death of an older person may free survivors to pursue goals that had been set aside, either because of the deceased person's health problems or because caregiving was required.

● SUICIDE

Suicide is a serious problem in the United States and is ranked as the tenth leading cause of death. Approximately 30,000 people a year commit suicide, and another 50,000 to 200,000 individuals intentionally injure themselves or attempt suicide each year (Ellis and Range 1989). Three major population groups are at high risk of committing suicide. One group, adolescents, was discussed in an earlier chapter (see Chapter 12). The other two groups are the elderly and Native Americans.

Although most elderly do not have suicidal thoughts, 25 percent of all reported suicides are committed by individuals sixty-five years and older (Blazer 1982). The national rate was 11.9 suicides per 100,000 population in 1980. For those over sixty-five years it was 17.7 per 100,000 population (National Center for Health Statistics [NCHS] 1983). The highest rate for the elderly is among older white males ages seventy-five to eighty-four (Belsky 1984). In 1980, white males over age eighty-five completed 50 suicides per 100,000, while white females completed 7. Nonwhite females completed 2 per 100,000, and nonwhite males completed 15 (NCHS 1983).

One possible explanation for the high rate of suicide among elderly white males is that they experience the greatest inconsistency between their ideal self-image and the realities of advancing age (Butler and Lewis 1982). As one ages, the role of worker is generally lost, chronic illness interferes with one's sense of control, and an individual may feel a loss of status. Lack of a supportive social network results in social isolation for most older white widowed males, which in turn would make suicide appear to be a reasonable and acceptable action (Stenback 1980; Holinger and Offer 1982; Robbins et al. 1977). The incidence of suicide is less among people who are married and those who stay in touch with their children and other family members (Robbins et al. 1977).

Since 1940 there has been a dramatic decline in suicide rates among the elderly, although their rates still remain the highest. Between 1960 and 1980, adolescents between fifteen and twenty-four years have demonstrated a twofold increase (McIntosh 1985). The probability of a successful act of self-destruction is higher among the elderly than among people of other ages (Maris 1981).

Native Americans have the highest national suicide rate of any ethnic or racial subpopulation. Also, their relative life expectancy is low compared to the general population (Harper, 1982; Hawton, 1986). However, rates have been

Native Americans have the highest suicide rate of any ethnic or racial subpopulation.

found to vary greatly from reservation to reservation and are strongly associated with the extent of social problems on the reservations (Davenport and Davenport 1987). Some common traits have been found across tribal groups. In many Indian communities, suicides tend to occur in clusters that take on epidemic proportions among particular groups of youth. The suicide of one young person (usually a male) may precipitate subsequent suicides and/or attempts in the same general community (Long 1986; Davis and Hardy 1986).

Native Americans are more at risk for suicide in youth than in old age, which is the opposite of the situation in the general population. Native American suicide is more frequently alcohol related, and violent methods—firearms and hanging—are more commonly used (May 1990). The peak age for suicide is from the late teens through the twenties.

The dominant white culture has attempted to make the Native Americans acculturate into the larger society and has not been completely successful. It has prevented the Native Americans from maintaining and developing their own culture and identity. Many Native Americans feel trapped between the two cultures, and they feel unsure of their destiny and identity. This, compounded with prejudice, discrimination, and low socioeconomic status, can cause the breakdown of the individual within his or her social environment (Davenport and Davenport 1987).

Others commit suicide for several different reasons. They may wish to *reunite* with someone previously deceased. A desperate longing may cause an individual to follow the dead, especially if the relationship was marked by extreme dependency. Another reason may be to achieve *rest or refuge* from unending problems. An ordinary good night's sleep may appear to be out of reach as depression deepens, so suicide appears to be the only solution. *Revenge* is another reason. Some people have a dominating, burning resentment and deep hurt. These individuals repeatedly feel that they are treated unfairly and that their achievements are not recognized. No matter how hard they try, love and appreciation are never shown to them. Low self-esteem is very evident in this situation. The combination of revenge fantasy and low self-esteem is very dangerous. Another reason for suicide is it can be a *penalty for failure*. That is, the victim feels he or she cannot fulfill certain self-expectations and holds himself or herself to blame. Finally, suicide can be a *mistake*. That is, the victim counted on being rescued. The individual may have wanted to live, but a mood, a desperate maneuver, and/or a misjudgment may have contributed to the death. Those individuals who use a suicide hot line are not completely convinced that they want to kill themselves. They experience conflicting life and death "tugs" at the same time (Kastenbaum 1986).

What are the characteristics of a suicidal person? First, more men than women commit suicide. The ratio ranges from 8:1 to 3:1 (men to women). Suicide among African-Americans is more rare than among whites by about half. White teenagers outnumber African-American teenagers two to one (Ellis and Range 1989).

Suicidal individuals are described as having "maladaptive" affect: that is, they are more likely to be depressed, irritable, excitable, arousable, energetic, and socially isolated. They have certain cognitive characteristics that separate them from nonsuicidal individuals. One such characteristic is a rigid cognitive style, that is, they are less flexible in their thinking, they have difficulty developing alternate solutions to their problems, and when placed in conditions of high stress, they are likely to become hopeless and thus engage in suicidal behavior. Other cognitive styles noted in suicidal individuals are field dependence and impulsivity. This is not to say that field-dependent and impulsive people are suicidal, but suicidal people may be field dependent and impulsive. Suicidal people hold negative expectations about the future (Ellis and Range 1989). Also, it is common for many who commit suicide to have the illusion that they will be around to witness the results of their suicide.

● FUNERALS

Funerals are a rite of passage for the dead and a show of support for the survivors. Such a leave-taking ceremony is purported to have a therapeutic value for the survivors by permitting them to grieve openly and to advance their acceptance of the reality of the death (Kalish 1985). Funerals help to establish the fact of death as an emotional reality for the surviving spouse as well as for the community. The pattern established by the funeral and memorial process enables the bereaved to function within a clear, well-organized framework. It allows society to complete its obligations to the deceased as well as support the survivors in their grief. A funeral, thus, helps immediate survivors, and society in general, to go on with their lives. A postfuneral gathering helps everyone concerned to begin to direct their attention to the continuation and renewal of life. Often, lively and lusty behavior after a funeral represent a partial release from tension and a need to show each other that life should go on (Kastenbaum 1986).

In most societies the period between death and the final disposal of the body involves a funeral and burial process. In our society the funeral and burial process has five phases. The first is the removal of the body, or separation of the dead from the living. The second phase is the visitation period. This may mean attending a wake or scripture service, or sitting shiva. Third is the funeral rite

Cremation is an ancient practice of Hindus and Buddhists.

Cremation
The process of returning a body to the elements through intense heat and evaporation.

itself. The procession from the place where the funeral is held to the place of the burial or disposal of the body is the fourth phase. And finally comes committing the body to its final disposal. Earth burial is still the most common form of body disposal (Kalish 1985).

Body disposal methods differ from society to society. **Cremation,** which is the process of returning a body to the elements through intense heat and evaporation, is an ancient practice. The Hindus and Buddhists have practiced it for thousands of years. Most religious groups, including the Roman Catholic church, permit it, but the Greek Orthodox church, Conservative and Orthodox Jews, Muslims, and some conservative Protestant groups oppose it. In 1985, cremation was used in 13.87 percent of the deaths in the United States. In Canada the rate was 25.84 percent, and in countries in Europe more than 50 percent of the dead were cremated (Morgan 1988). Cremation normally costs less than an earth burial.

S U M M A R Y

- Gender and social status contribute to mortality and life expectancy.
- It is common for family, friends, caregiving staff, as well as the dying individual, to evade the topic of death through mutual pretense.
- Interpersonal relationships affect patients' length of survival. Patients who maintain active and mutually responsive relationships survive longer than those who bring poor social relationships with them into the terminal stage of life.
- According to Kubler-Ross, the dying person may experience five stages: denial, anger, bargaining, depression, and acceptance.
- Recently there has been a movement in our society that supports letting each individual die an appropriate death. This means permitting each individual the opportunity to die as he or she wishes to die, at least to the extent that it is

Reproductive Loss

In the United States, approximately eight million infants a year die as newborns or stillbirths. These deaths become shrouded in silence. Society tends to treat reproductive loss as a "nonevent" because it is considered an unspeakable subject. Why is there such a conspiracy of silence? Our society has difficulty understanding that this traumatic event engenders feelings of profound grief. Society either may not recognize the loss or may regard it as a misfortune from which parents will recover quickly. Friends, neighbors, relatives, and others tend to disregard the infant as a real human being. They expect the grieving to be short-lived (Morgan 1988). They believe they will save the mother from pain if they never mention the baby. However, the effect of this misconception is to block the mother's grief from its healthy natural course. According to Nicol (1989), if a mother is not allowed to grieve naturally, her health suffers psychologically and physically. Nicol found that the pattern of health deterioration is similar to the effects of bereavement that women experience when their husbands die. That is, a stillbirth or the death of a neonate can have effects as severe on the mental and physical health of women as the loss of a husband.

Nicol (1989) identified four major factors that made bereaved mothers more vulnerable and less able to resolve their grief than others who are grieving a death. First, a crisis during the pregnancy, such as the death of a close relative or marital problems, seemed to interfere with a healthy grief resolution. The next two factors were a lack of support from the spouse or partner, as well as a lack of support from other family members. Compassionate, empathic support from people the mother can trust is very important. Without this support she will withdraw and isolate herself. Finally, the fourth factor that affected grief resolution was the mother never seeing and holding her baby. Mothers who did see and hold their babies were more able to reach healthy grief resolution.

Morgan (1988) notes that both parents should be encouraged to see the infant, to name him or her, and to accept the reality of the infant as a member of the family. The infant's photograph should be taken and saved with the baby's hospital bracelet. The National Funeral Directors Association (1981) recommends that parents hold and dress the infant, and place him or her in the casket. If parents do not recognize the existence and loss of the infant in this way, then they will have difficulty accepting the reality of the loss. Involving other loved ones such as grandparents and siblings will help those others acknowledge the humanness and loss of the infant.

Do fathers suffer the same way mothers do, or do they experience different feelings of loss? How can we get society to change its silence about this topic? How can family members help the parents' grief?

---

possible. Appropriate death may or may not involve passive, active, or voluntary euthanasia.

- The living will states conditions under which an individual, in good health and cognitively alert at the time of the signature, requests that no medically heroic methods be used to sustain his or her existence.
- The hospice movement is a system of care for the terminally ill. There are various models, including institutional care and home care. The family of the terminally ill patient is an integral part of the system.
- AIDS can be transmitted by intimate sexual contact and the sharing of IV needles. It can also be passed from a mother to a fetus during pregnancy. It is estimated that 1.0 to 1.5 million people have been affected by the AIDS virus.
- Healthy children's perception of death is related to their stage of cognitive maturation, according to Nagy's classic study and other more recent studies. Dying children perceive death differently than healthy normal children do.
- The bereaved child faces two sources of stress. First, he or she may be deprived of some of the normal support usually provided by the parents, because of their own involvement in the bereavement. Second, the child has to suffer through

his or her own bereavement response. The bereaved child may express his or her distress in ways that seem unrelated to the loss. The child who suffers loss by the death of one or both parents is likely to be more vulnerable to emotional and physical problems as an adult than the child who does not.

- Kastenbaum offers several guidelines for relating to children on the subject of death.

- The elderly have had many more death-related experiences than younger people have had. Five aspects of death awareness emerge as age increases: the anticipated life span is foreshortened; society realizes that the elderly have no future; desirable roles are closed to the elderly; the elderly are likely to see the future as requiring increasing effort; and changing health status can make an impact.

- In the United States, over 50 percent of all women over sixty-five are widows, and the proportion goes up to 70 percent among women over seventy-five. Widows outnumber widowers six to one among those sixty-five to seventy-five; the ratio is nearly five to one for those over seventy-five. Widows and widowers differ in their response to the death of their spouses.

- Bereavement is "a status of being deprived by loss." We are bereaved when a person close to us dies. Survivors have several behavioral responses to loss: anger, guilt, depression, anxiety and restlessness, and preoccupation with the image of the deceased. In the case of marital bereavement, the absence of an opportunity to prepare oneself emotionally will have a major impact on the intensity and duration of the trauma.

- Grief encompasses feelings engendered by the loss of a loved one and a process of adapting to the loss. Anticipatory grief is the initiating of grief and mourning in anticipation of someone's death. Grief work is the process in which the bereaved person slowly detaches his or her intense feelings from everything that linked him or her with the deceased. Mourning is grief and bereavement that is, in part, determined by custom and expressed through ritual.

- Suicide is ranked as the tenth leading cause of death in the United States. Three major population groups are at high risk for suicide: adolescents, the elderly, and Native Americans.

- People commit suicide for a variety of reasons: they may wish to reunite with a dead loved one, to achieve rest or refuge, to get revenge, to penalize themselves for failure, or to simply make a desperate move, never really intending to die.

- Funerals are rite of passage for the dead and a show of support for the survivors. Earth burial is the most common form of body disposal, but cremation is practiced by many ethnic and religious groups.

- Reproductive loss is often overlooked by the general public. The mother experiences grief that has gone unrecognized until recent years. This grief affects her relationship with the rest of her family.

R E A D I N G S

Brothers, J. (1990). *Widowed.* New York: Simon and Schuster.
    Dr. Joyce Brothers describes her own widowhood and offers advice to others on coping with a similar loss.
Kearl, M. C. (1989). *Endings.* New York: Oxford University Press.
    A presentation of death from a sociological as well as a psychological perspective.
Seibert, J. M. and Olson, R. A. (Eds.) (1989). *Children, Adolescents, & AIDS.* Lincoln, NE: University of Nebraska Press.
    A compilation of work by researchers, clinicians, and other professionals concerning the AIDS epidemic and children and adolescents.

Shneidman, E. S. (1984). *Death: Current perspectives*. 3rd ed. Mountain view, CA: Mayfield Publishing Co.

A variety of recent and contemporary writings concerning the myriad aspects of death and dying.

Books for Children

Clifford, E. (1980). *The Killer swan*. Boston: Houghton Mifflin.

Concerns suicide of a parent.

Jukes, M. (1985). *Blackberries in the dark*. New York: Alfred A. Knopf.

Death of a grandparent.

Rofes, E. (1985). *The kid's book about death and dying*. Boston: Little, Brown.

Glossary

A

Absurdity riddles Riddles in which an absurdity is positioned either in the question or in the answer. The question contains a blatant impossibility that, if mentally negated, allows the riddle to be answered logically.

Accommodation In Piaget's theory, a process in which previous experiences are modified to conform to new information, new environmental input, and/or new interactions. New categories are added.

Accumulation error theory A theory of aging involving the possibility that in the course of protein production, one or more of the components of the process will not function properly and will make a mistake resulting in an incorrect amino acid being inserted into a protein. Over the years these mistakes will accumulate and reduce the efficiency of the body or keep it from working altogether.

Active euthanasia Mercy killing; to actively aid in the death of a terminally ill person.

Activity theory A social theory of aging that implies that except for the inevitable changes in biology and in health, older people are the same as middle-aged people, with the same psychological and social needs.

Adaptation The inherent tendency to cognitively adjust to the environment through the processes of assimilation and accommodation.

Adolescence The psychosocial aspects of development in the years of life beginning with puberty and ending with the completion of general physical growth and maturation.

Adolescent egocentrism Adolescent's failure to differentiate between their own mental preoccupations and what others are thinking. They assume that others are as obsessed as they are with their behavior and appearance.

Age-grading The traditional society's system of social expectations regarding age-appropriate behavior.

AIDS-related complex (ARC) Chronic symptoms, such as fever, weight loss, diarrhea, and swollen lymph nodes, found in patients infected with AIDS.

Alternative Birth Center (ABC) Birthing rooms that are usually a part of or near a hospital or clinic, with emergency equipment and staff available on call. The birthing rooms are especially designed to care for uncomplicated births in a home-type setting.

Altruism The practice of acting unselfishly to help others.

Amenorrhea The cessation of menstruation.

Amniocentesis A fetal monitoring procedure in which a three-inch needle is inserted through the abdominal and uterine walls of the mother and into the amniotic sac, and a small amount of amniotic fluid is withdrawn. This procedure cannot be done until after the fifteenth week of pregnancy.

Amnion The inner membrane of the amniotic sac.

Amniotic sac A bag or envelope of clear fluid that surrounds and protects the embryo by functioning as a shock absorber. It maintains a constant temperature and allows the embryo the opportunity to move its primitive limbs.

Anal stage Freud's second stage of psychosexual development, in which there is a heightened sensitivity to the stimulation of the mucous membrane surrounding the anal area of the body. This stage lasts roughly from the second to the fourth year.

Animism A view, common in preschoolers, that nonliving objects are alive and human.

Anorexia nervosa An eating disorder characterized by an extreme reduction in food intake leading to a loss of at least 25 percent of original body weight.

Anoxia A condition in which an insufficient amount of oxygen reaches the neonate's brain.

Anticipatory grief The initiating of grief and mourning in anticipation of someone's death.

Anxiety Generalized, nonspecifiable fear; a reaction to an anticipated or imagined danger.

Apgar scale A scoring system used to evaluate and measure a neonate's physical condition at birth.

Appropriate death Permitting each individual the opportunity to die as he or she wishes to die, at least to the extent that this is possible.

Arousal Alertness.

Artificial insemination A procedure in which sperm from either a donor or the husband are injected into a woman's vagina with a syringe, with the intention of impregnating her.

Artificialism A view, common in preschoolers, that everything, including living things, can be made or built the same way.

Asocial state The stage of attachment that occurs during the first six weeks of life, when the very young infant lacks the capacity for social interaction.

Assimilation In Piaget's theory, a process in which information is incorporated and adapted to conform to the individual's already existing mental or intellectual structures or schemes.

Associativity The understanding that when three structures are combined, it does not matter what the order of the combination is.

Attachment Strong affectional ties that bind a person to his or her most intimate companions.

Attention The manner in which we focus on what we are doing.

Attention deficit-hyperactivity disorder (ADHD) A disorder in which a child has a high level of activity and is unable to inhibit it on command.

Authoritarian child rearing A parenting style in which the parent expects strict obedience from the child, and punishment and force are used.

Authoritative child rearing A parenting style in which parents give children reasons behind their decisions and permit verbal exchange, but the parents have the final say in the decisions.

Autoimmune theory A theory of aging that attributes aging to the development of antibodies that destroy normal cells. That is, human beings, as they age, show an increasing tendency to reject their own tissues.

Autonomous morality According to Piaget, a stage of morality in which children between nine and twelve years take their peers' intentions into consideration in evaluating their actions.

Autonomy vs. shame and doubt Erikson's second psychosocial crisis, in which the toddler will either learn independence and pride or feel a loss of self-control involving a sense of shame and compulsive doubt about himself or herself.

Autosomes The first twenty-two pairs of chromosomes in a human being.

B

Behaviorism A learning theory that focuses on the environment as a major determinant of human and animal behavior.

Behavior modification A behaviorism-based technique for eliminating or changing specific behavior.

Behaviorist theory of language development The theory that language is a product of environment and experience and can be explained as conditioned responses and/or imitation.

Bereavement A status of being deprived by loss.

Blastocyst During the germinal stage, the specialization of cells formed from the zygote that root in the uterine wall.

Body cells *See* Somatic cells

Body image How individuals perceive themselves, especially their bodies.

Bonding A period of heightened sensitivity of the new mother, during which she interacts with the neonate and begins to form a special attachment to him or her.

Bottle mouth A condition found in a two-, three-, or four-year-old child whose teeth have been destroyed by tooth decay. The cause of bottle mouth is prolonged exposure to sweetened liquids.

Braxton Hicks contractions Contractions of the uterus that occur several weeks before giving birth. This phenomenon is often called false labor.

Brazelton Neonatal Behavioral Assessment Scale A scale used to detect mild dysfunctions of the central nervous system and the development of behavioral responses during the neonatal period.

Breech delivery An infant born with the buttocks instead of the head delivered first. This is the case in about 3 to 4 percent of births.

Bulimia Uncontrollable binge eating often associated with self-induced vomiting, abuse of diuretics and laxatives, and a depressive mood after eating.

C

Case study A detailed description that focuses on one individual.

Cataract A condition of the eye in which the lens becomes increasingly opaque and a complete loss of vision ultimately results.

Caution Rigidity.

Centration Focusing, or centering, on only one feature or dimension of a situation at a time, to the exclusion of all others.

Cephalocaudal development A principle governing physical growth in which an individual develops from head to feet.

Cesarean section Removal of an infant from the uterus through an incision made in the abdominal wall and the uterus.

Chorion The outer membrane of the amniotic sac.

Chorionic villi sampling A prenatal diagnostic procedure that involves obtaining sample villi, which are hairlike projections in the chorion, and then examining the embryo's chromosomes for signs of birth defects. This procedure can be done after eight to twelve weeks' gestation.

Classical conditioning According to Pavlov, learning whereby a neutral stimulus elicits a certain response by repeated association with another stimulus that already elicits that response.

Classification Sorting objects into categories and classes.

Class inclusion *See* Combinativity.

Climacteric In women, the transition from the time reproductive ability begins to diminish, through the degeneration or involution of the ovaries and their various processes, to the final cessation of reproductive ability.

Cliques A type of peer group that is small, with an average of six members.

Cognitive-developmental theory of language development The theory that views language development as growing out of intellectual development, which is controlled by heredity and environment.

Cognitive styles The manner in which an individual takes in and responds to information.

Cohort People of the same age group who share common experiences or demographic traits, such as a school class or a whole generation.

Colic A catchall term that describes the symptoms of infants who have apparent extreme intestinal discomfort and cry a great deal because of it.

Collagen theory *See* Cross-link theory.

Collective monologue Egocentric speech among two or more children in which they give the impression of being engaged in a conversation but their statements and responses have little or no relationship to each other.

Colostrum A high-protein substance loaded with protective antibodies that is produced by the mother's breast shortly after a birth.

Combinativity The ability to reason simultaneously about the whole and the part, to group elementary classes into an encompassing class, and to reverse the process by reducing the broader class into its subordinate components.

Combinatorial logic A formal operation in which the adolescent can deal with problems in which many factors operate at the same time.

Concrete operational stage Piaget's third stage of cognitive development, in which the elementary-age child can mentally manipulate tangible and concrete information by using logical rules.

Conjugal family A nuclear family unit in which the husband-wife relationship is of primary importance.

Conjunctive faith In Fowler's theory, the sixth stage of moral development, in which the middle adult is ready to hear about beliefs other than his or her own. This stage tries to unify opposites in mind and experience.

Conservation The idea that a quantity or amount of something remains the same regardless of changes in its shape or position.

Continuity theory A retirement theory that assumes that occupational identity is not the central role for many workers.

Contrary-to-fact situations A contrary-to-fact premise constructed by an adolescent and proceeded with in argument as if the premise were correct. That is, the adolescent deals with the possible as well as the actual.

Coordination of secondary schemes In Piaget's theory, the fourth substage in the sensorimotor stage. It occurs between the eighth and twelfth months of age. Behaviors are now unquestionably intentional, and the infant can anticipate coming events. The infant is also capable of using new schemes in different situations to solve problems.

Correlational study A study in which researchers assess the extent to which variables appear to be related in some way. Correlation measures the strength and direction of the relationship between two or more variables.

Couvade A practice of allowing the father to go through the symptoms of childbirth with his wife.

Crawling The progression made by an infant in which he or she does not lift the abdomen from the floor while moving all four limbs.

Cremation The process of returning a body to the elements through intense heat and evaporation.

Crisis theory A retirement theory that assumes that retirement has negative and degrading effects because occupational identity is the basic legitimizing role for people in our society.

Critical periods Fixed times in the development of an organ, organ system, or anatomical structure, which, if interfered with, will permanently hamper further development of the organ, system, or structure.

Cross-cultural study A study that involves the comparison of individuals from two or more cultures. The principle behind this type of study is to determine whether certain behaviors or traits are the result of culture or of human nature. The results can make it possible, then, to generalize about human development under different cultural circumstances.

Cross-link theory A theory of aging that suggests living cells age when connective tissue binds together, becomes rigid, and loses its function.

Cross-sectional method A research method that investigates development by comparing different groups of people of different ages simultaneously.

Cross-sequential research Research combining the cross-sectional and longitudinal research methods. It begins with a cross-sectional study using several groups of people who are different ages. Then, months or years after the original testing, the same groups of people are tested again.

Crowd A type of peer group that is an association of two, three, or four cliques, with approximately fifteen to thirty members in all.

Crowning During the birth process, the point at which the widest diameter of the baby's head is at the mother's vulva.

Crystallized intelligence The sorts of skills one acquires through education and acculturation, such as verbal comprehension, numerical skills, and inductive reasoning.

Cytologic theory A theory of aging that sees the body as being victimized by additive effects of insults and injuries to individual cells.

D

Decenter The capability of considering two or more aspects of a problem simultaneously.

Deep structure According to Chomsky, the structure of language that involves the syntactical relationship between words.

Defended The personality type of elderly persons who are striving, ambitious, and achievement oriented, with high defenses against anxiety and the need to maintain tight controls over impulse life.

Defense mechanism A thought pattern that distorts one's perception in order to avoid an unbearable inner conflict.

Dependent variable A factor that is measured in an experiment and is controlled by one or more independent variables.

Detached grandparents Grandparents for whom intergenerational ties, by choice or by circumstance, play a small role in life.

"Deterioration of the immune system" theory A theory of aging in which viruses are seen as culprits that the body fights continuously with antibodies. The battle between antibodies and the invading viruses may injure cells and bring on degenerative diseases.

Development Those processes in an organism that are biologically programmed as well as those that are influenced and/or transformed by the environment.

Dick-Read method A natural childbirth method in which the key to childbirth is preparation, limited medication, and participation.

Difficult infant A temperament in which the infant tends to respond negatively, is slow to adapt to change, is rather intense, and is often irritable and unhappy.

Diffused identity No apparent personal commitment to occupation, religion, or politics.

Dilatation In childbirth, the enlargement of the cervix to permit the passage of the fetus. The cervix usually reaches ten centimeters in diameter.

Dilatation stage The first stage of the birth process, which begins with the first true labor contractions and ends with the complete dilatation of the cervix.

Disengagement theory A social theory of aging that argues that both society and the aging person mutually withdraw, with the aging individual accepting and perhaps desiring decreased interaction.

Disintegrated A personality type with gross defects in psychological functions, loss of control over emotions and deterioration in thought processes.

Dizygotic twins Fraternal twins, who develop from two ova fertilized at the same time by two sperm. The genetic relationship between these twins is the same as between any other siblings.

DNA (deoxyribonucleic acid) A complex chemical substance found in a gene. It is a hereditary code that determines the action or expression of that gene.

Dominant gene In a pattern of genetic inheritance, the one of a pair of genes that determines the trait and suppresses the expression of the other gene.

Dual-career families An intact family unit in which both parents work outside the home.

Dyscalcula The inability to perform operations of arithmetic.

Dyslexia The inability to read with understanding.

E

Easy infant A temperament in which the infant reacts with moderation, adapts easily to new situations, exhibits a positive mood, and enjoys being handled.

Echolalic babbling Babbling in which infants, at around nine months, begin to repeat or echo sounds and produce the intonational qualities of true speech.

Eclampsia The later, more serious stage of toxemia. Convulsions develop in the mother, which may cause fetal oxygen deprivation as well as endanger the life of the mother.

Ectoderm During the germinal stage, the outside layer of the blastocyst. This later forms the skin, teeth, hair, nails, and nervous system of the fetus.

Effacement The shortening of the cervical canal from a structure that is one or two centimeters in length to one in which no canal at all exists.

Ego According to Freud, the rational, reality component of the personality, which coordinates the impulses from the id and the societal pressures imposed by the superego.

Egocentric speech Speech in which children can concentrate on only one thing at a time, and have difficulty seeing things from another person's perspective.

Ego integrity vs. despair Erikson's final psychosocial stage, involving the elderly. The older person who exhibits ego integrity recognizes that he or she has led a meaningful, productive, and worthwhile life. When an individual has not resolved earlier crises successfully, he or she feels a sense of despair and cannot view life in a meaningful perspective. The individual is not ready to face death and feels bitter about his or her life.

Embryonic stage The second stage of prenatal development. It begins when the zygote attaches to the uterine wall and ends when the zygote's rudimentary organ systems and body parts take shape. The period of time involved is from the end of the second week to the end of the eighth week of gestation.

Embryo transfer A procedure that involves transplanting an embryo from the fallopian tube of the biological mother to the uterus of another woman who cannot conceive but who can carry the fetus to full term. This is a form of prenatal adoption.

Empathy The ability to experience the thoughts and feelings of others.

Encoding The identification or registration process involved in information processing.

Endoderm During the germinal stage, the inner layer of the blastocyst. This later develops into most of the body organs, including the liver, pancreas, and lungs.

Endogenous smiling Early infant smiling that is due to internal stimulation only, is present at birth, and occurs in the neonate during REM sleep and during those waking states in which rapid eye movements are present.

Engrossment The father-infant bond, which includes a feeling of preoccupation, absorption, interest, and the desire to touch, hold, and interact with the infant.

Euthanasia The act of painlessly putting to death someone who is terminally ill.

Exogenous smiling Smiling that develops in the first and second month after birth and is due to external stimulation.

Expansion A means adults use to imitate children's speech. They add words or parts of words to children's sentences to make the sentences grammatically correct.

Experimental method A carefully controlled method in which the factors that are believed to influence the mind or behavior are controlled.

Expressive movement The movement of preschoolers that expresses emotions and needs through motor activities, and curiosity through direct involvement.

Expulsion The second stage of the birth process, which begins with the complete dilatation of the cervix and ends when the baby emerges.

Extended family An integration of a complicated family structure resulting in families that may last for several generations.

Externalizer An individual who feels he or she has little control over events and attributes his or her successes and failures to luck or to the attitudes and actions of other people.

F

Fear An emotional state in anticipation of a dangerous or unpleasant stimulus; a reaction to imminent danger.

Fetal stage The third stage of prenatal development, during which the formation of the major organs and body parts occurs.

Fetoscopy A fetal monitoring procedure in which a tiny telescope is used to view the inside of the uterus.

Field dependence To respond globally to the most attention-directing features of the task of separating a figure from the field in which it is embedded.

Field independence The capability of isolating a figure from the field in which it is imbedded.

Fine motor development The development of small muscles, which predominantly involves muscles of the fingers, wrists, and ankles.

Fine motor skills Small-muscle skills that include the ability to reach with the hand, to grasp, and to manipulate objects.

Fluid intelligence Intelligence based mainly on the speed and effectiveness of neurological and physiological factors.

Fontanels Six soft spots on the head of a neonate, where the skull has not yet closed.

Forceps Curved, tonglike instruments shaped to fit on each side of a baby's head and used in the delivery of a baby.

Foreclosure An adolescent's choosing a premature identity, not exploring all of the identities that are available.

Formal operational stage Piaget's fourth and final stage of cognitive development, in which the adolescent and adult acquires the ability to think logically about abstract propositions and things he or she has not experienced before.

G

Gametes Human cells that are the sperm in males and ova in females.

Generativity vs. stagnation Erikson's seventh psychosocial stage, representing middle adulthood. Generativity emphasizes continuity with the preceding stages as well as with the next generation. Those who cannot support this continuity to the next generation may become overly absorbed in self and personal needs while ignoring the needs of others.

Gender conservation The ability of preschoolers to understand that their biological sex is irreversible.

Genes Independent units that determine inherited characteristics and remain constant even when passed from one generation to another.

Genetic counseling A service that helps prospective parents determine the likelihood or risk that their children will have genetic defects.

Genetic engineering A conscious manipulation that affects the frequency or expression of genes.

Genetic preprogramming A theory of aging that suggests there is a blueprint for the total life span "written in your genes."

Genital stage Freud's fifth stage of psychosexual development, which is viewed as synonymous with adolescence. It marks the beginning of mature adult sexuality.

Genotype An individual's genetic makeup; that is, the totality of the genes inherited from the parent cells.

Germinal stage The first stage of prenatal development. It begins at conception when the ovum is fertilized, and ends when the fertilized ovum implants itself in the lining of the uterine wall, which is about two weeks after conception.

Gestation The period of prenatal development. For humans it is nine and a half lunar months.

Grief Feelings engendered by the loss of a loved one and a process of adapting to the loss.

Grief work The process in which the bereaved person must slowly detach his or her intense feelings from everything that linked him or her with the deceased.

Gross motor development The development of large muscles, which predominantly involves muscles of the neck, back, shoulders, legs, and arms.

Gross motor skills Large-muscle skills that include upright postural body control and locomotion.

Growth hormone A pituitary product that controls, to a great extent, the speed of growth.

Growth spurt The most rapid phase of adolescent growth.

H

Heteronomous morality According to Piaget, a stage of morality in which children ages six to nine regard rules as unchangeable, even when they are lax in following the rules themselves. An infraction of the rules is judged according to the amount of damage done, regardless of whether it is accidental or intentional.

Heterozygous A gene pair that give different hereditary directions for a particular trait (for example, one dominant and one recessive gene).

Hitching A situation in which the infant may move about in a sitting position, using one leg to push the body along.

Holophrase A one-word sentence or phrase that conveys meaning.

Homozygous A gene pair that gives the same hereditary directions for a particular trait (for example, either the same two dominant genes or the same two recessive genes).

Hospice An institution and/or organization devoted to making the lives of dying people as dignified and comfortable as possible.

Hostile aggression Aggression oriented towards another person following some sort of threat or the belief that another person has behaved intentionally.

Humanistic psychology Theory that stresses the uniqueness of each human being and supports the idea that each individual has an inner drive to fulfill the best of his or her unique potential.

Hyperactivity *See* Attentive deficit–hyperactivity disorder

Hypothesis A specific prediction that is derived from a theory and confirmed or disproven by empirical investigation.

I

Id According to Freud, the part of an individual's personality that houses unconscious impulses, sexual impulses, the hunger drive, and aggressive urges.

Identity A sense of sameness and continuity that is sought after by adolescents. It involves a quest for personal discovery of "who I am" and a growing understanding of one's existence.

Identity-achieved adolescent The adolescent who has experienced a psychological moratorium and resolved crises on his or her own terms.

Identity vs. role confusion Erikson's fifth psychosocial stage, when adolescents begin defining themselves in terms of social, sexual, and occupational identities or they struggle to identify their role, resulting in an ill-defined concept of their identity.

Imaginary audience An audience imagined by adolescents because they are self-conscious and feel they are the focus of attention.

Impulsive A cognitive style in which an individual responds quickly, without thinking and without checking carefully to see if the response is correct.

Incongruity The dimension of humor in which the expectation of reality is not met.

Independent variable A factor that is manipulated to determine its influence on some behavior of the population being studied.

Indiscriminate attachment The second stage of attachment, which occurs between six weeks and six to seven months of age. Infants prefer human company and are likely to protest when an adult puts them down or leaves them alone.

Individuative-reflective faith In Fowler's theory, the fifth stage of moral development, in which the young adult is in a transition to finding a genuinely individual set of principles or beliefs.

Inductive discipline A method of discipline that consists of explaining reasons and justifications for the child to behave in a particular way.

Industry vs. inferiority Erikson's fourth psychosocial crisis, which occurs during the elementary years. The child either gains confidence to master social skills or perceives a lack of importance or inability to deal with the demands of his or her world.

Influential grandparents Grandparents who see their grandchildren often, are major figures in their grandchildren's lives, and tend to have a familistic value orientation.

Information processing The process in which the brain receives a stimulus, registers or identifies it, stores that information, and later retrieves it and applies it to new experiences.

Initiative vs. guilt Erikson's third psychosocial crisis, in which children learn to initiate activities and enjoy their accomplishments, which enables them to acquire direction and purpose. If initiative is discouraged, they will feel guilty for their attempts at independence.

Instrumental aggression Aggression that aims at the retrieval of an object, territory, or privilege.

Instrumental movement The movement of preschoolers in which they learn to use instruments or tools and thus are capable of increasing the range of motor activities available to them.

Integrated The personality pattern of well-functioning elderly persons who have a complex inner life and, at the same time, intact cognitive abilities and a competent ego.

Interactional synchrony The synchronization of neonates' body movements with the sound patterns of adult speech.

Internalization of sensorimotor schemes In Piaget's theory, the sixth substage of the sensorimotor stage. It occurs between eighteen and twenty-four months of age. The infant can now solve problems without having to physically explore their possibilities or solutions.

Internalizer An individual who believes that he or she is responsible for his or her own successes and failures.

Intimacy vs. isolation Erikson's sixth psychosocial crisis, involving young adults forming a commitment to each other so that a warm and meaningful relationship is established. When there is little or no intimacy, a sense of ostracism or isolation occurs, which can lead to unsuccessful and superficial relationships.

Intuitive-projective faith In Fowler's theory, the second stage of moral development, in which a child's imagination provides long-lasting information about protective or threatening powers surrounding him or her.

Intuitive thinking The second substage of preoperational thinking, in which the four- to seven-year-old is capable of some mental operations that involve classifying, quantifying, and relating of objects. However, the child cannot comprehend the underlying principles of these operations.

In vitro fertilization A procedure in which an egg from a woman is fertilized in a petri dish by her husband's sperm, then implanted in her womb approximately four days after the fertilization.

Invulnerable children Children who appear to be stress-resistant and retain mastery and control over their lives even when coping with poverty and emotional and social stress.

Irreversibility The fact that once a living thing dies, its physical body cannot be made alive again.

Irreversible thinking A limited form of thinking in which children have difficulty mentally retracing operations.

J

Jargonese *See* Echolalic babbling.

Jealousy A result of frustration over the desire to be loved best.

K

Kin Family members including grandparents, aunts, uncles, cousins, nieces, nephews, brothers, sisters, brothers- and sisters-in-law.

Kin-keepers Women who maintain contact and exchanges between generations.

L

Lamaze method Natural childbirth in which the mother uses various techniques of breathing and relaxation that ease the birth process and the father functions as a coach to help the mother's breathing techniques.

Language acquisition device (LAD) According to Chomsky, a mental structure that enables an infant to process sounds and speech patterns and that triggers milestones of speech. It helps explain the innate ability of the human brain to not only process words but understand the structure of language and the fundamental relationship between words.

Language ambiguity riddles Riddles in which a play on words can be located in either the question or the answer.

Lanugo A soft hair that covers the body of the fetus during the fifth and sixth months.

Latency stage Freud's fourth stage of psychosexual development, in which sexual feelings subside as the child attempts to resolve the Oedipal conflict. This stage begins around age seven.

Learning theories Theories of development that emphasize the importance of learning and the modifiability of the course of development.

Life review A process of self-reflection that results in a new perception of and relationship with one's own mortality.

Lightening Prior to the beginning of labor, the settling of the fetal head into the mother's pelvis or pelvic inlet, which is the space between the bones of the pelvis through which the child must pass to be born.

Living will A document to formalize and declare an individual's wishes in specifying treatment limitations in the event of an irreversible, serious, and long-term illness.

Longitudinal method A research method that involves studying the same individuals over a period of time to see the changes that occur with age.

Long-term memory Memory that retains information for the long run and contains more information than we can retrieve at any given time.

Love withdrawal A method of discipline in which the parent gives direct but nonphysical expression of anger or disapproval at the child's undesirable behavior.

M

Male climacteric A slow decline in the sexual potency of men during the sixties and seventies. Most men do not lose their ability to father children.

Maturational theories See Stage Theories.

"Mean time to failure" theory A theory of aging that suggests aging is a product of gradual deterioration of various organs. That is, organs deteriorate gradually and separately.

Meiosis A form of cell division involved in the production of gametes, or sex cells. Mature gametes, ova and sperm, have only one-half of the normal complement of chromosomes in their nuclei. Gametes undergo a reduction in the number of chromosomes carried in their nuclei so that when an ovum and sperm fuse, there will be forty-six chromosomes.

Memory span The number of individual items held in short-term memory.

Menarche The first menstrual period, occurring at the end of a girl's growth spurt. Menarche marks the definitive and mature stage of uterine growth, but it does not usually signify the attainment of full reproductive function.

Menopause The time in a woman's life during which menstruation ceases completely.

Mental images Mental representations, or "pictures in the mind," associated with fantasy thought.

Mesoderm During the germinal stage, the middle layer of the blastocyst. This later develops into muscles, the skeletal system, and the circulatory system.

Metacognition A structural feature of adolescent thought that enables the individual to think about thinking.

Mitosis The process in which somatic, or body, cells divide. All somatic cells in normal human beings contain 46 chromosomes that can be arranged into twenty-three pairs. With fertilization, the comparable chromosomes of the ovum and sperm match up with each other and are arranged into twenty-three pairs of chromosomes. The cells of the embryo, the fetus, and finally the human body will be formed from divisions of this fertilized ovum.

Molding A process during which soft bony plates of the skull (connected by cartilage) are squeezed together in the birth canal, causing the neonate's head to look misshapen and elongated.

Monozygotic twins Identical twins, who develop from the same fertilized ovum and thus have the same genotype.

Moratorium A state in which the adolescent is exploring and actively searching for alternatives and struggling to find an identity.

Mourning Grief and bereavement that is, in varying degrees, determined by custom and expressed through ritual.

Multiple attachment The final stage of attachment, when the infant starts becoming attached to people other than the mother, including the father, siblings, grandparents, and consistent babysitters.

Mutual pretense A context in which both the dying person and those relating to the dying person pretend they do not know the prognosis.

Myelination The process that facilitates the transmission of neural signals by coating the nerve fibers with a protective fatty sheath called myelin.

Mythic-literal faith In Fowler's theory, the third stage of moral development, in which children, adolescents, and some adults adopt specific beliefs and observances as part of their "faith community," literally without reflection.

N

Nativist theory of language development The theory that views language acquisition as a product controlled by biology and closely linked to the maturation of the brain.

Natural childbirth Preparation of the mother and father for labor and delivery, which allows for their active involvement in the childbirth process.

Naturalistic observation A research method that involves intense watching and recording of behavior as it occurs in the subject's natural habitat.

Negative identity A premature closure of adolescence; undesirable and dangerous.

Nonfunctionality The fact that all life-defining functions cease at death.

Nuclear family A family unit that consists of mother, father, and child(ren).

Nullifiability The awareness that structures can exist that leave others unchanged. That is, in every system there is one element that, when combined with other elements in the system, leaves the result unchanged.

O

Object permanence In Piaget's theory, the cognitive capacity to realize that an object exists even when it is out of sight.

Obsessional review To relive the events surrounding the death of a loved one.

Operant conditioning According to Skinner, a process in which a voluntary response is more or less likely to occur depending on the consequences.

Oral stage Freud's first stage of psychosexual development, in which the primary focus of stimulation is the mouth and oral cavity. This stage lasts from birth to one year.

Ordinal position The order in which a child is born into a family.

Organization In Piaget's theory, the process that enables experience and knowledge to be categorized and sorted out into meaningful segments or wholes that become more complex.

Organogenesis The basic formation of the fetus's major organs, organ systems, and body parts.

Osteoarthritis Changes in the bones of the joints.

Osteoporosis A physical condition in which bone marrow gradually disappears in the arms and legs and becomes concentrated in the bones of the trunk. A loss of calcium makes the bones more brittle, hollow, weak, and porous.

Ova Female gametes, or sex cells.

Overregularization The tendency of a child, when acquiring a grammatical rule, to apply the rule to situations that do not fit.

P

Passive-dependent The personality type that includes the succorance-seeking elderly (those who have strong dependency needs) and the apathetic elderly (those who are passive and have low role activity and medium or low life satisfaction).

Passive euthanasia To allow a person to die by withholding treatment and heroic measures.

Passive grandparents Grandparents who have regular contact with their grandchildren and are ready to offer assistence when needed but refuse to interfere in rearing them.

Peak height velocity (PHV) The peak of linear growth.

Permissive child rearing A parenting style in which parents behave in a kind, accepting, indifferent way toward their children and demand very little. The parents see their role as helping or serving their children.

Personal fable A belief in the uniqueness of one's feelings, thoughts, and experiences.

Phallic stage Freud's third stage of psychosexual development, sometimes called the *Oedipal stage,* in which psychic energy is invested in the genitals and pleasure is achieved through manipulating the genitals. This stage lasts roughly from the fourth to the sixth year.

Phenotype The visible expression of inherited traits, which depends on the genotype or how the environment has affected the expression of the genotype.

Placenta A critical organ that separates the infant's bloodstream from the mother's, provides nourishment to the embryo and later the fetus, provides immunizing agents that combat certain diseases, and acts as a filtering system.

Placental stage The third stage of the birth process, which includes the placental separation and the placental expulsion.

Planned mutations A theory of aging in which some genes have the specific function of causing mutations in other genes, which may have deleterious effects on the individual organism during its life span, thus accelerating the aging process.

Postretirement Life without a job, plus factors such as health, activity level, and perhaps having to live alone.

Power-assertive discipline A method of discipline that consists of enforcing standards of behavior with threats and punishment.

Preconceptual thinking The first substage of preoperational thinking, in which the two- to four-year-old uses symbolic thinking to a limited degree and tends to confuse his or her own thoughts with the thoughts of other people. He or she creates simple classifications that are necessary for identifying major objects and events.

Preeclampsia The first stage of toxemia, which occurs after the twenty-fourth week of pregnancy. A pregnant woman's blood pressure increases, she accumulates salt and water, and she develops swelling.

Preformationist A theory in which a human being existed preformed in either the sperm or the ova.

Premature Babies who are born before the thirty-seventh week of pregnancy and who weigh less than 2,500 grams (five and one-half pounds).

Preoperational thought Piaget's second stage of cognitive development. The preschool child engages in symbolic thought, which involves the child's emerging capability to use symbols, especially language, in his or her thinking. Preschoolers' reasoning is limited because of egocentrism, transductive reasoning, centering, and irreversible thinking.

Prepared childbirth *See* Natural childbirth

Preretirement The period that involves looking ahead to retirement, to what life in retirement will be like.

Preterm *See* Premature Small-for-dates Neonates who are clearly below their expected weight for their gestational age.

Primal faith In Fowler's theory, the first stage of moral development, in which a prelanguage sense of trust forms. A mutuality develops between parent and child to offset the anxiety that occurs from separations during infancy.

Primary circular reactions In Piaget's theory, the substage of the sensorimotor stage that begins after the first month and continues through fourth month. The infant's behavior is centered on his or her body rather than on external objects, and the behavior is endlessly repeated.

Propositional logic Logic that permits testing of hypotheses on purely a formal basis; that is, the kind of thinking required in scientific experimentation.

Proximodistal development A principle governing physical growth in which an individual develops from the midline out to the extremities.

Psychosexual theory Freud's theory of human personality development, which is based on fundamental instincts and drives. It involves three components of the personality (the id, ego, and superego) and five developmental stages (oral, anal, phallic, latency, and genital).

Psychosocial theory Erikson's theory of human development, which encompasses the social, cultural, and sexual aspects of development.

Puberty The morphological and physiological changes that occur in the growing child as the sex organs change from the infantile to the adult stage.

Q

Quickening During the second trimester, a period of activity in the womb that makes the mother aware of the fetus's presence.

R

Reality riddles Riddles based on a conceptual trick that remains within the context of reality.

Recall memory The ability to retrieve information about objects or events that are not present or currently happening.

Recessive gene In a pattern of genetic inheritance, the one gene in a pair of genes that is subordinate to the other, or dominant, gene. Two identical recessive genes must be present in order for a recessive trait to be expressed.

Recognition memory A retrieval system in which information is matched with stimulation information in the environment.

Recombinant DNA A form of genetic engineering that manipulates DNA by splitting and transferring genetic material from one species to another, creating life-forms unique to nature.

Reduction A means children use to imitate adult speech. Adult sentences are reduced to the number of words and the grammatical forms that the children can manage at their particular stage of language development.

Reflective A cognitive style in which the individual responds slowly and devotes a longer period of time to considering various aspects of a hypothesis.

Reflexes A range of built-in behavioral responses to particular kinds of stimuli.

Reflexive substage In Piaget's theory, the first substage of the sensorimotor stage. It begins at birth and continues through the first month of life. Neonates assimilate all stimuli through their reflex system.

Resolution The dimension of humor in which an individual can cognitively resolve a joke or riddle.

Retirement transition The period that involves leaving the job and taking on the role of a retired person.

Reversibility The understanding that for any operation there exists an opposite operation that can cancel it.

Rhythmical stereotypes Inborn behavior patterns that involve fairly rapid bursts of repetitious movements of the arms, legs, head, or torso. These rhythmicities occur in a predictable manner before voluntary behavior.

Rivalry A result of frustration over the desire to do best.

Role confusion The bewilderment adolescents feel in wondering who they are, where they belong, and where they are going.

Role diffusion Alienation and a lasting sense of isolation and confusion.

S

Sample A group of subjects selected from a population for study in order to estimate the characteristics of the population.

Schemes In Piaget's theory, structures for interpreting sensory input from the environment. Schemes begin as reflex actions, but through the processes of assimilation and accommodation, they become modified and provide the underlying patterns required in adapting to the environment.

Scooting *See* Hitching.

Secondary circular reactions In Piaget's theory, the substage of the sensorimotor stage that lasts from four to eight months of age. It consists of repetitive actions that center around the environmental consequences of those actions.

Second symbol system A set of symbols for symbols.

Secular trend The tendency for children to grow taller and mature at a faster rate over the past century.

Self-concept One's representation of one's own personality.

Self-demand feeding The practice of feeding infants when they are hungry rather than on a particular schedule determined by the parent and/or doctor.

Sensorimotor stage Piaget's first stage of cognitive development, in which infants develop concepts through their senses and motor abilities. The understanding of objects in their world is limited to the actions the infant performs on them.

Sensory memory A memory system of extremely short duration.

Separation anxiety A distressful behavior that occurs when a child is separated from a parent or significant caregiver. Separation anxiety is prominent between six months and three years of age.

Sex cells *See* Gametes

Sex chromosomes The twenty-third pair of chromosomes in a human being. Two X chromosomes determine a female, and an X and Y combination of chromosomes determines a male.

Sex cleavage The phenomenon of elementary school children segregating themselves into all-girl and all-boy groups.

Sexual identity Identity that proceeds from self-centered sexual preoccupations in early adolescence to mutual sexual relationships in late adolescence.

Short-term memory The immediate or working memory, with limited storage capacity.

Sign language The use of gestures and signs made with the fingers to represent words.

Slow-to-warm-up infant A temperament in which the infant reacts with a combination of mildly negative responses and slow adaptability to new stimuli.

Social identity Where one stands in relationship to others; an identity found through interaction with other people.

Socialized speech Conversation that enables the child to exchange thoughts with others, show a genuine interest in what others are thinking and saying, and use the interchange of ideas or collaborations to pursue common goals.

Social learning theory The theory that learning is a result of social interaction, including observing and imitating others.

Social survey A quantitative way of collecting information directly from people. Survey data are usually collected by interview or questionnaire.

Sociocenter The crowd joker, who is usually popular and outgoing and who maintains good feelings within the group and provides the group with a playful, congenial atmosphere.

Somatic cells Human cells that govern the formation of the human body, including the skin, bones, muscle, and organs.

Sonogram A picture from an ultrasound.

Specific attachment The third stage of attachment, which occurs at about seven months of age. The infant protests when separated from a particular individual, usually the mother.

Speed The rate of cognition.

Sperm Male gametes, or sex cells.

Stage theories Theories that emphasize the internal, self-directing quality of an individual's maturation, with sequential steps of development that form a logical hierarchy with one another.

Stage-three humor The humor of preschoolers that is based on appearances and perception.

States The level of arousal of an infant, such as asleep, drowsy, or alert.

Stranger anxiety A distressful behavior in which an infant reacts negatively to strangers.

Substage III–A The first substage of formal operational thinking. III–A is preparatory. Adolescents at this substage are capable of making correct discoveries and may handle certain formal operations.

Substage III–B The second substage of formal operational thinking. Adolescents at this substage are capable of advancing more inclusive laws and formulating more exquisite generalizations.

Superego According to Freud, the portion of one's personality that represents religious teachings, moral standards, and the ethics and mores of our parents and culture.

Superfecundity The technical term for dizygotic twins who are fathered by two different men.

Superfetation A rare occurrence when a second ovum is fertilized in the following reproductive cycle, producing fraternal twins with different gestation periods.

Surface structure According to Chomsky, the structure of language that involves the grammatical rules of language such as the order of words in a sentence.

Syntax The rules that govern the development of sentence structure.

Synthetic-conventional faith In Fowler's theory, the fourth stage of moral development, in which new cognitive abilities allow the adolescent to create a personal ideology of beliefs and values. The individual at this stage chooses a set of beliefs from those available.

T

Telegraphic speech The speech of toddlers, in which they put two or more words together to represent a larger sentence. It resembles a telegram. It is a patterned speech in which articles, auxiliary verbs, connecting verbs, and inflections are left out and content words are retained.

Teratogenic agent An environmental factor that interferes with the development of an embryo and is responsible for producing a physical defect in the embryo.

Terminal drop Sudden intellectual deterioration during a year or so immediately prior to a natural death.

Tertiary circular reactions In Piaget's theory, the fifth substage of the sensorimotor stage. It occurs between twelve and eighteen months of age. Infants experiment to discover new properties of objects and events and learn about the consequences their actions have on objects.

"The machine breaks down" A theory of aging in which the body cells, in the course of living, dividing, and growing, are subject to environmental influences as well as biochemical changes.

Theory A logical framework that attempts to explain a broad range of phenomena within a particular science.

Transductive reasoning Reasoning from one specific event to another, unrelated specific event.

Trust vs. mistrust Erikson's first psychosocial crisis, during which the infant will either establish a sense that the world is a safe place or develop a sense of suspicion and fear of those in his or her environment.

Type A behavior A pattern of personality traits including excessive competitive drive, aggressiveness, impatience, and a harrying sense of time urgency.

Type B behavior A pattern of personality traits opposite of Type A behavior. Type B personalities take time to ponder leisurely, weigh alternatives, and experiment.

U

Ultrasound A diagnostic tool used to detect abnormalities before birth. High-frequency sound waves are directed toward the fetus; they then bounce off the contours of the fetus's body, and a device transforms them into a fairly detailed picture called a sonogram.

Umbilical cord A cord that attaches the embryo and fetus to the placenta. It contains two arteries and a vein. The arteries remove waste products and carbon dioxide. The vein brings in oxygen and nutrients.

Universality The fact that all living things die.

Universalizing faith In Fowler's theory, the seventh stage of moral development, in which the person steps beyond individuality to a feeling of oneness with the power of being.

Unoccupied behavior According to Parten, a situation in which the child does not appear to be playing but watches whatever is taking place nearby.

V

Vernix caseosa A whitish, waxy substance that covers the fetus and protects the skin.

Voluntary euthanasia The act of killing oneself or letting oneself die when there is no hope of recovering from a terminal illness.

W

Wear and tear theory A theory of aging that views aging as a product of gradual deterioration, particularly in relation to bone or parts of the circulatory system.

Z

Zygote A single cell formed from the union of two gametes, a sperm and an ovum. A normal zygote contains forty-six chromosomes, twenty-three from the sperm and twenty-three from the ovum.

Bibliography

Abel, E. 1984. *Fetal alcohol syndrome and fetal alcohol effects*. New York: Plenum.

Abel, E. L. 1980. Fetal alcohol syndrome: Behavioral teratology. *Psychological bulletin*. 87, 29–50.

Abel, E. L. 1981. Behavioral teratology of alcohol. *Psychological bulletin* 90, 564–581.

Abraham, S., Johnson, C. L., and Najjar, M. F. 1979. *Weight and height of adults 18–74 years of age, United States: 1971–74*. Vital and Health Statistics, series 11, no. 211, DHEW publication no. (PHS) 79–1659.

Ackerman, B. P. 1981. Performative bias in children's interpretations of ambiguous referential communications. *Child development* 52, 1224–1230.

Addy, D. P. 1976. Infant feeding: A current view. *British medical journal* 1, 1268–1271.

Adler, J., and Carey, J. 1982. But is it a person? *Newsweek* 159 (January 11), 44.

Ager, S. 1986. Pressure myths result in babies. *Detroit free press* (May), 1B and 4B.

Ahammer, I. M., and Murray, J. P. 1979. Kindness in the kindergarten: The relative influence of role playing and prosocial television in facilitating altruism. *International journal of behavior development* 2, 133–157.

Ahlstrom, P. 1990. Physiological growth and development. In M. Story, ed. *Nutrition management of the pregnant adolescent*. Washington, D.C.: National Clearinghouse.

Ainlay, S. C., and Smith, D. R. 1984. Aging and religious participation. *Journal of gerontology* 39, 3, 357–363.

Ainsworth, M. D., and Bell, S. 1977. Infant crying and maternal responsiveness: A rejoinder to Gewirtz and Boyd. *Child development* 48, 1208–1216.

Ainsworth, M. D., Blehar, M., Waters, E., and Wall, S. 1978. *Patterns of attachment: A psychological study of the strange situation*. Hillsdale, N.J.: Erlbaum.

Ainsworth, M. D. S. 1973. Sensorimotor development of Ganda infants. In L. J. Stone, H. T. Smith, and L. B. Murphy, eds. *The competent infant*. New York: Basic Books.

Aldous, J. 1985. Structures, expectations, and functions, In V. L. Bengtson and J. Robertson, eds. *Grandparenthood*. Beverly Hills, Calif.: Sage Publications.

Altman, S. L., and Grossman, F. K. 1977. Women's career plans and maternal employment. *Psychology of women quarterly* 1, 365–376.

Altman, R., and Lewis, T. J. 1990. Social judgments of integrated and segregated students with mental retardation toward their same-age peers. *Education and training in mental retardation* 25, 2 (June), 107–112.

Altus, W. D. 1967. Birth order and its sequelae. *International journal of psychiatry* 3, 23–42.

Amato, P. R. 1986. Marital conflict, the parent-child relationship and child self-esteem. *Family relations* 35, 403–410.

Amato, P. R. 1987. Family processes in one-parent, stepparent, and intact families: The child's point of view. *Journal of marriage and the family* 49, 327–337.

American Association of Ophthalmology. 1970. *Dyslexia: Your child's reading disability*. American Association of Ophthalmology, 1100 17th Street NW, Washington, D.C. 20036. Pamphlet.

American Psychological Association. 1982. *Ethical principles in the conduct of research with human participants*. Washington, D.C.: American Psychological Association.

Ames, L. B. 1946. The development of the sense of time in the young child. *Journal of genetic psychology* 68, 97–125.

Anastasi, A. 1958. Heredity, environment, and the question "how?" *Psychological review* 65, 197–208.

Anastasi, A. 1985. Psychological testing: Basis concepts and common misconceptions. In A. Rogers and C. J. Scheirer, eds. *The G. Stanley Hall lecture series* Vol. 5. Washington, D.C.: American Psychological Association.

Anderson, C. W., Nagel, R. J., Roberts, W. A., and Smith, W. A. 1981. Attachment to substitute caregivers as a function of center quality and caregiver involvement. *Child development* 52, 53–61.

Anderson, J. V., and Van Nierop, M. R. 1989. *Basic nutrition facts*. East Lansing, Mich.: Cooperative Extension, Michigan State University.

Andersson, B. E. 1989. Effects of public day-care: A longitudinal study, *Child development* 60, 4, 857–866.

Andrews, L. 1984. Yours, mine, and theirs. *Psychology today* 18, 12, 20–29.

Angell, D. E. M. 1991. AIDS and babies remain a puzzle. *Lansing state journal* (May 28), 3D.

Angier, N. 1982. Helping children reach new heights. *Discover* 3, 35.

Anglin, J. 1977. *Word, object, and conceptual development*. New York: Norton.

Aniansson, A., and Gustafsson, E. 1981. Physical training in elderly men with special reference to quadriceps muscle strength and morphology. *Clinical physiology* 1, 87–98.

Annett, M. 1978. Genetic and nongenetic influences on handedness. *Behavior genetics* 8, 227–249.

Ansello, E. F. 1986. Male-female long-term relationships as a source of humor. In L. Nahemow, K. A. McCluskey-Fawcett, and P. E. McGhee, eds. *Humor and aging*. New York: Academic Press.

Antonucci, T. C. 1985. Personal characteristics, social support, and social behavior. In R. H. Binstock and E. Shanes, eds. *Handbook of aging and the social sciences*. New York: Van Nostrand.

Arbuthnot, J. 1975. Modification on moral judgment through role playing. *Developmental psychology* 11, 319–324.

Arehart-Treichel, J. 1978. America's teen pregnancy epidemic. *Science news* 113, 18 (May 6), 299–302.

Arehart-Treichel, J. 1982. Fetal ultrasound: How safe? *Science news* (June 12), 396–397.

Arey, L. B. 1974. *Developmental anatomy.* Philadelphia: W. B. Saunders.

Aries, P. 1962. *Centuries of childhood.* New York: Alfred A. Knopf.

Arlin, P. 1975. Cognitive development in adulthood: A fifth stage? *Developmental psychology* 11, 602–606.

Arlin, P. K. 1984. Adolescent and adult thought: A structural interpretation. In M. Commons, F. A. Richards, and C. Armon, eds. *Beyond formal operations.* New York: Praeger.

Arnon, S. S., et. al. 1979. Honey and other environmental risk factors for infant botulism. *Journal of pediatrics* 94:331.

Aronson, E., and Rosenbloom, S. 1973. Space perception in early infancy: Perception within a common auditory-visual space. In L. J. Stone, H. T. Smith, and L. B. Murphy, eds. *The competent infant.* New York: Basic Books.

Ascione, F., and Chambers, J. 1985. Videogame behavior. *Psychology today* 19 (September), 16.

Ashburn, S. S. 1986. Biophysical and cognitive development in young adulthood. In C. S. Schuster and S. S. Ashburn, eds. *The process of human development.* Boston: Little, Brown and Company.

Asher, S. R., and Renshaw, P. D. 1981. Children without friends: Social knowledge and social-skill training. In S. R. Asher and J. M. Gottman, eds. *The development of children's friendships.* Cambridge: Cambridge University Press.

Ashley, M. J. 1981. Alcohol use during pregnancy: A challenge for the 80's. *Canadian medical association journal* 125, 141–142.

Ashton, P. T. 1975. Cross-cultural Piagetian research: An experimental perspective. *Harvard educational review* 45, 475–506.

Astington, J. W., Harris, P. L., and Olson, D. R. 1988. *Developing theories of mind.* New York: Cambridge University Press.

Atchley, R. C. 1982. The process of retirement: Comparing women and men. In M. Szinovacz, ed. *Women's retirement.* Beverly Hills, Calif.: Sage Publications.

Atkin, C. 1978. Observation of parent-child interactions in supermarket decision making. *Journal of marketing* 42, 41–45.

Austrom, D. 1984. *The consequences of being single.* New York: American University Studies.

Averill, J. R. 1969. *Aging in a changing society.* 2nd ed. New York: Franklin Watts.

Azar, S. T., Robinson, D. R., Hekimian, E., and Twentyman, C. T. 1984. Unrealistic expectations and problem-solving ability in maltreating and comparison mothers. *Journal of consulting and clinical psychology* 52, 4, 687–691.

Azrin, M., and Foxx, R. 1981. *Toilet training in less than a day.* New York: Simon and Schuster.

Bachman, J. G., Bare, D. E., and Frankie, E. I. 1986. *Correlates of employment among high school seniors.* Ann Arbor, Mich.: Institute for Social Research.

Bachman, J. G., O'Malley, P. M., and Johnston, L. D. 1981. Smoking, drinking and drug use among American high school students: Correlates and trends, 1975–1979. *American journal of public health* 71, 59–69.

Bachrach, C. A., and Mosher, W. D. 1982. Voluntary childlessness in the United States: Estimates from the national survey of family growth. *Journal of family issues* (December).

Baecher, C. M. 1983. *Children's consumerism: Implications for education.* Paper presented at the Bush Center in Child Development and Social Policy, Yale University.

Baer, A. S. 1977. *The genetic perspective.* Philadelphia: W. B. Saunders.

Bailey, D. 1982. Sport and the child: Physiological considerations. In R. Magill, M. Ash, and F. Smoll, eds. *Children in sport.* Champaign, Ill.: Human Kinetics Publishers.

Bailey, D. A., Malina, R. M., and Mirwald, R. L. 1986. Physical activity and the growth of the child. In F. Falkner and J. M. Tanner, eds. *Postnatal growth neurobiology.* Vol. 2 of *Human growth: A comprehensive treatise.* 2nd ed. New York: Plenum Press.

Baillargeon, R., Spelke, E. S., and Wasserman, S. 1985. Object permanence in five-month-old infants. *Cognition* 20:191–208.

Bakeman, R., and Brownlee, J. R. 1980. The strategic use of parallel play: A sequential analysis. *Child development* 51, 873–878.

Baker, D. 1985. *Beyond rejection: The church, homosexuality and hope.* Portland, Oreg.: Multnomah Press.

Baldwin, A. L., Cole, R. E., and Baldwin, C. P. 1983. Parental pathology, family interaction, and the competence of the child in school. *Monographs of the Society for Research in Child Development* 47, no. 197.

Baldwin, D. A., and Markham, E. M. 1989. Establishing word-object relations: A first step. *Child development* (April) 60, 2, 381–398.

Baltes, P. B. 1985. The aging of intelligence: On the dynamics between growth and decline. *Scientific american.*

Baltes, P. B., and Schaie, K. W. 1975. The myth of the twilight years. In F. Rebelsky, ed. *Life: The continuous process.* New York: Alfred A. Knopf.

Baltes, P. B., and Willis, S. L. 1977. Toward psychological theories of aging and development. In J. E. Birren and K. W. Schaie, eds. *Handbook on the psychology of aging.* New York: Van Nostrand.

Bandura, A. 1969. *Principles of behavior modification.* New York: Holt, Rinehart and Winston.

Bandura, A. 1973. *Aggression: A social learning analysis.* Englewood Cliffs, N.J.: Prentice-Hall.

Bandura, A. 1977. *Social learning theory.* Englewood Cliffs, N.J.: Prentice-Hall.

Bandura, A. 1985. A model of causality in social learning theory. In M. Mahoney and A. Freedman, eds. *Cognition and therapy.* New York: Plenum.

Bandura, A., Grusec, J. E., and Menlove, F. L. 1967. Vicarious extinction of avoidance behavior. *Journal of personality and social psychology* 5, 16–23.

Bandura, A., and McDonald, F. J. 1963. The influences of social reinforcement and the behavior of models in shaping children's moral judgment. *Journal of abnormal psychology* 67, 274–281.

Bandura, A., Ross, D. M., and Ross, S. A. 1963. Imitation of film-mediated aggressive models. *Journal of abnormal and social psychology* 66, 3–11.

Bandura, A., and Walters, R. H. 1959. *Adolescent aggression.* New York: Ronald Press.

Bandura, A., and Walters, R. H. 1963. *Social learning and personality development.* New York: Holt, Rinehart and Winston.

Bank, S., and Kahn, M. D. 1982. *The sibling bond.* New York: Basic Books.

Bankart, C. P., and Anderson, C. C. 1979. Short-term effects of prosocial television viewing on play of preschool boys and girls. *Psychological reports* 44, 935–941.

Barclay, L. K. 1985. *Infant development.* New York: Holt, Rinehart and Winston.

Barnes, G. M., et al. 1986. Parental socialization factors and adolescent drinking behaviors. *Journal of marriage and the family* 48 (February), 27–36.

Barrett, D. E., Radke-Yarrow, M., and Klein, R. E. 1982. Chronic malnutrition and child behavior: Effects of early caloric supplementation on social and emotional functioning at school age. *Developmental psychology* 18, 541–556.

Barry, H., Bacon, M. K., and Child, I. L. 1963. A cross-cultural survey of some sex differences in socialization. *Journal of abnormal and social psychology* 67, 527–534.

Bart, P. 1971. Depression in middle-aged women. In V. Gornick and B. K. Moran, eds. *Women in sexist society*. New York: Basic Books.

Barth, P. R., Claycomb, M., and Loomis, A. 1988. Services to adolescent fathers. *Health and social work* (Fall), 277–285.

Bartlet, K. 1981. Study of twins results amazing. *Lansing state journal* (October 19), 3D.

Barton, J., et al. 1982. Social image factors as motivators of smoking initiation in early and middle adolescence. *Child development* 53, 1499–1511.

Baruch, G., Barnett, R., and Rivers, C. 1983. *Lifeprints: New patterns of love and work for today's women*. New York: McGraw-Hill Book Company.

Baruch, G. K. 1972. Maternal influences upon college women's attitudes toward women and work. *Developmental psychology* 6, 32–37.

Baruch, G. K. 1974. Maternal career-orientation in relation to parental identification in college women. *Journal of vocational behavior* 4, 173–180.

Baruch, G. K., and Barnett, R. 1986. Role quality, multiple role involvement, and psychological well-being in mid-life women. *Journal of personality and social psychology* 51, 578–585.

Basseches, M. 1980. Dialectical schemata: A framework for the empirical study of the development of dialectical thinking. *Human development* 23, 400–421.

Basseches, M. 1984. *Dialectical thinking and adult development*. Norwood, N.J.: Ablex.

Basseches, M. 1989. Dialectical thinking as an organized whole: Comments on Irwin and Kramer. In M. L. Commons, J. D. Sinnott, F. A. Richards, and C. Armon, eds. *Adult development*. Vol. 1 of *Comparisons and applications of developmental models*. New York: Praeger.

Bates, J. E. 1987. Temperament in infancy. In J. D. Osofsky, ed. *Handbook of infant development*. 2nd ed. New York: Wiley.

Bauchner, H., Zuckerman, B., McClain, M., Frank, D., Fried, L. E., and Kayne, H. 1988. Risk of sudden infant death syndrome among infants with in utero exposure to cocaine. *Journal of pediatrics* (November), 831–834.

Baumrind, D. 1967. Child-care practices anteceding three patterns of preschool behavior. *Genetic psychology monographs* 75, 43–88.

Baumrind, D. 1975. *Early socialization and the discipline controversy*. Morristown, N.J.: General Learning Press.

Baumrind, D. 1985. Research using intentional deception: Ethical issues revisited. *American psychologist* 40, 165–174.

Bayley, N. 1973. Behavioral correlates of mental growth: Birth to thirty-six years. In L. J. Stone, H. T. Smith, L. B. Murphy, eds. *The compentent infant*. New York: Basic Books.

Bayley, N. 1973. Comparisons of mental and motor test scores for ages 1–15 months by sex, birth order, race, geographical location, and education of parents. In L. J. Stone, H. T. Smith, L. B. Murphy, eds. *The competent infant*. New York: Basic Books.

Bayley, N., and Schaefer, E. S. 1963. Maternal behavior and personality development data from the Berkeley growth study. In R. E. Grinder, ed. *Studies in adolescence*. New York: Macmillan Company.

Beal, C. R., and Belgrad, S. L. 1990. The development of message evaluation skills in young children. *Child development* 61, 705–712.

Beal, C. R., and Flavell, J. H. 1982. The effect of increasing the salience of message ambiguities on kindergartners' evaluations of communi-

cative success and message adequacy. *Developmental psychology* 18, 43–48.

Bear, G. G., Clever, A., and Proctor, W. A. 1991. Self-perceptions of nonhandicapped children and children with learning disabilities in integrated classes. *Journal of special education* 24, 4, 409–426.

Beckwith, L. 1973. Relationships between infants' vocalizations and their mothers' behavior. In L. J. Stone, H. T. Smith, and L. B. Murphy, eds. *The competent infant*. New York: Basic Books.

Bee, H. L. 1987. *The journey of adulthood*. New York: Macmillan.

Beeson, B., and Williams, R. A. 1983. Preschool girls' play still sex-stereotyped. *Indiana daily student*. Cited in V. N. Edwards et al., eds. *Growing child research review*. (February 1984), 2, 6, 8.

Begley, S., and Carey, J. 1982. How human life begins. *Newsweek* 159 (January 11), 38–43.

Behrend, D. A. 1990. The development of verb concepts: Children's use of verbs to label familiar and novel events. *Child development* 61, 681–696.

Behrman, R. E., and Vaughn, V. C. 1982. In W. E. Nelson, ed. *Nelson textbook of pediatrics*. 12th ed. Philadelphia: Saunders.

Bell, A., Weinberg, M., and Hammersmith, S. K. 1981. *Sexual preference*. Indianapolis: Indiana University Press.

Bell, A. P., and Weinberg, H. S. 1978. *Homosexualities: A study of diversity among men and women*. New York: Simon and Schuster.

Bell, R. R. 1981. Friendships of women and of men. *Psychology of women quarterly* 5, 402–417.

Bell, S., and Ainsworth, M. D. 1972. Infant crying and maternal responsiveness. *Child development* 43, 1171–1190.

Bell, S. M. 1970. The development of the concept of object as related to infant-mother attachment. *Child development* 41, 291–311.

Bell, S. M., and Ainsworth, M. D. S. 1972. Infant crying and maternal responsiveness. *Child development* 43, 1171–1190.

Belle, D. 1982. *Lives in stress: Women and depression*. Beverly Hills, Calif.: Sage.

Bellugi, U. H. 1967. *The acquisition of the system of negation in children's speech*. Ph.D. dissertation, Harvard University.

Belsky, J. 1979. The interrelations of parent and spousal behavior during infancy in traditional nuclear families: An exploratory analysis. *Journal of marriage and the family* 41, 62–68.

Belsky, J. 1988. The "effects" of infant day care reconsidered. *Early childhood research quarterly*. Special issue: Infant day care (September), vol. 3 (3), 235–272.

Belsky, J., and Steinberg, L. D. 1978. The effects of day care: A critical review. *Child development* 49, 929–949.

Belsky, J., et al. 1985. Stability and change in marriage across the transition to parenthood: A second study. *Journal of marriage and the family* 47, 4 (November), 855–865.

Belsky, J., Roving, M. and Taylor, G. 1984. The Pennsylvania Infant and Family Development Project III: The origins of individual differences in infant-mother attachment. *Child development* 55, 718–728.

Belsky, J. K. 1984. *The psychology of aging: Theory, research and practice*. Monterey, Calif.: Brooks-Cole.

Bender S. D. 1989. *PMS: Questions and answers*. Los Angeles: The Body Press.

Benenson, J., and Dweck, C. 1986. The development of trait explanations and self-evaluations in the academic and social domains. *Child development* 57, 1179–1187.

Bengtson, V. L. 1985. Diversity and symbolism in grandparental roles. In V. L. Bengtson and J. F. Robertson, eds. *Grandparenthood*. Beverly Hills: Sage Publications.

Benin, M. H., and Nienstedt, B. C. 1985. Happiness in single- and dual-earner families: The effects of marital happiness, job satisfaction, and life cycle. *Journal of marriage and the family* 47, 4 (November), 975–984.

Benson, J. B., and Uzgiris, F. C. 1985. Effect of self-initiated locomotion on infant search activity. *Developmental psychology* 6 (November 21), 923–931.

Berg, W. K., and Berg, K. M. 1979. Psychophysiological development in infancy: State, sensory function, and attention. In J. D. Osofsky, ed. *Handbook of infant development.* New York: John Wiley and Sons.

Berk, S. F. 1985. *The gender factory: The apportionment of work in American households.* New York: Plenum Press.

Berlinsky, E., and Biller, H. 1982. *Parental death and psychological development.* Lexington, Mass.: Lexington Books.

Bermant, G., and Davidson, J. M. 1974. *Biological bases of sexual behavior.* New York: Harper and Row.

Berndt, T. J. 1982. The features and effects of friendship in early adolescence. *Child development* 53, 1447–1460.

Bernstein, A. C. 1976. How children learn about sex and birth. *Psychology today* 9, 8, (January), 31–35.

Berreuta-Clement, J., Schweinhart, L. J., Barnett, W. S., Epstein, A. S., and Weikert, D. P. 1984. *Changed lives: Effects of the Perry Preschool program on youths through age 19.* Ypsilanti, Mich.: High/Scope Press.

Bertelsen, A. 1985. Controversies and consistencies in psychiatric genetics. *Acta psychiatrie Scandinavia* 71, 61–75.

Berzonsky, M. D. 1982. Inter- and intraindividual differences in adolescent storm and stress: A life span developmental view. *Journal of early adolescence* 2, 211–217.

Biblow, E. 1973. Imaginative play and the control of aggressive behavior. In J. L. Singer, ed. *The child's world of make-believe: Experimental studies of imaginative play.* New York: Academic Press.

Bigler-Doughten, S., and Jenkins, R. M. 1987. Adolescent snacks: Nutrient density and nutritional contribution to total intake. *Journal of the American Dietetic Association* 87, 1678.

Biller, H. B. 1971. Father absence and the personality development of the male child. In S. Chess and A. Thomas, eds. *Annual progress in child psychiatry and child development.* New York: Brunner/Mazel Publishers.

Birren, J. E. 1974. Translations in gerontology from lab to life. *American psychologist* (November), 808–815.

Birren, J. E., and Renner, V. J. 1980. Concepts and issues of mental health and aging. In J. E. Birren and R. B. Sloane, eds. *Handbook of mental health and aging.* Englewood Cliffs, N.J.: Prentice-Hall.

Birren, J. E., Woods, A. M., and Williams, M. V. 1980. Behavioral slowing with age: Causes, organization, and consequences. In L. W. Poon, ed. *Aging in the 1980s.* Washington, D.C.: American Psychological Association.

Bischof, L. J. 1969. *Adult psychiatry.* New York: Harper and Row.

Bischof, L. J. 1976. *Adult psychology.* 2nd ed. New York: Harper and Row.

Bjorksten, J. 1974. Cross-linkage and the aging process. In M. Rockstein, M. L. Sussman, and J. Chesky, eds. *Theoretical aspects of aging.* New York: Academic Press.

Blackburn, J. A. 1984. The influence of personality curriculum and memory correlates on formal reasoning in young adults and elderly persons. *Journal of gerontology* 39, 207–209.

Blake, J. 1990. *Risky times.* New York: Workman Publishing.

Blau, D., and Berezin, M. A. 1975. Neuroses and character disorders. In J. G. Howells, ed. *Modern perspectives on the psychiatry of old age.* New York: Brunner/Mazel.

Blau, Z. S. 1981. *Aging in a changing society.* 2nd ed. New York: Franklin Watts.

Blazer, D. 1982. *Depression in late life.* St. Louis: Mosby.

Blewitt, P. 1983. Dog versus collie: Vocabulary in speech to young children. *Developmental psychology* 19, 602–609.

Blieszner, R., and Alley, J. M. 1990. Family caregiving for the elderly: An overview of resources. *Family relations* 39, 97–102.

Blieszner, R., and Shifflett, P. A. 1990. The effects of Alzheimer's disease on close relationships between patients and caregivers. *Family relations* 39, 57–62.

Block, J. D. 1980. *Friendship.* New York: Macmillan Publishing Company.

Block, J. H. 1979. *Personality development in males and females: The influence of different socialization.* Master Lecture Series of the American Psychological Association, New York.

Block, J. H. 1982. Another look at sex differentiation in the socialization behaviors of mothers and fathers. In J. Sherman and F. Denmark, eds. *Psychology of women: Future of research.* New York: Psychological Dimensions.

Block, J. H., and Block, J. 1980. The role of ego-control and ego-resiliency in the organization of behavior. In W. A. Collins, ed. *Development of cognition, affect, and social relations, Minnesota symposium on child psychology.* Vol. 13. Hillsdale, N.J.: Erlbaum.

Block, J. H., Block, J., and Morrison, A. 1981. Parental agreement-disagreement on child-rearing orientations and gender-related personality correlates in children. *Child development* 52, 965–974.

Block, M. R. 1982. Professional women: Work pattern as a correlate of retirement satisfaction. In M. Szinovacz, ed. *Women's retirement.* Beverly Hills, Calif.: Sage Publications.

Blok, J. H. 1978. The incidence of sudden infant death syndrome in North Carolina's cities and counties: 1972–1974. *American journal of public health* 68 (April), 367–372.

Blood, B., and Blood, M. 1978. *Marriage.* New York: Free Press.

Bloom, B. C. 1969. Letter to the editor. *Harvard educational review* 39, 419–421.

Bluebond-Langner, M. 1975. *Awareness and communication in terminally-ill children: Pattern, process, and pretense.* Unpublished doctoral dissertation, University of Illinois.

Bluebond-Langner, M. 1977. Meanings of death to children. In H. Feifel, ed. *New meanings of death.* New York: McGraw-Hill Book Company.

Blyth, D. A., Simmons, R. G., and Carlton-Ford, S. 1983. The adjustment of early adolescents to school transitions. *Journal of early adolescence* 3, 105–120.

Bogin, B., and MacVean, R. B. 1983. The relationship of socioeconomic status and sex to body size, skeletal maturation, and cognitive status of Guatemala City school children. *Child development* 54, 115–128.

Bohline, D. S. 1985. Intellectual and affective characteristics of attention deficit disordered children. *Journal of learning disabilities* 18 (December), 604–608.

Boldt, M. 1982. Normative evaluations of suicide and death: A cross-generational study. *Omega* 13, 145–157.

Borkan, G. A., Hults, D. E., Gerzof, S. G., Robbins, A. H., and Silbert, C. K. 1983. Age changes in body composition revealed by completed tomography. *Journal of gerontology* 38, 673–677.

Borland, D. C., Bergman, S., Keith, J. 1981. *The sibling relationship as an alternative to institutionalization: Some preliminary findings.* Paper presented at the twenty-first International Congress of Gerontology, Hamberg, Germany.

Bortz, W. M. 1982. Disuse and aging. *Journal of the American Medical Association* 248, 10, 1203–1208.

Boss, G. R., and Seegmiller, J. E. 1981. Age-related physiological changes and their clinical significance. *The Western journal of medicine* 135, 434–440.

Botwinick, J. 1984. *Aging and behavior: A comprehensive integration of research findings.* 3rd ed. New York: Springer.

Botwinick, J., and Storandt, M. 1974. *Memory, related functions and age.* Springfield, Ill.: Charles C. Thomas.

Bouchard, T. J., and McGue, M. 1981. Familial studies of intelligence: A review. *Science* 212 (May), 1055–1059.

Bowen, S. M., and Miller, B. C. 1980. Paternal attachment behavior as related to presence at delivery and preparenthood classes: A pilot study. *Nursing research* 29, 307.

Bower, T. G. R. 1967. The development of object-permanence: Some studies of existence constancy. *Perception and psychophysics* 2, 411–418.

Bower, T. G. R. 1977. *A primer of infant development.* San Francisco: W. H. Freeman and Company.

Bowlby, J. 1958. The nature of the child's tie to his mother. *International journal of psychoanalysis* 39, 350–373.

Bowlby, J. 1969. *Attachment.* Vol. 1 of *Attachment and loss.* New York: Basic Books.

Bowlby, J. 1973. *Separation.* Vol. 2 of *Attachment and loss.* London: Hogarth.

Bowling, A., and Cartwright, A. 1982. *Life after a death: A study of the elderly widowed.* New York: Tavistock.

Brackbill, Y. 1979. Obstetrical medication and infant behavior. In J. D. Osofsky, ed. *Handbook of infant development.* New York: John Wiley and Sons.

Brainerd, C. 1978. The stage question in cognitive-developmental theory. *Behavioral and brain sciences* 1, 173–213.

Brainerd, C. 1979. Concept learning and development. In Klausmar, H. J., ed. *Cognitive development from an information processing and a Piagetian view: Results of a longitudinal study.* Cambridge, Mass.: Ballinger.

Braisted, J. R., et al. 1985. The adolescent ballet dancer. *Journal of adolescent health care* 6, 365–371.

Braun, K. L., and Rose, C. L. 1987. Family perceptions of geriatric foster family and nursing home care. *Family relations* 36, 321–327.

Bray, D. W., and Howard, A. 1983. The AT&T longitudinal studies of managers. In K. W. Schaie, ed. *Longitudinal studies of adult psychological development.* New York: Guilford Press.

Brazelton, T. B. 1970. Effect of prenatal drugs on the behavior of the neonate. *American journal of psychiatry* 126, 9, (March), 1261–1266.

Brazelton, T. B. 1986. Development of newborn behavior. In F. Falkner and J. M. Tanner, eds. *Human growth: A comprehensive treatise.* Vol. 2, *Postnatal growth neurobiology.* New York: Plenum Press.

Brecher, E. M. 1984. *Love, sex, and aging.* Boston: Little, Brown and Company.

Breitmayer, B. J., and Ramey, C. T. 1986. Biological nonoptimality and quality of postnatal environment as codeterminants of intellectual development. *Child development* 57, 1151–1165.

Breitner, J. C. S. 1988. Alzheimer's disease: Possible evidence for genetic causes. In M. K. Aronson, ed. *Understanding Alzheimer's disease.* New York: Charles Scribner Sons.

Bremner, J. G. 1988. *Infancy.* New York: Basil Blackwell.

Bretherton, I. 1985. Attachment theory: Retrospect and prospect. In I. Bretherton and E. Waters, eds., Growing points of attachment theory and research. *Monographs of the Society for Research in Child Development* 50 (1–2, serial no. 209).

Brett, J. M. 1980. The effect of job transfer on employees and their families. In C. L. Cooper and R. Payne, eds. *Current concerns in occupational stress.* New York: John Wiley.

Brickman, A. S., McManus, M., Grapetine, W. L., and Alessi, N. 1984. Neuropsychological assessment of seriously delinquent adolescents. *Journal of the American Academy of Child Psychiatry* 23, 453–457.

Brightly, B. 1976. The effect of television: A look by preschoolers. In J. Travers, ed. *The new children: The first six years.* Stanford, Conn.: Greylock.

Brockington, C. F., and Lempert, S. M. 1966. *The social needs of the over-eighties: The Stockport survey.* Manchester, England: Manchester University Press.

Brody, E. M. 1981. "Women in the middle" and family help to older people. *The gerontologist* 21, 471–480.

Brody, E. M., and Schoonover, C. B. 1986. Patterns of parent care when adult daughters work and when they do not. *The gerontologist* 26, 372–381.

Brody, E. M., Johnsen, P. T., and Fulcomer, M. C. 1984. What should adult children do for elderly parents? Opinions and preferences of three generations of women. *Journal of gerontology* 39, 6, 736–746.

Brody, G. H., and Shaffer, D. R. 1982. Contributions of parents and peers to children's moral socialization. *Developmental review* 2, 31–75.

Bronfenbrenner, U. 1970. *Who cares for America's children?* Paper presented at the annual meeting of the National Association for the Education of Young Children.

Bronson, G. W. 1973. Fear of visual novelty: Developmental patterns in males and females. In L. J. Stone, H. T. Smith, and L. B. Murphy, eds. *The competent infant.* New York: Basic Books.

Bronson, W. 1981. *Toddlers' behavior with age-mates: Issues of interaction, cognitive and affect.* Norwood, N.J.: Ablex.

Brook, J. S., et al. 1983. Stages of drug use in adolescence: Personality, peer, and family correlates. *Developmental psychology* 19, 2, 269–277.

Brook, J. S., Whiteman, M., Gordon, A. S., and Cohen, P. 1986. Dynamics of childhood and adolescent personality traits and adolescent drug use. *Developmental psychology* 22, 403–414.

Brown, J. V., and Bakeman, R. 1980. Relationships of human mothers with their infants during the first year of life: Effect of prematurity. In R. W. Bell and W. P. Smotherman, eds. *Maternal influences and early behavior.* New York: S. P. Medical and Scientific Books.

Brown, R., and Bellugi, U. 1964. Three processes in the child's acquisition of syntax. *Harvard educational review* 2, 133–151.

Brown, R. T. 1982. A developmental analysis of visual and auditory sustained attention and reflection-impulsivity in hyperactive children. *Journal of learning disabilities* 15, 614–618.

Brozek, J., and Schurch, B., eds. 1984. *Malnutrition and behavior: Critical assessment of key issues.* Lausanne, Switzerland: Nestle Foundation.

Brunner, L. S., and Suddarth, D. S. 1984. *Testbook of medical-surgical nursing.* 5th ed. Philadelphia: Lippincott.

Brunnquell, D., Crichton, L., and Egeland, B. 1981. Maternal personality and attitude in disturbances of child rearing. *American journal of orthopsychiatry* 51, 680–691.

Bryan, J. H. 1975. Children's cooperation and helping behavior. In E. M. Hetherington, ed. *Review of child development research.* Vol. 5. Chicago: University of Chicago Press.

Budoff, P. W. 1983. *No more hot flashes and the other good news.* New York: Putnam.

Bullock, M. 1985. Animism in childhood thinking: A new look at an old question. *Developmental psychology* 21, 2, 217–225.

Bullough, V. L. 1981. Age at menarche: A misunderstanding. *Science* 213 (July 17), 365–366.

Burch, H. 1973. *Eating disorders: Obesity, anorexia nervosa, and the person within.* New York: Basic Books.

Burchard, J. D. 1979. Competitive youth sports and social competence. In M. W. Kent and J. E. Rolf, eds. *Social competence in children.* Vol. 3 of *Primary prevention of psychopathology.* Hanover, N.H.: University Press of New England.

Burke, R. M., and Weir, R. 1976. *Journal of marriage and the family* 38 (May), 279–287.

Burnside, I. M., Ebersole, P., and Monea, H. E., eds. 1979. *Psychosocial caring throughout the life span.* New York: McGraw-Hill.

Burnside, I. M., ed. 1981. *Nursing and the aged.* 2nd ed. New York: McGraw-Hill.

Burr, M. L., Milbank, J. E., and Gibbs, D. 1982. The nutritional status of the elderly. *Age and aging* 11, 89–96.

Buss, A., and Plomin, R. 1975. *A temperament theory of personality development.* New York: John Wiley and Sons.

Busse, E. W., and Maddox, G. L., eds. 1985. *The Duke longitudinal studies of normal aging, 1955–1980: Introduction and overview of findings.* New York: Springer.

Butler, R. N. 1968. The life review: An interpretation of reminiscence in the aged. In B. L. Neugarten, ed. *Middle age and aging.* Chicago: University of Chicago Press.

Butler, R. N., and Lewis, M. I. 1982. *Aging and mental health: Positive psychological and biomedical approaches.* 3rd ed. St. Louis: Mosby.

Butnarescu, G. F., and Tillotson, D. M. 1983. *Maternity nursing.* New York: Wiley Medical.

Butterfield, P. M. 1986. Women "at risk" for parenting disorder perceive emotions in infant pictures differently. *Infant behavior and development* 9, 56.

Byard, P. J., and Roche, A. F. 1984. Secular trend for recumbent length and stature in the Fels longitudinal growth study. In J. Borms, R. Hauspie, A. Sand, C. Susanne, and M. Hebbelinck, eds. *Human growth and development.* New York: Plenum Press.

Byrce, J. W., and Leichter, H. J. 1983. The family and television: Forms of mediation. *Journal of family issues* 4, 309–328.

Calderwood, D. 1965. Adolescents' views on sex education. *Journal of marriage and family* 27 (May), 291–298.

Cameron, R. 1984. Problem-solving inefficiency and conceptual tempo: A task analysis of underlying factors. *Child development* 55, 2031–2041.

Campos, J. J., Barrett, K. C., Lamb, M. E., Goldsmith, H. H., and Stenberg, C. 1983. Socioemotional development. In M. M. Haith and J. J. Campos, eds. *Infancy and developmental psychobiology.* 4th ed. New York: Wiley.

Cantor, M. H. 1983. Strain among caregivers: A study of experience in the United States. *The gerontologist* 23, 597–604.

Cantor, P. 1985. These teenagers feel they have no options. *People weekly* (February 18), 84–87.

Caplan, F., and Caplan, T. 1973. *The power of play.* Garden City, NY: Anchor Books.

Capsules. 1980. DES daughters. *Time* (March 24), 48–49.

Carew, J. 1980. Experience and the development of intelligence in young children. *Monographs of the Society for Research in Child Development* 45, (6–6, serial no. 187).

Carew, J. 1980. Experience and the development of intelligence in young children. *Monographs of the Society for Research in Child Development* 45, (1–2, serial no. 183).

Carey, S. 1977. The child as a word learner. In M. Halle, J. Bressman, and G. Miller, eds. *Linguistic theory and psychological reality.* Cambridge, Mass.: MIT Press.

Carlson, E. A. 1984. *Human genetics.* Lexington, Mass.: D.C. Heath and Company.

Carper, L. 1978. Sex roles in the nursery. *Harper's* (April).

Carrington, E. R. 1974. Editorial: Relationship of stilbestrol exposure in utero to vaginal lesions in adolescence. *Journal of pediatrics* 85, 295–296.

Carroll, J. L., and Rest, J. R. 1982. Moral development. In B. B. Wolman, ed. *Handbook of developmental psychology.* Englewood Cliffs, N.J.: Prentice-Hall.

Carroll, L. 1988. Concern with AIDS and the sexual behavior of college students. *Journal of marriage and the family* 50, 405–411.

Carter, A. S., Mayes, L. C., and Pajer, K. A. 1990. The role of dyadic affect in play and infant sex in predicting infant response to the still-face situation. Child development 61, 3, 764–773.

Carter, E. A., and McGoldrick, M. 1980. *The family life cycle: A framework for family therapy.* New York: Gardner.

Caruso, D. A. 1984. Infants' exploratory play. *Young children* 40, 1, (November), 27–30.

Case, R. 1985. *Intellectual development: Birth to adulthood.* New York: Academic Press.

Case, R., Kurland, D., and Goldberg, J. 1982. Operational efficiency and the growth of short-term memory span. *Journal of experimental child psychology* 33, 386–404.

Caspi, A., Elder, G. H., and Bem, D. J. 1987. Moving against the world: Life-course patterns of explosive children. *Developmental psychology* 23, 308–313.

Cate, R., Henton, J., Koval, J., Christopher, F. S., and Lloyd, S. 1982. Premarital abuse: A social psychological perspective. *Journal of family issues* 3, 79–91.

Cater, J. 1980. Correlates of low birth weight. *Child: Care, health, and development* 6, 267–277.

Cattel, R. B. 1963. The nature and measurement of anxiety. *Scientific American* 208, 3, 96–104.

Cattell, R. B. 1963. Theory of fluid and crystalized intelligence: A critical experiment. *Journal of educational psychology* 57, 253–270.

Cazden, C. B. 1972. Suggestions from studies of early language acquisition. In Courtney B. Cazden, ed. *Language in early childhood education.* Washington, D.C.: National Association for the Education of Young Children.

Center for Disease Control. 1990. *Morbidity and mortality report* 32. Atlanta, Ga.: U.S. Department of Health and Human Services/Public Health Services.

Cerella, J. 1985. Information processing rates in the elderly. *Psychological bulletin* 98, 67–83.

Cernoch, J. H., and Porter, R. H. 1985. Recognition of maternal axillary odors by infants. *Child development* 56, 6, 1593–1598.

Chall, J. S. 1964. *Learning to read: The great debate.* New York: McGraw-Hill.

Chambers, M. 1981. How the police target young offenders. *New York Times magazine* (September 20), 116–124.

Chambers, N., and Chamberline, L. J. 1976. How television is changing our children. *Clearing House* 50, 53–57.

Chaney, N. E., and Wadlington, W. B. 1988. Cocaine convulsions in a breast-feeding baby. *Journal of pediatrics* 112, 1, 134–135.

Chapman, A. J. 1975. Humorous laughter in children. *Journal of personality and social psychology* 31, 42–49.

Chapman, A. J. 1976. Social aspects of humorous laughter. In A. J. Chapman and H. C. Foot, eds. *Humour and laughter: Theory, research, and applications.* London: Wiley.

Chedd, G. 1981. Who shall be born. *Science* (January–February), 32–41.

Cherlin, A., and Furstenberg, F. F. 1985. Styles and strategies of grandparenting. In V. L. Bengtson and J. F. Robertson, eds. *Grandparenthood.* Beverly Hills, Calif.: Sage Publications.

Chess, S. and Thomas, A. 1986. The New York longitudinal study. In R. Plomin and J. Dun, eds. *The study of temperament: Changes, continuities, and challenges.* Hillsdale, N.J.: Erlbaum.

Chess, S., and Thomas, A. 1982. Infant bonding: Mystique and reality. *American journal of orthopsychiatry* 52, 213–222.

Chess, S., Thomas, A., and Birch, H. G. 1972. *Your child is a person.* New York: Viking Press.

Chevez, G. F., Mulinare, J., and Cordero, J. F. 1989. Maternal cocaine use during early pregnancy as a risk factor for congenital urogenital anomalies. *Journal of the American Medical Association* 262, 6, 795–798.

Children's Defense Fund 1990. *S.O.S. America! A children's defense budget*. Washington, D.C.: Children's Defense Fund.

Children's Defense Fund. 1989. *A vision for America's future*. Washington, D.C.: Children's Defense Fund.

Chilman, C. S. 1990. Promoting healthy adolescent sexuality. *Family relations* 39, 123–131.

Chinn, P. L. 1974. *Child health maintenance*. St. Louis: Mosby.

Choi, J. W. 1978. Exercise and participation in sports among persons 20 years of age and over: United States, 1975. *Advance data from vital and health statistics,* no. 19.

Chomsky, C. 1969. *The acquisition of syntax in children from 5 to 10*. Research monograph no. 57. Cambridge, Mass.: MIT Press.

Chomsky, N. 1975. *Reflections on language*. New York: Pantheon.

Chown, S. M. 1977. Morale, careers, and personal potentials. In J. E. Birren and K. W. Schaie, eds. *Handbook of the psychology of aging*. New York: Van Nostrand Reinhold Company.

Chown, S. M. 1981. Friendship in old age. In S. Duck and R. Gilmore, eds. *Personal relationships 2: Developing personal relationships*. New York: Academic Press.

Christopher, F. S., Fabes, R. A., and Wilson, P. M. 1989. Family television viewing: Implications for family life education. *Family relations* 38, 2, 210–214.

Chumlea, W. C. 1982. Physical growth in adolescence. In B. B. Wolman, ed. *Handbook of developmental psychology*. Englewood Cliffs, N.J.: Prentice-Hall.

Cicirelli, V. G. 1982. Sibling influence throughout the life span. In M. E. Lamb and B. Sutton-Smith, eds. *Sibling relationships: Their nature and significance across the life span*. Hillsdale, N.J.: Lawrence Erlbaum.

Cicirelli, V. G. 1983. Adult children and their elderly parents. In T. H. Brubaker, ed. *Family relationships in later life*. Beverly Hills, Calif.: Sage Publications.

Cicirelli, V. G. 1984. Marital disruption and adult children's perception of their siblings' help to elderly parents. *Family relations* 33, 613–621.

Clark, A. L., and Affonso, D. D. 1976. *Childbearing: A nursing perspective*. Philadelphia: Davis.

Clark, E. A., and Hanisee, J. 1982. Intellectual and adaptive performance of Asian children in adoptive American settings. *Developmental psychology* 18, 595–599.

Clark, H. H., and Clark, E. V. 1977. *Psychology and language: An introduction to psycholinguistics*. New York: Harcourt.

Clark, M., and Gosnell, M. 1981. Childbirth sitting up. *Newsweek* (March 2), 79.

Clarke-Stewart, A. 1986. Predicting child development from day-care forms and features: The Chicago Study. In D. Phillips, ed. *Predictors of quality childcare*. NAEYC Research Monograph Series 1.

Clarke-Stewart, A. 1987. Predicting child development from child-care forms and features: The Chicago Study. In D. A. Phillips, ed. *Quality in child care: What does research tell us?* Washington, D.C.: NAEYC.

Clarke-Stewart, K. A. 1982. *Day care*. Cambridge, Mass.: Harvard University Press.

Clarke-Stewart, K. A. 1988. The "effects" of infant day care reconsidered: Risks for parents, children and researchers. *Early childhood research quarterly*. Special issue: Infant day care. (September), vol. 3 (3), 293–318.

Clarke-Stewart, K. A., and Fein, G. G. 1983. Early childhood programs. In P. H. Mussen, ed. *Handbook of child psychology*. Vol. 2. New York: Wiley.

Clarren, S. K., and Smith, D. W. 1978. The fetal alcohol syndrome. *New England journal of medicine* 298, 1063–1067.

Clausen, J. A. 1972. The life course of individuals. In M. W. Riley, M. Johnson, and A. Foner, eds. *Aging and society*. Vol. 3. New York: Russell Sage Foundation.

Claussen, J. 1975. The social meaning of differential physical and sexual maturation. In S. Dragastin and G. Elder, Jr., eds. *Adolescence in the life cycle*. New York: Wiley.

Cleary, T. A., Humphreys, L. G., Kendrick, S. A., and Wesman, A. 1975. Educational uses of tests with disadvantaged students. *American psychologist* 30, 15–41.

Cleveland, P. H., Walters, L. H., Skeen, P., and Robinson, B. E. 1988. If your child has AIDS . . . Responses of parents with homosexual children. *Family relations* 37, 150–153.

Clingempeel, W. G., and Brand, E. 1985. Quasi-kin relationships, structural complexity, and marital quality: A replication, extension, and clinical implications. *Family relations* 34, 401–409.

Cockrum, J., and White, P. 1985. Influences on the life satisfaction of never-married men and women. *Family relations* 34, 4 (October), 551–556.

Cohen, D. 1972. *The learning child*. New York: Vintage Books.

Cohen, D. H. 1974. Is TV a pied piper? *Young children* 30, 1, 4–14.

Cohen, J., and Parmalee, A. 1983. Prediction of five-year Stanford Binet scores in preterm infants. *Child development* 54, 1242–1253.

Cohen, J., Simons, R. F., Fehilly, C. B., Fishel, S. B., Edwards, R. B., Hewitt, J., Rowlant, G. F., Steptoe, P. C., and Webster, J. M. 1985. Birth after replacement of hatching blastocyst cryopreserved at explanded blastocyst stage. *Lancet* (March 16), 1, 8429, 647.

Cohen, R., Schleser, R., and Meyers, A. 1981. Self-instructions: Effect of cognitive level and active rehearsal. *Journal of experimental child psychology* 32, 65–76.

Cohn, J. F., and Tronick, E. Z. 1983. Three-month-old infants' reaction to stimulated maternal depression. *Child development* 54, 185–193.

Coie, J. D., and Dodge, K. 1988. Multiple sources of data on social behavior and social status in the school: A cross-age comparison. *Child development* 59, 815–829.

Colby, A., Fritz, B., and Kohlberg, L. 1975. Relations between logical and moral judgment stage. Unpublished manuscript. Cambridge: Harvard University Press.

Cole, M. 1983. Culture and cognitive development. In P. H. Mussen, ed. *Handbook of child psychology* 4th ed. New York: Wiley.

Coleman, E., and Edwards, B. 1980. *Brief encounters*. Garden City, N.J.: Anchor.

Coleman, J. S., Campbell, E. Q., Hobson, C. J., McPartland, J., Mood, A. M., Weinfeld, F. D., and York, R. L. 1966. *Equality of educational opportunity*. Report from the U.S. Office of Education. Washington, D.C.: U.S. Government Printing Office.

Coleman, L. M., and Antonucci, T. C. 1983. Impact of work on women at midlife. *Developmental psychology* 19, 2, 290–294.

Coleman, L. M., Antonucci, T. C., Adelmann, P. K., and Crohan, S. E. 1987. Social roles in the lives of middle-aged and older black women. *Journal of marriage and the family* 49, 761–771.

Coleman, M., Ganong, L. H., and Gingrich, R. 1985. Stepfamily strengths: A review of popular literature. *Family relations* 34, 583–589.

Colen, B. D. 1982. The baby we thought we would never have. *Family circle* (April 27), 62.

Coll, C. T. G., Hoffman, J., and Van Houten, L. J. 1985. The social context of teenage childbearing: Effects on the infant's care-giving environment. *Journal of youth and adolescence* 16.

Collins, W., Sobol, B., and Wesby, S. 1981. Effects of adult commentary on children's comprehension and inferences about a televised aggressive portrayal. *Child development* 52, 158–163.

Collins, W. A. 1983. Social antecedents, cognitive processing, and comprehension of social portrayals on television. In E. T. Higgins, D. N. Ruble, and W. W. Hartup, eds. *Social cognition and social development: A sociocultural perspective.* Cambridge: Cambridge University Press.

Collins, W. A., and Getz, S. K. 1974. Children's social responses following modeled reactions to provocation: Prosocial effects of a television drama. *Journal of personality* 44, 488–500.

Comfort, A. 1980. Sexuality in later lie. In J. E. Birren and R. B. Sloane, eds. *Handbook of mental health and aging.* Englewood Cliffs, N.J.: Prentice-Hall.

Commons, M., et al. 1982. Systematic and metasystematic reasoning: A case for levels of reasoning beyond Piaget's stage of formal operations. *Child Development* 53, 1058–1069.

Condon, W. S. 1975. Speech makes baby move. In R. Lewin, ed. *Child alive.* London: Temple Smith.

Condon, W. S., and Sander, L. 1974. Neonate movement is synchronized with adult speech: Interactional participation and language acquisition. *Science* 183, 99–101.

Condry, J., and Keith, D. 1983. Educational and recreational uses of computer technology: Computer instructions and video games. *Youth and society* 15, 87–112.

Conger, R. D., McCarty, J. A., Yang, R. K., Lahey, B. B., and Kropp, J. P. 1984. Perceptions of child, child-rearing values, and emotional distress as mediating links between environmental stressors and observed maternal behavior. *Child development* 55, 2234–2247.

Conner, J. R., Jr., Diamond, M. C., and Johnson, R. E. 1980. Aging and environmental influences on two types of dendritic spines in the rat occipital cortex. *Experimental neurology* 70, 371–379.

Conniff, R. 1982. Supergene. *Science digest* (March), 63–65.

Consortium for Longitudinal Studies. 1983. *As the twig is bent.* Hillsdale, N.J.: Erlbaum.

Cooke, D. J. 1981. Life events and syndromes of depression in the general population. *Social psychiatry* 16, 4 (October), 181–186.

Cooke, D. J., and Greene, J. G. 1981. Types of life events in relation to symptoms at the climacterium. *Journal of psychosomatic research* 25, 1, 5–11.

Cooley, E. J., and Ayres, R. R. 1988. Self-concept and success-failure attributions of nonhandicapped students and students with learning disabilities. *Journal of learning disabilities* 21, 174–178.

Coonrad, D. 1981. *Fathering: The effect of father-absence on children's personality development.* Bloomington, Ind.: Debcon.

Coons, S., and Guilleminault, C. 1982. Development of sleep-wake patterns and non-rapid eye movement sleep stages during the first six months of life in normal infants. *Pediatrics* 69, 6, 793–798.

Coopersmith, S. 1967. *The antecedents of self-esteem.* San Francisco: W. H. Freeman.

Corah, N. L. 1979. Effects of perinatal anoxia after seven years. In J. D. Osofsky, ed. *Handbook of infant development.* New York: John Wiley and Sons.

Corballis, M. C. 1983. *Human laterality.* New York: Academic Press.

Corballis, M. C., and Morgan, M. J. 1978. On the biological basis of human laterality. *Behavioral and brain science* 2, 261–336.

Coren, S., et al. 1981. Lateral preference behaviors in preschool children and young adults. *Child development* 52, 443–450.

Corman, H. H., and Escalona, S. K. 1969. Stages of sensorimotor development: A replication study. *Merrill-Palmer quarterly* 15, 351–361.

Corrigan, D. C. 1978. Political and moral contexts that produced P.L. 94–142. *Journal of teacher education* (November/December).

Corso, J. F. 1977. Auditory perception and communication. In J. E. Birren and K. W. Schaie, eds. *Handbook of the psychology of aging.* New York: Van Nostrand Reinhold.

Cosgrove, M. D., Benton, B., and Henderson, B. E. 1977. Male genitourinary abnormalities and maternal diethylstilbestrol. *Journal of urology* 117, 220–222.

Cousins, N. 1979. *Anatomy of an illness as perceived by the patient.* New York: W. W. Norton and Co.

Couturier, L. C., Mansfield, R. S., and Gallagher, J. M. 1981. Relationship between humor, formal operational ability, and creativity in eighth graders. *Journal of genetic psychology* 139, 221–226.

Cowen, E. L., Pederson, A., Babigian, M., Izzo, L. D., and Trost, M. A. 1973. Long-term follow-up of early detected vulnerable children. *Journal of consulting and clinical psychology* 41, 438–466.

Cox, T. 1978. *Stress.* Baltimore, Md.: University Park.

Craig, G. J. 1980. *Human development.* Englewood Cliffs, N.J.: Prentice-Hall.

Craik, F. I. M. 1977. Age differences in human memory. In J. E. Birren and K. W. Schaie, eds. *Handbook of the psychology of aging.* New York: Van Nostrand Reinhold.

Craik, F. I. M., and Rabinowitz, J. C. 1985. The effects of presentation rate and encoding task on age-related memory deficits. *Journal of gerontology* 40, 309–315.

Crandall, V. C. 1973. Differences in parental antecedents of internal-external control in children and in young adulthood. Paper presented at the August meeting of the American Psychological Association, Montreal.

Crandall, V. C., Katkovsky, W., and Crandall, V. J. 1962. Motivational and ability determinants of young children's intellectual achievement behaviors. *Child development* 33, 643–661.

Crandall, V. C. 1965. Children's beliefs in their own control of reinforcements in intellectual-academic achievement situations. *Child development* 36, 91–109.

Crandall, V. J., et al. 1958. The development of social compliance in young children. *Child development* 29, 429–443.

Cratty, B. 1979. *Perceptual and motor development in infants and preschool children.* Englewood Cliffs, N.J.: Prentice-Hall.

Cratty, B. J. 1970. *Perceptual and motor development in infants and children.* New York: Macmillan Company.

Crnic, K. A., et al. 1983. Effects of stress and social support on mothers and premature and full-term infants. *Child development* 54, 209–217.

Crockenberg, S. 1986. *Maternal anger and the behavior of two-year-old children.* Paper presented at the International Conference on Infant Studies, Beverly Hills, California.

Cruickshank, W. M. 1977. *Learning disabilities in home, school, and community.* Syracuse, N.Y.: Syracuse University Press.

Crum, R. A., et al. 1983. Variety of props needed for make-believe play. *Perceptual and motor skills* 56, 947–955.

Crystal, H. A. 1988. The diagnosis of Alzheimer's disease and other dementing disorders. In M. K. Aronson, ed. *Understanding Alzheimer's disease.* New York: Charles Scribner's Sons.

Csikszentmihalyi, M., and Larson, R. 1984. *Being adolescent: Conflict and growth in the teenage years.* New York: Basic Books.

Cuber, J. F., and Harroff, P. B. 1963. The more total view: Relationships among men and women of the upper middle class. *Marriage and family living* 25, 140–145.

Cumming, E., and Henry, W. E. 1961. *Growing old: The process of disengagement.* New York: Basic Books.

Cummings, E. M. 1987. Coping with anger in early childhood. *Child development* 58, 976–984.

Cummings, E. M., Hollenbeck, B., Iannotti, R., Radke-Yarrow, M., and Zahn-Waxler, C. 1986. Early organization of altruism and aggression: Developmental patterns and individual differences. In C. Zahn-Waxler, E. M. Cummings, and R. Iannoti, eds. *Altruism and aggression*. New York: Cambridge University Press.

Cummings, E. M., Iannotti, R. J., and Zahn-Waxler, C. 1985. The influence of conflict between adults on the emotions and aggression of young children. *Developmental psychology* 21, 495–507.

Cummings, E. M., Iannotti, R. J., and Zahn-Waxler, C. 1989. Aggression between peers in early childhood: Individual continuity and developmental change. *Child development* 60, 887–895.

Cunningham, W. R., and Owens, W. A., Jr. 1983. The Iowa State study of adult development and abilities. In K. W. Schaie, ed. *Longitudinal studies of adult psychological development*. New York: Guilford.

Current Population Reports. 1984. *Marital status and living arrangements: March 1984*. Series P–20, no. 399, U.S. Department of Commerce, Bureau of the Census.

Curry, N. E., and Johnson, C. N. 1990. *Beyond self-esteem: Developing a genuine sense of human value*. Research Monograph of the National Association for the Education of Young Children. Vol. 4. Washington, D.C.: NAEYC.

Curtis, H., and Barnes, N. S. 1989. *Biology*. New York: Worth.

Curtis, R. L., Jr. 1975. Adolescent orientations toward parents and peers: Variations by sex, age, and socioeconomic status. *Adolescence* 10, 40 (Winter), 483–494.

Curtiss, S. 1977. *Genie: A psycholinguistic study of a modern-day wild child*. New York: Academic Press.

Cytrynbaum, S., et al. 1980. Midlife development: A personality and social systems perspective. In L. W. Poon, ed. *Aging in the 80s*. Washington, D.C.: American Psychological Association.

d'Anglejan, A., and Tucker, G. R. 1970. *The St. Lambert program of home-school language switch*. Montreal, Quebec: McGill University.

D'apolito, K. 1984. The neonate's response to pain. *Maternity-child nursing journal*, 9, 256.

Dacy, M. D. 1988. Cholesterol. *Mayo Clinic health letter* 6, 3 (March), 12.

Dale, N. J. 1980. *Evaluation of Medicaid foster family care pilot project*. Boston: Department of Public Welfare.

Dale, P. S. 1976. *Language development: Structure and function*. New York: Holt, Rinehart and Winston.

Daniels, A. K. 1987. Invisible work. *Social problems* 34, 403–415.

Darbyshire, J. O. 1984. The hearing loss epidemic: A challenge to gerontology. *Research on aging* 6, 384–394.

Darling-Fisher, C. S., and Tiedje, L. B. 1990. The impact of maternal employment characteristics on fathers' participation in child care. *Family relations* 39, 1 (January), 20–26.

Dasen, P. R. ed. 1977. *Piagetian psychology: Cross-cultural contributions*. New York: Gardner Press.

Datan, N. 1986. The last minority: Humor, old age, and marginal identity. In L. Nahemow, K. A. McCluskey-Fawcett, and P. E. McGhee, eds. *Humor and aging*. New York: Academic Press.

Davenport, J. A., and Davenport, J., III. 1987. Native American suicide: A Durkheimian analysis. *Social casework: The journal of contemporary social work* (November).

Davidson, P., Turiel, E., and Black, A. 1983. The effect of stimulus familiarity on the use of criteria and justification in children's social reasoning. *British journal of developmental psychology* 1, 49–65.

Davies, P. 1988. Alzheimer's disease and related disorders: An overview. In M. K. Aronson, ed. *Understanding Alzheimer's disease*. New York: Charles Scribner's Sons.

Davis, B. R., and Hardy, R. J. 1986. A suicide epidemic model. *Social biology* 33, 3–4, 291–300.

Davis, M. A., et al. 1985. Living arrangements and dietary patterns of older adults in the United States. *Journal of gerontology* 40, 4, 434–442.

Davison, A. N., and Dobbing, J. 1966. Myelination as vulnerable period in brain development. *British medical bulletin* 22, 40, 44.

de Mause, L. 1974. The evolution of childhood. In L. de Mause, ed. *The history of childhood*. New York: Psychohistory Press.

DeFoe, J. R., and Breed, W. 1988. Youth and alcohol in television stories, with suggestions to the industry for alternative portrayals. *Adolescence* 23, 91–92, 533–548.

Demirjian, A. 1986. Dentition. In F. Falkner and J. M. Tanner, eds. *Postnatal growth neurobiology*. Vol. 2 of *Human growth: A comprehensive treatise*. 2nd ed. New York: Plenum Press.

Dennis, W. 1966. Creative productivity between the ages of 20 and 80 years. *Journal of gerontology* 21, 1, 1–8.

Dennis, W. 1973. *Children of the crèche*. New York: Appleton-Century-Crofts.

Despert, J. L. 1946. Anxiety, phobias, and fear in young children. *Nervous child* 5, 8–24.

Deutsch, F. 1983. One-parent preschoolers rate an "A" in play. *Journal of social psychology*. (February) Cited in *Growing child research review*. (September 1983) 3, 1, 1–8.

DeVault, M. L. 1987. Doing housework: Feeding and family life. In N. Gerstel and H. E. Gross, eds. *Families and work*. Philadelphia: Temple University Press.

deVries, H. A. 1983. Physiology of exercise and aging. In D. S. Woodruff and J. E. Birren, eds. *Aging: Scientific perspectives and social issues*. 2nd ed. Monterey, Calif.: Brooks/Cole.

deVries, M. W., and Sameroff, A. J. 1984. Culture and temperament: Influences on infant temperament in three East-African societies. *American journal of orthopsychiatry* 54, 83–96.

Diaz, R. M. 1985. Bilingual cognitive development: Addressing three gaps in current research. *Child development* 56 1376–1388.

Dick-Read, G. 1972. *Childbirth without fear*. New York: Harper and Row.

Dickens, W. J., and Perlman, D. 1981. Friendship over the life cycle. In S. Duck and R. Gilmour, eds. *Personal relationships 2: Developing personal relationships*. New York: Academic Press.

Dickinson, G. E. 1978. Adolescent sex information sources: 1964–74. *Adolescence* 13, 52 (Winter), 653–658.

Dicks, H. V. 1973. Personality. In R. R. Sears and S. S. Feldman, eds. *The seven ages of man*. Los Altos, Calif.: William Kaufman.

Dierker, L. J., Pillay, S. K., Sorokin, Y., and Rosen, M. G. 1982. Active and quiet periods in preterm and term fetus. *Obstetrics and gynecology* 60 (July), 65–69.

Dietz, W. H., Jr. 1984. Obesity in infancy. In R. B. Howard and H. S. Winter, eds. *Nutrition and feeding of infants and toddlers*. Boston: Little, Brown and Company.

DiLeo, J. 1970. *Physical factors in growth and development*. New York: Teachers College Press.

DiLeo, J. H. 1967. Developmental evaluation of very young infants. In J. Hellmuth. *Exceptional infant*. Vol. 1. New York: Brunner/Mazel.

Dishion, T. J. 1990. The family ecology of boys' peer relations in middle childhood. *Child development* 61, 874–892.

Dishion, T. J., and Loeber, R. 1985. Male adolescent marijuana and alcohol use: The role of parents and peers revisited. *Journal of alcohol and substance abuse* 11 (1, 2), 11–25.

Dishion, T. J., Loeber, R., Stouthamer-Loeber, M., and Patterson, G. R. 1984. Skill deficits and male adolescent delinquency. *Journal of abnormal child psychology* 12, 37–54.

DiStefano, V. 1982. Athletic injuries. In R. Magill, M. Ash, and F. Smoll, eds. *Children in sport*. Champaign, Ill.: Human Kinetics Publishers.

Dodge, K. 1983. Behavioral antecedents of peer social status. *Child development* 54, 1386–1399.

Dodge, K. A. 1980. Social cognition and children's aggressive behavior. *Child development* 51, 162–170.

Dodge, K. A. 1986. Social information-processing variables in the development of aggression and altruism in children. In C. Zahn-Waxler, E. M. Cummings, and R. Iannoti, eds. *Altruism and aggression*. New York: Cambridge University Press.

Doherty, W. J., and Jacobson, N. S. 1982. Marriage and the family. In B. Wolman, ed. *Handbook of developmental psychology*. Englewood Cliffs, N.J.: Prentice-Hall.

Dohrenwend, B. S., and Dohrenwend, B. P., eds. 1981. *Stressful life events and their contexts*. New York: Neale Watson.

Donaldson, M., and Wales, R. 1970. On the acquisition of some relational terms. In J. Hayes, ed. *Cognition and the development of language*. New York: John Wiley and Sons.

Donohugh, D. L. 1981. *The middle years*. Philadelphia: Saunders Press.

Dorr, A. 1985. Contexts for experience with emotion, with special attention to television. In M. Lewis and C. Saarni, eds. *The socialization of emotion*. New York: Plenum.

Dorr, A., and Kunkel, D. 1990. Children and the media environment. *Communication research* 17, 1 (February), 5–25.

Doty, R. L., Shaman, P., and Dann, M. 1984. Development of the University of Pennsylvania Smell Identification Test: A standardized microencapsulated test of olfactory function. *Physiology and behavior* 32, 489–502.

Douvan, E. 1963. Employment and the adolescent. In F. I. Nye and L. W. Hoffman, eds. *The employed mother in America*. Chicago: Rand McNally.

Downey, G., and Moen, P. 1987. Personal efficacy, income, and family transitions: A longitudinal study of women heading households. *Journal of health and social behavior* 28, 320–333.

Drachman, D. A. 1980. An approach to the neurology of aging. In J. E. Birren and R. B. Sloane, eds. *Handbook of mental health and aging*. Englewood Cliffs, N.J.: Prentice-Hall.

Draz, R. M. 1985. Bilingual cognitive development: Addressing three gaps in current research. *Child development* 56, 1376–1388.

Drewes, L. M. 1983. Self appraisals of pregnant women: The effects of planned vs. unplanned pregnancy, first vs. additional child, and period of pregnancy. Vanderbilt University, Dissertation Abstracts International. Vol. 44 (1–B), 304.

Dreyer, P. H. 1982. Sexuality during adolescence. In B. B. Wolman, ed. *Handbook of developmental psychology*. Englewood Cliffs, N.J.: Prentice-Hall.

Dreyfuss-Brisac, C. 1979. Ontogenesis of brain bioelectrical activity and sleep organization in neonates and infants. In F. Faulkner and J. M. Tanner, eds. *Human growth: Neurobiology and nutrition*. Vol. 3 New York: Plenum Press.

Dubnoff, S. J., et al. 1978. *Adjustment to work*. Paper presented at the American Psychological Association, Toronto, Canada, August.

Duffty, P., and Bryan, M. H. 1982. Home apnea monitoring in "near-miss" sudden infant death syndrome (SIDS) and siblings of SIDS victims. *Pediatrics* 70, 69–75.

Duke Center for the Study of Aging and Human Development. 1978. *Multidimensional functional assessment: The OARS methodology*. 2nd ed. Durham, N.C.: Duke University Center for the Study of Aging and Human Development.

Duncan, G. J., and Liker, J. D. 1983. Disentangling the efficacy-earnings relationship among white men. In G. J. Duncan and J. N.

Morgan, eds. *Five thousand families: Patterns of economic progress*. Vol. 10. Ann Arbor, Mich.: University of Michigan, Institute for Social Research.

Duncan, G. J., and Morgan, J. W. 1981. Sense of efficacy and subsequent change in earnings: A replication. *Journal of human resources* 16, 649–657.

Duncan, J. W. 1985. The superiority theory of humor at work. *Small group behavior* 16, 4, 556–564.

Dunn, J., and Kendrick, C. 1982. Social behavior of young siblings in the family context: Differences between same-sex and different-sex dyads. In S. Chess and A. Thomas. *Annual progress in child psychiatry and child development*. New York: Brunner/Mazel.

Dunn, J., Kendrick, C., and MacNamee, R. 1982. The reaction of first-born children to the birth of a sibling: Mothers' reports. In S. Chess and A. Thomas. *Annual progress in child psychiatry and child development*. New York: Brunner/Mazel.

Dunphy, D. C. 1963. The social structure of urban adolescent peer groups. *Sociometry* 26, 230–246.

Dusek, D. E., and Girdano, D. A. 1987. *Drugs: A factual account*. 4th ed. NY: Random House.

Dweck, C. S. 1981. Social-cognitive processes in children's friendships. In S. R. Asher and J. M. Gottman, eds. *The development of children's friendships*. Cambridge: Cambridge University Press.

Eagan, A. B. 1986. Options for aging, *New age journal* (April), 54–59.

Eaker, E. D., and Castelli, W. P. 1988. Type A behavior and coronary heart disease in women: Fourteen-year incidence from the Framingham study. In B. K. Houston and C. R. Snyder, eds. *Type A behavior pattern*. New York: John Wiley.

Easterbrooks, M. A. 1989. Quality of attachment to mother and to father: Effects of perinatal risk status. *Child development* 60, 825–830.

Eastham, E., and Walker, W. 1977. Effect of cow's milk on the gastrointestinal tract: A persistent dilemma for the pediatrician. *Pediatrician* 60, 477.

Eaton, W. O., and Yu, A. P. 1989. Are sex differences in child motor activity level a function of sex differences in maturational status? *Child development* 60, 1005–1011.

Ebersole, P., and Hess, P. 1985. *Toward healthy aging*. St. Louis: C. V. Mosby Company.

Eccles, J. S., Adler, T. F., Futterman, R., Goff, S. B., Kaczala, C. M., Meece, J. L., and Midgley, C. 1983. Expectancies, values, and academic behaviors. In J. T. Spence, ed. *Achievement and achievement motivation*. San Francisco: W. H. Freeman.

Eccles, J. S., and Hoffman, L. W. 1984. Sex roles, socialization, and occupational behavior. In H. W. Stevenson and A. E. Siegel, eds. *Child development research and social policy*. Chicago: University of Chicago Press.

Eccles, J. S., and Midgley, C. 1990. Changes in academic motivation and self-perception during early adolescence. In R. Montemayor, eds *From childhood to adolescence: A transitional period?* Beverly Hills, Calif.: Sage Publications.

Eckerman, C. O., Davis, C. C., and Didow, S. M. 1989. Toddlers' emerging ways of achieving social coordinations with a peer. *Child development* 60, 2 (April), 440–453.

Eder, R. A. 1990. Uncovering young children's psychological selves: Individual and developmental differences. *Child development* 61, 849–863.

Eder, R. A., Gerlach, S. G., and Perlmutter, M. 1987. In search of children's selves: Development of the specific and general components of the self-concept. *Child development* 58, 1044–1050.

Edleson, J. L., and Brygger, M. P. 1986. Gender differences in reporting of battering incidences. *Family relations* 35, 377–382.

Edwards, C. P. 1982. Moral development in comparative cultural perspective. In D. A. Wagner and H. W. Stevenson, eds. *Cultural perspectives on child development.* San Francisco: Freeman.

Egeland, B., and Brunnquell, D. 1979. An at-risk approach to the study of child abuse: Some preliminary findings. *Journal of the American Academy of Child Psychiatry* 18, 219–225.

Egeland, B., and Sroufe, L. A. 1981. Developmental sequelae of maltreatment in infancy. In D. Cicchetti and R. Rizley, eds. *New directions in child development: Developmental approaches to child maltreatment.* San Francisco: Jossey-Bass.

Egeland, B., Jacobvitz, D., and Papatola, K. 1987. Intergenerational continuity of parental abuse. In R. J. Gelles and J. B. Lancaster, eds. *Child abuse and neglect: Biosocial dimensions.* New York: Aldine De-Gruyter.

Eichorn, D. H. 1963. Biological correlates of behavior. In H. W. Stevenson, J. Kagan, and C. Spiker. *Child psychology.* Chicago: University of Chicago Press.

Eisdorfer, C., and Wilkie, F. 1972. Auditory changes. *Journal of the American Geriatrics Society* 20, 377–382.

Eisdorfer, C., and Wilkie, F. 1973. Intellectual changes with advancing age. In L. F. Jarvik, C. Eisdorfer, and J. E. Blum, eds. *Intellectual functioning in adults.* New York: Springer Publishing Company.

Eisenberg, N. 1982. Social development. In C. B. Kopp and J. B. Krakow, eds. *The child: Development in a social context.* Reading, Mass.: Addison-Wesley.

Eisenberg, N. 1982. The development of reasoning regarding prosocial behavior. In N. Eisenberg, ed. *The development of prosocial behavior.* New York: Academic Press.

Eigenberg, N. 1987. Self-attributions, social interaction, and moral development. In W. Kurtines and J. Gewirtz, eds. *Moral development through social interaction.* New York: John Wiley and Sons.

Eisenberg, N., and Miller, P. A. 1987. The relation of empathy to prosocial and related behaviors. *Psychological bulletin* 101, 1, 91–119.

Eisenberg, N., and Neal, C. 1981. *Personality and social psychology bulletin* 7, 17–23.

Eisenberg, N., Lennon, R., and Roth, K. 1983. Prosocial development. *Developmental psychology* 19, 6, 846–855.

Eisenberg, R. B. 1976. *Auditory competence in early life: The roots of communicative behavior.* Baltimore, Md.: University Park Press.

Eisenberg, R. B. 1979. Stimulus significance as a determinant of infant responses to sound. In E. B. Thoman, ed. *Origins of the infant's social responses.* Hillsdale, N.J.: Lawrence Erlbaum Associates.

Elbers, L., and Ton, J. 1985. Playpen monologues: The interplay of words and babbles in the first words period. *Journal of child language* 3 (October 12), 551–565.

Elias, M. F. 1984. *Nursing and night walking in the first two years.* Paper presented at the International Conference on Infant Studies, New York.

Elkind, D. 1967. Egocentrism in adolescence. *Child Development,* 38, 1025–1034.

Elkind, D. 1970. Erik Erikson's eight stages of man. *The New York Times magazine* (April 5). Cited in *Readings in human development 77/78, Annual Editions.* Guilford, Conn.: Dushkin Publishing Group.

Elkind, D. 1977. Erik Erikson's eight ages of man. In *Readings in Human Development 77/78: Annual Editions.* Guilford, Conn.: Dushkin Publishing Group.

Elkind, D. 1978. *A sympathetic understanding of the child: Birth to sixteen.* 2nd ed. Boston: Allyn and Bacon.

Elkind, D. 1978. *The child's reality: Three developmental themes.* Hillsdale, N.J.: Lawrence Erlbaum Associates.

Elkind, D. 1981. *Children and adolescents.* New York: Oxford University Press.

Ellis, G. J. 1983. Television and the family: An emerging area. *Journal of family issues* 4, 275–278.

Ellis, J. B., and Range, L. M. 1989. Characteristics of suicidal individuals: A review. *Death studies* 13, 485–500.

Ellwood, D. T. 1988. *Poor support: Poverty in the American family.* New York: Basic Books.

Elster, A. B., and Panzarine, S. 1983. Teenage fathers: Stresses during gestation and early parenthood. *Clinical pediatrics* 22, 10 (October), 700–703.

Emde, R. 1985. The affective self. Continuities and transformations from infancy. In J. Call, E. Galenson, and R. Tyson, eds. *Frontiers in infant psychiatry II.* New York: Basic Books.

Emery, A. E. H. 1983. *Elements of medical genetics.* 6th ed. Edinburgh: Churchill Livingston.

Endres, J. B., and Rockwell, R. E. 1980. *Food, nutrition, and the young child.* St. Louis: C. V. Mosby.

Erickson, R. J. 1985. Play contributes to the full emotional development of the child. *Education.* (Spring) 105, 3, 261–263.

Erikson, E. H. 1963. *Childhood and society.* 2nd ed. New York: Norton.

Erikson, E. H. 1968. Generativity and ego integrity. In B. L. Neugarten, ed. *Middle age and aging.* Chicago: University of Chicago Press.

Erikson, E. H. 1968. *Identity: Youth and crisis.* New York: W. W. Norton and Company.

Eron, L. D., Huesmann, R., Brice, P., Fischer, P., and Mermelstein, R. 1983. Age trends in the development of aggression, sex typing, and related television habits. *Developmental psychology* 19, 71–77.

Ervin-Tripp, S. M. 1970. Discourse agreement: How children answer questions. In J. R. Hayes, ed. *Cognition and the development of language.* New York: John Wiley and Sons.

Espenschade, A. S., and Eckert, H. M. 1967. *Motor development.* Columbus, Ohio: Charles E. Merrill.

Etaugh, C. 1974. Effects of maternal employment on children: A review of recent research. *Merrill-Palmer quarterly* 20, 71–98.

Eubank, B. A. 1976. *Social involvement of preschool children within various exterior play areas.* Dissertation for the Degree of Ph.D., Michigan State University.

Evans, G. W., et al. 1984. Cognitive mapping and elderly adults: Verbal and location memory for urban landmarks. *Journal of gerontology* 39, 4, 452–457.

Eveleth, P. B., and Tanner, J. M. 1976. *Worldwide variation in human growth.* Cambridge: Cambridge University Press.

Fabes, R. A., Wilson, P., and Christopher, F. S. 1989. A time to reexamine the role of television in family life. *Family relations* 38, 3, 337–341.

Fabrizi, M. S., and Pollio, H. R. 1987. Are funny teenagers creative? *Psychological reports* 61, 751–761.

The Facts about AIDS. *Higher education advocate,* (August 31), Vol. IV, no. 13, National Education Association.

Fagot, B. 1982. Adults as socializing agents. In T. Field, A. Huston, H. Quay, L. Troll, and G. Finley, eds. *Review of human development.* New York: Wiley.

Fagot, B. I. 1974. Sex differences in toddlers' behavior and parental reaction. *Developmental psychology* 10, 554–558.

Fagot, B. I., and Kavanaugh, K. 1990. The prediction of antisocial behavior from avoidant attachment classifications. *Child development* 61, 3, 864–873.

Fantz, R. L. 1973. Visual perception from birth as shown by pattern selectivity. In L. J. Stone, H. T. Smith, and L. B. Murphy, eds. *The competent infant.* New York: Basic Books.

Farber, E. D., and Kinast, C. 1984. Violence in families of adolescent runaways. *Child abuse and neglect* 8, 295–299.

Farber, S. 1981. *Identical twins reared apart: A reanalysis.* New York: Basic Books.

Farber, S. 1981. Telltale behavior of twins. *Psychology today* (January), 58–80.

Farmer, A., McGuffin, P., and Gottesman, I. 1987. Twin concordance of DSM-III schizophrenia. *Archives of general psychiatry* 44, 634–641.

Farnham-Diggory, S. 1978. *Learning disabilities.* Cambridge: Harvard University Press.

Farnham-Diggory, S. 1984. Why reading? Because it's there. *Developmental review* 4, 62–71.

Faust, M. S. 1960. Developmental maturity as a determinant in prestige of adolescent girls. *Child development* 31, 173–184.

Feldlaufer, H., Midgley, C., and Eccles, J. S. 1988. Student, teacher, and observer perceptions of the classroom environment before and after the transition to junior high school. *Journal of early adolescence* 8, 133–156.

Feldman, M. A., Betel, J., and Rincover, A. 1986. Parent Education Project II: Increasing stimulating interactions of developmentally handicapped mothers. *Journal of applied behavior analysis* 19, 1, 23–38.

Feldman, M. A., Case, L., Towns, F., and Betel, J. 1985. Parent education project I: Development and nurturance of children of mentally retarded parents. *American journal of mental deficiency* 90, 3 (November) 253–258.

Feldman, S. S., and Aschenbrenner, B. 1983. Impact of parenthood on various aspects of masculinity and femininity: A short-term longitudinal study. *Developmental psychology* 19, 2, 278–289.

Ferree, M. M., 1976. Working-class jobs, housework and paid work as sources of satisfaction. *Social problems* 22, 431–441.

Feshbach, S. 1970. Aggression. In P. H. Mussen, ed. *Carmichael's manual of child psychology.* 3rd ed. New York: John Wiley and Sons.

Field, D. 1981. Can preschool children really learn to conserve? *Child development* 52, 326–334.

Field, T., and Reite, M. 1984. Children's responses to separation from mother during the birth of another child. *Child development* 55, 1308.

Figler, H. R. 1981. The midlife crisis. In H. E. Fitzgerald, ed. *Human development, 81/82.* Guilford, Conn.: Dushkin Publishing Group.

Fine, G. A. 1981. Friends, impression management, and preadolescent behavior. In S. R. Asher and J. M. Gottman, eds. *The development of children's friendships.* Cambridge: Cambridge University Press.

Fine, P. E., Adelstein, A. M., Snowman, J., Clarkson, J. A., and Evans, S. M. 1985. Long-term effects of exposure to viral infections in utero. *British medical journal* 290, 6467, 509–511.

Fischer, K. 1980. A theory of cognitive development: The control and construction of heirarchies of skills. *Psychological review* 87, 477–531.

Fischer, M. 1973. Genetic and environmental factors in schizophrenia. *Acta psychiatrie Scandinavia* 238, 1–158.

Fishbein, H. D., Lewis, S., and Kuffer, K. 1972. Children's understanding of spatial relations. *Developmental psychology* 7, 21–23.

Fisher, S. and Fisher, R. L. 1983. Personality and psychopathology in the comic. In P. E. McGhee and J. H. Goldstein, eds., *Handbook of humor research.* Vol. 2 of *Applied Studies.* New York: Springer-Verlag.

Fisher, S., and Fisher, R. L. 1981. *Pretend the world is funny and forever: A psychological analysis of comedians, clowns, and actors.* Hillsdale, N.J.: Erlbaum.

Fisichelli, V., and Karelitz, S. 1963. The cry latencies of normal infants and those with brain damage. *Journal of pediatrics* 62, 724–734.

Flavell, J. 1985. *Cognitive development.* 2nd ed. Englewood Cliffs, N.J.: Prentice-Hall.

Flavell, J. H. 1970. Cognitive changes in adulthood. In L. R. Goulet and P. B. Baltes, eds. *Life-span developmental psychology.* New York: Academic Press.

Flavell, J. H. 1977. *Cognitive development.* Englewood Cliffs, N.J.: Prentice-Hall.

Flavell, J. H. 1978. Developmental stage: Explanations or explanandum? *Behavioral and brain sciences* 1, 187.

Flavell, J. H. 1982. On cognitive development. *Child Development* 53, 1–10.

Flavell, J. H. 1985. *Cognitive development.* 2nd ed. Englewood Cliffs, N.J.: Prentice-Hall.

Flavell, J. H., Green, F. L., and Flavell, E. R. 1985. The road not taken: Understanding the implications of initial uncertainty in evaluating spatial directions. *Developmental psychology* 21, 207–216.

Fleming, A. T. 1980. New Frontiers in conception. *New York Times Magazine* (July 20).

Flerx, V. C., Fidler, D. S., and Rogers, R. W. 1976. Sex role stereotypes: Developmental aspects and early intervention. *Child development* 47, 998–1007.

Flewelling, R. L., and Bauman, K. E. 1990. Family structure as a predictor of initial substance use and sexual intercourse in early adolescence. *Journal of marriage and the family* 52, 171–181.

Fling, S., and Manosevitz, M. 1972. Sex typing in nursery school children's play interests. *Developmental psychology* 7, 146–152.

Flynn, C. P. 1987. Relationship violence: A model for family professionals. *Family relations* 36, 295–299.

Flynn, C. P. 1990. Relationship violence by women: Issues and implications. *Family relations* 39, 194–198.

Fogel, A. 1984. *Infancy: Infant, family, and society.* St. Paul, Minn.: West Publishing Company.

Foman, S. J. 1974. *Infant nutrition.* 2nd ed. Philadelphia: W. B. Saunders.

Foner, A., and Schwab, K. 1981. *Aging and retirement.* Monterey, Calif.: Brooks/Cole.

Forehand, R., Long, N., Brody, G. H., and Fauber, R. 1986. Home predictors of young adolescents' school behavior and academic performance. *Child development* 57, 1528–1533.

Forer, L. 1976. *The birth order factor.* New York: McKay.

Fowler, J. W. 1976. Stages in faith: The structural developmental approach. In T. Hennessy, ed. *Values and moral development.* New York: Paulist Press.

Fowler, J. W. 1981. *Stages of faith.* New York: Harper and Row.

Fowler, J. W. 1983. Stages of faith. PT conversation with James Fowler. *Psychology today* 17 (November), 56–62.

Frankel, K. A., and Bates, J. E. 1990. Mother-toddler problem solving: Antecedents in attachment, home behavior, and temperament. *Child development* 61, 3, 810–819.

Franks, D. D. 1981. Psychiatric evaluation of women in a surrogate mother program. *American journal of psychiatry* 138, 10, 1378–1379.

Fraser, B. J., and Fisher, D. L. 1982. Predicting students' outcomes from their perceptions of classroom psychosocial environment. *American educational research journal* 19, 498–518.

Frazier, E. 1969. *The Negro church in America.* New York: Schocken Books.

Freiberg, K. L. 1983. *Human development: A life-span approach.* Monterey, Calif.: Wadsworth Health Sciences Division.

Freud, A., and Dann, S. 1954. An experiment in group upbringing. In W. E. Martin and C. B. Stendler, eds. *Readings in child development.* New York: Harcourt Brace.

Freud, S. 1924. *A general introduction to psychoanalysis.* New York: Boni and Liveright.

Freud, S. 1938. *The basic writings of Sigmund Freud.* A. A. Brill, ed. and trans. New York: Modern Library.

Fried, P. A. 1982. Marijuana use by pregnant women and effects on offspring: An update. *Neurobehavioral toxology and teratology* 4, 451–454.

Fried, P. A., Watkinson, B., and Dillon, R. 1987. Neonatal neurological status in a low-risk population after prenatal exposure to cigarettes, marijuana, and alcohol. *Developmental and behavioral pediatrics* 8, 318–326.

Friedenberg, J. E. 1983. Learning to read two languages at once easier for bilingual children. *Growing child research review* 1, 4 (April), 1.

Friedman, M., and Rosenman, R. H. 1974. *Type A behavior and your heart.* New York: Alfred A. Knopf.

Fritz, M. 1985. Study: Cancer survival linked to marriage. *Lansing state journal* (November 5), 1D.

Frodi, A. 1984. When empathy fails: Aversive infant crying and child abuse. In B. Lester and Z. Boukydis, eds. *Infant crying: Theoretical and research perspectives.* New York: Plenum.

Frost, J. L., and Sunderlin, S. 1985. *When children play.* Wheaton, Md.: Association for Children's Education International.

Fry, W. F. 1974. Psychodynamics of sexual humor: Sexual views of humor. *Medical aspects of human sexuality.* 8, 9, (September), 77–80.

Fry, W. F., Jr. 1986. Humor, physiology, and the aging process. In L. Nahemow, K. A. McCluskey-Fawcett, and P. McGhee, eds. *Humor and aging.* New York: Academic Press.

Fry, W. F., Jr., and Rader, C. 1977. The respiratory components of mirthful laughter. *Journal of biological psychology* 19, 39–50.

Fry, W. F., Jr., and Rader, C. 1969. Humor in a physiologic vein. *News of physiological instrumentation* (July 3).

Fry, W. F., Jr., and Savin, M. 1982. *Mirthful laughter and blood pressure.* Paper presented at the Third International Conference on Humor, Washington, D.C.

Fry, W. F., Jr., and Stoft, P. E. 1971. Mirth and oxygen saturation levels of peripheral blood. *Psychotherapy and psychosomatics* 19, 76–84.

Fuhrmann, W., and Vogel, F. 1983. *Genetic counseling.* 3rd ed. New York: Springer-Verlag.

Furman, W., and Buhrmester, D. 1985. Children's perceptions of the personal relationships in their social networks. *Developmental psychology* 21, 1016–1024.

Furstenberg, F. F., and Nord, C. W. 1985. Parenting apart: Patterns of childrearing after marital disruption. *Journal of marriage and the family* 47, 4, 893–904.

Furstenberg, F. F., Jr. 1980. Burdens and benefits: The impact of early childbearing on the family. *Journal of social issues* 36, 1, 64–87.

Gabrielli, W. F., and Mednick, S. A. 1984. Urban environment, genetics, and crime. *Criminology: An interdisciplinary journal* 22, 4, 645–652.

Gadberry, S. 1980. Effects of restricting first graders' TV-viewing on leisure time use, IQ change, and cognitive style. *Journal of applied developmental psychology* 1, 45–57.

Gadow, K. D. and Sprafkin, J. 1987. Effects of viewing high- versus low-aggression cartoons on emotionally disturbed children. *Journal of pediatric psychology* 12, 3, 413–427.

Gadow, K. D., and Sprafkin, J. 1986. *Television violence and child behavior: The field experiments.* Paper presented at the meeting of the Royal College of Psychiatrists, Southampton, England.

Gallahue, D. L. 1982. *Understanding motor development in children.* New York: Wiley.

Galton, F. 1896. *Hereditary genius: An enquiry into its laws and consequences.* London: Macmillan.

Ganchrow, J. R., Steiner, J. E., and Daher, M. 1983. Neonatal facial expressions in response to different qualities and intensities of gustatory stimuli. *Infant behavior and development* 6, 189–200.

Garai, J. E., and Scheinfeld, A. 1968. Sex differences in mental and behavioral traits. *Genetic psychology monographs* 77, 169–299.

Garbarino, J., and Gilliam, G. 1980. *Understanding abusive families.* Lexington, Mass.: Lexington Press.

Gardner, D. B. 1964. *Development in early childhood: The preschool years.* New York: Harper and Row.

Garmezy, N. 1976. Vulnerable and invulnerable children: Theory, research, and intervention. *Catalog of selected documents in psychology* 6, 96.

Garmezy, N. 1983. Stressors of childhood. In N. Garmezy and M. Rutter, eds. *Stress, coping, and development in children.* New York: McGraw-Hill Book Company.

Garmezy, N., Masten, A., Nordstrom, L., and Ferrarese, M. 1979. The nature of competence in normal and deviant children. In M. W. Kent and J. E. Rolf, eds. *Primary prevention of psychopathology. Vol. III. Social competence in children.* Hanover, N.H.: University Press of New England.

Garn, S. M. 1966. Body size and its implications. In L. W. Hoffman and M. L. Hoffman, eds. *Review of child development research.* Vol. 2. New York: Russell Sage Foundation.

Gates, M. 1985. Healthgap: Blacks in U.S. face special problems caused by poverty and environment. *Lansing state journal* (October 29), 3C.

Gecas, V., and Schwalbe, M. L. 1986. Parental behavior and adolescent self-esteem. *Journal of marriage and the family* 48, 37–46.

Gelles, R. 1988. Violence and pregnancy: Are pregnant women at greater risk of abuse? *Journal of marriage and the family* 50 (August), 841–847.

Gelles, R. J. 1976. Abused wives: Why do they stay? *Journal of marriage and the family* 38, 659–668.

George, C., and Main, M. 1979. Social interactions of young abused children: Approach, avoidance, and aggression. *Child development* 50, 306–318.

George, L. K. 1984. The burden of caregiving: How much? What kinds? For whom? *Center reports on advances in research* 8, 2, 1–8. Durham, N.C.: Duke University Center for the Study of Aging and Human Development.

George, L. K., and Maddox, G. L. 1977. Subjective adaptation to loss of the work role: A longitudinal study. *Journal of gerontology* 32, 456–462.

George, L. K., Fillenbaum, G. G., and Palmore, E. 1984. Sex differences in the antecedents and consequences of retirement. *Journal of gerontology* 39, 3, 364–371.

Gerbner, G. 1980. Children and power on television: The other side of the picture. In G. Gerbner, C. J. Ross, and E. Zigler, eds. *Child abuse: An agenda for action.* New York: Oxford University Press.

Gerson, K. 1985. *Hard choices: How women decide about work, career, and motherhood.* Berkeley, Calif.: University of California Press.

Gesell, A. et al. 1974. *Infant and child in the culture of today.* New York: Harper and Row.

Gesell, A., and Ilg, F. L. 1946. *The child from five to ten.* New York: Harper and Row.

Gesell, A., et al. 1940. *First four years of life.* New York: Harper and Row.

Gesell, A., and Ames, L. B. 1947. The development of handedness. *Journal of genetic psychology* 70, 155–175.

Gibbs, J. C., Arnold, K. D., and Burkhart, J. E. 1984. Sex differences in the expression of moral judgment. *Child development* 55, 1040–1043.

Gibson, G. T., Baghurst, P. A., and Colley, D. P. 1983. Maternal alcohol, tobacco and cannabis consumptions and the outcome of pregnancy. *Australia and New Zealand obstetrics and gynecology* 3, 16–19.

Gilbert, A. 1983. Stress reduction through lifestyle. *Psychologia: An international journal of psychology in the orient* 26, 2 (June), 86–91.

Gill, R. L. 1976. *The effects of cartoon characters as motivators of pre-school disadvantaged children*. Ed.D dissertation, University of Massachusetts.

Gilligan, C. 1979. In a different voice: Women's conceptions of self and of morality. *Stage theories of cognitive and moral development: Criticisms and applications*. Harvard Educational Review, reprint no. 13.

Gilligan, C. 1982. *In a different voice: Psychological theory and women's development*. Cambridge: Harvard University Press.

Gispert, M., et al. 1984. Predictors of repeat pregnancies among low-income adolescents. *Hospital and community psychiatry* 35, 7 (July), 719–723.

Glenn, N. D., and Kramer, K. B. 1985. The psychological well-being of adult children of divorce. *Journal of marriage and the family* 47, 4 (November), 905–912.

Glenn, N. D., and McLanahan, S. 1981. The effects of offspring on the psychological well-being of older adults. *Journal of marriage and the family* 43, 409–421.

Glick, I. O., Weiss, R. S., and Parkes, C. M. 1974. *The first year of bereavement*. New York: John Wiley and Sons.

Glick, P. C. 1979. Children of divorced parents in a demographic perspective. *Journal of social issues* 35, 170–180.

Glick, P. C. 1984. Marriage, divorce, and living arrangements: Prospective changes. *Journal of family issues* 5, 1, 7–26.

Glick, P. C. 1989. Remarried families, stepfamilies, and stepchildren: A brief demographic profile. *Family relations* 38, 24–27.

Glick, P. C. 1990. Marriage and family trends. In D. H. Olsen and M. K. Hanson, eds. *2001: Preparing families for the future*. Minneapolis: National Council on Family Relations.

Glick, P. C., and Lin, S. L. 1986. More young adults are living with their parents: Who are they? *Journal of marriage and the family* 48, 1 (February), 107–112.

Globerson, T., Weinstein, E., and Sharabany, R. 1985. Teasing out cognitive development from cognitive style: A training study. *Developmental psychology* 21, 682–691.

Goble, F. 1971. *The third force*. New York: Pocket Books.

Godkewitsch, M. 1976. Physiological and verbal indices of arousal in rated humor. In A. J. Chapman and H. C. Foot, eds. *Humour and laughter: Theory, research, and application*. London: Wiley.

Goetting, A. 1986. The developmental tasks of siblingship over the life cycle. *Journal of marriage and the family* 48, 703–714.

Gold, D., and Andres, D. 1978. Comparisons of adolescent children with employed and nonemployed mothers. *Merrill-Palmer quarterly* 24, 243–254.

Gold, D. and Andres, D. 1978. Developmental comparisons between ten-year-old children with employed and nonemployed mothers. *Child development* 49, 75–84.

Gold, D. T., and Gwyther, L. P. 1989. The prevention of elder abuse: An educational model. *Family relations* 38, 8–14.

Gold, M., and Reimer, D. J. 1975. Changing patterns of delinquent behavior among Americans 13 through 16 years old: 1967–72. *Crime and delinquency literature* 7, 483–517.

Goldband, S. 1980. Stimulus specificity of physiological response to stress and the Type A coronary-prone behavior pattern. *Journal of personality and social psychology* 39, 670–679.

Goldberg, M. E., and Gorn, G. J. 1977. *Material vs. social preferences, parent-child relations, and the child's emotional responses*. Paper presented at the Telecommunications Policy Research Conference, Arleigh House, Va.

Goldberg, S. 1979. Premature birth: Consequences for parent-infant relationship. *American scientist* 67, 214–220.

Goldberg, S., and Lewis, M. 1973. Play behavior in the year-old infant: Early sex differences. In L. J. Stone, H. T. Smith, and L. B. Murphy, eds. *The competent infant*. New York: Basic Books.

Goldin-Meadow, S., and Mylander, C. 1985. Gestural communication in deaf children: The effects and noneffects of parental input on early language development. *Monographs of the Society for Research in Child Development* 49, (3–4, serial no. 207).

Goldman, A., and Goldblum, R. 1982. Anti-infective properties of human milk. *Pediatric update* 2, 359–363.

Goldsmith, H. 1983. Genetic influences on personality from infancy to adulthood. *Child development* 54, 331–355.

Goldstein, A. I., Dumars, K. W., and Kent, D. R. 1977. Minimizing the risk of amniocentesis for prenatal diagnosis. *Birth defects: Original article series 13*. No. 3D, 276–277.

Goldstein, R. 1981. On deceptive rejoinders about deceptive research: A reply to Baron. *IRB: A review of human subjects research* 3, 8, 5–6.

Golub, H. L., and Corwin, M. J. 1984. A physioacoustic model of the infant cry. In B. M. Lester and C. F. Z. Boukydis, eds. *Infant crying: Theoretical and research perspectives*. New York: Plenum.

Goodglass, H., Gleason, J. G., and Hyde, M. R. 1970. Some dimensions of auditory language comprehension in aphasia. *Journal of speech and hearing research* 13, 595–606.

Goodman, R. M. 1986. *Planning for a healthy baby*. New York: Oxford University Press.

Goossens, F. A., and vanIJzendoorn, M. H. 1990. Quality of infants' attachments to professional caregivers: Relation to infant-parent attachment and day-care characteristics. *Child development* 61, 3, 832–837.

Gordon, R., Range, L., and Edwards, R. 1987. Generational differences in reactions to adolescent suicide. *Journal of community psychology* 17, 268–274.

Gorlin, C. E., and Miley, T. 1984. Surrogate parenting. . . *The bench and bar of minnesota* 41 (January), 17–22.

Gorman, J. 1982. New hope for the childless. *Discover* (March), 62–65.

Gorn, G. J., Goldberg, M. E., and Kanungo, R. N. 1976. The role of educational television in changing the intergroup attitudes of children. *Child development* 47, 277–280.

Gorsuch, R., and Key, M. 1974. Abnormalities of pregnancy as a function of anxiety and life stress. *Psychosomatic medicine* (July–August), 36.

Gottesman, I. I. and Shields, J. 1982. *Schizophrenia: The epigenetic puzzle*. Cambridge: Cambridge University Press.

Gottesman, I. I., and Shields, J. 1973. *Schizophrenia and genetics: A twin study vantage point*. New York: Academic Press.

Gottfredson, D. C. 1985. Youth employment, crime, and schooling: A longitudinal study of a national sample. *Developmental psychology* 21, 3, 419–432.

Gottfried, A. W., and Bathhurst, K. 1983. Hand preference across time is related to intelligence in young girls, not boys. *Science* 221, 1074–1076.

Gottman, J., Gonso, J., and Rasmussen, B. 1975. Social interaction, social competence, and friendship in children. *Child development* 46, 709–718.

Gould, R. 1975. Adult life stages: Growth toward self-tolerance. *Psychology today* 8, 9 (February), 74–78.

Gould, R. 1978. *Transformations*. New York: Simon and Schuster.

Gove, F. 1983. *Patterns and organizations of behavior and affective expression during the second year of life*. Unpublished doctoral dissertation, University of Minnesota.

Granick, S., and Friedman, A. S. 1973. Educational experience and the maintenance of intellectual functioning by the aged: An overview. In L. F. Jarvik, C. Eisdorfer, and J. E. Blum, eds. *Intellectual functioning in adults*. New York: Springer Publishing Company.

Grant, J. P. 1982. *The state of the world's children: 1982–83*. New York: UNICEF and Oxford University Press.

Green, J., Bax, M., and Tsitsikas, H. 1989. Neonatal behavior and early temperament: A longitudinal study of the first six months of life. *American journal of orthopsychiatry* 59, (January), 82–93.

Green, S. K. 1981. Attitudes and perceptions about the elderly: Current and future perspectives. *International journal of aging and human development* 13, 99–119.

Greenberg, B. S., Buerkel-Rothfuss, N., Neuendorf, K. A., and Atkin, C. K. 1980. Three seasons of television family role interactions. In B. S. Greenberg ed. *Life on television*. Norwood, N.J.: Ablex.

Greenberg, M., and Morris, N. 1974. Engrossment: The newborn's impact upon the father. *American journal of orthopsychiatry* 44, 4, 520–531.

Greenberg, S. 1984. Early education for educational equity. In S. Klein, ed. *Handbook of educational equity*. Baltimore: Johns Hopkins University Press.

Greenberger, E., and O'Neill, R. 1990. Parents' concerns about their child's development: Implications for fathers' and mothers' well-being and attitudes toward work. *Journal of marriage and the family* 52, 621–635.

Greenberger, E., and Steinberg, L. 1986. *When teenagers work: The psychological and social costs of adolescent employment*. New York: Basic Books.

Greenberger, E., and Steinberg, L. 1981. The workplace as a context for the socialization of youth. *Journal of youth and adolescence* 10, 185–210.

Greenberger, E., Steinberg, L., and Vaux, A. 1981. Adolescents who work: Health and behavioral consequences of job stress. *Developmental psychology* 17, 691–703.

Greene, J. G., and Cooke, D. J. 1980. Life stress and symptoms at the climacterium. *British journal of psychiatry* 136 (May), 486–491.

Greenfield, P. M. 1984. *Mind and media: The effects of television, video games, and computers*. Cambridge, Mass.: Harvard University Press.

Greenfield, P. M., Bruzzone, L., Koyamatsu, K., Satuloff, W., Nixon, D., Brodie, M., Kingsdale, D. 1987. What is rock music doing to the minds of our youth? A first experimental look at the effects of rock music lyrics and music videos. *Journal of early adolescence* 7, 3, 315–329.

Greenland, S., Staisch, K., Brown, N., and Gross, S. 1982. The effects of marijuana use during pregnancy. *American journal of obstetrics and gynecology* 143, 408–413.

Greenspan, S., and Greenspan, N. T. 1985. *First feelings: Milestones in the emotional development of your baby and child*. New York: Viking.

Greif, G. L. 1985. Children and housework in the single father family. *Family relations* 34, 3 (July), 353–357.

Greif, G. L. 1986. Mothers without custody and child support. *Family relations* 35, 1 (January), 87–93.

Greulich, W. W. 1957. A comparison of the physical growth and development of American-born and native Japanese children. *American journal of physical anthropology* 15, 489–515.

Greven, P. 1977. *The protestant temperament*. New York: Alfred A. Knopf.

Grimby, G., and Saltin, B. 1983. The aging muscle. *Clinical psychology* 3, 209–218.

Groch, A. S. 1974. Joking and appreciation of humor in nursery school children. *Child development* 45, 1098–1102

Gross, T. F. 1985. *Cognitive development*. Monterey, Calif.: Brooks/ Cole.

Grzegorczyk, P. B., Jones, S. W., and Mistretta, C. M. 1979. Age-related differences in salt taste acuity. *Journal of gerontology* 34, 834–840.

Gudschinsky, S. 1977. Mother-tongue literacy and second language learning. In W. F. Mackey and T. Andersson. *Bilingualism in early childhood*. Rowley, Mass.: Newberry House Publishers.

Guntrip, H. 1973. Personality. In R. R. Sears and S. S. Feldman, eds. *Seven ages of man*. Los Altos, Calif.: William Kaufman.

Guntrip, H. 1973. Personality. In R. R. Sears and S. S. Feldman, eds. *Seven ages of man*. Los Altos, Calif.: William Kaufman.

Gupta, C., Yaffe, S. J., and Shapiro, B. H. 1982. Prenatal exposure to phenobarbitol permanently decreases testosterone and causes reproductive dysfunction. *Science* 216, 640.

Gusella, T. J., Tanzi, R. E., Anderson, M. A., Hobbs, W., Gibbons, K., Raschtchian, R., Gilliam, T. C., Wallace, M. R., Wexler, N. S., and Conneally, P. M. 1984. DNA markers for nervous system diseases. *Science* 225, (September), 1320–1326.

Guthrie, H. A. 1979. *Introduction to Nutrition*. St. Louis: Mosby.

Gutmann, D. 1975. Parenthood: A key to the comparative study of the life cycle. In N. Datan and L. H. Ginsberg, eds. *Lifespan developmental psychology*. New York: Academic Press.

Gutmann, D. 1977. The cross-cultural perspective: Notes toward a comparative psychology of aging. In J. E. Birren and K. W. Schaie, eds. *Handbook of the psychology of aging*. New York: Van Nostrand Reinhold Company.

Gutmann, D., Grunes, J., and Griffin, B. 1980. The clinical psychology of later life: Developmental paradigms. In N. Datan and N. Lohmann, eds. *Transitions of aging*. New York: Academic Press.

Gutmann, D. L. 1968. Aging among the highland Maya: A comparative study. In B. L. Neugarten, ed. *Middle age and aging*. Chicago: University of Chicago Press.

Guttmann, E. 1977. Muscles. In C. E. Finch and L. Hayflick, eds. *Handbook of the biology of aging*. New York: Van Nostrand.

Gwynne, P. 1976. Politics and genes. *Newsweek* (January 12), 50–52.

Haan, N., et al. 1968. Moral reasoning of young adults: Political-social behavior, family background and personality correlates. *Journal of personality and social psychology* 10, 183–201.

Haas, A. 1979. *Teenage sexuality: A survey of teenage sexual behavior*. New York: Macmillan.

Haas, A. D. 1975. She will carry another woman's baby. *Detroit free press* (August 17), 1C and 10C.

Hagestad, G. O. 1985. Continuity and connectedness. In V. L. Bengtson and J. F. Robertson, eds. *Grandparenthood*. Beverly Hills, Calif.: Sage Publications.

Hains, A. A., and Ryan, E. B. 1983. The development of social cognitive processes among juvenile delinquents and nondelinquent peers. *Child development* 54, 1536–1544.

Hale, L. E. 1978. The effects of intrauterine exposure of heroin and methadone on child motor development and learning potential. New York University, Dissertation Abstracts International. Vol. 39 (4–A), 2132.

Hale, S. 1990. A global developmental trend in cognitive processing speed. *Child development* 61, 653–663.

Hall, D. A. 1976. *The prime of Mrs. America: The American woman at forty*. New York: Putnam.

Hall, E. 1983. A conversation with Erik Erikson. *Psychology today* 17, 6, 22–30.

Hall, E. H., et al. 1972. Intellect, mental illness, and survival in the aged: A longitudinal investigation. *Journal of gerontology* 27, 2, 237–244.

Hallinan, M. 1981. Recent advances in sociometry. In S. Asher and J. Gottman, eds. *The development of children's friendships*. New York: Cambridge University Press.

Halme, J. 1985. In vitro fertilization. In M. G. Hammond and L. M. Talbert, eds. *Infertility*. 2nd ed. Ordell, N.J.: Medical Economics Books.

Halpern, W. 1983. Parental mortification and restitutional efforts upon the sudden loss of a child. In J. Schowalter, ed. *The child and death*. New York: Columbia University Press.

Halverson, C. F., Jr., and Waldrop, M. F. 1976. Relations between pre-school activity and aspects of intellectual and social behavior at age 7-½. *Developmental psychology* 12, 107–112.

Handel, W. W. 1984. Surrogate parenting, in vitro insemination and embryo transplantation. *Whittier law review* 6 (Summer), 783–788.

Hanratty, M. A., et al. 1969. Imitation of film-mediated aggression against live and inanimate victims. *Proceedings of the 77th Annual Convention APA,* 457–458.

Hanson, J. W., Streissguth, A. P., and Smith, D. W. 1978. The effects of moderate alcohol consumption during pregnancy on fetal growth and morphogenesis. *The journal of pediatrics* 92, 457–460.

Hanson, S. M. H. 1986. Healthy single parent families. *Family relations* 1, 125–132.

Hanson, S. M. H., and Sporakowski, M. J. 1986. Single parent families. *Family relations* 35, 1 (January), 3–8.

Hardy, J. B. 1973. Clinical and developmental aspects of congenital rubella. *Archives of otolaryngology* 98, 230–236.

Hardy, J. B., McCracken, G. H., Gilkeson, M. R., and Sver, J. I. 1969. Adverse fetal outcome following maternal rubella after the first trimester of pregnancy. *Journal of the American Medical Association* 207 (March 31), 2414–2420.

Hardyck, C., and Petrimovich, L. F. 1977. Left-handedness. *Psychological bulletin* 84, 385–404.

Harkaway, J. E. 1987. Family intervention in the treatment of childhood and adolescent obesity. In J. C. Hansen and J. E. Harkaway, eds. *Eating disorders.* Rockville, Md.: Aspen Publishers.

Harlow, L. L., Newcomb, M. D., and Bentler, P. M. 1986. Depression, self-derogation, substance use, and suicide ideation: Lack of purpose in life as a mediational factor. *Journal of clinical psychology* 42, 5–21.

Harper, B. C. 1982. Some snapshots of death and dying among ethnic minorities. In R. C. Manuel, ed. *Minority aging: Sociological and social psychological issues.* Westport, Conn.: Greenwood Press.

Harper, L. V., and Sanders, K. M. 1978. Preschool children's use of space: Sex differences in outdoor play. In M. S. Smart and R. C. Smart, eds. *Preschool children: Development and relationships.* New York: Macmillan.

Harrill, I., Smith, C., and Gangever, J. A. 1972. Food acceptance and nutritional intake of preschool children. *Journal of nutrition education* 4, 103–107.

Harriman, L. C. 1986. Marital adjustment as related to personal and marital changes accompanying parenthood. *Family relations* 35, 2 (April), 233–239.

Harris, C. S. 1983. The case of the vanishing twin. *Science* (March), 83.

Harris, J. R., and Liebert, R. M. 1984. *The child.* Englewood Cliffs, N.J.: Prentice-Hall.

Harris, L., et al. 1975. *The myth and reality of aging in America.* Washington, D.C.: National Council on Aging.

Harris, L., et al. 1981. *Aging in the eighties: America in transition.* Washington, D.C.: National Council on Aging.

Harris, P. L. 1974. Perseverative errors in search by young infants. *Journal of experimental child psychology* 18, 535–542.

Harris, P. L. 1983. Infant cognition. In P. H. Mussen, ed. *Handbook of child psychology* Vol. 2, 4th ed. New York: Wiley.

Harris, P. L. 1985. What children know about situations that provoke emotion. In M. Lewis and C. Saarni, eds. *The socialization of emotions.* New York: Plenum.

Harrison, W. M., Endicott, J., Nee, J., Glick, H., and Rabkin, J. G. 1989. Characteristics of women seeking treatment for premenstrual syndrome. *Psychosomatics* 30, 4. Washington, D.C.: American Psychiatric Press.

Hart, K. E. 1983. Physical symptom reporting and health perception among Type A and B college males. *Journal of human stress* 9, 4 (December), 17–22.

Harter, J., and Miner, C. 1979. *A cognitive-developmental understanding of emotions.* Paper presented at the Society for Research in Child Development, San Francisco, March 15–18.

Harter, S. 1981. A new self-report scale of intrinsic versus extrinsic orientation in the classroom: Motivational and informational components. *Developmental psychology* 17, 300–312.

Harter, S. 1982. The perceived competence scale for children. *Child development* 53, 87–97.

Hartley, E. L., et al. 1948. Children's perceptions of ethnic group membership. *Journal of psychology* 26, 387–398.

Hartley, R., and Goldenson, R. 1963. *The complete book of children's play.* New York: Thomas Crowell Company.

Hartrup, W. W., and Coates, B. 1967. Imitation of a peer as a function of reinforcement from the peer group and rewardingness of the model. *Child development* 38, 1003–1016.

Hartup, W. W. 1970. Peer interaction and social organization. In P. H. Mussen, ed. *Carmichael's manual of child psychology.* Vol. 2 3rd ed. New York: John Wiley and Sons.

Hartup, W. W. 1976. Peer interaction and the behavioral development of the individual child. In E. Schopler and R. J. Reichler, eds. *Psychopathology and child development.* New York: Plenum.

Hartup, W. W. 1983. Peer relations. In P. H. Mussen, ed. *Handbook of child psychology.* Vol. 4. New York: Wiley.

Harvey, E. B., Boice, J. D., Jr., Honeyman, M., and Flannery, J. T. 1985. Prenatal X-ray exposure and childhood cancer in twins. *New England journal of medicine* 312, 9 (February 28), 541–545.

Hatch, R. C., and Franken, M. L. 1984. Concerns of children with parents in nursing homes. *Journal of gerontological social work* 7, 3, 19–30.

Hauser, S., Liebman, W., Houlihan, J., Powers, S., Jacobson, A., Noam, G., Weiss, B., and Follansbee, D. 1985. Family contexts of pubertal timing. *Journal of youth and adolescence* 14, 317–338.

Havighurst, R. J. 1963. *Human development and education.* New York: McKay.

Havighurst, R. J. 1982. The world of work. In B. B. Wolman, ed. *Handbook of developmental psychology.* Englewood Cliffs, N.J.: Prentice-Hall.

Havighurst, R. J., Neugarten, B. L., and Tobin, S. S. 1968. Disengagement and patterns of aging. In B. L. Neugarten, ed. *Middle age and aging.* Chicago: University of Chicago Press.

Haviland, J. 1977. Sex-related pragmatics in infants. *Journal of communication* 27, 80–84.

Hawkins, A. J., and Belsky, J. 1989. The role of father involvement in personality change in men across the transition to parenthood. *Family relations* 38, 4, (October), 378–384.

Hawton, K. 1986. *Suicide and attempted suicide among children and adolescents.* Beverly Hills, Calif.: Sage.

Hay, D. F. 1984. Social conflict in early childhood. In G. Whitehurst, ed. *Annals of child development.* Vol. 1. London: JAI.

Hayes, H., White, B. L., and Held, R. 1973. Visual accommodation in human infants. In L. J. Stone, H. T. Smith, and L. B. Murphy, eds. *The competent infant.* New York: Basic Books.

Hayflick, L. 1980. The cell biology of aging. *Scientific American* 242, 58–65.

Hazen, N. L., and Black, B. 1989. Preschool peer communication skills: The role of social status and interaction context. *Child development* 60, 867–875.

Heald, F. P. 1975. Juvenile obesity. In M. Winick, ed. *Childhood obesity.* New York: John Wiley and Sons.

Heilbrun, A. B., Jr., and Frank, M. E. 1989. Self-preoccupation and general stress level as sensitizing factors in premenstrual and menstrual distress. *Journal of psychosomatic research* 33, 5, 571–577.

Heiman, M. 1965. Psychoanalytic observations on the relationship of pet and man. *Veterinary medicine small animal clinician.* 55, 713–718.

Heinonen, O. P., Slone, D., and Shapiro, S. 1977. *Birth defects and drugs in pregnancy.* Littleton, Mass.: Publishing Sciences Group.

Henry, W. E. 1975. The role of work in structuring the life cycle. In F. Rebelsky, ed. *Life: The continuous process.* New York: Alfred A. Knopf.

Henton, J., Cate, R., Koval, J., Lloyd, S., and Christopher, S. 1983. Romance and violence in dating relations. *Journal of family issues* 4, 467–482.

Herkowitz, J. 1978. Sex-role expectations and motor behavior of the young child. In M. V. Ridenour, ed. *Motor development: Issues and applications.* Princeton, N.J.: Princeton Book Company.

Herrmann, J., and Thomas, E. 1986. Transabdominal chorionic villus sampling as an office practice. *Lancet* 1, 8483, 747.

Herschel, M. 1978. Dyslexia revisited. *Human genetics* 40, 115–134.

Hertzog, C., Schaie, K. W., and Gribbin, K. 1978. Cardiovascular disease and changes in intellectual functioning from middle to old age. *Journal of gerontology* 33, 6, 872–883.

Hetherington, E. M. 1973. Girls without fathers. *Psychology today* 6 (February), 47–52.

Hetherington, E. M., Cox, M., and Cox, R. 1982. Effects of divorce on parents and children. In M. Lamb, ed. *Nontraditional families: Parenting and child development.* Hillsdale, N.J.: Erlbaum.

Hetrick, E. S., and Martin, A. D. 1985. Ego-dystonic homosexuality: A developmental view. In H. S. Hetrick and T. S. Stein, eds. *Innovations in psychotherapy with homosexuals.* Washington, D.C.: APA Press.

Hibbard, J. H., and Pope, C. R. 1987. Employment characteristics and health status among men and women. *Women and health* 12, 85–102.

Hildreth, G. 1948. Manual dominance in nursery school children. *Journal of genetic psychology* 73, 29–45.

Hill, J., Holmbeck, G., Marlow, L., Green, T., Lych, M. 1985. Menarcheal status and parent-child relations in families of seventh-grade girls. *Journal of youth and adolescence* 14, 301–316.

Hingson, R., Alpert, J. J., Day, N., Dooling, E., Kayne, H., Morlock, S., Oppenheimer, E., and Zuckerman, B. 1982. Effects of maternal drinking and marijuana use on fetal growth and development. *Pediatrics* 70, 539–546.

Hinton, J. M. 1979. Comparison of places and policies for terminal care. *Lancet* 8106, 29–32.

Hirsh-Pasek, K., Nelson, D. G., Jusczyk, P. W., and Wright, K. 1986. *A moment of silence: How the prosodic cues in motherese might assist language learning.* Paper presented at the International Conference on Infant Studies, Los Angeles, April.

Hodgman, C. H. 1983. Current issues in adolescent psychiatry. *Hospital and community psychiatry* 34, 6 (June), 514–521.

Hoff-Ginsberg, E. 1986. Function and structure in maternal speech: Their relation to the child's development of syntax. *Developmental psychology* 22, 155–163.

Hoffman, L. 1984. Work, family, and the socialization of the child. In R. Parke, ed. *Review of the child development research.* Vol. 7. Chicago: University of Chicago Press.

Hoffman, L., and Nye, F. I. 1974. *Working mothers.* San Francisco: Jossey-Bass.

Hoffman, L. W. 1979. Maternal employment: 1979. *American psychologist* 34, 10, 859–865.

Hoffman, M. L. 1970. Moral development. In P. H. Mussen, ed. *Carmichael's manual of child psychology.* Vol. 2. 3rd ed. New York: John Wiley and Sons.

Hoffman, M. L. 1975. Altruistic behavior and the parent-child relationship. *Journal of personality and social psychology* 31, 937–943.

Hoffman, M. L. 1975. Developmental synthesis of affect and cognition and its implications for altruistic motivation. *Developmental psychology* 11, 607–622.

Hoffman, M. L. 1975. Moral internalization, parental power, and the nature of parent-child interaction. *Developmental psychology* 11, 228–239.

Hoffman, M. L. 1975. Sex differences in oral internalization and values. *Journal of personality and social psychology* 32, 720–729.

Hoffman, M. L. 1976. Empathy, role-taking, guilt and development of altruistic motives. In T. Lickona, ed. *Moral development and behavior.* New York: Holt, Rinehart and Winston.

Hoffman, M. L. 1977. Moral internalization: Current theory and research. In L. Berkowitz, ed. *Advances in experimental social psychology.* Vol. 10. New York: Academic Press.

Hoffman, M. L. 1978. Toward a theory of empathic arousal and development. In M. Lewis and L. A. Rosenblum, eds. *The development of affect.* New York: Plenum.

Hogan, R. 1975. The structure of moral character and the explanation of moral action. *Journal of youth and adolescence* 4, 1–15.

Holahan, C. K., Holahan, C. J., and Belk, S. S. 1984. Adjustment in aging: The roles of life stress, hassles, and self-efficacy. *Health psychology* 3, 4, 315–328.

Holden, C. 1980. Identical twins reared apart. *Science* 207, 1323–1328.

Holiday, M. A. 1986. Body composition and energy needs during growth. In F. Falkner and J. M. Tanner, eds. *Postnatal growth neurobiology.* Vol. 2 of *Human growth: A comprehensive treatise.* New York: Plenum Press.

Holinger, P. C., and Offer, D. 1982. Prediction of adolescent suicide: A population model. *American journal of psychiatry* 139, 302–307.

Holmes, L. 1978. How fathers cause the Down Syndrome. *Human nature* 1, 10, 70–72.

Holmes, L. 1979. Genetic counseling for the older pregnant woman: New data and questions. *New England journal of medicine* 298, 25, 1419–1421.

Holmes, T. H., and Masuda, M. 1974. Life change and illness susceptibility. In B. S. Dohrenwend and B. P. Dohrenwend, eds. *Stressful life events: Their nature and effects.* New York: Wiley.

Holmes, T. H., and Rahe, R. H. 1967. The social readjustment rating scale. *Journal of psychosomatic research* 11, 213–218.

Honig, A. S. 1981. What are the needs of infants? *Young children* (November), 3–9.

Honig, A. S. 1986. Stress and coping in children (Part 2). *Young children,* 41, 5, 47–59.

Honig, A. S. 1988. Humor development in children. *Young children* 43, 4, 60–73.

Honzik, M. P., and Macfarlane, J. W. 1973. Personality development and intellectual functioning. In L. F. Jarvik, C. Eisdorfer, and J. E. Blum, eds. *Intellectual functioning in adults.* New York: Springer Publishing Company.

Hooper, F. H., Fitzgerald, J., and Papalia, D. 1971. Piagetian theory and the aging process: Extensions and speculations. *Aging and human development* 2, 3–20.

Hoopes, M. M., and Harper, J. M. 1987. *Birth order roles and sibling patterns in individual and family therapy.* Provo, Utah: Brigham Young University.

Hooyman, N. R., and Kiyak, H. A. 1988. *Social gerontology.* Boston: Allyn and Bacon.

Hopkins, J. R. 1977. Sexual behavior in adolescence. *Journal of social issues* 33, 2, 67–85.

Horn, J. L. 1970. Organization of data on life-span development of human abilities. In L. R. Goulet and P. B. Baltes, eds. *Life-span developmental psychology: Research and theory.* New York: Academic Press.

Horn, J. L. 1982. The theory of fluid and crystallized intelligence in relation to concepts of cognitive psychology and aging in adulthood. In F. I. M. Craik and S. Trehub, eds. *Aging and cognitive processes.* New York: Plenum.

Horn, J. L., and Cattel, R. B. 1966. Refinement and test of the theory of fluid and crystalized intelligence. *Journal of educational psychology* 57, 253–270.

Horowitz, F. D. 1962. The relationship of anxiety, self-concept and sociometric status among fourth-, fifth-, and sixth-grade children. *Journal of abnormal psychology* 65, 212–214.

Horowitz, M. J., Wilner, N., Marmar, C., and Krupnick, J. 1980. Pathological grief and the activation of latent self-images. *American journal of psychiatry* 137, 1157–1162.

Horsman, A., and Currey, J. D. 1983. Estimation of mechanical properties of the distal radius from bone mineral content and cortical width. *Clinical orthopedics and related research* 176, 298–304.

House, J. S., Strecher, V., Metzner, H. L., and Robbins, C. A. 1986. Occupational stress and health among men and women in the Tecumseh community health study. *Journal of health and social behavior* 27, 62–77.

Householder, J., Hatcher, R., Burns, W., and Chasnoff, I. 1982. Infants born to narcotic-addicted mothers. *Psychological bulletin* 92, 453–468.

Howard, L., and Polich, J. 1985. P300 latency and memory span development. *Developmental psychology* 21, 2, 283–289.

Howes, C. 1988. Relations between child care and schooling. *Developmental psychology* 24, 53–57.

Howes, C., and Olenick, M. 1986. Family and child-care influences on children's compliance. *Child development* 57, 202–216.

Howes, C., Rodning, C., Galluzzo, D. C., and Myers, L. 1988. Attachment and child care: Relationships with mother and caregiver. *Early childhood research quarterly* 3, 403–416.

Howes, C., and Stewart, P. 1987. Child's play with adults, toys, and peers: An examination of family and child-care influences. *Developmental psychology* 23, 423–430.

Hrncir, E. 1985. *Antecedents and correlates of stress and coping in school-age children.* William T. Grant Foundation Fifth Annual Faculty Scholars Program in Mental Health in Children.

Huba, G. J., and Bentler, P. W. 1984. Causal models of personality, peer culture characteristics, drug use, and criminal behaviors over a five-year span. In D. W. Goodwin, K. T. Van Dusen, and S. A. Mednick, eds. *Longitudinal research in alcoholism.* Boston: Kluwer-Nijhoff.

Hubbard, L. 1982. In search of 40 winks. *Modern maturity* 25, 72.

Hubert, N. C., and Wachs, T. D. 1985. Parental perceptions of the behavioral components of infant easiness/difficulties. *Child development* 56, 6, 1525–1537.

Hudson, J. I., et al. 1982. Bulimia related to affective disorder by family history and response to the dexamethasone suppressions test. *American journal of psychiatry* 139, 5 (May), 685–687.

Huebner, R., Risser, D., McGuinness, G., and Dougherty, L. 1980. The young infant's ability to produce discrete emotion expressions. *Developmental psychology* 16, 132–140.

Huesmann, L. R., Eron, L. D., Lefkowitz, M. M., and Walder, L. O. 1984. Stability of aggression over time and generations. *Developmental psychology* 20, 1120–1134.

Huesmann, L. R., Lagerspetz, K., and Eron, L. D. 1984. Intervening variables in the TV violence-aggression relation: Evidence from two countries. *Developmental psychology* 20, 746–775.

Hughes, R., Jr., Tingle, B. A., and Sawin, D. B. 1981. Development of empathic understanding in children. *Child development* 52, 122–128.

Humphreys, L. G. 1971. Theory of intelligence. In R. Cancro, ed. *Intelligence: Genetic and environmental influences.* New York: Grune and Stratton.

Humphreys, L. G. 1980. Methinks they do protest too much. *Intelligence* 4, 179–183.

Humphreys, L. G., Rich, S. A., and Davey, T. C. 1985. A Piagetian test of general intelligence. *Developmental psychology* 21, 5, 872–877.

Hunsberger, B. 1985. Religion, age, life satisfaction, and perceived sources of religiousness: A study of older persons. *Journal of gerontology* 40, 5, 615–620.

Hunter, F. T. 1985. Adolescents' perception of discussions with parents and friends. *Developmental psychology* 21, 3 (May), 433–440.

Hunter, F. T., and Youniss, J. 1982. Changes in functions of three relationships during adolescence. *Developmental psychology* 18, 806–811.

Huntley, T. 1986. Rejection feels like the worst fate. *Detroit free press* (May 25), F1–6.

Hurlock, E. 1980. *Developmental psychology.* 5th ed. New York: McGraw-Hill.

Hurlock, E. B. 1978. *Child development.* New York: McGraw-Hill Book Company.

Hurrelmann, K. 1989. *Human development and health.* Berlin, Germany: Springer-Verlag.

Huston, A. C. 1983. Sex typing. In P. H. Mussen, ed. *Handbook of child psychology.* (4th ed.) Vol. 4. New York: Wiley.

Huston, A. C., Carpenter, C. J., and Atwater, J. B. 1986. Gender, adult structuring of activities, and social behavior in middle childhood. *Child development* 57, 1200–1209.

Hyde, J. S. 1984. How large are gender differences in aggression? A developmental meta-analysis. *Developmental psychology* 20, 722–736.

Hynd, G. L., Obrzut, J. E., and Obrzut, A. 1981. Are lateral and perceptual asymmetries related to WISC-R and achievement test performance in normal and learning-disabled children? *Journal of consulting and clinical psychology* 49, 977–979.

Iannotti, R. 1985. Naturalistic and structured assessments of prosocial behavior in preschool children: The influence of empathy and perspective taking. *Developmental psychology* 21, 46–55.

Ideal weight for a long life adjusted upward in a survey. 1983. *New York times* (March 2), A21.

Ingalls, A. J., and Salerno, M. C. 1979. *Maternal and child health nursing.* St. Louis: C. V. Mosby Company.

Ingber, D. 1982. The violent brain. *Science digest* (April), 34 and 114.

Inhelder, B., and Piaget, J. 1958. *The growth of logical thinking from childhood to adolescence.* New York: Basic Books.

Institute of Medicine. 1985. *Preventing low birth weight.* Washington, D.C.: National Academy Press.

Irgens, L. M., Skjoerven, R., Peterson, D. R. 1988. Sudden infant death syndrome and recurrence in subsequent siblings. *Journal of pediatrics* 112, 3, 501.

Ivancevich, J. M., and Matteson, M. T. 1980. *Stress and work: A managerial perspective.* Glenview, Ill.: Scott, Foresman.

Izard, C. E. 1977. *Human emotions.* New York: Plenum.

Izard, C. E. 1979. *Emotions in personality and social psychopathology.* New York: Plenum.

Izard, C. E., Huebner, R. R., Risser, D., McGinnes, G. C., and Dougherty, L. M. 1980. The young infant's ability to produce discrete emotion expressions. *Developmental psychology* 16, 132–141.

Jackson, L. G., Wapner, R. A., and Barr, M. A. 1986. Safety of chorionic villus biopsy. *Lancet* 1, 8482, 674–675.

Jacobs, J. 1971. *Adolescent suicide.* New York: Wiley-Interscience.

Jacoby, S. 1974. Waiting for the end: On nursing homes. *New York Times magazine* (March 31), 13ff.

Jakobsson, I., and Lindberg, T. 1983. Cow's mild protein causes infantile colic in breast-fed infants: A double-blind crossover study. *Pediatrics* 71, 268.

Janson, P., and Martin, J. K. 1982. Job satisfaction and age: A test of two views. *Social forces* 60, 1089–1102.

Jarvik, L. F. 1973. Discussion: Patterns of intellectual functioning in the later years. In L. F. Jarvik, C. Eisdorfer, and J. E. Blum, eds. *Intellectual functioning in adults.* New York: Springer Publishing Company.

Jersild, A. T., and Holmes, F. B. 1935. Children's fears. *Child development monographs,* no. 20.

Jersild, A. T. and Holmes, F. B. 1935. Methods of overcoming children's fears. *Journal of psychology* 1, 75–104.

Jersild, A. T., Brook, J. S., and Brook, D. W. 1978. *The psychology of adolescence.* New York: Macmillan.

Jersild, A. T., Telford, C. W., and Sawrey, J. M. 1975. *Child psychology.* 7th ed. Englewood Cliffs, N.J.: Prentice-Hall.

Jessner, L., Weigert, E., and Foy, J. L. 1970. The development of parental attitudes during pregnancy. In E. J. Anthony and T. Benedek, eds. *Parenthood: Its psychology and psychopathology.* Boston: Little, Brown.

Johnson, A. L., et al. 1975. Evans County, Georgia, cardiovascular study: Race, sex, and weight influences of the young adult. *American journal of cardiology* 35, 523.

Johnson, C. L. 1982. Sibling solidarity: Its origin and functioning in Italian-American families. *Journal of marriage and the family* 44, 155–167.

Johnson, J. 1975. *Relationship between fantasy play, creativity, and intelligence in preschool children.* Paper presented at annual meeting of the American Psychological Association, Chicago.

Johnson, J. E., and McGillicuddy-Delisi, A. 1983. Family environment factors and children's knowledge of rules and conventions. *Child development* 54, 218–226.

Johnson, R. and Carter, M. M. 1980. Flight of the young: Why children run away from their homes. *Adolescence* 15, 58 (Summer), 483–489.

Johnson, T. G., and Goldfinger, S. E. 1981. *The Harvard Medical School health letter book.* Cambridge: Harvard University Press.

Johnston, F. E. 1986. Somatic growth in infancy and preschool years. In F. Falkner and J. M. Tanner, eds. *Postnatal growth neurobiology.* Vol. 2 of *Human growth: A comprehensive treatise* NY: Plenum Press.

Johnston, L. D., O'Malley, P. M., Bachman, J. G. 1986. *Drug use among American high school students, college students, and other young adults.* Rockville, Md.: National Institute on Drug Abuse.

Jones, C. 1981. Father to infant attachment: Effects of early contact and characteristics of the infant. *Research in nursing health* 4, 193.

Jones, J. M., and Harris, P. 1971. *Proceedings of the 79th Annual Convention of the American Psychological Association,* 381–382.

Jones, M. C., and Mussen, P. H. 1963. Self-conceptions, motivations, and interpersonal attitudes of early- and late-maturing girls. In R. E. Grinder, ed. *Studies in adolescence.* New York: Macmillan Company.

Joseph, L. 1980. *Allergy: Facts and fiction.* Chicago: Budlong Press.

Juel-Nielson, N. 1965. Individual and environment: A psychiatric-psychological investigation of monozygotic twins reared apart. *Acta psychiatrica et neurologica Scandinavica,* Monograph Supplement no. 183.

Justice, E. M. 1985. Categorization as a preferred memory strategy: Developmental changes during elementary school. *Developmental psychology* 21, 6, 1105–1110.

Kagan, J. 1964. Acquisition and significance of sex typing and sex role identity. In M. L. Hoffman and L. W. Hoffman, eds. *Review of child development research.* Vol. 1. New York: Russell Sage Foundation.

Kagan, J. 1965. Impulsive and reflective children: Significance of conceptual tempo. In J. D. Krumboltz, ed. *Learning and the educational process.* Chicago: Rand McNally.

Kagan, J. 1971. *Understanding children: Behavior, motives and thought.* New York: Harcourt.

Kagan, J. 1973. Continuity in cognitive development during the first year. In L. J. Stone, H. T. Smith, and L. B. Murphy, eds. *The competent infant.* New York: Basic Books.

Kagan, J. 1984. The idea of emotion in human development. In C. E. Izard, J. Kagan, and R. B. Zajonc, eds. *Emotion, cognition, and behavior.* New York: Cambridge University Press.

Kagan, J., and Kogan, N. 1970. Individual variation in cognitive processes. In P. H. Mussen, ed. *Carmichael's manual of child psychology.* Vol. 1. New York: John Wiley and Sons.

Kagan, J., and Moss, H. A. 1962. *Birth to maturity.* New York: John Wiley and Sons.

Kagan, J., Kearsley, R. B., and Zelazo, P. R. 1978. *Infancy: Its place in human development.* Cambridge, Mass.: Harvard University Press.

Kagan, J., Rosman, G. L., Day, D., Albert, J., and Phillips, W. 1964. Information processing in the child: Significance of analytic and reflective attitudes. *Psychological monographs* 78, 1, 578.

Kahana, B., and Kahana, E. 1975. Grandparenthood from the perspective of the developing grandchild. In F. Rebelsky, ed. *Life: The continuous process.* New York: Alfred A. Knopf.

Kahn, A., and Blum, D. 1982. Phenothiazines and sudden infant death syndrome. *Pediatrics* 70, 75–79.

Kail, R., and Hagen, J. 1982. Memory in childhood. In B. Wolman, ed. *Handbook of development psychology.* Englewood Cliffs, N.J.: Prentice-Hall.

Kaiser, S., Rudy, M., and Byfield, P. 1985. The role of clothing in sex-role socialization: Person perceptions versus overt behavior. *Child study journal* 15, 2, 83–97.

Kalish, R. A. 1985. The social context of death and dying. In R. H. Binstock and E. Shanas, eds. *Handbook of aging and the social sciences.* New York: Van Nostrand Reinhold Company.

Kalleberg, A. L., and Loscocco, K. A. 1983. Age differences in job satisfaction. *American sociological review* 48, 78–90.

Kallman, F. J. 1946. The genetic theory of schizophrenia: An analysis of 691 schizophrenic index families. *American journal of psychiatry* 103, 309–322.

Kallman, F. J. 1953. The genetic theory of schizophrenia. In C. Kluckhohn and H. A. Murray, eds. *Personality in nature, society and culture.* New York: Alfred A. Knopf.

Kane, T. R., et al. 1977. Humour as a tool of social interaction. In A. J. Chapman and H. C. Foot, eds. *It's a funny thing, humour.* Oxford, England: Pergamon Press.

Kaplan, H. B., Martin, S. S., and Robbins, C. 1984. Pathways to adolescent drug use: Self-derogation, peer influence, weakening of social controls, and early substance use. *Journal of health and social behavior* 25, 270–289.

Kappas, K. H. 1967. A developmental analysis of children's responses to humor. *Library quarterly* 37, 1, 67–77.

Karasek, R. A., Baker, D., Marxer, F., Ahlbom, A., and Theorell, T. 1981. Job decision latitude, job demands, and cardiovascular disease: A prospective of Swedish men. *American journal of public health* 71, 694–705.

Kardzic, V., and Marzulla, B. 1969. Deprivation of paradoxical sleep and brain glycogen. *Journal of neurochemistry* 16, 29.

Kastenbaum, R. 1985. Dying and death: A life-span approach. In J. E. Birren and K. W. Schaie, eds. *Handbook of the psychology of aging*. New York: Van Nostrand Reinhold Company.

Kastenbaum, R. J. 1977. *Death, society, and human experience*. St. Louis: C. V. Mosby Company.

Kastenbaum, R. J. 1986. *Death, society, and human experience*. Columbus, Ohio: Charles E. Merrill Publishing Company.

Katchadourian, H. 1977. *The biology of adolescence*. San Francisco: W. H. Freeman and Company.

Katkovsky, W., Crandall, V. C., and Good, S. 1967. Parental antecedents of children's beliefs in internal-external control of reinforcements in intellectual achievement situations. *Child development* 38, 765–776.

Katz, P., and Zigler, E. 1961. Self-image disparity: A developmental approach. *Journal of personality and social psychology* 5, 186–195.

Katzman, R. 1976. The prevalence and malignancy of Alzheimer disease. *Archives of Neurology* 33, 217–218.

Kavanaugh, R. D., and Jirkovsky, A. M. 1982. Parental speech to young children: A longitudinal analysis. *Merrill-Palmer quarterly* 28, 297–311.

Keasey, C. B. 1971. Social participation as a factor in the moral development of preadolescents. *Developmental psychology* 5, 216–220.

Keating, D. P. 1980. Thinking processes in adolescence. In J. Adelson, ed. *Handbook of adolescent psychology*. New York: Wiley.

Keith, J., and Nelson, C. 1991. The relationship between age and gender of the early adolescent and parent-child communication. *Journal of early adolescence* (in press).

Keith, P. M. 1985. Work, retirement, and well-being among unmarried men and women. *The gerontologist* 25, 4, 410–416.

Keith-Spiegel, P. 1972. Early conceptions of humor: Varieties and issues. In J. H. Goldstein and P. E. McGhee, ed. *The psychology of humor*. New York: Academic Press.

Kelly, J. B. 1982. Divorce: The adult perspective. In B. B. Wolman, ed. *Handbook of developmental psychology*. Englewood Cliffs, N.J.: Prentice-Hall.

Kempe, R. S., and Kempe, H. C. 1978. *Child abuse*. Cambridge, Mass.: Harvard University Press.

Kendler, K. S. 1983. Overview: A current perspective on twin studies of schizophrenia. *American journal of psychiatry* 140, 1413–1425.

Kendrick, C., and Dunn, J. 1980. Caring for a second baby: Effects on interaction between mother and firstborn. *Developmental psychology* 16, 4, 303–311.

Kennedy, C. E. 1978. *Human development: The adult years and aging*. New York: Macmillan Publishing Company.

Kennedy, S., Keicolt-Glaser, J. K., and Glaser, R. 1988. Immunological consequences of acute and chronic stressors: Mediating role of interpersonal relationships. *British journal of medical psychology* 61, 1, 77–85.

Kennell, J. H., Voos, D. K., and Klaus, M. H. 1979. Parent-infant bonding. In J. D. Osofsky. *Handbook of infant development*. New York: Wiley.

Kennell, J. N., and Klaus, M. 1982. *Parent-infant bonding*. St. Louis: C. V. Mosby.

Kent, R. D., and Bauer, H. R. 1985. Vocalizations of one-year-olds. *Journal of child language* 12, 3 (October), 491–526.

Keough, J. 1965. *Motor performance of elementary school children*. Los Angeles: University of California, Department of Physical Education Monographs.

Kessler, R., and McRae, J. 1982. The effect of wives' employment on the mental health of married men and women. *American sociological review* 47, 216–226.

Kidd, K. K., Kidd, J. R., and Records, M. A. 1978. The possible causes of the sex ratio in stuttering and its implications. *Journal of Fluency Disorders* 3, 13–23.

Kiecolt-Glaser, J., and Dixon, K. 1984. Postadolescent onset: Male anorexia. *Journal of psychosocial nursing* 22, 1 (January), 11–20.

Kiecolt-Glaser, J. K., Fisher, L. D., Ogrocki, P., Stout, J. C., Speicher, C. E., and Glaser, R. 1987. Marital quality, marital disruption, and immune function. *Psychosomatic medicine* 49, 1, 13–34.

Kihlstrom, J. F., Cantor, N., Albright, J. S., Chew, B. R., Klein, S. B., and Niedenthal, P. M. 1988. Information processing and the study of the self. In L. Berkowitz, ed. *Advances in experimental social psychology*. Vol. 21. Orlando, Fla.: Academic Press.

Killeen, J. D., Taylor, G., and Telch, M. 1986. Self-induced vomiting and laxative and diuretic use among teenagers. *Journal of the American Medical Association* 255, 11, 1447.

Kimmel, C. A., Wilson, J. G., and Schumacher, H. J. 1971. Studies on metabolism and identification of causative agent in aspirin teratogenesis in rats. *Teratology* 4, 15–24.

Kimmel, D. C. 1974. *Adulthood and aging: An interdisciplinary, developmental view*. New York: Wiley.

Kinsbourne, M., and Hiscock, M. 1983. The normal and deviant development of functional lateralization of the brain. In M. M. Haith and J. J. Campos, eds. *Infancy and developmental psychobiology*. New York: Wiley.

Kinstler, D. B. 1961. Covert and overt maternal rejection in stuttering. *Journal of speech and hearing disorders* 26, 1, 145–155.

Kistner, J., and Osborne, M. 1987. A longitudinal study of LD children's self-evaluations. *Learning disability quarterly* 10, 258–266.

Kitson, G. C., and Morgan, L. A. 1990. The multiple consequences of divorce: A decade review. *Journal of marriage and the family* 52, 913–924.

Klaus, M. H., Kennell, J. H., Plumb, N., and Zuehlke, S. 1970. Human maternal behavior at the first contact with her young. *Pediatrics* 46, 187–192.

Kleitman, N. 1969. *Basic rest-activity cycle*. Paper presented at the Association for the Psychophysiological Study of Sleep, Boston.

Kliot, D., and Silverstein, L. 1980. The Leboyer approach: A new concern for psychological aspects of childbirth experience. In B. Blum, ed. *Psychological aspects of pregnancy, birthing, and bonding*. New York: Human Sciences Press.

Knaub, P. K. 1986. Growing up in a dual-career family: The children's perceptions. *Family relations* 35, 3 (July), 431–437.

Knittle, J. L. 1972. Obesity in childhood: A problem in adipose tissue cellular development. *Journal of pediatrics* 81, 1048–1059.

Knittle, J. L. 1975. Basic concepts in the control of childhood obesity. In M. Winick, ed. *Childhood obesity*. New York: John Wiley and Sons.

Koch, H. 1980. Office visits for male genitourinary conditions: National ambulatory medical care survey: United States, 1977–78. *Advance data from Vital and Health Statistics,* no. 63.

Koch, H. L. 1955. Some personality correlates of sex, sibling position, and sex of sibling among five- and six-year-old children. *Genetic psychology monographs* 52, 3–50.

Kogan, N. 1983. Stylistic variation in childhood and adolescence: Creativity, metaphor, and cognitive style. In P. H. Mussen (Ed.), *Handbook of child psychology* (4th ed.) (Vol. 3): *Cognitive development* (J. H. Flavell and E. M. Markman, Eds.). New York: John Wiley, 630–706.

Kohlberg, L. 1966. A cognitive-developmental analysis of children's sex-role concepts and attitudes. In E. F. Maccoby, ed. *The development of sex differences*. Stanford, Calif.: Stanford University Press.

Kohlberg, L. 1969. Stage and sequence: The cognitive-developmental approach to socialization. In D. A. Goslin, ed. *Handbook of socialization theory and research*. Chicago: Rand McNally.

Kohlberg, L. 1978. Revisions in the theory and practice of moral development. In W. Damon, ed. *New directions in child development: Moral development*. San Francisco: Jossey-Bass.

Kohlberg, L. 1981. *The philosophy of moral development*. San Francisco: Harper and Row.

Kohlberg, L., and Zigler, E. 1967. The impact of cognitive maturity on the development of sex-role attitudes in the years 4 to 8. *Genetic psychological monographs* 75, 84–165.

Kohlberg, L., Levine, C., and Hewer, A. 1983. *Moral stages: A current formulation and a response to critics*. New York: Karger.

Kohlberg, L. A., Ricks, D., and Snarey, J. 1984. Childhood development as a predictor of adaptation in adulthood. *Genetic psychology monographs* 110, 91–172.

Kohn, R. R. 1977. Heart and cardiovascular system. In C. Finch and L. Hayflick, eds. *Handbook of the biology of aging*. New York: Van Nostrand Reinhold.

Kolata, G. B. 1981. Fetal alcohol advisory debated. *Science* 214, 642–645.

Kontos, S., and Fiene, R. 1987. Child care quality, compliance with regulations and children's development: The Pennsylvania study. In D. A. Phillips, ed. *Quality in child care: What does research tell us?* Washington, D.C.: NAEYC.

Koocher, G. 1973. Childhood, death, and cognitive development. *Developmental psychology* 9, 369–375.

Kopp, C. B., and Parmelee, A. H. 1979. Prenatal and perinatal influences on infant behavior. In J. D. Osofsky, ed. *Handbook of infant development*. New York: John Wiley and Sons.

Korner, A. F. 1980. Maternal deprivation: Compensatory stimulation for the prematurely born infant. In R. W. Bell and W. P. Smotherman, eds. *Maternal influences and early behavior*. New York: S. P. Medical and Scientific Books.

Kornharber, A., and Woodard, K. L. 1981. *Grandparents/grandchild: The vital connection*. Garden City, N.J.: Anchor.

Korones, S. B. 1981. *High-risk newborn infants: The basis for intensive nursing care*. 3rd ed. St. Louis: C. V. Mosby Company.

Korslund, M. K. 1962. Taste sensitivity and eating behavior of nursery school children. Unpublished master's thesis, Iowa State University.

Kosberg, J. I., and Cairl, R. E. 1986. The cost of care index: A case management tool for screening informal care providers. *The gerontologist* 26, 273–278.

Koyle, P. F. C., Jensen, L. C., Olsen, J., and Cundick, B. 1989. Comparison of sexual behaviors among adolescents having an early, middle and late first intercourse experience. *Youth and society* 20, 4, 461–476.

Kramer, D. A. 1983. Post-formal operations? A need for further conceptualization. *Human development* 26, 91–105.

Kramer, J., Hill, K., and Cohen, L. 1975. Infants' development of object permanence: A refined methodology and new evidence of Piaget's hypothesized ordinality. *Child development* 46, 149–155.

Kraus, A. S., Spasoff, R. A., Feattie, E. J., Holden, D. E. W., Lawson, J. S., Rodenberg, M., and Woodcock, G. M. 1976. Elderly application process: Placement and care needs. *Journal of the American Geriatric Society* 24, 165–172.

Krondl, M., et al. 1982. Food use and perceived food meanings of the elderly. *Journal of the American Dietetic Association* 80, 523–529.

Kubey, R., and Larson, R. 1990. The use and experience of the new video media among children and young adolescents. *Communication research* 17, 1 (February), 107–130.

Kubler-Ross, E. 1969. *On death and dying*. New York: Macmillan.

Kubler-Ross, E. 1975. *Death: The final stage of growth*. Englewood Cliffs, N.J.: Prentice-Hall.

Kubler-Ross, E. 1983. *On children and death*. New York: Macmillan.

Kuczynski, L. 1983. Reasoning, prohibitions, and motivations for compliance. *Developmental psychology* 19, 126–134.

Kuhl, P. K. 1983. Perception of auditory equivalence classes for speech in early infancy. *Infant behavior and development* 6, 263–285.

Kuhn, D. 1984. Cognitive development. In M. H. Bornstein and M. E. Lamb, eds. *Developmental psychology: An advanced textbook*. Hillsdale, N.J.: Erlbaum.

Kuhn, D., et al. 1977. The development of formal operations in logical and moral judgment. *Genetic psychology monographs* 95, 97–188.

Kuller, L. H., et al. 1984. Relationship of menopause to cardiovascular disease. *Behavioral medicine update* 5, 4 (Winter), 35–49.

Kunzinger, E. L., III. 1985. A short-term longitudinal study of memorial development during early grade school. *Developmental psychology* 21, 4, 642–646.

Kurdek, L. A., and Siesky, A. E., Jr. 1980. Effects of divorce on children—The relationship between parent and child perspectives. *Journal of divorce* 4, 85–99.

Kvale, J. N., and Bohlen, J. G. 1985. *Intimacy in families of patients with Alzheimer's disease*. Paper presented at the 38th Annual Scientific Meeting of the Gerontological Society of America, New Orleans, November.

LaBarbera, J. D., Izard, C. E., Vietze, P., and Parisi, S. 1976. Four- and six-month-old infants' visual responses to joy, anger, and neutral expressions. *Child development* 47, 535–538.

Labouvie-Vief, G., and Schell, D. A. 1982. Learning and memory in later life. In B. B. Wolman, ed. *Handbook of developmental psychology*.

Lachman, M. E., and Jelalian, E. 1984. Self-efficacy and attributions for intellectual performance in young and elderly adults. *Journal of gerontology* 39, 577–582.

Lack, S. A., and Buckingham, R. W. 1978. *The first American hospice: Three years of home care*. New Haven, Conn.: Hospice.

Ladd, G. W., and Oden, S. 1979. The relationship between peer acceptance and children's ideas about helpfulness. *Child development* 50, 405–408.

Lagoni, L. S., and Cook, A. S. 1985. Stepfamilies: A content analysis of the popular literature, 1961–1982. *Family relations* 34, (October), 521–525.

Lamaze, F. 1970. *Painless childbirth: The Lamaze method*. Chicago: Regnery.

Lamb, M., and Hwang, C. 1982. Maternal attachment and mother-neonate bonding: A critical review. In M. Lamb and A. Brown, eds. *Advances in developmental psychology*. Vol. 2. Hillsdale, N.J.: Erlbaum.

Lamb, M. E. 1977. Father-infant and mother-infant interaction in the first year of life. *Child development* 48, 167–181.

Lamb, M. E. 1977. The development of mother-infant and father-infant attachments in the second year of life. *Developmental psychology* 13, 639–649.

Lamb, M. E. 1984. Social and emotional development in infancy. In M. H. Bornstein and M. E. Lamb, eds. *Developmental psychology: An advanced textbook*. Hillsdale, N.J.: Erlbaum.

Lamb, M. E., and Elster, A. B. 1985. Adolescent mother-infant-father relationships. *Developmental psychology* 21, 5, 768–773.

Lamb, M. E., and Stevenson, M. 1978. Father-infant relationships: Their nature and importance. *Youth and society* 9, 277–298.

Lamb, M. E., and Thompson, R. A., Gardner, W., and Charnov, E. L. 1985. *Infant-mother attachment: The origins and developmental significance of individual differences in strange situation behavior*. Hillsdale, N.J.: Erlbaum.

Lambert, W. E. and Tucker, G. R. 1977. A home/school language switch program. In W. F. Mackey and T. Andersson, eds. *Bilingualism in early childhood*. Rowley, Mass.: Newberry House Publishers.

Lambert, W. E., and Tucker, G. R. 1972. *The bilingual education of children*. Rowley, Mass.: Newberry House.

Landy, S., et al. 1983. Teenage pregnancy: Family syndrome. *Adolescence* 18, 71 (Fall), 679–694.

Lane, K. E., and Gwartney-Gibbs, P. A. 1985. Violence in the context of dating and sex. *Journal of family issues* 6, 45–59.

Lang, A. M., and Brody, E. M. 1983. Characteristics of middle-aged daughters and help to their elderly mothers. *Journal of marriage and the family* 45, 193–202.

Langer, E. J., and Rodin, J. 1976. The effects of choice and enhanced personal responsibility for the aged: A field experiment in an institutional setting. *Journal of personality and social psychology* 34, 191–198.

Langevin, R., and Day, H. I. 1972. Physiological correlates of humor. In J. H. Goldstein and P. E. McGhee, eds. *The psychology of humor: Theoretical perspectives and empirical issues*. New York: Academic Press.

Langman, J. 1975. *Medical embryology*. 3rd ed. Baltimore: Williams and Wilkins.

LaRossa, R., and LaRossa, M. 1981. *Transition to parenthood: How infants change families*. Beverly Hills, Calif.: Sage.

LaRue, A., and Jarvik, L. F. 1982. Old age and biobehavioral changes. In B. B. Wolman, ed. *Handbook of developmental psychology*. Englewood Cliffs, N.J.: Prentice-Hall.

Lash, J. P. 1980. *Helen and teacher: The story of Helen Keller and Anne Sullivan Macy*. New York: Dell.

Lawry, J. A., Welsh, M. C., Jeffrey, W. E. 1983. Cognitive tempo and complex problem solving. *Child development* 54, 912–920.

Lazarus, R. S. 1981. The stress and coping paradigm. In C. Eisdorfer, D. Cohen, A. Kleinman, and P. Maxim, eds. *Models for clinical psychopathology*. Jamaica, N.Y.: Spectrum.

Lazarus, R. S., and Cohen, J. B. 1977. Environmental stress. In I. Altman and J. F. Wohlwill, eds. *Human behavior and environment: Current theory and research*. New York: Plenum.

Lazarus, R. S., and DeLongis, A. 1983. Psychological stress and coping in aging. *American psychologist* 245–254.

Lazarus, R. S., and Folkman, S. 1984. *Stress, appraisal, and coping*. New York: Springer.

Lazer, I., and Darlington, R. 1982. Lasting effects of early education: A report from the Consortium for Longitudinal Studies. *Monographs of the Society for Research in Child Development*. Serial no. 195. Vol. 47, nos. 2–3.

LeBow, M. 1984. *Childhood obesity*. New York: Springer.

Lee, G., and Clyde, R. W. 1974. Religion, socioeconomic status, and anomie. *Journal for the scientific study of religion* 13, 35–47.

Lee, G. R., and Ellithorpe, E. 1982. Intergenerational exchange and subjective well-being among the elderly. *Journal of marriage and the family* 44, 217–224.

Lee, R. R., Mancini, J. A., and Maxwell, J. W. 1990. Sibling relationships in adulthood: Contact patterns and motivations. *Journal of marriage and the family* 52, 431–440.

Lefkowitz, M. M. 1981. Smoking during pregnancy: Long-term effects on offspring. *Developmental psychology* 17, 192–194.

Legerstee, M., Pomerleau, A., Malcuit, G., and Feider, H. 1987. The development of infants' responses to people and a doll: Implications for research in communication. *Infant behavior and development* 10, 81–95.

Lehr, U. 1966. Problems and conflicts of middle age. *Probleme und ergebnisse der psychologie* 16, 41–45.

Lennenberg, E. H. 1967. *Biological foundations of language*. New York: John Wiley and Sons.

Lennon, M. 1982. The psychological consequences of menopause: The importance of timing of a strange life event. *Journal of health and social behavior* 23, 4 (December), 353–366.

Lerner, R., and Korn, S. 1972. The development of body-build stereotypes in males. *Child development* 43, 908–920.

Lerner, R. M., and Shea, J. A. 1982. Social behavior in adolescence. In B. B. Wolman, ed. *Handbook of developmental psychology*. Englewood Cliffs, N.J.: Prentice-Hall.

Lerner, R. M., and Weinstock, A. 1972. Note on the generation gap. *Psychological reports* 31, 457–458.

Lesser, H. 1977. *Television and the preschool child*. New York: Academic Press.

Lester, B. M. 1976. Spectrum analysis of the cry sounds of well-nourished and malnourished infants. *Child development* 46, 237–241.

Lester, B. M. 1984. A biosocial model of infant crying. In L. Lipsitt, ed. *Advances in infancy research*. New York: Ablex.

Lester, B. M. 1987. Prediction of developmental outcome from acoustic cry analysis in term and preterm infants. *Pediatrics* 80, 529–534.

Lester, B. M., and Dreher, M. 1989. Effects of marijuana use during pregnancy on new born cry. *Child development* 60, 765–771.

Leve, R. 1980. *Childhood*. New York: Random House.

Levenstein, P., Kochman, A., and Roth, H. 1973. From laboratory to real world: Service delivery of the mother-child home program. *American journal of orthopsychiatry* 43, 1.

Levi, L. 1965. The urinary output of adrenaline and nonadrenaline during pleasant and unpleasant emotional states. *Psychosomatic medicine* 27, 80–85.

Levin, J., and Levin, W. C. 1980. Ageism: Prejudice and discrimination against the elderly. Belmont, Calif.: Wadsworth.

Levin, W. C. 1988. Age stereotyping. *Research on aging* (March), 134–148.

Levinson, B., and Reese, H. W. 1967. Patterns of discrimination learning set in preschool children, fifth graders, college freshmen, and the aged. *Monographs of the society for research in child development* 32, 7.

Levinson, B. M. 1962. The dog as co-therapist. *Mental hygiene* 46, 59–65.

Levinson, B. M. 1964. Pets: A special technique in child psychotherapy. *Mental hygiene* 48, 243–248.

Levinson, B. M. 1967. The pet and the child's bereavement. *Mental hygiene* 51, 197–200.

Levinson, B. M. 1969. *Pet-oriented child psychotherapy*. Springfield, Ill.: Thomas.

Levinson, B. M. 1969. The value of pet ownership. *Proceedings of the 12th Annual Convention of the Pet Food Institute*. Washington, D.C.: Pet Food Institute, 12–18.

Levinson, B. M. 1972. *Pets and human development*. Springfield, Ill.: Thomas.

Levinson, D. J., et al. 1978. *The seasons of a man's life*. New York: Alfred A. Knopf.

Levy-Shiff, R. 1982. The effects of father absence on young children in mother-headed families. *Child development* 53, 1400–1405.

Lewis, M. 1973. Infants' responses to facial stimuli during first year of life. In L. J. Stone, H. T. Smith, and L. B. Murphy, eds. *The competent infant*. New York: Basic Books.

Lewis, M., Feiring, C., McGuffog, C., and Jaskir, J. 1984. Predicting psychopathology in six-year-olds from early social relations. *Child development* 55, 123–136.

Lewis, R. A., et al. 1978. Developmental transitions in male sexuality. *Counseling psychologist* 7, 4, 15–18.

Lieberman, M. A. 1975. Adaptive processes in late life. In N. Datan and L. H. Ginsberg, eds. *Life-span developmental psychology*. New York: Academic Press.

Lifschitz, M. A., Wilson, G. S., Smith, E. D., and Desmond, M. M. 1985. Factors affecting head growth and intellectual function in children of drug addicts. *Pediatrics* 75, 2, (February), 269–274.

Lifton, P. D. 1985. *Individual differences in moral development: A matter of anatomy of socialization?* Paper presented at the American Psychological Association, Los Angeles, August.

Lillard, A. S., and Flavell, J. H. 1990. Young children's preference for mental state versus behavioral descriptions of human action. *Child development* 61, 731–741.

Lind, J., Vuorenkoski, V., Rosenberg, G., Partanen, T. J., and Wasz-Hockert, O. 1970. Spectrographic analysis of vocal response to pain stimuli in infants with Down's syndrome. *Developmental medicine and child neurology* 12, 478–486.

Lindsay, R. 1985. The aging skeleton. In M. R. Haug, A. B. Ford, and M. Sheafor, eds. *The physical and mental health of aged women.* New York: Springer.

Lindzey, B., Loehlin, J., Manosevitz, M., and Thiessen, D. 1971. Behavioral genetics. *Annual review of psychology* 22, 39–94.

Linn, S., Schoenbaum, S. C., Monson, R. R., Rosner, B., Stubblefield, P. G., and Ryan, K. J. 1982. No association between coffee consumption and adverse outcomes of pregnancy. *New England journal of medicine* 306, 141–145.

Linton, M. 1980. Information processing and developmental memory: An overview. In R. L. Ault, ed. *Developmental perspectives.* Santa Monica, Calif.: Goodyear Publishing Company.

Lipsitt, L. P. 1979. Critical conditions in infancy. *American psychologist* 34, 10, 973–980.

Lipsitt, L. P., McCullagh, A. A., Reilly, B. M., Smith, I. M., and Sturner, W. O. 1981. Perinatal indicators of sudden infant death syndrome: A study of 34 Rhode Island cases. *Journal of applied developmental psychology* 2, 79–88.

Livson, F. B. 1981. Paths to psychological health in the middle years: Sex differences. In D. H. Eichorn, J. A. Clausen, N. Haan, M. P. Honzik, and P. H. Mussen, eds. *Present and past in middle life.* New York: Academic Press.

Locke, J. 1964. Some thoughts concerning education. In P. Gay, ed. *John Locke on education.* New York: Teachers College, Columbia University.

Loehlin, J. C., Horn, J. M., and Willerman, L. 1989. Modeling IQ change: Evidence from the Texas adoption project. *Child development* 60, 993–1004.

Loehlin, J. C., Willerman, L., and Horn, J. M. 1982. Personality resemblances between unwed mothers and their adopted-away offspring. *Journal of personality and social psychology* 42, 1089–1099.

Long, D. A. 1986. Suicide intervention and prevention with an Indian adolescent population. Issues in mental health nursing 8, 3, 247–253.

Long, V. O. 1986. Relationship of masculinity to self-esteem and self-acceptance in female professionals, college students, clients, and victims of domestic violence. *Journal of consulting and clinical psychology* 54, 323–327.

Longstreth, L. E., Longstreth, G. V., Ramirez, C., and Fernandez, G. 1978. The ubiquity of big brother. In M. S. Smart and R. C. Smart, eds. *School-age children.* New York: Macmillan.

Looft, W. R. 1971. Egocentrism and social interaction in adolescence. *Adolescence* 6, 24, 485–494.

Lorenz, K. 1963. *On aggression.* New York: Bantam.

Lovaas, O. I. 1977. *The autistic child: Language development through behavior modification.* New York: Halstead Press.

Lowery, C. R., and Settle, S. A. 1985. Effects of divorce on children: Differential impact of custody and visitation patterns. *Family relations* 34, 455–463.

Lowrey, G. H. 1973. *Growth and development of children.* 6th ed. Chicago: Year Book Medical Publishers.

Lowrey, G. H. 1978. *Growth and development of children.* 7th ed. Chicago: Year Book.

Lowrey, G. H. 1986. *Growth and development of children.* Chicago: Year Book Medical Publishers.

Lubic, R. 1981. Evaluation of an out-of-hospital maternity center for low-risk patients. In L. Aiken, ed. *Health policy and nursing practice.* New York: McGraw Hill.

Lucas, B., et al. 1985. Nutrition and the adolescent. In P. L. Pipes, ed. *Nutrition in infancy and childhood.* St. Louis: Times Mirror/Mosby.

McAnarney, E. R., et al. 1984. Adolescent mothers and their infants. *Pediatrics* 73, 3 (March), 358–362.

McAuley, W. J., and Blieszner, R. 1985. Selection of long-term care arrangements by community residents. *The gerontologist* 25, 188–193.

McCandless, B. R., and Evans, E. D. 1973. *Children and youth: Psychosocial development.* Hinsdale, Ill.: Dryden Press.

McCartney, K., Scarr, S., Phillips, D., Grajek, S., and Schwarz, J. C. 1982. Environmental differences among day-care centers and their effects on children's development. In E. Zigler and E. Gordon, eds. *Day care: Scientific and social policy issues.* Boston: Auburn.

Maccoby, E. 1984. Middle childhood in the context of the family. In W. A. Collins, ed. *Development during middle childhood—The years from six to twelve.* Washington, D.C.: National Academy Press.

Maccoby, E. E. 1980. *Social development.* New York: Harcourt Brace Jovanovich.

Maccoby, E. E., and Jacklin, C. N. 1974. *The psychology of sex differences.* Stanford, Calif.: Stanford University Press.

Maccoby, E. E., and Jacklin, C. N. 1980. Sex differences in aggression: A rejoinder and a reprise. *Child development* 51, 964–980.

McCord, J., et al. 1963. Some effects of paternal absence on male children. In R. E. Grinder, ed. *Studies in adolescence.* New York: Macmillan Company.

McCord, W., McCord, J. and Howard, A. 1961. Familiar correlates of aggression in nondelinquent male children. *Journal of abnormal social psychology* 62, 79–93.

McCoy, H., Moak, S., and Kenney, M. A. 1986. Snacking patterns and nutrient density of snacks consumed by southern girls. *Journal of nutrition education* 18, 2, 61.

McCready, W. C. 1985. Grandparents, diversity, and socialization. In V. L. Bengtson and J. F. Robertson, eds. *Grandparenthood.* Beverly Hills, Calif.: Sage Publications.

McCune, L., and Ruff, H. A. 1985. Infant special education: Interactions with objects. *Topics in early childhood special education* 5, 3 (Fall), 59–67.

McDavid, J. W., and Harari, H. 1966. Stereotyping of names and popularity in grade school children. *Child development* 37, 453–445.

McDevitt, T. M., Spivey, N., Sheehan, E. P., Lennon, R., and Story, R. 1990. Children's beliefs about listening: Is it enough to be still and quiet? *Child development* 61, 713–721.

MacDonald, R., and Parke, R. D. 1984. Bridging the gap: Parent-child play interaction and peer interactive competence. *Child development* 55, 1265–1277.

McFarland, C. E., Warren, L. R., and Crockward, J. 1985. Memory for self-generated stimuli in young and old adults. *Journal of gerontology* 40, 205–207.

Macfarlane, J. W., Allen, L., and Honzik, M. P. 1954. *A developmental study of the behavior problems of normal children between twenty-one months and fourteen years.* Berkeley: University of California Press.

McGhee, P. E. 1972. On the cognitive origins of incongruity humor: Fantasy assimilation versus reality assimilation. In J. H. Goldstein and P. E. McGhee, eds. *The psychology of humor.* New York: Academic Press.

McGhee, P. E. 1974. Cognitive mastery and children's humor. *Psychological bulletin* 81, 10, 721–730.

McGhee, P. E. 1976. Children's appreciation of humor: A test of the cognitive congruency principle. *Child development* 47, 420–426.

McGhee, P. E. 1976. Sex differences in children's humor. *Journal of communication* 26, 3 (Summer), 176–189.

McGhee, P. E. 1979. *Humor: Its origin and development.* San Francisco: W. H. Freeman and Company.

McGhee, P. E. 1986. Humor across the life span: Sources of developmental change and individual differences. In L. Nahemow, K. A. McCluskey-Fawcett, and P. E. McGhee, eds. *Humor and aging.* New York: Academic Press.

McGhee, P. E., and Duffey, N. S. 1983. The role of identity of the victim in the development of disparagement humor. *The journal of general psychology* 108, 257–270.

McGhee, P. E., and Lloyd, S. 1982. Social play fosters humor. *Journal of genetic psychology* (December). Cited in *Growing child research review* 2, 1 (September 1983), 1–8.

McGhee, P. E., Bell, N. J., Duffey, N. S. 1986. Generational differences in humor and correlates of humor development. In L. Nahemow, K. A. McCluskey-Fawcett, and P. E. McGhee, eds. *Humor and aging.* New York: Academic Press.

McGovern, M. M., Goldberg, J. D., and Desnick, R. J. 1986. Acceptability of chorionic villi sampling for prenatal diagnosis. *American journal of obstetrics and gynecology* 155, 25–29.

McGuffin, P., Farmer, A. E., Gottesman, I. I., Murray, R. M., and Reveley, A. M. 1984. Twin concordance for operationally defined schizophrenia: Confirmation of familiarity and hereditability. *Archives of general psychiatry* 41, 541–545.

McHale, S. M., and Huston, T. L. 1984. Men and women as parents: Sex role orientations, employment, and parental roles with infants. *Child development* 55, 1349–1361.

Macht, M. L., and Buschke, H. 1984. Speed of recall in aging. *Journal of gerontology* 39, 4, 439–443.

McIntire, M., and Angle, C. 1981. The taxonomy of suicide and self-poisoning. In C. Wells and J. Stuart, eds. *Self-destructive behavior in children and adolescents.* New York: Van Nostrand Reinhold.

McIntosh, J. L. 1985. Suicide among the elderly: Levels and trends. *American journal of orthopsychiatry* 55, 288–293.

Macklin, E., and Needle, R. 1987. *Epidemiology and prevention of HIV infection and AIDS.* Presentation at the National Council for Family Relations, Peachtree Westin, Atlanta, Ga., November 15.

McNeill, D. 1970. The development of language. In P. H. Mussen, ed. *Carmichael's manual of child psychology.* Vol. 1, 3rd ed. New York: Wiley.

Madden, D. J. 1985. Adult age differences in memory-driven selective attention. *Developmental psychology* 21, 4, 655–665.

Madden, D. J. 1985. Age-related slowing in the retrieval of information from long-term memory. *Journal of gerontology* 40, 2, 208–210.

Madden, J., Levenstein, P., and Levenstein, S. 1976. Longitudinal I.Q. outcomes of the mother-child home program. *Child development* 47, 1015–1025.

Magnus, P., Berg, K., Bjerkedal, T., and Nance, W. E. 1985. The heritability of smoking behavior in pregnancy, and the birth weights of offspring of smoking-discordant twins. *Scandinavian journal of social medicine* 13, 1, 29–34.

Magnusson, D., Stattin, H., and Allen, V. 1985. Biological maturation and social development: A longitudinal study of some adjustment processes from mid-adolescence to adulthood. *Journal of youth and adolescence* 14, 267–284.

Main, M., and George, C. 1985. Responses of abused and disadvantaged toddlers to distress in age-mates: A study in the day-care setting. *Developmental psychology* 21, 407–412.

Main, M., and Goldwyn, R. 1984. Predicting rejection of her infant from mother's representation of her own experience: Implications for the abused-abusing intergenerational cycle. *Child abuse and neglect: The international journal* 8, 203–217.

Makepeace, J. M. 1986. Gender differences in courtship violence victimization. *Family relations* 35, 383–388.

Makin, J. W., and Porter, R. H. 1989. Attractiveness of lactating females' breast odors to neonates. *Child development* 60, 803–810.

Maksimak, J., et. al. 1984. The infant at nutritional risk. In R. B. Howard and H. S. Winter, eds. *Nutrition and feeding of infants and toddlers.* Boston: Little, Brown and Company.

Malatesta, C., and Haviland, J. 1982. Learning display rules: The socialization of emotional expression in infancy. *Child development* 53, 991–1003.

Malatesta, C. Z. 1982. The expression and regulation of emotion: A life span perspective. In T. Field and A. Fogel, eds. *Emotion and early interaction.* Hillsdale, N.J.: Erlbaum.

Malina, R. M. 1979. Secular changes in growth, maturation, and physical performance. *Exercise and sport science reviews* 6, 203–255.

Maratsos, M. 1983. Some current issues in the study of the acquisition of grammar. In P. H. Mussen, ed. *Handbook of child psychology.* Vol. 3. New York: Wiley.

March of Dimes Birth Defects Foundation. 1984 *Genetic series: Rh disease.* White Plains, N.Y.: Public Health Education Information Sheet.

March of Dimes Birth Defects Foundation. 1983. *Be good to your baby before it is born.* White Plains, N.Y.: March of Dimes.

March of Dimes Birth Defects Foundation. 1990. *Birth defects.* White Plains, N.Y.: March of Dimes.

Marcia, J. E. 1966. Development and validation of ego identity status. *Journal of personality and social psychology* 3, 551–558.

Marcia, J. E. 1967. Ego identity status: Relationship to change in self-esteem, "general maladjustment," and authoritarianism. *Journal of personality* 35, 118–133.

Marcia, J. E. 1980. Identity in adolescence. In J. Adelson, ed. *Handbook of adolescent psychology.* New York: Wiley.

Maris, R. W. 1981. *Pathways to suicide.* Baltimore, Md.: Johns Hopkins Press.

Markman, E. M., and Gorin, L. 1981. Children's ability to adjust their standards for evaluating comprehension. *Journal of educational psychology* 73, 320–325.

Marshall, W. A. 1973. The body. In R. R. Sears and S. S. Feldman, eds. *The seven ages of man.* Los Altos, Calif.: William Kaufman.

Marshall, W. A., and Tanner, J. M. 1986. Puberty. In F. Falkner and J. M. Tanner, eds. *Human growth: A comprehensive treatise.* 2nd ed. Vol. 2, Postnatal growth neurobiology. New York: Plenum Press.

Marsiglio, W. 1988. Commitment to social fatherhood: Predicting adolescent males' intentions to live with their child and partner. *Journal of marriage and the family* 50, 2, 427–442.

Martin, A. D. 1982. Learning to hide: The socialization of the gay adolescent. In S. C. Feinstein, J. G. Looney, A. Schwartzberg, and J. Sorosky, eds. *Adolescent psychiatry: Developmental and clinical studies.* Vol. X. Chicago: University of Chicago Press.

Martin, A. D., and Hetrick, E. S. 1988. The stigmatization of the gay and lesbian adolescent. *Journal of homosexuality* 15, ½, 163–183.

Marx, C. M. 1984. Drugs excreted in breast milk. In R. B. Howard and H. S. Winter, eds. *Nutrition and feeding of infants and toddlers.* Boston: Little, Brown and Company.

Maslow, A. H. 1968. *Toward a psychology of being*. Princeton, N.J.: D. Van Nostrand.

Maslow, A. H. 1970. *Motivation and personality*. 2nd ed. New York: Harper and Row.

Matas, L., Arend, R. A., and Sroufe, L. A. 1978. The continuity of adaptation in the second year: Relationship between quality of attachment and later competence. *Child development* 49, 547–556.

Matthews, K. A. 1982. Psychological perspectives on the Type A behavior pattern. *Psychological bulletin* 91, 293–323.

Matthews, L. 1986. No one seems to notice as abuse runs rampant. *Detroit free press* (May 19), B–1.

Matthews, S. H., and Rosner, T. T. 1985. *Explanations for the division of filial responsibility between daughters in older families*. Paper presented at the annual meeting of the American Sociological Association, Washington, D.C., August.

Matthews, S. H., and Sprey, J. 1984. The impact of divorce on grandparenthood: An exploratory study. *The gerontologist* 24, 41–47.

Mawdsley, R. D. 1983. Surrogate parenthood: A need for legislative direction. *Illinois Bar journal* 71 (March), 412–417.

May, P. A. 1990. A bibliography on suicide and suicide attempts among American Indians and Alaska natives. *Omega journal of death and dying* 21, 3, 199–214.

Mayer, J. 1968. *Overweight: Causes, costs, and control*. Englewood Cliffs, N.J.: Prentice-Hall.

Mayer, J. 1975. Obesity during childhood. In M. Winick, ed. *Childhood obesity*. New York: John Wiley and Sons.

Mayes, L. C., and Carter, A. S. 1990. Emerging social regulatory capacities as seen in the still-face situation. *Child development* 61, 3, 754–763.

Mazess, R. B. 1982. On aging bone loss. *Clinical orthopaedics and related research* 165, 239–252.

Mednick, S. A., and Finello, K. M. 1983. Biological factors and crime: Implications for forensic psychiatry. *International journal of law and psychiatry* 6, 1, 1–15.

Mednick, S. A., Gabrielli, W. F., and Hutchings, B. 1984. Genetic influences in criminal convictions: Evidence from an adoption cohort. *Science* 224, 4651 (May), 891–894.

Medrich, E. A., Roizen, J. A., Rubin, V., and Buckley, S. 1982. *The serious business of growing up: A study of children's lives outside school*. Berkeley, Calif.: University of California Press.

Melton, G. B., and Pliner, A. J. 1986. Adolescent abortion: A psychological analysis. In G. B. Melton, ed. *Adolescent abortion*. Lincoln, Nebr.: University of Nebraska Press.

Menaghan, E. G. 1985. Depressive affect and subsequent divorce. *Journal of family issues* 6, 295–306.

Menaghan, E. G., and Merves, E. S. 1984. Coping with occupational problems: The limits of individual efforts. *Journal of health and social behavior* 25, 406–423.

Merton, R. K. 1968. *Social theory and social structure*. New York: Free Press.

Mervis, C. B., and Mervis, C. A. 1982. Leopards are kitty-cats: Object labeling by mothers for their thirteen-month-olds. *Child development* 53, 267–273.

Messaris, P. 1983. Family conversations about television. *Journal of family issues* 4, 293–308.

Meyer, M. B., and Comstock, G. W. 1972. Maternal cigarette smoking and perinatal mortality. *American journal of epidemiology* 96, 1–10.

Meyer, R. 1980. The development of girls' sex-role attitudes. *Child development* 51, 508–514.

Meyers, A. F., Sampson, A. E., Weitzman, M., Rogers, B. L., and Kayne, H. 1989. School breakfast program and school performance. *American journal of diseases of children* 143, 10, 1234–1239.

Micklos, J., Jr. 1982. A look at reading achievement in the United States: The latest data. *Journal of reading* 25, 760–762.

Midgley, C., Feldlaufer, H., and Eccles, J. S. 1989. Student/teacher relations and attitudes toward mathematics before and after the transition to junior high school. *Child development* 60, 981–992.

Mijuskovic, B. 1988. Loneliness and adolescent alcoholism. *Adolescence* 23, 91–92, 503–515.

Milgram, S. 1963. Behavioral study of obedience. *Journal of abnormal and social psychology* 67, 376.

Miller, B. 1981. Twins reunited after 21 years. *Lansing state journal* (October 26), 2D.

Miller, B. C., and Sneesby, K. R. 1988. Educational correlates of adolescents' sexual attitudes and behavior. *Journal of youth and adolescence* 17, 6, 521–530.

Miller, L. C. 1983. Fears and anxiety in children. In C. E. Walker and M. C. Roberts, eds. *Handbook of clinical child psychology*. New York: Wiley.

Miller, N. E. 1980. A perspective on the effects of stress and coping on disease and health. In S. Levine and H. Ursin, eds. *Coping and health*. New York: Plenum Press.

Miller, P. H., and Bigi, L. 1979. The development of children's understanding of attention. *Merrill-Palmer quarterly* 25, 235–250.

Miller, P. H., and Weiss, M. G. 1981. Children's attention allocation, understanding of attention, and performance on the incidental learning task. *Child development* 52, 1183–1190.

Mills, D. M. 1984. A model for stepfamily development. *Family relations* 33, 365–372.

Mills, J. L., Simpson, J. L., Driscoll, S. G., Jovanovic-Peterson, L., Van Allen, M., Aarons, J. H., Metzger, B., Bieber, F. R., Knopp, R. H., Holmes, L. B., Peterson, C. M., Witham-Wilson, M., Brown, Z., Ober, C., Harley, E., MacPherson, T. A., Duckles, A., and Mueller-Heubach, E. 1988. Incidence of spontaneous abortion among normal women and insulin-dependent diabetic women whose pregnancies were identified within 21 days of conception. *New England journal of medicine* 319, 25, 1617–1623.

Milne, A. A. 1927. *Now we are six*. New York: Dutton.

Milner, M. R., et al. 1985. Metabolic abnormalities in adolescent patients with anorexia nervosa. *Journal of adolescent health care* 6, 191–195.

Milunsky, A. 1977. *Know your genes*. Boston: Houghton Mifflin Company.

Mindel, C. H., and Vaughan, C. E. 1978. A multidimensional approach to religiosity and disengagement. *Journal of gerontology* 33, 1, 103–108.

Mirkin, M. P., et al. 1984. Parenting, protecting, preserving: Mission of the adolescent female runaway. *Family Process* 23 (March), 63–74.

Mirowsky, J., and Ross, C. E. 1986. Social patterns of distress. *Annual review of sociology* 12, 23–45.

Mischel, W. 1966. A social-learning view of sex differences in behavior. In E. Maccoby, ed. *The development of sex differences*. Stanford, Calif.: Stanford University Press.

Mischel, W. 1973. Toward a cognitive social learning reconceptualization of personality. *Psychological review* 80, 252–283.

Moerk, E. L. 1985. Analytic, synthetic, abstracting, and word-class defining aspects of mother-child interactions. *Journal of psycholinguistic research* (May) 14, 3, 263–287.

Moffitt, T. E. 1990. Juvenile delinquency and attention deficit disorder: Boys' developmental trajectories from age 3 to age 15. *Child development* 61, 898–910.

Mogul, S. L. 1980. Asceticism in adolescence and anorexia nervosa. *Psychoanalytic study of the child* 35, 155–175.

Moliter, N., Joffe, L., Barglow, P., Benveniste, R., and Vaughn, B. 1984. *Biochemical and psychological antecedents of newborn performance on* the Neonatal Behavioral Assessment Scale. Presentation at the International Conference on Infant Studies, New York.

Monagle, J. E. 1967. Food habits of senior citizens. Canadian journal of public health 58, 504–506.

Moncur, J. P. 1955. Symptoms of maladjustment differentiating young stutterers from nonstutterers. Child development 26, 91–96.

Money, J., Klein, A., and Beck, J. 1979. Applied behavioral genetics: Counseling and psychotherapy in sex-chromosomal disorders. In S. Kessler, ed. Genetic counseling: Psychological dimensions. New York: Academic Press.

Monge, R. H. 1975. Learning in the adult years: Set or rigidity. In F. Rebelsky, ed. Life: The continuous process. New York: Alfred A. Knopf.

Montagner, H. 1985. An ethological approach of the interaction systems of the infant and young child. (Second World Congress of Child Psychiatry, 1983, Cannes, France.) Neuropsychiatrie de l'enfance et de l'adolescence Feb-Mar., 33, 2–3, 59–71.

Montessori, M. 1964. The Montessori method. New York: Schocken Books.

Moore, C., Bryant, D., and Furrow, D. 1989. Mental terms and the development of certainty. Child development 60, 167–171.

Moore, K. L. 1983. Before we are born. Philadelphia: W. B. Saunders.

Moore, L. M., Nielsen, C. R., and Mistretta, C. M. 1982. Sucrose taste thresholds: Age related differences. Journal of gerontology 37, 64–69.

Moore, S. G., and Updegraff, R. 1964. Sociometric status of preschool children as related to age, sex, nurturance-giving, and dependence. Child development 35, 519–524.

Moore, T. W. 1975. Exclusive early mothering and its alternatives. Scandinavian journal of psychology 16, 256–272.

Morgan, E. 1988. Dealing creatively with death. Burnsville, N.C.: Celo Press.

Morin, S. F., Charles, K., and Malyon, A. 1984. The psychological impact of AIDS on gay men. American psychologist 39, 1288–1293.

Mortimer, J. T., and Finch, M. D. 1986. The effects of part-time work on adolescents' self-concept and achievement. In K. Borman and J. Reisman, eds. Becoming a worker. Norwood, N.J.: Ablex.

Moskowitz, B. A. 1978. The acquisition of language. Scientific American 239, 5 (November), 92–108.

Moss, H. A. 1973. Sex, age, and state as determinants of mother-infant interaction. In L. J. Stone, H. T. Smith, and L. B. Murphy, eds. The competent infant. New York: Basic Books.

Mueller, D. P., and Cooper, P. W. 1986. Children of single parent families: How they fare as young adults. Family relations 35, 1, 169–176.

Mulchahey, K. M. 1990. Adolescent pregnancy: Prevalence, health, and psychosocial risks. In M. Story, ed. Nutrition management of the pregnant adolescent. Washington, D.C.: National Clearinghouse.

Murphy, C. 1979. The effect of age on taste sensitivity. In S. Han and D. Coons, eds. Special senses in aging. Ann Arbor, Mich.: Institute of Gerontology, University of Michigan.

Murphy, C. 1982. Effects of aging on food perception. Journal of the American College of Nutrition 1, 128.

Murphy, L. B. 1937. Social behavior and child personality. New York: Columbia University Press.

Murphy, L. B., and Moriarty, A. E. 1976. Vulnerability, coping, and growth: From infancy to adolescence. New Haven, Conn.: Yale University Press.

Murphy, L. B., et. al. 1973. Sex differences in coping and development. In L. J. Stone, H. T. Smith, and L. B. Murphy, eds. The competent infant. New York: Basic Books.

Murray, A. D., Dolby, R. M., Nation, R. L., and Thomas, D. B. 1981. Effects of epidural anesthesia on newborns and their mothers. Child development 52, 71–82.

Murray, J. P. 1980. Television and youth: 25 years of research and controversy. Boys Town, Nebr.: The Boys Town Center for the Study of Youth Development.

Musante, L., MacDougall, J. M., Dembroski, T. M., and Van Horn, A. E. 1983. Component analysis of the Type A coronary-prone behavior pattern in male and female college students. Journal of personality and social psychology 45, 1104–1117.

Mussen, P. H., and Distler, L. 1959. Masculinity, identification and father-son relationships. Journal of abnormal social psychology 59, 350–356.

Mussen, P. H., and Haan, N. 1981. A longitudinal study of patterns of personality and political ideologies. In D. H. Eichorn, J. A. Clausen, N. Haan, M. P. Honzik, and P. H. Mussen, eds. Present and past in middle life. New York: Academic Press.

Mussen, P. H., and Jones, M. C. 1963. The behavior-inferred motivations of late- and early-maturing boys. In R. E. Grinder, ed. Studies in adolescence. New York: Macmillan Company.

Mussen, P. H., et al. 1970. Honesty and altruism among preadolescents. Developmental psychology 3, 169–194.

Mussen, P. H., et al. 1974. Child development and personality. New York: Harper and Row, Publishers.

Muuss, R. E. 1975. Theories of adolescence. New York: Random House.

Muuss, R. E. 1985. Adolescent eating disorder: Anorexia nervosa. Adolescence 20 (Fall), 79.

Myers, R. E., and Myers, S. E. 1979. Use of sedative, analgesic, and anesthetic drugs during labor and delivery: Bane or boon? American journal of obstetrics and gynecology 133, 1.

Nadelman, L. 1974. Sex identity in American children: Memory, knowledge and preference tests. Developmental psychology 10, 413–417.

Nadler, H. L., and Gerbie, A. 1970. Role of amniocentesis in the intrauterine detection of genetic disorders. New England journal of medicine 282, 596–599.

Nagy, M. H. 1948. The child's theories concerning death. Journal of genetic psychology 73, 3–27.

Nahemow, L. 1986. Humor as a data base for the study of aging. In L. Nahemow, K. A. McCluskey-Fawcett, and P. E. McGhee, eds. Humor and aging. New York: Academic Press.

National Center for Health Statistics. 1983. Advance report of final mortality statistics: 1980. Monthly vital statistics report 32.

National Center for Health Statistics. 1985. NCHS growth charts. Vital statistics. U.S. Department of Health, Education, and Welfare, August.

National Children and Youth Fitness Study. 1984. Washington, D.C.: Office for Disease Prevention and Health Promotion, U.S. Public Health Service.

National Coalition on Television Violence (NCTV). 1984. NCTV music video report. Washington, D.C.: National Coalition on Television Violence.

National Funeral Directors Association. 1981. Sudden infant death. Milwaukee, Wis.: National Funeral Directors Association.

National Indian Council on Aging. 1984. Indians and Alaskan Natives. In E. Palmore, ed. Handbook on the aged in the United States. Westport, Conn.: Greenwood Press.

National Institutes of Health. 1981. Caesarian childbirth. In Consensus development conference summary. 3, 6, Washington, D.C.: U.S. Government Printing Office.

Natterson, J. M., and Knudson, A. G. 1960. Observations concerning fear of death in fatally ill children and their mothers. Psychosomatic medicine 22, 456–466.

Needle, R. H., Su, S. S., and Doherty, W. J. 1990. Divorce, remarriage, and adolescent substance use: A prospective longitudinal study. Journal of marriage and the family 52, 157–169.

Neilon, P. 1973. Shirley's babies after fifteen years: A personality study. In L. J. Stone, H. T. Smith, L. B. Murphy, eds. *The competent infant.* New York: Basic Books.

Neimark, E. D. 1975. Longitudinal development of formal operational thought. *Genetic psychology monographs* 91, 171–225.

Neimark, E. D. 1982. Adolescent thought: Transition to formal operations. In B. B. Wolman, ed. *Handbook of developmental psychology.* Englewood Cliffs, N.J.: Prentice-Hall.

Nelson, K. 1973. Structure and strategy in learning to talk. *Monographs of the Society for Research in Child Development* 38, 1–2.

Nelson, K., Rescorla, L., Gruiendel, J., and Benedict, H. 1978. Early lexicons: What do they mean? *Child development* 49, 960–968.

Nelson, K. B., and Broman, S. H. 1977. Perinatal risk factors in children with serious motor and mental handicaps. *Annals of neurology* 2, 371–377.

Nelson, K. E. 1981. Experimental gambits in the service of language acquisition theory. In S. Kuczaj, ed. *Language development: Syntax and semantics.* Hillsdale, N.J.: Erlbaum.

Nelson, K. E., Denninger, M. M., Bonvillian, J. D., Kaplan, B. J., and Baker, N. 1983. Maternal input adjustments and nonadjustments as related to children's linguistic advances and to language acquisition theories. In A. D. Pellegrini and T. D. Yawkey, eds. *The development of oral and written languages: Readings in developmental and applied linguistics.* Norwood, N.J.: Ablex.

Neubauer, P. B., and Neubauer, A. 1990. *Nature's thumbprint.* New York: Addison-Wesley Publishing Company.

Neugarten, B. 1976. *The psychology of aging: An overview.* APA Master Lectures. Washington, D.C.: American Psychological Association.

Neugarten, B. 1979. Time, age, and the life cycle. *American journal of psychiatry* 136, 887–894.

Neugarten, B. L. 1968. The awareness of middle age. In B. L. Neugarten, ed. *Middle age and aging.* Chicago: University of Chicago Press.

Neugarten, B. L. 1975. Continuities and discontinuities of psychological issues into adult life. In F. Rebelsky, ed. *Life: The continuous process.* New York: Alfred A. Knopf.

Neugarten, B. L. 1978. The wise of the young-old. In R. Gross, B. Gross, and S. Seidman, eds. *The new old: Struggling for decent aging.* Garden City, N.Y.: Doubleday-Anchor.

Neugarten, B. L. 1982. The aging society. *National forum* (Fall), 42, 25–37.

Neugarten, B. L., and Weinstein, K. K. 1968. The changing American grandparent. In B. L. Neugarten, ed. *Middle age and aging.* Chicago: University of Chicago Press.

Neugarten, B. L., et al. 1968. Age norms, age constraints, and adult socialization. In B. L. Neugarten, ed. *Middle age and aging.* Chicago: University of Chicago Press.

Neugarten, B. L., et al. 1975. Women's attitudes toward the menopause. In F. Rebelsky, ed. *Life: The continuous process.* New York: Alfred A. Knopf.

Neugarten, B. L., Havighurst, R. J., and Tobin, S. 1968. Personality and patterns of aging. In B. L. Neugarten, ed. *Middle age and aging.* Chicago: University of Chicago Press.

Newcomb, M. D., Maddahian, E., and Bentler, P. M. 1986. Risk factors for drug use among adolescents: Concurrent and longitudinal analyses. *American journal of public health* 76, 525–531.

Newman, B. M. 1982. Mid-life development. In B. B. Wolman, ed. *Handbook of developmental psychology.* Englewood Cliffs, N.J.: Prentice-Hall.

Newman, H. H., Freeman, F. N., and Holzinger, K. J. 1937. *Twins: A study of heredity and environment.* Chicago: University of Chicago Press.

Newman, P. R. 1982. The peer group. In B. B. Wolman, ed. *Handbook of developmental psychology.* Englewood Cliffs, N.J.: Prentice-Hall.

Nichamin, S. J., and Windell, J. 1984. *A new look at attention deficit disorder.* Michigan: Minewa Press.

Nicol, M. 1989. *Loss of a baby: Understanding maternal grief.* Sydney, Australia: Bantam Books.

Nilsen, D. M. 1984. The youngest workers: 14- and 15-year-olds. *Journal of early adolescence* 4, 189–197.

NIMH. 1982. *Television and behavior: Ten years of scientific progress and implications for the eighties.* Vol. 1. Washington, D.C.: U.S. Printing Office.

Noble, E. 1980. *Having twins.* Boston: Houghton Mifflin Company.

Noelker, L. S., and Bass, D. M. 1989. Homecare for elderly persons: Linkages between formal and informal caregivers. *Journal of gerontology* 44, 63–70.

Noller, P., and Bagi, S. 1985. Parent-adolescent communication. *Journal of adolescence* 8, 125–144.

Nora, J. J., and Fraser, F. C. 1974. *Medical genetics: Principles and practice.* Philadelphia: Lea and Febiger.

Nora, J. J., Nora, A. H., and Wexler, P. 1981. Hereditary and environmental aspects as they affect the fetus and newborn. *Clinical obstetrics and gynecology* 24, 3, (September), 851–861.

Norman, M. 1978. Substitutes for mother. *Human behavior* (February), 18–22.

Norris, R. V., and Sullivan, C. 1983. *PMS—Premenstrual syndrome.* New York: Rawson Associates.

Norton, A. J., and Glick, P. C. 1986. One parent families: A social and economic profile. *Family relations* 35, 9–17.

Notman, M. T. 1984. Psychiatric disorders of menopause. *Psychiatric annals* 14, 6 (June), 448–453.

Nottelmann, E. D. 1987. Competence and self-esteem during the transition from childhood to adolescence. *Developmental psychology* 23, 441–450.

Nucci, L. 1981. Conceptions of personal issues: A domain distinct from moral or social concepts. *Child development* 52, 114–121.

Nucci, L. 1982. Conceptual development in the moral and conventional domains. *Review of educational research* 52, 92–122.

Nucci, L. P. 1985. Children's conceptions of morality, societal convention, and religious prescription. In C. G. Harding, ed. *Moral dilemmas: Philosophical and psychological issues in the development of moral reasoning.* Chicago: Precedent Publishing.

O'Brien, T. E., and McManus, C. E. 1978. Drugs and the fetus. *Birth and the family journal* 5, 2, 58–86.

O'Leary, K. D., Pelham, W. R., Rosenbaum, A., and Price, G. H. 1976. Behavioral treatment of hyperkinetic children: An experimental evaluation of its usefulness. *Clinical pediatrics* 15, 510–515.

O'Malley, T. A., Everett, D. E., O'Malley, H. C., and Campion, E. W. 1983. Identifying and preventing family-mediated abuse and neglect of elderly persons. *Annals of internal medicine* 98, 998–1004.

Ockleford, E. M., Vince, M. A., Layton, C., and Reader, M. R. 1988. Responses of neonates to parents' and others' voices. *Early human development* 18, 1, 27–36.

Offer, D. 1969. *The psychological world of the teen-ager.* Basic Books.

Oktay, J. S., and Volland, P. 1981. Community care program for the elderly. *Health and social work* 6, 41–47.

Olds, S. B., London, M. L., and Ladewig, P. A. 1988. *Maternal-newborn nursing.* Menlo Park, Calif.: Addison-Wesley Publishing Company.

Olejnik, A. B. 1980. Adult's moral reasoning with children. *Child development* 51, 1285–1288.

Oller, K. 1980. The emergence of the sounds of speech in infancy. In G. Yeni-Komshian and C. Ferguson, eds. *Child phonology*. Vol. 1. New York: Academic Press.

Olweus, D. 1979. Stability and aggressive reaction patterns in males: A review. *Psychological bulletin* 86, 852–875.

Olweus, D. 1980. Familial and temperamental determinants of aggressive behavior in adolescent boys: A causal analysis. *Developmental psychology* 16, 644–666.

Omark, D. R., Omark, M., and Edelman, M. 1975. Formation of dominance hierarchies in young children. In T. R. Williams, ed. *Psychological anthropology*. The Hague: Mouton.

Oppenheim, D., Sagei, A., and Lamb, M. E. 1988. Infant-adult attachments on the kibbutz and their relation to socioemotional development four years later. *Developmental psychology* 24, 427–433.

Orbach, H. L. 1961. Aging, religion: A study of church attendance in the Detroit metropolitan area. *Geriatrics* 16, 530–540.

Oren, D. L. 1981. Cognitive advantages of bilingual children relating to labeling ability. *Journal of educational research* 74, 164–169.

Orioli, R. 1985. Brain-body link getting closer look. *Lansing state journal* (June 25), 3C.

Ostensen, K. W. 1981. The runaway crisis: Is family therapy the answer? *The American journal of family therapy* 9, 3 (Fall), 3–12.

Osterweis, M., Solomon, F., and Green, M., eds. 1984. *Bereavement: Reactions, consequences, care*. Washington, D.C.: National Academy Press.

Ostrow, A. C. 1984. *Physical activity and the older adult: Psychological perspectives*. Princeton, N.J.: Princeton Book Company.

Ouellette, E. M., Rosett, H. L., Rosman, N. P., and Weiner, L. 1977. Adverse effects on offspring of maternal alcohol abuse during pregnancy. *New England journal of medicine* 297, 10, 528–530.

Owen, M. T., Easterbrooks, M. A., Chase-Lansdale, L., and Goldberg, W. A. 1984. The relationship between maternal employment status and the stability of attachment to mother and to father. *Child development* 55, 1894–1901.

Paddison, P. L., Gise, L. H., Lebovits, A., Strain, J. J., Cirasole, D. M., and Levine, J. P. 1990. Sexual abuse and premenstrual syndrome: Comparison between a lower and higher socioeconomic group. *Psychosomatics* 31, 3. Washington, D.C.: American Psychiatric Press.

Pagelow, M. D. 1984. *Family violence*. New York: Praeger.

Paige, D. M. 1988. *Clinical nutrition*. St. Louis: C. V. Mosby Company.

Paige, D. M., and Owen, G. M. 1988. Infants. In D. M. Paige, ed. *Clinical nutrition*. St. Louis: C. V. Mosby Company.

Palmer, F. H. 1978. The effects of early childhood intervention. *ERIC* Document 143427. American Association for the Advancement of Science.

Palmore, E., Fillenbaum, G. G., and George, L. K. 1984. Consequences of retirement. *Journal of gerontology* 39, 109–116.

Paluszny, M. J. 1977. Psychoactive drugs in the treatment of learning disabilities. In W. M. Cruickshank, ed. *Learning disabilities in home, school, and community*. Syracuse, N.Y.: Syracuse University Press.

Paneth, N., Kiely, J., and Walenstein, S. 1982. Newborn intensive care and neonatal mortality in low-birthweight infants. *New England journal of medicine* 307, 149–155.

Parisi, R. L., and Kayson, W. A. 1988. Effects of sex, year in school, and type of cartoon on ratings of humor and likability. *Psychological reports* 62, 563–566.

Parke, R., and Sawin, D. 1981. Father-infant interaction in the newborn period: A reevaluation of some current myths. In E. Hetherington and R. Parke, eds. *Contemporary readings in child psychology*. New York: McGraw-Hill.

Parke, R., and Sawin, D. 1980. The family in early infancy: Social interactional and attitudinal analyses. In F. Pedersen, ed. *The father-infant relationship: Observational studies in the family setting*. New York: Praeger.

Parke, R. D. 1978. Children's home environments: Social and cognitive effects. In I. Altman and J. F. Wohlwill, eds. *Children and the environment*. New York: Plenum Press.

Parke, R. D. 1979. Perspectives on father-infant interaction. In J. D. Osofsky, ed. *Handbook of infant development*. New York: John Wiley and Sons.

Parke, R. D., and Collmer, C. W. 1975. Child abuse: An interdisciplinary analysis. In E. M. Hetherington, ed. *Review of child development research*. Vol. 5. Chicago: University of Chicago Press.

Parke, R. D., and O'Leary, S. E. 1976. Father-mother-infant interaction in newborn period: Some findings, some observations and some unresolved issues. In K. F. Riegel and J. Meacham, eds. Vol. 2 of *Social and environmental issues. The developing individual in a changing world*. The Hague: Mouton.

Parke, R. D., and Slaby, R. G. 1983. The development of aggression. In E. M. Hetherington, ed., P. H. Mussen, series ed. *Socialization, personality, and social development*. Vol. 4 of *Handbook of child psychology*. 4th ed. New York: Wiley.

Parker, J. G., and Asher, S. 1987. Peer relations and later personal adjustment: Are low accepted children at risk? *Psychological bulletin* 102, 357–389.

Parker, P. J. 1983. Motivation of surrogate mothers: Initial findings. *American journal of psychiatry*, 140, 1, (January), 117–118.

Parker, S., and Bavosi, J. 1979. *Life before birth: The story of the first nine months*. Cambridge: Cambridge University Press.

Parkes, C. M., and Weiss, R. S. 1983. *Recovery from bereavement*. New York: Basic Books.

Parry, J. 1973. Ability. In R. R. Sears and S. S. Feldman, eds. *Seven ages of man*. Los Altos, Calif.: William Kaufman.

Parten, M. 1932. Social play among preschool children. *Journal of abnormal and social psychology* 27, 243–269.

Pasley, K., and Ihinger-Tallman, M. 1985. Portraits of stepfamily life in popular literature 1940–1980. *Family relations* 45, 527–534.

Patterson, G. R. 1980. Mothers: The unacknowledged victims. *Monographs of the Society for Research in Child Development* 45 (5, serial no. 186).

Patterson, G. R. 1982. *Coercive family process*. Eugene, Oreg.: Castalia.

Patterson, G. R. 1986. Maternal rejection: Determinant or product of deviant child behavior? In W. W. Hartup and Z. Rubin, eds. *Relationships and development*. Hillsdale, N.J.: Lawrence Erlbaum Associates.

Patterson, G. R., and Stouthamer-Loeber, M. 1984. The correlation of family management practices and delinquency. *Child development* 55, 1299–1307.

Paul, C. E. 1984. Policy and the work life of an older woman. In N. J. Osgood, ed. *Life after work*. New York: Praeger Publishers.

Paveza, G. 1987. Abuse among the elderly. *Gerontology news and views* 5, 4, 1–2.

Payne, F. D. 1980. Children's prosocial conduct in structured situations as viewed by others: Consistency, convergence, and relationships with person variables. *Child development* 51, 1252–1259.

Pearl, D., Bouthilet, L., and Lazar, S. J. eds. 1982. Report by the surgeon general on television violence. *Television and behavior: Ten years of scientific progress and implications for the eighties*. Washington, D.C.: U.S. Government Printing Office.

Pearlin, L. I. 1980. The life cycle and life strains. In H. M. Blalock, ed. *Sociological theory and research: A critical approach*. New York: Free Press.

Peck, R. F. 1960. *The psychology of character development*. New York: Wiley.

Pedersen, E., and Faucher, T. A. 1978. A new perspective on the effects of first-grade teachers on children's subsequent adult status. *Harvard educational review* 48, 1, 1–31.

Pedzek, K., and Stevens, E. 1984. Children's memory for auditory and visual information on television. *Developmental psychology* 20, 212–218.

Pellegrini, D. S., Masten, A. S., Garmezy, N., and Ferrarese, M. J. 1987. Correlates of social and academic competence in middle childhood. *Journal of child psychology and psychiatry* 28, 5, 699–714.

Perkins, H. W., and Harris, L. B. 1990. Familial bereavement and health in adult life course perspective. *Journal of marriage and the family* 52, 233–241.

Perlmutter, M. 1983. Learning and memory through adulthood. In M. W. Riley, B. B. Hess, and K. Bond, eds. *Aging in society: Selected reviews of recent research*. Hillsdale, N.J.: Erlbaum.

Petersen, A. 1985. Pubertal development as a cause of disturbance: Myths, realities, and unanswered questions. *Genetic psychology monographs* 111, 207–231.

Peterson, A., Ebata, A., and Graber, J. 1978. *Responses to developmental and family changes in early adolescence*. Paper presented at the annual meeting of the American Educational Research Association, Washington, D.C., April.

Peterson, G., et al. 1979. The role of some birth-related variables in father attachment. *American journal of orthopsychiatry* 49, 2, 330–338.

Pfeiffer, E. 1974. *Successful aging*. Durham, N.C.: Duke University Center for the Study of Aging and Human Development.

Pfeiffer, E. 1975. Successful aging. In L. E. Brown and E. O. Ellis, eds. *Quality of life: The later years*. Acton, Mass.: Publishing Science Group.

Pfeiffer, E. 1977. Psychopathology and social pathology. In J. E. Birren and K. W. Schaie, eds. *Handbook of the psychology of aging*. New York: Van Nostrand Reinhold Company.

Pfouts, J. H. 1980. Birth order, age-spacing, IQ differences, and family relations. *Journal of marriage and the family* 42, 3, 517–531.

Phillips, D., Scarr, S., and McCartney, K. 1987. Child care quality and children's social development. *Developmental psychology* 23, 537–543.

Phillips, D. P. 1977. Motor vehicle fatalities increase just after publicized suicide stories. *Science* 196 (June 24), 1464–1465.

Piaget, J. 1929. *The child's conception of the world*. Trans. J. and A. Tomlinson. New York: Harcourt, Brace.

Piaget, J. 1932. *The moral judgment of the child*. Trans. M. Gabain. New York: Harcourt.

Piaget, J. 1952. *The origins of intelligence*. Trans. M. Cook. New York: International Universities Press.

Piaget, J. 1955. *The child's construction of reality*. London: Routledge.

Piaget, J. 1959. The language and thought of the child. New York: Humanities Press.

Piaget, J. 1962. *Play, dreams and imitation in childhood*. C. Gategno and F. M. Hodgson, trans. New York: Norton.

Piaget, J. 1965. *The child's conception of number*. Trans. C. Gattegno and F. M. Hodgson. New York: Norton.

Piaget, J. 1968. *Six psychological studies*. Trans. A. Tenzer. New York: Vintage Books.

Piaget, J. 1970. *The child's conception of time*. Trans. A. J. Pomerans. New York: Basic Books.

Piaget, J. 1970. *The child's concept of movement and speed*. Trans. G. E. T. Holloway and M. J. MacKenzie. New York: Basic Books.

Piaget, J. 1972. Intellectual evolution from adolescence to adulthood. *Human development* 15, 1–12.

Piaget, J., and Inhelder, B. 1956. *The child's conception of space*. F. J. Langdon and J. L. Lunzer, trans. London: Routledge and Kegan Paul.

Piaget, J., and Inhelder, B. 1969. *The psychology of the child*. Trans. H. Weaver. New York: Basic Books.

Piazza, D. M. 1980. The influence of sex and handedness in the hemispheric specialization of verbal and nonverbal tasks. *Neuropsychologia* 18, 163–176.

Pien, D., and Rothbart, M. K. 1976. Incongruity and resolution in children's humor: A reexamination. *Child development* 47, 966–971.

Pillemer, K., and Finkelhor, D. 1988. The prevalence of elder abuse: A random sample survey. *The gerontologist* 28, 1, 51–57.

Pillemer, K. A. 1986. *Prevalence of elder abuse and neglect*. Paper presented at the Annual Scientific Meeting of the Gerontological Society of America, Chicago, November.

Pines, M. 1981. The civilizing of Genie. *Psychology today* 15, 9 (September), 28–34.

Pink, J. E. T., and Wampler, K. S. 1985. Problem areas in stepfamilies: Cohesion, adaptability, and the stepfather-adolescent relationship. *Family relations* 34 (July), 327–335.

Pinon, M. F., Huston, A. C., and Wright, J. C. 1989. Family ecology and child characteristics that predict young children's educational television viewing. *Child development* 60, 846–856.

Piotrokowski, C. S., Rapoport, R. N., and Rapoport, R. 1987. Families and work. In M. B. Sussman and S. K. Steinmetz, eds. *Handbook of marriage and the family*. New York: Plenum.

Pipes, P. 1981. Infant feeding and nutrition. In P. Pipes, ed. *Nutrition in infancy and childhood*. 2nd ed. St. Louis: Mosby.

Pitcher, E. G., and Schultz, L. H. 1984. *Boys and girls at play—The development of sex roles*. New York: Praeger.

Pleck, J. H. 1985. *Working wives/working husbands*. Beverly Hills, Calif.: Sage.

Polit, D. F., and LaRocco, S. A. 1980. Social and psychological correlates of menopausal symptoms. *Psychosomatic medicine* 42, 3 (May), 335–345.

Pope, H. G., Jr., et al. 1984. Anorexia and bulimia among 300 suburban women shoppers. *American journal of psychiatry* 1431, 2 (February), 292–294.

Popkin, B. M., Bilsborrow, R. E., and Akin, J. S. 1982. Breastfeeding patterns in low-income countries. *Science* 218, 1088–1093.

Post, F. 1973. Personality. In R. R. Sears and S. S. Feldman, eds. *The seven ages of man*. Los Altos, Calif.: William Kaufman.

Pratt, L. 1976. *Family structure and effective health behavior: The energized family*. Boston: Houghton Mifflin Company.

Prechtl, H. F. R., and Beintema, D. J. 1965. The neurological examination of the full term newborn infant. *Clinics in developmental medicine* 12. London: Heinemann (Philadelphia: Lippincott).

Prerost, F. J. 1980. Developmental aspects of adolescent sexuality as reflected in reactions to sexually explicit humor. *Psychological reports* 46, 543–548.

Price, D. W. W., and Goodman, G. 1990. Visiting the wizard: Children's memory for a recurring event. *Child development* 61, 664–680.

Pruitt, D. L., and Erickson, M. T. 1983. *A preliminary study of a predictive model for child abuse*. Paper presented at the Southeastern Psychological Association, Atlanta.

Puckett, J. M., Petty, R. E., Cacioppo, J. T., and Fischer, D. L. 1983. The relative impact of age attractiveness stereotypes on persuasion. *Journal of gerontology* 38, 340–343.

Pugliese, M. T., et al. 1983. Fear of obesity. *The New England journal of medicine* 309, 9 (September), 513–518.

Putallaz, M. and Gottman, J. M. 1981. Social skills and group acceptance. In S. R. Asher and J. M. Gottman, eds. *The development of children's friendships*. Cambridge: Cambridge University Press.

Putallaz, M., and Gottman, J. M. 1981. An interactional model for children's entry into peer groups. *Child development* 52, 986–994.

Putallez, M. 1987. Maternal behavior and children's sociometric status. *Child development* 58, 324–340.

Quay, H. C. 1982. Adolescent aggression. In T. Field (ed.), *Human development*. New York: John Wiley and Sons.

Rabbitt, P. 1977. Changes in problem solving ability in old age. In J. E. Birren and K. W. Schaie, eds. *Handbook of the psychology of aging*. New York: Van Nostrand Reinhold Company.

Radke-Yarrow, M., Zahn-Waxler, C., and Chapman, M. 1983. Children's prosocial dispositions and behavior. In P. Mussen, ed. *Carmichael's manual of child psychology*. Vol. 4. 4th ed. New York: Wiley.

Ragland, D. R., and Brand, R. J. 1988. Type A behavior and mortality from coronary heart disease. *The New England journal of medicine* 318, 2, 65–69.

Ramsey, D. S. 1985. Fluctuations in unimanual hand preference in infants following the onset of duplicated syllable babbling. *Developmental psychology* 21, 2 (March), 318–324.

Ramsey, S. H. 1986. Stepparent support of stepchildren: The changing legal context and the need for empirical policy research. *Family relations* 35, 3 (July), 363–369.

Rankin, J. L., and Collins, M. 1985. Adult age differences in memory elaboration. *Journal of gerontology* 40, 451–458.

Raphael, B. 1983. *Anatomy of bereavement*. New York: Basic Books.

Rapisardi, G., Vohr, B., Cashore, W., Peucker, M., and Lester, B. 1989. Assessment of infant cry variability in high risk infants. *International journal of otorhinolaryngology* 17, 19–29.

Rapoport, R., and Rapoport, R. 1971. *Dual-career families*. London: Penguin Books.

Redmond, A. M. 1988. Attitudes of adolescent males toward adolescent pregnancy and fatherhood. *Family relations* 337–342.

Reeder, S. J., and Martin, L. L. 1987. *Maternity nursing: Family, newborn, and women's health care*. 16th ed. Philadelphia: Lippincott.

Reeves, B. F. 1970. *The first year of Sesame Street: The formative research*. New York: Children's Television Workshop.

Reggie the Retiree. 1982. *Laughs and limericks on aging in large print*. Wells, Maine: Reggie the Retiree Company.

Reid, M., Landesman, S., Treder, R., and Jaccard, J. 1989. "My family and friends": Six-to-twelve-year-old children's perceptions of social support. *Child development* 60, 896–910.

Reif, G. 1985. *Fitness for youth*. Ann Arbor, Mich.: Department of Physical Education, University of Michigan.

Reisman, J. M. 1981. Adult friendships. In S. Duck and R. Gilmour, eds. *Personal relationships 2: Developing personal relationships*. New York: Academic Press.

Renick, M. J., and Harter, S. 1988. *Manual for the Self-Perception Profile for Learning Disabled Students*. Denver: University of Denver.

Repetti, R. L. 1988. Family and occupational roles and women's mental health. In R. M. Schwartz, ed. *Women at work*. Los Angeles: UCLA Institute of Industrial Relations.

Report of the American Academy of Pediatrics Task Force on Circumcision 1989. *American Academy of Pediatrics news* (March): 7.

Rest, J. R., and Thoma, S. J. 1985. Relation of moral judgment development to formal education. *Developmental psychology* 21, 4, 707–714.

Rheingold, H., and Cook, K. 1975. The contents of boys' and girls' rooms as an index of parent's behavior. *Child development* 46, 459–463.

Rhodewalt, F., et al. 1984. Type A behavior, perceived stress, and illness: A person-situation analysis. *Personality and social psychology bulletin* 10, 1 (March), 144–159.

Rice, M. 1983. The role of television in language acquisition. *Developmental review* 3, 211–224.

Richmond, A. 1971. *An introduction to Piaget*. New York: Basic Books.

Riegel, K. 1973. Dialectic operations: The final period of cognitive development. *Human development* 16, 346–370.

Riggs, B. L., Wahner, W. H., Dunn, W. L., Mazess, R. B., Afford, K. P., and Melton, L. J. 1981. Differential changes in bone mineral density of the appendicular and axial skeleton with aging. *Journal of clinical investigation* 67, 328–335.

Risman, B. J. 1986. Can men "mother"? Life as a single father. *Family relations* 35, 1 (January), 95–102.

Robbins, L. N., West, P. A., and Murphy, G. G. 1977. The high rate of suicide in older white men: A study testing ten hypotheses. *Social psychiatry* 12, 1–20.

Roberto, K. A., and Scott, J. P. 1986. Equity considerations in the friendships of older adults. *Journal of gerontology* 41, 2, 241–247.

Robertson, A. 1982. Day care and children's responsiveness to adults. In E. Zigler and E. Gordon, eds. *Day care: Scientific and social policy issues*. Boston: Auburn House.

Robertson, K. R., Gold, R. G., and Milner, J. S. 1984. *Convergent and discriminant validity of the Child Abuse Potential Inventory*. Paper presented at the Southeastern Psychological Association, New Orleans.

Robinson, E. B., and Barret, L. R. 1987. Self-concept and anxiety of adolescent and adult fathers. *Adolescence* (Fall), 611–615.

Robinson, E. J. 1981. The child's understanding of inadequate messages and communication failure: A problem of ignorance or egocentrism? In W. P. Dickson, ed. *Children's oral communication skills*. New York: Academic Press.

Robinson, E. J., and Whittaker, S. J. 1986. Children's conceptions of meaning-message relationships. *Cognition* 22, 41–60.

Roche, A., and Malna, R. 1983. *Manual of physical status and performance in childhood*. Vol. 1–2. New York: Plenum.

Roche, A. F. 1979. Secular trends in human growth, maturation, and development. *Monographs of the Society for Research in Child Development* 44, nos. 3–4.

Roche, A. F. 1986. Bone growth and maturation. In F. Falkner and J. M. Tanner, eds. *Human growth: A comprehensive treatise*. Vol. 2. New York: Plenum Press.

Roche, A. F., and Davila, G. H. 1972. Late adolescent growth in stature. *Pediatrics* 50, 6 (December), 874–880.

Rockstein, M., and Sussman, M. 1979. *Biology of aging*. Belmont, Calif.: Wadsworth.

Rockstein, M., Chesky, J. A., Sussman, M. L. 1977. Comparative biology and evolution of aging. In C. E. Finch and L. Hayflick, eds. *Handbook of the biology of aging*. New York: Van Nostrand.

Rode, S., Chang, P., Fisch, R., and Sroufe, L. 1981. Attachment patterns of infants separated at birth. *Developmental psychology* 17, 188–191.

Roff, M. F. 1974. Childhood antecedents of adult neurosis, severe bad conduct, and psychological health. In D. F. Ricks, A. Thomas, and M. Roff, eds. *Life history research in psychopathology*. Vol. 3. Minneapolis: University of Minnesota Press.

Rogel, M. J., et al. 1980. Contraceptive behavior in adolescence: A decision-making perspective. *Journal of youth and adolescence* 9, 6, 491–506.

Rogers, C. R. 1972. *Becoming partners: Marriage and its alternatives*. New York: Dell.

Rogers, C. R. 1977. Beyond education's watershed. *Educational leadership* 34, 623–631.

Rogers, D. 1982. *The adult years*. Englewood Cliffs, N.J.: Prentice-Hall.

Rogers, H., and Saklofske, D. H. 1985. Self-concepts, locus of control and performance expectations of learning disabled children. *Journal of learning disabilities* 18, 273–279.

Rogoff, B., Gauvain, M., and Ellis, S. 1984. Development viewed in its cultural context. In M. Bornstein and M. Lamb, eds. *Developmental psychology: An advanced textbook*. Hillsdale, N.J.: Erlbaum.

Rohr, F. J., and Lothian, J. A. 1984. Feeding throughout the first year. In R. B. Howard and H. S. Winter, eds. *Nutrition and feeding of infants and toddlers*. Boston: Little, Brown and Company.

Rohrbaugh, J., and Jessor, R. 1975. Religiosity in youth: A personal control against deviant behavior. *Journal of personality* 43, 136–155.

Roosa, M. W., et al. 1982. Teenage and older mothers and their infants: A descriptive comparison. *Adolescence* 17, 65, 1–17.

Rosen, L. N., Moghadam, L. Z., and Endicott, J. 1990. Relationship between premenstrual symptoms and general well-being. *Psychosomatics* 31, 1. Washington, D.C.: American Psychiatric Press.

Rosenkrantz, A. L. 1978. A note on adolescent suicide: Incidence, dynamics, and some suggestions for treatment. *Adolescence* 8, 50 (Summer), 209–214.

Rosenthal, D. 1963. *The Genain quadruplets*. New York: Basic Books.

Rosenthal, D. 1971. *Genetics of psychopathology*. New York: McGraw-Hill.

Rosenthal, R., and Jacobson, L. 1968. *Pygmalion in the classroom*. New York: Holt, Rinehart and Winston.

Rosett, H. L., and Sander, L. W. 1979. Effects of maternal drinking on neonatal morphology and state regulation. In J. D. Osofsky, ed. *Handbook of infant development*. New York: Wiley.

Ross, C. E., et al. 1983. Dividing work, sharing work, and in-between: Marriage patterns and depression. *American sociological review* 48, 809–823.

Ross, C. E., and Mirowsky, J. 1988. Child care and emotional adjustment to wives' employment. *Journal of health and social behavior* 29, 127–138.

Ross, D., and Ross, S. 1984. *Hyperactivity: Current issues, research, and theory*. New York: Wiley.

Ross, D. M., and Ross, S. A. 1976. *Hyperactivity: Research, theory, and action*. New York: Wiley-Interscience.

Ross, J. B., and McLaughlin, M., eds. 1949. *A portable medieval reader*. New York: Viking Press.

Rossman, I. 1977. Anatomic and body composition changes with aging. In C. E. Finch and L. Hayflick, eds. *Handbook of the biology of aging*. New York: Van Nostrand Reinhold.

Rossman, I. 1980. Bodily changes with aging. In E. W. Busse and D. G. Blazer, eds. *Handbook of geriatric psychiatry*. New York: Van Nostrand Reinhold.

Rothbart, M., and Derryberry, D. 1981. Development of individual differences in temperament. In M. Lamb and A. Brown, eds. *Advances in developmental psychology*. Vol. 1. Hillsdale, N.J.: Erlbaum.

Rotter, J. B. 1966. Generalized expectancies for internal versus external control of reinforcement. *Psychological monographs* 80, 1 (serial no. 609).

Rousseau, J. J. 1965. The child in nature. In W. Kessen, ed. *The child*. New York: John Wiley and Sons.

Rovee, C. K., Cohen, R. Y., and Shlapack, W. 1975. Life-span stability in olfactory sensitivity. *Developmental psychology* 11, 311–318.

Rubenstein, J., and Howes, C. 1983. Social-emotional development of toddlers in day care: The role of peers and individual differences. In S. Kilmer, ed. *Advances in early education and day care*. Vol. 3, 13–45. Greenwich, Conn.: JAI Press.

Rubin, K. H., et al. 1983. Play. In E. M. Hetherington, ed. *Handbook of child psychology*. Vol. 4. New York: John Wiley and Sons.

Rubin, R. 1984. *Maternal identity and the maternal experience*. New York: Springer Publishing.

Rubin, Z. 1980. *Children's friendships*. Cambridge: Harvard University Press.

Rutter, M. 1979. Protective factors in children's responses to stress and disadvantage. In M. W. Kent and J. E. Rolf, eds. *Social competence in children*. Vol. 3 of *Primary prevention of psychopathology*. Hanover, N.H.: University Press of New England.

Rutter, M. 1982. Socio-emotional consequences of day care for preschool children. In E. Zigler and E. Gordon, eds. *Day care: Scientific and social policy issues*. Boston: Auburn House.

Rutter, M. 1983. School effects on pupil progress: Research findings and policy implications. *Child development* 54, 1–29.

Ryff, C. D. 1982. Self-perceived personality change in adulthood and aging. *Journal of personality and social psychology* 42, 1, 108–115.

Safier, G. 1964. A study in relationships between the life and death concepts in children. *Journal of genetic psychology* 105, 283–294.

Saghir, M. T., and Robing, E. 1973. *Male and female homosexuality*. Baltimore, Md.: Williams and Wilkins.

Salameh, W. A. 1980. *The personality of the comedian: Theory of the tragicomic reconciliation*. Doctoral dissertation, University of Montreal.

Salend, S. J. 1984. Factors contributing to the development of successful mainstreaming programs. *Exceptional children* 50, 5, 409–416.

Salk, L. 1984. A high grade for Head Start programs. *A Letter from Dr. Lee Salk* 3, 1 (March), 1–8.

Salkind, N. J. 1981. *Theories of human development*. New York: D. Van Nostrand.

Saltz, E., and Brodie, J. 1982. Pretend-play training in childhood: A review and critique. In D. J. Pepler and K. H. Rubin, eds. *The play of children: Current theory and research*. Basel, Switzerland: S. Karger.

Saltz, E., and Johnson, J. 1974. Training for thematic fantasy play in culturally disadvantaged children: Preliminary results. *Journal of educational psychology* 66, 623–630.

Saltz, E., Dixon, D., and Johnson, J. 1977. Training disadvantaged preschoolers on various fantasy activities: Effects on cognitive functioning and impulse control. *Child development* 48, 367–380.

Sameroff, A. J., and Zax, M. 1973. Perinatal characteristics of the offspring of schizophrenic women. *Journal of nervous and mental disease* 157, 191–199.

Sampson, E. E. 1962. Birth order, need achievement, and conformity. *Journal of abnormal and social psychology* 64, 2, 155–159.

Sanders, C. M. 1982–83. Effects of sudden vs. chronic illness on bereavement outcome. *Omega, journal of death and dying* 13, 227–242.

Santrock, J. W., and Warshek, R. A. 1979. Father custody and social development in boys and girls. *Journal of social issues* 35, 112–125.

Sarason, S. B. 1983. Public law 94–142 and the formation of educational policy. In E. Zigler, S. L. Kagan, and E. Klugman, eds. *Children, families, and government: Perspectives on American social policy*. New York: Cambridge University Press.

Scanzoni, J., and Fox, G. L. 1980. Sex roles, family, and society: The seventies and beyond. *Journal of marriage and the family* 42 (November), 743–756.

Scanzoni, J. H. 1978. *Sex roles, women's work, and marital conflict: A study of family change*. Lexington, Mass.: Lexington.

Scarr, S. 1981. *Race, social class, and individual differences in IQ*. Hillsdale, N.J.: Lawrence Erlbaum.

Scarr, S. 1984. *Mother care, other care*. New York: Basic Books.

Scarr, S., and Salapatek, P. 1973. Patterns of fear development during infancy. In L. J. Stone, H. T. Smith, and L. B. Murphy, eds. *The competent infant*. New York: Basic Books.

Scarr, S., Webber, P. L., Weinberg, R. A., and Wittig, M. A. 1981. Personality resemblance among adolescents in biologically related and adoptive families. *Journal of personality and social psychology* 40, 885–898.

Scarr, S., and Weinberg, R. A. 1983. The Minnesota adoption studies: Genetic differences and malleability. *Child development* 54, 260–267.

Scarr, S., and Weinberg, R. A. 1981. IQ test performance of black children adopted by white families. *American psychologist* 36, 1159–1166.

Schaal, B. 1986. Presumed olfactory exchanges between mother and neonate in humans. In J. LeCamus and J. Cosnier, eds. *Ethology and psychology*. Toulouse, France: Privat, I.E.C.

Schachter, S., and Wheeler, L. 1962. Epinephrine, chlorpromazine, and amusement. *Journal of abnormal and social psychology* 65, 121–128.

Schaefer, C. E. 1969. Imaginary companions and creative adolescents. *Developmental psychology* 1, 747–749.

Schafer, H. R. 1971. *The growth of sociability*. Baltimore: Penguin.

Schaffer, H. R. and Emerson, P. E. 1973. Patterns of response to physical contact in early human development. In L. J. Stone, H. T. Smith, L. B. Murphy, eds. *The competent infant*. New York: Basic Books.

Schaffer, H. R., and Emerson, P. E. 1964. The development of social attachments in infancy. *Monographs of the Society for Research in Child Development* 29, 3 (serial no. 94).

Schaie, K. W. 1977–78. Toward a stage theory of adult cognitive development. *Aging and human development* 8, 129–138.

Schaie, K. W. 1983. The Seattle longitudinal study. A twenty-one-year investigation of psychometric intelligence. In K. W. Schaie, ed. *Longitudinal studies of adult psychological development*. New York: Guilford.

Schaie, K. W., and Geiwitz, J. 1982. *Adult development and aging*. Boston: Little, Brown and Company.

Schaie, K. W., and Hertzog, C. 1982. Longitudinal methods. In B. J. Wolman, ed. *Handbook of developmental psychology*. Englewood Cliffs, N.J.: Prentice-Hall.

Schaie, K. W., and Hertzog, C. 1985. Measurement in the psychology of aging. In J. E. Birren and K. W. Schaie, eds. *Handbook of the psychology of aging*. New York: Van Nostrand Reinhold.

Schaier, A. H., and Cicirelli, V. G. 1976. Age differences in humor comprehension and appreciation in old age. *Journal of gerontology* 31, 577–582.

Scheinfeld, A. 1972. *Heredity in humans*. New York: J. B. Lippincott.

Schiffman, S. 1979. Changes in taste and smell with age: Psychophysical aspects. In J. M. Ordy and K. R. Brizzee, eds. *Sensory systems and communication in the elderly*. New York: Raven Press.

Schlesinger, H. S., and Meadow, K. P. 1972. *Sound and sign: Childhood deafness and mental health*. Berkeley: University of California Press.

Schneider-Rosen, K., and Cicchetti, D. 1984. The relationship between affect and cognition in maltreated infants: Quality of attachment and the development of visual self-recognition. *Child development* 55, 648–658.

Schoenfield, D. 1982. Who is stereotyping whom and why? *The gerontologist* 22, 256–272.

Schonfield, D., and Robertson, B. 1966. Memory storage and aging. *Canadian journal of psychology* 2, 20, 228–236.

Schram, W., and Roberts, D. F. 1971. Children's learning from the mass media. In D. F. Roberts and W. Schramm, eds. *The process and effects of mass communication*. Urbana, Ill.: University of Illinois Press.

Schramm, D. G. J. 1935. Direction of movements of children in emotional responses. *Child development* 6, 26–51.

Schuckit, M. D., Goodwin, W., and Winokur, G. A. 1972. A study of alcoholism in half-siblings. *American journal of psychiatry* 128, 1132–1136.

Schumacher, E. F. 1979. *Good work*. New York: Harper Calophon Books.

Schuster, C. S., and Ashburn, S. S. 1986. *The process of human development: A holistic life-span approach*. Boston: Little, Brown and Company.

Schvaneveldt, J. D., and Ihinger, M. 1979. Sibling relationships in the family. In W. R. Burr, R. Hill, F. I. Nye, and L. L. Reiss, eds. *Contemporary theories about the family*. Vol. 1. New York: Free Press.

Schwartz, G. E. 1974. *Electromyographic studies during emotions*. Paper presented at the Annual Meeting of the American Psychosomatic Society.

Schwartz, D., Mayaux, M., Spira, A., Moscato, M., Jouannet, P., Czyglik, F., and David, G. 1983. Semen characteristics as a function of age in 833 fertile men. *Fertility and sterility* 39, 530–535.

Scott, J. P. 1983. Siblings and other kin. In T. H. Brubaker, ed. *Family relationships in later life*. Beverly Hills, Calif.: Sage Publications.

Scrimshaw, N. 1969. The effect of stress on nutrition in adolescents and young adults. In F. P. Heald, ed. *Adolescent nutrition and growth*. New York: Appleton-Century-Crofts.

Sears, R. 1957. Identification as a form of behavioral development. In D. B. Harris, ed. *The concept of development*. Minneapolis: University of Minnesota Press.

Sears, R., et al. 1953. Some child rearing antecedents of aggression and dependency in young children. *Monographs in genetic psychology* 47, 135–234.

Sears, R., Maccoby, E. E., and Lewin, H. 1957. *Patterns of child rearing*. New York: Harper and Row.

Sears, R. R. 1970. Relation of early socialization experiences to self-concept and gender role in middle childhood. *Child development* 41, 267–289.

Sears, R. R., Maccoby, E. E., and Lewin, H. 1957. *Patterns of child rearing*. New York: Harper and Row.

Seaver, W. B. 1973. Effects of naturally induced teacher expectancies. *Journal of personality and social psychology* 28, 333–342.

Sebald, H. 1986. Adolescents' shifting orientation toward parents and peers: A curvilinear trend over recent decades. *Journal of marriage and family* 48 (February), 5–13.

Segal, J., and Yahraes, H. 1979. *A child's journey*. New York: McGraw-Hill.

Seidel, H. M., Ball, J. W., Dains, J. E., and Benedict, G. W. 1987. *Mosby's guide to physical examination*. St. Louis: C. V. Mosby Company.

Seligmann, J. 1980. Pregnancy by proxie. *Newsweek* (July 7), 72.

Selman, R. L. 1976. Social-cognitive understanding: A guide to educational and clinical practice. In T. Lickona, ed. *Moral development and behavior: Theory, research, and social issues*. New York: Holt, Rinehart and Winston.

Selman, R. L. 1980. *The growth of interpersonal understanding*. New York: Academic Press.

Selman, R. L., and Byrne, D. F. 1974. A structural-developmental analysis of levels of role taking in middle childhood. *Child development* 45, 803–806.

Selye, H. 1976. *The stress of life*. New York: McGraw-Hill.

Serow, W. J. 1981. Population and other policy responses to an era of sustained low fertility. *Social science quarterly* 62, 323–332.

Shaeffer, M. B., and Hopkins, D. 1988. Miss Nelson, knock-knocks and nonsense: Connecting through humor. *Childhood education* 65, 2 (Winter), 88–93.

Shaffer, D. R. 1979. *Social and personality development*. Monterey, Calif.: Brooks/Cole.

Shanas, E. 1979. The family as a social support system in old age. *The gerontologist* 19, 2, 169–174.

Shannon, L. 1982. *Assessing the relationship of adult criminal careers to juvenile careers.* Washington, D.C.: Government Printing Office.

Sheldon, W. H. 1940. *The varieties of human physique: An introduction to constitutional psychology.* New York: Harper and Row.

Sheldon, W. H. 1944. Constitutional factors in personality. In McV Hunt, ed. *Personality and the behavior disorders.* Vol. 1. New York: Ronald.

Sherman, T. 1985. Categorization skills in infants. *Child development* 56, 6 (December), 1561–1573.

Shields, J. 1962. *Monozygotic twins.* London: Oxford University.

Shiels, M. 1980. How molecular biology is spawning an industry. *Newsweek* (March 17), 70–71.

Shirley, M. M. 1973. Motor development and maturational changes. In L. J. Stone, H. T. Smith, and L. B. Murphy, eds. *The competent infant.* New York: Basic Books.

Shock, N. W. 1952. Aging of homostatic mechanisms. In A. I. Lansing, ed. *Cowdry's problems of aging.* 3rd ed. Baltimore, Md.: Williams and Wilkins.

Shonkoff, J. P. 1984. The biological substrate and physical health in middle childhood. In W. A. Collins, ed. *Development during middle childhood: The years from six to twelve.* Washington, D.c.: National Academy Press.

Shuchter, S. R. 1986. *Dimensions of grief: Adjusting to the death of a spouse.* San Francisco: Jossey-Bass.

Sidney, K. H. 1981. Cardiovascular benefits of physical activity in the exercising aged. In E. L. Smith and R. C. Serfass, eds. *Exercise and aging: The scientific basis.* Hillside, N.J.: Enslow.

Siegal, M. 1984. Economic deprivation and the quality of parent-child relations: A trickle-down framework. *Journal of applied developmental psychology* 5, 127–144.

Siegal, M. 1985. *Children, parenthood, and social welfare in the context of developmental psychology.* Oxford, England: Clarendon.

Siegel, A., and Kohn, L. 1959. Permissiveness, permission and aggression: The effect of adult presence or absence on children's play. *Child development* 30, 1, 131–141.

Siegel, L. S., and Ryan, E. B. 1989. The development of working memory in normally achieving and subtypes of learning disabled children. *Child development* 60, 973–980.

Siegel, O. 1982. Personality development in adolescence. In B. B. Wolman, ed. *Handbook of developmental psychology.* Englewood Cliffs, N.J.: Prentice-Hall.

Siegler, I. C., and Costa, P., Jr. 1985. Health behavior relationships. In J. E. Birren and K. W. Schaie, eds. *Handbook of the psychology of aging.* New York: Van Nostrand Reinhold Company.

Siegler, R. S. 1986. *Children's thinking.* 2nd ed. Englewood Cliffs, N.J.: Prentice-Hall.

Siegler, R. S., and Richards, D. D. 1979. Development of time, speed, and distance concepts. *Developmental psychology* 15, 288–298.

Siegler, R. S., Liebert, D. E., and Liebert, R. M. 1973. Inhelder and Piaget's pendulum problem: Teaching preadolescents to act as scientists. *Developmental psychology* 9, 97–101.

Silber, S. J. 1981. *The male: From infancy to old age.* New York: Charles Scribner and Sons.

Simmons, R., et al. 1973. Disturbance in the self-image at adolescence. *American sociological review* 38 (October), 553–568.

Simmons, R. G., and Blyth, D. A. 1987. *Moving into adolescence: The impact of pubertal change and school context.* Hawthorne, N.Y.: Aldene de Gruylter.

Simon, A. 1980. The neuroses, personality disorders, alcoholism, drug use and misuse, and crime in the aged. In J. E. Birren and R. B. Sloane, eds. *Handbook of mental health and aging.* Englewood Cliffs, N.J.: Prentice-Hall.

Simons, C. J. R., McCluskey-Fawcett, K. A., Papini, D. R. 1986. Theoretical and functional perspectives on the development of humor during infancy, childhood, and adolescence. In R. Nahemow, K. A. McCluskey-Fawcett, and P. E. McGhee, eds. *Humor and aging.* New York: Academic Press.

Simpson, J. L., ed. 1976. *Disorders of sexual differentiation: Etiology and clinical delineation.* New York: Academic Press.

Singer, D. G. and Singer, J. L. 1980. Television viewing and aggressive behavior in preschool children: A field study. *Forensic pathology and psychiatry* 347, 289–303.

Singer, D. G. and Singer, J. L. 1980. Television viewing, family style and aggressive behavior in preschool children. In M. Green, ed. *Violence and the family: Psychiatric, sociological, and historical implications.* American Association for the Advancement of Science Symposium 47. Boulder, Colo.: Westview Press.

Singer, D. G., and Singer, J. L. 1977. *Partners in play.* New York: Harper and Row.

Singer, J. L. 1981. Introduction. *Cognitive and affective implications of television for the developing child.* Revised draft submitted to the Committee to Update the Surgeon General's Committee Report on Television. New Haven, Conn.: Yale University.

Singer, J. L., and Singer, D. G. 1981. *Television, imagination, and aggression: A study of preschoolers.* Hillsdale, N.J.: Erlbaum.

Singer, J. L., and Singer, D. G. 1982. Cognitive and emotional characteristics of the format of American television. In W. K. Agee, P. H. Ault, and E. Emery, eds. *Perspectives on mass communications.* New York: Harper and Row.

Singer, J. L., and Singer, D. G. 1979. Come back, Mister Rogers, come back. *Psychology today* 12, 10 (March), 56–60.

Singer, J. L., Singer, D. G., and Sherrod, L. R. 1979. *Prosocial programs in the context of children's total pattern of TV viewing.* Paper presented at the biennial meeting of the Society for Research in Child Development, San Francisco, March.

Sinnott, J. D. 1989. Life-span relativistic postformal thought: Methodology and data from everyday problem-solving studies. *Adult development.* New York: Praeger.

Sinnott, J. D. 1975. Everyday thinking and Piagetian operativity in adults. *Human development* 18, 430–443.

Siqueland, E. R., and DeLucia, C. A. 1973. Visual reinforcement of nonnutritive sucking in human infants. In L. J. Stone, H. T. Smith, and L. B. Murphy, eds. *The competent infant.* New York: Basic Books.

Skeels, H. M. 1966. Adult status of children with contrasting life experiences, *Monographs of the Society for Research in Child Development* 31 (serial no. 105), 3.

Skinner, B. F. 1953. *Science and human behavior.* New York: Macmillan.

Smart, M. S., and Smart, L. S. 1976. *Families: Developing relationships.* New York: Macmillan Publishing.

Smart, M. S., and Smart, R. C. 1977. *Children: Development and relationships.* New York: Macmillan Publishing Company.

Smeltzer, L. R., and Leap, T. L. 1988. An analysis of individual reactions to potentially offensive jokes in work settings. *Human relations* 41, 4, 295–304.

Smilgis, M. 1987. The big chill: Fear of AIDS. *Time* (February 16), 50–53.

Smith, A. 1986. *The body.* New York: Viking.

Smith, A. D. 1977. Adult differences in cued recall. *Developmental psychology* 13, 326–331.

Smith, B. D., Thompson, L. W., and Michaelewski, H. J. 1980. Averaged evoked potential research in adult aging: Status and prospects. In L. W. Poon, ed. *Aging in the 1980s.* Washington, D.C.: American Psychological Association.

Smith, K. F., and Bengtson, V. L. 1979. Positive consequences of institutionalization: Solidarity between elderly parents and their middle-aged children. *The gerontologist* 19, 438–447.

Smith, K. R., and Zick, C. D. 1986. The incidence of poverty among the recently widowed: Mediating factors in the life course. *Journal of marriage and the family* 48, 619–630.

Smith, P. K., and Connolly, K. 1986. Experimental studies of the preschool environment: The Sheffield project. In S. Kilmer, ed. *Advances in early education and day care,* 4. Greenwich, Conn.: JAI.

Smith, T., and Brehm, S. 1989. Person perception and the Type A coronary-prone behavior pattern. *Journal of personality and social psychology* 40, 1137–1149.

Smolak, L. 1986. *Infancy.* Englewood Cliffs, N.J.: Prentice-Hall.

Snow, M. E., Jacklin, C. N., and Maccoby, E. E. 1983. Sex-of-child differences in father-child interaction at one year of age. *Child development* 54, 227–232.

Society of Research in Child Development. 1972. *Ethical standards for research with children.* Chicago.

Society of Research in Child Development. 1973. Committee on ethics in research with children. *SRCD newsletter* (Winter), 3–4.

Solantaus, T., Rimpela, M., and Taipale, V. 1984. The threat of war in the minds of 12–18 year olds in Finland. *Lancet* 8380, 784–785.

Soldo, B. J., and Myullyluoma, J. 1983. Caregivers who live with dependent elderly. *The gerontologist* 23, 605–611.

Sondheimer, S. J., Turek, R. W., Blasco, L., Strauss, J., Arger, P., and Mennuti, M. 1985. Simultaneous ectopic pregnancy with intrauterine twin gestations after in vitro fertilization and embryo transfer. *Fertility and sterility,* 43, 2, (February), 313–316.

Sophian, C., and Yengo, L. 1985. Infants' understanding of visible displacements. *Developmental psychology* 21, 6, 9323–941.

Sorenson, R. C. 1973. *Adolescent sexuality in contemporary America.* New York: Worth Publishing Company.

Soules, M. R., and Bremner, W. J. 1982. The menopause and climacteric: Endocrinologic basis and associated symptomatology. *Journal of the American Geriatrics Society* 30, 9 (September), 547–561.

Spanier, G. 1990. Marital quality. In D. H. Olsen and M. K. Hanson, eds. *2001: Preparing families for the future.* Minneapolis: National Council on Family Relations.

Spanier, G. B., and Roos, P. A. 1985. Marital trajectories of American women: Variations in the life course. *Journal of marriage and the family* 47, 4 (November), 993–1003.

Sparks, D. L., and Hunsaker, J. C., III. 1991. Increased ALZ-50-reactive neurons in the brains of SIDS infants: An indicator of greater neuronal death? *Journal of child neurology* 6, 123–127.

Speece, M. W., and Brent, S. B. 1984. Children's understanding of death: A review of three components of a death concept. *Child development* 55, 1671–1686.

Speer, J. R. 1984. Two practical strategies young children use to interpret vague instructions. *Child development* 55, 1811–1819.

Spiegel, P. M. 1972. Theories of aging. In P. S. Timeras, ed. *Developmental physiology and aging.* New York: Macmillan Company.

Spirduso, W. W. 1975. Reaction and movement time as a function of age and physical activity level. *Journal of gerontology* 30, 435–440.

Spitz, R. A. 1949. The role of ecological factors in emotional development in infancy. *Child development* 20, 145–155.

Spitz, R. A., Emde, R. N., and Metcalf, D. R. 1973. Further prototypes of ego formation: A working paper from a research project on early development. In L. J. Stone, H. T. Smith, L. B. Murphy, eds. *The competent infant.* New York: Basic Books.

Spivak, G., and Shure, M. B. 1974. *Social adjustment in young children.* San Francisco: Jossey-Bass.

Sprafkin, J. N., Liebert, R. M., and Poulos, R. W. 1975. Effects of a prosocial televised example on children's helping. *Journal of experimental child psychology* 20, 119–126.

Sprague, J. 1983. Vision screening. In M. Krajicek and A. I. T. Tomlinson, eds. *Detection of developmental problems in children.* Baltimore: University Park Press.

Sprague, R., and Ullman, R. 1981. Psychoactive drugs and child management. In J. Kaufman and D. Hallahan, eds. *Handbook of special education.* Englewood Cliffs, N.J.: Prentice-Hall.

Spungen, L. B., Kurtzberg, D., and Vaughn, H. G. 1985. Patterns of looking behavior in full-term and low birth weight infants at 40 weeks post-conceptual age. *Journal of developmental and behavioral pediatrics* 6, 5, 287–294.

Squatting helps. 1985. *Lansing state journal* (October 22), 3–C.

Sroufe, L. A. 1975. Drug treatment of children with behavior problems. In F. D. Horowitz, ed. *Review of child development research.* Vol. 4. Chicago: University of Chicago Press.

Sroufe, L. A. 1979. Socioemotional development. In J. D. Osofsky, ed. *Handbook of infant development.* New York: John Wiley and Sons.

Sroufe, L. A. 1983. Infant-caregiver attachment and patterns of adaptation in preschool: The roots of maladaptation and competence. In M. Perlmutter, ed. *Minnesota symposia on child psychology* Vol. 16. Hillsdale, N.J.: Erlbaum.

Sroufe, L. A., and Waters, E. 1976. The ontogenesis of smiling and laughter: A perspective on the organization of development in infancy. *Psychological review* 83, 173–189.

Staffieri, J. R. 1967. A study of social stereotypes of body image in children. *Journal of personality and social psychology* 7, 101–104.

Staffieri, J. R. 1972. Body build and behavior expectancies in young females. *Developmental psychology* 6, 1, 125–127.

Staines, G. L., and Libby, P. L. 1986. Men and women in role relationships. In R. D. Ashmore and F. K. Del Boca, eds. *The social psychology of female-male relations: A critical analysis of central concepts.* New York: Academic Press.

Stamps, L. W. 1973. The effects of intervention techniques on children's fear of failure. *Journal of genetic psychology* 123, 85–97.

Stanovich, K. E. 1982. Individual differences in the cognitive processes of reading: 1. Word decoding. *Journal of learning disabilities* 15, 485–493.

Starr, B. D., and Weiner, M. B. 1981. *Sex and sexuality in the mature years.* New York: Stein and Day.

Stein, A. H., and Friedrich, L. K. 1975. Impact of television on children and youth. In E. M. Hetherington, ed. *Review of child development.* Vol. 5. Chicago: University of Chicago Press.

Steinberg, L. 1987. Impact of puberty on family relations: Effects of pubertal status and pubertal timing. *Developmental psychology* 23, 3, 451–460.

Steinberg, L., and Dornbusch, S. M. 1991. Negative correlates of part-time employment during adolescence replication and elaboration. *Developmental psychology* 27, 2, 304–313.

Steinberg, L., Greenberger, E., Garduque, L., Ruggiero, M., and Vaux, A. 1982. Effects of working on adolescent development. *Developmental psychology* 18, 385–395.

Steiner, B. W., et al. 1978. Flight into femininity: The male menopause? *Canadian Psychiatric Association journal* 23, 6 (October), 405–410.

Steinmetz, S. K. 1977–78. The battered husband syndrome. *Victimology* 2, 499–509.

Steinmetz, S. K., and Amsden, D. J. 1983. Dependent elders, family stress, and abuse. In T. H. Brubaker, ed. *Family relationships in later life.* Beverly Hills, Calif.: Sage Publications.

Stenback, A. 1980. Depression and suicidal behavior in old age. In J. E. Birren and R. B. Sloane, eds. *Handbook of mental health and aging.* Englewood Cliffs, N.J.: Prentice-Hall.

Stengel, G. B. 1983. Oral temperature in the elderly. *The gerontologist* 23, 306.

Stengel, R. 1985. The missing-father myth. *Time* 126, 23 (December 9), 90.

Stephan, C. W., and Corder, J. 1985. The effects of dual-career families on adolescents' sex-role attitudes, work and family plans, and choices of important others. *Journal of marriage and the family* 47, 4 (November), 921–929.

Stern, M., and Hildebrandt, K. A. 1984. *The behavioral implications of a prematurity stereotype: The effects of labeling on mother-infant interactions.* Paper presented at the meetings of the International Conference on Infant Studies, New York.

Sterns, H. L., Barrett, G. V., and Alexander, R. A. 1985. Accidents and the aging individual. In J. E. Birren and K. W. Schaie, eds. *Handbook of the psychology of aging.* New York: Van Nostrand Reinhold Company.

Stevens, G. L. 1986. *Selected aspects of humorous interaction among elderly participants and staff caregivers in community-based health support programs of the adult daycare type.* University of Maryland Baltimore Professional Schools.

Stevenson, H. W. 1971. Studies of racial awareness in young children. In W. W. Hartrup and N. L. Smothergill. eds. *The young child: Reviews of research.* Washington, D.C.: National Association for the Education of Young Children.

Stever, J., and Austin, E. 1980. Family abuse of the elderly. *Journal of the American Geriatrics Society* 28, 372–376.

Steward, J. L. 1960. The problem of stuttering in certain North American societies. *Journal of speech and hearing disorders, monograph supplement 6,* 1–87.

Stith, S., and Davis, A. 1984. Employed mothers and family day-care substitute caregivers: A comparative analysis of infant care. *Child development* 55, 1340–1348.

Stoller, S. A., and Field, T. 1982. Alteration of mother and infant behavior and heart rate during a still-face perturbation of face-to-face interaction. In T. Field and A. Fogel, eds. *Emotion and early interaction.* Hillsdale, N.J.: Erlbaum.

Stone, B., Cafferata, G. L., and Sangl, J. 1987. Caregivers of the frail elderly: A national profile. *The gerontologist* 27, 616–617.

Stone, L. J., Smith, H. T., and Murphy, L. B. 1973 *The competent infant.* New York: Basic Books.

Stone, M. L., Salerno, L. J., Green, M., and Zelson, C. 1971. Narcotic addiction in pregnancy. *American journal of obstetrics and gynecology* 109, 716–723.

Story, M. 1990. Nutrient needs during adolescence and pregnancy. In M. Story, ed. *Nutrition management of the pregnant adolescent.* Washington, D.C.: National Clearinghouse.

Straus, M. 1980. Victims and aggressors in marital violence. *American behavioral scientist* 23, 681–704.

Straus, M. A., and Gelles, R. J. 1986. Societal change and change in family violence from 1975 to 1985 as revealed by two national surveys. *Journal of marriage and the family* 48, 465–479.

Straus, M. A., Gelles, R. J., and Steinmetz, S. K. 1980. *Behind closed doors.* New York: Anchor Books.

Strayer, F. F., and Moss, E. 1987. *The development of social and representative tactics during early childhood.* Paper presented at the biennial meeting of the Society for Research in Child Development, Baltimore.

Strayer, F. F., and Strayer, J. 1975. *An ethological analysis of dominance relations among young children.* Paper presented at the biennial meeting of the Society for Research in Child Development, Denver, April.

Streib, G., and Schneider, C. 1971. *Retirement in American society.* Ithaca, N.Y.: Cornell University Press.

Streissguth, A. P., Barr, H. M., and Martin, D. C. 1983. Maternal alcohol use and neonatal habituation assessed with Brazelton scale. *Child development* 54, 1109–1118.

Streitfeld, P. P. 1978. Congenital malformation: Teratogenic foods and additives. *Birth and the family journal* 5, 7–19.

Strickberger, M. W. 1976. *Genetics.* 2nd ed. New York: Macmillan.

Strickler, M. 1975. Crisis intervention and the climacteric man. *Social casework* 56, 2 (February), 85–89.

Strober, M. 1982. Locus of control, psychopathology, and weight gain in juvenile anorexia nervosa. *Journal of abnormal child psychology* 10, 1, 97–106.

Stroebe, M. S., and Stroebe, W. 1983. Who suffers more? Sex differences in health risks of the widowed. *Psychology bulletin* 93, 279–301.

Stroebe, W., and Stroebe, M. S. 1987. *Bereavement and health: The psychological and physical consequences of partner loss.* Cambridge: Cambridge University Press.

Strube, M. J., Turner, C., Ceiro, D., Stevens, J., and Hincheg, F. 1984. Interpersonal aggression and the Type A coronary-prone behavior pattern: A theoretical distinction and practical implications. *Journal of personality and social psychology* 47, 839–847.

Sugar, M. 1983. Sexual abuse of children and adolescents. *Adolescent psychiatry* 11, 199–211.

Sund, R. B. 1976. *Piaget for educators.* Columbus, Ohio: Charles E. Merrill Publishing Company.

Sussman, N. 1976. Sex and sexuality in history. In B. J. Sadock, H. I. Kaplan, and A. M. Freedman, eds. *The sexual experience.* Baltimore, Md.: Williams and Wilkins.

Sutton-Smith, B. 1975. Children at play. In *Readings in Human Development, 73/74.* Guilford, Conn.: Duskin.

Svebak, S. 1975. Respiratory patterns as predictors of laughter. *Psychophysiology* 12, 62–65.

Svebak, S. 1977. Some characteristics of resting respiration as predictors of laughter. In A. J. Chapman and H. C. Foot, eds. *It's a funny thing, humour.* Oxford, England: Pergamon Press.

Svebak, S. 1982. The effect of mirthfulness upon amount of discordant right-left occipital EEG alpha. *Motivation and emotion* 6, 133–143.

Swerdloff, R. S., and Heber, D. 1982. Effects of aging on male reproductive function. In S. G. Korenman, eds. *Endocrine aspects of aging.* New York: Elsevier Biomedical.

Szegal, B. 1981. The relationship of area density and aggression in early childhood. *Magyar pszichologiai szemle* 38, 2, 153–160.

Szinovacz, M. E. 1984. Changing family roles and interactions. In B. B. Hess and M. B. Sussman, eds. *Women and the family: Two decades of change.* New York: Haworth Press.

Taft, L., and Cohen, H. 1967. Neonatal and infant reflexology. In Jerome Helmuth, ed. *Exceptional infant.* Vol. 1. New York: Brunner/Mazel.

Talbert, G. B. 1977. Aging of the reproductive system. In C. E. Finch and L. Hayflick, eds. *Handbook of the biology of aging.* New York: Van Nostrand Reinhold Company.

Talmadge, H., and Murphy, D. F. 1983. Innovative home care program offers appropriate alternative for elderly. *Hospital Progress* 64, 50–51.

Tan, L. 1985. Laterality and motor skills in four-year-olds. *Child development* 56, 119–124.

Tanguay, R., Dimirjian, A., and Thibault, H. W. 1984. Sexual dimorphism in the emergence of the deciduous teeth. *Journal of dental research* 63, 65.

Tanner, J. M. 1962. *Growth at adolescence.* 2nd ed. Oxford: Blackwell.

Tanner, J. M. 1963. The course of children's growth. In R. E. Grinder, ed. *Studies in adolescence.* New York: Macmillan Company.

Tanner, J. M. 1970. Physical growth. In P. H. Mussen, ed. *Carmichael's manual of child psychology.* Vol. 1. 3rd ed. New York: Wiley.

Tanner, J. M. 1978. *Education and physical growth.* 2nd ed. New York: International Universities Press.

Tanner, J. M. 1978. *Foetus into man: Physical growth from conception to maturity.* Cambridge: Harvard University Press.

Tanner, J. M. 1981. *A history of the study of human growth.* Cambridge: Cambridge University Press.

Tauber, M. A. 1979. Sex differences in parent-child interaction styles during a free-play session. *Child development* 50, 981–988.

Teachman, G., and Orme, M. 1981. Effects of aggressive and prosocial film material on altruistic behavior of children. *Psychological reports* 48, 3, 699–702.

Teachman, J. D., and Polonko, K. A. 1985. Timing of the transition to parenthood: A multidimensional birth-interval approach. *Journal of marriage and the family* 47, 4 (November), 867–879.

Terasaki, P. I., Gjertson, D., Bernoco, D., Perdue, S., Mickey, M. R., and Bond, J. 1978. Twins with two different fathers identified by HLA. *New England journal of medicine* 22, 11, (September 14), 590–592.

Terry, R. B., and Davies, P. 1980. Dementia of the Alzheimer type. *Annual review of neuroscience* 3, 77–95.

Tesch, S. A. 1983. Review of friendship development across the life-span. *Human development* 26, 266–276.

Testing fetuses. 1980. *Time* (March 24), 48.

Thal, L. J. 1988. Treatment strategies: Present and future. In M. K. Aronsen, ed. *Understanding Alzheimer's disease.* New York: Charles Scribner's Sons.

Thelen, E. 1981. Rhythmical behavior in infancy: An ethological perspective. *Developmental psychology* 17, 237–257.

Thelen, E. and Fisher, D. 1983. From spontaneous to instrumental behavior: Kinematic analysis of movement changes during very early learning. *Child development* 54, 129–140.

Thelen, E., and Fisher, D. 1982. Newborn stepping: An explanation for a "disappearing" reflex. *Developmental psychology* 18, 760–775.

Thomas, A., and Chess, S. 1977. *Temperament and development.* New York: Bruner/Mazel.

Thomas, A., Chess, S., and Birch, H. G. 1970. The origin of personality. *Scientific American,* 223 (August), 102–109.

Thomas, E. 1986. America's crusade. *Time* (September 15) 128, 11, 60–68.

Thomas, J. L. 1986. Age and sex differences in perceptions of grandparenting, *Journal of gerontology* 41, 3, 417–423.

Thomas, P. D., Hunt, W. C., Garry, P. J., Hood, R. B., Goodwin, J. M., and Goodwin, J. S. 1983. Hearing acuity in a healthy elderly population: Effects on emotional, cognitive, and social status. *Journal of gerontology* 38, 321–325.

Thompson, L., et al. 1985. Do parents know their children? The ability of mothers and fathers to gauge the attitudes of their young adult children. *Family relations* 34, 3 (July), 315–320.

Thompson, S. K. 1975. Gender labels and early sex role development. *Child development* 46, 2, 339–347.

Thorkildsen, T. A. 1989. Justice in the classroom: The student's view. *Child development* 60, 323–334.

Thorkildsen, T. A. 1989. Pluralism in children's reasoning about social justice. *Child development* 60, 965–972.

Thornburg, H. D., and Jones, R. M. 1982. Social characteristics of early adolescents: Age versus grade. *Journal of early adolescence* 2, 229–239.

Thornton, A. 1989. Changing attitudes toward family issues in the United States. *Journal of marriage and the family* 51, 873–893.

Thornton, A., and Freedman, D. 1983. The changing American family. *Population bulletin* 38 (October), 1–49.

Tiedje, L. B., Worman, C. B., Downey, G., Emmons, C., Giernat, M., and Lang, E. 1990. Women with multiple roles: Role-compatibility perceptions, satisfaction, and mental health. *Journal of marriage and the family* 52, 63–72.

Tieger, T. 1980. On the biological basis of sex differences in aggression. *Child development* 51, 943–963.

Tillinger, K. G. 1957. Testicular morphology: A histopathological study with special reference to biopsy findings in hypogonadism with mainly endocrine disorders and in gynecomastia. *Acta endocrinology* 30, 1.

Timiras, P. S. 1972. *Developmental physiology and aging.* New York: Macmillan Company.

Timiras, P. S. 1978. Biological perspectives on aging. *American scientist* 66, 605–613.

Tishler, C. L., McKenry, P. C., and Morgan, K. C. 1981. Adolescent suicide attempts: Some significant factors. *Suicide and life-threatening behavior* 11, 86–92.

Tomlinson, T. 1990. Case study: Conceiving children to use for tissue transplantation. *Medical humanities report.* Spring, Center for Ethics and Humanities in the Life Sciences, Michigan State University.

Tomlinson-Keasey, C. and Keasey, C. B. 1974. The mediating role of cognitive development in moral judgment. *Child development* 45, 291–298.

Tonna, E. A. 1977. Aging of skeletal and dental systems and supporting tissue. In C. E. Finch and L. Hayflick, eds. *Handbook on the biology of aging.* New York: Van Nostrand.

Torrance, N., and Olson, D. R. 1989. *Children's understanding of ambiguity and interpretation.* Paper presented at the annual meeting of the American Educational Research Association, San Francisco.

Torrey, E. F. 1985. *Surviving schizophrenia.* New York: Harper and Row.

Trevarthen, C. B. 1986. Neuroembryology and the development of perceptual mechanisms. In F. Falkner and J. M. Tanner, eds. *Human growth: A comprehensive treatise.* New York: Plenum Press.

Troll, L. E. 1983. Grandparents: The family watchdogs. In T. H. Brubaker, ed. *Family relationships in later life.* Beverly Hills, Calif.: Sage Publications.

Troll, L. E. 1985. *Early and middle adulthood.* Monterey, Calif.: Brooks/Cole.

Troll, L. E. 1985. The contingencies of grandparenting. In V. L. Bengtson and J. F. Robertson, eds. *Grandparenthood.* Beverly Hills, Calif.: Sage Publications.

Troll, L. E., and Bengston, V. 1982. Intergenerational relations throughout the lifespan. In B. B. Wolman, ed. *Handbook of developmental psychology.* Englewood Cliffs, N.J.: Prentice-Hall.

Tronick, E., and Field, T. 1986. *Maternal depression and infant disturbance.* New Directions for Child Development (no. 34). San Francisco: Jossey-Bass.

Tronick, E. Z., and Cohn, J. F. 1989. Infant-mother face-to-face interaction: Age and gender differences in coordination and the occurrence of miscoordination. *Child development* 60, 85–92.

Tronick, E. Z., and Gianino, A. F. 1986. The transmission of maternal disturbance to the infant. In E. Z. Tronick and T. Field, eds. *Maternal depression and infant disturbance.* New York: Wiley.

Troyer, W. G. 1973. Mechanisms of brain-body interaction in the aged. In L. F. Jarvik, C. Eisdorfer, and J. E. Blum, eds. *Intellectual functioning in adults.* New York: Springer Publishing Company.

Tuchmann-Duplessis, H. 1975. *Drug effects on the fetus.* Monographs on drugs. Vol. 2. Sydney, Australia: ADIS Press.

Turiel, E. 1978. Distinct conceptual and developmental domains: Social-convention and morality. In C. Keasey, ed. *Nebraska symposium on motivation.* Vol. 25. Lincoln, Nebr.: University of Nebraska Press.

Turner, J. 1980. *Made for life: Coping, competence, and cognition.* New York: Methuen.

Twitchell, T. 1970. Reflex mechanisms and the development of prehension. In K. Connolly, ed. *Mechanisms of motor skill development.* London: Academic Press.

Tynan, W. D. 1986. Behavioral stability predicts morbidity and mortality in infants from a neonatal intensive care unit. *Infant behavior and development* 9, 71–79.

U.S. Bureau of the Census 1987. *Statistical abstract of the United States: 1986.* 107th ed. Washington, D.C.: Government Printing Office.

U.S. Bureau of the Census. 1980. *1980 census of population.* General Population Characteristics, Chapter B.

U.S. Bureau of the Census. 1985. Marital status and living arrangements: March 1985. *Current population reports.* P–20, no. 410. Washington, D.C.: U.S. Government Printing Office, November.

U.S. Centers for Disease Control. 1989. *Morbidity and mortality weekly report* (February 3), 49–52.

U.S. Department of Commerce. 1981. *Social indicators.* Vol. 3. Washington, D.C.

U.S. Department of Labor. 1985. *The United Nations decade for women, 1976–1985: Employment in the United States.* Office of the Secretary, Women's Bureau, July.

U.S. National Center for Health Statistics. 1985. December 26, p. 5.

Uzgiris, I. C. 1973. Patterns of vocal and gestural imitation in infants. In L. J. Stone, H. T. Smith, and L. B. Murphy, eds. *The competent infant.* New York: Basic Books.

Uzgiris, I. C., and Hunt, J. M. 1975. *Assessment in infancy: Ordinal scales of psychological development.* Champaign, Ill.: University of Illinois Press.

Valdez-Depena, M. A. 1980. Sudden infant death syndrome: A review of the medical literature 1974–1979. *Pediatrics* 66, 4, 597–611.

Van Wieringen, J. 1978. Secular growth changes. In F. Falkner and J. Tanner, eds. *Human growth.* Vol. 2. New York: Plenum.

Vandenberg, B. 1980. Play, problem-solving, and creativity. In K. H. Rubin, ed. *Children's play.* San Francisco: Jossey-Bass.

Vandenberg, S. 1967. Hereditary factors in normal personality traits. In J. Wortis, ed. *Recent advances in biological psychiatry.* Vol. 9. New York: Plenum.

vanIJzendoorn, M. H., and Tevecchio, L. W. C. 1987. The development of attachment theory as a Lakatosian research program: Philosophical and methodological aspects. In L. W. C. Tavecchio and M. H. vanIJzendoorn, eds. *Attachment in social networks.* Elsevier Science Publishers.

Verbrugge, L. M. 1984. A health profile of older women with comparison to older men. *Research on aging* 6, 291–322.

Vernon, M. 1980. Education's Three Mile Island: P.L. 94–142. *Peabody journal of education* (October).

Vinton, K. 1983. *Humor in the workplace: It's more than telling jokes.* Santa Barbara, Calif.: Western Academy of Management.

Voydanoff, P. 1987. *Work and family life.* Beverly Hills, Calif.: Sage.

Voydanoff, P. 1990. Economic distress and family relations: A review of the eighties. *Journal of marriage and the family* 52, 1099–1115.

Voydanoff, P., and Donnelly, B. W. 1989. Economic distress and mental health: The role of family coping resources and behaviors. *Lifestyles: Family and economic issues* 10, 139–162.

Vukelich, C., and Kliman, D. S. 1985. Mature and teenage mothers' infant growth expectations and use of child development information sources. *Family relations* 34 (April), 189–196.

Vygotzky, L. S. 1962. *Thought and language.* Cambridge, Mass.: MIT Press.

Waechter, E. H., and Blake, F. G. 1976. *Nursing care of children.* 9th ed. Philadelphia: Lippincott.

Waldrop, M. F., and Halverson, C. F. 1972. Minor physical anomalies: Their incidence and relation to behavior in a normal and a deviant sample. In R. C. Smart and M. S. Smart, eds. *Readings in child development and relationships.* New York: Macmillan Company.

Waletzky, L. 1979. Breast-feeding and weaning: Some psychological considerations. *Primary care* 6, 2, 341–364.

Walker, L. E. 1984. *The battered woman syndrome.* New York: Springer.

Walker, L. J. 1984. Sex differences in the development of moral reasoning: A critical review. *Child development* 55, 677–691.

Wallerstein, J., and Kelly, J. 1980. *Surviving the breakup: How children actually cope with divorce.* New York: Basic Books.

Wallis, C. 1985. Children having children. *Time* 126, 23 (December 9), 78–90.

Walsh, R. P. 1983. Age differences in learning and memory. In D. S. Woodruff and J. E. Birren, eds. *Aging: Scientific perspectives and social issues.* 2nd ed. Monterey, Calif.: Brooks/Cole.

Walter, W. G. 1953. *The living brain.* New York: W. W. Norton.

Walters, J. K., and Stone, V. A. 1971. Television and family communication. *Journal of broadcasting* 15, 409–414.

Waltzer, H. 1982. Psychological and legal aspects of artificial insemination (A.I.D.): An overview. *American journal of psychotherapy* XXXVI, 1, (January), 91–102.

Wang, H. S. 1973. Cerebral correlates of intellectual function in senescence. In L. F. Jarvik, C. Eisdorfer, and J. E. Blum, eds. *Intellectual functioning in adults.* New York: Springer Publishing Company.

Warner, S. L. 1984. Humor and self-disclosure within the milieu. *Journal of psychosocial nursing and mental health services* 22, 4, 17–21.

Waters, C. B., Weinberg, J. E., Leake, R. D., and Fisher, D. A. 1982. Arginine vasopressin levels during a painful stimulus during infancy. *Pediatric research* 16, 569.

Waters, E., Wippman, J., and Sroufe, L. A. 1979. Attachment, positive affect, and competence in the peer group: Two studies in construct validation. *Child development* 50, 821–829.

Waters, H. S., and Andreassen, C. 1983. Children's use of memory strategies under instructions. In M. Pressley and J. R. Levin, eds. *Cognitive strategies: Developmental, educational, and treatment-related issues.* New York: Springer-Verlag.

Watson, E. S., and Engle, R. W. 1982. Is it lateralization, processing strategies, or both that distinguishes good and poor readers? *Journal of experimental child psychology* 34, 1–19.

Watson, J. B. 1928. *Psychological care of infant and child.* New York: Norton.

Watson, J. B., and Rayner, R. 1970. Conditioned emotional reactions. *Journal of experimental psychology* 3, 1–14.

Watson, J. S. 1973. Operant conditioning of visual fixation in infants under visual and auditory reinforcement. In L. J. Stone, H. T. Smith, and L. B. Murphy, eds. *The competent infant.* New York: Basic Books.

Weatherley, D. 1964. Self-perceived rate of physical maturation and personality in late adolescence. *Child development* 35, 1197–1210.

Weaver, R. H., and Cranley, M. S. 1983. An exploration of paternal-fetal attachment behavior. *Nursing research* 32, 68.

Wechsler, D. 1975. Intelligence defined and undefined: A relativistic appraisal. *American psychologist* 30, 135–139.

Weg, R. B. 1983. Changing physiology of aging: Normal and pathological. In D. S. Woodruff and J. E. Birren, eds. *Aging: Scientific perspectives and social issues.* 2nd ed. Monterey, Calif.: Brooks/Cole.

Weiffenbach, J. M., Baum, B. J., and Burghauser, R. 1982. Taste thresholds: Quality specific variation with human aging. *Journal of gerontology* 37, 372–377.

Weil, W. B., Jr. 1975. Infantile obesity. In M. Winick, ed. *Childhood obesity.* New York: John Wiley and Sons.

Weingarten, H. R. 1985. Marital status and well-being: A national study comparing first-married, currently divorced, and remarried adults. *Journal of marriage and the family* 47, 3 (August), 653–662.

Weinraub, M., Jaeger, E., and Hoffman, L. 1988. Predicting infant outcome in families of employed and unemployed and nonemployed mothers. *Early childhood research quarterly* 3, 361–378.

Weinstock, A., and Lerner, R. M. 1972. Attitudes of late adolescents and their parents toward contemporary issues. *Psychological reports* 30, 239–244.

Weintraub, S., Prinz, R., and Neale, G. 1978. Peer evaluations of the competence of children vulnerable to psychopathology. *Journal of abnormal child psychology* 6, 461–473.

Weisfeld, C. C., Weisfeld, G. E., and Callaghan, J. W. 1982. Female inhibition in mixed-sex competition among young adolescents. *Ethology and sociobiology* 3, 29–42.

Weisman, A. D., and Worden, J. W. 1975. Psychosocial analysis of cancer deaths. *Omega* 6, 61–65.

Welford, A. T. 1973. Ability. In R. R. Sears and S. S. Feldman, eds. *The seven ages of man.* Los Altos, Calif.: William Kaufman.

Wellman, H. M. 1986. A child's theory of mind: The development of conceptions of cognition. In S. R. Yussen, ed. *The growth of reflection.* New York: Academic Press.

Wells, C. E. 1978. Chronic brain disease: An overview. *American journal of psychiatry* 135, 1, 1–12.

Wender, P. H., and Klein, D. F. 1981. *Mind, mood, and medicine.* New York: Farrar, Straus, and Giroux.

Wertheimer, M. 1961. Psycho-motor coordination of auditory-visual space at birth. *Science* 134, 1692.

Wertz, P., Rohrbeck, C., Charner, I., and Fraser, B. 1987. *Intense employment while in high school: Are teachers, guidance counselors, and parents misguiding academically-oriented adolescents?* Washington, D.C.: George Washington University Graduate Institute for Policy Education and Research.

Wetherington, E., and Kessler, R. C. 1989. Employment, parental responsibility, and psychological distress: A longitudinal study of married women. *Journal of family issues* 10, 527–546.

Whipple, D. V. 1972. Human growth through the ages. In R. C. Smart and M. S. Smart, eds. *Readings in child development and relationships.* New York: Macmillan Company.

Whitbourne, S. K. 1985. *The aging body.* New York: Springer-Verlag.

Whitbourne, S. K. 1986. *Adult development.* New York: Praeger.

Whitbourne, S. K., and Weinstock, C. S. 1986. *Adult development.* New York: Praeger.

White, B. 1975. *The first three years of life.* Englewood Cliffs, N.J.: Prentice-Hall.

White, D. 1986. Treatment of mild, moderate, and severe obesity in children. *Canadian psychology* 27, 262–274.

White, R. B., and Gathman, L. T. 1973. The syndrome of ordinary grief. *AFP* 8, 2, 97–104.

White, R. W. 1979. Competence as an aspect of personal growth. In M. W. Kent and J. E. Rolf, eds. *Social competence in children.* Vol. 3 of *Primary prevention of psychopathology.* Hanover, N.H.: University Press of New England.

Whitehurst, G. J. 1982. Language development. In B. B. Wolman, ed. *Handbook of developmental psychology.* Englewood Cliffs, N.J.: Prentice-Hall.

Whiting, B., and Whiting, J. 1975. *Children of six cultures: A psychocultural analysis.* Cambridge, Mass.: Harvard University Press.

Whitt, J. K., and Prentice, N. M. 1977. Cognitive processes in the development of children's enjoyment and comprehension of joking riddles. *Developmental psychology* 13, 2, 129–136.

Who wants to live on Sesame Street? 1973. *Science news* 103, 12, 183.

Wichern, F., and Nowicki, S. 1976. Independence training practices and locus of control orientation in children and adolescents. *Developmental psychology* 12, 77.

Wilcox, A. J., Weinberg, C. R., O'Connor, J. F., Baird, D. D., Schlatteer, M. S., Canfield, R. E., Armstrong, E. G., and Nisula, B. C. 1988. Incidence of early loss of pregnancy. *New England journal of medicine* 319, 4, 189–194.

Wilkinson, D. 1980. *Information processing in reading.* New York: Wiley.

Williams, J. E., Bennett, S. M., and Best, D. L. 1975. Awareness and expression of sex stereotypes in young children. *Developmental psychology* 11, 635–642.

Williams, J. R., and Scott, R. B. 1973. Growth and development of Negro infants: IV. Motor development and its relationship to child rearing practices in two groups of Negro infants. In L. J. Stone, H. T. Smith, and L. B. Murphy, eds. *The competent infant.* New York: Basic Books.

Williams, R. B., and Barefoot, J. C. 1988. Coronary-prone behavior: The emerging role of the hostility complex. In B. K. Houston and C. R. Snyder, eds. *Type A behavior pattern.* New York: John Wiley.

Williams, T. 1986. *The impact of television.* New York: Academic Press.

Williams, T. M., Joy, L. A., Kimball, M. M., and Zabrack, M. L. 1985. Are most boys more aggressive than most girls? *Cahiers de psychologie cognitive* 5, 375.

Wilson, J. 1973. *Environmental birth defects.* New York: Academic Press.

Wilson, R. 1983. The Louisville twin study: Developmental synchronies in behavior. *Child development* 54, 298–316.

Wilson, R. S., and Harpring, E. B. 1972. Mental and motor development in infant twins. *Developmental psychology* 7, 277–287.

Winchell, D. S. 1977. *Children's humor and the acquisition of qualitative identity.* Ph.D. dissertation, Arizona State University.

Wingrove, C. R., and Alston, J. P. 1974. Cohort analysis of church attendance, 1939–1969. *Social forces* 53, 324–331.

Winick, M., ed. 1975. *Childhood obesity.* New York: John Wiley and Sons.

Winn, M. 1977. *The plug-in drug.* New York: Viking Press.

Wiswell, T. E., Miller, G. M., Gelston, H. M., Jr., Jones, S. K., and Clemmings, A. F. 1988. Effect of circumcision status on periurethral bacterial flora during the first year of life. *Journal of pediatrics* 113, 3, 442–446.

Witkin, H. A., and Goodenough, D. R. 1976. *Field dependence revisited.* Research Bulletin 76–39. Princeton, N.J.: Educational Testing Service.

Wolfe, D. 1985. Child-abusive parents: An empirical review and analysis. *Psychological bulletin* 97, 462–482.

Wolfenstein, M. 1954. *Children's humor.* Glencoe, Ill.: Free Press.

Wolff, P. H. 1966. The causes, controls and organization of behavior in the neonate. *Psychological issues* 5, 1 (Monograph 17): 496–503.

Wolff, P. H. 1973. The natural history of crying and other vocalizations in early infancy. In L. J. Stone, H. T. Smith, and L. B. Murphy, eds. *The competent infant.* New York: Basic Books.

Wolkenberg, F. 1987. Out of darkness. *New York Times magazine* (October 11), 62–82.

Wolman, B. B. 1978. *Children's fears.* New York: Grosset and Dunlap.

Wolpe, J. 1973. *The practice of behavior therapy.* 2nd ed. New York: Pergamon Press.

Wolpe, J. 1981. Behavior therapy versus psychoanalysis. *American psychologist* 36, 159–164.

Wolvin, A., and Coakley, C. G. 1988. *Listening.* 3rd ed. Dubuque, Iowa: W. C. Brown.

Wood, C., Downing, B., Trounson, A., and Rogers, P. 1984. Clinical implications of developments in in vitro fertilisation. *British medical journal* 289, 6450, 978–980.

Wood, C., McMaster, R., Rennie, G., Trounson, A., and Leeton, J. 1985. Factors influencing pregnancy rates following in vitro fertilization and embryo transfer. *Fertility and sterility* (February), 245–250.

Worthington-Roberts, B. 1985. Nutritional considerations for children in sports. In P. L. Pipes, ed. *Nutrition in infancy and childhood.* St. Louis: Times Mirror/Mosby.

Wright, J., and Hamilton, R. 1978. Work satisfaction and age: Some evidence for the job change hypothesis. *Social forces* 56, 1140–1158.

Wright, P. H. 1982. Men's friendships, women's friendships and the alleged inferiority of the latter. *Sex roles* 8, 1–20.

Yakolev, P. I., and Lecours, A. R. 1967. The myelogenetic cycles of regional maturation of the brain. In A. Minkowski, ed. *Regional development of the brain in early life.* Oxford, England: Blackwell.

Yalisove, D. 1978. The effect of riddle structure on children's comprehension of riddles. *Developmental psychology* 14, 2, 173–180.

Yarrow, L. J., et al. 1973. Dimensions of early stimulation and their differential effects on infant development. In L. J. Stone, H. T. Smith, and L. B. Murphy, eds. *The competent infant.* New York: Basic Books.

Yarrow, M. R., and Waxler, C. Z. 1976. Dimensions and correlates of prosocial behavior in young children. *Child development* 47, 118–125.

Yerushalmy, J. 1972. Infants with low birth weight born before mothers started to smoke cigarettes. *American journal of obstetrics and gynecology* 112, 277–284.

Young, W. 1982. *The effect of humor on memory.* Paper presented at the Third International Conference on Humor.

Young-Browne, G., Rosenfield, H. M., and Horowitz, F. D. 1977. Infant discrimination of facial expressions. *Child development* 48, 555–562.

Youniss, J. 1974. Operations and everyday thinking. *Human Development* 17, 386–391.

Youniss, J. 1980. *Parents and peers in social development: A Sullivan-Piaget perspective.* Chicago: University of Chicago Press.

Zajonc, R. B. 1975. Dumber by the dozen. *Psychology today* 8, 8 (January), 37–43.

Zaporozhets, A. V., and Elkonin, D. B., eds. 1971. *The psychology of preschool children.* Cambridge, Mass.: MIT Press.

Zeanah, C. H., Keener, M. A., and Anders, T. F. 1986. Adolescent mothers' prenatal fantasies and working models of their infants. *Psychiatry* 49 (August), 193–203.

Zeits, C. R., and Prince, R. M. 1982. Child effects on parents. In B. B. Wolman, ed. *Handbook of developmental psychology.* Englewood Cliffs, N.J.: Prentice-Hall.

Zelazo, P. 1976. From reflexive to instrumental behavior. In L. Lipsitt, ed. *Developmental psychobiology: The significance of infancy.* Hillsdale, N.J.: Erlbaum.

Zeskind, P. S. and Ramey, C. T. 1981. Preventing intellectual and interactional sequelae of fetal malnutrition: A longitudinal, transactional, and synergistic approach to development. *Child development* 52, 213–218.

Zeskind, P. S., and Ramey, C. T. 1978. Fetal malnutrition: An experimental study of its consequences in two caregiving environments. *Child development* 49, 1155–1162.

Zierler, S. 1985. Maternal drugs and congenital heart disease. *Obstetrics and gynecology* 65, 2, (February), 155–165.

Zigler, E., and Turner, P. 1982. Parents and day-care workers: A failed partnership? In E. Zigler and E. Gordon, eds. *Day care: Scientific and social policy issues.* Boston: Auburn House.

Zillman, D. 1982. Cognitive and affective influences: Television viewing and arousal. In D. Pearl, L. Bouthilet, and J. Lazar, eds. *Television and behavior: Ten years of scientific progress and implications for the 1980s: Technical reviews.* Vol. 2. Washington, D.C.: Government Printing Office.

Zimiles, H., and Lee, V. E. 1991. Adolescent family structure and educational progress. *Developmental psychology* 27, 2, 314–320.

Zimmerman, B. N. 1980. Human questions vs. human hurry. *American journal of nursing* 80, 719.

Zion, L. L. 1965. Body concept as it relates to self concept. *Research quarterly of the American Association of Health, Physical Education, and Recreation* 36, 490–495.

Zuckerman, B., Frank, D. A., Hinson, R., Amaro, H., Levenson, S. M., Kayne, H., Parker, S., Vinci, R., Aboagye, K., Fried, L. E., Cabral, H., Timperi, R., and Bauchner, H. 1989. Effects of maternal marijuana and cocaine use on fetal growth. *New England journal of medicine* 320, 12, 762–768.

Zuckerman, D., Singer, D. G., and Singer, J. L. 1980. Television viewing, children's reading and related school behavior. *Journal of communications* 30, 166–74.

Zussman, R. 1987. Work and family in the new middle class. In N. Gerstel and H. E. Gross, eds. *Families and work.* Philadelphia: Temple University Press.

Index

Hormones
    and birth defects, 82
    female, 369–370
Hospice, 503–505
Hospitalization, correlation with
    personality disorders, 274
Hospitals, competition with home birth
    procedures, 111–112
Hostile aggression, 231–232
Hot flashes, 408, 409
Human growth hormone, genetically
    engineered, 56
Human immunodeficiency virus (HIV),
    incidence of infection by, 505
Humanistic psychology, 19–22
Human papillomavirus, 114
Humor
    development during adolescence,
        325–326
    development in the preschool years,
        203–207
    in early adulthood, 375–376
    infant's and toddler's development,
        149–150
    in late adulthood, 465–467
    in middle adulthood, 418–421
    in middle childhood, 259–262
    stages of infant's and toddler's
        development of, 151–153
Hunter's syndrome, 50
Huntington's chorea, 46
    marker for, 56
Hushbeck, Judy, 495
Hyaline membrane disease, 102–103
Hydrochloric acid secretion in late
    adulthood, 452
Hyperkinesis, 62–63, 254–255
Hypnosis, and stress reduction, 423
Hypothesis, defined, 2

I

Id, 12
Idealism in middle adulthood, 429–430
Idealization of dead spouses, 516
Identical twins, and studies of heritability,
    57–58
Identity
    and cognitive and moral development,
        323
    development in adolescence, 333, 336
    and development of anorexia in
        adolescence, 310–311
    in early adulthood, 362
    and intimacy in early adulthood, 382
    and self-reflection in the elderly, 477
    and sexual experience in adolescence,
        343–344
Identity diffusion, 335
Identity versus role confusion stage of
    development, 15

Ideology, political, in middle adulthood,
    417–418
Imaginary audience, construct in
    adolescence, 320–321
Imaginary friends, 221
Imagination, and faith, 416
Imitative speech in the preschool years,
    198
Immunoglobin E, and allergies, 63
Imperial Cancer Research Fund, research
    on sex chromosomes, 44
Impotence in late adulthood, 457
Impulsive behavior
    in middle childhood, 250
    and suicide in adolescence, 341
Incentives in observational learning, 270
Incipient cooperation stage of
    development, rule-orientation during,
    285
Incongruity
    and humor, 152–153
    and humor in the preschool years,
        203–204
    infant's reactions to, 152
Independence
    and anorexia in adolescence, 311
    as a stage in early adulthood, 386
Independent living in late adulthood, 452
Independent variables, 23
Indiscriminate attachment in an infant's
    and toddler's development, 165
Individuality, 161–165
Individualized education program (IEP) for
    the handicapped, 263
Individual stage of development,
    rule-orientation during, 285
Individuating-reflexive stage of
    development, 324–325
Individuative-reflective faith stage, 416
Inductive discipline, 287
Industry versus inferiority stage of
    development, 15, 268
Infant day care, risks of, 178
Infant mortality, 154–156
Infants and toddlers, development of,
    132–153
Inferences, and previous learning in middle
    childhood, 252
Inflation, and retirement, 398
Influential grandparenting, 487
Information processing, and middle
    childhood development, 251–252
Inheritance patterns, Mendelian, 39
Initiative versus guilt stage of
    development, 15
    in the preschool years, 212
Innovation in Social Policy, Center for,
    355
Insistent communicator (television), 236
Institutional care for the elderly, 481–482
Instrumental aggression, 231

Instrumental movement in the preschool
    years, 190
Instrumental relativist orientation, 278
Integrated personality in the elderly, 474
Intellectualization, and stress management, 423
Intelligence
    and behavioral deviance, 274
    and brain structure, 367
    effects of heredity and environment on,
        57–59
    and gender-role stereotypes, 292
    and humor in early adulthood, 375–376
    in late adulthood, 461–464
    measurement of, 252–253
    in middle adulthood, 413–414
    and self-esteem, 271
Intelligence quotient (IQ), 253
    of hyperactive children, 255
Interactional synchrony in neonates, 118
Interactionist model of language
    development, 145–146
Interactions
    caregiver-child, in day care centers, 227
    parental, and socialization of children, 220
    parent-infant, 173
Interactions, parent-child, and
    temperament, 163–164
Interactive capacities, neonatal, 102
Internalization of sensorimotor schemes,
    Piaget's theory of, 144–145
Internalizers, 251
Internal locus of control
    in adolescence, 336
    and anorexia nervosa, 312
Internal organs, development in
    adolescence, 305
Interpersonal concordance in moral
    development, 278
Intimacy
    and clique membership, 350–351
    in early adulthood, 373
    and humor, 419
    with offspring in middle adulthood, 435
Intimacy versus isolation stage of early
    adulthood, 382
Intimacy versus isolation stage of
    development, 15
Intravenous drug use, and AIDS infection,
    506–507
Intrinsic contributions to work satisfaction,
    398
Introspection in adolescence, 318
Intuitive-projective faith stage, 415
Intuitive thinking in the preschool years,
    190–191
Invasion of privacy, and research, 28
In vitro fertilization, 55
Iodide, and birth defects, 81
Irony, and humor in adolescence, 325
Irrational-conscientious stage of
    development, 430

Nutrition
in adolescence, 308–314
for adolescent pregnant women,
346–347
and dental health in late adulthood, 452
and gender in early adulthood, 370
and infant's and toddler's development,
137–140
in late adulthood, 452–455
maternal, and prenatal development,
84–85
and premature birth, 104

O

Obesity
in adolescence, 309–310
hereditary and environmental factors in,
63–64
in middle childhood, 243–244
Objective concepts versus subjective
concepts, 320
Objectivity
in child rearing, 7
and humor in adolescence, 326
Object permanence
Piaget's theory of, 143–144
and separation anxiety, 167
Observational learning, 9, 269–270
Obsessional review of a spouse's death,
516
Occupational identity in adolescence, 334
Occupational status
in early adulthood, 395–396
and retirement age, 491
Oedipal stage of psychosexual
development, 13
Old-old stage of development, 448–449
Onlooker stage of social interaction, 222
Operant conditioning, 7
Operation, defined (Piaget), 19
Opportunistic infections, 505
Oral contraceptives, and cardiovascular
disease, 366–367
Oral stage of psychosexual development,
13
Ordinal position
and language development, 202–203
and socialization in the preschool years,
217–218
Organization, Piaget's theory of, 141–142
Organizational capacities regarding
physiologic responses to neonatal state
control, 102
Organizational capacities regarding state
control, neonatal, 102
Organogenesis, second trimester of
prenatal development, 74
Orientation, and stage of moral
development, 278
Original sin theory, 5

Ortho Pharmaceutical, 368
Osteoarthritis in late adulthood, 451
Osteoporosis
in late adulthood, 450–451
in middle adulthood, 404
Ova, 37, 38
Overfeeding in infancy, 140
Overregularization of speech forms in the
preschool years, 200–201
Overwork, and premature birth, 104
Oxygen debt, and endurance during early
adulthood, 364

P

Palmar grasp in neonates, 120
Parental imperative, 432
liberation from in the elderly, 476
Parent-child relationships, correlation with
peer relationships, 283–284
Parenthood, 434–435
anticipating, 90–91
in early adulthood, 393–395
Parents
abuse by, and stress, 480
as companions, 287
death of, 513
and early childhood programs, 227
Parents Anonymous, 173
Parten, Mildred, 221–222
Passive-dependent personality in the
elderly, 475
Passive euthanasia, 502
Passive grandparenting, 487
Pathological symptoms, due to mid-life
role changes, 432
Pavlov, Ivan, 6
Peak experiences, 20
Peak height velocity, and culture, 304
Peck, Robert, 428, 430
Peers
death of, 514
and drug abuse, 338
evaluation of the learning disabled, 254
and gender-role development in middle
childhood, 291
groups of, 350–351
and identity in adolescence, 333–334
and middle childhood development, 268
and moral development in adolescence,
324
networks and anorexic behavior, 312
preschoolers' relationships with,
222–224
and sexual activity in adolescence, 344
and socialization in adolescence, 350–
352
and socialization in middle childhood,
281–284
and social learning theory of
adolescence, 336–337

Pepsin levels in late adulthood, 452
Performance stage of career development
in early adulthood, 396
Perkins Institute for the Deaf and Blind,
11
Permanence of an intimate relationship,
383
Permissive child rearing in the preschool
years, 216
Personal fable of adolescence, 322
Personality
and body build in the preschool years,
185
changes in the elderly, 473–475
and drug abuse, 339
and environment, 59–63
and power, 285
Personality development
in adolescence, 332–337
in early adulthood, 382–389
in the elderly, 472–477
infant's and toddler's, 159–179
in middle adulthood, 428
in middle childhood, 268–270
in the preschool years, 212–216
Personal philosophy in middle adulthood,
414–418
Perspective-taking
in adolescence, 323
and delinquency, 341
Pets, and socialization, 224
Phallic stage of psychosexual development,
13
Phenobarbital, and birth defects, 81–82
Phenotype, 37
Phenylketonuria (PKU), 48
Physical activity
and obesity, 310
and stress reduction, 423
See also Exercise
Physical and cognitive development in
preschool years, 181–208
Physical characteristics
heritability of, 63–64
of neonates, 112
in the preschool years, 185
Physical development, 132–141
in adolescence, 298–314
in early adulthood, 363–370
in late adulthood, 449–460
in middle adulthood, 404–411
in middle childhood, 240–244
and organized competitive sports, 293
in the preschool years, 182–190
Physical environment, and quality of child
care, 176–177
Physical growth
effects of medication for hyperactivity,
256
factors affecting in the preschool years,
187–188

Physical punishment, and aggressive
    behavior in preschool children,
    232–233
Physiological changes
    in middle childhood, 240–242
    in the preschool years, 183–187
Physiological functioning of neonates,
    113–117
Piaget, J., 18–19, 23, 141–145, 147, 193,
    245–246
    on development of humor, 149–150
Piagetian test, and the WISC-R, 253
Pickens, T. Boone, 443
Pituitary, and the menstrual cycle, 369
PKU. See Phenylketonuria
Placenta, 72–73
Placental stage of delivery, 99–100
Placenta previa
    and cesarean section delivery, 107
    and premature birth, 104
Placing reflex in neonates, 120
Planned mutations theory of aging, 460
Planning defects, and dyscalcula, 257
Plantar grasp in neonates, 120
Plato, 2–3, 36, 56
Play
    and humor, 153
    in the preschool years, 204
    sexually stereotyped, in the preschool
        years, 213
    and social development, 284–285
    and socialization, 224–226
Pleasure
    as a dimension of well-being, 389
    infant's and toddler's development of
        experience of, 151
Pneumocystis carinii pneumonia (PCP), 506
Political thought in middle adulthood,
    417–418
Polydactyly, 79
Population of mature adults, 448
Population Crisis Committee, 368
Positive conditioning to manage fear in
    preschoolers, 229
Postconventional justice reasoning, 415
Postconventional stage of moral
    development, 279
Postexperiment test, 23
Postpartum depression, 100
Postretirement, 490
Power-assertive discipline, 287
Powerlessness, and anorexia, 310–311
Preconceptual thinking in the preschool
    years, 190
Preconventional stage of moral
    development, 278
Preeclampsia, 87
Preformationism, 36
Pregnancy
    incidence among adolescents, 345
    and nutrition, 370

repeated teen-aged, 347
    teenaged, 368
Premarital pregnancy, and divorce rate,
    436
Premature infants
    defined, 102
    development and maturation of,
        103–105
Prematurity, incidence of, 102–103
Premenstrual syndrome, 378–379
Prenatal development, 69–95
Preoperational thought
    in the preschool years, 190–195
    stage of, 18
Preparation for an economic career stage of
    early adulthood, 395
Prepared childbirth (natural childbirth),
    109–111
Preretirement, 490
Preschool years, physical and cognitive
    development in, 181–208
Preservation of inappropriate procedures,
    and dyscalcula, 257
Primal faith stage, 415
Primary circular reactions, Piaget's theory
    of, 142–143
Problem finding behavior in early
    adulthood, 375
Problem solving
    in early adulthood, 370–371
    infant's and toddler's pleasure in, 151
    in late adulthood, 461
Productivity in middle adulthood, 428
Progesterone, 369, 378
Promiscuity, and pregnancy in
    adolescence, 345
Propositional logic, development of in
    adolescence, 316
Prosocial behavior
    age and gender correlations with, 282
    in preschool children, 233–234
Prosocial reasoning, 281
Prostate gland, 409
Protest stage of separation anxiety, 167
Proximodistal development, 133
Psychiatric disorders
    family variables correlated with, 274
    and premenstrual distress, 379
Psychological development, and anorexia
    nervosa, 312–313
Psychological risk, and peer acceptance,
    283
Psychological tasks of adolescents, and
    obesity, 309
Psychopathic personality, 430
Psychosexual theory, 12–13
Psychosocial development
    in early adulthood, 382–400
    in the elderly, 468
    in middle adulthood, 428–445
    in middle childhood, 268–295

in the preschool years, 212–237
Psychosocial stage theory, 14–17
Psychosocial theory of development,
    160–161
    in adolescence, 332–337
    in middle adulthood, 428
Ptyalin secretion in late adulthood, 452
Pubertal development
    female, 301
    male, 302–303
Puberty, 299–303
    defined, 298
    timing and social development, 307–308
Pulmonary system in late adulthood,
    451–452
Punishment
    and obedience orientation, 278
    and repetition of behaviors, 9
Puns, 260

Q

Quickening, 74

R

Race
    and AIDS associated with intravenous
        drug use, 506–507
    and divorce rate, 436
    and humor in racist jokes, 421
    and incidence of single-parent families,
        437
    and infant mortality rates, in the U.S.,
        155
    and mortality in adolescence, 353
    and rate of gross motor development,
        135
    and sexual activity in adolescence, 344
    and skin and hair changes in late
        adulthood, 451
    and suicide, 521
    and suicide rates, 519
    and susceptibility to SIDS, 127
Radiation, and birth defects, 79–80
Rapid eye movement (REM) sleep, 115–116
Rational-altruistic stage of development,
    430
Raub, William, 32
Reality riddles, 260
Reasoning in early adulthood, 370–371
Recall memory in late adulthood, 465
Recessive genes, 36
    for abnormal conditions, 47–49
    Mendelian patterns of inheritance, 49
Recognition memory in late adulthood,
    465
Recombinant DNA, and genetic
    engineering, 55–56
Red-green color blindness, 50

Reduction, and language development in the preschool years, 199
Reflection in middle childhood, 250
Reflexes
    in neonates, 119
    survival and grasping, in neonates, 122
    survival, in neonates, 119
Reflex grasp, 135
Reflexive substage, Piaget's theory of, 142
Regional differences in family size, 394
Regular sleep of neonates, 113
Reinforcement of behaviors, 7, 9
Rejection
    and the ability to form friendships, 283
    and running away from home, 349
Relationship abuse in early adulthood, 399
Relaxation, and stress reduction, 423
Religion
    development during adolescence, 322
    of the elderly, 489
    and family agreement with adolescents, 354
    individuating-reflexive stage in, 324–325
    medieval Christian theory of development, 3–4
    and moral development in adolescence, 324
    and morality in middle adulthood, 415
Remarriage
    and grandparents' rights, 487
    and social development in stepfamilies, 289–290
Reproductive loss, 523
Reproductive systems
    in early adulthood, 367–370
    in middle adulthood, 407–408
Research, ethics in, 28–29
Resolution, and humor in the preschool years, 203–204
Responsibility, and moral development, 280
Rest as a reason for suicide, 520
Retirement, 489–491, 494
    as a career stage, 397–398
    transition, 490
Revenge as a reason for suicide, 520–521
Reversibility, concept in middle childhood, 247
Rh factor, and prenatal development, 86
Rhode, Deborah, 93
Rhogam (anti-Rh immunoglobulin), 86
Rhythmical stereotypes, and infant's and toddler's development, 133–134
Riddles, and cognitive maturity, 260–261
Rights
    development of concepts of, 279
    of grandparents, 487
Right to Die, Society for, 503
Rigidity, and cognitive functioning in middle adulthood, 413
Risk
    of cardiovascular disease, 406

of careers for women, 389
in development of life skills, 353
in failure of nurturance in infancy, 167–171
in having mentally retarded parents, 173
of impaired health, and preventive programs, 442–443
and impulsive behavior, 250
for inadequate cognitive development in the preschool years, 195–197
psychological, and peer acceptance, 283
Risk-taking behavior
    and the personal fable of adolescence, 322
    sexual, 345–346
Ritalin for treating hyperactivity, 256
Rivalry in preschool children, 233
Robinson, John, 482
Roe v. Wade, 94
Rogers, Carl, 21–22, 383
Role conflict, and stress at work, 423
Role confusion in adolescence, 332–333
Role diffusion in adolescence, 334–335
Role models, 355
    in dual-career families, 440–441
    teachers', and students' achievement, 285–286
Role-taking
    and delinquency, 341
    development in middle childhood, 276–277
    Hogan's theory of development, 281
    and maturity, 323
Rooting reflex in neonates, 119–120
Rootless runaways, 349
Rote, and social speech, 258–259
Rouse, Fenella, 503
Rousseau, Jean-Jacques, 5
Rozansky, Phyllis, 174
RU-486, 368–369
Rubella, and birth defects, 79
Rule codification state of development, 285
Rules
    awareness of importance of, and moral development, 281
    of language, 199–200
    and stage of development, 284
Runaways, 349–350
Russell, Louise, 442

S

Saguaro High School (Scottsdale, Arizona), 356
Saint Christopher's Hospice, 504
Sample for a study, 25
Sandwich generation of daughters, 479–480
Saunders, Cicely, 504
Scales, Peter, 355

Schizophrenia, hereditary components of, 61
School adults, and pressure toward peer group relationships, 351–352
School experiences
    and psychosocial development, 268
    and social development, 285–287
Schroeder, Patricia, 31
Scofield, Giles, 503
Scooting, 134
Script of events in the preschool years, 194–195
Secondary circular reactions, Piaget's theory of, 143
Secondary reinforcer, mother as, 161
Secular trend
    in adolescence, 306
    in height and weight, 63
    and physical growth in the preschool years, 187–188
    and sexual behavior in adolescence, 343–344
Security, defining as the absence of anxiety, 230
Sedative drugs, and stress reduction, 423
Selective investment in grandchildren, 487
Self-actualization as the goal of human development, 20
Self-admiration in adolescence, 321
Self-awareness in the elderly, 477
Self-concept
    academic, 287
    development in the preschool years, 214–216
    and learning disabilities, 254
    in middle childhood, 270–271
    of overweight children, 243
    and timing of puberty, 307–308
Self-criticism in adolescence, 321
Self-defense
    and humor, 262
    in humor in late adulthood, 467
Self-demand feeding for infants, 116
Self-disclosure in humor, 419
Self-efficacy, and mental health in the elderly, 476
Self-esteem
    in adolescence, 337
    and communication with parents, 357
    conditions leading to, 214–215
    and divorce, 437
    and employment, 439
    factors that contribute to, 270–271
    and friendship patterns, 283
    and friendships of the elderly, 488
    and group activity in adolescence, 334
    and new surroundings, 351
    and parental treatment, 22
    and premenstrual distress, 379
    and sexual activity in adolescence, 345
    and suicide, 520–521